CROSS-CULTURAL
PERSPECTIVES OF
MATE-SELECTION
AND MARRIAGE

CONTRIBUTIONS IN FAMILY STUDIES

A Coat of Many Colors: Jewish Subcommunities
in the United States
EDITED BY ABRAHAM D. LAVENDER

Passing: The Vision of Death in America
EDITED BY CHARLES O. JACKSON

CROSS-CULTURAL PERSPECTIVES OF MATE-SELECTION AND MARRIAGE

Edited by GEORGE KURIAN

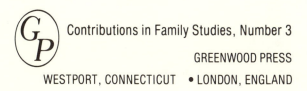

Contributions in Family Studies, Number 3

GREENWOOD PRESS

WESTPORT, CONNECTICUT • LONDON, ENGLAND

Library of Congress Cataloging in Publication Data
Main entry under title:

Cross-cultural perspectives of mate-selection and
    marriage.

    (Contributions in family studies ; no. 3 ISSN 0147-1023)
    Bibliography: p.
    Includes index.
    1. Mate selection—Addresses, essays, lectures.
2. Family—Addresses, essays, lectures. 3. Youth—
Sexual behavior—Addresses, essays, lectures.
I. Kurian, George. II. Series.
HQ734.C93   301.42   78-19306
ISBN 0-313-20624-4

Library of Congress Catalog Card Number: 78-19306
ISBN: 0-313-20624-4
ISSN: 0147-1023

First published in 1979

Greenwood Press, Inc.
51 Riverside Avenue, Westport, Connecticut 06880

Printed in the United States of America

10 9 8 7 6 5 4 3 2 1

To my brother, Dan

Contents

PART III: DIVORCE AND REMARRIAGE

Introduction

Students of family sociology have a choice of any number of textbooks as well as books of readings that deal primarily with the American family. Only occasionally, however, are ethnic families or family studies approached from a comparative perspective.

One of the earliest comparative studies with emphasis on the family was Margaret Mead's *Coming of Age in Samoa,*[1] a study of Samoan and American adolescent and adult behavior. Another interesting study is Ruth Benedict's *Patterns of Culture,*[2] which compares three types of ethos. Undoubtedly, the most significant pioneering work in cross-cultural studies, however, is *Social Structure* by G. P. Murdock.[3] In his classic work, Murdock analyzes 250 world societies, with primary emphasis on the study of the family and kinship. No study has yet matched the comprehensiveness of this one.

One of the best known books with a cross-cultural perspective on family studies is M. F. Nimkoff's *Comparative Family Systems,*[4] in which well-known scholars describe a number of family systems. While the work focuses on no particular theme, it contains the best analytic introduction to comparative family studies. Another publication of some significance is *The Family in Cross-Cultural Perspective* by William N. Stephens;[5] this work is based on a review of literature on family customs from an anthropological view. Another study is Marvin Sussman and Betty E. Cogswell, *Cross-National Family Research,*[6] a collection of articles mostly from the papers presented at the World Sociology Congress in Varna, Bulgaria, in 1970. Although the quality of most of the papers is good, the study suffers from a lack of a coordinated theme.

The above-mentioned works are perhaps the most significant of a rather small body of publications that employ a cross-cultural approach to family studies. It can also be asserted with some confidence that anthropologists have done more work in this area than sociologists, although the great majority of anthropologists devote most of their attention to kinship studies.

Comparative studies can deal with two or more societies, or with the same society at two or more periods of time. "In view of the variability of human cultures and the imperfect consensus among students of the family with respect to definitions of terms such as the family, it is probably more accurate to speak of certain behavior patterns as near-universals rather than as universals."[7]

In a number of societies, certain family practices are characteristic of particular socioeconomic conditions. For example, extended families with the attendant authority patterns, marriage customs, and the like found in all societies where agriculture is the main occupation, whereas small nuclear family types are typical in modern industrial urban societies.

All of the books mentioned above, have a general base through which they attempt to include every aspect of family life. In no case is the attempt very successful inasmuch as there are limits to generalization, especially in cross-cultural studies where some variables may not always have equal validity for comparison. Indeed, some claim that a common failing of comparative researchers on the family is their tendency to study phenomena out of context. "The virtue of comparative data is that findings derived from them are applicable to a larger universe."[8]

In order to gain the maximum advantage from a cross-cultural approach, this book deals only with mate-selection and marriage. Comparisons are between traditional societies and modern societies, and the emphasis is on the significance of social change.

Today, more than during any other period in history, we are living in a world that is getting smaller. Communications and travel have made it possible for people of different nations to have easy access to each other, and the awareness of economic opportunities elsewhere has promoted migrations from one country to another for short periods and more often, for permanent settlement. In a historical sense, the most recent settlements have taken place in North America, South America, Australia, New Zealand, and some Western European nations. The acceptance of these new immigrants by the dominant majority has often been slow and sometimes difficult, owing in part to the majority's ignorance of the newcomers' sociocultural values. The study of the family from a cross-cultural perspective will undoubtedly provide a better understanding of the various world cultures and may ultimately facilitate the process of assimilation of new immigrants by revealing the richness of their culture to the host society.

In an attempt to provide an outlet for studies of the family from a cross-cultural perspective, in 1970 I began publication of a journal devoted to comparative family studies entitled the *Journal of Comparative Family Studies*. The journal publishes sociological as well as anthropological articles dealing with various cultures. Some issues of the *Journal* have been devoted to special themes, one of the most significant of which was "Comparative Perspectives on Marriage and the Family."[9]

A careful study of all the articles published since 1970 demonstrates the need for focus on one or two aspects of family life. Hence it is that this book deals only with mate-selection, marriages, and divorces. All of the articles were originally published in the *Journal of Comparative Family Studies* between 1970 and 1977.

This book contains three sections, namely, Premarital Attitudes, Mate-Selection and Marriage, and Divorce and Remarriage. The subjects of the articles range from traditional family types to modern urban families. Some articles describe one family type only while others compare one or more types. This approach may be valuable both for the academic who is specializing in one aspect of family life and for the general reader.

It is my hope that this book will be a worthwhile contribution to family studies in general and to comparative family studies in particular.

Notes

1. Margaret Mead, *Coming of Age in Samoa*, New York: William Morrow, 1928.
2. Ruth Benedict, *Patterns of Culture*, Boston: Houghton Mifflin, 1934.
3. George P. Murdock, *Social Structure*, New York: Free Press, 1949.
4. Meyer F. Nimkoff, *Comparative Family Systems*, Boston: Houghton Mifflin, 1965.
5. William N. Stephens, *The Family in Cross-Cultural Perspective*, New York: Holt, Rinehart and Winston, 1965.
6. Marvin Sussman and Betty E. Cogswell, *Cross-National Family Research*, Leyden, Netherlands: E. J. Brill, 1972.
7. Nimkoff, pp. 6.
8. Ibid., p. 8.
9. Eugene Lupri and Gunther Luschen, "Comparative Perspectives on Marriage and the Family," Special Issue, *Journal of Comparative Family Studies*, Spring 1972.

PART I

PREMARITAL ATTITUDES

Premarital relations have been undergoing tremendous changes in recent years. In Western societies, including most parts of Europe and North America which represent the so-called urban industrial society, premarital heterosexual contacts have become easy with parents exhibiting much less influence than earlier. This liberalism is having a great impact on societies influenced by the process of modernization.

The articles presented here represent a good cross-section of various cultures, including premarital views in both traditional and modern societies. The traditional view on premarital sexual relations is a continuum from strict nonactivity enforced by the community through social pressure, and even social sanctions against transgressors, to equal permissiveness for both sexes.

All the studies in this section deal with student attitudes. The first three articles focus on two traditional cultures, India and China. The third of these, in which Chinese students are compared with American students, highlights the contrast between traditional and modern urban-industrial societies. The fourth study is a comparison between Ghanaians, who live in a traditional authoritarian society, and the British, who are part of a modern urban-industrial society. The next two studies compare English-speaking American students with French students, and English Canadians with French Canadians. Finally, a comprehensive study of student opinion in nine cultures is presented.

With regard to the traditional view, India represents one extreme of the continuum. Premarital heterosexual contacts are very limited in this country, especially in its rural areas and small towns. The segregation of sexes at the school level and even, to some extent, at the university level, prohibits easy contacts. Since arranged marriages are still the accepted norm, the families discourage close contact between the sexes.

In the large urban areas of India, such as New Delhi, Bombay, Calcutta, Madras, and Bangalore, there are increasing opportunities for premarital contacts. However, this relative freedom is in no way comparable to the freedom found in modern Western societies. India's young people, especially students, would prefer freer contacts and greater decision-making power. Some well-known studies confirm this attitude. For example, Ross reports that "there is a decided desire on the part of the young people interviewed to have more choice in the selection of their marriage partners than the older married interviewers had actually had."[1]

Students who attend universities in India's urban areas are showing increasing interest in heterosexual contacts. According to Cormack,

> No subject is of greater moment than "Sex" on any campus we visited. A few campuses permit "dates" during daytime, most do not even permit casual conversation between boys and girls. . . . The love marriage has become a favorite cinema theme and audience applaud love's triumph. Students admit enjoying foreign films largely because of the physical contact and kissing that is taboo—but titillating—in India.[2]

In Western societies, which allow the sexes the freedom to choose a compatible mate, it is presupposed that the contacts will be many and also that sufficient time will be devoted to clarifying this compatibility. Indian youths are increasingly being given the right of decision without the means to make it, or they are being given the means without the right of decision.

There is some evidence that the attitude of Indian parents is changing. In a study which I recently conducted among the educated middle and upper middle classes of India, I found that "children between twelve and sixteen years of age were expected to be put under some control according to the majority of respondents, but 29.6% said the children should not be allowed to meet or associate with members of the opposite sex. This is a conservative attitude, which indicates there are still people who feel freedom for teenagers means disaster. However, 65.8% were willing to give freedom under supervision."[3]

The first article in this book, the Raos' "*Arranged Marriages*" deals with the gradual changes in attitudes in India. Following a survey of traditional ideas about marriage, they cite some of the literature attesting to the changes. One of the most significant works cited is that by B. V. Shah of two hundred students, which reveals that only two students would leave the decision of mate-selection to the parents. Nearly two-thirds (66.5 percent) of the study population chose their brides jointly in consultation with the parents.

The Rao study shows that about half of the student sample wanted a definite say in mate-selection, although they preferred that their parents actually arranged the marriage. About 20 percent of the students wanted to know their future spouse for periods ranging from seven months to two years. In general, an overwhelming majority of the students desired more freedom in choosing a spouse and to make their feelings known.

Premarital heterosexual contacts in India are still limited. Clearly, then, the conservative traditional attitude is very much in evidence there.

The next study, that of Chinese students, is also of special interest, inasmuch as, between them China and India share two of the world's oldest civilizations. A note of caution is in order here: not too much should be read from the results of the study of Chinese students since such studies are done outside the People's Republic of China. However, it is important to note that in the People's Republic of China, "with urban living, a pattern of freer association between the sexes emerged and romantic love is threatening to replace parental arrangement as the basis for marriage."[4] While premarital sexual contacts are not discouraged in China, there is continuous emphasis on not marrying at too early an age. A late marriage means fewer children, which is a major consideration in a nation with a population of over 800 million. Compared to the prerevolutionary times, that is, before 1949, young people today have more freedom and marriages arranged by the parents have less meaning.

The second article, a comparative study among 264 American students, 56 Chinese students en route by plane to study in the United States, and 153 students in Hong Kong, revealed that, when male and female respondents were combined, there was a male-female double standard concerning premarital sex among all three groups. Chinese students were found to hold to a double standard more than the American students, while the respondents in the airplane sample seemed the most egalitarian.

The great difference in attitude between the Chinese and American samples toward premarital sexual permissiveness and activity suggests that the Chinese are not completely westernized regarding sexual attitudes and behaviors. The least permissive were members of the Buddhist faith or those who held religious values. While there is a trend towards sexual permissiveness among the young Chinese, the traditional restrictive standards still have much support.

The third study examines attitudes among young people in Hong Kong and makes comparisons with the United States and Taiwan. Niney-four percent of the Hong Kong respondents, versus only 58 percent of the Taiwanese respondents, expected to be able to choose their spouses. The wide gap in percentages can be attributed basically to the more traditional family life in Taiwan compared to the large cosmopolitan way of life in Hong Kong. Dating and courtship were rarely found in Taiwan, thereby making free choice difficult. Relations between the sexes were reported to be more informal and easier in Hong Kong than in Taiwan. There were more opportunities for heterosexual contacts in Hong Kong through dances, public camps, and community centers. Although the freedom of relations between the sexes was not found to be as complete in Hong Kong as in Western societies and dating seemed to begin later, it was common to see mixed groups of unchaperoned young people on country walks, at barbecues, or at the beach.

Another dimension of premarital life considered in Part I is that which bears directly on marriage decisions. Expectations for the marital relationship have a lot to do with the quality of marriage itself. Presented here are a few studies which look at marriage decisions from different perspectives. The first such study is a comparative one between Ghanaian and British women students. The article basically deals with the changing status of African women: specifically, how do they view the idea of careers after marriage? The comparison is of particular interest since these two societies with very different cultural backgrounds should show the variability in attitudes, even though all the respondents were educated.

In the study, 165 Ghanaian students were compared to 157 British students. The girls in both societies planned to marry but the Ghanaians intended to marry at a slightly later age and to have more children, at an earlier age, than the British. In contrast, apparently the British gave priority to the establishment of a satisfactory marital relationship. Ghanaians not only intended to continue working after marriage but also were much more inclined than the British to be working mothers, despite their desire to have twice as many children as the British. In addition, Ghanaian girls were found to have a more pragmatic attitude toward matrimonial difficulties than the British girls.

The remaining three studies in this section are concerned with Western family systems, and all suggest the subtle differences between various Western societies. The first study compares French and American college students with regard to the qualities desired in spouses. The American sample consisted of 172 males and 196 females and the French of 131 males and 137 females.

Even when the educational level of the two samples was identical, there were unexpected differences in attitudes. French males were not as concerned as the American to marry a woman who was religious, respectful of authority, and interested in family planning and saving. They also expected their spouses to have experience in sex before marriage. Interestingly, French men showed greater egalitarianism in husband-wife relationships in all spheres of domestic activity. They were pragmatic, and their idealized spouse was not a traditional submissive stereotype. They expressed a preference for an aggressive wife with independent views. Physical appearance was more important for them than for the Americans. The French thought she should be popular and be liked by their mother.

French women also expressed a greater preference than the Americans for an egalitarian spouse, agreeing with their men as regards equality in all aspects of domestic activities. They also wanted their spouse to accept their career or community involvement desires and were less idealistic than their American counterparts about desirable qualities in the husband. Husbands, they felt, should have the same political beliefs and a comparable sex drive; the French are probably more politically conscious than Americans. They also wanted a more aggressive husband compared to Americans. Unlike French men, however, they were less concerned about physical appearance and were more discriminating about premarital sex than men. They, too, expected a socially popular husband.

In general, the French were found to be more egalitarian than the Americans, possibly because the French sample lived near Paris and was thus more cosmopolitan than the American sample. They also represented a better quality student, since they were volunteers for the study. The American subjects were mainly "captives" in that they were tested, for the most part, in large classes. While the American group is typical of American students, the French group is not, by the elitest nature of the sample. These French groups may be trend-setters for the less elite. In both samples, the men showed more concern about the traditional submissive role of the spouse, a finding which reflected the higher status of men relative to women in both societies.

The next study, by Charles W. Hobart, compares English-speaking and French-speaking Canadian students with regard to the shift towards more egalitarian marital roles, the degree of influence when the mother works, urban versus rural background, education, social class, and other social background factors on marital attitudes. The samples included university as well as trade school students. There were 497 English-speaking university students and 203 trade school students. The French-speaking sample totaled 162 university students and 242 trade school students.

For the English-Canadian students, it was assumed "(1) that women tend to accept egalitarianism before men do and (2) that university students tend to accept egalitarianism before trade-school students do." On the basis of these assumptions, it appears that egalitarianism was more completely accepted in the education area than in the other two—namely personal characteristics and social participation—since all male-female samples showed the same high level of acceptance.

The data on authority and employment and support revealed that the women were generally significantly less traditional than the men. In the authority area, women were more egalitarian than men, but in the household area, men were more egalitarian than women which probably indicates women's defensive attitudes in this area of responsibility.

Among the French-Canadian students, males were consistently less egalitarian than female students, with tradeschool students even less so.

English-speaking students widely believed that married women should have equal work opportunities following marriage whenever there were no young children, and that authority and household responsibilities should be divided.

In terms of general egalitarianism, the data suggest that the English sample was more egalitarian, but with regard to employment of the wife, the English were less egalitarian than the French-speaking students. For all times, male-female sex differences were larger for the French than for the English samples, since women in both samples were consistently more egalitarian than the men, and the English-speaking men were more egalitarian, generally, than their French counterparts.

One language group, the French Canadian, was consistently more egalitarian in its orientation toward marriage than the other. Compared with English-speaking respondents, French Canadian women are pioneers in advocating egalitarian and permissive orientations, while the French Canadian men are the most traditional of all.

The French sample tended to have more egalitarian attitudes toward employment of the wife than did the English, and the French women students had more egalitarian attitudes in many areas than the English women. Interestingly, this finding is consistent with Bernard Murstein's study of French and American students. In both studies, the French respondents were from large urban areas like Paris and Montreal which provided the proper environment for liberal attitudes.

The final study in this section deals with attitudes toward marital infidelity. In a nine-culture comparison of student opinion comprising a large university in Sweden, Denmark, and Belgium, respectively; two Negro colleges in the Deep South; a state, a Catholic and a Mennonite-oriented college, respectively, all in the Midwest; a Mormon University in the West; and a university in Taiwan, a grand total of 2,764 cases were included. Since most of the students were unmarried, only attitudes could be studied.

More than half of all respondents indicated unqualified disapproval of marital infidelity. In fact, there was twice as much disapproval of extramarital sex than of premarital sex. The women were more conservative than the males regarding both premarital and extramarital coitus. Significantly, the cross-cultural pattern was relatively stable for premarital and extramarital coitus based on males as well as female respondents. The Asian culture was more conservative regarding premarital and especially extramarital sex than the American and European cultures: Denmark, followed by Sweden, was the most liberal or permissive.

There was considerably less disapproval of extramarital coitus among the sexually experienced in the total sample. Furthermore, the association of premarital sex experience with permissiveness concerning postmarital infidelity seemed to be strongest in the most conservative and weakest in the most liberal cultures.

Another important consideration has to do with the commitment variable, that is, with the question of how attitudes are affected by differing levels of involvement that are assumed for the extramarital relationship. On a cross-sexual and cross-cultural basis, more males than females approved of extramarital coitus at each of the commitment levels. The Scandinavian cultures gave the highest approval, followed by Southern Negro college respondents. The three American religious cultures, together with the Taiwanese, gave the lowest approval.

About twice as many males as females approved of the traditional double standard, a finding which perhaps is understandable in view of the fact that this standard puts fewer restrictions on the male, which was true for all nine cultures. Southern Negro and Taiwanese samples most favored the double standard, and the Mennonite and Danish samples the least. However, it is interesting that with the two sexes and nine cultures combined, respondents favored the single over the double standard by nearly five to one. The traditional double standard ranked higher for married males seeking sexual release during long periods away from their spouse than it did when premarital coitus was considered. Compared to the studies made in 1958 and 1968, single-standard permissiveness has increased for Denmark, the midwestern U.S. university, and the Mormon university respondents. Also, no female respondent approved the traditional double standard for a love relationship with another married person.

The study found that half of all respondents disapproved of extramarital coitus under all circumstances, and about one-fourth similarly disapproved of premarital coitus. Rejection of extramarital coitus was higher with female respondents than male respondents. Overall, five times more respondents identified themselves with the single standard than with the traditional double standard, which gives greater sexual freedom to the male. Compared with males, females were found to give less approval to extramarital coitus and to place a substantially greater emphasis upon the single standard. As is easily evident, this one study is probably the most comprehensive cross-cultural study on this subject to date.

Some of the emerging patterns from these studies are of significance, although it must be cautioned that there are only limited clear-cut trends since different sets of variables are involved in these studies. One of them concerns the double standard in sexual freedom. More males apparently favored the double standard than females. Here again traditionalist-oriented cultures have more of a double standard than modern societies. Another point worth comparing is permissiveness which is of some concern in any discussion of premarital life. Here again modern societies led by Scandinavian countries, showed the highest level of permissiveness. As a general rule, however, it seems that males in the study were more in favor of sexual permissiveness than females.

A third point of comparison is egalitarianism in all spheres of activity, domestic as well as public. The more modern and educated the society, the greater the acceptance of male-female egalitarianism; thus, the burden of providing such conditions is mostly on the males.

Notes

1. Aileen D. Ross, *The Hindu Family in Its Urban Setting*, Toronto: University of Toronto Press, 1961, p. 252.

2. Margaret Cormack, *She Who Rides a Peacock*, Asia Publishing House, Bombay: 1961, p. 100.

3. George Kurian, *Structural Changes in the Family in Kerala, India*, in *Socialization and Communication in Primary Groups*, edited by Thomas R. Williams, World Anthropology Series, The Hague: Mouton Publishers, 1975, p. 76.

4. Gerald R. Leslie, *The Family in Social Context*, New York: Oxford University Press, 1976, p. 124.

Arranged Marriages: An Assessment of the Attitudes of the College Students in India*

V. V. PRAKASA AND V. NANDINI RAO**

Introduction

Based on Hindu Scriptures, marriage system in India was well established in Vedic period (4000-1000 B.C.)[1], and has been closely adhered to by a vast majority of the population ever since. India is complex and her people are so different in terms of language, caste, customs, and beliefs that it is difficult to make generalizations about the family life. However, arranged marriage system seems to cross all caste lines, regional boundaries and language barriers. From ancient times, marriage is considered as a ritual and a sacramental union. Marriage is an indispensable event of Hindu life and the person who is unmarried is considered unholy. From the religious point of view, the unmarried remains incomplete and is not eligible for participation in some social and religious activities. Marriage is indissoluble and except in a very few exceptional cases the importance of marriage transcends not only the entire family but also the past ancestral line as well as the future generations (Altekar, 1962; Basham, 1963; Kapadia, 1966; Ross, 1961; Prabhu, 1963). Usually parents in collaboration with other elderly kinsmen, friends, or occasionally 'go-betweens' start planning their children's marriage well ahead of time. Upon the decision as to when they should marry the parents initiate, scout around and negotiate with the other potential partner for a prolonged period of time.

There are certain traditional norms which prescribe to the parents of girls as well as boys their responsibilities in getting their children married. The Hindu view of life has always greatly emphasized progeny, whereby the fathers and their ancestors were assured of a happy after-life and the ancestral line was continued to the future members who are yet to come into being. Since the family system in India is largely regulated by patrilineal descent[2], the customs and traditions demand parents of male children to see that their sons are married and have male children to continue and preserve their ancestral line for generations to come. On the other hand, with respect to the norms governing the

---

[1]No common agreement is found in the literature on specific years of Vedic period. Kapadia (1966) gives the chronological order of Vedic period as outlined by different authorities in the field.

---

[2]Expections to patrilineal descent are Nayyars in Kerala, and Khasis and Garos in Assam.

*This is a revised paper presented at the Annual meeting of the Southern Sociological Society, Washington, D.C., April, 1975.

**Jackson State University, Jackson, MS 39217

parents of girls, as Basham put it "that a father who did not give his daughter in marriage before her first menstruation incurred the guilt of one procuring abortion (a very grave sin, worse than many kinds of murder) for every menstrual period in which she remained unmarried" (1963: 167). As the family's honor and status in the community depends to a large extent on the fulfillment of responsibility by the parents, they would like their daughters happily married before they pass their prime marriageable age.

Marriage was treated as an alliance between two families rather than a mere union of two individuals. In selecting a bride, the parents of the groom certainly consider such things as the girl's family background, economic position, general character, family reputation, the value of the dowry, the effect of alliance on the property, and other family matters (Kurian, 1974; Cormack, 1961; Shah, 1961). Greater emphasis was placed specifically on the characteristics of fitness and adjustability of the bride in the joint family. Hence it is only logical for the parents to assume the responsibility of selecting spouses for their sons because the bride was part of the whole family environment rather than a wife only to her husband.

The traditional normative pattern did not provide any opportunity to the prospective spouses to participate in the decision-making process of their own marriage. In fact, they were never to see each other until the wedding day. Lack of participation in the process of marital choice does not mean the prospective bride and groom either disregard or minimize the importance of marriage. The seriousness with which the marriage ritual is taken by youth is all the more reason why they are not entrusted with the responsibility of making self selection and why the parents' judgments are accepted. This practice is quite different from North American and European countries where young men and women are expected to date, court and fall in love, and then make the decision on their own to get married with or without parental consent depending on their age and closeness of their relations with the parents. But, in India as Ross put it "love was not necessary as a basis for marriage selection, nor was courtship a necessary prelude for testing the relationship" (1961: 251). Love was regarded as an uncontrollable and explosive emotion which makes a young person blind to reality, reason and logic. The family's stability may even be jeopardized since the emotions might lead one to marry an unsuitable person not only to his temperament but to the entire joint family. As Kalidasa, the Indian poet, remarked that "young people seek pleasures" (Auboyer, 1965: 176), the Hindu system regarded mate selection by self choice as undesirable and feared that freedom of choice might upset the process of adjustment of the bride in her new family. Goode rightly observed the prevalent sentiments of the parents regarding individual mate selection. "The young person could not be relied upon to follow the rules exactly. With limited social experience and no opportunity to travel, he or she could not locate the few eligible persons to be found in a population of several thousands distributed among villages. Even if this was possible, the individual might not respond emotionally to the eligible person or be able to persuade them to agree to a marriage" (1963: 210).

There seems to be a close relationship between the type of family and the type of marriage in most of the societies. Societies having a nuclear family as the norm emphasize romance as the basis for a marriage. In a society like India where the joint family system is the norm, marriages are largely arranged by parents and elders. The arranged marriage is said to have the following effects: (1) it helps maintain the social stratification system in the society; (2) it gives parents control over the family members; (3) it enhances the chances to preserve and continue the ancestral line; (4) it provides opportunity to strengthen the kinship group; (5) it allows the consolidation and extension of family property and (6) it enables the elders to preserve the principle of endogamy (Goode, 1963: Fox, 1975; Chekki, 1968).

Over the years, all the social institutions in India have undergone constant and gradual changes and modifications. Although the family is the most conservative institution only next to religion, it is not left untouched by the process of modernization. Reseach has been conducted to examine the impact of industrialization, urbanization, and increased education on the traditional family structure (Cormack, 1961; Goode, 1963; Gore, 1969; Kapadia, 1966; Ross, 1961). Following the tradition of theorizing by western and American writers about the relationship between these forces of change and the family system, it is assumed that they would encourage the people to develop individualistic attitudes which would more likely enhance the possibility of making independent decisions on matters related to their marriage practices.

A group of writers contend that the Indian family system is experiencing change slowly yielding its rigidity to flexibility, exhibiting loss of firm grip over the traditional patterns of mate selection, and demonstrating the adaptive strategy of allowing freedom to the young to a certain extent (Goode, 1963; Gore, 1969; Shah, 1961; Ross, 1961). Goode is convinced that India exhibits a number of changes in family relations and concludes that "even in mate selection choices, the winds of change may be felt, and there is a movement in the direction of giving greater freedom to the young. This change is especially important because the Hindu arranged marriage was the keystone to all the other family patterns that characterized Indian society for so long" (1963: 207-208).

However, some writers argue that the findings reveal no significant departure from the traditional method of mate selection under the present social conditions and observe that the Indian family system is maintaining its basic character adhering to traditional patterns of life (Kurian, 1961, 1971, 1974; Singer, 1958; Vatuk, 1972). In fact, one writer argues that Taya Zinkin's statement made in 1958 that "India is a country of arranged marriages. Only aboriginals and modern elite marry for love" holds true even today (Kurian, 1971).

Although arranged marriages are still a way of life, modifications in arranged marriages are observed in recent times in large urban areas and among the educated youth. It does not mean that the young people have assumed the full responsibility of self selection of their mates. But the boys and girls are given an opportunity to participate in the decision-making process of mate selection and to meet their future spouse if both families of potential bride and bridegroom are satisfied about the wisdom of going ahead with the proposal. "On a prearranged day, the boy will visit the girl's family accompanied by one or two married male relatives . . . At present it has been increasingly possible for the boy and girl to have a brief conversation by themselves, which is the only form of courting allowed. In a few families in large urban centers, they are allowed to see each other after the formal engagement. However, unchaperoned courtship is very rarely approved" (Kurian, 1974: 357). In spite of these recent changes, Kurian insists that the sacramental nature of marriages is still dominant in India where arranged marriages continue to exist. Most youth believe that parents and close relatives will strive their best to find the most suitable match.

The major purpose of this research is to examine the relationship between the forces of modernization and the attitudes of the college students toward mate selection. It is assumed of course, that the younger generation tends to be more receptive toward change than the other generations and hence the younger people would serve as a barometer to assess the changes in the family structure, especially arranged marriages. In addition, at higher educational institutions, students are exposed to an intellectual atmosphere and introduced to novel ideas pertaining to different normative patterns of behavior. Hence, students are selected to determine the degree to which they have changed in their attitudes toward traditional arrangement of marriages.

Review of Related Literature

A very limited number of studies are conducted to find out the influence of various aspects of modernization on traditional arranged marriages. Special attention will be given to observe whether the overtly expressed attitudes are translated into reality. Ross (1961), in the study of Bangalore residents, found that there is a definite desire on the part of the single young people to have more choice in selecting their marriage partners than the older married people. Of all the single women interviewed, 37 percent wanted complete choice, another 37 percent, some choice and only 26 percent did not want any choice in selecting their husbands. In contrast, 43 percent of young unmarried men wanted complete choice, 50 percent, some choice and only 7 percent wished no part in selecting their spouse. In general, a high proportion of respondents prefer to have more choice in their marriage partners. Ross concludes that "instead of the former practice of parents and relatives making the complete decision or giving their children the opportunity of selecting from a group of picked candidates, now the young people themselves tend to select the person they want to marry, and ask their parent's approval of their choice" (1961: 253).

In his study of 125 Syrian christians of Kerala, Kurian (1961) revealed that nearly two-thirds of marriages are "arranged by the parents with consent of respondents." Nearly one-fourth of the respondents selected their own spouse with the consent of parents and only 7 percent of the sample reported that their marriages were "arranged according to the ideas of parents." Only two respondents made their "own choice without consent of parents." In terms of rural-urban differences, the number of people whose marriages are controlled by parents is slightly more in the rural group over the urban residents. In general, the majority of the respondents enjoyed some degree of freedom in the selection of their spouse reflecting "the slackening of the rigid traditional authority patterns" (Kurian, 1961: 67).

In his recent study of 240 families in Kerala State, Kurian (1974) attempted to find out the qualities that were considered important among wives and husbands, the strength of religions and caste endogamy, and the relative opportunity that the respondents had to acquaint themselves with their future spouse. About 82 percent of the sample wanted marriage within the same religion, 89 percent with individuals of similar economic standards, and nearly 92 percent within the same caste which underscores the relative strength of traditions in mate selection. The male respondents were also asked whether they saw their wives before marriage, and if they saw them, did they have a chance to speak to them. Fifty percent of them had met and spoken to their wives before marriage. In terms of qualities that were considered important in a wife, Kurian listed them in order of importance as follows: good character, obedience, ability to manage home, good cook, take an active part in social and political affairs, education, religion, depending entirely on the husband for major decisions, fair complexion, good companion with similar intellectual interest, and beauty (Kurian, 1974: 355).

The study of Aggarwala (merchant) community in Delhi by M. S. Gore (1968) reveals that 56 percent of respondents feel that marriages should be arranged by elders without consulting either the boy or girl concerned. However, 42 percent of the sample think that marriages must be arranged by parents after the parties involved are consulted. Only two percent of the respondents express that marriages should be decided upon by the boys and girls concerned. A high percentage of urban residents tend to think that marriages should be arranged by parents with consultation of parties involved when compared to rural residents.

Education was considered a major differentiating factor in the attitudes of respondents toward arranged marriages in Gore's study. He found that 73 percent of the respondents without a formal education as against 9 percent with graduate education hold to the traditional arrangement of marriages by elders. That means the more educated a respondent is, the more likely he is to give more freedom to the boy or girl concerned. In summary, he concludes that high education and urban residence are directly related to the attitudes of the respondents in regard to the freedom of choice of the parties to the marriage concerned.

In his study of 200 college male students, B. V. Shah (1961) attempted to examine the attitudes toward the selection of brides and the considerations behind mate selection. Data reveals that only two students would leave the decision of selecting their spouse to the parents. However, nearly two-thirds (66.5 percent) of the respondents select their brides jointly in consultation with the parents. One of the important aspects of the study is that although they would not agree to a match they disapprove of, they would also not finalize a match their parents disapprove of. Thus, they give equal importance to their parents' judgment with regard to the selection of marriage partners. Nearly one-third of the students gave more weight to their decision and would select their spouse even against the wishes of their parents. This fact reveals a tendency toward change in the attitudes of college students·in terms of the degree of freedom they would like to have in selecting their bride.

In his study of teachers, Kapadia finds that nearly 38 percent of the sample claim that they had a choice in selecting their own spouses, but after analyzing the responses he concludes that "the whole data failed to give any idea about the freedom an individual has in the selection of his marriage partners" (Kapadia 1954: 74-75). The Indian Institute of Public Opinion (1955) survey reveals that 29 percent of rural population and 31 percent of urbanites of West Bengal feel that a young man should follow his own inclination if he would like to marry a girl of his own choice. Reviewing the studies of Ross, Kapadia and Indian Institute of Public Opinion, Goode concludes that "the active sentiment in favor of freedom of choice is still fairly low, and the reality of its expression most minimal" (1963: 217).

Cormack (1961) in her study of college students, found that the winds are blowing toward greater freedom. Although 78 percent of the students think that their marriage should be arranged by parents with their consent, about one-fifth of the students favor love marriages. The study also reveals that the traditional normative pattern, which prohibited a prospective bride and groom to see each other until the wedding day, is becoming 'obselete' in most urban areas and among college educated youth.

The traditional arrangement of marriage by the parents of a bride and groom involved has changed to some extent in urban areas. Parents and relatives, mediators, and match-makers are being replaced by anonymous channels of communicatioh. In large urban areas in India and in some foreign countries such as England, U.S.A., Canada and others, one finds advertising in newspapers for a suitable partner a more useful and convenient communication procedure to reach a large segment of the population of their national origin. Kurian observes that advertising has become an established method of finding out a suitable partner (Kurian, 1971: 304). He gives a number of examples of matrimonial advertisements published in a newspaper in Canada to support his argument that both males and females use this method to find prospective spouses. Cormack (1960) also observes that the practices of marriage advertisements is growing in most metropolitan cities in India. They are considered the last, desperate resort to get married. The newspapers have become modern "go-betweens." As many people do not trust the information given in the advertisements, they practice a kind of modified arranged marriage system by checking out the accuracy of the information. Gist also observed how traditional methods of selecting a marriage partner through parental arrangement lost much of its compulsiveness in the city in India and documented how mass media was providing channels through which a wider range of marital choice was made (1953: 54).

The preceding literature indicates a trend toward more freedom among college youth. A vast majority of the students would like their parents to consult them before any final decision is taken over their marriage. Urbanization and education seem to have brought changes in the attitudes of not only college students but also of parents. Also seen in the recent past is the embryonic development of new channels of communication replacing the traditional mechanisms which permitted parents and relatives to arrange marriage for their children. As Vatuk (1972) observed in her study that in recent days the participation and approval of the boys and girls involved are actively sought by the parents.

Methods

Data were collected in the Summer of 1973 from a sample of 182 college students who are classified as juniors and seniors in two colleges of Hyderabad, India: Women's College, Osmania University and Agricultural University. Questionnaires were administered to students by the teachers of these institutions following a brief appraisal of the mechanics of administering the instrument. With regard to the measurement of attitudes toward mate selection, we resorted mostly to the scales developed by J. Henry Korson. Students were asked to respond to a series of questions that would reflect their attitudes toward the traditional and current norms of arranged marriages in India. Background information pertaining to socio-economic and demographic characteristics was also collected to examine the influence of the forces of modernization on the process of mate selection.

For analytical purposes, two categories were established on the basis of fathers' education. The fathers who had high school education or less were collapsed into "low education" category and the fathers who had more than high schooling were grouped under "high education" category. Similarly, for father's income variable, "low income" category consisted of fathers whose annual income was less than 5,000 rupees and "high income" category formed the rest of the parents. On the size of the family variable, the families with 6 or less members were classified into "small family" and the rest were grouped under "large family" category. In dischotomizing the preceding variables, a median was used as the cutting point. For the 'type of community' variable, based on the definition of the Census of India, the students coming from a community of less than 5,000 population were classified as "rural" residents and the students whose community had a population of 5,000 or more were classified as "urban" residents. The students belonging to Kshatriya, Vaisya, and Sudra castes and untouchables were grouped under "non-Brahmin" category.

Findings

In order to determine the degree of change in an arranged marriage system, the students were asked to evaluate the traditional pattern of parents' selecting their future spouse by giving five options. Table I indicates that only about 9 percent of the students expressed strong approval and felt that the present system of marriage should continue unchanged . However, females, Muslims, urban residents, nuclear family members, and the students whose father's education was high and whose father's income was low tended to show strong approval in greater proportion than their counterparts. Fifteen percent of the sample chose the second option which permitted them to generally approve the current system with more freedom to help make the final choice, alhough females, Muslims, urban residents, joint family members, the members of large family size and the students whose father's education was low showed more positive responses to this alternative than their counterparts.

TABLE I

ATTITUDES TOWARD PRESENT SYSTEM OF PARENTS SELECTING SPOUSE FOR THE CHILDREN

(In percentage)

ITEM	N-182	SEX		RELIGION		CASTE		RESIDENCE		FAMILY TYPE		FAMILY SIZE		FATHER'S EDUCATION		FATHER'S INCOME	
		M	F	H	M	B	NB	R	U	J	N	S	L	L	H	L	H
1) I very much approve and feel the system should continue unchanged	8.8	2.8	10.5	6.4	15.9	4.0	5.9	5.1	10.3	4.1	11.0	7.4	3.3	6.0	13.8	9.9	1.7
2) I generally approve although I would like more freedom to help make the final choice	15.0	8.3	16.9	11.8	22.7	12.0	13.7	10.2	17.6	22.4	11.9	11.1	19.7	20.9	10.3	16.9	13.8
3) I should like to be consulted by my parents so that I can make my feelings known	13.7	16.7	19.4	18.2	18.2	18.0	17.6	38.5	12.1	14.3	20.2	14.8	19.7	23.9	16.7	21.1	19.0
4) I feel I should have ultimate power over the final selection	6.9	5.6	7.3	9.1	2.3	18.0	3.9	2.6	8.5	6.1	7.3	9.3	8.2	4.5	10.3	5.6	10.2
5) I feel that although my parents will be consulted, the final choice should be left to me	42.5	63.9	36.3	49.1	25.0	40.0	56.9	43.6	40.3	40.8	43.0	55.6	47.5	40.3	42.3	39.4	53.4
6) No answer	8.1	2.8	9.7	5.4	15.9	6.0	2.0	0.0	11.2	12.2	6.4	1.8	1.6	4.5	7.7	7.0	1.7

In the third option, 18.7 percent of the students wanted their parents to consult them so that they can make their feelings known. The most significant difference was observed when 38.5 percent of rural residents as against 21.1 percent of urban residents indicated this attitude. Differences were also found with nuclear family members, the members of large family size, and the students of highly educated fathers making this choice in higher proportions as compared to their counterparts. Of all the options, the fourth one which would offer the students the "ultimate power over the final selection" received the smallest approval of about 7.0 percent. The major difference was when 18.0 percent of the Brahmins made this choice as against only 3.9 percent of non-Brahmins. Hindus, urban residents and the students whose father's education was high, showed somewhat more positive agreement to have ultimate power in higher proportion. This option indicates that a very small segment of the total sample completely deviated from the traditional marriage system to the extent of exercising autonomous decision-making independent of the parents.

The fifth option which allowed the students to consult their parents and also allowed the final decision to be left to the students, received a high response of 42.5 percent from the students. However, it is observed that a significant proportion of males, Hindus, non-Brahmins, the students from high income parents, members of small families, preferred to have the final choice in the mate selection. The finding that a high proportion of non-Brahmins wished to have final choice in the mate selection is contrary to our expectation. The absence of direct control by parents, relative independence enjoyed in educational institutions, and the novelty of new ideas to which the non-Brahmin students are exposed to for the first time in their family tradition may have contributed to this departure from their expected behavior.

On the basis of the fourth and fifth option it can be argued that about half of the students opined that they should have a definite say over the decision-making process of mate selection. It is also fair to interpret on the basis of the second and third options that one-third of the student body expressed the feeling that they should be consulted by their parents so that they can make their feelings known. The most significant finding of the study is that only a small proportion (8.8 percent) of the sample approved the traditional system of arranged marriage.

As the impact of the forces of modernization on the attitudes of the college youth is only slowly being felt, it is difficult to argue that the attitudes of the students can be taken as measures of their behavior in reality. Hence, the students were asked to respond to the question "to what extent will your parents arrange your marriage for you?" Table II shows the response of the students on four alternative choices. The first option received a favorable response from 10.3 percent of the students indicating that their parents would arrange their marriages without consulting them. In fact, this choice received the smallest percentage of approval than any other option. It is interesting to note that not a single male student expected his parents to arrange a marriage without consulting him, while 13.3 percent of the females indicated that their parents would not consult them at the time of arranging their marriages. Muslims, urban

TABLE II

ATTITUDES TOWARD "WHAT EXTENT WILL YOUR FAMILY ARRANGE YOUR MARRIAGE FOR YOU" (In percentages)

ITEM	N-182	SEX		RELIGION		CASTE		RESIDENCE		FAMILY TYPE		FAMILY SIZE		FATHER'S EDUCATION		FATHER'S INCOME	
		M	F	H	M	B	NB	R	U	J	N	S	L	L	H	L	H
1) Arrange my marriage without consulting me	10.3	13.3	13.3	3.7	26.1	2.1	6.1	5.5	13.0	14.9	7.5	7.4	10.0	6.4	15.4	13.5	5.1
2) Arrange my marriage but I will have some voice in choosing who my mate will be	30.8	19.4	34.2	26.2	32.6	27.1	24.5	30.5	31.5	25.5	33.0	22.2	26.7	32.2	30.8	24.3	32.8
3) Arrange my marriage but I will take initiative in suggesting who my mate should be	17.9	36.1	12.5	22.4	8.7	12.5	28.6	36.1	9.2	19.1	17.9	11.1	31.7	32.2	10.3	18.0	22.4
4) Consider the mater but in the end accept my own choice of mate	31.4	41.7	28.3	40.2	10.9	50.0	36.7	25.0	33.3	29.8	32.1	46.3	30.0	35.8	34.6	28.4	34.5
5) No answer	9.6	2.8	11.7	7.5	15.2	8.3	4.1	2.8	13.0	10.6	9.4	1.8	1.7	3.2	8.9	14.9	5.2

residents, joint family members, the students of highly educated fathers and the students of low income families indicated this choice in higher proportion than their counterparts.

Nearly 31 percent of the students reported that their parents would arrange their marriage but also feel that their parents would give them some voice in choosing their mates. An examination of the data for possible differences among the respondents reveals that a comparatively high percentage of females, nuclear family members and the students of high income families expected the parents to arrange their marriage after hearing their opinion relative to the choice as to who the mate should be.

The third option drew the second highest response of 17.9 percent from the students. This option would give the students initiative in suggesting who their mate should be. It is interesting to note the wide difference between the male and female students, and also between rural and urban residents. Thirty-six percent of the male students compared to 12.5 percent of female and 36.1 percent of the students from rural background as against 9.2 percent urban residents made this choice. In addition, the students of large family size and the respondents whose father's education was high, wished to take initiative in suggesting a future mate in higher proportion than their counterparts.

The fourth option, which indicates that the parents will "consider the matter but in the end accept my own choice of mate," received the highest response of 31.4 percent from the student body. This choice shows greater differences among the respondents. A high percentage of males, Hindus, Brahmins, urban residents, the members of small family size and the students whose father's education was high expressed willingness to make suggestions as to who their mate should be, as to their counterparts. The students who did not answer the question constituted 9.6 percent of the sample.

On the basis of these response patterns, it appears that more and more students would like to have some choice and wish to take initiative in suggesting their future mate, although they prefer their parents to arrange their marriage. In general, the findings thus far suggest that students prefer to have the opportunity of expression in selecting their future mate rather than the decision itself.

It is interesting to observe the difference in the attitudes toward the "present system of parents selecting a spouse for the children" and "to what extent the parents will arrange your marriage for you" among non-Brahmin students. While a substantial number of them would like to have a final choice in the mate selection, a comparatively smaller number of non-Brahmins feel that their choice of mate will be accepted by their parents. It may be due to the fact that they are cognizant to the traditional parental authority and social influence which is difficult to encounter.

In order to determine the roles the students and their parents are expected to play when the time comes for the students to marry, eight alternative choices were provided. Table III shows the percentage distribution of the student responses. With respect to the first option, 7 percent of the sample indicated that

TABLE III

ATTITUDE TOWARD "WHEN THE TIME COMES FOR YOU TO MARRY"
(In percentages)

ITEM	N-182	SEX		RELIGION		CASTE		RESIDENCE		FAMILY TYPE		FAMILY SIZE		FATHER'S EDUCATION		FATHER'S INCOME	
		M	F	H	M	B	NB	R	U	J	N	S	L	L	H	L	H
1) Select a spouse who is completely unknown to you	7.0	0.0	9.1	3.4	16.3	2.0	4.0	5.1	7.6	6.5	3.1	6.0	3.1	6.1	8.9	8.1	3.3
2) Select a spouse who is related to you	7.0	11.1	5.8	6.5	9.3	2.0	12.0	12.8	4.8	15.2	3.7	4.0	6.2	12.1	3.8	9.5	5.0
3) Select a spouse who is the son/daughter of a close friend	2.8	2.5	2.8	2.8	2.3	4.1	2.0	5.1	1.9	4.4	1.8	0.0	3.1	4.5	1.3	5.4	26.7
4) Consult you in choosing a spouse	22.9	36.1	19.0	20.6	23.3	18.4	24.0	35.9	20.0	21.7	23.2	24.0	20.3	19.7	26.6	20.2	3.3
5) Will you have a ultimate power in choosing your spouse	6.5	5.6	4.1	5.6	2.3	2.0	6.0	0.0	5.7	2.2	5.6	10.0	1.6	1.5	3.8	1.4	3.3
6) Will you consult with your parents but make the final choice yourself	23.6	27.8	22.3	30.8	9.3	34.7	28.0	28.2	21.0	21.7	24.1	26.0	23.4	27.3	20.2	24.3	21.7

TABLE III

ATTITUDE TOWARD "WHEN THE TIME COMES FOR YOU TO MARRY" – Continued
(In percentages)

ITEM	N-182	SEX		RELIGION		CASTE		RESIDENCE		FAMILY TYPE		FAMILY SIZE		FATHER'S EDUCATION		FATHER'S INCOME	
		M	F	H	M	B	NB	R	U	J	N	S	L	L	H	L	H
7) Will you make a completely independent choice	5.1	11.1	3.3	6.5	0.0	8.2	6.0	5.1	5.7	10.9	2.8	6.0	6.2	6.1	5.1	4.1	8.3
8) I am uncertain what will happen but will probably leave it to my parents	21.0	2.8	26.4	21.5	20.9	24.5	16.0	7.7	24.8	13.0	25.0	22.0	28.1	19.7	22.8	18.9	23.3
9) No opinion	6.4	2.8	7.4	2.8	16.3	4.1	2.0	0.0	3.6	4.4	7.4	2.0	7.8	3.0	7.6	8.1	5.0

their parents will select a spouse who is completely unknown to them. In terms of the differences it is noticed that no male student responded favorably to this choice while 9.1 percent of the females made this choice. In addition, 16.3 percent of Muslims as against 3.4 percent of Hindus expected their parents to select a spouse completely unknown to them.

In the second option the students were asked to indicate whether their parents would select a spouse who is related to them. In this case, 7.0 percent of the students favored this choice. Non-Brahmins, rural residents, the joint family members and the students whose father's education was high made this option in higher proportion than their counterparts. The third option, which indicates that their parents would select a son/daughter of a close friend, brought forth the smallest percent of 2.5 percent approval.

The fourth option, which indicates that the parents would consult them in choosing their spouse when the time comes for them to marry, received the second highest percentage (22.9) approval of the student body. There appears to be some difference among the students as the responses of males, rural residents, and the students of low income parents were higher over their counterparts. A high percentage of rural residents and students whose father's education was low feel that their parents would consult them in choosing a spouse. A plausible explanation for this finding, which is contradictory to the predicted relationship, is an awareness of the less educated and rural parents the importance of higher education, the conception of independence associated with it, and the idea of differential life styles of the educated influencing them to frequently consult with their children regarding the mate selection. The fifth choice, which offered the students the possibility of having veto power in choosing their future spouse, drew only 6.5 percent response of all the students.

The highest percentage (23.6) of approval of the sample was accorded to the sixth option which indicated that the students would consult their parents but make the final choice themselves. It is observed, however, that the highest percent of response for this alternative was received from Hindus, rural residents and the students of high educated parents. Only 5.1 percent of the students selected the seventh choice which indicated that the students would make a completely independent mate choice. Comparatively, a high percentage of males, Hindus and the members of the joint family system wanted to make an independent choice.

The last option, which indicated that the students are uncertain as to what will happen but would probably leave the decision to their parents, brought forth a response of 21.0 percent of the sample. A high proportion of females, Brahmins, urban residents, nuclear family members and the members of large family size indicated that they would most likely leave it to their parents as they were uncertain. Only 6.4 percent of the students did not answer this question.

No matter who makes the decision pertaining to the youth marriages, all people are expected to marry in India because of religious and social obligations imposed on them. Traditionally, the prospective bride and the groom were never to see each other before their marriage. In order to determine the degree of

TABLE IV

ATTITUDE TOWARD DESIRABILITY TO HAVE THE OPPORTUNITY TO MEET FUTURE SPOUSE
(In percentages)

ITEM	N-182	SEX		RELIGION		CASTE		RESIDENCE		FAMILY TYPE		FAMILY SIZE		FATHER'S EDUCATION		FATHER'S INCOME	
		M	F	H	M	B	NB	R	U	J	N	S	L	L	H	L	H
1) Alone	27.7	29.4	27.3	36.7	8.5	40.4	27.1	23.9	25.0	24.1	31.5	28.8	31.3	26.7	32.5	22.8	42.4
2) With mutual friends	19.1	26.5	17.3	17.4	22.0	15.4	22.9	34.8	14.3	18.5	15.7	21.2	17.0	20.0	16.9	13.9	18.6
3) With family members present	23.7	35.3	20.9	23.9	25.4	21.2	29.2	26.1	25.0	33.3	21.3	28.8	26.9	25.3	20.5	27.8	18.6
4) Not necessary to meet my future spouse before Marriage	19.7	5.9	23.0	14.7	28.8	15.4	14.6	10.9	24.1	16.7	21.3	13.5	14.9	20.0	21.7	21.5	13.6
5) No opinion	9.8	11.5	7.3	15.7	7.7	6.2	4.3	11.6	7.4	10.2	7.7	9.0	8.0	8.0	8.4	13.9	6.8

change in this respect, the students were asked to indicate whether they believed it to be desirable to have the opportunity to meet their future spouse before marriage and were given four alternative choices to respond. Table IV reveals that 27.7 percent of the students wanted to have the opportunity to meet their spouse 'alone' before marriage. Significant differences were observed when a comparatively higher percentage of Hindus, Brahmins, the nuclear family members and the students of high income families made this choice as against their counterparts. Surprisingly, no major difference was observed between the male and the female students.

The second option, which offered the students the opportunity to meet their future spouse in the presence of mutual friends, brought forth 9.1 percent of response from the student body. Comparatively, a high percentage of the males, non-Brahmins and rural residents made this choice. When offered the opportunity of meeting future spouses in the presence of family members, 23.7 percent of the student body gave approval to this choice. In terms of the differences, it is observed that a high proportion of males, non-Brahmins, the joint family members and the students whose father's income is low chose this option.

The last option, which indicated that it was not necessary to meet a future spouse before marriage, was accorded an approval of 19.7 percent of the sample. A large percentage of females, Muslims, urban residents and the students of low income parents did not feel it necessary to meet future spouses, thus revealing some significant differences among the students.

Traditionally, the young people were not given the opportunity to see each other before marriage. To determine the extent of change in this regard, the students were asked to indicate the optimum length of time for knowing the future spouse before marriage. Table V shows the response distribution on four alternative choices. About one-third of the respondents reported that it was not necessary to know the future spouse before marriage, thus upholding the traditional norm. Females, Brahmins, urban residents, the students whose father's education was high and the respondents of low income parents decided to go along with the traditional practice of not knowing the future spouse in high proportions.

The second highest response of 28.0 percent of the students was given to the second option which indicates that the respondents would like to know their future spouse for a period of up to six months. The breakdown of the responses reveals that a high percentage of Hindus, rural residents, the nuclear family members, the students of less educated fathers, and the respondents whose father's education was high made this choice when compared to their counterparts.

Nearly ten percent of the student body indicated a preference for knowing their future spouses for a period of 7-12 months before marriage. Major differences were observed on two demographic characteristics of the students. Males and rural residents made this choice in higher proportions than their counterparts.

TABLE V

OPTIMUM LENGTH OF THE TIME FOR KNOWING FUTURE SPOUSE
(In percentages)

ITEM	N-182	SEX		RELIGION		CASTE		RESIDENCE		FAMILY TYPE		FAMILY SIZE		FATHER'S EDUCATION		FATHER'S INCOME	
		M	F	H	M	B	NB	R	U	J	N	S	L	L	H	L	H
1) Not necessary to know	33.7	27.8	35.2	33.0	36.7	30.2	26.5	17.8	43.9	36.4	33.3	34.6	39.3	37.8	37.9	28.2	17.0
2) 0-6 months	28.0	27.8	28.1	29.4	21.7	29.4	24.5	42.2	21.4	16.4	30.6	36.5	32.8	31.9	24.9	17.9	39.0
3) 7-12 months	9.7	16.7	7.9	11.0	8.3	11.8	14.3	17.8	8.4	7.2	10.8	13.5	13.1	11.1	8.0	41.0	38.9
4) One to two years	11.4	8.3	12.2	11.0	13.3	11.8	10.2	11.1	14.3	16.4	9.9	17.7	9.8	13.9	10.3	6.4	3.4
5) No opinion/ No Answer	17.1	19.4	16.6	15.6	20.0	7.8	24.5	11.1	17.1	23.6	15.3	7.7	11.5	15.3	19.5	6.4	1.7

The third option, which would give the students the opportunity of knowing a future spouse for a period of 1 to 2 years, received a response of 11.4 percent from the students. No major differences were observed in the students' response pattern. A total of 17.1 percent of the student body did not express any opinion on this question. On the basis of these responses, it would appear that about half of the sample would like the opportunity of knowing a future spouse for some period before marriage, thus indicating a change in the attitudes of the students regarding the norms governing the behavior of the prospective bride and the groom before marriage.

Summary and Conclusions

The study was conducted to examine the relationship between the forces of modernization and the arranged marriages. It was assumed that the industrialization, urbanization, high rate of literacy, increased geographical mobility and the expanded occupational structure will affect the attitudes of the college students toward the traditional arrangement of the marriages.

It would appear that change is evident in many aspects of the marriage system. In general, an overwhelming majority of the students wanted more freedom in selecting a future spouse and also wanted their parents to consult them before selecting a spouse so that they can make their feelings known. About half of the sample preferred to take the decision into their own hand and then consult their parents before the marriage is arranged. It suggests that they would like to have some voice in choosing their own mates. A great majority of the students liked to have the opportunity to meet their future spouse before marriage, thus indicating a departure from the tradition which did not allow the prospective bride and the groom to see each other before marriage. A majority of the students also indicated that they wanted to know their future spouse for some time before their marriage, instead of not having any acquaintance as in the traditional days.

Throughout the study it is evident that the liberal views are supported by the male students and the traditional ones are mainly chosen by the female students. Families in India provide greater protection to a girl, do not allow her to go outside alone, socialize her to be a good housewife rather than a career woman, do not encourage her to pursue higher education, and give very little freedom to be independent. Traditionally, it is widely believed that as a child she is protected by her parents, as a married woman she is protected by her husband and as an old person she is protected by her children. For these reasons, it is not surprising to understand why the female students tend to hold on to the traditional marriage system. Boys are given more freedom than the girls even from their childhood. Over the last decades they were encouraged to get a higher education and were encouraged to experience the outside world. As a result, it can be understood why higher proportions of male students manifest greater independence in their attitudes.

The study also reveals that Muslims expressed more conservative attitudes when compared to Hindus pertaining to the present system of marriage. This can be explained by the fact that the proportion of the female students among

Muslims is higher than the male students which resulted in more traditional responses. The fact that the Hindu students are liberal can be explained by the flexibility and "otherness" of Hindu religion. As Spear put it "Hinduism has been likened to a vast sponge, which absorbs all that enters it without ceasing to be itself . . . Hinduism has shown a remarkable power of assimilating as well as absorbing; the water becomes part of the sponge" (1968: 33).

Although the study reveals no significant differences among Brahmin and non-Brahmin students in their attitudes, a trend is observed among them. Non-Brahmin students seem to be more liberal as more of them want to make final the choice in selecting their future spouse. In contrast, when asked to what extent the family would arrange their marriages, a majority of the Brahmins expect their parents would accept their choice of mate. Similarly, Brahmin students would take initiative in consulting their parents but make the final choice themselves when the time comes for them to marry. This independence can be explained by the fact that the Brahmins traditionally are better educated and are employed in non-agricultural occupations in higher proportion when compared to non-Brahmins. The majority of the Brahmin students also wanted to have the opportunity to meet their future spouse alone. But when the opportunity for knowing the future spouse was given, a comparatively large number of Brahmins did not feel it necessary to know the future spouse before marriage.

Residence and the family type have not produced signigicant differences in the attitudes of the college students. However, as a majority of them seen to be liberal in mate selection, it can be argued that the modern values and new life styles may be slowly entering into the rural areas and the joint families, resulting in somewhat uniform attitudes. As the Indian Society is becoming urbanized and industrialized there seems to be a growing recognition of more liberal and individualistic attitudes in the rural areas and the joint families.

The evidence from the study reveals that the small family members are more likely to be liberal in their attitudes when compared to members of the large family which is in the expected direction. The members of the small family expressed a desire for final choice in their mate selection and felt that their parents would accept their own choice of mate.

The level of the father's income seems to be playing an important role in shaping the student's attitudes. The students whose father's income is high show more liberal attitudes in mate selection. They also feel that their parents would accept their own choice of mate and also welcome the opportunity to know their future spouse for some time before the marriage. In contrast, the students whose father's income is low tend to be traditional in their attitude toward arranged marriages.

The father's level of education failed to provide any definite influences on the attitudes of their children who are attending college for higher education. In fact, the data did not even reveal any trend among the respondents. The finding seems to be contrary to a number of studies which documented the influence of education on the attitudes. But as we did not examine the attitudes of parents with different levels of education on arranged marriages, we cannot generalize that evidence to the college students whom we studied. As a matter of fact, the finding that a great majority of the students tend to be liberal in their attitude toward the present system of marriage seems to support the hypothesis advanced by Goode who argues that education which stresses the individualism and equality has more influence on the attitudes than the industrialization itself (1963: 204).

The study reveals that father's education, family type, father's income, and residence have not produced uniform changes in the attitudes of the college students. This result is in contrast to hypothesized relationships which can be explained by Ogburn's (1922) 'cultural lag' thesis which states that two or more interrelated cultural elements can change at different rates of speed. It implies that the college student's attitudes on one dimension of arranged marriage is indicative of a trend toward modernization, whereas on the other dimensions, traditionalism is maintained.

In general, the study supports the thesis that the forces of modernization are resulting in liberal attitudes toward mate selection among the college students. These attitudes are significantly different from the traditional practice of parents selecting a spouse for the child. Further research should be conducted to examine the relationship between covert attitude and overt behavior. Attention should be also directed to assess the social climate that might prevent these attitudes from materializing into reality, the non-functional effects of modernization on the traditional family system, and the impact of social and geographical mobility on arranged marriages.

REFERENCES

Altekar, A. S.
    1962   The Position of Women in Hindu Civilization. Delhi: Motilal Banarsidass.
Auboyer, Jeannine
    1965   Daily Life in Ancient India. New York: MacMillan Company.
Basham, A. L.
    1963   The Wonder That Was India. New York: Hawthorn Books, Inc.
Chekki, D. A.
    1968   "Mate Selection, Age at Marriage, and Propinquity Among the Lingayats of India."
              Journal of Marriage and the Family, 30,(November): 707-711.
Conklin, George H.
    1974   "The Extended Family as an Independent Factor in Social Change." Journal of
              Marriage and the Family, 36, (November): 798-804.
Cormack, Margaret L.
    1961   She Who Rides a Peacock. New York: Praeger.
Fox, Greer Litton
    1975   "Love Match and Arranged Marriage in a Modernizing Nation: Mate Selection in
              Ankara, Turkey." Journal of Marriage and The Family, 37, (February): 180-193.
Gist, Noel P.
    1953   "Mate Selection and Mass Communication in India." Public Opinion Quarterly, 17
              (Winter): 481-495.
Goode, William J.
    1959   "The Theoretical Importance of Love." American Sociological Review, 24,
              (February): 38-47.
    1963   World Revolution and Family Patterns. New York: The Free Press.
    1964   The Family. New York: Prentice-Hall.

81-225

Gore, M. S.
    1969   Urbanization and Family Change. Bombay: Popular Prakash.
Kapadia, K. M.
    1959   "The Family in Transition." Sociological Bulletin, 9 (September).
    1966   Marriage and Family in India. 3rd Edition, Bombay: Oxford University Press.
Korson, J. Henry
    1969   "Student Attitude Toward Mate Selection in a Muslim Society: Pakistan." Journal of
              Marriage and The Family, 31, (February): 153-165.
Kurian, George
    1961   The Indian Family in Transition: A Case Study of Kerala Syrian Christians. Mouton
              and Company.
    1971   "Marriage and Adjustment in a Traditional Society: A Case Study of India." in
              Mahfooz A. Kanwar, The Sociology of Family. Hamden, Connecticut: Linnett Books.
    1974   "Modern Trends in Mate Selection and Marriage with Special Reference to Kerala" in
              George Kurian (ed.), The Family in India: A Regional View. The Hague: Mouton.
Merchant, M. T.
    1935   Changing Views of Marriage and Family. Madras: B. G. Paul.
Ogburn, William F.
    1952   Social Change. New York: Huebsch.
Prabhu, P. H.
    1963   Hindu Social Organization. Bombay: Popular Prakash.
Ross, Aileen D.
    1961   The Hindu Family in its Urban Setting. Toronto: University of Toronto Press.
Shah, B. V.
    1961   "Gjarati College Students and Selection of Bride." Sociological Bulletin, 11
              (March-September): 121-140.
Singer, Milton
    1958   "The Indian Joint Family in Modern Industry." in Milton Singer and Bernard S. Cohen
              (editors), Structure and Change in Indian Society. Chicago: Aldine Publishing
              ₍Company.
Spear, Percival
    1968   India, Pakistan, and the West. London: Oxford University Press.
Vatuk, Sylvia
    1972   Kinship and Urbanization. Berkeley: The University of California Press.

Premarital Sexual Permissiveness of College Students in Hong Kong

VERNON RASCHKE AND ANGELINA LI*

Although Hong Kong is a British colony it is a Chinese community with 98% of its population of Chinese origin whose ways of thinking and acting are rooted in Chinese culture. Since World War II the process of modernization—urbanization and industrialization—as well as westernization have affected most aspects of social life in Hong Kong, including the family. Researchers have noted the impact of these changes on many aspects of family life, including: parent-child relations (Wong, S, L., 1970; Liu, 1966), parental influence over occupational choice (Podmore and Chaney, 1973), family interactions and husband-wife relations (Liu, 1966; Mitchell, 1972), family planning (Mitchell, 1972), nuclear vs. extended family orientations (Wong, F. M., 1972), norms and preferences regarding premarital interactions and mate selection (Podmore and Chaney, 1972; Stoodley, 1967).

While all these studies of family norms, values and behaviors in Hong Kong do indicate that the family has indeed been affected by modernization and Westernization, they also indicate that the family in Hong Kong remains strongly influenced by traditional Chinese culture. The present study compares the premarital sexual permissiveness of college students in Hong Kong and college students in the United States. Much sociological research indicates that sexual attitudes like all attitudes are learned (Reiss, 1967, pp. 23-24); therefore, we expect that persons growing up in cultures as diverse as Hong Kong and the American midwest would have different attitudes toward premarital sexual permissiveness.

After checking to see whether Reiss' (1967) Premarital Sexual Permissiveness scales work as Guttman scales in a culture as different from the United States as Hong Kong, this research seeks to test the following hypotheses:

1. Although English-speaking college students in Hong Kong have been influenced by western ideas (Wong, S. L., 1970) they are still likely to be strongly influenced by their parents regarding mate selection (Stoodley, 1967), to accept parental authority (Cansdale, 1969), to accept sex segregation in the schools (Podmore and Chaney, 1972), and to interact with the other sex in groups rather than privately in pairs. Hence, we hypothesized that the students in Hong Kong would be less sexually permissive, less sexually active, and hold more of a double standard concerning premarital sex than American students.

*Dept. of Sociology, Old Dominion University, Norfolk, Virginia, U.S.A.

2.   That students from Hong Kong studying in America will be somewhere between the American students and the Chinese students living in Hong Kong in their level of premarital sexual permissiveness because the students from Hong Kong studying in America will be influenced by both the less permissive Chinese values and the more permissive American values.

3.   That certain determinants of sexual permissiveness found by Ira Reiss and others to hold for Americans will also hold for the college students in Hong Kong. We hypothesize this not only because we expect these determinants of premissive-ness to hold universally, but also because the Hong Kong students in our sample were all from English-speaking colleges and hence can be expected to be more like American students in attitudes and values than students in Chinese-speaking colleges in Hong Kong.

The specific determinants of premarital sexual permissiveness to be tested are:

(a)   Males will be more permissive than females (Reiss, 1967, p. 98).

(b)   Older students will be more permissive than young students (Reiss, 1967, p. 125).

(c)   Respondents who have younger siblings will be less permissive because responsibility for those siblings will be a retardant to their level of permissiveness (Reiss, 1967, pp. 153-155).

(d)   Reiss (1967, pp. 165-168) found that respondents whose parents are more highly educated and whose families have higher incomes are more permissive regarding premarital sex. We expect this to be especially true of the respondents because of the likelihood that higher status families in Hong Kong have been more influenced by western ideas and ways of living than lower status families (Wong, S. L., 1970).

(e)   Reiss (1967, p. 168) found that students who live with their parents were less permissive than students who did not live with their parents. Again, we expect this to be especially true of students in Hong Kong who live with their parents because their parents would be better able to influence these respondents to maintain traditional Chinese values.

(f)   Even though Chinese students are more likely to date in groups than in single pairs and less likely to be going steady or to be engaged than American students (Stoodley, 1967, p. 778; Podmore and Chaney, 1972, p. 235) we expect to find that the more actively the student is involved in the courtship process the more permissive he/she will be (Reiss, 1967, pp. 82-85).

(g)   We hypothesize that as in the United States (Clayton, 1971) the students who are sexually active will be more permissive regarding premarital sex than those who are not sexually active.

(h)   Although the role of religion as a determinant of sexual permissiveness in the United States seems to be changing (Walsh, et al., 1974) most researchers still find that being religious, however that is defined or measured, is associated with lower levels of sexual permissiveness (Raschke, 1972, p. 2). Therefore, we expect that Chinese students who report being Christian will be less permissive than those reporting that they are atheists.

(i) Respondents who attended English-speaking grade and high schools will be more permissive than those who attended Chinese-speaking grade aud high schools because the English schools are considered less traditional and conservative than Chinese schools (Wong, S. L., 1970).

Method

The data for the American students were collected from the students of a large introductory sociology class of non-sociology majors at the University of Minnesota, Minneapolis, in November 1971. This resulted in an American sample of 264 American, never-married, Caucasian students between the ages of 18 and 22. Henceforth this sample will be referred to as the "American sample."

The data for the Hong Kong students who attended American universities and colleges were collected on the plane during a chartered flight from Hong Kong to Oakland, California, in January 1973. There were 56 students on the flight who completed the questionnaire. After excluding married students and those over 22 years of age this resulted in a sample of 26 never-married, Chinese students between the ages of 18 and 22 who were from Hong Kong attending American schools. Henceforth, the "Airplane sample."

The data for the Hong Kong students attending schools in Hong Kong were collected in January 1973, at the University of Hong Kong, Hong Kong Baptist College, and New Asia College, all of which are English-speaking schools. Altogether 173 questionnaires were completed in Hong Kong. This resulted in a sample of 153 never-married, Chinese students between the ages of 18 and 22 who attended school in Hong Kong; henceforth, the Chinese sample."

The principal instrument used was Reiss' (1967) seven-item Premarital Sexual Permissiveness Scale. Other variables measured were nationality, religious preference, city of residence, class in school, age, sex, number of siblings, type of elementary and high school attended, parents' education and income, whether the respondent lives with parents while in school and out of school, amount of courtship participation, whether the respondent had petted to orgasm during the past year, and whethear the respondent had sexual intercourse during the past pear.

Before going to Hong Kong the investigator pretested the instrument using four students who were recently from Hong Kong and attending an American college to see whether the items concerning sexual attitudes and behaviors would be meaningful to Chinese students. The instrument was found to meaningful in that these students felt that the terminology used in the items to designate behaviors and relationships would be understood by the students in Hong Kong and that these behaviors and relationships were experienced by students in Hong Kong.

Statistical procedures used in the analysis were comparisons of means, Guttman scale analysis, Pearson's product-moment correlation, and step-wise multiple regression.

The data used here is ordinal data for Guttman sexual permissiveness scales, as well as for some of the control variables. Most of the control variables were dichotomous and coded "0" and "1" so that regression analysis could be used as an equivalant to analysis of variance and covariance (Cohen, 1968). The reasons for using linear regression and correlation techniques instead of specifically ordinal measures of association include: (1) the use of more powerful, sensistive, better developed, and interpretable statistics with known sampling error, (2) the retention of more knowledge about the characteristics of the data, and (3) greater versatility in statistical manipulation (e.g., partial and multiple correlation and regression, analysis of variance and covariance, and most pictorial presentations) (Labovitz, 1970). Labovitz (1967, 1970) has demonstrated that treating any ordinal data as interval usually results in very little error and that scales such as the Guttman and Likert scales used in the present research really produce data that lies somewhere between ordinal and interval data (Somers, 1962); and interval techniques may be applied with even greater confidence in such cases.

Richard Boyle (1971) writes that errors occurring because of ordinal data being used as interval data are not likely to be great because they are due to coincidences of error, rather than magnitudes of error in estitmating intervals. He also points out that:

> Since most sociological research works with rather low-order correlations, this suggests that the dangers of assuming equal intervals are in addition to being conservative, not likely to be huge. (Boyle, 1971, p. 435).

Findings

We found that Reiss' Permissiveness scales did work as Guttman scales for the Chinese respondents. From Table 1 we see that for all the samples the

TABLE 1   GUTTMAN SCALE STATISTICS FOR REISS' PREMARITAL PERMISSIVENESS SCALES

	American Sample	Airplane Sample	Chinese Sample
Sample Size	264	26	153
FOR THE MALE REFERENT ITEMS :			
Coefficient of reproducibility	.98	.95	.92
Minimum marginal reproducibility	.75	.66	.67
Percent improvement	.23	.29	.25
Coefficient of scalability	.91	.84	.76
FOR THE FEMALE REFERENT ITEMS :			
Coeffieient of reproducibility	.97	.97	.93
Minimum marginal reproducibility	.74	.67	.66
Percent improvement	.23	.30	.27
Coefficient of scalability	.90	.90	.79

In each of the three samples some of the items were endorsed by either more or less than the commonly accepted (Guttman, 1974, pp. 159-160) 20 to 80% of the respondents. However, in the Chinese and Airplane samples there were at least six of the seven items endorsed by 20 to 80% of the respondents; with the American sample five of the seven items were endorsed by 20 to 80% of the respondents. Mirande and Hammer (1974) argue that the statistics of internal consistency of Reiss' 12-item Premarital Sexual Permissiveness scales are inflated by the extreme endorsement marginals of some of the items. Reiss (1974) responded that the coefficient of scalability being above .60 is one means of insuring that the coefficient of scalability is not artificially inflated.

The item order for the 7-item Sexual Permissiveness scales used in the present research remained the same for all three samples; this gives added support for the validity of these scales.

commonly accepted minimum criteria for Guttman scales were met; namely, that the coefficient of reproducibility be at least .90 and the coefficient of scalability be above .60.

From Table 2 we see that the Chinese sample scored much lower on sexual permissiveness than the American sample and the Airplane sample scored very

TABLE 2   MEAN PREMARITAL SEXUAL PERMISSIVENESS SCORES

	American Sample	Airplane Sample	Chinese Sample
Sample Size	264	26	153
Percent male	45.4	50.0	41.8
Mean scores for male referent items (Range=0—7)	4.63	4.31	2.90
Mean scores for female referent items (Range=0—7)	4.41	4.23	2.53
Difference between the mean for male referent items and the mean for female referent items	.22	.08	.37

close to the American sample. Looking at the difference between the permissiveness scores for the male and female referent items we see that the difference was .22 for the American sample, .08 for the Airplane sample, and .37 for the Chinese sample. This indicates that for all three samples, when male and female respondents are combined, there is a male-female double standard concerning premarital sex and that the Chinese students hold to more of a double standard than the American students while the students forming the Airplane sample seem to be most egalitarian.

When we separated the males from the females in the samples and made these comparsions to see how males regarded premarital sexual permissiveness for males and for females and to see how females regarded premartial sexual permissiveness for both males and females we found even greater differences regarding the double standard. The male and female Chinese students were found to hold more of a double standard than the male and female American students while the male and female students from Hong Kong studying in the United States were the most egalitarian. (It must be remembered, however, that the Airplane sample is quite small.)

Table 3 shows that the Chinese sample is much less sexually active than the American sample. The fact that there are such great differences between the

TABLE 3   PERCENT WHO PETTED TO ORGASM OR HAD COITUS DURING
THE PAST YEAR

	American Sample	Airplane Sample	Chinese Sample
Sample Size	264	26	153
Percent who petted to orgasm during the past year	61.7	65.4	13.8
Percent who had coitus during the past year	42.6	42.3	5.9

Chinese and American samples regarding premarital sexual permissiveness and activity seems to indicate that the Chinese are not at all completely Westernized regarding sexual attitudes and behaviors. Interestingly, the Airplane sample was as sexually active as the American sample. This may be partly accounted for by the fact the Airplane students live so far from their homes and parental supervision while attending school. Again we must bear in mind that the Airplane sample of 26 is too small to be very reliable.

The remainder of our findings concern the Chinese sample only:

(a) Males were found to be more permissive than females for both male and female referent items. Being male correlated .42 (p. < .001) and .35 (p. <. 001) with the male and female referent permissiveness items, respectively.

(b) Older students, as indicated by being in the upper classes of school, were more permissive than younger students. Class in school correlated .18 (p. < .05) and .21 (p. < .01) for the male and female referent items, respectively.

(c) No significant relationships were found between premarital sexual permissiveness and having younger siblings. Perhaps this is because so few (5.9%) Chinese students have engaged in premarital sex during the past year that they don't see premarital sexual activity as a realistic threat to their younger brothers and sisters and hence are not concerned about protecting them from it.

(d) No significant relationships were found between parental levels of education and permissiveness. However, family income was positively related to permissiveness as hypothesized. Family income correlated .20 (p. < .05) and .22 (p. < .05) with the male and female referent permissiveness scales, respectively. It is possible that it is parental income, rather than the number of years of formal education parents have received, which is the better indicator of westernization.

(e) No significant relationships were found between sexual permissiveness and whether the respondents lived with their parents. The reason no significant relationships were found may be that nearly all of the respondents (87%) did live with their parents while attending college.

(f) Courtship participation was considered high if the respondent reported dating one person exclusively, being engaged to be married, or was living with a friend of the opposite sex to whom he/she was not related; this represents 21% of the sample. Courtship participation was considered low if the respondent reported dating several different people regularly, dating different people occasionally, dating one person occasionally, or never dating; 79% were low on courtship participation. While high courtship participation was positively correlated with sexual permissiveness the findings were not significant.

(g) We found that whether or not the respondent had petted to orgasm during the past year or had sexual intercourse was positively correlated with permissiveness. Petting to orgasm correlated .28 (p. < .001) and .27 (p. < .001) with permissiveness for the male and female referent items, respectively. Having had sexual intercourse correlated .34 (p. < .001) and .22 (p. < .01) with permissiveness for the male and female referent items, respectively.

(h) We had hypothesized that atheists would be more permissive regarding premarital sex than Christians. Table 4 shows that this hypothesis was not

TABLE 4   MEAN PREMARITAL SEXUAL PERMISSIVENESS SCORE
                                              BY RELIGIOUS PREFERENCE

Religious Preference	Mean Permissiveness Scores
Christian (N = 54)	3.00
Atheist (N = 55)	2.98
Agnostic (N = 5)	3.40
Buddhist (N = 8)	2.00
Other (N = 31)	2.74

supported, in fact, the Christians are slightly more permissive than the atheists. The reason for this may be that the underlying determinant here is not religion but traditionality. The Buddhists are the most traditional and the least permissive group. Those who claimed to be atheist or agnostic were probably students who had rejected the traditional Buddhism of their parents but were still influenced by the traditionalism of their parents in other areas of life. Unfortunately, we did not ask the respondents to give the religion of their parents or their own religious history so that this could be checked out further.

(i) We hypothesized that students who had attended English grade and/or high schools would be more permissive than those who attended Chinese schools because the English schools are probably more westernized and because the more traditional Chinese families would be more likely to send their children to Chinese schools. However, no significant relationships were found between premarital sexual permissiveness and whether or not the respondent attended English or Chinese grade and/or high school. The reason no significant relationships were found may be that all the respondents were presently attending English-speaking colleges and 75% had also attended English-speaking high schools. Although 80% of the respondents had attended Chinese-speaking elementary schools, most of the respondents had been oriented toward English-speaking schools since the beginning of high school. To more adequately test the hypothesis that students attending English-speaking schools are more permissive than those attending Chinese-speaking schools we would need a sample of students currently attending a Chinese-speaking college.

Finally, we used step-wise multiple regression to find out what are the most important determinants of sexual permissiveness. Those independent variables were retained which explained at least 1% of the variance in the permissiveness scores.

From Table 5 we see that the three most important determinants of both male and female referent sexual permissiveness are, in order: respondent's sex, exper-

TABLE 5   MULTIPLE REGRESSION TABLES

		Dependent variable :	
		Male referent permissiveness scores	
Independent variables :			
	Beta	Pearson's r	F
Respondent is male	.391	.40	31.69[2]
Had coitus last year	.275	.33	15.82[2]
Year in school	.232	.20	11.36[2]
Percent of variance accounted for : $R^2 = .30$			

		Dependent variable :	
		Female referent permissiveness scores	
Independent variables :			
	Beta	Pearson's r	F
Respondent is male	.408	.40	32.73[2]
Had coitus last year	.269	.23	14.43[2]
Year in school	.156	.22	4.82[1]
Percent of variance accounted for : $R^2 = .26$			

[1]probability is less than .05
[2]probability is less than .01

ience of premarital intercourse, and year in college. These three independent variables account for .30% of the variance in the male referent premarital sexual permissiveness scores and .26% of the variance in the female referent scale scores.

Conclusion

This research comparing American and Chinese students has found that Reiss' Premarital Sexual Permissiveness Scales worked as Guttman scales for the Chinese students, that Chinese students in Hong Kong are less permissive and less active concerning premarital sex, and that the majority of determinants of premarital sexual permissiveness found by Reiss and others to hold for Americans also hold as determinants of permissiveness for Chinese students. Those determinants of sexual permissiveness which did not hold in a statistically significant manner for Chinese students were, however, in the predicted direction for the most part.

It must be remembered that the samples used were not randomly selected and that the use of inferential statistics in this research was for heuristic, rather than strictly scientific purposes.

We also found that the Chinese students who were studying in America tended to adopt American standards of sexual behavior and attitudes regarding premarital sex.

REFERENCES

Boyle, Richard P.
    1971   "Path Analysis and Ordinal Data." In H.M. Blalock (Ed.,), Causal Models in the Social Sciences. Chicago: Aldine-Atherton, pp. 432-452.

Cansdale, J.S.
    1969   "Cultural Problems of Chinese Students in a Western Type University." In I.C. Jarvie (Ed.), Hong Kong: A Society in Transition. London: Routledge & Kegan Paul, pp. 345-360.

Clayton, Richard R.
    1971   "Religiosity and Premarital Sexual Permissiveness: Elaboration of the Relationship and Debate." Sociological Analysis, Vol. 32:81-96.

Cohen, Jacob
    1968   "Multiple Regression as a General Data-Analytic System." Psychological Bulletin, Vol. 70, No. 6, pp. 426-443.

Guttman, Louis L.
    1974   "The Basis for Scalogram Analysis." In Gary M. Maranell (Ed.), Scaling: A Source book for Behavioral Scientists. Chicago: Aldine Publishing Co., pp. 142-171.

Labovitz, Sanford
    1967   "Some Observations on Measurement and Statistics." Social Forces, (Dec), Vol. 46, pp. 151-160.

Labovitz, Sanford
    1970   "The Assignment of Numbers to Rank Order Categories." American Sociological Review, Dec. Vol. 35, pp. 515-524.

Liu, William T.
    1966   "Family Interactions Among Local and Refugee Chinese Families in Hong Kong." Journal of Marriage and the Family, Vol. 28 (August), pp. 314-323.

Mirande, Alfred M., and Elizabeth L. Hammer
  1974   "Premarital Sexual Permissiveness: A Research Note." Journal of Marriage and the Family, May, Vol. 36, No. 2, pp. 356-358.

Mitchell, Robert E.
  1972   "Husband-Wife Relations and Family Planning Practices in Urban Hong Kong." Journal of Marriage and the Family, Vol. 34 (February), pp. 139-146.

Nie, Norman H., Dale H. Bent, and C.H. Hull
  1970   Statistical Package for the Social Sciences. New York: McGraw-Hill Book Company.

Podmore, David, and David Chaney
  1972   "Attitudes Toward Marriage and the Family Amongst Young People in Hong Kong, and Comparisons with the United States and Taiwan." Journal of Comparative Family Studies, Autumn, Vol 3(2), pp. 228-238.

Podmore, David, and David Chaney
  1973   "Parental Influence on the Occupational Choice of Young Adults in Hong Kong, and Comparisons with the United States, the Philippines and Japan." International Journal of Comparative Sociology, Vol. XIV (1-2), p. 104-113.

Raschke, Vernon J.
  1972   Religiosity and Sexual Permissiveness. Unpublished Ph.D. thesis, University of Minnesota.

Reiss, Ira L.
  1965   The Social Context of Premarital Sexual Permissiveness. New York: Holt, Rinehart & Winston.

Reiss, Ira L.
  1974   "Comments on 'Premarital Sexual Permissiveness'." Journal of Marriage and the Family, August, Vol. 36, No. 3, pp. 445-446.

Somers, Robert H
  1962   "A New Asymmetric Measure of Association." American Sociological Review, Dec, Vol. 27, pp. 799-811.

Stoodley, Bartlett H
  1967   "Normative Family Orientations of Chinese College Students in Hong Kong." Journal of Marriage and the Family, Vol. 29 (November), pp. 773-782.

Walsh, Robert, William Tolone, Wilbert Leonard, Marry Ferrel, and Dovie Bryant
  1974   "An Eight Year Study of Attitudes About Sexual Permissiveness." An unpublished paper delivered at the National Council on Family Relations meeting in St. Louis, MO, October 1974.

Wong, Fai-Ming
  1972   "Modern Ideology, Industrialization and Conjugalism: The Hong Kong Case." Internatio nal Journal of Sociology of the Family, Vol. 2(2), pp. 139-150.

Wong, Shau-Lam
  1970   "Social Change and Parent-Child Relations in Hong Kong." In Reuben Hill and Rene Konig (Eds.), Families in East and West. Paris: Mouton, pp. 167-174.

Attitudes Towards Marriage and the Family Amongst Young People in Hong Kong, and Comparisons with the United States and Taiwan§

DAVID PODMORE ‡ AND DAVID CHANEY †

A link between industrialisation and a particular set of attitudes has been claimed by sociologists of the "convergence" school such as A. Inkeles. Inkeles has argued that the environment created by large scale bureaucratic industrial systems moulds the values, attitudes and perceptions of individuals.[1] These values, attitudes and perceptions are standardised from one industrial society to another, despite the randomising influences of traditional cultural patterns. In his more recent work[2] Inkeles has presented evidence—based on 6,000 interviews with men from six developing countries in three continents—to show that "there is a set of personal qualities which reliably cohere as a syndrome and which identify a type of man who may validly be described as fitting a reasonable theoretical conception of modern man."[3] Inkeles goes on to argue that " what defines a man as modern in one country also defines him as modern in another,"[4] and that " one must be struck by the exceptional stability with which variables such as education, factory experience and urbanism maintain the absolute and relative strength of their impact on individual modernisation despite the great variation in the culture of the men under-going the experience and in the levels of development characterising the countries in which they live."[5]

This view, that there is an underlying logic in the process of industrialisation which means that industrial societies (and developing societies as they industrialise) become more and more similar in terms of both their social structures and the attitudes and values of their members, has attracted a number of social scientists.[6] W. E. Moore has summarised this " convergence " approach : " The essential idea is that a commercial-industrial system imposes certain organisational and institutional requirements not only on the

§The research on which this paper is based was carried out when the authors were members of the Department of Sociology, University of Hong Kong, and was financed by a grant from the Nuffield Foundation through the Centre of Asian Studies, University of Hong Kong. Acknowledgement is made to Frank H. H. King, Director of the Centre and to Andrew L. C. Lu, formerly of the Centre of Asian Studies, Hong Kong now of the Social Research Centre, Chinese University of Hong Kong.

‡Lecturer in Sociology, Department of Industrial Administration, University of Aston, England.

†Lecturer in Sociology, Department of Sociology and Social Administration, University of Durham, England.

economy but also on many other aspects of society."[7] Industrial societies, he has argued, will increasingly share a " common culture."[8]

In our view, the approach taken by "convergence" theorists such as Moore and Inkeles does not distinguish with sufficient clarity between *structural features* (institutions), *attitudes* (of individuals) and the *adaptive processes* (for example a stress on individualism or achievement-orientation) which result from individuals' adjustment to structural changes. We content that the structural features of industrial societies may become more similar, i. e. converge, whilst attitudes and adaptive processes may remain diverse, although we do not deny the interdependency of structure, attitudes and adaptive processes such that there is in the long term a strain towards consistency.

Not all sociologists share the " convergence" view. H. Blumer has written that : "... the evidence points clearly to the conclusion that industrialisation, by its very make-up, can have no definite social effect."[9] J. H. Goldthorpe[10] has similarly argued against the " convergence " view, whilst in his recent work Moore has expressed doubts about the creation of a common culture by the industrialisation process and now argues that industrial societies are characterised by a variety of social structures.[11] Plural social structures will persist in industrial societies as a result of the wide cultural variations between societies prior to industrialisation and because societies industrialise at different time-periods, using different models—" capitalist", " socialist ", " mixed " etc.[12] R. Bendix traces the genesis of the opposed " convergence " or common culture approach to the technological determinism of Karl Marx and Thorstein Veblen,[13] and against Marx and Veblen quotes Joseph Schumpeter : " Social structures, types and attitudes are coins that do not readily melt..."[14]

We do not wish to consider here the detailed arguments of the opposing schools of thought in the " convergence—divergence " debate.[15] We believe that industrialisation lessens cultural differences in that associated with industrialisation are changes in values, attitudes and beliefs in a common direction, that is, values etc., become more " modern ". Industrial technology in effect limits the possibilities open to societies. On the specific question in which we are interested, for example, Moore has written that " Both mate selection and parent-child relationships are affected by the " individualism " that industrialisation fosters, even in societies with a collectivist ideology. Marriage by arrangement......is virtually certain to disappear.....and voluntary mate selection to appear in its stead ... some " tension " between the generations, even before children leave their parental families, is virtually inevitable,"[16] Moore is writing here about structural changes and adaptive processes rather than attitudes themselves, but the point he is making is well taken—that industrial technology has consequences for social processes as well as for social institutions.

At this stage we will distinguish between those often-abused terms " industrialisation", " modernisation " and " westernisation." When using the term " industrialisation " we are referring to a purely economic process, removed from non-economic and secondary connotations[17]. " Modernisation" involves the acquisition by a society of the social-structural features which characterise industrial societies, whilst " modern attitudes " are those essential to the acceptance of the industrial way of life, though not necessarily *caused* by industrialisation. A difficulty in any discussion of industrialisation and modernisation in developing countries lies in a third concept, that of "westernisation", since norms, values and attitudes may be modern (i. e. associated with the imperatives of the industrial way of life) without being westren (i. e. similar to those found in Westren European societies). To a considerable extent, of course, the categories of modern and western overlap, but it is possible to envisage norms, values and attitudes which are modern but not western. In China, the revolution is modernising society whilst consciously rejecting westernisation. (This observation is not true of the Soviet Union).

There is considerable evidence from Japan of the emergence of particular social-structural features and a normative structure which are modern, in that they are associated with an industrial system, but are definitely not western.[18] Similarly it may be that societies can be identified as having adopted many of the social-structural characteristics, norms, values and attitudes associated with Western European Societies without having also adopted widespread industrial technology.

We were able to test the broad proposition mentioned above in the course of a survey (carried out in 1969) of young people in Hong Kong. 1,123 young people aged 15–29 were interviewed, a representative sample of those living in the metropolitan areas of Hong Kong and Kowloon. In our questionnaire a number of attitude items derived from an earlier study by R. M. Marsh and A. R. O'Hara, using Asian and United States subjects, were included.[19] The items were concerned with attitudes towards marriage and family behaviour, and the results are discussed below.

Marsh and O'Hara's study was based on samples of United States and Taiwanese students. We hypothesised that young people in Hong Kong would be more modern in their attitudes than the Taiwanese students, but less modern than those in the United States.[20] This hypothesis is derived from our observation that Hong Kong is a more industrialised society than Taiwan, but less so than the United States, using three general indicators (see below). In view of the possibility, already mentioned, that societies may be modern in terms of having similar social structural characteristics, etc., but without having reached the same degree of industrial development, we formulated a second hypothesis that Hong Kong respondents and Taiwanese students will display generally *similar* attitudes, despite the different extent to which each society is industrialised. We argue that respondents' attitudes will reflect the strong influence of western life-styles in the two societies. We are very conscious of the pervasiveness of western, and more particularly American, culture and life-styles in both Taiwan and Hong Kong, especially amongst educated elite groups (this is probably true for much of South-East Asia).[21] In the last 20 years their special geo-political situations have forced Taiwan and Hong Kong into a close association with the United States and into an increasing dependence on American culture. This factor of westernisation and orientation towards the United States may, we suggest, be more important in determining attitudes in the short term than the influence of modernisation.   This is why we have formulated an alternative hypothesis. Although macro-social changes such as modernisation may be influential over a long period of time, attempts to understand a particular situation at a particular time are most successful when such special factors are also taken into account.

In order to test our first hypothesis, some general indicators are necessary of the relative extent of industrialisation in the United States, Hong Kong and Taiwan.   Most economists agree about the particular economic features which are associated with industrial societies e. g. a high average per capita income ; a technology based on the use of inanimate power ; and occupational structure containing a high proportion of white-collar and managerial employees.

We have chosen three economic indices, for all of which the United States is more highly-industrialised than Hong Kong, which in turn is more highly industrialised than Taiwan.[22]

(1) Occupational Structure

Colin Clark has argued that the distribution of a country's employed population between primary, secondary and tertiary occupations is a useful index of the extent to which that country is industrialised.[23]   The more industrialised the society, the more important the tertiary sector of the economy.   This is, of course, a crude index and it has been criticised, particularly as applied to relatively primitive economics, but it will serve our needs here.[24]

TABLE 1

Distribution of Employed Population (percentages)

	Primary Occupations	Secondary Occupations	Tertiary Occupations
United States	7	32	60
Hong Kong	5	45	50
Taiwan	43	23	33
		(Data for 1966)	

Sources :   *United States*—U. S. Bureau of the Census: *Statistical Abstract of the United States, 1967* (Washington, D. C., 1967)

Hong Kong—Commissioner for Census and Statistics : *Report of the By-Census, 1966* (Hong Kong, 1968)

Taiwan—United Nations: *Economic Survey of Asia and the Far East, 1968* (Bangkok, 1969)

(2) The Application of Inanimate Power

The widespread use of inanimate power in the process of production (and elsewhere) has long been regarded as a characteristic feature of industrial society.[25]   Of the prodigious use of electric energy, gas and more recently, nuclear energy in the industrial societies Raymond Aron writes : " Modern societies seem to belong to a completely new type, precisely because of their energy potential ".[26]

Table 2 shows the per capita production of electrical energy in 1968 in the United States, Hong Kong and Taiwan.

TABLE 2

Electrical Energy Produced
(kilowatt hours per capita per annum)

United States	8260
Hong Kong	1005
Taiwan	745

(Data for 1968)

Source: *United Nations Statistical Year Book 1969* (New York, 1970)

(3) Wealth

The more industrialised a society, the higher the per capita Gross Domestic Product. Cross-national comparisons of wealth are notoriously unreliable, but Table 3 gives an approximate indication of the per capita G. D. P. for three societies.

TABLE 3

Per Capita Gross Domestic Product (in US)

United States	4280	(Data for 1968)
Hong Kong	680	(Data for 1969)
Taiwan	304	(Data for 1969)

Sources : *United States*—U. S. Bureau of the Census: *Statistical Abstract of the United States, 1969* (Washington, D. C. 1969)

Hong Kong and Taiwan—data quoted by Lee Kuan Yew, Prime Minister of Singapore, in an address to the 75th Congregation of the University of Hong Kong 18 February 1970. See:

University of Hong Kong Gazette Vol. XVII, No. 4, p. p. 50-54, 19 February 1970.

Comparison of the United States, Taiwanese and Hong Kong Responses

Marsh and O'Hara contrasted traditional Chinese patterns of family and marriage with modern Western patterns, using the well-established sociological generalisations shown in Table 4.[27]

During the period 1954–58, Marsh and O'Hara administered a questionnaire to students in two universities in Taipei, Taiwan, and in 1959 to students at the University of Michigan in the United States. The questionnaire was composed of items derived from the six contrasting patterns of family life listed above. We repeated Marsh and O'Hara's questions to our sample of young adults living in the urban areas of Hong Kong and Kowloon. The pattern of response for American and Taiwanese students and our young adults is shown in Table 5. Marsh and O'Hara's data indicate that Americans display more modern attitudes than Taiwanese—the differences for all items are significant at the 5% level or better. As expected, American students also show more modern attitudes than the Hong Kong respondents, differences for all items are again significant at the 5% level. Our hypothesis that Hong Kong respondents would be more modern than Taiwanese is supported for items 4 and 6 only, where the differences are significant at the 5% level. For

TABLE 4

Contrasting Patterns of Marriage and Family Life

" Traditional Chinese " Pattern	" Modern Western " Pattern
1. Parental control of the selection of a spouse.	1. Greater freedom from parental control.
2. Separation of the sexes, from puberty to marriage, in formal education and other spheres.	2. Increasingly frequent, intimate and open interaction between the sexes.
3. Absence of dating, courtship and engagement as the institutionalised transition from the family of orientiation to the family of procreation.	3. Dating, courtship, and engagement and their gradual diffusion to progressively younger groups.
4. Irrelevance of romantic love as an institutionalised basis of selection.	4. Romantic love institutionalised as the basis of marriage.
5. Patrilocal residence, as an ideal.	5. Separate local residence of each couple, both ideally and actually.
6. Subordination to the husband's parents and family, and especially of the wife to her mother-in-law.	6. The couple's relatively greater independence of the husband's parents and family and the wife's of her mother-in-law.

(adapted from Marsh and O'Hara, op. cit. p. p. 1–2)

item 5, however, Hong Kong respondents give a significantly more traditional response than those in Taiwan.   Our alternative hypothesis, that Hong Kong and Taiwanese respondents would display similar attitudes, is confirmed for items 1, 2 and 3.   Controlling for education—the Taiwanese respondents were University students and we identified as sub group of similar educational attainment amongst our Hong Kong respondents—merely confirmed these findings.

TABLE 5

Attitudes Towards Marriage and the Family
(percentages agreeing with the statement)

	United States Respondents	Taiwanese Respondents	Hong Kong Respondents
(i) *Romantic Love Ideal*			
1. " Marriage should be based on love; there should be love before marriage."	98	92	91
(ii) *Separation of the Sexes*			
2. " Sexes should not be separated at social gatherings."	96	87	82
3. " Sexes should not be separated in primary schools."	94	84	79
4. " Sexes should not be separated in secondary schools."	95	45	65
(iii) *Nuclear Family Ideal*			
5. " Newly-married couples should not live with their parents."	99	59	50
(iv) *Independent Choice of Spouse*			
6. " I expect to be able to choose my husband / wife independently."	98	58	94
N =	651	238	1,123

For all items the differences between United States and Taiwanese respor lents, and United States and Hong Kong respondents, are significant at the 5% level or better.   I he differences between Taiwanese and Hong Kong respondents are significant at the 5% level for items 4, 5 and 6.

We attempt to account for the discrepancies between the expected and actual results in terms of special aspects of social life in Hong Kong and Taiwan, which we discuss below. The six items in Table 5 are discussed under four headings—romantic love ideal; seperation of the sexes; nuclear family ideal; and independent choice of spouse.

(i) Romantic Love Ideal (Item 1)

Similar proportions of Taiwanese and Hong Kong respondents support the statement on the romantic love ideal.

(ii) Separation of the Sexes (Items 2, 3, 4)

There is little difference between Hong Kong and Taiwanese respondents with regard to separation of the sexes at social gatherings and in primary schools (items 2 and 3). Item 4 needs further discussion, however, Marsh and O'Hara explain the relatively low proportion (45%) of Taiwanese respondents who are against the separation of the sexes at secondary school in terms of the competition for education in Taiwan: " there is. . . . great pressure to study during middle school years, and social and romantic diversions are regarded as undesirable ".[28] The Hong Kong educational system is, however, also highly competitive, yet 65% of all Hong Kong respondents are against segregation of the sexes at secondary school. This finding can be understood in terms of the structure of secondary education in Hong Kong and Taiwan. Hong Kong's secondary schools are already co-educational to a considerable extent[29], whilst in Taiwan, as Marsh and O'Hara note " there is virtually no such thing as co-education." [30] In responding to the statement on the segregation of the sexes at secondary school, it is likely that Hong Kong and Taiwanese respondents are merely reflecting their own experience and what they know to be the experience of most of their peers.

(iii) Nuclear Family Ideal

Fewer Hong Kong respondents than Taiwanese favoured the nuclear family ideal and the difference is significant at the 5% level. This difference may be a reflection of the serious housing shortage in Hong Kong which makes it almost inevitable that newly weds live with parents or close relatives immediately after marriage. (Nearly a third (29%) of our married respondents lived with their parents).

For this item alone amongst the six items discussed, there are important differences in attitudes associated with the sex of the respondents. As Marsh and O'Hara found in Taiwan so we found in Hong Kong—females are more likely than males to favour the setting up of a separate home on marriage (Table 6). The differences between Hong Kong and Taiwanese respondents remained even after we controlled for education. Marsh and O'Hara explained this difference between the sexes in terms of the patrilocal pattern of residence typical in Chiness society which has the effect of separating the wife from her family of orientation and placing her amongst strangers in her husband's parents' home. The subordinate role which the newly married wife would be expected to occupy (in traditional Chinese society) in her husband's parents' home has, of course, been noted on many occasions.[31]

TABLE 6

Nuclear Family Ideal
" Newly-married couples should not live with their Parents "
(percentages agreeing)

	Male	Female	Total
Hong Kong Respondents	46	54	50
Taiwanese Respondents	51	69	59

The differences between male and female respondents are significant at the 5% level or better in both cases.

(iv) Independent Choice of Spouse (Item 6)

A very much higher proportion of Hong Kong respondents (94%) than Taiwanese (58%) expected to be able to choose their spouse independently. Marsh and O'Hara noted that in traditional China it was the parents in higher socio-economic groups who exercised greatest control over the selection of marriage partners for their children.[32] Since the Taiwanese respondents are all university students, it may be assumed that their parents are largely in the upper socio-economic groups. The parents of Hong Kong respondents are drawn from a wider range of socio-economic groups, so it might be argued that this factor contributes to the expectation of greater freedom of mate selection in Hong Kong.[33] The difference between the Hong Kong and Taiwanese responses for this item is so great that a full explanation must be sought elsewhere. Marsh and O'Hara explained the low proportion of Taiwanese respondents who expected to be able to choose their spouse independently in terms of the absence of institutional arrangements for free choice. Dating and courtship were rarely found in Taiwan and in these circumstances free choice of marriage partner could not exist. Relations between the sexes are more informal and easy in Hong Kong than in Taiwan. In Hong Kong there are many institutionalised situations in which the sexes mingle freely—not only in school but also at Government-sponsored dances, youth camps and community centres. Although the freedom of relations between the sexes is not as complete as in Western society and dating seems to begin later, it is common to see mixed groups of unchaperoned young people on country walks, holding barbecues or at the beach (a situation which has been described to us as " group dating.")[34]

B. H. Stoodley found a similar pattern amongst post-secondary students in Hong Kong : " Most boy-girl interaction took place as temporary nucleations within larger mixed groups".[35] The discrepancy between the Hong Kong and Taiwan responses may therefore be explained in terms of the absence of any socially-approved mechanism for exercising free choice in Taiwan and its presence in Hong Kong.

Our findings are not conclusive. Items 1, 2 and 3 in Table 5 support the alternative hypothesis that Hong Kong and Taiwanese respondents will reveal generally similar attitudes. Items 4 and 6 support the first hypothesis, but item 5 refutes it. For each of these items there are significant differences between the Hong Kong and Taiwanese responses. These differences may be accounted for at least in part in terms special aspects of social life of Hong Kong and Taiwan which cut across other modernizing tendencies, i. e. the effects of government education policies which influence attitudes towards the segregation of the sexes in secondary schools (item 4), an acute housing shortage which makes very difficult the establishment of independent households by young couples immediately after marriage (item 5) and the existence (or otherwise) of institutionalised means of exercising a free choice of marriage partner (item 6).

NOTES AND REFERENCES

1. Inkeles, A., 1960-1, "Industrial Man: The Relation of Status to Experience, Perception and Value" *American Journal of Sociology* Vol. 66, pp. 1-31

2. See, for example: Smith, D. J. and A. Inkeles, 1966. "The OM Scale: A Comparative Socio-Psychological Measure of Individual Modernity " *Sociometry* Vol. 29, p. p. 353-77, and Inkeles, A 1969-70. "Making Men Modern: On the Causes and Consequences of Individual Change in Six Developing Countries " *American Journal of Sociology* Vol. 75, p. p. 208-25

3. Inkeles, 1969-70, op. cit. p. 210

4 Ibid P. 212

5. Ibid P. 225

6. See, for example, Kerr C. et al, 1962, *Industrialism and Industrial Man*, London, Heinemann (especially Chapters 2 and 10) and, more recently, Galbraith, J. K., 1967. *The New Industrial State* London, Hamish Hamilton (particularly Chapter 35)

7. Moore, W. E., 1965. *The Impact of Industry* Englewood Cliffs, Prentice-Hall, p. p. 11-2

8. See Moore, W. E., 1955, "Creation of a Common Culture " *Confluence* Vol. 4, p. p. 229-38. Moore has since modified his position considerably—see below

9. Blumer, H. 1960. "Early Industrialisation and the Labouring Class" *Sociological Quarterly* Vol. 1, p. 9

10. Goldthorpe, J. H, "Social Stratification in Industrial Societies " in Halmos, P. (ed.) 1964., *The Development of Industrial Societies* Sociological Review Monograph No. 8 Keele University of Keele

11. Moore, W. E., 1965, p. p. 14-9

12. For a full discussion, see Feldman, A. S. and W. E. Moore, 1962. "Industrialisation and Industrialism: Convergence and Differentiation" *Transactions of the Fifth World Congress of Sociology* Vol. 2, p. p. 151-69 London, International Sociological Association

13. Bendix, R., 1964. *Nation Building and Citizenship* New York, Wiley, p. p. 5-10

14. Ibid, p. 8 (The quotation is from Schumpeter, J. 1947. *Capitalism, Socialism and Democracy* New York, Harper, p. 12)

15. For a recent review of some of the literature see: Weinberg, I., 1969. "The Problem of Convergence in Industrial Societies" *Comparative Studies in Society and History* Vol. 11, p. p. 1-15

16. Moore, W. E., 1963. *Social Change* Englewood Cliffs, Prentice-Hall p. 102

17. We have "shrunk" the term in accordance with the valuable suggestion of J. P. Nettl and R. Robertson in their book *International Systems and the Modernisation of Societies* London, Faber and Faber, 1968. (p. p 38-42)

18. See, for example, on the Japanese family : Wilkinson, T. O. 1962. " Family Structure and Industrialisation in Japan " *American Sociological Review* Vol. 27, p. p. 678-82 and Vogel, E. F. 1965. *Japan's New Middle Class* Berkeley, University of California Press. On Japanese industry: Odaka, K. 1963, " Traditionalism, Democracy in Japanese Industry" *Industrial Relations* Vol. 10, p. p. 95-103; Karsh, B. and R. E. Cole 1968, " Industrialisation and the Convergence Hypothesis: Some Aspects of Contemporary Japan" *Journal of Social Issues* Vol. 24 No. 4 p. p. 45-64 and Matsushima S. " Labour Management Relations in Japan" in Halmos, P. (ed.) 1966. *Japanese Sociological Studies* Sociological Review Monograph No. 10, Keele, University of Keele

19. Marsh, R. M. and A. R. O'Hara 1961-2. " Attitudes Toward Marriage and the Family in Taiwan " *American Journal of Sociology* Vol. 67, p. p. 1-8

20. Marsh and O'Hara showed that Taiwanese respondents originating from Hong Kong were more modern in their attitudes than those from mainland China or Taiwan itself (op. cit. p 5). An anecdote in Francis L. K. Hsu's book *Under the Ancestors' Shadow*, London, Routledge and Kegan Paul, 1949, neatly makes the point about the modernising influence of Hong Kong. Writing of a town in Yunnan in the West of China he says: " It was still vividly told in 1943 that a young returner from Hong Kong, who had walked along the street hand-in-hand with his bride had been drenched with human excrement poured over their heads According to the custom of the community such liberty was not allowed..." (p. p. 27-28)

21. Amongst elite groups, the well-educated in particular show considerable orientation towards things American. For example only 2,000 of 10,000 secondary school children interviewed for the Urban Family Life Study of the Chinese University of Hong Kong said that they wished to remain in Hong Kong after completing their studies. Most wanted to emigrate to the United States or Canada. It should be noted that the fieldwork for this study was carried out in 1966-68 during a period when the Colony was wracked by civil disorders. For a perceptive discussion of these disorders see Jarvie, I. C. " A Postscript on Riots and the Future of Hong Kong" in Jarvie, I. C and J. Agassi (eds.) 1969. Hong Kong : *A Society in Transition* London, Routledge.

22. We are aware of the dangers inherent in this procedure of generalising to a whole society from relatively crude data which may be characteristic of only a segment of the total population. (For a useful discussion of the problems of developing indices of industrialisation see Inkeles, 1960-1, op. cit. p. p. 3-4). However, we are not developing sophisticated indices, we are merely attempting to place the three societies in a "more-less-little" relationship to each other with regard to the extent of industrialisation.

23. Clark, C., 1951. *The Conditions of Economic Progress* London, Macmillian p. p. 395-439.

24. See, for example, the criticisms made by Bauer, P. T. and B. S. Yamey, 1951 " Economic Progress and Occupational Distribution" *Economic Journal* Vol. 61, p. p. 741-56

25. See the discussion in Weber, M. 1947 *The Theory of Social and Economic Organisation* New York, Oxford, p. 245.

26. Aron, R., 1967. *18 Lectures on Industrial Society* London, Weidenfeld and Nicolson, p. 79

27. There are numerous accounts of the structure and functions of the traditional Chinese family, e. g. Lang, O., 1946. *Chinese Family and Society* New Haven, Yale University Press, Part 1; Winch, R. F. 1963 *The Modern Family* New York, Holt, Rinehart and Winston Chapter 2 and Lee, Shu-Ching 1953, " China's Traditional Family, Its Characteristics and Disintegration" *American Sociological Review* Vol. 18, p. 272-80. The generalisations in Table 4 however, represent an "ideal type" of traditional Chinese family seldom, if ever, found in reality—of. Hsu, Francis, L. K. 1943. "The Myth of Chinese Family Size" *American Journal of Sociology* Vol. 48, p. p. 555-62 and Freedman, M. 1961. "The Family in China, Past and Present" *Pacific Affairs* Vol. 34, p. p. 323-36. For a brief summary of the main features of the modern western family see Goode, W. J. 1964. *The Family* Englewood Cliffs, Prentice-Hall, p. p. 51-2, also Firth, R. " Family and Kinship in Industrial Societies ' in Halmos, (ed.) 1964 op cit.

28. Marsh and O'Hara, op. cit. p. 8.

29. 74.3% of Hong Kong's secondary pupils attend co-educational schools whilst 13.8% go to boys' schools and 11.9% go girls' schools. (Personal communication from the Education Department, Hong Kong Government, September 15, 1970). Primary education is almost wholly co-educational - 93.5% of primary pupils attend co-educational schools.

30. Marsh and O'Hara, op. cit. p. 8.

31. See, for example, Freedman, op. cit. (p. 328) where he refers to "the unhappy position of the daughter-in-law" cut off by marriage from her own family.

32. Marsh and O'Hara, op. cit. p. p. 5-6.

33. We did not collect data on the occupation of the fathers of our respondents, but a rough indication of the socio-economic standing of our sample can be obtained from the occupations of those 47.1% (527) of young adult respondents who normally worked. 34.2% were in white collar occupations, 11.9% in service and miscellaneous jobs; 53.9% in manual jobs.

34. On this point we estimate that the situation in Hong Kong today is similar to that in the "more traditional" of the Western societies where, as Goode has noted, "In Spain and Italy a respectable girl no longer requires chaperone when she goes out." Goode, W. J. 1963 *World Revolution and Family Patterns* New York, Free Press, p. 31. For a discussion of the social relations between well-educated young men and women students at Hong Kong University see: J. S. Cansdale "Cultural Problems of Chinese Students in a Western type University" in Jarvie, I. C. and J. Agassi (eds.) op. cit. especially p. p. 357-8.

35. Stoodly. B. A., 1967. "Normative Family Orientations of Chinese College Students in Hong Kong" *Journal of Marriage and the Family* Vol. 29, p. p. 773-82 (quotation from p. 778).

A Question of Matrimonial Strategy?
A Comparison of Attitudes Between Ghanaian
and British University Students*

KENNETH LITTLE**

Introduction

Christine Oppong has studied what she terms power relationships among families of senior civil servants in Ghana. She found that twice as great a proportion of husbands of housewives as of working wives asserted they were dominant in the home. On the other hand, the tendency was for wives who were shouldering a larger share of the financial responsibility with their husbands also to share more frequently in 'decision-making'. There was *no* significant difference between the power relationship of couples in which wives do not work and those of couples in which wives work but make a relatively low contribution to domestic expenses. There was, however, a significant difference between couples in which the wife makes a nil or low contribution, on the one hand, and couples in which the wife makes a medium or high contribution, on the other. In other words, joint financial provision was associated with joint decision-making, and it is not merely a question of the wife's influence increasing with her experience. Further, although couples in which the wife's educational level most closely approximated that of her husband were most likely to share in decision-making, neither the educational nor the status factor was in itself conclusive. The wives of doctors, for example, were relatively well educated but most of them were housewives alone and in this group as a whole it was mostly the husband who decided things. Teachers, on the other hand, were remarkable for their joint decision-making and joint provision for household needs. Yet teachers have a somewhat lower status than doctors. (1974, *passim*)

There is, in fact, evidence that other educated West African women as well as Ghanaians, want a companionate type of marriage. They wish to be regarded in it as partners (see, *inter alios*, Harrell-Bond 1975 and Little, 1966). If, therefore, the realization of this objective does depend largely upon circumstances of the above kind, to what extent do wives consciously or unconsciously set out to acquire economic resources of their own? How do they themselves regard the idea of having careers and what are the implications for marriage and the family?

* The research basic to this article was supported by the award of a Leverhulme Research Fellowship and grants from the Noel Buxton Trust and the Carnegie Trust for Universities of Scotland. The author wishes to express his sincere thanks for this assistance.
**African Urban Studies, University of Edinburgh, Scotland.

Volume VII Number 1, (Spring 1976)

A questionnaire was designed to elucidate these matters and, its being impracticable to obtain a sufficient sample of married women, this was distributed among unmarried women students at the University of Ghana.[1] 165 forms were wholly or partially completed and information gained in this way concerning these girls' attitudes. They are asked, *inter alia,* their reasons for studying, how they regarded the idea of working after marriage and while bringing up children; the way in which they expected to dispose of or use their earnings, etc. In addition, in order that the Ghanaians' position might be seen in perspective, a group of Edinburgh University women students were asked to answer a slightly abbreviated version of the same questionnaire. The latter sample numbered 157 and represented, of course, only a small fraction of Edinburgh's total enrollment of female students. The Ghanaian sample, on the other hand, constituted some 40 per cent of all women students on the Legon campus; but neither group was randomly selected.

It will be noted that the number of replies cited varies. This is because some respondents left some questions unanswered. It is difficult to know precisely why this happened more often in the Ghanaian case. It may have been due partly to the questionnaire having been administered in somewhat different ways. Thus, at Edinburgh the whole exercise was undertaken in the students' classrooms, but at Legon many of the forms were distributed individually and completed in the students' own time.

Therefore, being no other means of overcoming the drawback, n in the tables signifies the number of actual replies to a given question. It also provides a base upon which means and percentages (shown in brackets) have been calculated.

Summarization

It will be convenient if, before considering the implications of the above data, we quickly summarize the principal points emerging. The first is that the Ghanaian girls apparently have very positive reasons of an economic kind for being at "university". Thus, whereas 75% of them say they have chosen their courses in preparation for a specific occupation or profession, only 40 per cent of the British sample have replied to the same effect. Also, whereas 84 per cent of the Ghanaians say they intend to enter a salaried occupation or profession immediately after completing their training, this is the expressed intention of only 55 per cent of the British girls. The latter, instead, lay stress on the idea of improving their general education (Tables 4 and 5). Also, most of the Ghanaians say that the most important considerations in choosing a job are its monetary reward and prospects of promotion. Only 22 per cent of them compared with 54 per cent of the British intimate that it is 'interest' in the chosen subject that attracts them most (Table 6).

The girls' responses leave little doubt that most of them, Ghanaian and British alike, intend to marry. However, although a slightly larger proportion of the

---

[1] I have to thank most sincerely Dr. D.K. Fiawoo, Sociology Department, University of Ghana, for the arrangements he made in this connection. Dr. Fiawoo also provided some very helpful comments on the data obtained, but the present writer accepts full responsibility for the way in which they have been interpreted.

Ghanaians than the British have already decided on this step, they expect to take it at a slightly latter age than the British among whom the proportion with a particular young man already in view is smaller (Tables 7 and 8). Further, and more predictably, the Ghanaians apparently hope or plan to have more children than the British—on the average 4 as against 2. In addition, whereas the Ghanaians wish to have children as soon as possible after marriage, this intention was shared by only one out of every five of the British.[2] Indeed, not only were nine out of every ten of the Ghanaians, compared with 26 per cent of the British, apparently reluctant to wait for more than two years, but there was an obvious difference in attitudes towards this matter. The Ghanaians mostly said that one would be able to do best for children while still young oneself and that it was medically safer to have one's children at this stage. The British, by contrast, apparently gave priority to the establishment of a satisfactory marital relationship (Tables 14, 15 and 16).

TABLE 1

AGE				ACADEMIC STATUS		QUALIFICATIONS SOUGHT	
Ghanaian n=165		British n=157		Ghanaian n=153	British n=157	Ghanaian n=151	British n=157
Yrs.		Yrs.					
18	11 (6)	17	1 (1)	1st yr. 65 (42)	1st yr. 36 (24)	Degree 119 (79)	Degree 156 (99.9)
19	17 (10)	18	19 (12)	2nd yr. 48 (31)	2nd yr. 99 (63)		
20	31 (18)	19	65 (42)	3rd yr. 36 (24)	3rd yr. 5 (3)	Certificate/ Diploma 32 (21)	Dip. in Social Admn. 1
21	26 (16)	20	38 (24)	4th yr. 3 (2)	4th yr. 16 (10)		
22	31 (18)	21	10 (6)	5th yr. 1 (1)	Post. grad. 1 (—)		
23	17 (10)	22	14 (9)				
24	10 (6)	23	3 (2)				
25	8 (5)	24	2 (1)				
26	4 (3)	25	— ⎤				
27	2 (1)	26	1 ⎟				
28	2 (1)	27	1 ⎬ (3)				
29	1 (1)	30	1 ⎟				
30	4 (3)	32	1 ⎟				
31	1 (1)	38	1 ⎦				
Mean=21.8		Mean=20					

[2]It might be argued that this Ghanaian desire to have children sooner after marriage is due to the group being on the average nearly two years older than the British. On the other hand, there is a good deal of overlapping in respect of age. Thus, although 85 per cent of the Britsh girls are between the ages of 18 and 22 inclusive, 68 per cent of the Ghanaians fall within this same bracket.

TABLE 2

Father's Occupation					Mother's Occupation				
	Ghanaian n=158		British n=153			Ghanaian n=159		British n=154	
Administrative/ Managerial	31	(20)	44	(29)	Administrative/ Managerial	19	(12)	8	(5)
Businessman	27	(17)	7	(5)	Businesswoman	33	(21)	3	(2)
Civil Servant	21	(13)	10	(6)	Civil Servant	—	—	7	(4)
Clerical	7	(4)	2	(2)	Clerical/Secretarial Recept.	—	—	30	(20)
Diplomat	1	(0.7)	—	—	Farmer	13	(8)	—	—
Farmer	16	(10)	9	(6)	Housewife	53	(33)	64	(42)
Fisherman	1	(0.7)	—	—	Miscellaneous	—	—	3	(3)
Minister of Religion	4	(2)	—	—	Nurse	11	(8)	6	(3)
Miscellaneous	—	—	6	(5)	Petty Trader	19	(12)	—	—
Police/Security Officer	3	(2)	2	(1)	Professional	1	(—)	11	(8)
Professional	35	(22)	37	(24)	Religious Leader	1	(—)	—	—
Salesman	1	(0.7)	—	—	Seamstress	5	(3)	—	—
Teacher	—	—	9	(6)	Teacher	14	(9)	8	(11)
Technician/artisan/ craftsman	11	(7)	25	(16)	Technician/artisan crafts	—	—	3	(2)

TABLE 3

Fathers's Education					Mother's Education				
Ghanaian n=155			British n=145		Ghanaian n=160			British n=119	
University	41	(27)	University and approx. equivalent	70 (47)	University	5	(3)	University	34 (28)
Teacher Training College	14	(9)	Secondary	74 (51)	Teacher Training College	25	(16)	Teacher Training College	18 (16)
Secondary	50	(32)	Primary only	1 (1)	Secondary	25	(16)	Secondary	66 (55)
Middle	34	(22)			Middle	48	(30)	Primary only	1 (1)
Elementary	5	(3)			Elementary	26	(16)		
No formal education	6	(4)			No formal education	28	(17)		
Other	5	(3)			Other	3	(2)		

TABLE 4   REASONS FOR TAKING COURSE CHOSEN

	Ghanaian n=153		British n=156	
To take up specific occupation or profession	114	(75)	63	(40)
To improve general education	33	(21)	82	(52)
Other reasons	6	(4)	7	(5)
Gain qualifications for advanced course	—	—	4	(3)

TABLE 5   IS IT THE INTENTION TO ENTER A SALARIED OCCUPATION OR PROFESSION IMMEDIATELY AFTER COMPLETION OF TRAINING FOR IT?

	Ghanaian n=162		British n=157	
Yes	136	(84)	87	(55)
No	10	(6)	26	(17)
Don't Know	16	(10)	44	(28)

TABLE 6   WHAT DOES RESPONDENT FEEL IS THE MOST IMPORTANT CONSIDERATION IN DECIDING ON AN OCCUPATION OR PROFESSION?

	Ghanaian n=175		British n=156	
Travel Opportunities	10	(5)	15	(10)
Lots of free time	6	(4)	7	(4)
Money is good	46	(26)	18	(12)
Chance to meet important people	5	(3)	3	(2)
Respect of people	12	(7)	7	(4)
Good prospects of promotion	40	(23)	21	(13)
Interest in job	38	(22)	83	(54)
Opportunity to help others	9	(5)	1 ⎫	(1)
Other reasons	9	(5)	1 ⎭	

TABLE 7   IS IT THE RESPONDENT'S INTENTION (a) TO MARRY? IF SO, (b) AT
                 WHAT AGE WOULD THE RESPONDENT LIKE OR
                 INTEND TO MARRY?

	A Ghanaian n=160		British n=149		Age Group	B Ghanaian n=147		British n=139	
Yes	145	(91)	121	(81)	15—19	—	—	2	(1)
No	10	(6)	3	(2)	20—24	47	(32)	59	(43)
Don't Know	5	(3)	25	(17)	25—29	95	(66)	72	(52)
					30–34	4	(2)	5	(3)
					35+	1	(1)	1	(1)

TABLE 8   DOES THE RESPONDENT HAVE ANY YOUNG MAN AT PRESENT
                 SPECIFICALLY IN VIEW FOR MARRIAGE?

	Ghanaian n=147		British n=144	
Yes	69	(47)	46	(32)
No	78	(53)	98	(68)

TABLE 9   (a) DOES THE RESPONDENT INTEND TO CARRY ON EITHER HER JOB
                 OR TO EARN MONEY IN SOME OTHER WAY AFTER MARRIAGE?
                 (b) IF SO, DOES SHE INTEND TO WORK ON A FULL-TIME OR
                 PART-TIME BASIS?

(A)	Ghanaian n=153		British n=146		(B)	Ghanaian n=138		British n=133	
Yes	138	(90)	131	(90)	Full-Time	123	(89)	104	(79)
No	6	(4)	4	(2)	Part-Time	13	(10)	24	(16)
Don't Know	9	(6)	11	(8)	Don't Know	2	(1)	5	(4)
No Answers	12		11						

TABLE 10 — REASONS FOR CONTINUING TO WORK

	Ghanaian n=172		British n=100	
Put education into effect	36	(21)	4	(4)
Counteract boredom and relief from household duties	13	(7)	26	(26)
Economic reasons	35	(20)	7	(7)
General uncertainty of economic conditions	10	(6)	—	—
Uncertainty of personal future in relation to prospective spouse	10	(6)	—	—
Desire to be relatively 'free' and 'independent'	34	(20)	23	(23)
Altruistic	10	(6)	1	(1)
Personal satisfaction and self-expression	21	(13)	39	(39)
Other reasons	3	(1)		

TABLE 11 — IF RESPONDENT'S HUSBAND COULD FULLY SUPPORT HER AND HER CHILDREN IN REASONABLE COMFORT, WILL SHE STILL WISH TO ENGAGE IN PAID EMPLOYMENT?

	Ghanaian n=156		British n=140	
Yes	139	(89)	95	(68)
No	9	(6)	19	(13)
Don't Know	8	(5)	26	(19)

TABLE 12 — REASONS FOR (a) AFFIRMATIVE and (b) NEGATIVE ANSWERS TO THE PRECEDING QUESTION

(A)	Ghanaian n=158		British n=90		(B)	Ghanaian n=5		British n=18	
Personal fulfilment	21	(13)	51	(55)	Devote time to home and children	2	(45)	10	(56)
Economic	36	(23)	6	(7)	Dependent on circumstances	3	(55)	2	(11)
Retain relative independence within marriage	54	(35)	14	(16)	Would consider voluntary work	—	—	6	(33)
Offset boredom	21	(13)	17	(19)					
Use of education and training	19	(21)	2	(2)					
Support of parents, sisters, brothers, etc.	7	(4)	—	—					
Contribution to community	—	—	1	(1)					

TABLE 13   DOES RESPONDENT THINK (a) THE MAN SHE WILL MARRY WILL WANT HER TO CARRY ON EITHER HER JOB OR EARN MONEY IN SOME OTHER WAY AFTER MARRIAGE? REASONS (b) FOR EXPECTING THAT HE WILL

(A)					(B)				
	Ghanaian n=157		British n=146			Ghanaian n=94		British n=57	
Yes	97	(60)	78	(53)	Economic reasons	62	(66)	14	(25)
No	3	(2)	7	(5)	Husband will respect wishes or can be persuaded	19	(20)	20	(35)
Don't Know	57	(38)	61	(42)	Waste of training and personal satisfaction	10	(10)	12	(21)
					Would not marry if husband disagreed with work	—	—	8	(14)
					Other reasons	3	(2)	3	(6)

TABLE 14   DOES THE RESPONDENT INTEND/HOPE TO (a) HAVE CHILDREN? IF SO, THE NUMBER (b) THAT SHE PLANS/HOPES TO HAVE

(A)					(B)				
	Ghanaian n=160		British n=145		No. of Children	Ghanaian n=225		British n=135	
Yes	145	(91)	112	(77)	0	5	(1)	—	—
No	10	(6)	11	(8)	1	—	—	5	(4)
Don't Know	5	(3)	22	(15)	2	21	(10)	78	(58)
					3	56	(25)	30	(22)
					4	111	(49)	18	(13)
					5	17	(8)	—	—
					6	16	(7)	3	(2)
					7	—	—	—	—
					8	—	—	1	(1)

TABLE 15   DOES RESPONDENT WISH (a) TO HAVE CHILDREN AS SOON AS POSSIBLE AFTER MARRIAGE? IF NOT, (b) HOW MANY YEARS WOULD RESPONDENT LIKE TO WAIT BEFORE STARTING TO HAVE CHILDREN?

	(A)				(B)				
	Ghanaian n=152		British n=121		No. of Years	Ghanaian n=25		British n=131	
Yes	124	(82)	26	(21)	1	5	(20)	5	(4)
No	28	(18)	95	(79)	2	17	(68)	27	(22)
					3	3	(12)	34	(26)
					4	—	—	32	(25)
					5	—	—	17	(13)
					6	—	—	8	(6)
					7	—	—	1	(—)
					8	—	—	4	(3)
					9	—	—	1	(—)
					10	—	—	2	(1)

TABLE 16   REASONS GIVEN FOR AFFIRMATIVE REPLY (a) and FOR NEGATIVE REPLY (b) TO THE ABOVE

(A)					(B)				
	Ghanaian n=113		British n=13			Ghanaian n=25		British n=83	
Will be able to do one's best for children before too old and obviate age gap	44	(40)	5	(39)	Enjoy life with husband first	6	(28)	26	(31)
Important part of marriage	10	(10)	5	(39)	Adjust to partner first	9	(34)	21	(24)
To provide background for educ. before returning to work	17	(15)	2	(16)	Establish economic stability	8	(31)	24	(30)
Medically safer	37	(32)	1	(6)	Wish to continue work for a while	2	(7)	12	(15)
Miscellaneous	5	(3)	—	—					

TABLE 17   DOES RESPONDENT INTEND/HOPE TO CARRY ON HER JOB AFTER
                  SHE HAS HAD CHILDREN? (a) IF SO, ON A FULL-TIME BASIS
                  OR PART-TIME BASIS? (b)

(A)	Ghanaian n=156		British n=125		(B)	Ghanaian n=139		British n=99	
Yes	147	(94)	85	(68)	Full-time	89	(61)	38	(38)
No	5	(3)	40	(32)	Part-time	50	(39)	59	(60)
Don't Know	4	(2)	—	—	Don't Know	—	—	2	(2)

TABLE 18   REASONS GIVEN FOR WORKING FULL-TIME (a) AND PART-TIME (b)

(A)	Ghanaian n=69		British n=16		(B)	Ghanaian n=50		British n=47	
Part-time not available in chosen profession	5	(7)	1	(6)	Spend more time with husband and children	48	(96)	32	(68)
Use of qualifications	16	(23)	3	(19)	Outside interest for short time	—	—	8	(17)
Self-satisfaction and outside interest	19	(27)	9	(56)	Economic	—	—	1	(2)
Economic	29	(43)	—	—	Other reasons	2	(4)	6	(13)
Other reasons	—	—	3	(19)					

TABLE 19   WHAT ARRANGEMENTS DOES RESPONDENT EXPECT TO MAKE FOR
                  THE CARE OF HER CHILDREN WHILE SHE IS ABSENT
                  FROM THE HOUSE?

	Ghanaian n = 148		British n = 83	
Hire a maidservant	33	(22)	6	(7)
Bring in a friend/relative	30	(19)	8	(10)
Allow children to accompany her to work	1	(1)	6	(7)
Leave children daily with relatives	7	(5)	—	—
Day Nursery/Child Care Centre	70	(40)	47	(56)
Have mother's service	6	(4)	—	—
Work during school hours	—	—	13	(16)
Other reasons	1	(1)	3	(4)

TABLE 20   WHAT DOES RESPONDENT INTEND TO DO WITH WHATEVER
                  MONEY, SALARY OR WAGES SHE EARNS?

	Ghanaian n = 142		British n = 136	
Joint account with husband	11	(8)	54	(40)
Keep some and pay rest into joint account with husband	33	(24)	58	(43)
Keep part for self, rest spent on relatives, husband and children	53	(37)	12	(9)
Keep part for self, part save and rest on children	11	(8)	10	(7)
Keep part for self, rest for own relatives and children	33	(23)	—	—
Dependent on circumstances	—	—	1	(1)

(ANSWERED BY GHANAIAN GIRLS ONLY)

TABLE 21   IF RESPONDENT KEEPS ALL OR SOME OF THE MONEY SHE EARNS,
                  TO WHICH OF THE FOLLOWING USES DOES SHE
                  INTEND TO PUT IT ?

n = 125		
Education of own children	17	(14)
Education of own children and relatives' children	28	(22)
Education of children and acquisition of property	43	(35)
Solely on the acquisition of property	10	(8)
Saving towards setting up own business	14	(11)
Presents for own and husband's relatives	9	(7)
Self, children and own relatives	4	(3)

In addition most of the Ghanaians say they want to continue in jobs after marriage. This announcement is in line with the attitudes of Ghanaian school girls, as reported by Masemann (1974). However, although most of the British students express similar intentions, only 68 per cent of them compared with 94 per cent of the Ghanaians intend to carry on working after the arrival of children. In this regard, too, 61 per cent of the Ghanaians compared with 38 per cent of the British were apparently prepared to work full-time.

Finally only 32 per cent of the Ghanaians compared with 83 per cent of the British girls apparently intend to share their earnings with husbands. 61 per cent of the Ghanaians seemingly propose instead to spend at least a part of such money on themselves, their children and their relatives as well as on their husbands.

Discussion

As explained, the main purpose of this enquiry is to elucidate the attitude of educated Ghanaian women towards the idea of being working wives and mothers. Many such women want to be treated by husbands as partners and there is evidence that this objective is more readily achieved when the wife as well as the husband plays a bread-winning role. In order, therefore, to assess the extent to which the women themselves are alive to this and intend to deal with it realistically, a group of Ghanaian women was compared with a British sample of broadly similar educational status. From this comparison it appeared that Ghanaian and British girls alike were aware of the intellectual and social benefits of University training. What emerged even more strongly, however, was that the Ghanaians seemingly were much more disposed than the British to regard it as a monetary asset and an instrument for economic purposes. A corollary of this was that the Ghanaians not only intended to continue working after marriage, but were much more inclined than the British to be working mothers. This was despite the fact that in addition to wanting twice as many children as the British, the Ghanaians also wished to begin a family much sooner after marriage.

A major difficulty to be contended with throughout is that of representativeness, because neither group was randomly selected. This makes it obligatory both here and in the discussion following to move sociologically with considerable caution. However, without disregarding this essential *caveat*, what can we perhaps deduce from the above apparently clear differences? Do they imply, for example, that educated young Ghanaian women are indeed very career minded? If so, the first question to be answered is whether basically the Ghanaian standpoint is dissimilar from the British one. Thus, it might be argued that, wider cultural considerations apart, both the Ghanaians and the British girls either belong to or are likely to move into a broadly 'middle class' stratum of society. Admittedly, in the Ghanaian case, the mothers' educational background is low by comparison with that of the British girls. On the other hand, in terms of both education and the relatively high ranking occupations of the fathers, the two groups are broadly similar. Also, although on the average the British girls are nearly two years younger than the Ghanaians, it is possible that any consequent differences in intellectual maturity is cancelled out by the much larger proportion of the British girls seeking degrees rather than diplomas. In addition, contrary perhaps to expectations, few of the Ghanaians apparently intend to leave their children in the care of relatives. Mostly they, as well as the British, intend to use day nurseries.[3]

What, however, cannot be regarded as similar at all is the encompassing economic situation of the two groups. True, the rising cost of living is something that British middle class families as well as Ghanaians have to face. However, although Ghanaian senior civil servants enjoy free medical care for man, wife and children, car loans, access to subsidized housing, pensions, etc., these people constitute by comparison with most others a very privileged class. For the generality of urban wage-earners, there are no such perquisites or statutory safe-

---

[3]Day nurseries tend to supplement maid service because, with the growing national emphasis on primary education for all, there are fewer illiterate relatives available from the rural areas. (Communicated by Dr. Fiawoo).

guards in the event of ill-health, unemployment or retiral from the labour market. Consequently, since there is in Ghana no counterpart of the British welfare state, it is to anticipate the proverbial rainy day that the Ghanaian girls demonstrate extra willingness to continue working. This is the more likely because of those who intended to work full time. Some 66 per cent said either they wished to use their qualifications or gave economic reasons. In other words, especially since most mothers are ambitious for their children, one assumption could be that a wife's contribution is to be seen as a constructive way of reinforcing the family's financial position.

Another reason not unrelated to this is perhaps reflected in the Ghanaians' intention to spend money earned on relatives and relatives' children. Quite often, the university girl owes the additionel educational opportunities she has enjoyed to kinsfolk and so has a corresponding duty to reciprocate. School fees for the younger members of the family may have to be paid, anniversaries remembered, loans made to indigent aunts and uncles and so on. Educated men naturally incur debts of a similar kind. Not all of them, however, are willing or able to discharge their wives' obligations as well as their own. It is possible, therefore, that this eventuality as well has been anticipated in some of the Ghanaian answers.

Thus, we can perhaps understand the above obvious differences between the Ghanaian and the British responses in terms of dissimilar environments. The Ghanaians, it seems evident, are much more economically motivated than are the British. But this, it may be argued, represents merely a realistic reaction to the general position of the family. It has to fend for itself in circumstances that arise less often in the British situation and for which in consequence the British girls have less need to prepare.

However 'rational' as may be this more 'economic' attitude of the Ghanaians they do appear to have as well a somewhat different conception of the marital relationship itself. For example, although a smaller percentage of the Ghanaians than the British expect that a prospective husband will want them to continue working, by far the most common reason they give for his consent is financial. Only 20 per cent compared with 35 per cent of the British consider that he will agree because it is the wish of his wife (Table 13). Indeed, whereas eight of the British respondents declare that they would not marry a man who objected, this kind of attitude is not expressed by any of the Ghanaians. It also seems significant that many of the Ghanaian replies imply more interest in the idea of bearing children than in the uxorial role. Thus, although most of the British sample as well as the Ghanaians, hope to become mothers, very few of the British girls concerned plan to start a family before they have been married for at least four years. They explain that they wish to settle down first and to establish a satisfactory home life with their husbands. The Ghanaians, by contrast, want to have their children much sooner. True, about 10 per cent of them suggest that to have children early may help marriage itself. but only the small minority favouring postponement take their relationship with prospective husbands explicitly into account. Most of the sample deal with the matter from the standpoint of their children's welfare, or of their own health (Tables 15 and 16).

It also seems evident that personal as well as economic factors are behind the greater desire of the Ghanaians to continue working. This is implied in the intention of nearly nine out of every ten to remain in jobs even in the event of their husbands being able to provide a reasonable amount of comfort and support (Tables 11 and 12). Also, whereas 23 per cent of the latter group give "outside interests and a little independence" as a general reason for continuing work, the Ghanaian reaction in this regard is consistently both stronger and more specific. Thus, in addition to stressing that their aim is 'freedom' and 'independence', they express in some ten cases considerable doubt about the reliability of spouses in general. To the latter kind of uncertainty, the British make no reference at all (Tables 10 and 12).

Attitudes towards the idea of combining outside employment with the rearing of children, too, are different. Thus, although most of the Ghanaians and the British alike apparently intend to carry on full-time work after marriage, the percentage of the latter group drops to 68 per cent when it is a question of working after the arrival of children. By contrast, not only do nearly all the Ghanaians say they intend to continue in jobs but the proportion of those who apparently propose to work full-time is twice as large as the proportion of the British girls expressing this intention (Tables 9 and 10, 17 and 18). The Ghanaian replies also suggest a much stronger desire than the British to engage in paid employment even in the event of husbands providing adequate standards of comfort and support (Table 11).

Finally, how do the respondents intend to dispose of whatever salary, wages or money they earn ? Including those who propose to keep back something, a proportion as high as 83 per cent of the British compared with only 32 per cent of the Ghanaians intend to pay into a joint account with their husbands. Mostly the Ghanainas apparently intend, instead, to spend such money on their own children and their relatives as well as on themselves. Concern for relatives was also signified to some extent in replies to an extra question that the Ghanaian group alone was asked to answer. These indicated that the use to which money kept back would be specifically put would be mostly on educating the girls' own and their relatives' children. It appeared that these girls also had quite strongly in mind the employment of such funds for particular purposes of their own (Tables 20 and 21).

There is thus in respect of attitudes towards the marital relationship much more variation among the Ghanaian girls than the British. True, so far as can be judged, a large proportion of the Ghanaians view it in the some positive way as the British. They apparently expect, in other words, that the relationship with prospective husbands will be satisfactory and that both spouses will co-operate in the mutual task of home building. However, as we have just shown, a not inconsiderable proportion cf the Ghanaians do not have this kind of outlook. Instead, they appear to regard the marital relationship impersonally and are much more individualistic in their interpretation of it.

How is this difference to be explained ? Questionnaires do not always reveal respondents' true feelings and so perhaps the British girls have merely conveyed what they consider to be normative behaviour in relations between husband and wife. However, even if the Ghanaians have been franker in their replies, their attitude is too ambivalent to be so easily accounted for. It suggests the operation of factors that do not apply in the British case.

In fact a good deal of study has been made elsewhere of the Ghanaian situation in this regard, and so it may be helpful to look at the above Ghanaian attitudes in terms of the relevant structure of the Ghanaian society itself. By this is meant that the latter girls often have to contend with difficulties that do not confront the British girls at all. These difficulties derive from the clash between the traditional family system and modern marriage. (See inter alia, Busia 1950; Little 1974; Omari 1962; Dinan n.d.; Tetteh 1967; *Ideal Woman* and other African women's magazines). This is liable to affect the educated wife's position adversely in various ways. For example, if her husband has a good job he may feel obliged to provide less well-off nephews and nieces with as good an education as the couple's own children. Since a fifth of a man's income may be spent in this way or in other forms of assistance, the amount of housekeeping money available to his own wife is correspondingly depleted. In addition to the effect of this conflict of loyalties, there are also repercussions on the wife's position should the husband's financial circumstances be reversed, and he himself require kinship support. Perhaps his business has collapsed or he has for political reasons been passed over for promotion, got seriously into debt, or even been dismissed from his job. In such an event, he can usually rely upon his relatives' help, but at a price decided upon by them. This may well involve some control over his personal life, including the activities of his wife as well as his own.

Further, since conservatively minded kinsfolk are more concerned with procreation than the husband-wife relationship, the husband's people are as likely to encourage as to condemn his relations with other women. This consideration is the more significant because, although educated young men profess to regard 'love' as important for marriage, their idea of this emotion does not necessarily have an exclusive connotation. (Jahoda, 1959). True, it appears that a majority of the educated young men look upon polygamy with disfavour; and specially if socially ambitious, have as their aim statutory marriage, i.e. one contracted in church and/or before a registrar. However, as Omari has remarked, monogamy tends to be functionally associated with concubinage and mistress relations (1962). In other words, although few educated men have plural marriages, a substantial proportion made extra-marital arrangements whose effect is not dissimilar from polygamy.[4] The 'good-time' girls and others available for such liaisons are not usually to be regarded as prostitutes. They do expect, nevertheless, their services to be remunerated and so it is the practice of patrons and protectors to pay rentals and provide 'chop money' and other forms of assistance in cash or in kind. There is thus a further drain on household resources and even on the wife's own savings.[5] This is

---

[4] One of the main reasons for this situation is that the urban social system holds out visions of luxury and material comfort far beyond the reach of girls whose earnings as salesgirls, typists, and in other poorly paid occupations barely satisfy their basic needs let alone the aspirations aroused. Consequently, these young women—many of them rural migrants—depend on men to supplement their incomes.

[5] See also footnote 7 next page.

especially the case when such relationships take on a more or less permanent form and are productive of children. Indeed, there may already be 'outside' children to support because it is by no means uncommon for a man to marry by customary law before he is sufficiently established to obtain an educated wife. These customary law wives are usually put away prior to the statutory marriage taking place, but his relationship is invariably continued with any sons and daughters they may have borne. (Little, 1974, *et. alii*).

Also, although the educated woman gains some legal advantages through marriage by statute, there are some important drawbacks as well. Thus, despite her being now entitled to sue an adulterous husband for divorce, public opinion will not necessarily support such an action. Divorce proceedings tend to be protracted as well as expensive, and obviously there will be little materially to gain in the event of her husband being unable to pay adequate alimony or of his defaulting. Socially, too, she will drop in status, and since the ground on which she sued will naturally be known this is more than likely to discourage further educated suitors for her hand (Little, 1974). Also, how does she stand in the event of her husband's decease? If there is anything unusual about the circumstances in which he died, the widow's in-laws may accuse her of witchcraft and on this pretext seize immediately every article of property they can lay hands on. Since in patrilineal systems they have a claim to the children, a customary law wife may be given to the support and protection of her late husband's people; but these in-laws do not regard a woman married by statute as their responsibility. Instead, they may even occupy the deceased man's house, citing family laws of inheritance as the excuse. Admittedly, this is more likely to happen when the husband dies intestate, but a widow rendered homeless is not necessarily better off even if her husband has willed her money. What he left is likely to be needed for herself and her children, and there may not be enough for the costs of legal action.[6]

These difficulties of educated women are commonplace not only in Ghana, but in West Africa as a whole. They are frequently discussed and referred to with resentment when such women meet at conferences as well as in ordinary conversation.[7] Indeed, both the blandishments of male seducers and the infidelity of husbands are one of the most constant themes in the correspondence columns and short stories printed by women's magazines.[8]

---

[6]The Ghanaian women's magazine *Ideal Women* provides instances of this situation.

[7]At one such formal gathering the delegates concerned were mostly community workers, leaders of women's associations and so on. These women came from the Francophone countries as well as Anglophone ones and the purpose was to discuss problems of social welfare, including family planning, up-to-date methods of hygiene and the rearing of children. These matters were keenly debated but one speech won by far the greatest acclaim. It invited the audience to deal effectively with husbands whose practice it was to squander their wives' earnings on girl friends.

[8]See, *inter alia*, the Ghanaian magazine *Ideal Women* and the Nigerian magazine *Woman's World*. Present space does not permit the citation of examples, but it is significant that although editors of and contributors to these journals usually disapprove of husbands' infidelity, there is relatively little forthright criticism. Instead, wives are urged to be "understanding" and "tolerant" of sexual peccadiloes so long as a husband's liaisons are conducted with a reasonable amount of consideration for his wife's position. There is also the implication that an etiquette attaches to extra-marital relations and that this applies to the part played in such *affaires* by women as well as by men.

It is not strange, therefore, that the educated wife should seek ways of dealing with an unsatisfactory marriage, of offsetting insecurity and of safeguarding her own children. True, since we have now to return to the original question of careers, it must be remembered that Ghanaian women have a tradition of working to support themselves. It might, therefore, be argued that the urge shown by the present data simply repeats this *motif*: it merely brings up to date the time-honoured occupation of market-trading as a means of accumulating capital for more ambitious schemes. In other words, university experience has not detracted from this tradition. Instead, university training has been assimilated to it; making these women students even more career-minded than popular stereotypes of the entrepreneurial female trader.

However, what we have also to bear in mind are Oppong's findings and the educated woman's desire for a 'modern' type of union. These are important because the attitudes described as 'ambivalent' are also purposive. Instead, therefore, of being opposable they may simply express what is in effect a differential adaptation to ambiguities in the educated married woman's position. By this is meant that the tendency to regard the matrimonial situation in different ways is not entirely emotional. It involves a deliberate, although not necessarily conscious, strategy[9] whereby the women concerned prepare simultaneously for what Elizabeth Bott (1957) has usefully called a joint conjugal role relationship and a segregated role relationship. Bott applied the former term to the kind of family in which husband and wife spend as much time together as possible; all major decisions are taken together and the spouses help one another even in minor household matters. When, on the other hand, roles are segregated, both spouses participate in activities with people outside their own elementary family. Each will get some emotional satisfaction from these external relationships and will be likely to demand correspondingly less of the spouse.

What, therefore, is meant in the present case is that like the British girls the Ghanaians have hopes of marriage as a co-operative effort on the part of husband and wife. Unlike the British sample, however, the Ghanaians feel at the same time a good deal of doubt about the realization of this prospect. Consequently, to the extent that they anticipate not only disillusion, but having also to deal with practical problems of economic as well as social insecurity, their attitude towards marriage is pragmatic. This being the case, the well-marked decision of the Ghanaians to earn money and to carry on jobs as working mothers is not necessarily taken for its own sake. Rather is it to be seen as a form of insurance against a somewhat unpredictable future. It is made in order to provide oneself with greater personal latitude in the event of extra ground being required for monoeuvre.

If, therefore, despite their statistical limitations the data reported above can be accepted as evidence, the position of Ghanaian educated women is intricate. It is complex because these women do not reject the uxorial role in favour of

---

[9]Space does not permit a consideration of 'tactics' within the context of generalship; but *Ideal Woman* provides its women readers with much detailed advice in this regard.

careers but perform it in ways which—if required,—are instrumental to the achievement of alternative objectives.

REFERENCES

BOND, Barbara Harrell
    1975   *Modern Marriage in Sierra Leone.* The Hague, Mouton.

BOTT, Elizabeth
    1957   *Family and Social Network*, London: Tavistock Publications.

DINAN, Carmel,
    n.d.   Unpublished ms. A Study of the 'Single' Girl in a West African City.

JAHODA, Gustav
    1959   "Love, marriage and social change. Letters to the advice column of a West African newspaper." *Africa*, Vol. 29, No. 2.

LITTLE, Kenneth
    1966   "Attitudes towards marriage and the family among educated young Sierra Leoneans". In P.C. Lloyd (ed.) *New Elites of Tropical Atrica.* London: Oxford University Press for International African Institute.

    —
    1974   *African Women in Towns: An Aspect of Africa's Social Revolution.* Cambridge: Cambridge University Press.

MASEMANN, Vandra
    1974   'The Hidden Curriculum of a West African girls' boarding school'. *Canadian Journal of African Studies*, 8(3).

OMARI, Peter
    1962   "Changing attitudes of students in West African society towards marriage and family relationships." *British Journal of Sociology*, Vo. II, No. 3.

    —
    1962   *Marriage Guidance for Young Ghanaians.* Edinburgh, Nelson.

OPPONG, Christine
    1970   "Conjugal power and resources: an urban African example." *Journal of Marriage and the Family.* November.

    —
    1973   "Norms and Variations: A Study of Ghanaian Students' Attitudes to Marriage and Family Living". In C. Oppong (ed.) *Legon Family Research Papers.* Institute of African Studies, University of Ghana.

    —
    1974   *Marriage among a Matrilineal Elite.* Cambridge, Cambridge University Press.

TETTEH
    1967   "Marriage, Family and Household" in Birmingham, W., Neustadt J. and Amaboe, E.N. (eds.) *A Study of Contemporary Ghana* Vol. 2, Evanston, Ill, Northwestern University.

Qualities of Desired Spouse:
A Cross-Cultural Comparison Between
French and American College Students

BERNARD I. MURSTEIN*

What do people want in a marriage partner? Presumably, tastes vary not only from individual to individual but from nation to nation. Or do they? The fact is that we possess very little quantitative information on either count. There have been a series of items of qualities desired in a spouse which have been presented to American college students on a number of occasions (Powers, 1971). Men have generally rated highly characteristics such as emotional stability, pleasing disposition, desires a home and children, whereas women have given top priority to emotional stability, ambition, and pleasing disposition, in that order.

Such research suffers from a number of limitations. First, the small number of items chosen comes from the researcher and reflects his experience, judgment, and values rather than those of the subjects. Second, these lists may omit items with low social desirability such as "adequate sex-drive" or "sexually compatible" which are, nevertheless, important expectations in marriage. They may overemphasize vague generalities such as "desires home and children," which is probably true of most women and hence is rather undifferentiating as an item.

The author earlier (Murstein, 1976) developed a scale entitled the Marriage Expectation Test(MET). Development of the scale commenced by reviewing many of the better known tests and item lists describing ideal spouses and engagement success. In addition, engaged persons were interviewed, and their opinions solicited. Finally the author added items from his own experience in the field to arrive at a pool of 262 items. Through several factor analyses (Murstein, 1966) these were whittled down to a 132 item male scale and 137 item female scale in which the first 78 items are common to both sexes.

Such a test, by offering a representative series of items to be evaluated by students in a five point scale (very important to not at all important), is more apt to indicate the consciously acknowledged characteristics subjects are seeking in a spouse than a ten to twenty item check list. Rather than focusing on single items, factor analysis offers more stable clusters of associated items or dimensions of marital expectation.

* My thanks to Leo Schneiderman, Gilbert Nass, and Michael Gordon for aid in recruiting subjects and to Jacqueline McGinty, Marianne Calo, Frank Fulchierro, Laurie Riddett, and Jane Arabian who tested, scored, and computed the data. Jerry Lamb was kind enough to develop the program for the analyses. Ted L. Huston, Regina Roth, and Robert G. Ryder generously gave the manuscript the benefit of their criticism.
**Department of Psychology, Connecticut College, New London, Connecticut 06320 U.S.A.

Our intent was to factor analyze the MET for an American college population and examine the first nine factors extracted from both a male and female sample. This would then be compared with data from a different western national population (France) for similarity and differences in factorial structure. Last, item analyses would be done for each item to determine differences in expectations between the American and French samples.

It was predicted that French college students would be more traditional and less egalitarian concerning spousal roles than United States students for two reasons. First, spousal egality depends, in part, on a high level of industrialization, so that dependence on physical strength, such as is involved in hunting and large scale agrarian societies, is minimized. Although both the United States and France qualify as industrialized societies, the degree of industrialization of the United States exceeds that of France. Second, historically speaking, the ideology regarding equality of the sexes has been more pronounced in the United States than in France. Pioneer conditions resulted in a relatively high status for American women, while French women lagged behind French men (Murstein, 1974). Women achieved the right to vote a generation earlier in the United States, and the Woman's Rights Movement has been much more vigorous and influential there.

Factor Analysis of the American Population

Population

The MET was administered to students drawn from classes and dormitories from four Connecticut colleges and universities (two private, two state universities). There were 172 male and 196 female subjects, the mean and standard deviation for the men's ages being 19.98 and 1.62 years respectively; that of women was 19.21 and 1.32. Approximately one third of the subjects were volunteers, the others coming from sociology and psychology classes.

Test

The MET instructions called for the subject to examine the items according to his realistic rather than socially desirable expectations in a spouse. If the item described his expectations very closely, he was to put a 5 next to it, if the item were generally true but not always, he put a 4. If he was unsure or thought the item applicable some times but not others, he put a 3 next to it. If the items were generally untrue but not always so, he put a 2. If the items were completely opposite to his expectations, he scored it 1.

Results

Factor analyses were done separately by sex by the principal components method and the Kaiser varimax rotation. It was arbitrarily decided to extract nine factors which seemed a convenient number to work with in an essentially exploratory study. According to one criterion of when to stop factoring (Harman, 1967), the cutoff point should be when the eigenvalues drop below 1. In the analyses we did, this cutoff was reached only after the forty-second factor had been extracted. There are, in short, a plethora of factors for our sample, but we shall consider only the first nine. The percent of variance accounted for by our nine factors for women is only 36, the first factor extracted for the women accounts for only 9.39 percent of the total variance and the ninth factor accounted for only 2.18 percent. For men, the situation was much the same, the nine factors accounted for 38 percent of the variance, with the first factor accounting for 11.32 percent of the total variance and the ninth factor for 2.07 percent.

Significant loadings were defined as 1.96 times the standard error of the factor. In practice this meant that loadings of .35 or greater were considered as significant. Because of space limitations, the items significantly loaded for each factor cannot be presented here[1]. However, a brief description of the factors and their highest loadings, which defined them, can be presented. For simplicity of exposition, the factors are described from the point of view of high positive loadings.

Women's Loadings

The first factor for women is labelled *Popular and Socially Minded*. The husband described by women gets along well with friends, parents, and just about anyone. Factor 2 is quite clearly the *Patriarchal-Dominant Male Stereotype*. The male envisioned would play the dominant role in running the family, while the wife would stay at home doing the cooking and housekeeping and raising the children. The third factor is defined by a man who is calm, reacts pleasantly to suggestions, listens well, is responsible, but is not jealous and overpossessive. It is labelled *Even-Tempered, Well-Balanced*. Factor 4 is most strongly represented by items relating to free sexual expression before marriage, but also contains items relating to anti-religious and authority feelings. It seems appropriate to call it *Free Sexual Expression; Anti-Church*.

The fifth factor describes a man who is muscular, taller than his girlfriend, has a good physique, is not fat, is in good physical condition, and is strong and sexually attractive. In addition, his family is of higher social standing and has more money than that of his girlfriend; accordingly, this factor is called *Physical Appearance and Status*.

The sixth factor involved a man who loves his girlfriend and does not feel unloved himself. He is not passive and unaggressive, appreciates a good homemaker, and is in favor of mutual respect for each other's religious, political, and ethical beliefs. Also, he is in good physical condition, finds it hard to spend leisure time together with his girlfriend, is patient with her, can accept disappointment, and can maintain emotional balance and control. Last, he does not insist that his wife be at least three years younger than him. The organization of all these variables under one rubric is not as obvious as with other factors, but by relying on the heaviest loadings, we may call this factor *Loving and Tolerant*.

Factor 7 depicts a man whom his girlfriend can respect, and who both respects and admires his girlfriend. Affectionate, he does not take advantage of her, but confides in her and appreciates what she does for him. He listens to his partner, helps solve her problems, and is admired by her. We call this factor *Admirable and Respected*. The eighth factor is called *Responsible and Controlled* because it is most highly loaded for a man who does not fly off the handle for every little thing, and who accepts the responsibility of being a spouse. He believes education is important for women and can exercise self-control and be strict if necessary. The ninth and last factor deals with a man who expects his wife to care for the children only when they are babies. He will decide about the children's lives and future, and he is not particularly appreciative of her staying home and caring for him and the children. He thinks it is her duty to take full responsibility for their care and training while he is concentrating on his job. The factor is called *Relegates Child Care to Wife*.

Men's Loadings

For men, the first factor was called *Traditional-Submissive* because it loaded highly for items in which the woman catered to a patriarchal, nineteenth-century type of husband. This desired woman, for example, would believe that the husband should decide whether or not she would work. He would be "boss", decide all "masculine" matters, and make all the decisions, while she adhered to the traditional exclusively domestic role.

We call the second factor the *Nurturant Madonna* because of her sterling qualities. Among her multitude of virtues is the fact that she does not fly off the handle at every little thing, she accepts the responsibility of being a spouse, is attentive, not suspicious, forgiving, insightful, keeps promises, does not always have to have her way, is dependable. Need I go further?

Our third factor depicts a woman who has lots of friends, joins in the fun and humor at parties, is the life of the party, has likable friends, is popular socially, is liked by her boyfriend's friends, mixes socially, is a good dancer, and is popular with men. This factor is therefore the female counterpart of the male factor of *Popular and Socially Minded,* without items relating to interaction with the parents. Those items referring to the fact that both the mother and father of the girlfriend like the man, and both of his parents like her, occur in Factor 4 which is called *Family Approved.*

Factor 5 describes a woman who is efficient, will *not* yield her point of view in order to avoid argument, can take criticism well, and can criticize herself. She likes responsibility, wants to make a plan for saving, doesn't mind a good argument, is critical of her boyfriend, can be strict, is not shy, and is a good, neat, and orderly homemaker. It is labelled *Efficient, Non-Defensive and Outspoken.* The sixth factor is exactly the counterpart of the male *Free Sexual Expression* with the exception that the anti-church component is omitted.

Factor 7 is related to appearance, both physical and social, as was the women's fifth factor labelled "physical appearance and status." Instead of wealth and social status accompanying physical appearance as desiderata which was the case in the women's expectations, the men have substituted orderliness, craves my company, good homemaker, good manners, and does not smoke excessively. The physical side of the picture is represented by good figure, well-developed breasts, and good looking legs. The factor is called *Physical and Social Appearance.*

The eighth factor envisions a woman who, if she works, will relinquish half of the housework to her hubby. She will know as much as he does about family finances, will not be worried if she earns as much as he does, has more education than he, will have sexual relations anytime he wants to, but will also expect him to do the same. Such men expect an *Egalitarian Relationship with Spouse*. The last factor concerns itself with a woman who makes the man feel passionate and is passionate herself. In short, she is a good lover. Additionally, however, she can confide in the man, is admired by him, but is not more intelligent than he. She radiates confidence, is forgiving and listens to and helps the man solve his problems. It is not easy to cluster these items under a meaningful label, but we shall call it *Passionate and Man-Oriented*.

Discussion of Factors

Inspection of the factors leads to one inescapable conclusion. They are concerned with the central issues which traditionally have influenced marital choice and apparently still do today. Shall one marry a family approved, popular spouse or a non-conformist; shall it be the traditional, domestic woman and patriarchal male marriage or a more egalitarian one? Will it be sex before marriage or afterwards; and looks and status or psychological compatibility? The dimensions invite future research. Scales could be constructed from the higher loadings on each factor and marriage types categorized by noting which kinds of individuals were drawn to which.

How general are these dimensions of marital expectation? To get some idea of generalizability, a sample of French students was studied.

Factor Analysis.of French METs

The MET was translated into French, and a graduate student from France left 200 of the forms for men and 200 for women with students at several colleges and universities in and around Paris. About one-third of these were either not returned or improperly filled out for one or more items and had to be discarded. As a result, 131 male and 137 female METs were factor-analyzed. The mean and standard deviation of the ages of the students was men mean 21.42, S.D. 2.36; women mean 21.71, S.D. 4.23.

Surprisingly, the first nine factors extracted for both French men and French women account for more of the total variance than is the case for American men and women for whom the test was designed; thus where nine factors acconted for 38 percent of the total variance for American men, nine factors for the French men accounted for 48 percent of the variance. For women, the difference was even greater. Whereas 36 percent of the variance is acconted for by the 9 American women's factors, the same number of factors accounted for 49 percent of the total variance for the French women. Apparently, the criteria for selection are less complex, relatively speaking, for French as opposed to American college students, and for French women in particular.

It is possible to compare the similarity of the French and American factorial structure for similarity; however, before doing this it should be noted that the ages and schooling of the subjects are not identical. Table 1 shows a significant difference in the ages and years of college schooling of American and French women and in the ages of American and French men. It is impossible to say whether these differences in age and schooling necessarily influenced the marital expectations, but they serve as a caution that the factor analyses may be of different populations apart from nationality. Later in the paper these differences will be controlled for before undertaking the item analyses.

TABLE 1

MEANS AND STANDARD DEVIATIONS FOR AGE AND YEAR IN

COLLEGE FOR AMERICAN AND FRENCH MALE AND FEMALE SUBJECTS

Variable Compared	Groups Compared	American Mean	S. D.	French Mean	S. D.	t
Age	American Men vs French Men	19.98	1.62	21.42	2.63	4.47**
	American Women vs French Women	19.21	1.32	21.71	4.23	6.69**
Year in School	American Men vs French Men	2.65	.96	2.96	1.77	1.90
	American Women vs French Women	2.21	.90	3.50	1.22	10.81**

**p .01

The factorial structure of the American and French populations may be compared by use of the coefficient of congruence[2] which is somewhat analogous to a coefficient of correlation (Harman, 1967). The French male factors were correlated with the American male factors and the matrix of coefficients of congruences for men is depicted in Table 2 and for women in Table 3.

TABLE 2

COEFFICIENTS OF CONGRUENCE BETWEEN FACTORS OF MARITAL EXPECTATION OF A SPOUSE BY AMERICAN AND FRENCH MEN

French Men's Factors	American Men's Factors								
	I Traditional-Submissive	II Nurturant Madonna	III Popular and Socially Minded	IV Family Approved	V Efficient, Non-Defensive, Outspoken	VI Free Sexual Expression	VII Physical and Social Appearance	VIII Egalitarian Relationship With Spouse	IX Passionate and Man-Oriented
I Socially Adequate Madonna	31	(58)	47	37	41	-05	41	12	32
II Traditional-Submissive	(82)	10	14	32	-15	11	46	-09	01
III Family Approved	19	52	23	(57)	35	05	43	15	29
IV Social and Oriented Away From Home	-12	-18	(33)	-11	05	11	-07	25	-07
V Free Sexual Expression and Anti-Church	-30	-09	-03	-33	-10	(47)	-04	00	14
VI Responsible, Personally Adequate Madonna	12	(41)	03	-02	24	-02	14	21	14
VII Controlled and Socially Inclined	02	(44)	32	12	31	-04	13	17	31
VIII Cooperative and Physically Appealing	10	(33)	27	31	20	24	(33)	(33)	21
IX Subservient	06	-02	-18	-12	-10	-03	(30)	-03	-21

Note: Decimal points have been omitted.

TABLE 3

COEFFICIENTS OF CONGRUENCE BETWEEN FACTORS OF MARITAL EXPECTATION OF A SPOUSE BY AMERICAN AND FRENCH MEN

French Women's Factors	American Women's Factors								
	I Family Approved, Popular, and Socially Minded	II Patriarchal-Dominant Male Stereotype	III Even-Tempered, Well-Balanced	IV Free Sexual Expression and Anti-Church	V Physical Appearance and Status	VI Loving and Tolerant	VII Admirable and Respected	VIII Responsible and Controlled	XI Man Who Delegates Child Care to Wife
I Socially Adequate, Rational, Greek God	(56)	03	42	08	36	32	39	36	16
II Wife Aider	21	-36	25	-01	(31)	14	14	03	-11
III Emotionally Stable, Responsible and Warm	32	-04	(49)	-05	09	31	37	18	04
IV Family Approved, Well-Bred	(62)	19	29	-32	50	18	25	09	09
V Spouse-Oriented	06	15	03	-06	16	31	(42)	19	-12
VI Physically Appealing	22	11	02	21	(48)	-05	16	-05	10
VII Egalitarian and Respects Wife's Career	09	-56	(24)	04	00	05	20	05	-14
VIII Free Sexual Expression and Anti-Church	-08	-28	-24	(55)	-02	05	-05	03	13
IX Patriarchal Dominant Male Stereotype	14	(56)	-00	-32	29	00	02	-05	20

Note: Decimal points have been omitted.

Comparison of French and American Male Factors

Inspection of Table 2 shows that the first French factor for men's expectations "Socially Approved Madonna" correlated at least moderately (.40 or higher) with four American male factors. The highest correlation (.58) was with the second American factor "Nurturant Madonna." The factors are similar in that both groups of men want a veritable fountain of goodness and attentiveness in their wives. The differences stem from the fact that the American men emphasize the nurturant aspect of the madonna, whereas the French men give little ground here in favor of desiring a spouse in whom social competence is fused with personal involvement in her spouse.

The second French male factor is the desire for a "Traditional-Submissive" spouse. This shows a very high correlation (.82) with the American male factor 1, also labelled "Traditional-Submissive," The third French male factor "Family Approved" correlates moderately well (.57) with the fourth American factor, also so labeled. The correlation was not higher mainly because other items on both factors not pertaining to family approval did not covary very much. The French "Family Approved" spouse has many desirable characteristics, which may be why the parents like her so much. Not surprisingly, therefore, this factor also correlates substantially (.52) with the American male factor II, "Nurturant Madonna."

The fourth French factor "Social and Oriented Away From Home" is a very motley, undefined factor and does not correlate substantially with any American male factor. The fifth French factor is much clearer and is called "Free Sexual Expression and Anti-Church" because the desire is for a sexually oriented and experienced bride and there is an anti-church attitude. It correlates .47 with the similarly labeled American factor 6, the relative lowness of the correlation again presumably being due to lower loaded items not relating to sex or religion.

Factor 6 for the French men is labeled "Responsible, Personally Adequate Madonna," and it correlates highest (.41) with the second American factor "Nurturant Madonna." There is a slight difference in emphasis, with the French factor describing a desirable woman who is nonetheless particularly capable and self-sustaining, whereas the American factor involves the woman focusing more on the man.

The seventh French factor is called "Controlled and Socially Inclined" and correlates highest (.44) with the American factor 2, "Nurturant Madonna." The correlation results from the overlap of an even tempered socially competent woman common to both factors. The eighth French factor "Cooperative and Physically Appealing" and the ninth factor "Subservient" do not correlate substantially with any American male factor.

Comparison of French and American Female Factors

The first French women's factor "Socially Adequate, Rational, Greek God" correlates moderately well (.56) with the American women's first factor "Family Approval, Popular, and Socially Minded." The communality resides in the social adequacy desired in the male. The second French women's factor involves a husband eager to aid his wife around the house. No comparable American factor was found. The third French factor "Emotionally Stable, Responsible, and Warm" showed a moderate association (.49) with the third American factor "Even-Tempered, Well-Balanced." It may be seen that the factors are most similar in the perception of *personality characteristics* that the helpful ideal-husband would possess, but the American factor makes no mention of *actual help* around the house.

Factor 4 for the French women "Family Approved, Well Bred" correlates fairly well (.62) with American Factor 1, "Family Approved, Popular, and Socially Minded" having family approval common to both. The same French factor correlates moderately (.50) with the American factor 5, "Physical Appearance and Status."

The fifth French women's factor, "Spouse-Oriented," correlates moderately (.42) with the American factor "Admirable and Respected." What is common to both factors is the appreciation of the wife by the husband. French women's Factor 6, "Physically Appealing," is most related (.48) to American Factor 5, "Physical Appearance, Status." For the American women, physical appeal and wealth go together, but the dimension is exclusively physical for the French women.

The seventh French factor "Egalitarian and Respects Wife's Career" is negatively correlated (-.56) with the second American factor "Patriarchal-Dominant Male Stereotype." The labels make it clear why the two are negatively related. Inspection of the data indicates that the negative correlation is not artifactual (i.e., it is not due merely to reflection of signs in the extraction of the factors). The highest loadings in each factor are not the same but represent true opposites — the French stressing egalitarianism between husband and wife, the American opting for a traditional patriarchal role for the spouse.

The eighth French factor "Free Sexual Expression and Anti-Church" has an American counterpart (.56) in the similarly labeled American female Factor 4. Last, the ninth French women's factor, "Patriarchal-Dominant Male Stereotype," corresponds fairly closely (.56) to the American female Factor 2 of the same label.

Cross-Cultural Comparison for Factors

To facilitate the discussion, a comparison of best correlating positive factors is shown in Tables 2 and 3 by considering each French factor and circling the American factor with which it is most highly, positively correlated. Due to ties, 11 coefficients are actually circled for men (Table 2) and 9 for women (Table 3). Inspection of these tables indicates considerable but not overwhelming similarity between both of the men's and the women's groups. The highest similarity occurs between the men's groups for "Traditional-Submissive" spouse. Three factors among the French men (4, 8, 9) and two among the American men (8, 9) had no substantive correlations (arbitrarily defined as .40). It is probable, however, that the fact that Factors 8 and 9 were the last two extracted and that they account for little variance is responsible for the lack of association.

Turning to the women, the highest correlation was between the fourth French factor "Family-Approved, Well-Bred" and the first American factor "Family Approved, Popular, and Socially Minded." A slightly greater number of the women's factors showed no substantive positive correlation (French 2, 7; American 6, 8, 9). The French dimension of "Wife Aider" and "Egalitarian and Respects Wife's Career" is not related to any American women's dimensions, and the American "Loving and Tolerant," "Responsible and Controlled" and "Relegates Child Care to Wife" have no clear French counterpart. The last two or three factors are by definition, the weakest. What stands out therefore is the French woman's concern about help in the house, which concern is not shared by the American woman. In order to examine the actual position of the subjects from the different cultures on these items rather than their dimensional concerns, it is necessary to do an item analysis.

Differences in Expectations of French and Americans

American men vs. French men

Because the two groups of men had differed significantly in age and showed a strong direction towards a significant difference in schooling, it was decided to compare the largest possible subsample of American and French men who were not significantly different on either of these characteristics. This was achieved by comparing the number of men in each year of schooling and using the sample with the smallest number of men as the matching criterion; thus, all French graduate students were eliminated since no such students were represented in the American sample. In the first year of college, there were initially 24 American men and 40 French men. The American men, therefore, were the matching criterion. Twenty-four first year French men were randomly selected from the pool of 40; the same thing was done for each of the three succeeding years of schooling.

As a result of this *expicit* matching, the years of college were indentical for the men of both countries (M.2.53, S.D. 1.12). Age was not explicitly selected, but by virtue of the schooling selection, the ages of the 89 French and 89 American men showed no significant difference (American M.20.24, S.D. 1.89; French M.20.70, S.D. 1.75 (t = 1.39, n.s.)).

An identical selection procedure resulting in identical schooling for the 80 American and 80 French women (M.2.82, S.D. 0.90). The respective ages were also not significantly different (American M.20.06, S.D. 1.09; French M.20.21, S.D. 1.05 (t = 1.07, n.s.)).

The 89 French and American men were compared for differences in item response for each of the 132 items of the male form of the Marital Expectation Test. Because of the large number of comparisons, only these items different at the .01 level or better were regarded as significant. In view of the factorial similarity, it might be expected that the differences would not be extreme; however, this was not the case. Some 43 of the 132 items differentiated the subjects. Inspection of the data indicated that French men differ from American men in some unanticipated ways. They want a wife who is less religious, less respectful of authority, and less interested in planning and saving. This partner is not as concerned about the responsibilities of being a spouse, is more likely to smoke, and is much freer than The American counterpart regarding sex (she thinks sex is O.K. with anyone you "like," wants sex before marriage, and does not have conventional sex standards).

The French men also want a more egalitarian relationship with the wife. They are less likely to expect their wives to delegate financial responsibility solely to them, to have them decide whether the wife will work, or to let them concentrate on their job, while leaving the child care to the wife. Moreover, they are more willing to share household tasks and to agree that the husband is not boss.

There is also a pragmatic, non-idealized quality to their desires regarding a spouse. They are more concerned about a normal heredity, but less concerned about marrying an admirable, physical strong and emotionally-stable spouse who confides all to the husband.

Their idealized spouse departs considerably from the traditional-submissive stereotype. She is much tougher and aggressive than her American sister. Comparatively speaking, she does not mind a good argument, but talks back and does not let others dominate her, including her spouse. She feels she *must* always have her way, is not dependent but decisive, likes responsibility, is not shy, can be strict if necessary, and does *not* react pleasantly to suggestions. Seemingly contradictory is the fact that although she does not enjoy competition per se and yields her point to avoid argument, she is more competitive with her husband than with others. But it may be that competition and argument are negatively value loaded as compared to expressive even aggressive ordinary debate. Moreover, being competitive with hubby may be a way of expressing egalitarianism, which French men favor.

Physical appearance, however, is more paramount for the French than for the American men. They also are more likely to emphasize that the spouse be no taller than they, and that she have a good figure and good legs.

Somehow this more aggressive, demanding French woman must achieve her goals without sacrificing her popularity, for this is important to French men. His mother must like and accept her, she should be popular socially, popular with men, and, in short, she should be the life of the party. To summarize, the French men compared to American men want an *aggressive, sexy, unidealized, egalitarian, unconventional, but socially popular spouse.*

French Women vs. American Women

Overall, the expectations of the 80 French women seem more similar to the French men's expectations than to the expectations of the 80 American women. Some 49 of the 137 items were significantly different at the .01 level or better. Like the French men, the French women very much wanted a more egalitarian spouse than did the American women. There are such a multitude of examples of this that we shall list only a sample of the items reflecting this expectation. A tendency to expect the husband to grant equality in decisions over financial matters is accompanied by expectations that the husband will help around the house, will aid with the dishes, and will not relegate *care* of the children to the wife, while reserving *decisions* about their life to himself. He will accept her desire for a career even if it means combining a career with motherhood. Her interest in community affairs and lack of desire to be a good homemaker will not disturb him any more than the fact that she may earn as much as he.

As with the French men, the French woman is less idealistic about the qualities of a husband than her American counterpart. She is less apt to admire him and has less need of his admiring her. Her ideal is more nervous, less cooperative, has less of a sense of humor, is less sexually attractive, less patient, and less able to accept disappointment and adjust to change. However, it is more important that he have the same political beliefs and a comparable sex drive.

The French woman also desires a more aggressive spouse than the American woman. Relatively speaking, he does not mind a good argument, is less respectful of authority, is bothered by not having his own way, likes responsibility, is straightforward and direct, and does not react pleasantly to suggestions. As with the French men's expectations, however, directness and aggressiveness are separated from competitiveness. The French ideal husband will not enjoy competition as much as the American men, and also will be less likely to compete with his wife.

Physical appearance and unconventionality, unlike the case with French men, do not appear differentiating for French women. However, in the area of sex, we find the French woman more accepting of sex with a liked person, a fiancé, and in general, before marriage. On the other hand, they are less likely to require a husband who makes them feel passionate or to enjoy one who wants to make love whenever *he* feels like it.

Again, as with French men, a popular, socially poised spouse is more valued than by American women. The husband should be a good dancer, popular socially, and not lacking in social graces. It is not as necessary, however, that he enjoy being with people. In sum, the ideal French husband differs from the American one in being more *egalitarian, pragmatic and less idealized, more aggressive, less conventional on sex matters, and more popular socially.*

Discussion

Despite the expectation that the French would be more traditional and less egalitarian concerning spousal roles than the Americans, the data indicate a much greater egalitarian viewpoint regarding the expectation of a future spouse for both French men and French women. In interpreting our findings, the first question to deal with is, how much of the differences found are due to intercultural factors, and how much to different sampling techniques and different strata being sampled? It is clear that there are considerable differences in the latter categories even when the subjects show no significant differences for age and year in school. The majority of the French students, for example, came from various colleges in Paris, with some coming from the University at

Nanterre. The American subjects, however, came mainly from a northeastern state university, supplemented by a few from private colleges. The French group, therefore, was somewhat more cosmopolitan. In addition, the opportunity to go to college in France is much more restrictive than in the United States and more dependent on excelling in examinations than is the case for the American state university, which contributed most of our subjects. Further, the American subjects were mainly "captives" in that they were tested for the most part in large classes. The French subjects, however, were approached in their rooms and were all volunteers.

Analysis of these differences may provide a lead as to the unexpected results. The American group may be more typical of American students, whereas the Parisians may be an extremely selected elite which is atypical with respect to the rest of France. Whether our French data reflect an elitish image by highly educated college students in general, or only the atypical liberality of the Parisian volunteer collegiate population is a point which can only be determined by testing other collegiate populations. However, since philosophies as well as fashions generally travel from the elite down to the less elite, it may well be that the Parisian students represent a trend of marital orientation for urban, collegiate populations, if not the France of tomorrow.

Last, inspection of the factors and items indicates a considerable sex difference that transcends cultural differences. Despite the greater concern about egality between men and women, the sexes still show some differences in their spousal expectations, and these follow traditional lines. Women in both cultures show more factors concerned with interpersonal relationship and the interaction between the husband and wife — what Talcott Parsons would call "expressive concerns."

Men show more concern about the traditional-submissive role of the spouse, and her passion potential. They also emphasize more her social stimulus attributes, and give somewhat less emphasis to her interactional qualities. Although this is a question of emphasis rather than sharp contrasts, it appears that relative to women they emphasize the "object" qualities of the intended spouse more than the interactional qualities. Perhaps this is due to the greater status of men in both societies, which makes them less dependent on marriage for their emotional and interpersonal gratifications. It should be interesting to see whether these traditional concerns persist in the face of increasing change in the status and sex-role behavior of the sexes.

---

[1]Copies of the male and female versions of the MET may be obtained by enclosing $1.00 payable to the Psychology Department, Connecticut College, New London, Conn. 06320, U.S.A. to cover the cost of reproduction. Copies of the MET and the complete factor analysis and item analysis, significant differences, etc., for both the French and American samples (slightly less than 50 pages) may be obtained by enclosing a check for $3.50.

---

[2]It will be recalled that only the first 78 of the items were common to both sexes. Hence it is impossible to compare the two sexes for similarity of factorial structure.

REFERENCES

Harman, H. H.
  1967   Modern Factor Analysis. (2nd ed.). Chicago: The University of Chicago Press.
Murstein, B. I.
  1966   "Phychological determinants of marital choice." Progress Report NIMH 08-405-02.
Murstein, B. I.
  1974   Love, sex, and marriage through the ages." New York: Springer.
Murstein, B. I.
  1976   Who will marry whom? Theories and research in marital choice. New York: Springer.
Powers, E. A.
  1971   "Thirty years of research on ideal mate characteristics: What do we know?" International Journal of Sociology of the Family 1: 1-9.

Orientations to Marriage Among Young Canadians

CHARLES W. HOBART§

Future historians must surely identify the twentieth century as the period during which women gained a slow but increasingly complete emancipation from the second class status that had been their lot in North America. At the turn of the century they were disfranchised; their property rights and their freedom of access to gainful employment were inferior to those of men.[1] Their sexual freedom, too, was inferior, as the well-known double standard and some of the Kinsey research clearly testify (Kinsey, et al, 1948, 1953). By 1971 there were many indications that these restrictions had been significantly mitigated (Hobart, 1971).

The major developments of this century are quickly outlined. The employment opportunities accompanying World War I reinforced women's sense of the limitations of their traditional status and their ambitions for a

§Professor of Sociology, Department of Sociology, The University of Alberta, Canada,

[1]This is shown by certain provincial and federal laws in force prior to 1900, see, British Columbia, e. g. (Married Women's Property Act, R. S. B. C., 1888, 51 Vic., c. 80 ; Dower Act, R. S. B. C., 1897, 60 Vic,, c. 63) ; Alberta, e. g. (Property and Civil Rights Act, Ord., 1884, 47 Vic., no. 26 ; Married Women's Real Estate Act, Ord., 886, 49 Vic., no. 6 ; Personal Property of Married Women, R. S. O., 1889, 52 Vic., no. 16, 1898, c. 47); Ontario, e. g (An Act Respecting Certain Separate Rights of Property of Married Women, C. S. U. C., 1859, 22 Vic., c. 73 ; *Ontario Statutes Annotations, R. S. O., 1960* (Toronto : Canada Law Bank Co., 1961) p. 378, citing " Married Women's Real Estate Act, " C S. U. C, 1859, c 85 ; Property Act of Married Women, R. S. O., 1887, 50 Vic., c. 132, Dower Act, c. 133, Married Woman's Real Estate Act, c. 134) ; New Brunswick, e. g. (Married Woman's Property Act, S. N. B., 1896, 58 Vic., c. 24) ; Newfoundland, e. g. (Married Woman's Property Act, R. S. N., 1883); Nova Scotia, e. g. (Married Woman's Property Act, 1898, 52 Vic., c. 22, Dower Act, c. 23) ; Prince Edward Island, e. g. (Married Woman's Property Act, 1896, Journ. P. E. I.). This may also be inferred from amendments to the above laws, and passage of later statutes pertaining to the property rights of women. For the statutes passed after 1900, see, British Columbia, e. g (Married Woman's Property Act, S. B C., 1915, 5 Geo. V, c. 41, as amended ; Mother's Pension Act, S. B. C., 1920, 10–11 Geo. V, c 61) ; Alberta, e. g. (Henrietta Muir Edwards, ed., *Legal Status of Women of Alberta* : *As shown by Extracts from Dominion and Provincial Laws* (2nd ed ; Edmonton: Issued by Attorney General, 1921), p. 26, citing " Dower Act ", S. A., 917, p. 28, citing " Personal Property Act ", C. O., 1911, c. 47, sec. 1, no. 20 of 1890 ; " Real Estate Act ", S. A., 1906, c. 9, sec. 10 ; " Intestate Succession Act ", S. A., 1920, sec. 3 (a) (c), c. 19, S. A., 1906 ; p. 31, citing " Married Woman's Relief Act ", S. A., c. 19, 1910, as amended ; p. 72, citing " Dominion Lands Act ", S. C., 1908, c. 20 ; An Act Respecting the Transfer and Descent of Land, 1906, S. A., c. 19, 1922, c. 10); Saskatchewan, e. g. (Married Woman's Property Act, 1907, S. S., 7 Ed III, c 18); Manitoba, e. g. (Married Woman's Property Act, 1913, 3 Geo. V, c. 123 ; Devolution of Estates Act, c. 48 ; Ontario, e g. (Property Rights of Married Women, R. S. O., 1914, 9 Ed. VII, c. 149, as amended ; Dower Act, 1914, S. O., 9 Ed. VII, c. 39) ; Quebec, e. g. (Property Rights of Married Women, C. C. Q. S., 1931, art. 986, 1954, art. 986, as amended ; Women's Property Rights, Q. S., 1909, 9 Ed. VII, c. 30 ; Woman's Contract Rights, C. C. Q. S., 4 Ed. VII, art 1301, as amended) ; New Brunswick, e. g. (Act Respecting Dower, C. S. N. B., 1903, 6 Vic., c. 77) : Newfoundland, e. g (Property Rights of Married Women Act, R S. N , 1952, c. 143, as amended); Prince Edward Island, e. g. (Married Woman's Property Act, 1903, 3 Ed. VII, c. 9).

changed future, thus strengthening the suffragette demands that gained the franchise for women in 1918 in Canada,[2] and in 1920 in the United States.[3]

If the Crash of 1929 and the Great Depression that followed closed factories in every major centre and drove women back into the home, it drove men—up to 26 per cent of the male work force in Canada at the height of the Depression[4]—into the streets, making them unable to provide for their families. Thus the justification for masculine dominance of the family based on economic support was broken as never before, particularly so as some wives were able to get work and support their families when their husbands could not.

World War II was more desperately fought than was the First World War; accordingly the needs for female labor on the farm, in the factory, and in the armed forces as well was greater. Thus its emancipating effect was correspondingly great, and this effect has been prolonged in attenuated form to the present day, particularly in the United States. A nostalgic demand to return to "normalcy" after the war—including returning women to the home —was soon terminated by the Cold War, the Berlin Crisis, and wars in Korea and Viet Nam. These influences were of course weaker in Canada because Canada was less involved in these wars and also because massive immigration after the war brought millions of men and women here who had more conservative traditional conceptions of sex roles than most native-born Canadians.[5] But this conservativism was powerfully counteracted in English speaking Canada at least, by the heavy impact of American Mass Media.[6] Thus it appears that the egalitarianism pressures which have been building in the United States since about 1950 have been communicated with almost undiminished power to Canada, though the socio-economic conditions here are not so urgently conducive.

[2]Elections Act, S. C., 1918, 8–9 Geo. V. c. 20. This Act amended sec. 62 (p) of the Wartime Election Act, S. C., 1917, 7–8 Geo. V. c. 39, which limited the franchise to women having close relatives in the armed forces.

[3]U. S. const. amend. XIX, sec. 177 (1920). *August 26, 1920 May 24, 1918.*

[4]Canada, Department of Trade and Commerce, *The Canada Yearbook*, 1940 (Ottawa: King's Printer, 1940), subsections 1, 2, and 4 pp. 750, 751, and 759 ; see also Canada, Department of Labour, *The Labour Gazette*, 1934 (Ottawa : King's Printer, 1934) XXXIV, 49–65.

[5]Immigration figures cited in (Canada, Department of Manpower and Immigration, *Immigration Statistics : Canadian Immigration Division*, 1967 (Ottawa : King's Printer, 1967) p. 4, show that during the years 1951 to 1960, 1,521,679 people entered Canada. This represented 10.8% of the total population in 1951. The years of peak immigration were 1957 and 1953, when 282,164 and 168,868 people entered respectively. (1967 when 222,876 people entered; 1966 when 194,743 entered).

[6]The most recent figures on television content reported by the Committee on Broadcasting, *Report of the Committee on Broadcasting.* Robert M. Fowler, chairman (Ottawa : Queen's Printer, 1965), pp. 32–36, show that in a study of television programs shown from 6 : 00 p. m. to midnight in four typical Canadian cities during March, 1964, 51% to 78% of all programs available to viewers were of American origin. The proportion of American programs broadcast by Canadian stations is limited to the Canadian Broadcasting Act (S. C., 1958, 7 Eliz. II, c. 22) ruling, that 55% of daily television program content must be Canadian produced. However, on the average, 54% of Canadian homes can receive American television programs directly from U. S. stations. The most recent information on magazine distribution available here is found in the *Report of the Royal Commission on Publications to the Governor General in Council*, M. Grattan O'Leary, chairman (Ottawa : Queen's Printer, 1961), p. 36, which used borrowed figures reported in the A. B. C. Publisher's Statements, *Audit Bureau of Circulation New Bulletin*, June 30, 1960, to estimate that 75% of the consumer magazines sold in Canada in the month of June, 1960 were of American origin.

Several recent studies have investigated changes in allocation of role responsibilities in American married couples (Hobart, 1958, 1960; Blood and Wolfe, 1960). Such research has rarely been done in Canada and the few studies that exist are severely limited in scope. Thus this study was designed, just at the time when concern for women's liberation was becoming urgent, to discover what changes are taking place in young Canadian's conceptions of appropriate division of responsibilities between husbands and wives. The issue is important because the opportunities Canadian women have to play a bigger part in public life depends on their being relieved of at least some of their traditional duties.

Specifically the research was designed to answer the following questions: is there evidence of a shift towards more egalitarian definition of marital roles? and if so, is it more pronounced in certain areas of married life? What influences make for more traditional or egalitarian orientations? What is the influence of coming from a family in which the mother worked, of urban vs. rural background, of education, social class and other social background factors on marital role conceptions?

THE SAMPLE

The samples which supplied the data on which this study is based consisted of English and French speaking university and trade school students. The English speaking university samples were drawn by randomly sampling third and fourth year students at the Universities of Alberta and Waterloo. First and second year students were excluded since we wanted members to have had opportunity to emancipate themselves from the moral influences of home and community. Of the 726 students drawn in the first sample and a later re-sample, 558 were contactable and eligible (under 27 years of age, of European or North American ancestry, and not belonging to a religious order). Of these 497 or 89 per cent returned usable questionnaires.

In selecting a trade school sample in Alberta it was necessary to include first and second year students because there were few third and no fourth year students enrolled. Accordingly all of the second and third year, and a random sample of first year students were selected to be contacted. Of the 298 students drawn in the first sample and a later resample, 253 were contactable and eligible, and of these 203 or 80.2 percent returned usable questionnaires. The main reason for the lower rate of return from trade school students was that a larger proportion of them—26 per cent as compared with 7 per cent of Alberta university students, could only be contacted by mail, and many of them were in apprenticeship positions, away from Edmonton.

These students were contacted by telephone or by mail and asked to participate in a study of changing orientations to courtship and marriage. They were asked to come to a conveniently situated room on campus to fill out a questionnaire. Upon arrival they were given a questionnaire and seated at widely spaced desks to assure privacy. When a respondent had completed the questionnaire he placed it in a plain envelope and returned it to the assistant, and was then asked to cross his name off the appointment list. Those missing an appointment were telephoned again that same evening and asked to set a new appointment time.

The French-Canadian data were collected by a research assistant at the University of Montreal and a trade school in the same city. Here questionnaires were delivered at the residences of the randomly selected university sample members, and returned through the mail. In the trade school they were administered in selected classes.

The rate of return at the University of Montreal was very much lower than at the English speaking schools. One hundred and sixty two questionnaires were returned by 370 students who received them giving a rate of return of 43.8 per cent. One important reason for this was that questionnaires were mailed out to a resample of Montreal students only shortly before the lengthy mail strike of the summer of 1968. Apparently many students, knowing that the questionnaire could not be immediately mailed back, simply did not bother to fill it out. At any rate only 27 out of the 100 person resample returned their questionnaires. No data are available on what proportions of students in the Montreal trade school classes were absent when the questionnaire was filled out, or refused to fill it out. Returns were actually received from 242 trade school students.

It is clear that while the English samples are adequately representative of the student populations from which they were drawn, this is not true of the French-Canadian samples. No claims of representatives are made; the French data are included for their suggestive value only.

THE QUESTIONNAIRE

Several sections of the lengthy questionnaire are relevant to this paper; those dealing with marriage role expectations, child rearing procedures, and the background and prior social experience of the respondent. Sixty-seven questions about the marriage role obligations of husbands and wives were selected from the Hobart Marital Role Expectation (Hobart, 1956) and the Dunn Marriage Role Expectation Inventories (Dunn, 1960) and were scored according to the technique suggested by Dunn. Sample items included:

" In my marriage I expect that if there is a difference of opinion the husband will decide where to live."

"In my marriage I expect that if the wife prefers a career to having children, the husband will accept that decision and cooperate."

Sample members responded to these items using six point Likert type response categories.

Many background items were also included in the questionnaire to provide information on the antecedents of variations in attitude. These included generation of Canadian residence, areas of residence, amount of physical mobility the respondent had experienced, occupation and amount of education of the respondent's parents, denominational membership and devoutness of the respondent and his parents, his grades in school. his attitudes toward his parents, self rating of his attractiveness. his success in attainment of his goals, his perception of the clarity of sexual norms, his current living arrangements, opportunities for entertaining opposite sex members alone, etc. Scales found in the questionnaire included a Protestant Ethic Scale designed to measure the respondent's commitment to work production values vs. leisure values, (Johnson, n. d.) and items from Dean's Alienation Scale (Dean, 1961).

A first draft was pretested on 200 students in a university class, and some deletions and rewordings were made on the basis of the responses received. It was originally anticipated that the French language questionnaire would be a verbatim translation of the English original. However, unauthorized changes and deletions were made by the research assistant. These will be noted as relevant.

ANALYSIS OF THE DATA

Following receipt of the completed questionnaries, the data were coded for computer analysis. The findings described in this paper required two kinds of analysis. The descriptive section of this paper required only frequency distributions of appropriate items. The analytic section seeks to discover background influences associated with differential acceptance of and acquaintence with trial marriage. Here the procedure used permitted identification of " pure " independent and dependent variables and determining the independent contribution of a predictor to the variance in the criterion. " Pure " indices were obtained by factor analysis of the available measures, identification of statistically significant and conceptually meaningful factors, and calculation of factor scores for each factor for each respondent.

The independent contribution of a predictor to the variance in the criterion was assessed using step regression analysis. This permits identification of the significance of the independent association of the predictor and the criterion measures, and also the proportion of the variance in the latter which is independently accounted for by the former.

A disadvantage of this procedure is that factor analysis requires 100 per cent complete data, so that the more variables one includes in the factor analysis, the greater the number of schedules which cannot be used in the analysis because they are not fully complete. In the present study 43 out of 70 possible predictor variables were used in the factor analysis for the English language data with the result that the sample was reduced from 700 to 528 subjects. A check in regard to these variables was made to determine whether these 528 were an unbiased sample of the total 700, and the absence of bias was established at or beyond the 5% confidence level.

For the French language data, 41 predictor variables were factor analyzed resulting in a sample reduction from 404 to 220 subjects. This reduced set was found to be an unbiased sample of the larger group at the 5% confidence level.

THE FINDINGS : ENGLISH CANADIAN DATA

In this section are found the descriptive findings, consisting of attitudes toward various traditionalism—egalitarianism and role of the wife issues for the English and French language samples. The results of the factor and regression analyses, exploring the antecedents of these attitudes are presented thereafter.

Traditionalism—Egalitarianism

The 67 marital role conception items are about equally divided between those dealing with the role of the husband and the wife and between items reflecting a traditional definition of roles and those reflecting an egalitarian definition of roles. The items relate to seven areas : personal characteristics, education, social participation, care of children, homemaking, employment and support, and authority. They are scored so as to give subscores for each of these seven areas, and a total score which is reflective of the overall traditionalism or egalitarianism of the respondent.

In this section we shall present information on the personal characteristics, education, and social participation sub scores and on the total score, for the total sample and the school subsamples, by sex of respondent. Since there are no norms available for any of the Dunn Inventory scores we cannot determine whether our sample members are distinctively traditional or egalitarian in their orientation, but we can make comparisons between subsamples of our total sample. The relevant data are found in Table I which shows the distribution of the various Dunn Inventory scores for the total and the school subsamples, by sex. Higher scores signify more egalitarian, and lower scores signify more traditional orientations.

TABLE I

Personal Characteristics, Education, and Social Participation Sub-Scores,
and Total Role Scores for English Sample Members, by School and Sex

		Total Sample			U. of A.			U. of W.			Trade School		
		Total	M	F	Total	M	F	Total	M	F	Total	M	F
Personal Characteristic Sub-Score*	43+	40%	a 32%	48%	45%	a 37%	53%	41%	a 30%	51%	32%	b 24%	38%
Education Sub-Score*	26+	36	a 30	42	41	38	44	35	b 28	41	31	a 20	40
Social Participation Sub-Score*	40+	35	a 21	46	39	a 25	53	35	a 24	47	29	a 23	36
Total Role Score*	260+	29	a 19	38	31	b 25	38	34	a 17	49	21	a 12	29
Number of Cases (no less than)		662	319	342	279	147	132	177	87	90	189	90	99

* Higher scores signifies more egalitarian orientation
a — signifies that differences between males and females are significant at the 1% level of confidence
b — signifies that differences between males and females are significant at the 5% level of confidence

The data show that for the three subscores as well as for the total score, the female sample members were consistently significantly more egalitarian than the male sample members. In regard to the personal characteristics of husbands and wives subscore the university samples were more egalitarian than the trade school sample, and this was true of the male and female components of each as well. By contrast, for the education area, the differences between the school samples were due solely to the differences between the male sample members, while the differences between the universities and the trade school in regard to the social participation scores were due to differences between the female members of the samples.

These data suggest some inferences about recency of impact of the egalitarian orientation in various areas. Two assumptions must be made, both largely substantiated by our data: (1) that women tend to accept egalitarianism before men do, and (2) that university students tend to accept egalitarianism before trade-school students do. Granted these assumptions, it appears that egalitarianism is more completely accepted in the education area than in the other two, since all the female samples show the same high level of acceptance, and since the University of Alberta males show about the same level of acceptance as do the females. The social participation area appears most resistant to the impact of egalitarianism, since all the male samples are at the same low level of acceptance of an egalitarian orientation here, and since there are sizable differences between the female samples with some reflecting little acceptance of egalitarianism. The personal characteristics area falls between these two, since the two female university samples show high egalitarianism tendencies, but the trade school female sample does not, and the male samples have significantly lower scores than the female samples.

The Role of the Wife

Information on the expected role of the wife includes three area scores from the Dunn Inventory—the household responsibility, authority, and employment and support areas—and several other questionnaire items dealing with issues relating to employment of the wife. These data are summarized in Table II for the total and the school samples, by sex of respondent.

The data show only one significant difference among the sex and school subsample comparisons, involving the household management area. The authority area, and employment and support area data show that women were generally significantly less traditional than were the men. School comparisons show that trade school women are less egalitarian than those in University, in regard to the employment and support area.

Responses to the first single item indicator were as follows:

" In my marriage I want the wife to be :

(1) housewife and mother to our children only (18 per cent)

(2) employed, but only after the children are in high school (37 per cent)

(3) able to pursue a work career, with children taken care of by babysitters as necessary (10 per cent)

(4) primarily a career woman who has babies only if they will not handicap her career, and may be childless (2 per cent)

(5) I don't know, I'm quite confused (33 per cent)

TABLE II

Indices Relating to Attitudes toward the Role of the Wife, for English Sample Members, By School and by Sex

		Total Sample			U. of A.			U. of W.			Trade School		
		Total	M	F	Total	M	F	Total	M	F	Total	M	F
Household management sub-score*	36+	30%	33%	28%	32%	34%	30%	30%	29%	32%	27%	32%[b]	22%
Authority sub-score*	42+	40	33[a]	46	39	35	42	44	35[a]	53	37	28[a]	45
Employment and support sub-score*	33+	22	16[b]	27	26	18[b]	33	28	18[a]	37	11	10	12
Wife's role-housewife & mother only		20	26[b]	15	16	21	11	18	23	13	29	36[b]	23
Wife's role-employed only after children in high school		37	31[b]	42	39	33[b]	45	37	32[b]	42	34	27[b]	40
Not willing for wife to work after we have children		58	60	55	51	55	47	50	51	50	75	77	72
Wife take better job? Yes, definitely		28	39[a]	18	29	38[a]	21	25	42[a]	11	28	38[a]	20
Numbers of Cases (no less than)		662	319	342	279	147	132	177	87	90	189	90	99

* Higher scores signifies more egalitarian orientation.

a—signifies that differences between males and females are significant at the 1% level of confidence

b—signifies that differences between males and females are significant at the 5% level of confidence

Men responded (1) significantly more often than women, and women responded (2), (3) or (4) more often than men.

In response to the question, "How do you feel about the wife's working following your marriage?" 58% said they were not willing for the wife to work after children came. Tradeschool students were significantly less willing for mothers to work than either of the two university samples, but there were not differences between men and women.

A final question relevant to the role of housewife asked:

"What decision would you press for if in your marriage the wife had the opportunity to take a higher ranking or higher paying job than the husband's job? Why?"

About two third of the sample members said the wife ought to take the job, 37 per cent qualifying their affirmative answers ('yes, if we needed the money'). Eleven per cent qualified their negative answers ('no, unless we were desperate') and 22 per cent said the wife definitely should not take the job. Significantly more men than women in all of the samples gave definite affirmative answers. There were no differences between the school samples.

The reasons given by respondents (too detailed to enumerate here) show that women were more likely to be defensive in approaching the issue posed by the question, while men were more likely to be expensive. Women significantly more often said the wife could take the job, only if, the money was badly needed, or said the wife should not take the job because she should not threaten the husband. Men significantly more often said women should be equal or should have a chance to exercise their capabilities.

Again it is possible to rank these areas in terms of differential impact of egalitarianism. More general egalitarianism is found in the authority area— where women in all three schools were significantly more egalitarian than their male classmates, and there were no differences between women at different schools—than in the employment and support area, where only university women were significantly more egalitarian than their male classmates, and technical school were less egalitarian than university women. The authority area thus falls in the same middle egalitarianism range as the personal characteristics area, while the employment and support area falls in the same low egalitarianism range as the social participation area.

However, the household management shows a second different pattern, similar to the pattern of responses to the single item questioning whether the wife should take a better job than her husband. For the latter, men at all three schools made more egalitarian responses than their female classmates, and for the former, only the technical school men made more egalitarian responses than female students, while there were no differences between the men. We infer that areas deomonstrating the *first* pattern are areas where men feel threatened by egalitarianism, whereas the *second* pattern is characteristic of areas where women feel threatened or defensive. It is plausible that women might feel defensive about men taking responsibility in the household management area; or threatened by their anticipation of a husband's response should they take a better job than his.

RESPONSES OF FRENCH CANADIAN SAMPLE MEMBERS

In making the French translation, the French-Canadian research assistant, without authorization, reduced response alternatives of the Marital Role Expectation Inventory and of the Shobin Parent Attitude Survey from six to four. This change makes no difference in comparing proportions of students the two samples who agree or disagree with various items. However, the scores for various scales and subscales of the Marital Role Expectation Inventory and the Shobin Parent Attitude Survey differ. Responses in the English language schedule were scored by weighing the six response alternatives in sequence from one to six. For the French language schedules " entirely in agreement " was scored as I, " partially in agreement " as 3. " partially in disagreement " as 4, and " entirely in disagreement " as 6, or the reverse, depending on whether the item as stated was pro- egalitarian or pro-traditionalism.* These two scoring procedures may not be commensurable, and this should be borne in mind when comparisons between French and English samples are tentatively made.

---

* If responses were equally distributed across all six categories for the English Canadian respondents and across all four categories for the French Canadian respondents, these scoring procedures would give identical total scores.

Traditionalism–Egalitarianism

The data in Table III suggest that the English sample members may be more egalitarian in their conceptions of marital roles than the French sample members. On all three of the subscores, as well as for the total score, the French sample scored lower than the English. The differential between these two as particularly large for the education subscore, where 55 percent of the English as compared with 41 percent of the French sample members scored under 23, as well as for the total score.

TABLE III

Personal Characteristics, Education and Social Participation Sub-Scores and Total Role Scores for French Sample Members, by School and by Sex with Comparison Data for English Sample

	Total French Sample			Total English Sample			University of ††† Montreal			Trade School		
	Total	M	F	Total	M	F	Total	M	F	Total	M	F
Personal Characteristics Score† Under 39	56%	67%^a	46%	28%	35%^a	21%	32%	34%	28%	72%	88%^a	56%
Education Score† Under 23	41	55^a	27	32	39^a	25	18	26^b	10	57	75^a	39
Social Participation Score† Under 34	39	52^a	25	25	30^a	20	22	26	18	50	70^a	30
Total Role Score† Under 240	49	65^a	32	43	51^a	35	31	44^a	16	60	78^a	40
Numbers of Cases	376	185	191	662	319	342	158	74	84	218	111	107

† Higher score signifies more egalitarian orientation.

††† School information not available for 32 respondents.

a Signifies that differences between males and females are significant at the 1% level of
confidence.

b signifies that differences between males and females are significant at the 5% level of
confidence.

The data show that male French students were consistently less egalitarian in their orientations than the female students on all three subscores and that trade school students were consistently less egalitarian than the university students, for all areas. However, the spread in egalitarianism between the male and the female students was less wide among the university than among the trade school students.

Given the same assumptions as were made with the English language data, it is again possible to rank these areas in terms of differential impact of egalitarianism on them. The pattern is the reverse of that found for the English data, since the education area reflects the least spread of egalitarianism, among the French speaking students, and the personal characteristics and social participation areas reflect more egalitarianism, though neither to the extent of the education area among the English speaking respondents.

The Role of the Wife

In interesting contrast to the pattern of French-English sample contrasts seen in the previous section, the data in Table IV suggest that in defining the wife's role the French sample was generally more egalitarian than the English sample. French-Canadian women were more egalitarian than men, and university students more egalitarian than trade school students on all subscores.

TABLE IV

Indices Relating to Attitudes Toward the Role of the Wife, for French Sample Members, by School and by Sex, with Comparison Data from English Sample

	Total French Sample			Total English Sample			University of *** Montreal			Trade School		
	Total	M	F	Total	M	F	Total	M	F	Total	M	F
Household Score* Under 31	31%	33%	28%	36%	35%	37%	21%	24%	18%	38%	42%	35%
Authority Score* Under 38	35	a 52	18	36	a 40	31	23	a 33	11	44	a 67	21
Employment and Support Score* Under 27	28	a 38	17	42	a 48	37	20	a 30	8	33	b 42	22
Wife's Role–Housewife and Mother Only	17	a 29	5	20	b 26	15	6.4	a 11.5	0.0	24	a 40	6
Wife's Role Employed only after children in high school	34	a 29	39	37	b 31	47	34	33	34	32	a 26	40
Not Sure About What the Wife's Role Should Be	26	a 28	23	31	33	30	28	33	21	25	25	25
Wife's Role–A Career Under Any Conditions	23	14	33	12	10	13						
Not willing For Wife to Work After We Have Children	59	56	61	58	60	55	39	41	36	70	65	76
Wife Should be Free to Choose Whether or not to Take a Better Job Than Her Husband's Yes Definitely	47	47	48	28	a 39	18	56	55	58	43	42	43
Would let Wife Choose Whether or Not She Worked	22	40	4	9	17	1						
Numbers of Cases	371	191	180	662	319	342	158	85	73	213	106	107

* High score signifies more egalitarian orientation

*** School information not available for 32 respondents

a Signifies that differences between males and females are significant at the 1% level of
                                                                                                confidence.

b Signifies that differences between males and females are significant at the 5% of level
                                                                                                confidence.

Responses to the first single item indicator were as follows:

" In my marriage I want the wife to be:

(1) Housewife and mother to our children only (17 per cent)

(2) Employed at productive and interesting work, but only after the children are in high school (34 per cent)

(3) Able to pursue a work career under any conditions (23 per cent)

(4) I don't know (26 per cent)

These data show little commitment to the traditional conception of the wife as housewife and mother, since only one in six chose this limited role. Men were five times as likely as women to choose this response, as the data in Table IV shows and women twice as often as men felt a woman should be able to pursue a career under any conditions.

The second question asked " How do you feel about the wife's working following your marriage?" The responses were as follows:

(1) I would approve of her working only before we have children (39 percent)

(2) I would not approve of her working under any circumstances (4 percent)

(3) I would approve under any circumstances (7 per cent)

(4) I would approve if we needed the money (16 per cent)

(5) I would leave my wife free to choose (22 per cent)

(6) I would leave my husband free to choose (4 per cent)

(7) Others (9 per cent)

The responses also show a rather liberal orientation to the question of the wife's working. The women very much more often than the men said they would approve of the wife's working under any circumstances, if they needed the money while the men much more often said they would leave the decision to the wife. (See Table IV).

The last question asked : " If the wife had the opportunity to take a position which was more important and more remunerative than that of the husband, the latter should let the wife make her own decision." An over-whelming 77 per cent of the respondents agreed with this statement, 47 per cent agreeing " entirely." The responses of men and women were similar.

The information reviewed in this section suggests that the attitude of French-Canadian students toward the role that the wife should play in marriage may be more emancipated than that of English speaking students. One cannot be sure because of differences in scoring procedures. But this does not mean that there is consensus between French-Canadian young men and women. On all the indicators the women were found to have a more egalitarian orientation than men.

These areas may also be ranked in terms of the differential impact of egalitarianism that the respondent's scores reflect. The rankings of the employment and authority areas are the same as for the English speaking respondents, with the former reflecting less egalitarianism than the latter. However instead of presenting quite a different pattern of differential egalitarianism, as the household management area did for the English data, the pattern for the French speaking respondents is the same as the employ-ment area. That is, instead of seeming less accepting than men of the suggestion that they should share household chores with men, as were the English language women, the French language women were more accepting of egalitarianism than the men in this as in other areas.

Predictors of Marital Role Attitudes: English Canadian Data

Identification of the predictors of marital role attitudes involved factor analysing the independent and dependent variables used in this study. The dependent variables included all of the scores and individual items mentioned in the previous pages. The independent variables included the usual social background items as well as others relating to roles played by the respondent's mother, and his courtship experience.

The English and the French language data were factor analysed separately. Then factor scores were calculated for each factor for each subject, and step regression analyses were performed using selected variables, and factor scores as criteria, and the independent variable factor scores as predictors, for the two sets of data. Step regression analysis provides a measure of the independent contribution of a predictor to the variance of a criterion variable. None of the inter-item correlations in the correlation matrix exceed .68 and the principle axis method was used which yields orthogonal factors. Thus here need be no concern about multicolinearity in regard to either the factor analysis or the step regression analysis.

The predictive variables used for the English speaking sample were 15 factor scores obtained as follows. Forty-three independent variables were factor analysed using the varimax rotation procedure. This resulted in identification of the following fifteen factors having eigen values larger than one. The *courtship involvement* factor loaded on current courtship status, and most advanced courtship status experienced by the respondent. The *conventionality* or similarity to reference figures factor loaded on perceived similarity of own sex standards to those of parents and friends. The *SES* factor loaded on occupation and education of respondent's father. The *university* vs. *trade school* enrollment factor loaded on variables dealing with occupational aspiration, high school marks and age. The *religiosity* factor loaded on frequency of church attendance and devoutness. The *courtship precosity* factor loaded on age at first data and first single date. The *family solidarity* factor loaded on ratings of relationships with the mother and relationships with the family. The *sex identity* factor loaded heavily on this index. The *mobility* factor loaded on geographic mobility and duration of residence variables. The *peer-parent-ego consistency* factor loaded on variables dealing with the perceived consistency of peers, parents, best friends and self in regard to sexual norms. The *alienation* factor loaded on non-achievement of goals and alienation measures. The *fast living* factor loaded on liquor consumption, self-attractiveness and perception of school and family controls as strict. The *sex education* factor loaded on two items dealing with this area. The *generation* factor loaded on generation of Canadian residence. And finally the *sex norm confusion* factor loaded on items dealing with confusion in this area and adequacy of the Church's teaching concerning sex.

The dependent variables were also the factor analysed using the varimax rotation procedure. Rather than attempt any *a priori* grouping of these, the decision was made to include all of the independent indices, whether they related to marital role attitudes, or to other aspects of courtship and marriage not considered here, into the same pool of items to be factor analysed. Of the total set of dependent variables, 19 were selected for factor analysis.

Six factors were identified having eigen values greater than one. Two of these factors are of interest here. The *traditionalism in role definition* factor loaded heavily on the Dunn Inventory total score and the authority sub–score, and less heavily on several other sub–scores of the Inventory. The *employment of wife* item loaded heavily on the question asking whether the wife should take a job better than her husband, and less heavily on the employment sub–score of the Dunn Inventory.

Factor scores were calculated for these factors, and these scores were used as criteria in regression analyses using the independent variable factor scores as predictors. Ten other dependent variable indices were also analysed using the regression analysis procedure. Of the total of 12 indicators, five deal generally with traditionalism—egalitarianism in role definition, and seven deal with role of the wife.

Traditionalism—Egalitarianism in Marital role Definition

The results of the regression analyses of the predictive factors using six indicators of traditionalism—egalitarianism as criteria are found in Table V.

TABLE V

Proportions of Variance[1] in Indices of General Egalitarianism in
Marital Role Definition explained by independent variable
Factor Scores, for English Sample Members.

Independent Factors	Egalitarianism Factor	Total Role Egalitarianism Score	Personal Characteristics Egalitarianism	Social Life Egalitarianism	Education Egalitarianism
1. Courtship Involvement		+ 1.2			+ 2.9
2. Conventionality			− .71	− .51	
3. Socio-Economic Status					
4. University or Trade School	w+ 1.9	u+ 1.9	u+ 1.7	u+ 1.7	
5. Religiosity		− 1.2			− 2.2
6. Courtship Precosity	+ 1.9	+ 1.6	+ .5	+ 1.0	
7. Home Influence Family Solidarity					
8. Masculinity-Femininity	f+ 1.4		f+ 1.0		f+ 1.6
9. Geographical Mobility	+ .6	+ .7	+ 1.7		
10. Peer-Parent Consistency	.6				
11. Alienation					
12. Fast Living			− 1.3	− .6	
13. Adequacy of Sex Education		+ .8			+ 2.3
14. Generation					
15. Confusion Regarding Sex Norms					
16. Mother's Influence					
Total Variance Explained	5.8	8.0	6.9	3.8	9.0
Numbers of Cases	518	528	528	528	528

[1]Reporting only those significantly different from zero, at or beyond the 5% confidence level.

The data show that very little of the variance in these criteria is explained by the predictors available, the best being the education sub-scale score, 9 percent of whose variance was predicted. Only 4 percent of the variances on the social life and authority scores were explained. If we look over the whole table for the best predictors of the five criteria we find that in no case is more than 3 percent of the variance of a criterion explained by a predictor. In all but three of the 29 significant associations between a criterion and a predictor less than 2 percent of the variance was predicted. The most powerful predictor is university attendance which is directly associated with egalitarianism for four of the criteria, but in all cases less than 2 percent of the variance is predicted. It is remarkable that the socio-economic status, family solidarity, mother's influence and generation factors were not significantly predictive for any of the criteria.

The implication of this lack of findings appears to be that egalitarianism is so widely disseminated throughout the English Canadian culture that it is not distinctively associated with any particular social class, or religiosity, or family solidarity grouping of people. That is, in terms of this variable the various sub-cultures in English speaking Canadian society are quite homogeneous. It is not possible to predict from our data that in some subcultures one will learn a more traditionalist orientation while in others one will grow more egalitarian. Clearly there is a range of perspectives in regard to traditionalism—egalitarianism— the wide range of scores that we obtained from sample members on the various scales and sub-scales used in this study demonstrate that. But whether the individual person adopts a more traditional or more egalitarian orientation appears to depend on influences other than those sociologists usually find associated with such normative and value commitment variables.

Role of the Wife

The data in Table VI show that the indicators of role of the wife are as unpredictable as the egalitarianism role indicators. The proportions of variance explained by the predictive factors ranged from 3 to 14 percent for the indicators used. The criterion whose variance was best explained was the item dealing with the circumstances under which the wife should work, perhaps the most controversial one. The least well explained criterion was the household responsibilities indicator ; apparently there is general consensus that housework should be shared between husband and wife. The best single predictor of all seven criteria was the school enrollment factor which predicts 6 percent, 3 percent and 2 percent respectively of the variance in the wife work item, the employment sub-scale and the egalitarianism factor criteria.

Again, one concludes that beliefs that married women should have work opportunities following marriage equal to those of men, whenever there are no young children, and that authority and household responslbilities should be divided, are widely distributed among the English speaking sample students. It is not possible among our data to identify a background predictor that will discriminate the more traditional from the more egalitarian respondents. It is particularly noteworthy that neither the mobility factor, which is loaded on the rural-urban background variable, nor the socio-economic status factor, which is loaded on the father's occupation and father's education items, explain any appreciable variance in any of the criteria. Whether one thinks the wife should play housewife or working wife roles, and how the husband and wife should divide authority, and household duties, depends less on one's background than on one's personal choice, experience in advanced courtship, and university attendance, according to these data.

TABLE VI

Proportions of Variance[1] in Indices of the attitude concerning the Role Appropriate to the Wife explained by independent variable Factor Scores, for English Sample Members.

Independent Factors	Wife Employment Factor	Egalitarian Division of Household Responsibilities	Egalitarian Division of Authority	Employment and Support Egalitarianism	Wife's Role Egalitarian Definition	Approve of Wife's Working	Wife Should Take Better Job
1. Courtship Involvement	+ 2.4	+ .5		+ .6		+ 1.8	+ 1.7
2. Conventionality				− .8	+ .5	− .5	− .7
3. Socio-Economic Status	− .5		− 1.2				
4. University or Trade School		+ .6		u+ 3.2		u+ 5.8	
5. Religiosity	− 2.2		− .8	− 3.1		− .6	− 1.9
6. Courtship Precosity			+ 1.1	+ .8		+ .6	
7. Home Influence Family Solidarity						− .9	
8. Masculinity-Femininity	m+ 2.1						m+ 2.5
9. Geographical Mobility			+ .5			+ .5	
10. Peer-Parent Consistency						− 2.0	
11. Alienation				+ .8	− 3.4	+ .6	
12. Fast Living		+ .6				+ .5	
13. Adequacy of Sex Education						+ .7	
14. Generation							
15. Confusion Regarding Sex Norms							− .6
16. Mother's Influence		1.2					
Total Variance Explained	7.2	2.9	3.6	9.3	3.9	14.5	7.4
Numbers of Cases	518	528	528	528	528	528	528

[1]Reporting only those significantly different from zero, at or beyond the 5% confidence level.

THE FRENCH CANADIAN DATA

Fortyone independent variables for the French Canadian data were factor analyzed using the same procedures as for the anglophone data. The following fourteen factors were identified. The *religiosity* factor loaded on variables reflecting the respondent's church attendance and attitudes toward its teachings. The *courtship experience* factor loaded on indices of the current courtship status of the respondent and the most advanced status he had ever experienced. The *age* factor loaded on this variable and several others reflective of age. The *socio-economic status* factor loaded on items dealing with father's occupation and educational attainment. The *family solidarity* or *influence* factor loaded on respondent's ratings of his relationships with his father and mother, and happiness of family relationships. The *alienation* factor loaded on the alienation and anomie variables. The *family devoutness* factor loaded on ratings of the religious devoutness of the respondent's father and mother. The fast-popularity-with-the-opposite-sex factor loaded heavily on variables dealing with the respondent's liquor consumption, his ratings of his own attractiveness, his age at first dating, and his knowledge of couples living commonlaw together. The *sex identity* factor loaded heavily on this index. The *peer-parent consistency* factor loaded on respondent's ratings of the similarity between the sexual staindards of his parents, and his peers and best friends. The *mobility* factor loaded on geographic mobility and duration of residence. The *perceived similarity to peers* factor loaded on the respondent's ratings of the similarity of his sex norms to those of his peers and best friend. The *home discipline* factor loaded on a home discipline rating item. The working mother factor loaded on whether or not the mother worked.

Similarly 18 dependent variables, including a number not relevant to this paper, were factor analyzed. Of the 6 factors which were identified only two are relevant here. They are essentially identical with the two factors identified in factor analysis of the English language data. The traditionalism *in marital roles* factor loaded heavily on the three scores from the Dunn Marital Role Inventory. The *wife employment factor* loaded heavily on items dealing with the role of the wife, conditions of her employment, and whether or not she should take a better job than that of her husband.

Again, factor scores were calculated and these were used as criteria in regression analyses using the independent variable factor scores as predictors. Ten other dependent variable indices were also analyzed using the step regression analysis procedure.

Predictors of Traditionalism-Egalitarianism in Marital Role Definition

In remarkable contrast to the findings for the English-language sample, the data in Table VII show that substantial portions of the variance in all five of the traditionalism-equalitarianism criteria were explained by the predictive factors available. The proportions ranged from a low of 24 percent in the case of the social life subscale, to a high of 33 percent for the total role score. Clearly the influence affecting internalization of these role conceptions differ for the French and English-language groups in our sample.

TABLE VII

Proportions of Variance[1] in Indices of General Egalitarianism
in Marital Role definition explained by Independent variable
Factor Scores, for French Sample Members.

Independent Factors	Role Egalitarianism Factor	Total Role Egalitarianism Score	Personal Characteristics Egalitarianism	Social Life Egalitarianism	Education Egalitarianism
1. Religiosity of Respondent	− 9.5	− 7.9	− 16.1	− 5.9	− 2.5
2. Courtship Experience					
3. Age	+ 1.4	+ 3.4	+ 3.8	+ 2.9	+ 2.4
4. Socio-Economic Status	+ 2.8		+ 1.4		+ 3.3
5. Family Solidarity	− 1.1	− 2.1		.9	− 2.1
6. Alienation					
7. Family Devoutness					
8. Fast Popularity with Opposite Sex	+ 1.4		+ 1.0	+ 1.0	
9. Masculinity-Femininity	+f 12.2	+f 17.5	f+ 7.8	f+ 11.9	f+ 10.9
10. Peer-Parent Ego Norm Consistency					
11. Mobility		+ .8	+ .8	+ 1.1	
12. Preceived Similarity to Peers More Strict					+ 2.9
13. Home Discipline					
14. Mother Worked					+ 1.0
Total Variance Explained	28.4	31.7	30.9	23.7	25.1
Numbers of Cases	216	220	220	220	220

[1]Reporting only those significantly different from zero, at or beyond the 5% confidence level.

Cues to the nature of these differences are found in the proportions of variance explained by the various predictive factors. The two most powerful predictors for the five of the criteria are the sex identity (masculinity-feminity) and the religiosity factors. The proportion of variance predicted by the sex identity factor ranges from a low of 8 percent for the personal characteristics, to a high of 18 percent for the total role score criteria, while the range for the religiosity factor is from a low of 2.5 percent for the education to a high of 16 percent for the personal characteristics criterion. Female responses were more egalitarian and high religiosity was associated with the traditionalism. The only other noteworthy predictor is the age factor which consistently explains 2 or 3 percent of the variance, and is directly associated with more egalitarian responses.

In contrast, to the findings for the English sample, the relationship factors (fast popularity, and courtship experience) are *not* significantly predictive of any of the criteria. Similarly the family influence factors are not substantially predictive of the variables.

If we examine the predictive patterns for the five criteria in detail we find a somewhat inverse relationship between the predictive power of the religiosity and sex identity factors. The former predicts 16 percent of the variance in the personal characteristics criterion and is inversely associated with egalitarianism, as compared with 8 percent for the latter. In regard to the education criterion, however, the religiosity factor predicted (inversely) only 2.5 percent of the variance, while the sex identity factor predicted 11 percent of the variance and it is the females who make the more egalitarian responses. Accordingly we may suggest that the education and social life areas are seen as having minimal moral implications, since religiosity explains little of the variance in each of these criteria, while the personal characteristics area of marital role expectations appear to have significant moral implications since religiosity explains a substantial proportion of the variance. There are good and bad personal characteristics, these data seem to suggest. A distinctively feminist perspective is apparently somewhat better able to develop in areas where this moral definition is lacking.

In any case, the data show that in contrast to the data for the English-language sample, the French students are still influenced by powerful cultural influences with distinctive orientations toward the marital role issues for which we have indicators. Two of these are a feminist influence, which is egalitarian in orientation, and a Church influence, which is traditional in orientation.

Role of Wife

The data in Table VIII show that the variances in the seven role-of-wife criteria are far better explained by the predictors than were these same criteria in the case of the English data, but the proportions explained are not so high as for the egalitarianism criteria just considered. For two of the criteria in the table, the household responsibilities score based on marital role inventory items, and the " wife take better job " item, only 7 percent of the variance is explained. At the other extreme 22 percent of the variance in the authority score, 19 percent of the variance in the employment score, and 19 percent of the variance in responses to the " wife's role " item are explained by the predictors.

As in the case of the data for the Traditionalism-Egalitarianism area, the three consistently most powerful predictors in order of significance are the sex identity, religiosity, and age factors. However the proportions of total variance explained by each decline to a low of 1 percent for each, from a high of 16 percent for sex identity, 6 percent for religiosity, and 4 percent for age. The family solidarity factor explained 5 percent of the variance in two criteria dealing with the issue of the wife's employment.

TABLE VIII

Proportions of Variance[1] in indices of attitude concerning the
Role appropriate to the Wife explained by independent variable Factor
Scores, for French Sample Members.

Independent Factors	Wife Employment Factor	Egalitarianism Approach to Household Responsibilities	Egalitarian Division of Authority	Employment & Support Egalitarianism	Egalitarian Approach to Wife's Role	Approve Wife's Working	Wife Decide on Taking Better Job
1. Religiosity of Respondent	−1.1	−2.0	−4.0	−5.8	−1.9	−2.4	−1.1
2. Courtship Experience						+.9	
3. Age	+2.0	+2.0	+2.0	+1.2	+1.2	+3.6	
4. Socio-Economic Status							−1.0
5. Family Solidarity	−1.8	1-3		−2.0	−5.3	−5.0	
6. Alienation	+2.2				+1.3		+.7
7. Family Devoutness	−1.2						
8. Fast Popularity with Opposite Sex					−.7	−1.3	
9. Masculinity-Femininity	f+ 1.2	f+ 1.3	f+ 16.2	f+ 9.1	f+ 4.5		f+ 1.6
10. Peer-Parent Ego Norm Consistency					+1.1		
11. Mobility	+2.3				+.8		+1.1
12. Perceived Similarity to Peers More Strict	+1.1				+2.0		
13. Home Discipline				−1.1			
14. Mother Worked	+1.2						+1.2
Total Variance Explained	14.1	6.6	22.2	19.2	18.8	13.2	6.7
Numbers of Cases	216	220	220	220	220	220	220

[1]Reporting only those significantly different from zero, at or beyond the 5% confidence level.

In general the data show that there are fairly strong cultural influences defining the authority, employment and support, and wife's role issues, as indicated by the substantial proportions of variance in these criteria that are explained. There is less sharp definition of specific wife employment issues, and there is no definition of the household responsibility issue.

None of these issues is very strongly religiously (morally) defined. Perhaps because responses to the wife's role and wife's employment items raise the issue of conflict between the mother and worker roles of the wife, these responses are more powerfully predicted by the family solidarity factor than by any other criterion.   About one third of the explained variance in each of the two responses is accounted for by this factor.   Responses to issues regarding relative authority of husband and wife and who is to work and provide for family support are most powerfully predicted by sex identity.   More than two thirds of the variance in the first, and one half the variance in the second are explained by this factor, pointing to the salience of these issues for the female students in the French speaking sample.   That these issues are yet morally defined, however, is shown by the fact that 6 percent of the variance in the employment and support, and 4 percent of the variance in the authority criteria, are explained by the religiosity factor.

Although the age factor was significantly associated with six of the seven criteria that we are here concerned with, in only one case did it predict more than 2 percent of the explained variance.   Age was directly associated with approval of the wife's working, and it accounted for 4 percent of the variance.

In summary it should be pointed out that the religiosity factor was not as powerfully predictive of the criteria considered in this section as in the case of the preceding sections; activities appropriate to the wife were not as strongly morally defined as the area considered earlier.   However, sex identity was powerfully predictive of many criteria, pointing to the growth of new feminist, egalitarian conceptions which challenge the traditional definitions of the role appropriate to the wife.

Conclusions from Analysis of English and French Canadian Data

The indices of orientation to marriage used in the present study related to marital interaction and responsibility in terms of egalitarianism, with special reference to personal characteristics, social life, significance of education and role alternatives of the wife.   It is not possible to make statements about the relative egalitarianism or permissiveness of the sample as a whole since adequate comparison data from other groups are not available.   Comparisons between French and English members of the sample are tentatively made because of differences in the wording and some of the response categories used in the two questionnaires.   One of the most fruitful uses of the data is to test the ability of various independent variables to predict variance in the criterion items, thus identifying differences in attitude forming influences between some of the subsamples studies on the criterion.

The available data suggest some interesting contrasts between the French and the English-language samples.   In terms of general egalitarianism, the data suggest that the English sample was distinctly more egalitarian.   However, on several items relating to the conditions of employment of the wife, the English were less egalitarian than the French speaking respondents.   For almost all the items, the male-female sex differences were larger for the French than for the English samples, since the women in both samples were consistently more egalitarian than the men and the English speaking men were more egalitarian, generally, than their French counterparts.

We cannot conclude that one language group is consistently more egalitarian in its orientation toward marriage than the other. The English speaking sample members were the more egalitarian in areas concerned with personal characteristics of marriage partners, social life and education expectations. In the area of the wife's role, including her authority, housework and gainful employment, the French speaking respondents were more egalitarian. However, this was entirely a result of the high egalitarianism of the women. The French men were more traditional than were the English speaking men.

Thus in several areas, French Canadian women are pioneers in advocating egalitarian and permissive orientations, in comparison with English speaking respondents while French Canadian men are the most traditional of all.

We have found evidence of the differential impact of egalitarianism in different marital role areas, as follows. Among English speaking respondents the impact of egalitarianism was most strongly seen in the education area, and least seen in the social participation and employment areas, with the personal characteristics and authority areas in between. In addition to these areas reflecting male conservativism, the household management was found to reflect female conservativism, with men making more egalitarian responses than women, among the English respondents. Among French speaking respondents there was no area reflecting as much egalitarianism as the education area among the English, where only trade school men were significantly less egalitarian than other sex-school categories. However the personal characteristics, social participation, and authority areas had response patterns suggesting medium egalitarianism, and the education, household management, and employment and support area scores suggest low spread of egalitarianism. No area was found reflecting female conservativism, among the French respondents, comparable to the household management area for the English speaking respondents.

One of the most interesting findings of this study is the magnitude of the difference in the explainable variance in the indicators of these marital role issues. In general at least 18 or 20 percent of the variance for most items was explained by the predictive factors in the French data, but no more than 7 to 10 percent of the variance as explained for these items in the English data. These data indicate that there are much more powerfully entrenched definitions of orthodox orientations in the French Canadian culture than in the Anglo-Canadian culture. Wide variations in the responses of Anglo-Canadian students were found but it is not possible to predict these variations on the basis of knowledge of their background characteristics. Thus background characteristics do not identify subcultures that define orthodoxies related to marital role expectations.

The pattern of predictive relationships for the French sample data is in marked contrast. Of the 12 indicators considered in this study, in 8 cases for the French data the variance predicted in the criterion by the predictive variables exceeded 19 percent, while this was true for none of the indicators for the English data. The reason for this much higher degree of predictability of the French student responses in these areas is easily seen. For seven of the twelve items the sex identity factor was the most powerful predictor and for two it was the second most powerful. For two items the religious factor was the most powerful predictor and for five it was the second most powerful. Thus for these areas there are very substantial differences between the men and women in the French student sample, and crucial issues in these areas are still significantly morally (religiously) defined for a substantial minority.

Two aspects of these data suggest that the revolution in sex roles in marriage is more advanced among the English than among the French speaking students. First, among the English, religiosity is little predictive of attitudes on relevant issues ; thus traditional moral definitions of these issues have broken down. Second, during the early stages of a feminist revolt one would expect sizeable differences between male and female perspectives among *avant garde* elements of the population, such as students. These differences are in fact found in the French but not in the English speaking sample members, generally speaking, suggesting that the " revolution" is sufficiently advanced among the latter for it to have affected men as well as women.

However, this is an oversimplified picture since (1) the French sample members tended to have more egalitarian attitudes toward employment of the wife than did the English members, and (2) the French women students had more egalitarian attitudes in many areas than the English women. The reasons for these findings are not clear. Perhaps the first may be explained by larger differences on value issues between the French and English Canadian cultures. A reason for the second point may be that during any period of conflict the attitudes of the two sides tend to polarize, with each taking a more extreme position.

SOURCES CITED

Blood, Robert O. Jr. and Donald M. Wolfe, 1960. *Husbands and Wives*, New York : Free Press of Glencoe.

Dean, Dwight G., 1961. "Alienation : Its Meaning and Measurement," *American Sociological Review*, Vol. 26 pp. 753-758.

Dunn, Marie S., 1960. "Marriage Role Expectations of Adolescents", *Marriage and Family Living*, Vol. 22, p. 100.

Hobart, Charles W., 1956. "Disagreement and Non-Empathy During Courtship," *Marriage and Family Living*, Vol. 18, pp. 317-322.

Hobart, Charles W., 1958. "Disillusionment in Marriage and Romanticism", *Marriage and Family Living*, Vol. 20, pp. 156-162.

Hobart, Charles W., 1960. "Attitude Changes During Courtship and Marriage", *Marriage and Family Living*, Vol. 22, pp. 352-359.

Hobart, Charles W., 1971. "Sexual Permissiveness in Young English and French Canadians", Forthcoming in the Journal of Marriage and the Family.

Johnson, Benton, n. d. "The Comparative Value Project", National Institute of Mental Health, Grant No. 4309-Rl. United States Government.

Kinsey, A. C., W. B. Pomery, and C. E. Martin, 1948. Sexual Behaviour in the Human Male, Philadelphia : Saunders.

Kinsey, A. C., W. B. Pomery, C. E. Martin and P. H. Gebhard, 1953. Sexual Behaviour in the Human Female. Philadelphia : Saunders.

Attitudes Toward Marital Infidelity:
A Nine-Culture Sampling of
University Student Opinion

HAROLD T. CHRISTENSEN *

This paper is a sequel to another on a similar topic published about a decade ago (Christensen, 1962). In that, the writer made cross-cultural comparisons of attitudes toward marital infidelity, drawing from questionnaire data gathered in 1958 at three universities located in each of three western societies. They were: sexually-permissive Denmark, the Midwestern region of the United States, and sexually-restrictive Mormon country in the Intermountain region of western United States. Major findings reported at that time include the following: the Danish sample reflected the most permissive attitudes and the Intermountain sample the most restrictive attitudes; male attitudes toward marital infidelity were more permissive than were those of the female; approval of marital infidelity was higher for love-absent liaisons than for love affairs, and lowest approval was for love affairs between persons each of whom was married to someone else; and finally, the single sex standard was favored far more than the double sex standard, but the latter, when it was approved, received stronger support as applied to premarital relations than when extramarital relations were being considered.

This 1958 study was replicated in 1968 at the same three universities. In addition, the 1968 study was expanded to include samples from several other colleges and universities located in Europe and the United States; and was extended once more in 1970 to encompass a university in Taiwan. The analysis to follow comes from the more recent and more extensive data based upon this second round. It is to retest some of the earlier findings, but in a broader cross-cultural perspective and with particular attention to the question of mental and family health. Furthermore, the present report goes beyond the earlier one in a number of ways. Among these is the testing of attitudinal shifts over time, which has been made possible by the acquisition of 1968 data.

*Professor, Department of Sociology and Anthropology, Purdue University, West Lafayette, Indiana, U.S.A.

The section of the questionnaire relevant to marital infidelity was stated as follows:

Under which of the following circumstances would you approve of *sexual infidelity after marriage* (Consider husbands and wives separately; and for each, please check *all* items with which you agree).

Approve for husbands	Approve for wives	
_____	_____	Never under any circumstances.
_____	_____	If he or she has fallen in love with an unmarried person.
_____	_____	If he or she has fallen in love with another married person.
_____	_____	If he or she feels the need for sexual release (with prostitutes or others) during periods of long absence from the spouse.

A similar section relating to premarital coitus immediately preceded this one in the questionnaire, but it of course had different approval alternatives. In both sections respondents were given the opportunity to write in additional reasons or conditions for approving, but the "Other" category was so little used that it has been ignored for present purposes.

The nine samples from which data were drawn for the present analysis may be briefly described as follows: (1) a large state-supported University in Denmark; (2) a large state-supported university in Sweden; (3) a large Catholic oriented university in Belgium; (4) combined data from two relatively small state-supported and mainly Negro-enrolled colleges in the deep south; (5) a large state-supported university in the Midwest; (6) a large Catholic-oriented and mainly male-enrolled university in the Midwest; (7) a small Mennonite-oriented college in the Midwest; (8) a large and heavily Mormon-enrolled university of the Intermountain west; and (9) a large state-supported university in Taiwan. For the most part, questionnaires were administered to sociology and other social science classes, with anonymity assured and with the option of non-participation made plain. The response rate was nearly one-hundred percent. The resulting overall sample amounted to 2764 cases.[1] The breakdowns of this combined sample, by sex and for the nine cultures, are shown below in the first two columns of Table 1.

---

[1]For convenience in analysis, the 1970 Taiwanese sample is treated as if it were drawn along with the others in 1968. Also, since the Midwest II sample picked up only 12 females, that category for that sample has been eliminated from all of the tables. Still again, the relatively small samples from the two southern Negro colleges were combined to produce larger N's; but a preliminary testing of selected items had shown them to be quite similar.

An alphabetical list of collaborators in the data-gathering process follows: George R. Carpenter, Chen-lou Chu, William V. D'Antonio, Wilfried A. Dumon, Christina F. Gregg, A.M. van der Heiden, Georg Karlsson, J. Howard Kauffman, Shirley S.L. Liu, Erik Mannicke, Eugene G. Sherman, Kaare Svalastoga, and Jan Trost. Of these, Carpenter, Gregg, and Liu were involved also in data analysis. They, at different times, worked with me as graduate students and their research efforts resulted in advanced degrees -- the Ph.D. for the first two and the M.S. for the third. Jean H. Hicks also received her M.S., but by analyzing data already at hand from one of these samples.

Since these are not probability samples and also since the cell N's, in some instances, are relatively small, no statistical tests of association or significance have been applied. Furthermore, since most of the student respondents were unmarried, there was no possibility of studying actual behavior -- only attitudes. Essentially the study is exploratory. It applies the comparative method to look for clues in the understanding of marital infidelity, but it does not lay claim to definitive answers.

Table 1. Percentages Giving Unqualified Disapproval to Premarital and to Extramarital Coitus

By Sex and Culture for 1968

Sample Location and Type		Number of Respondents		Percentages Giving Unqualified Disapproval[1]			
				To Premarital Coitus		To Extramarital Coitus	
		Males (1)	Females (2)	Males (3)	Females (4)	Males (5)	Females (6)
Europe							
Denmark (state U.)	(1)	134	61	0.0(9)[2]	0.0(9)[2]	8.2(9)[2]	6.6(9)[2]
Sweden (state U.)	(2)	206	250	.5(8)	.4(8)	29.6(7)	32.8(8)
Belgium (Catholic U.)	(3)	260	120	16.2(6)	27.5(5)	53.5(6)	59.2(6)
United States							
South (Negro, state)	(4)	104	175	12.5(7)	14.3(7)	25.0(8)	36.0(7)
Midwest I (state U.)	(5)	245	238	20.8(5)	26.9(6)	55.5(5)	76.9(4)
Midwest II (Catholic U.)	(6)	291	—	23.7(4)	—	64.6(2)	—
Midwest III (Mennonite)	(7)	82	145	65.9(1)	69.0(2)	86.6(1)	93.8(1)
Intermountain (Mormon culture)	(8)	115	105	46.1(2)	57.1(3)	60.9(3)	76.2(5)
Asia							
Taiwan (state U.)	(9)	106	127	33.0(3)	84.3(1)	56.6(4)	85.0(3)
Total	(10)	1543	1221	20.6	31.9	49.4	59.5

[1]Those who checked "never under any circumstances" for *both* males and females.
[2]Numbers in parentheses give rank order, in this and in subsequent tables.

The Conservative Stance Compared Across Cultures

As explained above, respondents were asked to check specified approval categories for both premarital and extramarital coitus and to do this separately for males and for females. Although this paper focuses upon extramarital coitus, Table 1 shows the premarital also, for purposes of comparison. Pictured here are percentages of those who took the most conservative stance; in other words, who indicated that they would not approve premarital and/or extramarital coitus for either males or females regardless of the circumstances. The following points may be observed:

1. Overall, for the nine cultures combined, more than half indicated unqualified disapproval of marital infidelity (line 10, columns 5 and 6).

2. Proportionately more disapproved of extramarital sex than disapproved of premarital sex, about twice as many in fact (more than 50 percent compared with around 25 percent). This may be seen in the bottom line of the table. But one can also observe that the direction of difference is the same in each of the nine cultures. There are no exceptions.

3. Proportionately more females took the conservative stance than did males. This is generally true for both premarital and extramarital coitus. The minor exceptions shown for Scandinavia (line 1, columns 3 through 6; and line 2, columns 3 and 4) perhaps may be explained on the basis of a previously reported relationship between permissive sex norms and male-female convergence (Christensen, 1966:66-67; 1969: 217; Christensen and Gregg, 1970).

4. The cross-cultural pattern appears to be a relatively stable one, whether the comparison is for premarital or extramarital coitus or is based upon male or female respondents. This may be seen by comparing the rank ordering of the last four columns. While there is some irregularity, this is not great; the striking fact is the overall consistency among ranks.

5. Four of the samples show up as the most conservative or restrictive: Midwest III is first in this regard; with Midwest II, Taiwan, and Intermountain following in close succession. Thus, conservatism concerning premarital and extramarital sex (the latter especially) seems to be associated with Asian culture in contrast to American and European culture, and with the Mennonite, Catholic, and Mormon religious cultures.

6. Two of the samples show up as the most liberal or permissive: Denmark outdistanced all others in this regard and Sweden came in second. With reference to premarital sex these two cultures appear to be of the same mold, but with extramarital sex they differ considerably. Nevertheless, Scandinavian culture, as represented by these samples, is clearly at the permissive end of our restrictive-permissive continuum.

7. The remaining three samples are in the middle. Midwest I is located at dead centre and the other two are on the permissive side of center. South, which is an American Negro sample, is next to the Scandinavian in permissiveness; in fact, it appears to be almost as permissive as Sweden on attitudes toward extramarital sex. Belgium,

which is both Catholic and European, is more permissive than the American Catholic (Midwest II) but less permissive than the other two European samples (Denmark and Sweden). Perhaps its in-between position reflects both the conservative Catholic and the liberal European norms.

Table 2. Percentages of the Sexually Experienced Giving Unqualified Disapproval to Extramarital Coitus, Compared with Total Respondents

By Sex and Culture for 1968

Sample Location and Type		Number with Sexual Experience[1]		Percentage Disapproving[2]		Percentage Point Difference from Total Respondents[3]	
		Males (1)	Females (2)	Males (3)	Females (4)	Males (5)	Females (6)
Europe							
Denmark							
(state U.)	(1)	126	57	7.1	7.0	1.1(6)	-.4(5)
Sweden							
(state U.)	(2)	174	201	28.2	30.4	1.4(5)	2.4(4)
Belgium							
(Catholic U.)	(3)	33	16	33.3	*	20.2(1)	*
United States							
South							
(Negro, state)	(4)	96	112	26.0	41.1	-1.0(7)	-5.1(7)
Midwest I							
(state U.)	(5)	121	81	45.5	79.0	10.0(4)	-2.1(6)
Midwest II							
(Catholic U.)	(6)	96	—	49.0	—	15.6(3)	—
Midwest III							
(Mennonite)	(7)	3	19	*	*	*	*
Intermountain							
(Mormon culture)	(8)	42	33	45.2	72.7	15.7(2)	3.5(2)
Asia							
Taiwan							
(state U.)	(9)	9	1	*	*	*	*
Total	(10)	700	520	31.3	43.8	18.1	15.7

[1]Those who had had premarital coitus by the time of the survey.
[2]Those who checked "never under any circumstances" for *both* sexes.
[3]Columns 3 and 4 of Table 2 subtracted from columns 5 and 6 of Table 1, respectively.
*N's too small (less than 30) for percentages to be shown.

Premarital Coitus as a Factor

One might hypothesize a positive relationship between premarital and extramarital coitus, based upon two assumptions: that each of these experiences will tend to select out the same liberal element of the population; and that experience in premarital sex will tend to make participants more liberal concerning all sex, including the extramarital. Table 2 has been constructed as a test of this assumed relationship. The first two columns show the numbers in each sample who had experienced premarital coitus; the next two columns, the percentages of these sexually experienced who gave unqualified disapproval of extramarital coitus; and the last two columns, the *differences in disapproval* between the total samples and the subsamples characterized by premarital sexual experience.

It is to these differences (columns 5 and 6) that attention is now focused. Quite obviously the hypothesis has found support, for disapproval of extramarital coitus is considerably lower among the sexually experienced as compared with the total sample. Overall it is about 18 percentage points lower with males and nearly 16 percentage points lower with females. Since proportionately fewer of the sexually experienced disapprove, it is apparent that more of them approve -- indicating an above-average permissiveness regarding extramarital coitus.

Table 3. Percentages Approving Extramarital Coitus Under Specified Conditions for Males and Females Alike

By Sex and Culture for 1968

Sample Location and Type		For Sexual Release During Long Separation[1]		Love Involvement With Unmarried Person[2]		Love Involvement With Married Person[3]	
		Males (1)	Females (2)	Males (3)	Females (4)	Males (5)	Females (6)
Europe							
Denmark (state U.)	(1)	68.7(1)	80.3(1)	74.6(1)	72.1(1)	66.4(1)	68.2(1)
Sweden (state U.)	(2)	39.3(2)	30.8(2)	25.7(3)	21.2(2)	22.8(2)	19.6(2)
Belgium (Catholic U.)	(3)	13.5(6)	1.7(7)	6.5(7)	6.7(4)	4.6(7)	4.2(4)
United States							
South (Negro, state)	(4)	24.0(3)	12.0(3)	26.9(2)	11.4(3)	15.4(3)	7.4(3)
Midwest I (state U.)	(5)	14.3(5)	2.5(6)	12.7(4)	2.9(5.5)	11.0(4)	2.1(7)
Midwest II (Catholic U.)	(6)	10.3(8)	—	7.6(6)	—	5.5(6)	—
Midwest III (Mennonite)	(7)	0.0(9)	.7(9)	0.0(9)	.7(8)	0.0(9)	0.0(8.5)
Intermountain (Mormon culture)	(8)	14.8(4)	2.9(5)	9.6(5)	2.9(5.5)	7.0(5)	3.8(5)
Asia							
Taiwan (state U.)	(9)	11.3(7)	4.7(4)	3.8(8)	0.0(9)	2.8(8)	0.0(8.5)
Total	(10)	21.2	13.5	17.2	11.1	14.1	9.7

[1]"If he or she feels the need for sexual release (with prostitutes or others) during periods of long absence from the spouse."
[2]"If he or she has fallen in love with an unmarried person."
[3]"If he or she has fallen in love with another married person."

Furthermore, this association of premarital sex experience with permissiveness concerning post-wedding infidelity seems to be strongest in the most conservative and weakest in the most liberal cultures. It is to be noted that smallness of the subsamples (numbers with premarital coital experience) did not permit comparisons for the Belgium Catholic females, nor for either males or females in the Mennonite and Taiwanese groups. But of the remainder, it was the Catholic males (in both Belgium and America) and the Mormon males and females who showed the largest differences; and it was the American Negro and Scandinavian respondents who showed the smallest differences. As a matter of fact, some of the differences in these last-named cultures are actually in the negative direction (though of low magnitude).

Commitment as a Variable

Another important consideration has to do with the commitment variable; that is, with the question of how attitudes are affected by differing levels of involvement that are assumed for the extramarital relationship. Three such involvement or commitment levels were set up for the respondents to consider and their responses are shown in Table 3. The first or lowest level assumes no commitment in the sexual relationship by either party and only a non-affectional and/or commercial involvement sufficient to obtain release from sexual tension. The second level assumes love, at least by the married person, with the other party unencumbered by marriage and therefore free to reciprocate. The third level also assumes love on the part of the married person, but with the other party not legally free to reciprocate because of a marriage commitment to someone else. Thus the last two levels, in contrast to the first, assume at least a one-sided affectional commitment, but the last level further assumes a *competing marital commitment*. It is to be noted that at each level the married party experiences competition with his commitment to his spouse, but on the last level this competing commitment is two-sided -- putting the extramarital relationship in double jeopardy, so to speak.

I had hypothesized that commitment would have a restraining effect upon approval of extramarital coitus. This finds support in the data of Table 3. With minor exceptions, percentages giving single-standard approval declined from the sexual-release category, to the unmarried-person category, to the married-person category. This was generally true within each of the nine cultures and for both male and female respondents. Overall, about 18 percent approved sexual release during long separation, 14 percent approved a love-sex involvement with an unmarried person, and 12 percent approved a love-sex involvement with another married person (line 10).

Furthermore and as might be expected, the cross-sex and cross-cultural pictures are essentially the same as they were in Table 1 -- except that the percentages and ranks run in opposite directions, since there the concern was with disapproval whereas here it is with approval. More males than females approve extramarital coitus at each of the commitment levels. The Scandinavian cultures give highest approval, the three American religious cultures, together with the Taiwanese, give lowest approval, and -- as before -- the Southern Negro falls next to the Scandinavian in permissiveness, while the Belgium Catholic is interstitial between the American Catholic and the European non-Catholic cultures. Some exceptions may be observed in certain of the columns, but they are few.

A somewhat comparable analysis of attitudes concerning *premarital* coitus has demonstrated a positive relationship between approval and the level of the commitment that is assumed, whereas here it is a negative one. Approval of premarital coitus was shown to be lowest for persons who were dating casually and randomly, next for persons in love and going steady, and highest for persons in love and formally engaged to be married (Christensen and Carpenter, 1962a:31). But the two situations are qualitatively different. Before marriage, each advance in involvement or commitment can be seen as justification for greater sexual intimacy, since a wedding may be the assumed end. But after the wedding, sexual intimacy with someone other than one's spouse may be seen as competitive with the marital relationship, and where two spouses from different marriages are involved it can compete against *both* of the already-established relationships. This competitive aspect of extramarital coitus seems to be the reason why approval in this case is negatively related to the assumed commitment level.

Residues of the Double Standard

Up to this point in the discussion we have been concerned only with single-standard approval or disapproval; that is, with cases in which respondents answered the same way for both males and females. Actually the single-standard stance involved the majority of all respondents in each of the samples. There are, however, residues of the double standard which differ considerably across sex lines and among the nine cultures. Percentages of respondents who adhered to the traditional double standard (approve for males but not for females) are presented in Table 4, separately for each of the commitment levels. Reverse double standard adherents were too few in number to be included in the analysis (see table footnote).

First, it will be observed that the relationship between double-standard approval and the commitment level is a negative one: as commitment level goes up, approval of the double standard in extramarital coitus goes down. This is true generally in each of the cultures. The overall comparison gives approximately 10 percent approval for the sexual-release category, less than 3 percent for the unmarried-person category, and only 2 percent for the married-person category (line 10). It will be noted that the big drop is between the sexual-release category (which essentially describes prostitution) and the other two (which associate extramarital sex with love). Extramarital coitus with prostitutes or others who can give sexual release to the male during periods of long separation is the practice which gains highest approval. Overall, about one out of every ten approve that.

It will be further noted that, proportionately, about twice as many males as females approve the traditional double standard; which perhaps is understandable since this standard puts fewer restrictions upon the male. This sig-

Table 4. Percentages Approving the Traditional Double Standard for Extramarital Coitus[1]

By Sex and Culture for 1968

Sample Location and Type		For Sexual Release During Long Separation		Love Involvement With Unmarried Person		Love Involvement With Married Person	
		Males (1)	Females (2)	Males (3)	Females (4)	Males (5)	Females (6)
Europe							
Denmark							
(state U.)	(1)	1.5(8)	0.0(8.5)	1.5(7)	0.0(7)	1.5(6)	0.0(5)
Sweden							
(state U.)	(2)	9.7(5)	4.4(7)	3.4(4)	.4(3.5)	2.9(3)	0.0(5)
Belgium							
(Catholic U.)	(3)	6.9(7)	7.5(4)	.8(9)	0.0(7)	.4(9)	0.0(5)
United States							
South							
(Negro, state)	(4)	44.2(1)	12.0(1)	22.1(1)	8.0(1)	20.2(1)	6.9(1)
Midwest I							
(state U.)	(5)	18.8(3)	9.2(3)	4.5(3)	.4(3.5)	2.4(4)	0.0(5)
Midwest II							
(Catholic U.)	(6)	8.6(6)	—	1.7(6)	—	.7(8)	—
Midwest III							
(Mennonite)	(7)	1.2(9)	0.0(8.5)	1.2(8)	0.0(7)	1.2(7)	0.0(5)
Intermountain							
(Mormon culture)	(8)	10.4(4)	4.8(5)	2.6(5)	0.0(7)	1.7(5)	0.0(5)
Asia							
Taiwan							
(state U.)	(9)	26.4(2)	9.4(2)	4.7(2)	.8(2)	4.7(2)	0.0(5)
Total	(10)	12.8	6.6	3.8	1.4	3.0	1.0

[1]Represented here are those who approved extramarital coitus for males but not for females. The opposite of this -- approval for females but not for males (the reverse double standard) -- involved only 5 males and 24 females in the "Sexual Release" category, 6 males and 22 females in the "Unmarried Person" category, and 5 males and 17 females in the "Married Person" category. Whether in error or not, these numbers are so small that they can be ignored in the present analysis.

nificantly greater male approval for the traditional standard which favors him is found without exception: in each of the nine cultures and at each of the three commitment levels.

Since the relationship to commitment level is a negative one for *both* single-standard approval (Table 3) and double-standard approval for extramarital coitus (Table 4), it may be tentatively concluded that the marriage commitment reduces approval of the permissive single and the traditional double standards in much the same way. In other words, when love is introduced into the equation, and then when there is an additional assumption that the sex partner also is married, percentages approving extramarital coitus go down whether the respondent is thinking of freedom for both sexes or just for the male.

The cross-cultural picture in Table 4 portrays the Southern Negro and Taiwanese samples to be highest on the double sex standard, and the Mennonite and Danish samples to be lowest. (Other differences may be noted also but present comment will be limited to these four cultures, located at the two extremes.) Since previously the Mennonite and Taiwanese samples have been shown to be highly restrictive, and the Danish and Southern Negro samples to be highly permissive, one is led to wonder which two of them are now deviant with reference to double versus single standard. In the following section, when Table 5 is discussed, it will be shown that sex-norm permissiveness and emphasis upon a single standard are positively related

Table 5. Two Indices of the Single Sex Standard for Extramarital Coitus

By Sex and Culture for 1968

Sample Location and Type		Ratio of Single Standard to Double Standard[1]			Ratio of Permissive Single Standard to Restrictive Single Standard[2]		
		Males (1)	Females (2)	Total (3)	Males (4)	Females (5)	Total (6)
Europe							
Denmark (state U.)	(1)	41.71(1)	*	61.57(2)	25.55(1)	33.75(1)	27.73(1)
Sweden (state U.)	(2)	6.54(4)	7.46(4)	6.99(4)	2.97(2)	2.18(2)	2.52(2)
Belgium (Catholic U.)	(3)	8.46(3)	5.73(7)	7.41(3)	.46(6)	.21(4)	.38(4)
United States							
South (Negro, state)	(4)	.89(9)	1.75(9)	1.22(9)	2.65(3)	.88(3)	1.38(3)
Midwest I (state U.)	(5)	3.14(7)	6.28(6)	4.10(7)	.68(4)	.10(6)	.35(6)
Midwest II (Catholic U.)	(6)	6.10(5)	—	6.10(6)	.36(7)	—	.36(5)
Midwest III (Mennonite)	(7)	23.67(2)	*	69.67(1)	**	.01(9)	.01(9)
Intermountain (Mormon culture)	(8)	4.82(6)	10.00(3)	6.32(5)	.51(5)	.13(5)	.31(7)
Asia							
Taiwan (state U.)	(9)	1.18(8)	4.56(8)	2.10(8)	.32(8)	.06(8)	.15(8)
Total	(10)	4.12	6.26	4.81	1.06	.58	.83

[1]Calculated by dividing (1) total number of items that were evaluated identically for males and females by (2) total items with infidelity approved for males but not females plus total items with infidelity *dis*approved for females but not males. Numbers in parentheses give rank order.

[2]Calculated by dividing (1) total number of items approved for both sexes by (2) total items disapproved for both sexes.

*In these instances, no items were evaluated as double standard so no index could be calculated.

**In this instance, no items were evaluated as permissive single standard so no index could be calculated.

-- with the Southern Negro and Mennonite samples standing out as notable exceptions: the first by combining high permissiveness with double-standard emphasis and the second by combining low permissiveness with single-standard emphasis. It seems probable, therefore, that these two are the deviant cases. For reasons not yet entirely understood, the Southern Negro seems to stress the double sex standard much more than would be expected from such a permissive culture (compare Denmark, for example); and the Mennonite seems to stress the single sex standard much more than would be expected from such a restrictive culture (compare Taiwan, for example).

Additional Aspects of the Single Standard

Table 5 has been designed to again get at some of the points previously discussed, although in slightly different ways, and to permit examination of certain additional aspects of the single sex standard. Two separate indices are presented. The first expresses the way single standard and double standard are interrelated; and the second, the way two different types of single standard -- with the double standard temporarily ignored -- are interrelated.

The first index (columns 1, 2, 3) protrays the single standard in terms of its ratio to the double standard. The higher the ratio, the greater the acceptance of the single standard over the double standard and vice versa. Since the picture in this instance is in terms of single-standard emphasis, while in Table 4 it was on double-standard emphasis, one would expect similar though opposite-direction patterns in the two tables. This is what was found. Earlier it was observed that males are stronger than females on the double standard while now we see females stronger than males on the single standard. Furthermore, even the rank ordering across cultures is approximately reciprocal in the two instances; with, for example, the Southern Negro and Taiwanese samples first portrayed as highest on the double standard and now lowest on the single standard, and with the Mennonite and Danish samples first portrayed as lowest on the double standard and now highest on the single standard. Although the measures presented in the two tables are not precisely the same, there is an approximate complementarity and so the results may be taken as mutually reinforcing.

It is interesting to note that with the two sexes and nine cultures combined, respondents favored single over double standard by nearly five to one (line 10, column 3). A special but comparable calculation for approval of *premarital* coitus produced an index of 4.21, or slightly more than four to one. Furthermore, the premarital index was lower than the extramarital index in seven of the nine cultures (Sweden and Southern Negro being the two exceptions). This means that the single standard is stressed relatively more with respect to extramarital coitus than with respect to premarital coitus (where the double standard is stronger, in a relative sense).

An additional special calculation of this ratio for each of the three commitment levels produced overall indices of 1.77 for the sexual-release category, 5.29 for the unmarried-person category, and 5.79 for the married-person category. This confirms the cross-category generalization previously made from Table 4. Double-standard approval goes down *and* single-standard approval goes up as one moves from lowest commitment to highest commitment. When the index for premarital coital approval is added in (see previous paragraph), the picture is like this:

Level of Competing Commitment	Description of the Relationship	Ratio of Single to Double Standard
(1) Lowest	Neither married, and so no competing commitment	Second
(2) Second	One married, no love involvement in the extramarital liaison	Lowest
(3) Third	One married, love involvement in the extramarital liaison	Third
(4) Highest	Both married, love involvement in the extramarital liaison	Highest

It will be noted that the traditional double standard ranks higher (shown here as relatively lower single standard) for married males seeking sexual release during long periods away from spouse than it does when premarital coitus is considered. Nevertheless, *both* of these categories give greater acceptance to the double standard than do the last two where love and then an additional marriage become factors in considering the extramarital liaison.

The second index shown in Table 5 portrays the permissive single standard as a ratio of the restrictive single standard (columns 4, 5, 6). The higher the ratio, the greater the stress that single-standard advocates put upon permissiveness over restrictiveness in viewing extramarital coitus. Certain categories or cultures may be permissively single standard, others restrictively single standard, and it is important to understand the difference.

The ratio, as calculated, actually understates the relative stress given to the restrictive single standard, since in the structuring of the questionnaire there was only one response category for it, but three for the permissive single standard (the three commitment levels of Table 3) and respondents could check two or even all three of them. Thus, while the table makes clear that the restrictive single standard generally is more accepted for extramarital coitus than is the permissive single standard, the magnitudes of these differences are surely greater than those suggested here. The overall ratio of .83 (line 10, column 6), for example, would be even lower than this were it not for the data limitation just explained. Nevertheless, the index should be valid for comparative purposes as it stands.

As expected, female ratios for the most part turned out to be lower than male ratios. They are lower overall and in most of the cultures when these are considered separately. Not only do females hold to the single standard more than the males (columns 1, 2), but they are inclined much more than males to hold to a *restrictive* single standard (columns 4, 5).

The cross-cultural picture can be summarized best by examining column 6 and comparing it with column 3. It will be noted that the two sets of rankings -- with two exceptions -- are remarkably close to each other. This suggests a relationship between permissiveness and single-standard adherence, and, conversely, between restrictiveness and double-standard adherence. The cultures that tend to be both permissive and single standard are Denmark, Sweden and Belgium; while those that tend to be both restrictive and double standard are Taiwan, Intermountain, Midwest I, and Midwest II. This apparent relationship between permissiveness and the single standard is similar to, if not identical with, the author's earlier reported finding for premarital coitus of a positive association between permissive sex norms on the one hand and male-female convergence in sexual attitudes and behavior on the other hand (Christensen, 1966: 66-67; 1969: 217; Christensen and Gregg, 1970). While single sex standard, as measured here, may not be precisely the same thing as the attitude and/or behavior convergence of males and females as measured in the earlier study, at least the phenomena are similar and these parallel findings do seem to support each other.

The two exceptions mentioned above are: (1) Southern Negro, which combines high permissiveness with emphasis on the *double* standard. Reasons for this possibly lie in racial history and tradition plus contemporary discrimination, as these apply to Black Americans. (2) Midwestern Mennonite, which combines low permissiveness with emphasis on the *single* standard. Reasons for this, also, would seem to lie in the history and present conditions or belief systems peculiar to this very conservative religious culture. (3) A third exception to the apparent association of single sex standard with sex norm permissiveness -- although not one based upon cross-cultural comparisons -- is the female in contrast with the male. As discussed two paragraphs above, she combines low permissiveness with emphasis on the *single* standard -- the same as the Mennonite group from the cross-cultural comparison. Undoubtedly, differences in biological risk as well as a more conservative socialization cause the female to be more restrictive in sexual matters. It also seems likely that the contemporary feminist movement is causing her to reject the double standard more than does her male counterpart, because she sees it as working to her own disadvantage. A more complete understanding of each of these three "exceptions" should make a fruitful field for future research.

Increasing Permissiveness Over Time

A final question has to do with movement in attitudes regarding extramarital coitus: Are they changing and, if so, what is the direction and tempo of this change, and how does it compare as between males and females and across the cultures studied? As explained earlier, in three of the cultures the questionnaire (which was more widely used in 1968) had been administered previously in 1958 at the identical universities. It therefore was possible to make a time analysis for these three and the results are presented in Table 6. What is shown is decade differences in percentage points for both the permissive single standard and the traditional double standard, and for each of the three levels of commitment regarding extramarital coitus.

Table 6. Trends in Approval of Extramarital Coitus, 1958-1968

By Sex for Three Cultures

(1958 percentages subtracted from 1968 percentages[1])

Sample Location and Type		For Sexual Release During Long Separation		Love Involvement With Unmarried Person		Love Involvement With Married Person	
		Males (1)	Females (2)	Males (3)	Females (4)	Males (5)	Females (6)
I. Permissive Single Standard							
Denmark (state U.)	(1)	35.1(1)	51.2(1)	47.8(1)	44.2(1)	44.3(1)	44.9(1)
Midwest I (state U.)	(2)	4.9(3)	-1.7(3)	6.1(3)	1.5(3)	5.8(3)	.7(3)
Intermountain (Mormon culture)	(3)	10.5(2)	2.1(2)	8.5(2)	2.9(2)	5.9(2)	2.4(2)
Total	(4)	50.5	51.6	62.4	48.6	56.0	48.0
II. Traditional Double Standard							
Denmark (state U.)	(5)	-3.9(3)	-5.8(3)	-.5(3)	-2.3(3)	.8(2)	0.0
Midwest I (state U.)	(6)	3.3(1)	2.2(1)	1.7(1)	-.3(1)	1.0(1)	0.0
Intermountain (Mormon culture)	(7)	.8(2)	-.6(2)	1.6(2)	-1.4(2)	.7(3)	0.0
Total	(8)	.2	-4.2	2.8	-4.0	2.5	0.0

[1]The 1968 percentages are shown in Tables 3 and 4. Nineteen fifty-eight percentages may be obtained, if desired, by simply subtracting the figures shown here from the corresponding 1968 percentages.

It will be noted that single-standard permissiveness did increase between 1958 and 1968. This was true for both males and females and within each of the three cultures and as applied to each of the three commitment levels -- with but one exception (line 2, column 2). With respect to double-standard permissiveness, however, no clear trend is apparent. The percentage-point differences in this case (Part II of the table) are all small and there are nearly as many instances with a decrease as with an increase. Since single-standard permissiveness went up and double-standard permissiveness remained nearly constant, one would expect the *ratio* of single to double standard to show an increase. This expectation was confirmed by a special calculation of 1958 ratios, which were then subtracted from the corresponding 1968 ratios (shown in Table 5, column 3). Ratio *differences* over the decade were found to be 49.93 for Denmark, .28 for Midwest I, and 1.87 for Intermountain.

Cross-cultural comparisons may be observed further in Table 6. Fairly consistently, Denmark has the largest, Intermountain next, and Midwest I the smallest increase in single-standard permissiveness. But the ordering is the reverse of this when it comes to the relatively small fluctuations over time in double-standard permissiveness. It is interesting that the greatest movement with respect to both increasing permissiveness and shifting to the single standard is with the two extremes: the most permissive (Denmark) and the most restrictive (Intermountain) cultures.

Gender comparisons reveal males to be slightly higher in the shift toward permissiveness (Part I of the table) and females higher in the shift toward the single standard (Part II of the table). As a matter of fact, *no* female respondent approved the traditional double standard for a love relationship with another married person (column 6) in *either* 1958 or 1968; and, with one exception (line 6, column 2), *fewer* females approved for the remaining categories in 1968 than did in 1958. Certainly it can be said that females, more than males, are increasingly rejecting the double standard.

Summary

Probably because it implies unfaithfulness or infidelity, extramarital sex generally has been viewed more seriously than premarital sex, which means that the sanctions that societies have imposed upon it have tended to be the more severe (see, for example, Kinsey et al., 1948: 583-594; 1953: 409-445; Murdock, 1949: 265 and passim). It was no surprise, therefore, to find better than half of the respondents of this present study disapproving extramarital coitus under all circumstances as compared with just about one-fourth similarly disapproving of premarital coitus. Rejection of extramarital coitus was higher with female respondents than male respondents and higher in some of the sample cultures than others -- with disapproval ranging all the way from nine-tenths to less than one-tenth. The cross-sex and cross-cultural patterns, nevertheless, remained remarkably stable whether it was premarital or extramarital percentages that were being compared.

Opinion statements have been taken here as reflecting the value positions of individual respondents, and each cluster or composite of individual positions as representing the norm of the particular group or culture being considered. At one point in the analysis, permissiveness regarding extramarital coitus was found to be associated with the single sex standard which means treating males and females alike. Overall, approximately five times more identified themselves with the single standard than with the traditional double standard which gives greater sexual freedom to the male. Yet the nine cultures differed considerably in this regard and, with two exceptions, it was the permissive norms that were also high on single standard and the restrictive norms that were also high on double standard. The exceptions are the Southern Negro culture, which appears to be strongly double standard in spite of being highly permissive, and the Mennonite culture, which appears to be strongly single standard in spite of being highly restrictive. More research is needed to see if this apparent positive relationship between permissiveness and the single standard holds up in other cultures, as well as to explain exceptions such as those found here.

Throughout most of this paper, both norm permissiveness-restrictiveness and single-versus-double standard have been considered as dependent variables; and the attempt has been to determine what forces may be operating to influence them. Five different independent variables have been examined: (1) the norms of the respondent's resident culture; (2) whether the respondent is male or female; (3) the respondent's personal life style as reflected by whether or not he has experienced premarital coitus; (4) the level of commitment in, or competing with, the nonmarital sexual liaison being considered; and (5) generational trends as determined by the passage of time.

Attitudes toward marital infidelity were found to vary greatly across the nine cultures studied. Permissiveness turned out to be highest in Scandinavia (Denmark and Sweden) with the Southern Negro and Belgium samples following close behind; and norm restrictiveness turned out to be highest in the Taiwanese and the religiously-oriented American samples (Mennonite, Catholic, and Mormon). Furthermore, the cross-cultural ordering of single versus double standard followed this same general pattern -- although, as has been pointed out, Southern Negro and Mennonite stood out as notable exceptions in this regard. Ethnic, racial, and religious factors seem to be operating within the various cultures to determine the special qualities of the sex norms of each.

Gender differences have been found to be rather consistent, regardless of the culture or the item being considered. Compared with males, females were found to give less approval to extramarital coitus and to combine this with a substantially greater emphasis upon the single sex standard. Furthermore, females showed greater movement between 1958 and 1968 toward the single standard than did males. But it is a *restrictive* single standard that the females typically seem more interested in, not a permissive single standard. Movement on the latter was found to be greater for males.

Since premarital coitus may be presumed to select out persons with permissive views on sex, and also -- through this intimate experience -- to incline them even farther toward the more liberal value positions, it might be expected that there will be a certain amount of carry-over to the married state. Kinsey and his associates (1948, 1953) found support for this expectation; it was the premaritally experienced who turned to extramarital coitus in largest numbers. And this present investigation has come up with a comparable finding, although at the level of attitudes alone; it was the respondents with premarital experience who expressed the most permissive views toward extramarital coitus. Furthermore, this relationship generally was found to be strongest in the most restrictive cultures.

As to the commitment variable, it was found that approval of extramarital coitus decreased with each assumption of greater involvement. It was highest for a married person seeking simple release from sexual tension during spousal absence, and lowest for a married person falling in love with another married person other than his own spouse. This is thought to be because the extramarital involvement competes against the marital commitment and vice versa. In the pre-marriage state, however, there is no such conflict of interests. New heterosexual relationships there are essentially non-competitive; and this is why, in the first place, premarital coitus is approved overall more than extramarital coitus, and, in the second place, why for the premarital, approval percentages increase with each higher level of involvement or commitment whereas for extramarital coitus they decrease. It was found, also, that double-standard approval tends to be higher for premarital than for extramarital coitus; and that, within the extramarital category, it tends to go down and single-standard approval to go up with each increase in *competing* commitment. Extramarital relationships that involve spouses from two separate marriages are the most rejected, and the rejection tendency is nearly the same whether for husbands or for wives.

Attitudinal comparisons between 1958 and 1968 revealed a general increase in permissiveness toward extramarital coitus -- which, of course, parallels a similar increase, previously reported, for permissiveness in premarital coitus (Christensen and Gregg, 1970). It is to be noted, however, that this trend toward permissiveness was a single-standard trend; double standard approval -- proportionately low to begin with -- did not change much over the decade. Another way of saying this is that permissiveness and single standard increased together, so that both received great acceptance at the end of the decade as compared with the beginning. This finding of an apparent association between permissiveness and the single sex standard, when compared over time, reinforces the very same finding that was reported above when the comparison was across cultures.

REFERENCES

Christensen, Harold T.
    1962   "A cross-cultural comparison of attitudes toward marital infidelity." International Journal of Comparative Sociology 3 (September): 124-137.
    1966   "Scandinavian and American sex norms: some comparisons, with sociological implications." The Journal of Social Issues 22 (April): 60-75.
    1969   "Normative theory derived from cross-cultural family research." Journal of Marriage and the Family 31 (May): 209-222.
Christensen, Harold T. (ed.)
    1964   Handbook of Marriage and the Family. Chicago: Rand McNally and Company.
Christensen, Harold T., and George R. Carpenter
    1962a   "Timing patterns in the development of sexual intimacy." Marriage and Family Living 24 (February): 30-35.
    1962b   "Value-behavior discrepancies regarding premarital coitus in three western cultures." American Sociological Review 27 (February): 66-74.
Christensen, Harold T., and Christina F. Gregg
    1970   "Changing sex norms in America and Scandinavia." Journal of Marriage and the Family 32 (November): 616-627.

Kinsey, Alfred C., Wardell Pomeroy and Clyde Martin
   1948   Sexual Behavior in the Human Male.   Philadelphia: W.B. Saunders Co.
Kinsey, Alfred C., Wardell Pomeroy, Clyde Martin and Paul Gebhard
   1953   Sexual Behavior in the Human Female. Philadelphia: W.B. Saunders Co.
Murdock, George Peter
   1947   Social Structure. New York: Macmillan.
Neubeck, Gerhard (ed.)
   1969   Extramarital Relations. Englewood Cliffs, N.J.: Prentice-Hall, Inc.
Whitehurst, Robert N.
   1971   "Violence potential in extramarital sexual responses." Journal of Marriage
             and the Family 33 (November): 683-691.

PART II

MATE-SELECTION AND MARRIAGE

This section begins with a discussion of a theoretical article on the subject of mate-selection and marriage and is followed by an examination of more particularized studies in this research area. The article on theory, based on data collected in Belgium, Denmark, Finland, France, Germany, Ghana, Greece, Japan, the United States, and Yugoslavia, is of special relevance to the cross-cultural theme of this book. According to the author, Hyman Rodman, it "provides a unique opportunity for a cross-cultural view of the findings and for attempting a general theoretical explanation. Although cross-cultural comparisons have their pitfalls, they offer the great advantage of steering the behavioural scientist away from provincial theories based upon information from a single society or a single type of society." This statement underlines the great value of cross-cultural studies, which in a sense is an added justification for the present endeavor.

As many studies of marital power reveal, the husband's occupational and educational status is positively associated with his power. Data from different countries show a great deal of variability in this power.

With regard to the wife's working status and her power, most of the studies that Hyman Rodman refers to indicate that working wives have more marital power than nonworking wives. Rodman's article shows that the relationship between the comparative status and power of husband and wife is unmistakable. Husbands who have greater education, belong to more organizational groups, or are more involved in their church and their jobs than their wives have more power in the marriage. "Although most of the data show a positive correlation between a husband's status and power, the data for Greece and Yugoslavia show a negative correlation." These findings are a good example of the advantages of cross-cultural research in different societies. They preclude any sweeping generalization on the status-marital power correlation.

According to the theory of resources, "the greater one's resources, the greater's one's power." As quoted in the Rodman article, Blood and Wolfe state that "the husband's average power score generally increased with increases in his education, income, and occupational status. Similarly, the husband's decision-making powers were enhanced when the wife was more dependent upon her husband. When the wife worked, she gained power because she was supplying valued resources for the family."

The data which apply to industrially developed countries might not apply to less-developed countries. For example, the more highly educated the Greek man, the likelier he is to promote a more egalitarian status for his wife, despite his traditional patriarchal culture.

"Education may play its major role as a resource variable or as a cultural variable, depending upon the particular community or society under consideration. The stress placed here upon cultural differences stems from the attempt to deal simultaneously with apparently discrepant findings from different societies." It seems that two conflicting tendencies are operative: in one, higher status increases a man's marital power, and in the other, it decreases his marital power.

Based on the theory of behavior as a function of situations and norms, several major arguments regarding marital power emerge. In Belgium, Denmark, France, the United States, and West Germany, marital decision-making is generally characterized by an egalitarian ethic and by a flexible outlook on the precise degree of decision-making that husband and wife exercise. In Greece and Yugoslavia, the marital decision-making norms are more patriarchal and less flexible.

Rodman's study also deals with the exchange of resources in a cultural context and cites the contributions of, among others, Marcel Mauss, Howard Becker, Alvin W. Gouldner, John W. Thibaut, Harold H. Kelley, George C. Homans, David M. Heer, Robert Blood, Donald M. Wolfe. According to some of these researchers, the balance of power in the marital relationship is related to how the resources obtained within the marriage compare to those that can be obtained in an exchange outside of it. "The more resources a person is contributing to the marital relationship, the more he generally stands to gain from an alternative relationship and, therefore, the more power he will be able to exercise within the marital relationship."

Rodman also suggests that "physical power, physical attractiveness, leadership qualities, and sexual control are areas in which the cultural setting can have an important influence over the exchange process. The cultural context may permit or forbid the use of these resources in bargaining for marital power." For example, neither a man's greater physical power to intimidate his wife nor a woman's manipulation of sexual favors is a legitimate resource if the spouses are not allowed to use them as such by their representative cultures.

"Even if the norms about marital decision-making are reasonably clear, adjustments between husband and wife still have to be worked out in the process of marital interaction. The formal structure of marital authority is complemented by an informal structure of marital power."

Rodman divides societies into four ideal types. The first is the *patriarchy*, in which there are strong patriarchal family norms, a high level of paternal authority, and no variation in paternal authority from one stratified group to another. Societies in which the men hold formal positions of authority are generally considered patriarchal. India possesses many characteristics of the patriarchal society, and although many changes are clearly under way there, especially in the urban areas, paternal authority remains very strong. In studies which I have conducted in India, the changes in decision-making reflect a diminution in patriarchal authority: "Almost all the respondents have commented that for one or more major decisions other family members influence their decisions. But while other family members exert some influence over the actual decisions, only the immediate family—wife, father, mother and brother, in that order—seem to be primarily involved in the decision-making process."[1]

Rural areas in India with low-level literacy exemplify the ideal-type patriarchy. However, in urban areas and in rural areas with high literacy rates and a higher standard of living, Rodman's second stage, *modified patriarchy*, exists. The modified patriarchy is a society in which patriarchal family norms have been modified by egalitarian norms at the upper strata, so that paternal authority is inversely correlated with social class. Rodman suggests that "Greece and Yugoslavia would also typify this kind of modified patriarch, in which patriarchal norms are retained in the lower classes, while 'modern,' equalitarian norms are adopted from the top down." Thus, the low-income man does not suffer any loss of authority, and it is only the upper-income man, adopting more equalitarian patterns, who modifies the patriarchal tradition.

The third type is the *transitional equalitarian* society, in which egalitarian norms are replacing patriarchal norms. Germany and the United States are examples of this stage. Unlike the first two types of societies, in this stage a man achieves esteem and power through educational, occupational, and income channels, and not simply by tradition. Thus, the lower-class man in this society may have difficulty exercising what he considers his legitimate authority and may use physical power to get his way.

The fourth type, *equalitarianism*, is characterized by a high level of power sharing by the husband and wife. Denmark and Sweden approach this kind of egalitarianism.

Similar findings to Rodman's were made in a recent study conducted by Greer Fox in Turkey:

This study of power in Turkish marriages suggests, as has been noted in studies of other developing nations, that the husband's absolute power diminishes when either the husband or the wife comes from backgrounds that evince increasing contact with the modern world of modern ideas as channeled through education, experience in urban centers, and no-agricultural occupations.[2]

Van der Geest's 1976 study of conjugal roles in rural Ghana shows that women have far more power than outward appearances would suggest:

We should not draw the precipitate conclusion that segregation of con-jugal roles necessarily implies subservience on the part of the wife. Out-ward male dominance appears perhaps to be a cloak to cover the lack of real male power, and female deference is often nothing more than a sop thrown to the men to satisfy their pride while the women carry on the handling of their own affairs.[3]

The nature of the power structure within the marital relaitonship has relevance to the overall structure of the family, including patterns of com-munication, prestige, and affection within the family. It also has an impor-tant bearing on the patterns of socialization and discipline of children within the family.

Rodman's theoretical article is followed by a number of studies on specific aspects of mate-selection and marriage. The papers are so arranged as to reflect the transition from tradition to modernity. Since Asia represents the classical traditional family society, Asian families are discussed first.

Mate-selection and marriage practices in Asia have been changing for quite some time. Thus, two extremes coexist there. On the one extreme, marriages are arranged by the parents, with or without the consent of their children. At the other, the young people have complete freedom of choice in marrying, and may or may not obtain the consent of their parents.

In traditional families, especially in Asia, marriages represent the alliance of two families. Therefore, the bride and bridegroom are expected to fit well into the traditions of their respective families. In Malaya,

Ideally, both male and female should be industrious and capable within their respective traditional sphere; he should show evidence of becoming a good provider and she should hold promise of competence as housewife and mother—Parity and balance of all qualities are highly desirable, but compensating strengths can be found for many weaknesses.[4]

In all patrilineal family systems, which are the predominant family types in the world, the girl must spend her married life with her husband's family. Therefore, it is especially important that the girl adjust well to the new family.

In most traditional family systems, especially in Asia, there is an interest in arranging marriages to well-known families. For this reason, "the family tree is carefully scrutinized and approved before marriage takes place."[5]

"The match is initiated by relatives and friends, and very seldom by the parents themselves in order to avoid the embarrassment of rejection. This precaution is for the benefit of both the girl's parents and the boy's parents. If the initial approach is favorable, more active steps are taken. The parents are eager to find out all available details about the girl and the boy. The girls are subjected to these enquiries more thoroughly than boys."[6] In Japan, the qualities of the young man and woman who are going to get married are thoroughly scrutinized by both sets of parents. In a study by Ezra Vogel, "Both families discussed the matter thoroughly and quietly investigated each other through friends and in some cases private detectives."[7]

In most traditional societies, female chastity is highly valued. Through the close-knit family system, girls are closely supervised, and it is virtually guaranteed that they will have relatively little premarital relations.

The traditional family system in India also places great value on the male's premarital chastity (this is the Hindu concept of "Brahamchari"). In contrast, covert or even open double standards exist in other cultures. Gri Raj Gupta's study, "Love, Arranged Marriage, and the Indian Social Structure," suggests that many people believe that their life's mate is predestined, that they are "right for each other"; hence, any voice in the selection is impossible for them and they "must succumb to the celestial forces of the universe. . . . Generally, love is considered a weak basis for marriage because its presence may overshadow suitable qualities in spouses." According to Gupta,

Love, as a pre-marital manifestation, is thus thought to be a disruptive element upsetting the firmly established close ties in the family, a transference of loyalty from the family of orientation to a person, and a loss of allegiance of a person, leaving the family and kin group in disdain for personal goals.

Practical considerations in the choice of the mate are emphasized in India. The prospective wife should possess good character, be able to manage the home and cook well, take active part in social and political affairs, be educated, religious, and dependent entirely on her future husband for major decisions, have a fair complexion and beauty, and share similar intellectual interests with her spouse.[8] For the man, his family's social and economic status, his education, and his earning potential take precedence over all personal qualities. Similar practical aspects are emphasized in Japan. In one case in Vogel's study of the Japanese family,

> Because there was not a diffuse close relationship between the couple, their families relied on objective criteria such as the family's status and wealth, the health, life expectancy and strength of the family line, the appearance of the girl and the economic prospects of the young man. Recently, they rely increasingly on level of education and the quality of the school as a basis for judgement.[9]

The need to reinforce family ties is the paramount consideration in traditional family systems. According to a respondent in Gupta's study:

> Young people do not know what love is; they are, if at all, infatuated which is very transitory and does not entail considerations of good marital life. If my son marries, I wish to see that the girl is well-raised, obedient, preserves the family traditions, ready to bear the hardships with us, and to nurse us in our old age.

The idea that the arranged marriage exploits women is not quite valid. According to Giri Raj Gupta, it is difficult to assume that the arranged marriage is related to the low status of women since man is also a party to it. It should also be emphasized that modified arranged marriages, whereby young people have an opportunity to accept or reject the choice, is now quite widespread in India. In a sense, this change has offset much of the criticism leveled at this well-founded tradition. Manisha Roy's very insightful discussion of arranged marriages in India further broadens one's understanding of the tradition.[10]

Some of the new directions in mate-selection in India were reported in two recent studies. While arranged marriages are still widespread, some people advertise for prospective spouses in newspapers. The increasing mobility of people from rural to urban areas not only within the same state, but also to different regions and even outside India, has widened the choice of mates even within the same linguistic-caste groups. This trend has been noted both in India and in Canada.[11]

A recently published study of advertisements in South India produced some interesting conclusions. According to Rao and Sudarsen: "The most frequently mentioned qualities show that traditional considerations such as caste, religion, personal characteristics, family background and income continue to have great importance in the selection of marriage partners. In the present sample a few advertisers reveal a progressive tendency by giving less importance to caste, religion, horoscope and *gōtrā*. The present study also claims to disprove the notion that only people who are unmarriageable resort to newspaper advertisements: This study shows that a high proportion of the advertisors belonged to the upper class and had a relatively high level of education."[12]

Another recent study shows that the number of intercaste marriages and love marriages is increasing in India: "The data suggest that inter-caste marriages are tolerated with little difficulty because although they break traditional rules requiring caste endogamy, they do not come into direct conflict with other concepts involving social stratification and family structure which are characteristic of upper and upper-middle class Bengali society."[13] This study also shows that those who make love marriages apparently retain normal contact with their families and that some even stay in joint-families. The author concludes with the claim that "although most marriages continue to be both arranged and caste-endogamous, few members of the urban elite now view inter-caste marriage as an impossibility."[14]

The next study also deals with a traditional society, namely that of Pakistan. Arranged marriages are also the norm in Pakistan. All members of the family render whatever assistance is necessary to those more directly involved in mate-selection. In Muslim families, marriage is a civil contract. As noted by Henry Korson, during the last generation all Muslim societies have undergone extensive social changes, especially with regard to the status of women.

Endogamous marriages are found in many Muslim societies. For example, Korson notes from a study in Lebanon that "60 percent of the marriages in one village in Lebanon are arranged within the kin group, largely for the purpose of consolidating property holdings which in turn supports the status system." In a study among Muslims in India which Korson refers to, "marriages arranged with kinsmen are the only alternative to spinster-hood or the loss of honor."

Korson proposes thirteen reasons for endogamous marriage; two of the most important are to conserve economic resources and to strengthen family ties. Another consideration is that in a society with limited heterosexual contacts, the only opportunities for such contacts are limited to cousins, which also might encourage endogamy.

During the last generation, there has been a decline in marriages between cousins. One important reason is the population shift from India to Pakistan, and another is the rural-urban migration which has disrupted established communities. It is expected that in time modern education in Pakistan will create greater individualism and a shift away from the traditional norm of family-centered decisions.

The third study in this section, also on a traditional society, is Joseph's paper on a Muslim society in Morocco. According to Joseph, at least some portions of Berber society can be characterized as bilateral, that is, "decision making among the Berbers is part of an ongoing sexual dialectic between men and women." Although the father, independent of external restraints, is expected to select a marriage mate for his son or daughter, females have some influence in mate-selection and devise strategies to this end. This is the main theme of Joseph's study.

Historically, Berber tribesmen arranged marriages based primarily on their desire to foster or cement relationships with other men, who were or could become allies. This motivation was much the same as that in other cultures which arranged marriages. By establishing matrimonial links with nonrelated families or reaffirming ties with kinsmen, the Berbers seek to elevate their social position or to reinforce their present standing. Marriages are arranged to bring reciprocal advantages to the males. In addition, most of the ceremonial and public aspects of the marriage arrangements from the preliminary ceremonial protocols through the final exchange of bride price and gifts—are conducted exclusively by males. The bridegroom's father approaches the bride's father and also negotiates the bride price.

Through the creation of informal power blocs, women can also exert influence. The usual avenue by which they attain influence is through their sons in competition with their husbands. Female social status among the Berbers varies with age; as a mother grows older, her son rises in power and as the son gains status so does his mother. This pattern is comparable to that in many other traditional family systems in Asia as well as in Europe. While the girls in Berber society are brought up in a sexually segregated environment, when they grow up their mobility cannot be completely restricted. The status of older women, especially those with children and grandchildren, improves. Of equal importance in building their political influence is their linkages with other women.

Not only older women but also young unmarried women take a political interest in mate-selection. While they are not supposed to have heterosexual contacts, when they participate in economic activities to help the family they are not completely segregated:

As girls move along the pathways from their homes to get water, they usually pick up female age mates occupied with the same task. Boys also follow in groups but they carefully maintain a distance between themselves and the females. If a boy is interested in a particular girl and has been led to believe through his female relatives such as a sister or from other sources, that the girl likes him, he will "walk her home."

In arranging a marriage, the son prefers to talk with a third party rather than directly with his father. The mother often becomes a broker. As the mother, she has a particular interest in her son's marriage: she can increase her own status by establishing affinal ties through the recruitment of a daughter-in-law and that woman's female kin. She will seek to establish a good marriage which will promote her son's status and at the same time improve her own political position. In fact, if one looks carefully at family systems in traditional societies, the subtle influence of women in major decisions like arranging a marriage is quite evident. Joseph's study confirms this role.

The next study in Part II, a paper on women's strategies in modern marriages in Anglophone West Africa, has some similarities to the study of the Berber family system. As is true among the Berbers, while the men in West Africa are supposed to be dominant in marriage decisions, women play a crucial role.

The position of the West African woman in marriage is examined from the viewpoint of a social anthropologist. Little explains the traditional and other obstacles in the way of those women who seek a more compassionate type of marriage. He also describes the tactics advocated by the women's magazines and explains what strategies are in fact open to women in this regard. Special attention is paid to the wife's use of economics and other resources and to the women's pragmatic approach.

Much of Little's article derives from information in women's magazines. These magazines reflect both the male and female point of view, providing an important clue to the matrimonial situation. Moreover, unlike some of their Western counterparts, these West African magazines convey an acute sense of realism. The compassionate marriage that many educated women now desire is not achieved without a great deal of forethought. Its attainment requires that a woman employ certain tactics in her dealings with the opposite sex.

In finding a suitable partner, a woman is cautioned not to be too conservative in her behavior. The prudent would-be wife, however, must survey the potential field with care. This she may do by drawing on information from relatives and girl friends. She will naturally be told to keep clear of married men and be warned in particular against "sugar daddies." To widen the range, a girl must reside in one of the larger cities, and she should join an association—a youth club, drama group, or church organization. If the association includes young men, she might even enroll for evening studies.

A girl can do some pursuing, but not openly. In addition, she must take care that the man never feels he can take her for granted; instead, he should be given the idea that if he does not take the initiative, other men will.

The magazines also stress that men are always attracted to women who have poise. It is in fact clear that, although men may fear the university graduate, they want their wives to have some education. She should be sophisticated and sufficiently at ease to impress her husband's social superiors.

These magazines also focus on marital relationships, often pointing out the "unreliability" and "infidelity" of men. In marriage, the wife is encouraged to keep her husband's interest alive. She should seek to satisfy her husband's sexual needs but should not be too demanding herself. Female as well as male contributors to the magazines go out of their way to stress the wife's subordinate position. Husband and wife should respect each other, and the wife should show greater respect to her husband. Even if he is unfaithful, he should not be emulated.

More and more women in West Africa tend to postpone marriage until after they have established themselves in their own right. Educated women tend to make better marriages. As a symbol of elite behavior, a man should not treat his wife as an inferior in public. Few husbands like their wives to work outside the house; among other things, they dislike the idea of her being under another man's authority. When a wife does work, the husband demands complete sharing of economic resources.

Even in urban areas, woman's position is rather ambiguous because, as Little points out, "community ideas of women's role have not kept pace with other structural changes."

The next article in Part II concerns another country in the traditional category—the People's Republic of China. Lucy Jen Huang's paper gives the official view on mate-selection and marriage. Since foreigners are not allowed to conduct sociological investigations in China, the sociologist must depend on official documents or information from refugees.

Huang reports that the Communist party has continually inveighed against the traditional concept of marriage. It has severely criticized "the 'survival philosophy' in which one would live only for fame, position, money, marriage and childbirth as too pitiful, selfish and ugly," for, according to the party, the only true happiness is the happiness of the people. The Communist view of happiness is based on "spiritual rather than private interest; it is based on collective welfare rather than individual happiness, and it champions service for the people and the revolution over the cause of self-actualization and the welfare of one's own family."

Regime leaders have emphasized the importance of selecting a mate with political enthusiasm. As a warning against bourgeois ideology and selfish sentiment, they have often published plays and novels illustrating the errors of the bourgeois way of life. Since the early years of the Communist regime, young people have been criticized for marrying as soon as they reached the legal age—eighteen for women and twenty for men. According to the dean of the Department of Health of Peking Medical College, the best age for a girl to marry from the standpoint of physiological and intellectual maturity, is between twenty-three and twenty-seven, and for a man between twenty-five and twenty-nine.

The official view is that a husband is impressed not with his mate's traditional role as wife and mother but rather with her new role as productive worker and committee woman. Marital happiness is secured by the wife's sharing her husband's dedication to the socialist cause. Unfortunately, many women had to experience a political struggle and a new awakening in order to achieve the approved concept of marital happiness. As a result of the regime's emphasis on public service rather than on personal interest as the basis of marital happiness, Chinese wives began to enjoy unprecedented sexual equality and freedom.

According to the government, political compatibility is one of the most important ingredients in the marital relationship. Marital happiness rests not upon physical beauty but upon political equality. The true beauty is that of political equality, sentiment, thinking, and acting.

Despite official policy, the prerevolutionary tradition of arranged marriages by families with the help of a go-between persists. In that tradition, extensive inquiries were made as to the suitability of the prospective spouses, and young men and women had little say in the matter. Since patrilocal residence was the usual pattern, the girl was under the control of her mother-in-law. The extended family had much influence on the members of the family.

In the present-day People's Republic of China, the state encourages the nuclear family structure. Nationalization of the land holdings of traditionally wealthy families has also favored nuclear families. The new law specifically supports free-choice marraiges. "The marriage law ordered that all marriages be freely formed with the thought of family alliances; it also set up an administrative structure-marriage registration to enforce this provision."[15] The law also provided equal rights to all members of the family, and in divorce proceedings husbands and wives were given equal custody of children.

The only groups which seem to have real free choice in marriage are professional and white collar workers in urban areas and the politically active youths in rural areas. The geographically mobile who are leaders in the new society are apparently influenced little by tradition; they have neo-local residence emphasizing husband-wife conjugal relations over extended family kinship. Many, however, are unable to escape their extended family ties. For a woman, as Salaff points out, "her patrilocal residence after marriage, however, is indicative of residual parental control over the new couple."[16] This pattern is more prevalent in rural areas where the mother-in-law can more easily exert her influence.

The couple has even less independence when the family becomes involved in marriage, especially in the case of non-elite village youth. "Most non-elite village youths have to contend with many social pressures to follow village custom where there is corresponding lack of support from friends and relatives for new social patterns."[17]

A news report which appeared in the *New York Times* in the early 1970s shows that tradition is still relatively strong in the People's Republic of China:

When a young Hong Kong businessman from a family in Chiu Chow decided to marry recently, his family insisted that his bride should come from their ancestoral home in the Swatow area of China's Kwantung province. Although Peking officially discourages such old customs as arranged marriages, a relative living in China had no difficulty in finding a bride, and the Chinese authorities provided a permit for her to go to Hong Kong.

The ease with which the betrothal was effected reflects the persistence of traditional patterns of social life in many areas of China, especially regarding women.[18]

A similar case was reported in Canada in 1975. After China and Canada established diplomatic relations, a Chinese family in Vancouver was able to arrange a marriage for their son to a girl from the People's Republic. The Peking government granted the bride an exit permit, and the marriage was celebrated in Vancouver, amidst great publicity in the mass media including Canada's national TV news.

While the traditional extended family is yielding to the conjugal family, it will be many years, if ever, before the modern free choice marriage is accepted.

The next article in Part II shifts from country by country traditional culture studies to an examination of the correlation between marriage ceremonies and wealth and family alliances. Rosenblatt's and Unangst's study is based on data from a number of societies. The authors agree with Jack Goody of Cambridge University that (1) the value of marriage prestations is correlated with the degree to which rights over persons are transferred as a concomitant of marriage and (2) the importance of alliances is associated with the magnitude of prestations. (Goody's article ["Marriage Prestations, Inheritance and Descent in Pre-Industrial Societies," *Journal of Comparative Family Studies*, Autumn 1970, 37-54], while an important work, is not included here because of its specialized theme and also because it is given some attention in the Rosenblatt study.)

The hypothesis of the Rosenblatt-Unangst study is that where marriage is responsible for large dowry or bride-wealth or gift transfers, or where marriage has implications for rights to substantial land or livestock, it is more likely that ceremonies will be present and will be relatively elaborate.

One advantage of public commitments is that they are likely to be stronger and more enduring than private commitments; it is relatively difficult to back down on a commitment witnessed publicly. In traditional cultures, where marriages are arranged by the family, extensive publicity contributes to marital stability—providing the couple voluntarily agreed to the marriage. Marriage ceremonies also minimize potential problems over inheritance and wealth transfer.

As shown in this study, when the wealth to be transferred in the marriage agreement is substantial, it is more likely that ceremonies will be held. It is unlikely that a culture would adopt or long retain a ceremony that was not functionally linked to other aspects of the culture.

As part of the study, the authors investigated the relationship between ceremonies and herding and agriculture activities. Among their conclusions was that agriculture and herding may enable the accumulation of surplus of wealth and larger population concentrations, either of which promotes ceremonies directly. Economic surplus also, makes it possible "to establish dowry, bridewealth, or substantial gift exchange, which may in turn promote ceremony." Based on available data, however, the authors were unable to establish causation for ceremonies. They conclude that ceremonies can be interpreted as a device for publicizing and (thereby protecting) rights and agreements, and for committing members of both groups being united by marriage to these rights and agreements.

The next study in Part II focuses on female age at marriage in the rural and semi-urban areas of four Latin American countries—Mexico, Costa Rica, Colombia, and Peru. Latin American countries can be considered to be between the extremes of traditional societies and modern societies. In rural areas, traditions are stronger, while in urban areas, especially among the middle and upper classes, the population is moving towards the Western European and North American marital pattern.

In an age of great concern about increasing population pressure in economically backward areas, this study is of special importance. Age at marriage has been an important variable in fertility studies because of its predominant effect on family size, especially in countries where there is little voluntary control of fertility. Later age at marriage significantly decreases fertility levels.

The population sample for this study consisted of approximately three thousand women in each of the four countries. The mean actual ages for the sample varied from 17.72 in Mexico to 19.10 in Peru. The mean age increased with the women's level of urbanization and education. It was found that women who lived in towns larger than 2,500 and whose early socialization took place in a city married at a later age. In addition, the ideal age for marriage was usually higher than the actual age of marriage by as much as two years. The ideal age also increased with level of urbanization and education, and the highest mean ideal was among the most educated women. The gap between ideal and actual age decreased with education and urbanization.

This study has particular significance to emerging patterns in family life. In China, for example, the government encourages late marriage. In India, legislation was passed in early 1978 "which has laid down that in future girls shall not marry until they are 18 and boys until they are 21. The present ages are 15 and 18, respectively."[19] Fertility patterns definitely influence from traditional to modern families. Small families can better adjust to the modern environment, and this small-size pattern can be found among educated and urbanized families in all traditional societies.

The next paper deals with contemporary Poland, a society which is rapidly accepting the concept of freedom of choice in marriages. Traditionally, Polish marriages were between members of the same social class and of similar economic statuses. The parents made the final choice, and individuals had little or no voice in mate-selection.

In earlier times, the urban family being a consumptive unit, was less concerned than the rural family about land as a productive unit. Moreover, the parent-child relationship in urban areas was more democratic than that in rural areas. As a result, the urban youth had more freedom in marriage decisions. With the increasing mobility from rural to urban areas, greater education, and the process of social equalization, the traditional structure has disappeared. Since personal wealth is no longer as important in contemporary Poland, young people have far greater opportunities to become acquainted without interference from the older generation.

Parental influence in marital choice is now slight or nonexistent. Most "modern" parents try not to express their opinions about their children's marital decisions. The more traditional parents sometimes express their opinions, but their children generally ignore them. Numerous marriages are consummated contrary to parental wishes. Thus, this study provides a valuable view of the continuum from traditional attitudes to modern values.

Matchmakers are not needed in urban areas except for people who move from rural areas and have no friends in the city.

With regard to motivation for mate-selection, this study reveals that among both there is significantly greater emotional than either familial or economic motivation. Indeed, the emotional motivation may be the main factor in modern marriages. By age category, the younger the person involved, the more likely the marriage was motivated by emotions.

The study also demonstrated a definite shift from the traditional segregation of the spouses' respective roles to partnership, especially by men. The basic family function in modern relations is the satisfaction of emotional needs. The two significant "modern" values of marriage are (1) the ability to move out of the parental home and thus become economically emancipated and (2) the ability to set up one's own home.

Attitudes in marital sex are of great interest to social scientists. Robert Bell's study compares attitudes among Negro women in the United States, Great Britain, and Trinidad. An important variable affecting the attitudes of these respective peoples is that U.S. and Trinidadan blacks are living in an environment where their ancestors were slaves and thus have a negative status in society, whereas the West Indians who migrated to Great Britain have generally been able to attain higher economic status than the other two groups.

While Trinidad has no racial ghettos, most of its blacks belong to the lower social class; in the United States, there is a combination of racial discrimination and low social class status. Bell hypothesizes that views of marital sex are similar, i.e., lower class, in the United States and Trinidad, while those of the West Indians in Great Britain are conventional and middle class.

West Indian women in Great Britan had a more positive definition and view of marriage; the respective figures were 60 percent for the British black versus 48 percent for the U.S. and 28 percent for the Trinidadan. Overall, however, there was little positive identification with marriage in all groups, with the least negativism in Great Britain.

While middle-class families generally condemn illegitimacy, black families are not that concerned; almost two-thirds of the study population had one child before marriage. In no group did a majority express negative attitudes towards unmarried women with children; however, they preferred to get married for the sake of the children.

The U.S. and Trinidadan blacks had generally lower expectations in marriage than the British because the lower class generally assigns less importance than the middle class to sexual behavior. And, too among the lower classes sex is more open and does not usually have the highly emotional and psychological dimensions that it does among the middle classes.

More women in Great Britain suggested that sex in marriage was of equal importance to husband and wife than did the other two groups of women. The middle-class black viewed infidelity as a threat to marital stability, especially when the woman was the unfaithful party. Lower-class black women in the United States felt they had the same sexual rights as the men; whatever the husband or boyfriend did with another women, they had the same right to do with another man. In Trinidad, however, the women were more conservative in this respect, probably because of their Roman Catholic faith.

With regard to the women's attitude to male infidelity, the conservative single standard was expressed mostly in England, thereby reflecting middle-class values. The United States had more of a double standard, while in Trinidad, the women seemed to expect men to stray.

The main finding of this study is that sexual behavior in marriage is strongly influenced by class position. Thus it was that women in the United States and Trinidad followed their lifelong socialization to sexual values, whereas the women in Britain were resocialized into the middle-class values and as a result strongly identified with, and followed, the new values.

The next article, a discussion of Jewish-Gentile intermarriages, together with the following one by Thomas Monahan, provides an appropriate conclusion to this section. Statistically, compared to endogamous marriages, intermarriages account for only a very small part of the population.

In the study of Jewish-Gentile marriages in Manitoba, Canada, Frideres et al. examine four characteristics: identity (religious and ethnic), alienation, self-esteem, and anxiety. Their first hypothesis is that the offspring of inter-religious married couples will have lower religious and ethnic identity than those from intrareligious marriages. Their findings partly upheld the hypothesis, with a moderate relationship existing between type of marriage and degree of religious identity.

Their second hypothesis is that the offspring from interreligious marriages will score higher in alienation than those from intramarriages. Study results, however, showed that the relationship was not that strong. In addition predictability of anxiety and self-esteem from type of marriage was found to be very limited; "type of marriage" had little impact as regarding these two factors.

The findings suggest that the assumption that the nominal faiths of spouses indicate the degree of conflict between spouses is highly questionable. The present sample revealed that most of the marriages were rather highly congruent in terms of spouses' religious and ethnic identities; none of the marriages fell into the category of low congruence. Individuals whose religious and ethnic identities were highly incongruent might decide not to marry or if they did marry, they might not remain together for an extended time period, without reducing the incongruity. The findings also show that interreligious marriages did not affect the children differently than intrareligious marriages.

Canada is experiencing an increase in interethnic marriages. Studies of immigrant groups also indicate that, although there is a relatively high rate of endogamy within the first generation, this pattern begins to change in the second and third generations.[20] It also seems that Asians and Italians, who are stereotypically considered "clannish," are not so when it comes to intermarriage. On the other hand, the British show one of the highest incidence of endogamy.[21] Recently, in the centennial celebrations of Japanese immigration in Canada, newspapers reported that among the third-generation Japanese or the Sanseis, as they are known, a significant number marry non-Japanese.

A 1976 study conducted in Singapore revealed several interesting aspects of interethnic marriage. The sociological variables examined were previous marital status, religion, age, and socioeconomic status. It was found that interethnic marriages are more likely to take place between (1) those who have been married before; (2) those who have already married across religious lines; and (3) those from the lower or upper occupational groups. As regards age, when remarriage cases are excluded, the age differences in marriage are not significant; this particular finding is quite different than findings for other societies.[22]

The subject of interethnic marriages continues to fascinate social scientists, especially the questions of why people marry, how successful the marriages are, and what is the future of the children from such marriages. Because society considered the interethnic marriage to be "atypical" or even "deviant," only a very small minority marry across racial lines, even in multiracial societies where interactions have taken place for generations. In a sense, then, it becomes more difficult to make generalizations. Monahan, among others, has recognized some of the problems inherent in the study of interethnic marriages: "A controlled comparison of the intermarriages as to age at first marriage, age difference, birthplace, area of residence, non-residence, previous marital status, type of ceremony, and occupational level, illustrates the difficulty in deriving only one generalization applying to all races."[23]

The last study in Part II, Thomas Monahan's examination of interracial marriage in Maryland, Virginia, and the District of Columbia, covers marriages between both Negroes and whites and other racial minorities. Monahan traces the history of the laws against interracial marriages in the South from the colonial and slavery periods, when the southern states placed severe restrictions or absolutely prohibited such marriages, to 1967 when the U.S. Supreme Court finally invalidated these miscegenation laws. While the District of Columbia never passed any legislation forbidding interracial marriages, the Maryland and Virginia systems were probably followed down to the 1860s. Thus, Negro-white marriages in the District were permitted by custom if not by law. Any attempt to pass legislation prohibiting interracial marriage in the District consistently failed.

The removal of restrictions on interracial marriages in Maryland and Virginia had no significant effect on such marriages in the District of Columbia. In fact, in 1973 there was an increase. A somewhat different picture emerges when one examines the marriages of whites and Negroes separately. A sizable proportion of the intermarriages of whites are with the Oriental and other non-Negro races. For the years 1965-1970, 27 percent of the mixed marriages of whites were with other races and 73 percent with Negroes.

Before 1900, there wre few mixed marriages, and nearly all of these were between whites and Negroes. In the years following, persons of other races, the men especially, began to intermarry with white women. In the latter part of the 1930s, an increasing number of Filipino men and women (prohibited by law from marriage with whites in Maryland and Virginia) started marrying whites in the District. After 1940, races other than the Negro and Filipino also began strongly to affect the intermarriage picture in the District.

After June 1967, with the outlawing of miscegenation laws in all the states, interracial couples no longer needed to come to the District of Columbia to marry. District records show that in the period 1968-1970 about 3.3 percent of all marriages were interracial. These included the marriages of whites to Korean, Chinese, Japanese, and American Indians. The 1968-1970 data suggest that white men, more often than white women, were choosing Japanese, Korean, and Filipino mates, but in the case of the Negro, American Indian, and miscellaneous other races, the white female was more likely to intermarry with these races. The study concludes that, in terms of marriages contracted, minority races are very much involved in racial mixtures.

About 5 percent of Negro marriages are interracial, which is a large percentage considering the total Negro population. Even whites are experiencing increasing proportions of intermarriages with Negroes and other races. Hence, interracial marriage in the United States can no longer be called a "rare phenomenon."

Monahan, an acknowledged authority on interracial marriages, demonstrates the increasing significance of such unions. With large numbers of nonwhite ethnic groups in urban North America, interracial marriages will have an increasing influence on society. For example, in Canada, the proportion of the foreign-born population has increased since the liberalization of immigration in 1962, while the traditional immigration from Great Britain dropped from 42.8 percent for the period before 1946 to 20.9 percent during 1966-1971. The number of migrants to Canada from other European countries increased in the 1961-1971 period, and marked upward trends occurred for Asiatic and Commonwealth countries excluding the United Kingdom, such as India, Pakistan, and the West Indies. The foreign-born from Asiatic and other Commonwealth countries together accounted for only 8.8 percent of the total foreign born in 1971; the corresponding proportion for those born in Italy alone was 11.7 percent.[24] Clearly, the increase in the number of foreign-born will have an influence on marriage patterns in Canada.

One interesting aspect of mate-selection is that while there is a movement away from traditional arranged marriages, even in Poland where the changes are most evident, parents still attempt to influence the lives of their children. Though these attempts are seldom successful, they indicate the persistence of tradition.

Notes

1. George Kurian, *Structural Changes in the Family in Kerala, India* in *Socialization and Communication in Primary Groups*, edited by Thomas R. Williams, World Anthropology Series, The Hague: Mouton Publishers, 1975, p. 66.

2. Greer Litton Fox, "Another Look at the Comparative Resources Model: Assessing the Balance of Power in Turkish Marriages," *Journal of Marriage and the Family*, Vol. 35, No. 4, Nov. 1973, p. 728.

3. Sjaak van der Geest, "Role Relationship Between Husband and Wife in Rural Ghana," *Journal of Marriage and the Family*, Vol. 38, No. 4, Aug. 1976, p. 577.

4. Heather Strange, "Continuity and Change: Patterns of Mate Selection and Marriage Ritual in a Malay Village," *Journal of Marriage and the Family*, Vol. 38, No. 3, Aug. 1976, pp. 562-563.

5. S. C. Dube, "Men's and Women's Role in India, a Sociological View," in *Women of Asia*, UNESCO, 1960, p. 58.

6. George Kurian, ed. *Modern Trends in Mate Selection and Marriage with Special Reference to Kerala, in The Family in India—A Regional View,* The Hague: Mouton Publishers, 1974, p. 355.

7. Ezra Vogel, *The Japanese Family in Comparative Family Systems*, edited by M. F. Nimkoff, Boston: Houghton Mifflin, 1965, p. 292.

8. Kurian, "Modern Trends in Mate Selection and Marriage in Kerala."

9. Vogel, *The Japanese Family*, p. 293.

10. Manisha Roy, *Bengali Women*, Chicago: University of Chicago Press, 1975, pp. 73-123.

11. Kurian, *Modern Trends in Mate Selection*, pp. 358-359.

12. P. Venkata Rao and V. Sudarsen, "Continuity and Change in Marital Choices: A Note on Marital Advertisements in South India," *Social Action*, Vol. 28, No. 1, Jan.-Mar., 1978, p. 60.

13. Lauren A. Corwin, "Caste and Class and the Love-Marriage: Social Change in India," *Journal of Marriage and the Family*, Vol. 39, No. 4, Nov. 1977, p. 823.

14. Ibid., p. 831.

15. Janet W. Salaff, "The Emerging Conjugal Relationships in the People's Republic of China," *Journal of Marriage and the Family*, Vol. 35, No. 4, Nov. 1973, p. 707.

16. Ibid., p. 709.

17. Ibid., p. 710.

18. "Women Still Far Away from Equality in Modern China," *New York Times*, reprinted in the *Calgary Herald*, Calgary, Alberta, Canada, September 19, 1973.

19. *The Canadian India Times*, Ottawa, March 16, 1978, p. 2.

20. S. P. Wakil, "Marriage and Family in Canada," *Journal of Comparative Family Studies*, Monograph—1976, p. 26.

21. Ibid., p. 28.

22. Eddie C.Y. Kuo and Riaz Hassan, "Some Social Concomitants of Interethnic Marriage in Singapore," *Journal of Marriage and the Family*, Vol. 38, No. 3, Aug. 1976, p. 558.

23. Thomas P. Monahan, "Marriage Across Racial Lines in Indiana," *Journal of Marriage and the Family*, Vol. 35, No. 4, Nov. 1973, p. 639.

24. M. V. George, "Place of Birth and Citizenship of Canada's Population," 1971 Census of Canada, Statistics Canada, Ottawa, April 1978, pp. 18-20.

Marital Power and the Theory
of Resources in Cultural Context*

HYMAN RODMAN

Comparable information on marital power has been collected in Belgium, Denmark, Finland, France, Germany, Ghana, Greece, Japan, United States, and Yugoslavia. This provides a unique opportunity for a cross-cultural view of the findings and for attempting a general theoretical explanation. Although cross-cultural comparisons have their pitfalls, they offer the great advantage of steering the behavioral scientist away from provincial theories based upon information from a single society or a single type of society.

This paper extends an earlier analysis of the same subject (Rodman, 1967). It summarizes several methodological issues raised by the studies on marital power. The major purposes of the paper, however, is to summarize the data on marital power, and to formulate a general theoretical explanation.

It should be borne in mind that the power relationship between husband and wife is but one aspect of a total relationship. As in any other relationship, such as a work or friendship relationship, one could also study the division of labor, the communication system, the distribution of prestige, and the affectional-emotional ties. Moreover, the husband and the wife may be part of a larger kinship (or friendship) group in which children and possibly many others are part of the system of relationships (cf. Strodtbeck, 1958; Kandel and Lesser, 1970; Liu *et al.*, 1970; Troll, 1970). As a result, focussing upon the power relationship of husband and wife is tapping only a small portion of a complex set of relationships. The studies we are relying upon, however, have not consistently collected information on most of these other dimensions.

Methodological Issues

Many methodological issues are raised by the studies of marital power, but since these have been discussed by others, and are in any case not unique, we will deal with only several issues briefly.

First of all, the method by which the information is obtained may influence the results (Safilios-Rothschild, 1969a, 1970; Blood *et al.*, 1970;

---

*A grant from the Institute of Life Insurance aided in the completion of the study. The research assistance of Jane Brackett and the helpful comments of David Heer and Denise Kandel are acknowledged.

Olson, 1969; Strodtbeck, 1958; Liu *et al.,* 1970; cf. D'Antonio and Erickson, 1962). Some studies have measured power by observing it in an experimental setting, while others have relied upon interviews and questionnaires. Among the latter, some have obtained their information from a wife or child only, while others have obtained their information from husband and wife. There are strong indications that the method by which the information is obtained influences the results. The comparisons made in this paper, which ignore the method of obtaining the information, are therefore highly tentative.

There is also the issue of the cultural equivalence of the questions asked and the words used in the different societies (Lupri, 1969a; Blood and Takeshita, 1964; Safilios-Rothschild, 1970). A particular decision may be highly relevant to marital power in one society and irrelevant in another. As a result, the investigators have generally avoided a simple duplication of each other's questions, and have attempted to develop culturally equivalent questions. This indicates sensitivity to the issue, but it does not assure the comparability of the data.

Other issues in decision-making center around the possible delegation of power, its variation from decision to decision, and its change through time (Wolfinger, 1960; Safilios-Rothschild, 1970). Spouse A may make certain decisions because spouse B has delegated that power to A while retaining veto power. If A makes certain everyday decisions, while ultimate power rests with B, it is not clear how respondents will answer questions about who "makes the decisions". The results obtained may, therefore, be somewhat ambiguous, and they may be contingent upon the decisions that were investigated (Centers *et al.,* 1971) and the time of the investigation.

Finally, information is not ordinarily available as to what it means to an individual to be able to make certain decisions. For example, decisions about the frequency of sexual intercourse or about whether the wife works may have high salience for one spouse and relatively low salience for another. Consequently, one spouse may be willing to forego power in several other areas for power in an area of importance. Husbands and wives may each have their own sphere of power (Bott, 1957: 64). Wilkening and Lupri (1965) point out that, among farm families, Hessian (German) women have more power than Wisconsin (U.S.A.) women in decisions about land and livestock because these decisions are of greater consequence to them. And Netting (1969) reports that Kofyar (Nigeria) women, who live in a society that is formally male-dominated, nevertheless have considerable power:

> In things that matter to a Kofyar woman, she retains considerable control. Where she lives, when she works, and with whom she sleeps are subject to her own choice. She cannot be ordered to work, restricted in economic matters, regulated in extramarital affairs, or constrained from changing spouses. (p. 1043.)

In order to facilitate the presentation of the data, methodological issues will not be raised in the sections that follow. Despite the problems, we will assume that the data on marital power are sufficiently comparable to warrant discussion. (For a contrasting position, and a much more elaborate discussion of the methodological problems, see Safilios-Rothschild, 1970.)

Husband's Status and Husband's Power

A finding that is common to many studies of marital power is that the husband's status is positively associated with the husband's power. There are data in Table 1 based on three German studies, four U.S.A. studies, and one study each from Belgium and Japan, that document that relationship.[1] But the data in Table 1 also demonstrate that there is a great deal of variability.

TABLE 1

CROSS-NATIONAL URBAN DATA ON HUSBAND'S SOCIAL STATUS AND HUSBAND'S MARITAL POWER*

	Cologne, Germany. König, 1957: % with marked paternal authority (by combined social class index)	Münster, Germany Lamousé, 1969: % with marked paternal authority (by husband's income)	Urban sample, West Germany. Lupri, 1969a: husband's mean power score (by husband's income)	Boston area, U.S.A. Heer, 1963a: % both partners agree husband usually wins out (by husband's occupation)	Detroit area, U.S.A. Blood & Wolfe, 1960: husband's mean power score (by husband's education)
Husband's Social Class					
High 53			5.79		5.46
		36.1			
30			5.60		5.70
		43.8			
25			5.51	39	5.41
		37.8			
8			4.94		5.17
		31.4			
19			4.88	22	4.73
25			4.50		4.87
Low					

*Because of variations in how the percentages or power scores were computed from study to study, they are not comparable across countries, and only the trends within each country should be noted. Additional details on how the social class variable was measured can be found in each study. The original studies should also be consulted for a more complete presentation of the available data.

TABLE 1 (Continued)

	Boston area, U.S.A. D. G. McKinley, 1964: % father main source of authority (by combined social class index)	Urban sample, U.S.A. Kandel and Lesser, 1971: husband's mean power score (by husband's occupation)	Los Angeles, U.S.A. Centers et al., 1971: husband's mean power score (by husband's education)	Paris & Bordeaux, France. Michel, 1967: husband's mean power score (by husband's education)	Urban sample, Denmark. Kandel and Lesser, 1971: huband's mean power score (by husband's occupation)
Hus-band's Social Class					
High	64	3.05	3.01	2.04	3.13
		3.16	2.97	2.01	3.24
	61	3.06	3.00	1.96	3.23
		3.10	2.96	1.95	3.23
		3.04	2.80		3.18
	48	2.50	2.71		3.11
			3.41		
Low					

TABLE 1 (Continued)

	Tokyo, Japan. Blood, 1967: husband's mean power score (by husband's income)	Louvain, Belgium. Leplae, 1968: husband's mean power score (by husband's education)	Athens, Greece. Safilios-Rothschild, 1967: husband's mean power score (by husband's education)	Kragujavac, Yugoslavia. Buric and Zecevic, 1967: husband's mean power score (by husband's education)
Hus-band's Social Class				
High	5.7	2.93	2.57	1.76
	5.5	2.97	2.58	1.88
	5.1	2.83	2.75	1.97
	5.1	2.75	2.98	2.65
				2.79
Low				

The investigators represented in Table 1 have published considerably more information than is included in that table. They have typically reported variations in husband's power by several status criteria, as well as by other variables. They have sometimes also reported information on other samples. Table 1 is, therefore, highly selective, but it does include information on those studies that have provided the broad outlines for the correlation between husband's status and husband's power. As is evident from the table, the social class variables I have selected from the investigators' work is husband's occupation, education, or income, or a combined index based upon these variables.

Although husband's status is positively (but sometimes nonsignificantly) associated with husband's power for many of the studies reported in Table 1, there are a number of reversals in the data. There is at least one reversal in the data selected from König, Lamousé, Lupri, Blood and Wolfe, Centers et al., Kandel and Lesser (Denmark), and Leplae. The Kandel and Lesser data on the U.S.A. show even more reversals. These curvilinear tendencies need to be strongly emphasized, including their occurrence in the Blood and Wolfe study that so many researchers are trying to replicate, because they are too often ignored. They will be discussed later in the paper.

Wife's Working Status and Wife's Power

Several studies have examined marital power in relation to the wife's working status. The findings in most of these studies indicate that working wives have more marital power than non-working wives. This is reported for Germany by Lamousé (1969) and Lupri (1969a), for Greece by Safilios-Rothschild (1967), for the United States by Blood and Wolfe (1960), Heer (1963a), and Papanek (1969), for France by Michel (1967), for Denmark and the United States by Kandel and Lesser (1971), for Yugoslavia by Burić and Zečević (1967), for Japan by Blood (1967), for Puerto Rico by Weller (1968), and for Ghana by Oppong (1970). These data refer to summary scores based upon a variety of decisions. But there are variations from decision to decision, and on some decisions there are no differences between working and non-working women, while in some working wives have less power than non-working wives (Blood, 1963a; Safilios-Rothschild, 1970). Working women are especially likely to acquire more power regarding major economic decisions (Blood, 1963a; Burić and Zečević, 1967).

When wives work their husbands are likelier to do more of the housework (Blood and Wolfe, 1960; Silverman and Hill, 1967; Michel, 1970; Safilios-Rothschild, 1970). Working wives also usually have fewer children. Weller (1968) reports lower fertility among working women (cf. Freedman et al., 1959; Gendell, 1963), and greater influence by the working woman regarding decisions about additional children. Working women want fewer children and have fewer children (Michel, 1970).

Relative Status of Husband and Wife

A few studies report data on marital power in relation to the comparative status of husbands and wives. Comparative educational status is
ordinarily used, but some studies also report data by comparative income,
occupational involvement, and organizational participation. These data
indicate that comparative status is an important variable — generally,
spouses with higher relative status or with greater work or organizational
participation have more power than comparable spouses with lower
status or participation.

Similar findings on comparative status are reported by Haavio-Mannila
(1970) for Finland, by Blood and Wolfe (1960) and Komarovsky (1964)
for the United States, by Michel (1967) for France, by Lupri (1969a)
for German, by Burić and Zečević for Yugoslavia (1967), and by Kandel and Lesser for Denmark and the United States (1971).

TABLE 2

HUSBAND'S POWER, BY COMPARATIVE STATUS OF HUSBAND AND WIFE*

	Wife more	Equal	Husband more
Comparative Education	4.80	5.08	5.28
Comparative Organizational Membership	5.05	5.14	5.36
Comparative Church Attendance	4.72	5.21	5.70
Comparative Work Participation	2.67	4.46	5.28

*Source: Robert O. Blood, Jr. and Donald M. Wolfe, 1960, Tables
10, 11, 12, and 13. The scores report husband's overall power based
upon wives' answers about eight decisions — higher scores represent
more husband power. The data on comparative education are based
upon families in which the husband had a high-blue-collar occupation.
The data on comparative work participation are selected from a
more detailed breakdown.

Some of the data reported by Blood and Wolfe for the United States
are summarized in Table 2. The relationship between comparative status
and power is unmistakable. Husbands who have more education or
organizational memberships than their wives have more power. Similarly, the more the husband is involved in church attendance and work
participation — in comparison to his wife — the more power he has.

Some Divergent Findings

I have emphasized the overall consistency of the findings for Denmark,
France, Germany, Greece, United States, Yugoslavia, and also, at some
points, for Belgium, Ghana, Finland, Japan, and Puerto Rico. This may
have suggested to some readers that a great deal of cross-cultural evidence supports the generalizations made so far between marital power

and either husband's status, wife's working status, or comparative status of husband and wife. There are, however, some crucial and interesting differences that need to be focussed upon.

Although most of the data show a positive correlation between husband's status and husband's power, the data for Greece and Yugoslavia (see Table 1) show a negative correlation. In addition, when one looks closely at some of the studies that show an overall positive correlation between husband's status and power, there are indications of curvilinear relationships and of weak relationships that are not statistically significant. Some of these divergent findings can be seen in Table 1.

These divergent findings are a concrete example of the advantages of cross-cultural research with varying societies. They preclude the generalization that husband's status is positively associated with husband's marital power — a generalization that might have been made without modification if we were using only data based upon Germany and the United States. The divergent findings, especially for Greece and Yugoslavia, present a challenge to the cross-cultural investigator. They call for a modification of the generalization and offer the hope that we may inductively be able to arrive at a generalization that has greater explanatory power.

The Theory of Resources

The theory of resources, Dahl (1968:409) points out, "is an ancient, distinguished, widespread, and persuasive mode of explanation" which holds that "the greater one's resources, the greater one's power". It has been applied to societies and classes as well as to individuals and groups. Curiously, in the encyclopedic articles on authority (Peabody, 1968) and power (Dahl, 1968), the family is listed as an area of application at the beginning of both articles and at the end of one, but there is no discussion of power or authority in the family in the body of either article.

Blood and Wolfe (1960) found that the theory of resources provided the best explanation for their findings on the U.S.A. The husband's average power score generally increased with increases in his education, income, and occupational status. These variables were conceptualized as resources which the husband was able to use within the marital relationship in order to gain greater decision-making power. Similarly, the husband's decision-making powers were enhanced when the wife had preschool-age children, because under these circumstances the wife was more dependent upon her husband. When the wife worked she gained power because she was supplying valued resources for the family. Further, Blood and Wolfe (1960:37) state that

it is desirable to compare the wife and the husband on the same characteristics, for then the comparative resourcefulness and competence of the two partners can be discovered. Once we know which partner has more education, more organizational experience, a higher status background, etc., we will know who tends to make most of the decisions.

The data on Germany, and to a lesser extent the data on Belgium, Finland, Ghana, Denmark, France, and Japan, provide some additional support for the theory of resources. In several of these societies, the husband's status is positively correlated with his power; the wife's power rises when she is working; and the comparative status of husband and wife has an important influence upon the distribution of power. Since the husband's status, or the wife's working position, or comparative status can be seen as indicators of resources, the theory of resources provides us with an excellent start for developing a more comprehensive theory to explain the available data.

In König's (1957:125) pioneering study, he provided empirical data to suggest that "the German family . . . seems to have followed the same trend as the other family types in the industrially developed countries of Western Europe". This leaves open the question of the distribution of marital power in less developed countries. Michel (1967), for example, in presenting French data that also lend some support to the theory of resources, cautioned that there might be differences in less developed countries where occupational and educational status may have different significance.

Resources in Cultural Context

The specification that the data apply to industrially developed countries and might differ in less developed countries was well-founded. In Greece and Yugoslavia, rather than finding a positive correlation, we find that the husband's occupational, or educational, or income status is negatively correlated with the amount of power he exercises within the family. For example, husbands at the highest educational levels in Germany, France, Denmark, and the U.S.A. generally have the highest average power scores; in Greece and Yugoslavia, husbands at the highest educational level have the lowest average power score.

From the perspective of the developed societies, education, income, and occupational status are resources, and the comparative amount of such resources possessed by husband and wife are important in determining the distribution of power. But the reversal of the relationships for the Greek and Yugoslavian data forces us to reconsider our view of education, income, and occupation. They are not merely resource variables in a power struggle, but are also positional variables in the social structure. The different positions they represent may involve differing patterns of socialization and may, for example, represent a greater or lesser likelihood of learning attitudes favorable toward the equalitarian distribution of power. This is particularly true of education: the more highly educated the Greek man, as pointed out by Safilios-Rothschild (1967), the likelier is he to hold attitudes that would lead to a more equalitarian status for his wife.

In Greece and Yugoslavia, therefore, we are not dealing so much with resources in a power struggle, but with the learning of a new role. The more education a man has, the likelier is he to grant his wife more authority, despite a traditional patriarchal culture.

Education may play its major role as a resource variable or as a cultural variable, depending upon the particular community or society under consideration. The stress placed here upon cultural differences stems from the attempt to deal simultaneously with apparently discrepant findings from different societies. Blood and Wolfe also considered the possible influence of cultural factors in explaining the U.S.A. data, but found them wanting. They examined the influence of several variables that might indicate a greater acceptance of an authoritarian tradition — farm families, immigrant families, older couples, uneducated couples, and Catholic couples. But these families did not show a more patriarchal pattern of decision-making. It was after testing for the influence of such cultural factors in the U.S.A. that Blood and Wolfe turned to the theory of comparative resources. In the present discussion we have access to other data that do indicate the importance of cultural expectations, including data on the U.S.A. from Centers *et al.* (1971). It seems that comparative resources play an influential role in the United States and other developed societies because of several underlying cultural factors: (1) the transition toward an equalitarian marital ethic; (2) a high degree of flexibility about the distribution of marital power; and (3) the importance that education, occupation, and income have in defining a man's status.

It appears that there are two conflicting tendencies operating — in one, higher status increases a man's marital power, and in the other it decreases his marital power. To the extent that a man's higher status operates as a valued resource that gives him more leverage within the marital relationship, it increases his power. To the extent that it operates to place the man in a patriarchal society in closer touch with equalitarian norms, it decreases his marital power. To the extent that both influences are operating simultaneously, we may find a curvilinear relationship or a weak relationship between a man's status and his marital power.

König's data indicate that although the highest percentage with strong paternal authority are found in the highest class, and although paternal authority declines as we descend the status ladder, there is an upswing at the bottom, presumably because traditional emphasis upon paternal authority remains stronger at the bottom of the social class scale. The data by Lamousé indicate a general positive correlation, except that there is a decline in the amount of paternal authority in the very top status level for which data are reported; Kandel and Lesser's data also show this decline. The Blood and Wolfe data reported in Table 1 indicate both the increase in paternal authority at the bottom and the decrease at the very top, despite the generally positive association that exists.

It seems evident that these data reflect the joint influence of resources on the one hand and of cultural or subcultural differences regarding power on the other. Two interesting sets of data provide further confirmation — one based on a blue-collar sample in the United States, and the other on a middle-class sample in Japan. Although dealing with relatively homogeneous samples, both studies report that husbands of lower status exercised more power within the family. In the United States sample (Komarovsky, 1964: 224) the higher blue-collar workers had less power than the lower blue-collar workers; in the Japanese sample (Blood, 1967) the blue-collar men had more power that the white-collar men. Both Komarovsky and Blood suggest that the explanation lies in the greater adherence to patriarchal authority at the lower status levels, and Komarovsky (1964:225-7) presents data that confirm these different attitudes toward marital power (cf. Burić and Zečević, 1967; Haavio-Mannila, 1969). Thus, in societies where there is evidence that a husband's higher status is correlated with his higher marital power, there are also indications that normative differences between the social classes can introduce a curvilinear relationship.

Situations, Norms, and Behavior

In an ad hoc and inductive way, a "theory of resources in cultural context" has been elaborated in order to place the findings on power structure in Belgium, Denmark, France, Ghana, Germany, Greece, Japan, U.S.A., and Yugoslavia into theoretical context. We found that the "theory of resources" was reasonably adequate for the German and U.S.A. data but less adequate for the Danish and French data. In modifying the theory to account for the Greek and Yugoslavian data we have expanded its explanatory power. The "theory of resources in cultural context", inductively developed to account for much of the reported data, requires further specification through testing on additional communities. Lupri (1969a), Oppong (1970), and Kandel and Lesser (1972) offer further relevant discussions of the theory.

Now that we have developed the theory of resources in cultural context inductively, let us turn around and approach it deductively. A debate that once raged among psychologists had to do with whether behavior was an automatic reaction to stimulus influences or whether there were certain mediating processes in the organism between the stimulus and the behavior or response. A parallel debate among sociologists had to do with whether behavior was an automatic outcome of situational influences or whether there were certain mediating cultural processes that provided normative guidelines for behavior in particular environmental situations. Most psychologists realized that the naked stimulus was clothed in the prior experiential history of the organism, and in this sense the response was influenced by stimulus and organism interaction. Most sociologists realized that the naked environmental situation was draped with normative guidelines and that behavior was influenced by the interaction between the situation and the norms. Similarily, to tie in the ad hoc theory we have developed, we might say that the naked theory of resources has to be set within a cultural context; in this way it is possible to state explicitly that decision-making behavior is influenced by the interaction between resources and cultural definitions. In fact, of course, though the words and perspectives are different, the psychological S-O-R theory, the sociological theory of situation, norms, and behavior, and the theory of resources in cultural context are all getting at the same general formula for predicting behavioral outcomes. There is a stimulus or a situation; there is an organism with prior experience which may include learned cultural or normative dispositions; and the response or behavior that ensues is influenced by these factors in interaction with each other.

A restatement of the findings in terms of the theory of behavior as a function of situation and norms summarizes several of the major arguments:

1. In Belgium, Denmark, France, U.S.A., and West Germany the norms about marital decision-making have two major characteristics that are of special relevance. They tend to favor, in general, an equalitarian ethic, and they tend to be flexible about the precise degree of decision-making that should be exercised by husband and wife. As a result of this normative framework, the situation of interaction between husband and wife, including their comparative resources, comes into play and has an influence over the behavioral outcome. As a result there are positive relationships between a husband's resources and his power score, or between the comparative resources of husband and wife and their power scores.

2. In Greece and Yugoslavia the norms about marital decision-making are more patriarchal in character and less flexible. As a result, the normative guidelines place constraints upon the possible influence of situational conditions or resources. It is therefore among those groups that have learned "modern" norms regarding marital decision-making — such as groups at the higher educational levels — that there is the greatest possibility for the increased participation of women.

A theoretical statement about marital power can be formulated: The balance of marital power is influenced by the interaction of (1) the comparative resources of husband and wife and (2) the cultural or subcultural expectations about the distribution of marital power. Similar statements, referring to the interaction of comparative resources and cultural expectations, could also be made about the distribution of power in other areas. It should be kept in mind that cultural values may influence the definition of resources and their exchange value.

The Exchange of Resources in Cultural Context

The theory of exchange and reciprocity in social relationships has had a long history. Marcel Mauss (1954), Howard Becker (1956), Alvin

W. Gouldner (1960), John W. Thibaut and Harold H. Kelley (1959), and George C. Homans (1961), among others, have dealt with the idea of exchange and reciprocity in social interaction. Heer (1963b) has introduced exchange theory into the discussion of marital decision-making (cf. Blood, 1963b; Heer, 1963c). According to this position, the balance of power is related to the comparative value of the resources obtained within the marital relationship to the value of the resources that could be obtained in an exchange outside the marital relationship. The theory of resources proposed by Blood and Wolfe and the theory of exchange proposed by Heer are closely related. The former emphasizes the comparative resources each person brings to the marital relationship: the more resources a person has in comparison to his spouse, the more power he will have. Heer's emphasis is upon a comparison of the value of the resources obtained within the marital relationship to that obtainable outside. Since he explicitly related this to the resources each spouse has available for exchanging, it is similar to the theory of resources. The more resources a person is contributing to the marital relationship, the more he generally stands to gain from an alternative relationship and, therefore, the more power he will be able to exercise within the marital relationship.

The important contributions by Heer and by Blood and Wolfe were based upon data for the United States and helped to illuminate that data. The Greek and Yugoslavian data, however, cannot be dealt with in strictly "resource" or "exchange" terms. They add a comparative perspective to the discussion of marital power and permit a modification of earlier theoretical statements that specifically takes the cultural component into account. The theory of resources in cultural context, as elaborated here, is still highly tentative, and much remains to be done in getting measures of the strength of cultural expectations about marital authority or of the nature of the interaction between cultural expectations and comparative resources as they influence the distribution of power.

Another way of contrasting "resource theory" and "exchange theory" would lead us back to methodological issues, and will only be mentioned briefly. *Resources* can be identified as the commodities that are exchanged, while *exchange* can refer to the process by which these resources are exchanged. In focusing upon resources, one would single out the major items that are involved in the exchange process without observing the process. One would look, for example, at indices of social class such as education, in order to discuss societal trends. By focussing upon the exchange, one would single out the actual process of exchange (ideally through observation), perhaps by studying influence techniques (Safilios-Rothschild, 1969). In this way it would be possible to collect data on patterns of exchange and influence. It would also be possible to see the idiosyncracies of the process, the influence of personality variables, the individual rather than merely the cultural values attached to specific resources (cf. Wolfe, 1959; Lenski, 1966).

Physical power, physical attractiveness, leadership qualities, and sexual control are areas in which the cultural setting can have an important influence over the exchange process. The cultural context may permit or forbid the use of these resources in bargaining for marital power. For example, man's greater physical power would not be a legitimate resource if he is culturally forbidden to beat or intimidate his wife. Similarly, a woman's ability to grant or withhold sexual favors would not be a legitimate resource if she is culturally expected to submit to the sexual desires of her husband. Nevertheless, there may be a substantial gap between the cultural expectation and the actual exchange process. In some or even many cases, despite cultural restrictions over such matters as the use of physical power or of sexual bargaining, these resources become important in the marital exchange process and may have an important bearing upon the distribution of marital power (cf. Safilios-Rothschild, 1969a; Whitehurst, 1971).

The distinction between authority and power can be clarified at this point, although it should be recognized that these concepts are variously defined (Dahl, 1968; Peabody, 1968). Authority refers to the exercise of influence over others by virtue of one's position; the norms specify that a person in that position is the leader. Power refers to the exercise of influence over others without normative support — through fear or charisma, for example. Either power or authority can change toward the other with changes in the degree of legitimacy. Insofar as the cultural norms are unclear about who exercises legitimate authority within the marital relationship, decision-making becomes problematic and the development of the power structure becomes highly relevant. It is perhaps because of the decline in traditional authority (Nisbet, 1968-69) that the area of marital power has recently become of such interest and has generated so many studies.

Even if the norms about marital decision-making are reasonably clear, adjustments between husband and wife still have to be worked out in the process of marital interaction. The formal structure of marital authority is complemented by an informal structure of marital power. The latter is based upon the expected patterns of authority as well as a host of other factors that enter into the relationship — for example, personality dominance, the strength of each partner's love for the other, and comparative income and education. Some of these resources have greater generalizability than others, and this would have a bearing upon their possible value in other relationships. Income, for example, would be highly generalizable, and could readily be used in other relationships. In contrast, A's greater love for B (than B's for A) is highly specific, and could not readily be used by B as a resource in another relationship. The classification of resources by Foa (1971) is helpful in examining the question of marital power.

The process of exchanging resources for marital power has many similarities to the exchange process in other areas. For example, marital power in one area may be traded for power in another area, just as legislators may trade votes or influence in one area that is of less importance to them for votes or influence in other areas that are of greater importance. It is only by focussing upon the exchange process that we can obtain information about the bargaining and compromises that are carried out with respect to marital decision-making.

Four Ideal Types of Society

In an attempt to simplify the understanding of the varying cross-national data on marital power, I have tentatively devised a typology of four kinds of societies. These may also represent four stages of societal development. As a typology it is not meant to be comprehensive, but only to order the data we presently have on marital power.[2] The data, for the most part, permit comparisons within a society but not across societies. As a result, the assumptions I will make about the overall level of patriarchal and equalitarian family norms in different societies need to be tested against other data.

Stage 1. Patriarchy. A society with strong partiarchal family norms, with a high level of paternal authority, and with no variation in paternal authority from one stratified group to another.

Most societies for which we have information are patriarchal, in the sense that men hold the formal positions of authority. This was amply documented by Zelditch (1955) who found few societies that are exceptions to the rule that men are predominantly the instrumental leaders within the nuclear family. But once we look beyond the formal situation the picture may change drastically (Komarovsky, 1964; Vogel, 1963). It was in fact the attempt of most studies of marital power to go beyond the formal, normative allocation of authority and get at the informal, actual distribution of marital power. In this they had considerable success, as attested to by the differences found within each society. But respondents' answers to questions are to some unknown degree influenced by formal expectations, and relatively little information emerges in the studies about informal interaction within families.

Which societies are in Stage 1? Some of the societies judged by Zelditch to have men in roles of instrumental leadership would undoubtedly also have strong patriarchal norms and would approach the ideal type of patriarchy considered here. India, in general, shows many characteristics of a patriarchal society, and although there are clearly many changes under way, especially in urban areas, paternal authority still remains very strong. Of course, social and personality differences can still make a difference in particular instances (Ross, 1961). Without exactly comparable data, however, one can only speculate that Indian society approaches our ideal-type patriarchy, or perhaps is transitional to Stage 2 in urban areas.

Stage 2. Modified Patriarchy. A society with patriarchal family norms that have been modified by equalitarian norms at the upper strata, so that paternal authority is inversely correlated with social class.

Greece and Yugoslavia would typify this kind of modified patriarchy, in which patriarchal norms are retained in the lower classes while "modern", equalitarian norms are adopted from the top down. In addition, some of the curvilinear relationships reported for Germany, the U.S.A., and elsewhere, also indicate that certain segments of the overall class structure in these societies approach a modified patriarchy.

In Stage 2 societies, as in Stage 1, the man's power is ascribed. He has legitimate authority within his family by virtue of his maleness. As Safilios-Rothschild (1967:349) points out, "In Greece as in many other developing countries, in contrast to industrialized nations, the worth of a man cannot be measured in terms of his earning capacity". The low-income man does not therefore suffer any loss of authority, and it is only the upper-income man, adopting more equalitarian marital patterns, who modifies the patriarchal tradition.

Stage 3. Transitional Equalitarianism. A society in which equalitarian family norms are replacing patriarchal norms, in which there is normative flexibility about marital power, and in which paternal authority is positively correlated with social class.

Germany and the U.S.A. typify this kind of transitional equalitarianism. There is evidence that both Germany (König, 1957; Lupri, 1965) and the U.S.A. (Dyer and Urban, 1958; Mowrer, 1969) are, in fact, undergoing the transition from a patriarchal to an equalitarian family ethic. Due to the normative ambiguity about marital authority, the situation in these societies can be characterized as a "power struggle" in which additional resources bring additional power. In consequence, occupational, educational, and income resources have the greatest impact in these societies, and husband's status is positively associated with husband's power.

One aspect of these societies is the greater emphasis that is placed upon the husband-father's breadwinner role. Unlike Stage 1 and Stage 2 societies, a man's esteem and power are not ascribed, but are achieved through educational, occupational, and income channels. This places the lower-class man at a distinct disadvantage, because he is unable to fulfill the key role of provider. He is handicapped in precisely those areas that are most highly valued by the society as a whole and by his own family (Liebow, 1967; Rodman, 1968b). This has consequences for the structure of lower-class families and for the development of a subculture of poverty (Rodman, 1968a, 1971). It also means that a lower-class man may have difficulty in exercising what he regards as his legitimate authority (Parsons, 1969), and this increases the likehood that he will use physical power as a resource within the family in order to try to get his way.

Stage 4. Equalitarianism. A society with strong equalitarian family norms, with a high level of husband-wife sharing of power, and with no variation in authority patterns from one stratified group to another.

Under these circumstances the equalitarian norms have become so well established throughout the whole society that we do not find any correlation between husband's power and husband's status. Denmark and Sweden approach this kind of equalitarianism. The data on Denmark show no relationship between husband's status and husband's power, and unpublished data on Sweden indicate that over 90% of all decisions are jointly made (Trost, cited in Safilios-Rothschild, 1970:547). Both of these societies exhibit marked equalitarian trends and have developed social welfare policies that provide strong support to the family at all social class levels. The equalitarian character of Danish family patterns, more marked than those in the U.S.A., have been documented by Kandel and Lesser (1969, 1970).

Concluding Remarks

Now that we have reviewed some of the cross-national data on marital power structure, and some of the variables that influence power structure, let us ask about the importance of studying power structure. It clearly has relevance for the overall structure of the family, including patterns of communication, prestige, and affection within the family. It is related to a country's labor force size and birth rate through the proportion of women who decide to work. It also has an important bearing upon the patterns of socialization and discipline of children within the family. Each of these issues is worth further study and such study will perhaps be stimulated by the availability of this unique set of cross-national data on power structure.

We pointed out that the exchange of resources in cultural context accounts for the distribution of marital power. Where the norms are sufficiently flexible to permit a "power struggle" we found the husband's status positively correlated with the husband's power, as in Germany, U.S.A., and other societies. If the norms are strongly patriarchal throughout the society, we have speculated that there will be no correlation between husband's status and marital power structure. Where the norms are patriarchal, but modified by an infusion of equalitarian norms at the upper strata, we found a negative correlation between husband's status and husband's power, as in Greece and Yugoslavia. When the norms become strongly equalitarian throughout the society, and if there is a strong system of progressive welfare legislation, we have suggested that there will be no relationship between husband's status and husband's power, as in Denmark and Sweden. Further, we found that a wife's working status usually increases her marital power, and that the comparative status of husband and wife have a strong bearing upon marital power structure. These latter findings need to be qualified in terms of the normative situation regarding the distribution of marital power (Hoffman, 1963; Safilios-Rothschild, 1970).

The differences in the findings, depending upon the source of information, can be a serious source of difficulty. Safilios-Rothschild (1970:548) has pointed out that Greek working wives, but not their husbands, say they have more decision-making power than nonworking wives:

> Thus, while the Greek women's answers support the "resource theory", the Greek men's answers do not. Does this mean that the "resource theory" or the "theory of resources in cultural context" is a "wife-specific" sociological theory?

The answer lies in a search for the explanation of the different perceptions of the men and women, something that Safilios-Rothschild .has herself tackled. Sex differences might then help to specify or to modify the resource theory, in the same way that class, race, or nationality differences may contribute to the development and modification of a theory. Nevertheless, it is clear that better measures of marital power are needed in order to provide us with greater assurance of the validity of our findings.

Finally, we might ask whether there is a universal tendency for the development of marital power patterns: Do small groups, such as families, inevitably develop a differentiated structure, including a differentiated power structure (Bales and Slater, 1955)?

Let us approach this question with a quotation:

> In the future, one of the things characterizing new family experiments, and families in general, will be a change in the way family members view each other. We shall not think in terms of power relationships. The idea that one person is the major influence will not be important; we shall have dropped the head-of-the-household concept. We shall find ourselves learning from our children. We shall find women increasingly making a place for themselves in such a way that they will refuse to be subservient to men. (Farson, 1969:60.)

Does this herald a brave new world, or is it a formula for a nightmare? The answer depends upon whether this future family is flexible about the development of its power structure or is without structure in the area of power.

We know "the major broad functional value of norms — that they serve as substitutes for the exercise of personal influence and produce more economically and efficiently certain consequences otherwise dependent upon personal influence processess" (Thibaut and Kelley, 1959:130). Without a normatively organized distribution of power there is a greater likelihood of emotional disturbance (Schuham, 1970; cf. Westley and Epstein, 1969). It may well be that cultural guidelines about the distribution of power will show flexibility, and that individual families will then work out the distribution of power in a rational manner. Whether from a cultural level or from an interactional level, the evidence suggests that normative patterns of marital power will develop or the family will be characterized by pathology.

FOOTNOTES

[1]Since the tabular data for Belgium do not correspond with the textual data, further references to Belgian data will be restricted. For Japan, since the sample is entirely middle class, the range of occupational, educational, and income differences is limited, and further references to the Japanese data will also be restricted.

[2]Information about the variance of the data on marital power could help to assess the relative importance of the cultural norms or the exchange of resources for determining marital power.

REFERENCES

Bales, Robert F. and Phillip E. Slater, 1955. "Role differentiation in small decision-making groups". Pp. 259-306 in Talcott Parsons and Robert F. Bales, Family Socialization and Interaction Process. Glencoe, Ill.: Free Press.

Becker, Howard, 1956. Man in Reciprocity. New York: Praeger.

Blood, Robert O., Jr., 1963a. "The employment of wives". Pp. 282-305 in F. Ivan Nye and Lois W. Hoffman (eds.), The Employed Mother. Chicago: Rand-McNally.

——, 1963b. "The measurement and basis of family power: a rejoinder". Marriage and Family Living 25 (November): 475-477.

——, 1967. Love Match and Arranged Marriage: A Tokyo-Detroit Comparison. New York: Free Press.

Blood Robert O., Jr. and Yuzura John Takeshita, 1964. "Development of cross-cultural equivalence of measures of marital interaction for U.S.A. and Japan". Transactions of the 5th World Congress of Sociology 4, Louvain, International Sociological Association. PP. 333-344.

Blood, Robert O., Jr. and Donald M. Wolfe, 1960. Husbands and Wives. Glencoe, Ill.: Free Press.

Blood, Robert O. Jr., et al., 1970. "Comparative analysis of family power structure: problems of measurement and interpretation". Pp. 525-535 in Reuben Hill and René König (eds.), Families in East and West, Paris: Mouton.

Bott, Elizabeth, 1957. Family and Social Network. London: Tavistock.

Buric, Olivera and Andjelka Zečevic, 1967. "Family authority, marital satisfaction, and the social network in Yugoslavia". Journal of Marriage and the Family 29 (May): 325-336.

Centers, Richard et al., 1971. "Conjugal power structure: a re-examination". American Sociological Review 36 (April): 264-278.

Dahl, Robert A., 1968. "Power". International Encyclopedia of the Social Sciences 12: 405-415.

D'Antonio, William V. and Eugene C. Erickson, 1962. "The reputational technique as a measure of community power." American Sociological Review 27 (June): 362-376.

Dyer, William G. and Dick Urban, 1958. "The institutionalization of equalitarian family norms." Marriage and Family Living 20 (February): 53-58.

Farson, Richard E., 1969. "Behavioral science predicts and projects." Pp. 55-76 in Richard E. Farson et al., The Future of the Family. New York: Family Service Association.

Foa, Uriel G., 1971. "Interpersonal and economic resources." Science 29 (January): 345-351.

Freedman, R. et al., 1959. "Expected family size and family size values in West Germany." Population Studies 2 (November): 136-150.

Gendell, Murray, 1963. Swedish Working Wives. Totowa, N.J.: Bedminister Press.

Gouldner, Alvin W., 1960. "The norm of reciprocity: a preliminary statement." American Sociological Review 25 (April): 161-178.

Haavio-Mannila, Elina, 1969. "Some consequences of women's emancipation." Journal of Marriage and the Family 31 (Febuary): 123-134.

———, 1970. Personal communication.

Heer, David M., 1963a. "Dominance and the working wife." Pp. 251-262 in F. Ivan Nye and Lois W. Hoffman (eds.), The Employed Mother. Chicago: Rand-McNally.

———, 1963b. "The measurement and basis of family power: an overview." Marriage and Family Living 25 (May), 133-139.

———, 1963c. "Reply." Marriage and Family Living 25 (November): 477-478.

Hoffman, Lois W., 1963. "Parental power relations and the division of household tasks". Pp. 215-230 in F. Ivan Nye and Lois W. Hoffman (eds.), The Employed Mother. Chicago: Rand-McNally.

Homans, George C., 1961. Social Behavior: Its Elementary Forms. New York: Harcourt Brace.

Kandel, Denise and Gerald S. Lesser, 1969. "Parent-adolescent relationships and adolescent independence in the United States and Denmark". Journal of Marriage and the Family 31 (May): 348-358.

———, 1970. "The internal structure of families in the United States and Denmark". Presented at the 7th World Congress of Sociology, Varna, Bulgaria.

———, 1972. "Marital decision-making in American and Danish urban families: a research note". Journal of Marriage and the Family 34 (February): 134-138.

Komarovsky, Mirra, 1964. Blue-Collar Marriage. New York: Random House.

König, René, 1957. "Family and authority: The German father in 1955". Sociological Review 5 (July): 107-127.

Lamousé, Annette, 1969. "Family roles of women: a German example". Journal of Marriage and the Family 31 (February): 145-152.

Lenski, Gerhard E., 1966. Power and Privilege: A Theory of Social Stratification. New York: McGraw-Hill.

Leplae, Claire, 1968. "Structure des Taches Domestiques et du Pouvoir de Decision de la Dyade Conjugale". Pp. 13-49 in Pierre de Bie et al., La Dyade Conjugale. Bruxelles, Belgique: Editions Vie Ouvriere.

Liebow, Elliot, 1967. Tally's Corner: A Study of Negro Streetcorner Men. Boston: Little Brown.

Liu, William T. et al., 1970. "Conjugal power and decision making: a methodological note". Presented at the 7th World Congress of Sociology, Varna, Bulgaria.

Lupri, Eugen, 1965. "Industrialisierung und Strukturwandlungen in der Familie: ein Interkultureller Vergleich." Sociologia Ruralis 5 (November): 57-76.

———, 1969a. "Contemporary authority patterns in the West German family: a study in cross national validation." Journal of Marriage and the Family 31 (February): 134-144.

———, 1969b. "Theoretical and methodological problems in cross-national research." Sociologia Ruralis 9:99-113.

Mauss, Marcel, 1954. The Gift (translated by Ian Cunnison). New York: Free Press.

McKinley, Donald G., 1964. Social Class and Family Life. Glencoe, Ill.: Free Press.

Michel, Andrée, 1967. "Comparative data concerning the interaction in French and American families." Journal of Marriage and the Family 29 (May): 337-344.

———, 1970. "Working wives and family interaction in French and American families." International Journal of Comparative Sociology 11 (June): 157-165.

Mowrer, Ernest R., 1969. "The differentiation of husband and wife roles." Journal of Marriage and the Family 31 (August): 534-540.

Netting, Robert McC., 1969. "Women's weapons: the politics of domesticity among the Kofyar." American Anthropologist 71 (December): 1037-1046.

Nisbet, Robert A., 1968-69. "The twilight of authority." Public Interest (Nos. 13-17): 3-9.

Olson, David H., 1969. "The measurement of family power by self-report and behavorial methods." Journal of Marriage and the Family 31 (August): 545-550.

Oppong, Christine, 1970. "Conjugal power and resources: an urban African example." Journal of Marriage and the Family 32 (November): 676-680.

Papanek, Miriam L., 1969. "Authority and sex roles in the family." Journal of Marriage and the Family 31 (May): 359-363.

Parsons, Anne, 1969. Belief, Magic, and Anomie. New York: Free Press.

Peabody, Robert L., 1968. "Authority." International Encyclopedia of the Social Sciences 1:473-477.

Rodman, Hyman, 1967. "Marital power in France, Greece, Yugoslavia, and the United States: A cross-national discussion." Journal of Marriage and the Family 29 (May): 320-324.

———, 1968a. "Class culture." International Encyclopedia of the Social Sciences 15:332-337.

———, 1968b. "Family and social pathology in the ghetto." Science 161 (August): 756-762.

———, 1971. Lower-Class Families. New York: Oxford University Press.

Ross, Aileen D., 1961. The Hindu Family in its Urban Setting. Toronto: University of Toronto Press.

Safilios-Rothschild, Constantina, 1967. "A comparison of power structure and marital satisfaction in urban Greek and French families." Journal of Marriage and the Family 29 (May): 345-352.

———, 1969a. "Family sociology or wives' family sociology? A cross-cultural examination of decision-making." Journal of Marriage and the Family 31 (May): 290-301.

———, 1969b. "Patterns of familial power and influence." Sociological Focus 2 (Spring): 7-19.

———, 1970. "The study of family power structure: a review 1960-1969." Journal of Marriage and the Family 32 (November): 539-552.

Schuham, Anthony I., 1970. "Power relations in emotionally disturbed and normal family triads." Journal of Abnormal Psychology 75 (February): 30-37.

Silverman, William and Reuben Hill, 1967. "Task allocation in marriage in the United States and Belgium." Journal of Marriage and the Family 29 (May): 353-360.

Strodtbeck, Fred L., 1958. "Family interaction, values, and achievement." Pp. 135-194 in David C. McClelland et al., Talent and Society: New Perspectives in the Identification of Talent. Princeton, N.J.: Van Nostrand.

Thibaut, John W. and Harold H. Kelley, 1961. The Social Psychology of Groups. New York: Wiley.

Troll, Lillian E., 1970. "Issues in the study of generations." Aging and Human Development 1 (no. 3): 199-218.

Vogel, Ezra, 1963. Japan's New Middle Class: The Salary Man and His Family in a Tokyo Suburb. Berkeley and Los Angeles: University of California Press.

Weller, Robert H., 1968. "The employment of wives, dominance and fertility." Journal of Marriage and the Family 31 (August): 437-442.

Westley, William A. and Nathan B. Epstein, 1969. The Silent Majority: Families of Emotionally Healthy College Students. San Francisco: Jossey-Bass.

Whitehurst, Robert N., 1971. "Violently jealous husbands." Sexual Behavior 1 (July): 32-41.

Wilkening, E. A. and Eugen Lupri, 1965. "Decision-making in German and American farm families." Sociologia Ruralis 5: 366-385.

Wolfinger, Raymond E., 1960. "Reputation and reality in the study of 'community power'." American Sociological Review 25 (October): 636-644.

Wolfe, Donald M., 1959. "Power and authority in the family." Pp. 99-117 in Dorwin Cartwright (ed.), Studies in Social Power. Ann Arbor, Michigan.: University of Michigan Institute for Social Research.

Zelditch, Morris, Jr., 1955. "Role differentiation in the nuclear family: a comparative study." Pp. 307-351 in Talcott Parsons and Robert F. Bales, Family, Socialization and Interaction Process. Glencoe, Ill.: Free Press.

Love, Arranged Marriage
and the Indian Social Structure*

GIRI RAJ GUPTA**

Marriage is an immemorial institution which, in some form, is found everywhere. Mating patterns are closely associated with marriage, more so with the social structure. It's not the institution of marriage itself, but the institutionalization of mating patterns which determine the nature of family relationships in a society. Primitive societies present a wide array of practices ranging from marriage by capture to mutual love and elopement. Yet, the people who marry through customary practice are those who are eligibles, who consciously followed the established norms, and who did the kind of things they were supposed to do. The main purpose of marriage is to establish a family, to produce children, and to further the family's economic and social position. Perhaps, there are some transcendental goals too. Generally, women hope for kind and vigorous providers and protectors and men for faithful mothers and good housekeepers; both undoubtedly hope for mutual devotion and affection too. Irrespective of the various ways of instituting marriage, most marriages seem to have these common goals.

There are few works commenting on mating patterns in India. Though some monographs on tribal and rural India have treated the subject, nevertheless, serious sociological attention has only infrequently been given. The present paper attempts to explain the variables as a part of the cultural system which help in promotion and sustenance of the arranged marriage, particularly in the Hindu society in India. In addition, the paper also critically analyzes the present day mating patterns which relate to precautionary controls working against the potentially disintegrative forces of change; especially those endangering family unity, religious structure, and the stratification system.

Romantic Love vs. Conjugal Love

One is intrigued by the cultural pattern in India where the family is characterized by arranged marriage. Infatuation as well as romantic love, though, is reported quite in abundance in the literature, sacred books, and scriptures, yet is

*Data presented in this paper were gathered as a part of a larger field-study on Marriage and Social Structure in India during 1963-67 and Summer 1974. This is the first part and revised version of a paper presented at the Annual Meeting of the National Council of Family Relations and American Council of Marriage and Family Counsellors held in St. Louis, October 22-26, 1974. I am indebted to Steven M. Cox for his constructive criticism of an earlier draft of this paper.
**Giri Raj Gupta is Professor in the Department of Sociology and Anthropology, Western Illinois University, Macomb, Illinois, 61455, USA.

not thought to be an element in prospective marital alliance (see, Meyer, 1953: 322-339).

Sanskrit or Hindi terms like *sneh* (affection) and *prem* or *muhbbat* carry two different meanings. *Sneh* is non-sensual love, while *prem* is a generic term connoting love with god, people, nation, family, neighbour, and, of course, lover or beloved. In fact, there is a hierarchy of relationships. In Urdu literature, concepts like *ishque ruhani* (love with the spirit), *ishque majazi* (love with the supreme being), and *ishque haqiqi* (love with the lover or beloved) are commonly referred to love relationships. Interestingly, the humans supposedly reach the highest goal of being in love with god through the love they cherish among humans. Great love stories in mythology and history illustrate the emotion, as opposed to reason, which characterize the thoughts and acts of persons in love. The quality of the emotions may be characterized best by the altruistic expressions of a person for the person in love. Most people in India do not go around singing of their love as one might imagine after watching Indian movies and dramatic performances. Even the proximity, intimacy, freedom, and permissiveness characterized in such media are rarely commonplace in the reality of the day to day life. In general, to verbalize and manifest romantic expressions of love is looked upon as a product of poets' or novelists' fantasies. Yet, at least theoretically, to be in love with someone is a highly-cherished ideal.

In one of the most ancient scriptures, Rgveda, it was wished that a person's life be of a hundred-year duration. The Hindu sages in their theory of purushar-thas suggested four aims of life: *dharma*, righteousness, which provides a link between animal and god in man; *artha*, acquisitive instinct in man, enjoyment of wealth and its manifestations; *kama*, instinctive and emotional life of man and the satisfaction of sex drives and aesthetic urges; and *moksha*, the end of life and the realization of an inner spirituality in man (see, Kapadia, 1966: 25).

The Hindu scriptures written during 200 B. C. to 900 A. D. mention eight modes of acquiring a wife known as Brahma, Daiva, Arsha, Prajapatya, Asura, Gandharva, Rakshasa, and Paisacha. Only the first four are known as *dharmya*, i. e. according to religion. An exchange of gifts between the subjects' families marks the wedding ceremony, but no dowry is paid. In the Asura form payment of the bride price is the main element, while Rakshasa and Paisacha, respectively, pertain to the abduction and seduction of a girl when she is unconscious. The Gandharva marriage refers to a marriage by mutual choice. The Hindu Law givers differ in their opinions and interpretations of this kind of marriage; some called it the best mode of marriage, while others viewed it stigmatic on religious and moral grounds. However, there is no reliable data to support or justify the popularity of anyone of these modes of marriage. The first four kinds pertain to arranged marriages in which the parental couple ritually gives away the daughter to a suitable person and this ideal, continues to be maintained in the Hindu society. Opposed to these are four others, three of which were objected to by the script-writers in the past and viewed as illegal today, though nevertheless, they happen. The Gandharva mode, though opposed to the accepted norm, is nearest to what may be variously termed as "free-choice", "romantic", or "love" marriage. Yet through the ages Hindu revivalism and other socio-religious and economic factors discredited the importance of Gandharva marriage.

Diversified sects of Muslims and Christians view marriage as a civil contract as opposed to a sacrament. However, marriages are arranged most often with the consent of the subjects. The Muslims, at least theoretically, permit polygamy according to Islamic law; however, they prefer monogamy. As opposed to Hindu and Christian communities it is customary that the boy's party initiates a marriage proposal (see Kapadia, 1966: 209-214; Kurian, 1974: 357-358, 1975).

Most Indian marriages are arranged, although sometimes opinions of the partners are consulted, and in cases of adults, their opinions are seriously considered. Another aspect of this pattern is that individuals come to believe that their life mate is predestined, their fate is preordained, they are "right for each other", they are helpless as far as choice is concerned and therefore must succumb to the celestial forces of the universe. That the entire syndrome, typical for the society, represents a complex set of forces working around and upon the individual to get married to a person whom one is destined to love. It is also believed to be good and desirable that critical issues like the choosing of a life partner should be handled by responsible persons of family and kin group. However, it is generally possible that persons in love could marry if related prohibitions have been effectively observed.

Generally, love is considered a weak basis for marriage because its presence may overshadow suitable qualities in spouses. Therefore, arranged marriages result from more or less intense care given to the selection of suitable partners so that the family ideals, companionship, and co-parenthood can grow, leading to love. Ernest Van Den Haag writes about the United States:

> "A hundred years ago, there was every reason to marry young—though middle-class people seldom did. The unmarried state had heavy disadvantages for both sexes. Custom did not permit girls to be educated, to work, or to have social, let alone sexual freedom...........And, though, les srestricted than girls shackled to their families, single men often led a grim and uncomfortable life. A wife was nearly indispensable, if only to darn socks, sew, cook, clean, take care of her man" (1973:181).

Goode views romantic love paradoxically, and calls it the antithesis of "conjugal love," because marriage is not based upon it, actually a couple strives to seek it within the marital bond (1959:40). The latter, presumably, protect the couple against the harmful effects of individualism, freedom and untoward personality growth. It may be worthwhile here to analyze the structural conditions under which mating relationships occur and to see how they relate to various values and goals in Indian society.

A study conducted in 1968, on 240 families in Kerala, a state which has the highest literacy rate in India, reveals that practical consideration in the selection of mates rather than free-choice or romantic love becomes the basis of marriage. In order of importance, the study reports that the major qualities among the girls considered important are: good character, obedience, ability to manage home, good cook, should take active part in social and political affairs, educated, religious, depending entirely on husband for major decisions, fair complexion, good companion with similar intellectual interests and beauty (Kurian 1974: 335). Among the boy's qualities, his appearance, charm, and romantic manifestation do not count much, while the social and economic status of his family, education and earning potential, overshadow his personal qualities (Kurian, 1974: 355; see also Ross 1961: 259).

The Kerala study further illustrates some interesting trends, such as: that only 59 percent of the respondents thought that meeting the prospective wife before marriage contributes to marital happiness. The parental preferences about the nature of choice of spouse of their children showed that 5.8 percent wanted to arrange the marriage without consulting sons and daughters, while 75.6 percent wanted to arrange the marriage with the consent of sons and daughters, 17.3 percent were willing to allow free choice to their children with their approval, and only 1.3 percent will allow freedom of choice without parental interference (Kurian, 1974: 358). In fact, what Srinivas observed over three decades ago in Mysore was that "romantic love as a basis of marriage is still not very deep or widely spread in the family mores of India today," has not yet changed much (see Srinivas, 1942:60).

The dilemma of a boy who had fallen in love with a girl from a lower caste is reported from a study of Bangalore, a city of about a million people:

> My love affair has caused me great trouble, for my intense love of the girl and the devotion to my parents cannot be reconciled. My parents don't like our engagement, and I cannot displease them, but on the other hand I cannot give up my girl who has done so much for me. She is responsible for progress and the bright future which everyone says is ahead of me. The problem is my greatest headache at the present time (Ross, 1961: 269).

During my own field-work during 1963-67, in Awan, a community of about three thousand people in Rajasthan state, having extensive and frequent urban contacts, it took me no time to figure out that a question inquiring about "romantic" or "love" marriage would be futile, because people simply laughed it away. Parental opinion was reinforced by several other considerations. One man, a community elite, remarked:

> Young people do not know what love is; they are, if at all, infatuated which is very transitory and does not entail considerations of good marital life. If my son marries, I wish to see that the girl is well-raised, obedient, preserves the family traditions, ready to bear the hardships with us, and to nurse us in our old age.

Love, a pre-marital manifestation, is thus thought to be a disruptive element in upsetting the firmly established close ties in the family, a transference of loyalty from the family of orientation to a person, and a loss of allegiance of a person, leaving the family and kin group in disdain for personal goals.

Continued loyalty of the individual to the family of orientation and kin group is the most cherished ideal in the Indian family system. To preserve this ideal, certainly the simplest recourse is child marriage or adolescent marriage. The child is betrothed, married, and most often placed in a job and generally provides the deference demanded by the elders. Though this pattern does not give much opportunity to the individual to act freely in matrimonial affairs, it maintains a close link of the couple with the father's household which requires much physical, social and emotional care throughout the family cycle and particularly in old age. The relationships in the extended joint family are all important.

The Hindu scriptural texts prescribe that a person should go through *grahsta-shrama* (a stage of householder's life) which includes procreation of children. The status system gives high prestige to the parents of large familes. Kinship and religious values stress the need for a male heir. Large families provide security, both in economic and social terms, for the old and the destitute and the ill in a country where old age pensions, disability, sickness benefits, and unemployment as well as medical insurance are either nonexistent or inadaquate. When a family has several children, their marriages have to be spaced for economic as well as social reasons, which in turn necessitates early marriages.

Similar to other indigenous civilizations, a high value is placed upon chastity, especially female virginity in its ideal form. Love as play or premarital activity is not encouraged. Rather, elders consider it as their most important duty to supervise nubile girls. Marriage is an ideal, a duty and a social responsibility usually preceded by highly ritualized ceremonial and festive events illustrating gradual involvement, especially of the female preparatory to the initiation of her marital role. Interestingly, all these ritual activities are role oriented (such as contributing to the long and prosperous life of the prospective husband) rather than person oriented (such as taking vows for the success of a person who is in love). This is one of those most pertinent factors which infuses longevity to the marital bond. The upper caste ideal that a girl could be ritually married only once in her lifetime and destined to marry the same person in lives to come continues to determine explicit and categorical aversion among girls to premarital interactions with strangers. Paradoxically, though, there is an implicit assumption that a person's marriage to a person of the opposite sex is governed by supreme celestial forces; in actual practice, mundane realities usually settle a marriage.

The early marriage of the person does not permit much personal independence and is further linked with another structural pattern in which the kinship rules define a class (caste, subcaste, regional group) of eligible future spouses. In other words, in the interest of homogamy and sanctity of the kin group, marriage should occur early. Thus, this would eliminate the chances of an unmarried adult to disregard a link with his or her kin group and caste. Problems arise at times when a person goes across the narrow limits of a group, often losing his chances of obtaining the usual support from the family, the kin group, and the caste. However, transgressions of basic family norms by an individual which may cause loss of identity, rejection, and an aggravated departure from the value system are rare. Often it is circumventing rather than contradicting the system which provides clues to change.   Under such a pattern, elders negotiate and arrange marriages of their children and dependents with a likelihood of minimum generational conflict reinforcing greater chances of family unity.   Adolescent physical and social segregation is marked by a greater emphasis on the learning of discrete sex roles idealizing, at least theoretically, parental roles.

As found in Western cultures, the youth culture frees the individual from family attachments thus permitting the individual to fall in love; and love becomes a substitute for the interlocking of kinship roles.   The structural isolation of the Western family also frees the married partners' affective inclinations, that they are able to love one another (Parsons, 1949:187-189).   Such a pattern is absent in the Indian family system.

Contrary to this, in India, marriage of a boy indirectly strengthens his bonds with the family of orientation.   It is one of the major crises which marks his adulthood and defines his responsibilities towards his parents and the kin group. His faith and sentimental involvement in the family of orientation is an acknowledgment of the usual obligations incurred in his raising and training.   A pervasive philosophy of individualism appears to be spreading and suggests a trend toward free mate choices, equality for women, equal divorce rights, and taking up of traditionally known ritually inferior but lucrative occupations; this militantly asserts the importance of the welfare of the person over any considerations of the continuity of the group.   The trend toward conjugal family systems, widespread as it is, is generally confined to the urbanized regions (Gore, 1958; Kapur, 1970) Moreover, these changes where they appear on one hand, are viewed as social problems and as symptoms of the breakdown of time-honored ways; on the other, they are looked at as indicators of personal achievement, individual fulfilment, and family prestige.

Socialization

The cultural pattern demands that a child in India cannot isolate himself from his parents, siblings, and other members of the extended family.

The maturation process is rarely fraught with problems or turmoil associated with parent and adolescent children as they all learn to play new roles and feel new feelings.   A child's expanding world gradually gives a mature sense of responsibilities to share in most of the important decisions in his life cycle.   Covert parent-child conflict is shadowed by affection and sentimental ties helping the adolescents to achieve desirable balance between rebellion and conformity, individual wishes and feelings of the parents.   Occasionally, this causes some problems. Since parents make decisions about most significant aspects of the family, including the marriage of their children, passive, indifferent, and sometimes negative feelings develop in the children as they seek to be dependent on other members of the family.

The family in India is known for its cohesive function, especially providing for the emotional needs of its members. Most often, this function is effectively performed by the extended kin group which, in fact, is a segment of the caste or subcaste. Adults, as well as children, must have love and security in order to maintain emotional stability under the stresses of life and in order to meet the emotional demands made upon them by the crises. In addition to providing the positive emotional needs of its members by personal sacrifices done by the members on a regular basis throughout the life cycle of the family, it also provides a safe outlet for negative feelings. Conflicts arising from interpersonal relations are generally handled by the older members, and care is taken by them to ensure that roles and responsibilities are clearly defined. Conflicts are resolved and mitigated by a general concern in the group favoring the emotional satisfaction of the individual. A person throughout his adolescence is never isolated from the family. Thus, not only generations, but extended and local units of kin groups are forced into a more intensive relationship. The affectional ties are solidified by mutual care, help in crises situations, and assistance provided. This often destroys negative feelings. Several rituals, rites, and ceremonial occasions reinforce the unity of the family (Dube, 1955:131-158; Gupta, 1974:104-116). In general, a person substantially invests his emotions and feelings in his family and kin group, denial of which may be hazardous to his psyche. Such a deep involvement of the individual causes his emotional dependence on the family and acceptance to its wishes in most of the crucial decisions and events in his life, including marriage.

Premarital Interaction and Mate Selection

India is perhaps the only sub-continent which provides a wide variety of mate selection processes from an open to a very closed system, from marriage by capture in the primitives to the arranged marriage among Hindus and Muslims. Moreover, rules prohibiting certain classes of persons from marrying one another also vary, such as three to four clan avoidance rules in central and northern parts to preferential cross-cousin or maternal uncle and niece marriages in the south. In other words, rules regarding the definition of incest or areas of potential mates vary substantially. Most people in the Northern states, for example, prohibit marriage between persons of similarly named clans and extend this rule to several other related clans, such as of mother's clan, mother's mother clan, and father's mother clan. The people bearing these clan names may be living several hundred miles away, however, but are usually thought to be related. From this point of view, then, the ideal mate for any person could also be a stranger, an outsider, but an individual related to him in distant terms or imagined way. A person living across a state belonging to one's caste has a greater chance of being an eligible for a prospective mate than a person belonging to some other caste living next door. Caste is thus an extended kin group and, at least theoretically, membership in which is related through various kinds of kinship ties. Marriage alliances within the *jati* (caste or sub-caste) reinforces kinship and family ties and cause a sort of evolution of the class system. Class generally determines future marital alliances within the caste. The resources assessed by a family in seeking a marital alliance from another family play a crucial role in determining the decision about the alliance. The voices of the significant members of the family are crucial in making a marriage since newly-wed couples are barely into adulthood and have neither the material nor psychological resources to start a household of their own. Later in their married life when they have resources, they may still consider the opinions of the significant members because the disadvantages of not adhering to such opinions are greater than the annoyances of living together.

A Sociological Paradigm of Arranged Marriages

Recent research on the changing aspects of the family in India (Collver, 1963; Conklin, 1974; Desai, 1964; Gore. 1965; Gould, 1968; Gupta, 1974; Hooja, 1968; Kapur, 1970; Kurian, 1961, 1974; Orenstein, 1959, 1961, 1966; Ross, 1961; Shah, 1974; Singer, 1968) suggests that there has been little change in the joint family system in India, which is a vanguard of the arranged marriage.

The above discussion gives us to understand that what is needed in our approach to arranged marriage is a frame of reference which is more fully on the sociological level. As a step toward this goal, a general theoretical approach to the arranged marriage or "conjugal love" relationship has been formulated which, it is believed, takes account of the historical, cultural, and psychological levels, and brings into central focus the sociological level. The following tentative theoretical formulation is proposed only as a first attempt to outline what sociological factors are generally responsible to the growth of "conjugal love" as opposed to "romantic love". By any conservative estimate, love marriages occur in only less than one percent of the population.

1. It is important to note that arranged marriages are closely associated with "closed systems" wherein the hierarchies are very intricate and more than one factor such as historical origins, ritual positions, occupational affiliations, and social distance determinants play significant roles in defining the in-group and the out-group, particularly in marital alliances. In such systems, group identity is marked by strong senses of esoteric values, and such values are preserved and reinforced by attributes which distinguish a group in rank and its interaction with others. That is, most proximate ties of the individuals ought to be within their own group.

2. Continuity and unity of the extended family is well-preserved since all the significant members of the family share the mate-selection decision make-up which involves several persons who are supposedly known to have experience and qualifications to find a better choice as against the free choice of the subject. Obviously, this leads to lower age at marriage and, in turn, strengthens the predominance of the family over the individual choice.

3. Any possible problems emerging from a couple's functioning in marital life become problems for the whole family. Advice and counselling from the members of the extended family to improve the couple's relationship, weathering life's storms, or even sharing in crises are reinforced by the shared responsibilities. This is also partly responsible for denouncing the idea of divorce and forces working against it. This is not to say that this, in fact, resolves all the conflicts in marriage.

4. As long as the social system is unable to develop a value system to promote individualism, economic security outside the family system, and a value system which advances the ideals of nuclear family, the individuals in such a

system continue to demand support from the family which, in turn, would lead to re-emphasizing the importance of arranged marriage. Forces of modernization supporting the "romantic ideal" would continue to find partial support in such a system as long as the sources of moral and material support for the individual are based in the extended/joint family system.

5. It is difficult to assume that arranged marriage is related to the low status of woman since man is also a party to it. If the concept of "free choice" is applicable to either sex, perhaps it will not support the ideal of arranged marriage. Apparently, an individual who opts for free choice or a "love marriage" is likely to dissociate from his/her family, kin group, caste and possibly community which he/she cannot afford unless he/she has been ensured tremendous support from sources other than these conventional institutions.

6. Arranged marriages, in general, irrespective of caste or class categories, help in maintaining closer ties with several generations. Families in such a system are an insurance for the old and the orthodox, a recluse for the devout and the defiant, a haven for the invalid and the insipid.

7. The demographic situation in India, as in most developing societies, is also a contributing factor, among others, to the early arranged marriages. After independence, India has made many advancements in science, technology, and medicine. The life expectancy which was 29 years in 1947, is now 54 years. However, the vicious circle of early child marriage, early pregnancy, high mortality rate, and replacement of the population are closely interwoven to ensure society from extinction. While the value system notoriously maintains this chainwork, the declining mortality rate further accentuates early marriages to shelve off the economic burden of the family by spacing weddings. The family protects and insulates from ruining itself by arranging marriages as early as possible and for using its resources for status aggrandizement.

Since the changes in Indian society often present a welter of traditional and modern, conventional as well as prestige and glamour-oriented marital role models with significant changes in the value system, it is quite probable that in the long run, "romantic ideal" will pervade the system. Whether such changes will be a part of a continuum, i.e. revitalization of the mythological past or acceptance of the ideals of the modern West, preserving tenacity and positive elements of its own against the swaggering forces of change, has yet to be seen.

REFERENCES

Chekki, D.A.
 1968 "Mate Selection, Age at Marriage and Propinquity Among the Lingayats of India". Journal of Marriage and the Family 30 (November): 707-711.

Collver, Andrew
 1963 The Family Cycle in India and the United States. American Sociological Review 28: 86-96.

Conklin, George H.
 1974 "The Extended Family as an Independent Factor in Social Change: A Case from India". Journal of Marriage and Family 36 (November): 798-804.

Cormack, Margaret
    1953   The Hindu Woman. New York: Bureau of Publications, Columbia University.
Desai, I.P.
    1964   Some Aspects of Family in Mahuva, Bombay: Asia Publishing House.

Dube, S.C.
    1955   Indian Village. New York: Cornell University Press.

Goode, William J.
    1959   "The Theoretical Importance of Love". American Sociological Review 24:
             38-47.
    1963   World Revolution and Family Patterns. New York: Free Press.

Gore, M.S.
    1968   Urbanization and Family Change. Bombay: Popular Prakashan.

Gupta, Giri Raj
    1974   Marriage, Religion and Society: Pattern of Change in an Indian Village. New York:
             Halsted Press.

Hate, C.A.
    1970   "Raising the Age at Marriage". The Indian Journal of Social Work 30: 303-309.

Hooja, Swarn
    1968   "Dowry System among the Hindus in North India: A Case Study". The Indian
             Journal of Social Work 38: 411-426.

Kapadia, K.M.
    1966   Marriage and Family in India. (Third Edition). London: Oxford University
             Press.

Kapur, Promilla
    1970   Marriage and the Working Woman in India. Delhi: Vikas Publications.

Karve, I.
    1965   Kinship Organization in India. Bombay: Asia Publishing House.

Klass, Morton
    1966   "Marriage Rules in Bengal". American Anthropologist 68: 951-970.

Kurian, George
    1961   The Indian Family in Transition. The Hague: Mouton.
    1974   "Modern Trends in Mate Selection and Marriage with Special Reference to Kerala".
             pp. 351-367 in G. Kurian (ed.) The Family in India—A Regional View. The Hague:
             Mouton.
    1975   "Structural Changes in the Family in Kerala, India". in T.R. Williams (ed.)
             Psychological Anthropology. The Hague: Mouton.

Madan, T.N.
    1965   "Family and Kinship: A Study of the Pandits of Rural Kashmir. New York: Asia
             Publishing House.

Mandelbaum, David G.
    1970   Society in India. (Volume I & II) Berkley: University of California Press.

Meyer, Johann J.
    1953   Sexual Life in Ancient India. New York: Barnes & Noble.

Orenstein, Henry
    1959   "The Recent History of the Extended Family in India". Social Problems 8: 341-
             350.
    1961   "The Recent History of Family in India." Social Problems 8 (Spring): 341-350.
    1966   "The Hindu Joint Family: The Norms and the Numbers". Pacific Affairs 39 (Fall-
             Winter): 314-325.

Parsons, Talcott
  1949   Essays in Sociological Theory. Glencoe, Illinois: Free Press.

Ross, Aileen D.
  1961   The Hindu Family in its Urban Setting.   Toronto: University of Toronto Press.

Shah, A.M.
  1974   The Household Dimension of Family in India.   Berkeley: University of California
            Press.

Singer, Milton
  1968   "The Indian Joint Family in Modern Industry" in Milton Singer and B.S. Cohn (eds.)
            Structure and Change in Indian Society. Aldine Publishing Co., Chicago.

Srinivas, M.N.
  1942   Marriage and Family in Mysore. Bombay: New Book Co.

Van Den Hagg, Ernest
  1973   "Love or Marriage". pp. 181-186 in Marcia E. and Thomas E. Lasswell (eds.) Love,
            Marriage and Family: A Developmental Approach.   Glenview, Illinois: Scott,
            Foresman and Co.

Vatuk, Sylvia
  1972   Kinship and Urbanization. Berkeley: University of California Press.

*Note : The observation that "Diversified sects of Muslims and Christians view marriage as a civil
        contract as opposed to a sacrament" does not hold good universally.   In India, at any
        rate, for all Christians, to whichever denomination they belong, marriage is a sacrament.

                                                                                —Editor

Endogamous Marriage in a Traditional Muslim Society: West Pakistan. A Study in Intergenerational Change

J. HENRY KORSON*

INTRODUCTION

The traditional system of mate selection in Muslim societies has been a marriage arranged by the families of the principals, usually with the consent of the couple. In Muslim societies, marriage is a civil contract, not a sacrament.

In traditional Muslim societies, when it is felt that the proper time has come for a young man or woman to marry, the adult women of the family—mother, sisters, aunts, and even cousins (as well as male relatives)—will combine to search out the best possible prospect (Korson, 1968a). Furthermore, all members of the family feel a certain responsibility toward those more directly involved in the search and are expected to render whatever assistance is necessary. Although the preliminary screening and negotiations will often be made by the women, the final decision must await the approval of the fathers of the principals, or other male head of the family. The details that go into the wedding preparations themselves, of course, are usually left to the women.

Traditionally, the Islamic ideal calls for the three-generational, patriarchal, patrilineal, and patrilocal extended family which, in turn, might claim strong ties to a biraderi, or larger kin group, or even a tribal group. [1]

* Professor, Department of Sociology, University of Massachusetts, Amherst, Massachusetts, U. S. A.

* The author is indebted to the United States Educational Foundation in Pakistan and the University of Massachusetts Research Council for the financial support of this project, and to Drs. M. S. Jillani, A. Kiani, A. Syed, S. Hashmi and H. Papanek for helpful suggestions.

[1] *Biraderi* is a term derived from the Persian *Birader*, brother, hence, brotherhood. Although there is not complete agreement concerning its definition, consanguineal ties are stronger than affinal ties. "The size of the biraderi is as large as the distance at which one can recognize one's relatives" (Wakil, 1970: 700). Underlying the complex system of favors and obligations is an intricate, but highly functional system of gift-giving (see Eglar, 1960),

From the Western point of view, the Status of Muslim women has always been considered to be low, while only in the last generation or two have women, in substantial numbers, begun to approach the degree of egalitarianism that is considered to be the ideal in the West. For example, in the matter of arranging a marriage in West Pakistan (and in many other Muslim societies), it is required that a *Nikahnama*, or marriage contract, be written and signed by both parties, the details of which have been arranged by the fathers or other male heads of the respective families. In addition, a sum of money—dower (*mehr, mahar,* or *meri'ah*) is pledged as a gift to the bride by the bridegroom (Korson, 1967). Dower is irrevocable. It provides a form of economic security for the woman, should the marriage fail and a separation or divorce occur. After marriage, the bride cannot rescind her rights to the dower, although the husband is free to increase the amount, should he choose to do so (Korson, 1968b).

Although Islam presents the picture of a male–dominated society, with the major aspects of decision–making in the hands of males, women do enjoy the security of the "women's world" to which they have been socialized and which they have learned to accept. It has been said, for example, that the greatest social cleavage in Muslim societies has not been between social classes or racial groups, but the social distinctions made between the sexes that are considered the norms of Muslim society. There seems to be little need at this time to offer examples for the distinctions made between the two sexes, but suffice it to say that in the last generation all Muslim societies have witnessed extensive social change, most especially as it relates to the status of women. Although progress has been uneven, laws have been passed which not only provide greater social welfare benefits and protection to women (even the franchise), but educational and even occupational opportunities outside the home. For example, in West Pakistan, which is still considered one of the more conservative Muslim societies, approximately 50 percent of all graduate students at the University of Karachi are women.

Perhaps one of the most important concepts that distinguishes Muslim from Western societies is that of individualism. Although family identification is important in the West, a man is more likely to be judged as an individual in terms of his achievement in adult life. A person is known not only as an individual in a Muslim society, but also by his family and the family's connections, and these are frequently more important. The kinds of ties that are forged by marriages arranged between two families have farreaching consequences. Family connections and the reputation of the family are the currency of social interaction for the members of the Muslim family.

Individualism is a concept not in tune with the Muslim ethos, because individual ambition and success are translated to mean improving the position of the whole family, whether in financial, social, or prestige terms. Older children are expected to assist their younger siblings to achieve their goals in education, in the search for occupational placement, or even in the selection of marriage partners. The Muslim who succeeds in business or in some other field of endeavor might find himself under obligation to employ or even support to the limit of his abilities more and more relatives.

Intergenerational continuity provides the kind of support for the individual in need that is usually absent in the Western nuclear family, and the abrasive, if not shattering experience of independently finding one's own way—which in the West is condoned as a welcome part of the maturation process—is often absent in the Muslim family. The extended family and even more so, the biraderi in Muslim society, plays the supportive role of the "great umbrella' with protection for all who qualify by kinship. "Muslims place great emphasis on kinship. Traditional reciprocities between grandparents and grandchildren, uncles and aunts, and nieces, nephews, and cousins, as well as those between members of nuclear family units, create close family ties." (Blitsten, 1963:200). Patrilineal and patriarchal in character, family continuity through the male line is considered to be one of the greatest importance. "Endogamy permits the maintenance of descent group ties while discouraging alliances with other descent groups" (Farber, 1966:40)

The extended family is here defined as one of three or more generations living in one household, or within one compound, with the grandfather actively serving as the family head, and with married sons and their families, as well as unmarried sons and daughters. This form appears to be the epitome of the patriarchal, patrilocal and patrilineal family, with the family head as the power-center and the major decision-maker. The joint family, on the other hand, is usually limited to two generations, and consists of two or more brothers, married or unmarried, with their children and unmarried sisters living in one household, or within a compound. The oldest son usually assumes the headship upon the death or disability of the father. Married sons, of course, are not required to live with the family head, but, once again, this appears to be the ideal to be achieved.

Although the extended family is viewed as the ideal form in Pakistani society, in 1958 only 17.3 percent of all families in Karachi were of the extended type, and another 15.1 percent of the joint type, for a total of 32.4 percent of all family types in the city (Hashmi, 1964). Nevertheless, it would appear that the influence of the extended family type is far stronger than the figures above would indicate, largely because the data above were the result of a *household* survey. Although the great majority of families were of the nuclear type, many extended and joint families live in very close proximity to each other, so that constant visiting of family members is very evident with the result that the influence of the extended family is ever-present as a source of social control, and as a socializing force for the young (Ghani, 1963 : 324 ; Goode, 1963 : 123–9).

Endogamous marriage among Muslims is frequently referred to in the literature, but there is little empirical evidence showing its extent, depth of influence in a society, or, indeed, whether the practice in increasing, decreasing, or is continuing at a stable rate. Peters (1963 : 188), indicates that 60 percent of the marriages in a Lebanese village are arranged within the kin-group, largely for the purpose of consolidating property holdings, which, in turn, supports the status system. Land ownership is a vital indicator of social rank.

Jacobson found, in her study of the Muslims in an Indian village, that " marriages arranged with kinsmen are the only alternative to spinsterhood or the loss of honor " (1970 : 212). Her findings stressed the suitability of prospective marriage partners largely in socio-economic class terms.

Antoun found, in his study of an Arab village in Jordan, that endogamous marriages were used to maintain and solidify political power, and to preserve property within the kin-group. It also guarantees modesty of the women and thereby secures the honor and status of her father's group (1968 : 671–97).

FINDINGS

In an effort to determine to what degree, if any, intergenerational changes in cousin marriage might be detected and measured, stratified samples of graduate students were taken in 1965 of all the departments in the College of Arts and Sciences at the two major universities in West Pakistan, the University of Karachi, and the University of the Punjab at Lahore. Since various terms are used by Pakistanis to describe the relationship of the spouses chosen by their siblings or parents, a variety of options was offered to the respondents so that they could chose one that best fitted their understanding of the relationship. The term biraderi is frequently used to describe a kin-group relationship either by blood or marriage, and for this reason the term " cousin " or " relative " was frequently chosen, with no further definition.

Of the total sample of 765 graduate students, 758 reported a total of 2,165 brothers for an average of 2.8 per student, while 755 students reported a total of 2,004 sisters for an average of 2.65 per student. On the assumption that the students' mothers had completed their child-producing period, this would indicate an average of 6.45 children per family, counting the respondent. All of the respondents were unmarried.

Of the respondents' brothers, 620, or 28.6 percent had married. Of these, 160, or 25.8 percent had married relatives of one degree or another ; 79, or 12.7 percent had married first cousins ; 9, or 1.4 percent had married second cousins ; and the balance had married more distant relatives.

Of the respondents' sisters, 913, or 45.6 percent had already married. Of these 76 or 8.3 percent had married first cousins ; 18 or 2.0 percent had married second cousins ; and the balance, 9.3 percent, had married relatives of various degrees of relationship. Of all the respondents' siblings who had married, 23.3 percent had married relatives of one degree or another.

TABLE I

Percentage of those Married to Relatives*

Graduate Students'	Married to	First Cousins	Second Cousins	Other	Total
Brothers		12.7	1.4	11.7	25.8
Sisters		8.3	2.0	9.3	19.6
Parents		18.7	6.1	16.4	41.2

*Since there were no significant differences in the responses of the students from Karachi and Lahore, the two samples were combined.

Data on the parents show that 41.2 percent of the students' parents were related before marriage; 51.1 percent were not related before marriage; while 2.9 pecent of the students offered no answer to this question. A breakdown of these results showed little difference among the Karachi males, Karachi females, and the Lahore males, with 46.3 percent, 49.2 percent, and 45. 8 percent, respectively, whie the Lahore females showed a 29.2 percent response.

A breakdown of these responses showed that a total of 18.7 percent of the parents were first cousins. The responses from the Karachi males, females, and the Lahore males were very close : 19.4, 19.5, and 19.2 percent, respectively, while the Lahore females indicated a lower percentage of 8. 3 percent of their parents were first cousins before marriage. A total of 6.1 percent of the students indicated that their parents were second cousins before marriage, with no significant differences showing among the four subsamples. The balance of 16.4 percent showed various degrees of relationship before marriage.

Returning to the respondents' siblings for a moment, it should be noted that 57.2 of the respondents' brothers had already married, while 91.1 percent of the respondents' sisters had already married. The mean age of the Karachi male students was 22.6; for Karachi females, 21.3; for the Lahore males, 22.2; and the Lahore females, 21.2 years. The significance of the age factor will be discussed below.

AGE OF MARRIAGE

Age at marriage is a significant factor in this study because an earlier study demonstrated that the mean age at first marriage for middle and upper class Karachi women was 19.9 and 21.7 years, respectively, while the mean age at first marriage for Karachi males 27.2 and 27.9 years for the middle and upper classes, respectively (Korson, 1965). This would indicate a mean–age differential between the sexes of 7.3 and 6.2 years for the middle and upper classes. This conforms to the norm in West Pakistan.

Although the study referred to above was limited to Karachi, there seems little reason to assume that age at first marriage among the middle and upper classes in Lahore is significantly different from that found in Karachi.

Since almost all university graduate students come from middle and upper class families in Pakistan, in all likelihood it will not be too long before the women students' families arrange a marriage for them. Although it can be assumed that, as in other societies, the more education women achieve the later the age at first marriage, the Pakistan female graduate students may also delay marriage, but limited employment opportunities for women do not encourage many to become career women as they are found in the West (Korson, 1970). It is valid to assume, then, that the women graduate students will not wait long for their marriage to be arranged. The male graduate students, on the other hand, will probably wait several years before entering marriage, since the age differential between the sexes at marriage is several years,

The major reasons for the age differential at first marriage appear to be largely economic. A commitment of dower from the bridegroom to the bride at the time of marriage is not only traditional, but is required by law, and the amount pledged and its method of payment are incorporated in the marriage contract, which is then registered at the local Union Council of the bride's residence. Furthermore, it usually takes several years before a male university graduate is in a sufficiently secure position to take on the financial responsibilities of marriage.

REASONS FOR ENDOGAMOUS MARRIAGE

Open-end questions, as well as interviews with students and non-students, revealed the following major reasons in support of endogamous marriages in Muslim societies, and, most especially, in West Pakistan.

1. The granting of dower by the bridegroom to the bride is universally found in all Muslim societies. Should the principals be related, then the bride's family will request a smaller amount of dower because they know their daughter will be well cared for, and the element of risk in an exogamous marriage is reduced. There is no strong preference for either cross-cousin or parallel-cousin marriage.

2. Under the system of patrilocal residence, the bride will reside in the husband's home where she will be expected to make the necessary adjustments in order to please her father- and mother-in-law (especially the latter) who are also her uncle and aunt. In addition to the dual roles of niece and cousin, at marriage she takes on new roles—those of daughter-in-law and sister-in-law, The girl knows that at marriage she will leave her family of orientation with its secure social world and enter her husband's household where she is expected to develop a congenial relationship with the women of the family—especially with her mother-in-law. Since the girl has probably known these relatives all her life, her success as a wife will be measured by her ability to please her husband and produce hoped-for sons. Role fulfilment for the new bride, then, must await developments which are not always achieved by every bride. There is also the expectation that the girl will be well-treated by her relatives, while that may not be the case if "she is given to a strange family."

3. Social and cultural similarities are important factors, especially as it is the women who must make the adjustment within the family circle which helps keep the peace. Even such matters as food preparation are considered important in the process of adjustment for the new wife. Knowledge of the wife's family and their idiosyncrasies is always a valuable asset which helps in the adjustment process. The character, temper and morals of the girl are always a matter of concern to the husband's family, and an intimate knowledge of the girl's (as well as the boy's) family is considered a great asset. Such information is usually lacking or not readily available about a girl from another kin group or community. In fact, unfavourable factors may be deliberately disguised or hidden in order to further the chances of making a match for a girl (or boy) with undesirable characteristics.

4. Family honor plays a significant role in cousin marriages. A family which has been able to marry off a daughter to a cousin is then under

obligation to the son-in-law's family, and when a brother of the bride reaches an eligible age and a sister of the bridegroom is also of an eligible age for marriage, there is an obligation on the part of the bridegroom's family to accept the girl in marriage. Family ties and obligations are thus strengthened. Should the family with the first bridegroom look elsewhere for a bride when an eligible girl is available, this would cause a split in the two families, with resultant ill feelings and no sense of obligation on the part of family members to assist in times of need. This concept of functional exchange is considered to be central to the whole system of endogamous marriage.

5. "The paternal cousin has the right to the girl. If he exercises that right and obtains the girl (for no more than wedding expenses) he owes support to his uncle (her father) in any factional fight" (Goode, 1963:95). Under the Arab kinship system, Goode cites the preference for marrying the father's brother's daughter and points up the fact that a man had a *right* to marry the daughter (Goode, 1963:95). Although patrilateral cousin marriage is preferred, almost any relative will do, should there be a lack of eligible persons of the same age or socioeconomic status.

6. Conservation of economic resources is frequently cited as a major reason for endogamous marriages. In rural areas the continued ownership of land without the threat of fragmentation because of inheritance rights is matched in urban areas where family ownership of a business or real estate holdings is maintained within the patrilineage.

7. "Keeping the blood pure." Blood, among Muslims, always seem to be described in terms of patrilineal idiom. From this flows the idea that children's loyalty to the kin group will be maintained when parents are related. "Kin groups represent, so to speak, the second line of defense" when a person is in danger or trouble, or when he needs help in the performance of an economic task or ceremonial obligation. Because of extended kinship ties he can call on kinsmen for assistance, while he, on the other hand, is also under reciprocal obligation to lend assistance when called upon. This holds most especially for members of consanguineal kin groups (Murdock, 1949:43).

8. Even where *purdah* is no longer practised, the only opportunity a girl will have to meet eligible men outside the nuclear family will be cousins and not only can an intimate friendship develop but even a romantic attachment. Furthermore, it is likely that the parents of the couple have already agreed to a betrothal long before the time for marriage has arrived. In the earlier years, cousins are frequently regarded as "brothers" and "sisters"—an indication of the close relationship between the families. Such a relationship will frequently develop into a romantic attachment that is comparable to the dating process in the West.

9. Endogamous marriage serves an informal political function because family ties continue to be strengthened. Although Pakistani Muslims do not recognize a caste system as it functions in Hindu society, nevertheless, a semi-caste system based on occupational endogamy, common place of origin, or religious sectarianism is readily apparent The extended family in Pakistan

permits the function of socialization of the children to be shared by many family members of various age groups, and a child's loyalty will flow to all members of the larger kin group and not be limited to his nuclear family (Bell and Vogel, 1960:6—7).

10. In an urban setting entrepreneurial expansion will call for more employees, and relatives are preferred over non–relatives. Endogamous marriages will provide trustworthy partners and employees and will insure a secure level of living for the bride. Both parallel– and cross–cousin marriage is practised with no strong preference for either type manifested.

11. Class differentials in social control of the young probably play an important role. Middle and upper class families, because of property holdings, have greater economic and political power and can therefore, more readily sanction and control the behavior of their young. Furthermore, the young find the same economically secure base more attractive as a reason for conforming to the norms of their parents. The young of the lower class, on the other hand, have less to lose by non-conforming behavior, and, in fact, may seek out new opportunities in other communities, thereby weakening family ties.

12. Bertocci has suggested that classes in any society manifest different patterns of behaviour and life styles. and that these are characterized by unequal access to goods and services. This thesis is demonstrated by marriage patterns which may be seen to unite families along horizontally stratified lines (Bertocci, 1971:40).

13. Finally, the *Koran* specifically prohibits a man from marrying his mother, daughters, sisters, paternal or maternal aunts, nieces, foster mothers, foster sisters, mothers–in–law, step-daughters, and daughters–in–law (Dawood. 1956:357). There are no prohibitions against the marriage of cousins, regardless of degree of relationship.

CONCLUSION

This has been an exploratory study based on limited data, and is by no means intended to be definitive. It is apparent that the practice of cousin marriage in Pakistan has declined in the last generation. The most important reason that can be assigned to this decline in one generation is the disruption caused by the shifting of Muslim and Hindu populations following Partition of the subcontinent in 1947. In the twenty-four years that have elapsed since Partition, many thousands of Muslims left their homes in what is India today and migrated to the two wings, West and East Pakistan, largely to the major cities which provided greater opportunities for employment and where families had relatives to receive them. For example, in 1959, only 16.6 percent of the population of Karachi was native-born (Hashmi, 1965:4). The 1941 census indicates that Karachi had a population of 387,000, but in 1961 the city had grown to 1,917,000, a fivefold increase (Hashmi, 1965:13). The population of Karachi continues to grow, and the estimate in 1971 is 3,200,000.

Not only have many thousands of Muslims emigrated from India to what is Pakistan today, but there has also been a significant rural-urban shift in population with the growth of industry and commerce in the major cities. This great migration movement has inevitably had the effect of disrupting long-established community and biraderi ties, thereby reducing the number of eligible cousins who could serve as potential mates. Furthermore, it seems reasonable to assume that the kind of mobility created by increased industrialization and urbanization undoubtedly aided the drift toward the conjugal family, although the writer has no evidence to substantiate this statement.

Although social change in some areas of the social life of the society occurs more readily and with less resistance than in others, next to the religion, the institution of the family is slowest to change, and traditional norms are more apt to be defended by the older generation. The presence of the three-generational extended family, which is considered the ideal in West Pakistan, makes social change away from the traditional norms more difficult to accomplish. With grandparents and aunts and uncles present in a household, it is much more difficult for the younger generation to effect any change that runs counter to the traditional norms of a society, and it is unlikely that young people approaching the age of marriage would find many allies among the older generation, should they seek to exert any pressure upon their parents in terms of gaining greater freedom in decision making in the area of mate selection. The presence of grandparents and aunts and uncles offers constant reinforcement of the more conservative views of the parents. Also, in terms of organization, the nuclear family predominates in the West, and young members of nuclear families are apt to have greater independence and opportunity for decision-making than are their counterparts in joint and extended families more commonly found in West Pakistan. At least they are less apt to be confronted with the presence of other relatives in the household who may wish to intervene or pass judgment on their wishes, actions, or behavior.

An earlier study based on the same samples of graduate students indicated that, when the time came for the graduate students to marry, 12.7 percent felt their parents would select a relative as their spouse (Korson, 1969). It is even possible that their future spouses have already been chosen by their parents, although no formal betrothal has been announced.

In any case, social change in the family will not come rapidly in West Pakistan. Should a young couple be attracted to each other, an arrangement would have to be made for a member of the boy's family to approach the girl's family with a proposal that the two families consider the possibility and desirability of union by the marriage of the principals. A marriage arranged by the families continues as a *sine qua non*, even among educated families. There may be a trend toward democratization in mate selection in West Pakistani families by permitting greater participation of the principals in making the final choice, but it is more likely that the statement that "the criteria for a successful marriage are not necessarily companionship and love, but fertility, permanence and the alliance of two family groups" (Shah, 1960) still holds. There is no question but that cultural intrusion from the West will continue to influence both the younger generation as well as their parents, but for the foreseeable future it is unlikely that rapid change in the process of mate selection can be predicted.

Today all students are caught up in the whole process of modernization and the rapid social change of their nation. The rationalization of agriculture and industry by the introduction of modern technology has brought some social change and will inevitably bring more. One of the basic social institutional differences between West Pakistan and the West is that of family formation. Mate selection in West Pakistan is based on the traditional norms of the individual's obligations and responsibilities to the family and, through marriage, to contribute to the alliance of two families to extend and reinforce the influence of both. In the West, mate selection has as its major goal individual happiness based on the concepts of romance and individualism.

Since higher education in West Pakistan is modeled along Western lines, it is inevitable that the knowledge and rational understanding that accompany not only the natural sciences but also the social sciences as embodied in Western practices will make themselves felt. It is predicted that modernization in West Pakistan will, in time, reflect a greater trend toward individualism and away from the traditional norms of family centered decisions.

Although this study is limited to university graduate students who come of middle and upper class families, the question raised at this point is: are the strong kin-ties manifested by preference for cousin marriage also found to the same degree among lower class families? Furthermore, is there a correlation between the strength of kin-ties (and the preference for cousin marriage) and economic status? One can speculate that the upper class does have economic sanctions to maintain control of the young, while the youth in lower class families might, indeed, have greater freedom in decision making because they have less to lose. But these are questions that call for additional research in this very challenging area of social change.

REFERENCES

Antoun, Richard T., 1968. "On Modesty of Women in Arab Muslim Villages : A Study in the Accommodation of Traditions," American Anthropologist, 70, 4, August, Pp. 671-97.

Bell, Norman W., and Ezra F. Vogel, (eds.), 1960. A Modern Introduction to the Family, Glencoe, Illinois : The Free Press.

Bertocci, Peter J., 1971. Social Stratification in Rural East Pakistan, Unpublished paper.

Blitsten, Dorothy, 1963. The World of the Family, New York : Random House.

Dawood, N. J. 1956. trans., The Koran, London, Penguin Books.

Eglar, Z., 1960. A Punjabi Village in Pakistan, New York, Columbia University Press.

Farber, Bernard (ed.), 1966. Kinship and Family Organization, New York : Wiley.

Ghani, Anna, 1963. "Combining Career and Marriage," in Barbara Ward, Women in the New Asia, Paris : UNESCO.

Goode, William J., 1963. World Revolution and Family Patterns, New York : Free Press.

Hashmi, Sultan S., Masihur R. Khan, and Karol J. Krotki, 1964. The People of Karachi, Data From a Survey, Statistical Paper No. 2, Karachi : Pakistan Institute of Development Economics.

Hashmi, Sultan S., 1965. The People of Karachi, Demographic Characteristics, Karachi, Pakistan Institute of Development Economics.

Jacobson, Dorothy A., 1970. Hidden Faces, Hindu and Muslim Purdah in an Indian Village. New York, Unpublished dissertation, Columbia University.

Korson, J. Henry, 1965. "Age and Social Status at Marriage : Karachi," Pakistan Development Review, V, 4, (Winter) : pp. 586—600.

Korson, J. Henry, 1967. " Dower and Social Class in an Urban Muslim Community," Journal of Marriage and the Family, 29, (August), pp. 527-533.

Korson, J. Henry, 1968a " Residential Propinquity as a Factor in Mate Selection in an Urban Muslim Society." Journal of Marriage and the Family, 30, (August), pp. 518-527.

Korson, J. Henry, 1968b. " The Roles of Dower and Dowry as Indicators of Social Change in Pakistan," Journal of Marriage and the Family, 30, (November), pp. 696-707.

Korson, J. Henry, 1969. " Student Attitudes Toward Mate Selection in a Muslim Society : Pakistan," Journal of Marriage and the Family, 31, (February), pp. 153-165.

Korson, J. Henry, 1970. " Career Constraints Among Women Graduate Students in a Developing Society : West Pakistan," Journal of Comparative Family Studies, 1, (Autumn), pp. 82-100.

Murdock, George P., 1949. Social Structure, New York, Macmillan Co.

Peters, E., 1963. Aspects of Rank and Status Among Muslims in a Lebanese Village, in, The Mediterranean Countryman, ed., J. Pitt-Rivers, Paris Mouton.

Shah, Khalida, 1960. " Attitudes of Pakistani Students Toward Family Life," Marriage and Family Living, 22, 2, May, pp. 156-61.

Wakil, P , 1970. " Explorations Into the Kin-Networks of the Punjabi Society : A Preliminary Statement, Journal of Marriage and the Family, 32, 4, pp. 700-7.

Sexual Dialectics and Strategy in Berber Marriage*

ROGER JOSEPH**

Introduction

Few acconts of Berber society in Morocco have examined the political role of women in making decisions. Most studies have reflected the model of Berber males in which women are relegated to the role of pawns in a strategy of male manipulation. The purpose of this paper is to demonstrate that Berber society, at least some realms, can be characterized as having a bilateral nature. Decision making among the Berbers is part of an ongoing sexual dialectic between men and women. The synthetic nature of this dialectic can be seen by examining the relationship between the normative models of mate selection held by males and the antithetical behavior employed by females. By recognizing that females have and pursue political interests, it is possible to examine the means by which they forward these interests.

The mechanics of mate selection shall be utilized as the methodological framework for pursuing this problem. The normative model elicited from male informants is that the father, independent of external restraints, selects a marriage mate for his son or daughter. This normative model is, however, contradicted by the political concerns females have in influencing the selection of a mate and the strategies they employ to gain their own ends. The synthetic model which emerges is one of negotiation between men and women.

Two Strategies: Norms and Interaction

Because the models employed to analyze political organization have differential explanatory consequences, it is useful to examine the two strategies employed in studies of Berber society. The two models may be characterized as the formalist and the interactionist. Each has a particular focus; the former on discrete kinship units and the latter on individual dyadic relationships. The formalist position relies upon normative structure; the interactionist upon how individuals manipulate norms for their own purposes. The one model produces a highly ordered and rigid world of political organization; the other a relatively atomized world of individualism. Taken in combination, however, the two models reveal an interplay between norms and acts. One of the consequences

* Data upon which this paper is based was collected during eighteen months of field work in the Rif Mountains of Morocco in 1965-66. Field work was sponsored by a grant from the Wenner-Gren Foundation. The author wishes to thank Terri Joseph and his colleagues and students at the American University of Beirut for many helpful suggestions.
**Department of Anthropology, California State University, Fullerton, Fullerton, California, U.S.A.

of   investigating the inferface of the two models is that it reveals the influence
that women play in the power arena.

The formalist approach places an emphasis upon the unilineal aspects of
Berber social units. Gellner argues that "from the viewpoint of any group, its
composition can be specified without ambiguity, and without any danger of using
criteria of membership which might cut across each other" (1969:42). This
systemic approach produces unambiguous systems; it also underplays the role of
women. "In the social structure, women, handed around in marriage from one
lineage to the next . . . provided links of alliance in which they themselves being
passive instruments of policy, had little or no choice or voice and these links
were continuously reinforced through subsequent marriages (Hart 1972:38).

The interactionists, however, do not see political action as stemming from
segmentary collectives, but rather as a product of individualistic concerns.
Geertz argues that "Moroccan integration comes down to mediating relations
among a field of competing individuals, each with a somewhat different basis of
power and each scrambling to make his way within the general rules of the game
by his own wit and resources" (1972:37).

The model that emerges from this approach is one of manipulation and
fluidity. There are "virtually no corporate groups which can demand the
undivided allegiance of their members in every social situation" (Rosen
1972:227). Unlike the formalists whose model constitutes a world of
unambiguous organizational units, the model used by Geertz and Rosen is one in
which individuals negotiate their social order amidst a field of ambiguity in
which each bond is distinctive. The tactic of this paper is to examine this
apparent contradiction between the normative view (one of belief) and the
interaction view (one of acts). While only one decision process will be examined,
that of selecting a mate, the bilateral nature of influence may be assumed to
occur in other areas of political decision making.

Formal Normative Model

As stated earlier in this paper, the formal normative model of Berber social
structure emerges from an analysis of group interrelationships within the context
of lineage organization. Berber tribesmen of the Rif Mountains did indeed
confirm that marriage linkages were historically motivated by the desire of men
to foster or cement relationships with other men, who were or could become
allies. In an acephalous society which was afflicted by constant feuding and
lacking integrative institutions, save the market place (Benet 1957:210-13), such
mctivation was logical as well as plausible. Whether normative explanations
were, even in the days of lineage feuding, more than rationales for a dialectic
remains to be seen. Coon (1931:133) noted that even when "pacification" by
European powers was still indeterminate, parents desired to arrange marriages
for their children before the latter were old enough to have preferences and insist
upon them strongly. Berber males still utilize this motive for setting up early
marriages for their children although they are less quick to offer it as an
explanation of their own marriages. How an adult male views the circumstances
that led to his marriage is determined to some extent by how he feels about his

wife. An unhappy man will say his father forced him into marriage. If satisfied, he will talk about how after great trials he was able to overcome parental pressures. Fathers still insist, however, that they alone arrange their children's marriages.

The ideological model upon which marriage contracts are based is one in which men consolidate their political position by incorporating other men into their alliance system through the exchange of women. Men seek to elevate their own social position or reinforce their present standing by establishing matrimonial links with non-related families, or reaffirming ties with kinsmen. This strategy follows a marriage pattern reported in the literature of the Middle East in which, from the standpoint of the lineage, marriage is contracted inwardly with relatives and outward toward strangers. There are a number of "causal explanations" or rationales for either type of marriages. By marrying a relative:

1. There are no arguments over which family is superior;

2. Ego's family is acquainted with the girl and has an idea of what sort of a person she is;

3. Property arrangements are simpler;

4. Ego's family knows the girl and presumably likes her — this reduces the potential for friction which could occur between the outsider and the women of ego's household;

5. As an agnate of the family, ego's wife would be less likely to shame the family or bring its honor into question through inappropriate behavior or gossip;

6. If ego is fighting with his wife the common family relatives will pressure him into treating her better in order to maintain family solidarity;

7. As a corollary of (6), family unity will decrease the possibility of divorce.

There are, however, a countervailing set of factors which serve as rationales for marrying an outsider:

1. It is socially and economically advantageous to spread out one's contacts through alliance with non-kin;

2. Although property arrangements are more complicated there is a greater possibility of bringing additional property into the family through a marriage with an outsider;

3. Ego's family has more power over his wife since she does not have any natural allies within the household.

Since marriages move freely in both directions it can be argued that the reasons for kin marriage are equally offset by the reasons for marrying an outsider. It might also be argued, however, that these "explanations" are rationales given after the fact and that the selection of mates rests upon other deterministic factors.

Two such considerations are population size and social class. Girls usually get married between the ages of fourteen and twenty. Thus, in any localized, interacting social group (whether it be the *dchar* or a structurally more inclusive unit) the availability of women of marriageable age will be numerically restricted. In addition, at the upper social levels, especially among the *shorfa* or priestly class, marriage tends to become more restrictive in an effort to maintain lineage purity (Joseph, 1974a).

Within the ideological construct of the formal normative model, the only individual other than the father who is recognized as having any discriminatory powers in the selection of a mate is the son. Young men can utilize the traditional obligatory ritual or *'ar* upon their fathers by sacrificing a sheep outside the family home. A much simpler tactic, however, is to threaten to divorce the woman a father wishes Ego to marry. If a father, by the conventions of Berber ideology, has the ability to force a son into marriage, the son, by the same conventional system, has the right to divorce his wife. The logic behind the formal model is contradicted if an alliance is dissolved by divorce. Thus, within the male ideology there is some room for maneuvering by sons.

One of the most appealing aspects of the formal model is that it satisfactorily explains most of the overt behavior connected with marriage negotiations. Marriages are indeed arranged in an ordered manner which brings reciprocal advantages to men. In addition, most ceremonial and public aspects of the marriage arrangements are conducted exclusively by males from the preliminary ceremonial protocals through the final exchange of bride price and gifts. It is the father of the potential groom or his male representative who approaches the father of the potential bride. It is between these men that negotiating over bride price takes place and a contract is formalized. The males of the groom's family collect the goods to be exchanged and, with the exception of the dowry which goes to the bride, these goods are turned over to the males of the bride's family. The vast majority of public social interaction that precedes a marriage contract is done exclusively by males. The model that emerges from this interaction suggests that only male interests are served by marriage. Fathers have politically valid reasons for arranging a particular marriage but mothers do not; sons have affective involvement with mates but daughters do not. Two obvious questions arise. If males have such motives, why don't females; if females do have similar motives how can they pursue them?

Berber Female Society

Analysis of the social role of women in the Middle East has been hampered by two factors. The first of these derives from the difficulty of male ethnographers to have any significant opportunities to participate in or observe female activities. The anthropologist not only records almost exclusively male social life but also has recourse only to male explanations of relationships. The second factor is that anthropologists have generally failed to probe the logical question that given these male relational networks, why is it that women do not have corresponding realms of social relationships? Nelson, in an excellent paper on Middle Eastern political structure (1974) has argued that indeed such networks do exist. Power, as she points out, is not an exclusive concern of males; "women's relevance structures intersect with those of men at many points" (Nelson, 1974:553). One of these points of intersection is the nexus between power and influence. According to Nelson (1974:554), we must recognize "the ongoing dialectical process of social life in which both men and women are involved in a reciprocity of influence *vis- α -vis* each other."

One means by which women can exert a reciprocity of influence is through the creation of informal power blocs. These blocs among Berber women are similar to those created by men in that they coalesce around the personal ability of women to acquire allies through neighbors and friends as well as through their consanguineal and affinal relationships with other females. It is the category of affines which is especially important when discussing the consequences of marriage; just as matrimonial linkage can be seen as a male device for marketing for allies, it is equally true that the same basic strategy accomplishes similar results for females. Khuri (1970) demonstrated that the relationship between mother and daughter-in-law is a critical one in a successful Middle Eastern marriage. It is necessary, however, to take his argument beyond the psychological level and to account for the sociological meaning of such a marriage among females. Such a meaning is rooted in the fact that this relationship expands a mother's influence by recruiting a new set of female affinal allies through her daughter-in-law.

The political milieu in which women exert influence possesses many of the features of the male political world, although it is not quite a mirror reflection of the latter. The female political structure has a ranking order if not a hierarchy. Factors which may determine the degree of a woman's influence are social class, numbers of clients and supporters, economic status, and personality. Women also have recourse to spells and charms (Joseph, 1974b).

The major difference between the two political worlds of men and women, however, is that while men rise to political influence through a balance between obtaining influence through their fathers and at the same time competing with them, *women usually gain influence through their sons and in competition with their husbands.* Young Berber men rise in status by overtly demonstrating their influence. Since most public displays of influence are managed by males, sons must overtly manifest competitiveness with fathers in order to forward their own claims to political power. Women, however, can only display their influence through covert means and one such means is to utilize their sons as allies. A women's influence, then, is in part dependent upon her adult male children.

Female social status among the Berbers varies with age. As the mother grows older her sons rise in power; as the son gains status so does his mother. One area in which this can be seen is the interface between sexual seclusion and age, which can be charted in a bell-shaped curve (See Figure 1). A mechanism of seclusion is rooted in preserving sexual propriety and has meaning only when sexual segregation is socially significant. Thus, infants and pre-puberty children are not secluded from each others' company. As a girl enters her teens segregation becomes more pronounced but work tasks taking the girl outside the house make it impossible for parents to supervise such seclusion. When a young woman marries both her husband and her father share in responsibility for her

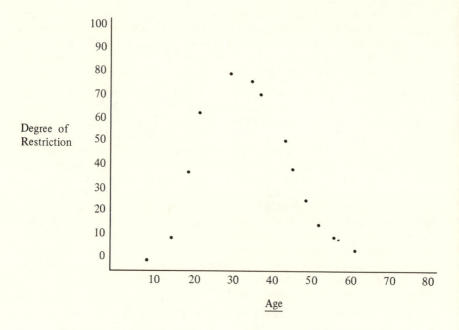

Figure 1: Projected Social/Sexual Restriction of Females

honor, and her seclusion becomes more marked. Bearing children and the necessities of nursing and child care bind the married woman closely to home. As she grows older, however, she becomes less restricted in her physical mobility and acquires more contacts in the female sub-society which increases her status. By the time she is thirty-five or forty years of age her eldest children are of marriageable age, and her older children can relieve her of much of the domestic chores. By the time a woman is fifty she will have built a considerable network of female allies and be actively engaged in broadening this circle. It is in this context that women ally themselves with their sons and often become political councilors for these men.

Women build their political influence not only through their sons but also, and of equal importance, through their linkages with other women. The relationship of mother to ego's wife is a crucial one in expanding a woman's political network which can be viewed as a sort of kindred of her own consanguinial relatives, her affines, and other neighborhood friends. These sub-societies serve as communication systems, and the control of such systems gives women a great deal of influence. Nelson (1974:'558) summarizes this aspect of political life very concisely:

Simultaneously, the woman as daughter, sister, wife, and mother acts as an "information broker," mediating social relations within the family and larger society. The implications for power (reciprocity of influence) are obvious in that by these networks of relationships, the woman is in a position to channel or withhold information to male members of the kindred. And in this position the woman influences decision-making about alliances, actually sets up marriage relations, and informs male members of the household what is going on in other homes.

Once one takes into account the political role of women, the formal normative model becomes less satisfactory and a greater degree of bilaterality emerges. As shown in the following diagram (Figure 2a) the formal model need only establish a correspondence of interest between males. By incorporating female interests, a four-section matrix emerges. In Diagram 2b females #3 and #4 not only have political interests separate from males #1 and #2, but they also influence the final selection of a mate by acting as a conduit of information between one another. Callender and El Guindi in discussing the role that young women play in acquiring a husband, the subject of the next section of this paper, observed the working of this among the Kenuz of the Egyptian Nubia (1971:47):

> The most effective technique . . . was the aid of their mothers and other female relatives who continuously canvassed males who were potential husbands and, either in person or acting through men, exerted relentless pressure on them invoking for this purpose any obligation they could manipulate.

Female Juveniles

Not only do older Berber women take a political interest in mate selection but young unmarried women also participate. While girls ideologically are proscribed from having contact with marriageable males, the economic conditions of peasant subsistence make this impossible except in the wealthiest families. Young women from an early age up until the time they are married are charged with household tasks such as gathering firewood, washing clothes, and obtaining the family's water supply. All these activities take young women away from their homes and outside the supervision of adults. As Coon points out, young boys and girls "have ample opportunity to become acquainted with each other and to form preferences for particular individuals of the opposite sex" (1931:132).

Since the Berber settlement pattern is one of dispersed households, it is a daily necessity for members of the family to collect water supplies. This task is exclusively a female activity and is almost always carried out by unmarried girls. Each day girls travel to rivers, wells, or springs. The fact that at certain times of the day unmarried women travel towards and congregate around a water source is known to the young unmarried males who often travel in the same direction. As girls move along the pathways from their homes to water, they usually pick up female age mates occupied with the same task. Boys also follow in groups but they carefully maintain a distance between themselves and the females.

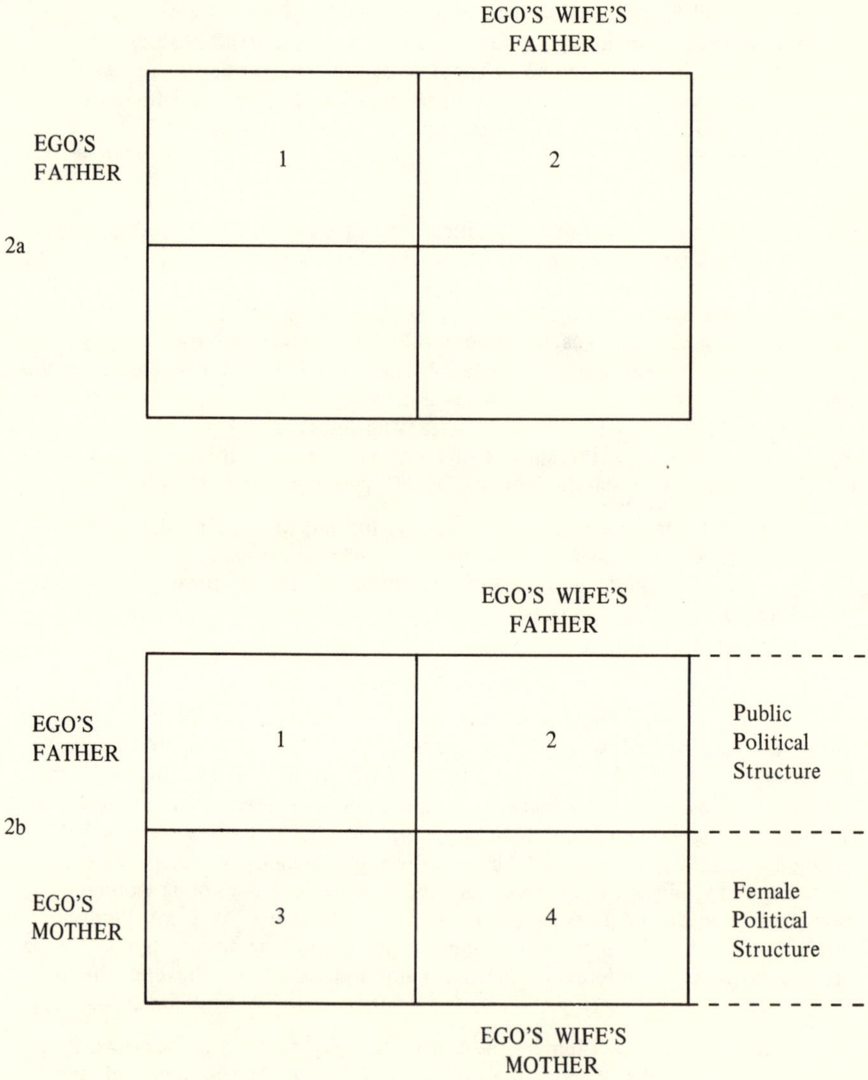

EGO'S WIFE'S
FATHER

EGO'S FATHER	1	2
2a		

EGO'S WIFE'S
FATHER

	EGO'S WIFE'S FATHER		
EGO'S FATHER	1	2	Public Political Structure
2b EGO'S MOTHER	3	4	Female Political Structure

EGO'S WIFE'S
MOTHER

Figure 2

If a boy is interested in a particular girl and has been led to believe through his female relatives such as a sister or from other sources, that the girl likes him, he will "walk her home." The social etiquette of such a display of affection calls for the boy to walk several yards behind the girl he is accompanying. It is entirely up to the girl whether she wishes to encourage or discourage a young man and it is she who controls the "social distance" which separates the two.

Unmarried girls, far from playing the passive role that Berber normative ideology assigns them, have several means by which they attempt to encourage or discourage young males. They can elicit assistance from their sisters, mothers, and other female relatives in attracting the interest of a particular male; they also attempt to gain their ends through manipulating supernatural forces with charms and other magic. Their most effective technique, however, is to utilize a public forum, the wedding ceremony itself. Such ceremonies are liminal events in which ordinary role playing is suspended or even reversed (Turner, 1974). At these ceremonies the unmarried girlfriends and relatives of the bride and groom publically perform dances and sing personally composed songs. The dances demonstrate the sexual appeal of the young woman and the songs allow her to appeal to or reject certain males (Joseph, 1975). Girls are allowed wide latitude in their songs and a girl "exercises her judgment in rejecting or accepting a suitor without bowing to, or even consulting her father" (T. B. Joseph, 1975).

The Role of the Mother

While women communicate their disposition towards males by allowing individual men to accompany them in the task of fetching water and by utilizing personally composed songs at the wedding ceremonies, it is usually the task of a young man to encourage actual negotiations. Since there is an ideological preference for the father to arrange a marriage, the son rarely communicates directly with his father. Rather than having a confrontation, a young man will use a third party or broker between himself and his father. The most useful broker is his mother who stands at a pivotal point in terms of the three categories of relationships involved in a marriage (Figure 3). As the mother, she has a particular interest in her son's marriage. As a woman, she has access to other women through her personal political network and is in a position to know information about ego's potential bride that is unavailable to men. Finally, as the wife of ego's father, she has an influential role in making household decisions. In her structural position the mother has access to all the involved parties. Each of the relationships can be used by her to exert influence, channel or withhold communication, and manipulate.

It is the mother who can increase her own status by establishing affinal ties through the recruitment of a daughter-in-law and that woman's female kin. It is this woman who seeks to establish a "good" marriage which will promote her son's status and consequently improve her own political position. She is located in the female communication network and has more sources of information regarding potential mates than any other person in the family. It is the mother who can supply intimate information to her husband about a potential bride; information which can bolster or destroy a candidate's standing depending on

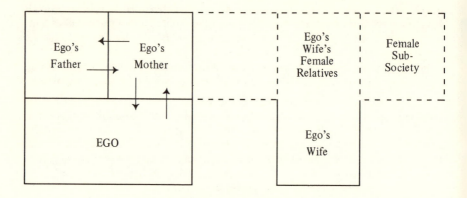

<u>Figure 3</u>

how the mother chooses to manipulate the information. While Berber men are the custodians of honor, women are the molders of a person's reputation. In a society in which relationships are flexible and fluid, women possess much influence in shaping the direction and quality of these relationships.

Summary

Berber society can be characterized as possessing a normative ideology in which political decision making is the province of males. Such an ideology lies at the basis of the formalists' model of Berber social structure. The experiential life of Berbers, however, allows for a considerable amount of individualistic manipulation and a resulting fluidity of social relationships. It is this latter fact which stands at the base of the interactionists' position. If these two models are placed in opposition to each other, a third model of dialectical process emerges. This latter model is particularly useful in studying political processes because it demonstrates the underlying bilateral nature of Berber political structure. This bilaterality emerges when the true interests and means for developing these interests among females is isolated. As there exist mechanisms by which fathers and sons pursue their goals, there also exists a complementary set of means by which women pursue their own interests. Berber society makes room for women in the power arena, even though the means females utilize are often more covert than overt.

BIBLIOGRAPHY

Benet, Francisco
   1957   "Explosive Markets: The Berber Highlands." In Trade and Market in the Early Empires. Karl Polanyi, Conrad Arensberg and Harry Pearson (eds.). Gleneve: Free Press.

Coon, Carleton
    1931   Tribes of the Rif. Cambridge: Harvard African Studies, Peabody Museum, Vol. IX.
Callander, Charles and Fawzi El Guindi
    1971   Life-Crisis Rituals among the Kenuz. Cleveland: Case Western Reserve Press.
Geertz, Clifford
    1968   Islam Observed. Chicago and London: University of Chicago.
    1972   "The Wet and the Dry: Traditional Irrigation in Bali and Morocco." In Human
            Ecology, Vol. 1, No. 1.
Gellner, Ernest
    1969   Saints of the Atlas. Chicago: University of Chicago.
Hart, David
    1972   "The Tribe in Modern Morocco: Two Case Studies." In Arabs and Berbers. Ernest
            Gellner and Charles Micaud (eds.). Lexington, Massachusetts: D. C. Heath.
Joseph, Roger
    1974a   "Choice or Force: A Study in Social Manipulation." In Human Organization, Vol. 33,
            No. 4.
    1974b   "The Idiom of Fatalism in North Africa." In Manifest, Vol. 2.
    1975   "Berber Marriage as Liminal Ceremony." Paper delivered at the California Folklore
            Society.
Joseph, Terri B.
    1975   "Berber Wedding Songs." Paper delivered at the California Folklore Society.
Khuri, Fuad
    1970   "Parallel Cousin Marriage Reconsidered: A Middle Eastern Custom that Nullifies the
            Effects of Marriage on the Intensity of Family Relations." In Man, Vol. 5.
Nelson, Cynthia
    1974   "Public and Private Politics: Women in the Middle Eastern World." In American
            Ethnologist, Vol. 1, No. 1.
Rosen, Lawrence
    1972   "Rural Political Process and National Politics." In Rural Politics and Social Change in
            the Middle East. Richard Antoun and Iliya Harik (eds.). Bloomington and London:
            Indiana University Press.
Turner, Victor
    1974   Dramas, Fields and Metaphors. Ithaca and London: Cornell University.

Women's Strategies in Modern Marriage in Anglophone West Africa: An Ideological and Sociological Appraisal*

KENNETH LITTLE**

In contemporary Africa, political independence and economic development have enlarged the scope of activities in which women may engage. This is particularly evident in the cities. Not only do most women possess the franchise but to an increasing extent women now hold senior posts in government, in the civil service and the professions. Many women also find jobs in the modern sector in nursing and in teaching and there are now opportunities for them in journalism, catering, banks, stores and offices. Thanks also to the emergence of a whole new class of elite men, the marriage market has correspondingly widened.

The difficulty is, however, that the number of girls completing a secondary (high) school course is still relatively small. The disadvantage is considerable because women wishing for position in this more 'open' society have naturally to compete with men as well as with other women. Also, although much official lip service is paid to women's 'progress' and their contribution to the nation, traditional ideas of status continue for practical purposes to be influential. Men retain control of most major institutions and it is, in fact, arguable that urban women, in particular, are more rather than less dependent upon their husbands.[1] True, the women's own movements have made important gains in matrimonial legislation but a frontal attack's success tends to depend upon women acting *en masse* and upon its serving male political purposes.[2] It is somewhat rarely practicable in other circumstances. Consequently, in order to secure their *individual* objectives, women have often to resort to a less direct kind of tactic. They find this expedient in most of the above fields, but we are concerned here specifically with the matrimonial situation of 'literate' and of 'educated' women.[3]

*The author wishes to express his sincere thanks to the Leverhulme Trust for an award that helped substantially with the preparation of this article. He is also grateful for the helpful comments made on the original draft of the article, including those at the Seminar under the auspices of the Department of Social Anthropology, Queen's University, Belfast.
**African Urban Studies, University of Edinburgh, Scotland.
[1]Schwarz (1972) is a leading protagonist of this contention.
[2]Among the increasing documentation of this point see, in particular, Riviere's description of collaboration between African women and male politicians (1968, *passim*).
[3]We distinguish for sociological reasons between persons whose education is elementary and those whose schooling extends up to or beyond the secondary stage.

This is complex because considerable value continues to be attached to the procreation of children. Women gain esteem through their production and for men it is a sign of virility. The difference is that whereas men and society generally still tend to condone male sexual activity outside as well as within marriage itself, women are expected to remain faithful to a single partner. (Harrell-Bond, 1975; Little 1973; Omari 1962 *et alii*). For such extra-marital liaisons there are plenty of 'good-time' girls available, ready to provide 'sex' in return merely for expensive presents and entertainment. Also, other attractive young women are willing to be an elite man's mistress if the only alternative is to marry someone of their own or a lower social position. It is not unusual for such women to bear their patron children, and a prospective husband may also have had children by illiterate women, married by customary law, before he was sufficiently established to contemplate 'legal' marriage. Relationships with the latter women have probably been broken off. But the bond with the children invariably continues, and a man may spend almost as much money on these outside children as well as on irregular unions as on his legal wife and her children. Indeed, instead of being called mistresses or concubiness, these women are often referred to simply as 'outside' wives. (*ibid., passim.*)

That educated women object to this double standard there is no doubt. It is frequently referred to with considerable resentment in ordinary conversation and also when such women meet at conferences. Thus, at one such formal gathering the delegates concerned were mostly community workers, leaders of women's associations and so on. These women came from the Francophone countries as well as Anglophone ones and the purpose was to discuss problems of social welfare, including family planning, up-to-date methods of hygiene and the rearing of children. However, although these matters were keenly debated, one speech won by far the greatest acclaim. It invited the audience to deal effectively with husbands whose practice it was to squander their wives' earnings on girl friends.

The women's discontent and sense of insecurity is also a very frequent theme in women's magazines. To *Ideal Woman (Obaa Sima)*, for example, a correspondent wrote:

'I am so miserable that I want to die. I am a 38 year old mother of four. I married a divorcee twelve years ago. My husband is such a flirt that it is difficult to describe him.

He had a child with a certain girl four years ago (who has had a child by another man also). He promised at that time not to have anything more to do with that girl. Recently I have heard that the girl has been delivered of another child again by my husband.

Apart from this girl he has a child with another girl at his home town. My worry is that my eldest child has just entered secondary school and the rest are very young. I fear that the way he is going about having children here and there, my children may suffer in the future.

He spends very little money on me and the children, and always gives the excuse that he has a "lot" of responsibilities. What shall I do to keep my sanity...?' (July 1974).

This kind of difficulty is amply documented in the sociological literature of Harrell-Bond, *op. cit;* Little, *op. cit. et alii.* However, we have cited *Ideal Women* in this connection because although designed specially for women, magazines of this kind frequently include articles and short stories by men. Since in consequence they reflect the male as well as female point of view their pages provide an important clue to the way in which the matrimonial situation referred to is ideologically conceived. Moreover, unlike some of their Western contemporaries, these West African magazines also convey an acute sense of realism. True, they include stories of romantic love that have a happy ending; but they also make it clear that wedding rings do not necessarily guarantee more than a socially and legally recognized status. They stress that, given the sociological situation described, the companionate marriage that many educated women now desire is not achieved without a great deal of forethought. Its attainment requires certain tactics on the woman's part which, if she is wise, she will use in dealings with the opposite sex.

The problem, indeed, starts with courtship because, as indicated, there are different rules of conduct. Thus, while it is socially accepted that young men are entitled to their 'fling', a girl seeking a high status husband needs to be very circumspect, especially when her own family background is humble. Such a man's relatives are likely to demand a very exacting standard of behaviour, even though he himself will probably feel entitled to sexual intercourse during the courtship. So long as the parties concerned are known to be 'going steady' there may be little or no public objection to this. Nor may it greatly matter if the girl becomes pregnant provided her fiance accepts the responsibility. If, however, marriage does not follow, the girl's social reputation will be seriously jeopardized. She will not be ostracised by other men, but her prospects of making an equally favourable marriage may be considerably diminished. This is likely to happen even if it was the girl herself who broke the engagement off. In this case it will probably be said that she is either too "proud" or too "fickle" to make a satisfactory wife. Nor is chastity necessarily the solution. It will preserve her good name but, at the cost perhaps, of driving a promising suitor straight into the arms of less prudish rivals. Consequently, as one of Bond's university informants remarked, "In order to get a good husband, you have to be good, but you also have to be careful not to be *too* good." (*op. cit.*p. 158).

It follows from this that it is prudent for the would-be wife to survey the potential field with care.[4] This may be done by drawing on relatives' and girl friends' general pool of information. She will naturally be told to keep clear of married men and warned in particular against 'sugar daddies'. Sugar daddies are depicted as old enough to be one's father and even grandfather, bald, and with protruding bellies. Such men, it is said, are very dangerous. Although rich enough to

---

[4]A few girls, however, simply advertise for help to see them through their education, and offer marriage as part of the bargain.

provide a girl with everything she wants, they have no intention of marrying her and will leave her in the lurch if she becomes pregnant.[5] Not only does *Ideal Woman* emphasise this, but it is also a constant theme in the Ghanaian *Chit Chat*, the Nigerian *Woman's World*, and the Sierra Leone *Sierra Fashion*. Indeed, according to one of these articles, a girl needs to be on her guard from the age of thirteen. Men of all sorts will be showing her favours thereafter, including:

> the young handsome school boy who offers to be your guide at sports meeting or debates; the young clerk who meets you at a party or in the street and attaches himself to you like moth to fire; the young, pleasant faced man who offers you a lift in his gleaming sports car with stereo rodio and music, to or from school, or while going out on a visit, and subsequently dates you.[6]

The acid test, nevertheless, is personal experience gained by enlarging one's circle of male acquaintances, but discreetly. These magazines also stress that one's place of employment should be selected with care because in banks, stores and hospitals, there are plenty of other girls to attract male attention. The offices of engineers, contractors and architects on the other hand, are mostly staffed by men. Naturally, therefore, a girl must reside in one of the larger cities.[7] Also, to widen the range further, she should join an association—a youth club, drama group, or church organisation—and, if the class includes young men, might even enrol for evening studies. She should also take up those out-door activities that interest men, such as tennis and swimming, but *not* 'politics' as this is not ordinarily regarded as "women's business" at all. Rather should she, as one correspondent of *Ideal Woman* put it—be "dumb" in male company—this is her "secret weapon for attracting the eligible males".

The next step is very much more delicate. It requires extra caution because having found the 'right' kind of person, it is necessary not only to attract him but in the process to establish the 'right' kind of relationship. This means that although approachable, the girl must be 'conventional' to the extent of letting the man know that she has no secrets from her family. Also, although she herself may in fact undertake some of the pursuing, this must never be done openly. There must never arise an occasion in which the man feels he can take the girl for granted. Instead, he should be given the idea that if he does not take the initiative other men will.

This, however, must be done without appearing to be actually free with one's favours,[8] and preferably within the context of Platonic friendship. It may require a good deal of preliminary spade-work, and so *Ideal Woman* suggests the following tactical procedure:

---

[5]In one of *Woman's World's* short stories entitled *The Sugar Daddy*, the heroine tries to terminate her pregnancy and then commits suicide.

The other side of the picture is that the "sugar daddy" has to pay heavily for his pleasures. "For him love is an ocean of emotions, entirely surrounded by expenses." *Ideal Woman*, October 1973.

[6]"Beware of Men", *Woman's World*, January 1975.

[7]The dismay of a young secretary who has been posted "upcountry" is depicted in one of *Ideal Woman's* short stories.

[8]A short story suggests that although to have more than one string to one's bow may be strategic in the Western world this kind of tactic is unlikely to work in Ghana (Ideal Woman, August 1971, p. 28).

If the man you have found does not ask you out, plan a birthday party. Invite some 20 people as well as him and include young married couples, engaged couples, a few popular male and female relatives and two friendly unattached girls.

While avoiding any impression of extravagance, provide plenty of inexpensive drinks[9] and simple dishes you have prepared yourself. Show that you are a good hostess by moving freely among your guests; but don't talk too much or attempt to show off your own clothes or achievements. And don't spend too much time with the man himself. Instead, as soon as you see that his interest is aroused, be very pleasant to your other male guests. Then, when you detect the slightest sign of jealousy switch your attention back to him.

At the end of the party, thank all the guests and make sure he is the last one you thank. Raise your head and look right into his eyes.

When he does ask for a 'date', don't be in a hurry to accept. Say you are busy that evening, but will be free in three days time. Be sure, however, that he has your telephone number.

Then, when he calls ask where he proposes to take you, and make a definite suggestion if he leaves it to you. Propose a cinema, play or a concert, but don't suggest an expensive night club. If you do he may not invite you again. When the evening is over, ask him to escort you home; but on parting don't allow any 'goodnight' kisses—and don't stay out late in any circumstances. Impress on him that your parents would not like this and let him meet one member of your family, preferably your mother. Also when he does start taking you out, do not accept more than one date a week; and the next time you meet talk about yourself and what, in the meantime, you have been doing. This may spur him on by making him want to feel more important to you. At this stage, however, don't mention the friendship to your other relatives. It would be disastrous if any member of your family were to ask him whether he was going to marry you or not. Instead, try to consolidate your position as the one woman he would like to be his life's companion.

This can be done by being 'feminine'. In other words, walk, talk and even laugh in a feminine manner, pay special attention to your dress and wear the particular clothes he admires most. Also, invite him to dinner and if you are not already a good cook, start lessons straight away and practise in private until you are perfect.[10] Perhaps your talent may lie in dress-

[9]..."Ato took her to the bar... and was very impressed that she ordered only soft drinks. "Why, you are not like any of the girls I have met..." "You are a sweet Colo (old-fashioned) girl," Ato told her (*Ideal Woman*, August, 1971, p. 18).

[10]Girls wanting a husband need to demonstrate these domestic arts, says a male contributor to *Sierra Fashion*. "All women should know how to cook and prepare a house". Instead he finds "many beautiful and well-dressed ladies" who spend all their time gadding around Freetown. "Tell me, Madam Editor, do you expect a lady to prepare any food at home after eating a plate of rice at an hotel? Do you expect a lady who eats in an hotel to think of buying pots, spoons, cups, plates and so on for the house? Do you expect from (sic) a lady who has made an appointment to meet at an hotel to find time to prepare the house?"

making. If so, let him know about this drawing his attention to the dresses you have made yourself. It is also most important to show interest in his own work and so try to learn about it. Whatever happens, don't be easily offended, and never be critical of him. Instead, flatter your Mr. 'Right' now and then, and laugh over his jokes, however dry they may seem.

The following general rules should also be observed—instead of talking a lot about yourself let the man find out for himself. Do not break a date unless it is absolutely unavoidable, and try to be punctual. Since he should feel free to move about, do not be too possessive when you are out or show jealousy. If he is flirtatious type the idea that women find him irresistible may urge him on. Above all, since he should feel that it is he who is doing the chasing—that he has to woo and win you—do not admit by your actions that you are serious about marriage for the immediate future. On the other hand, while indicating that you are satisfied with work, let him also know that you are prepared to settle down when the right person presents himself. He will then have to decide if he is the very person you need. When he does try to convince you that he is and when there's no further doubt at all about his intentions, hesitate no longer. Say "yes" as soon as he poses the question because—if you don't—he may never ask again.

This dialogue will be between the two of you, but now is the moment to bring in the family. And so direct him to them so that a *formal* approach for your hand in marriage can be made by his own people. The status of wife is yours when these negotiations have been satisfactorily concluded and the appropriate ceremonies also carried out. (*Ideal Woman*, December 1971, January, February and March, 1972).

These magazines also stress that men are always attracted to women who have poise; and it is in fact clear that, although they may fear the university graduate, men want their wives to have *some* education. Indeed, one of the most common complaints made by ambitious young men is that their traditionally oriented parents want them to marry illiterate girls. (Little, 1973, p. 139, and *passim;*)[11] Consequently in addition to taking adequate care of her physical appearance, the would-be wife needs enough savoir-faire to entertain visitors in a 'modern' way. She should be sophisticated enough and sufficiently at ease to impress her husband's social superiors *(ibid passim)*'.

In fact, since many of the new class of elite men were themselves reared by illiterate relatives, the present situation demands quite often more of wife than of

---

[11]A correspondent who agrees with this attitude wrote in *Woman's World*, July 1974: 'A chat with a man reveals he has made a bad choice. His wife is unadaptable to social changes. She is a semi-literate who cannot contribute intelligently to any discussion. Apart from her narrow scope in her job, her head is completely blank and vacant in any other field. She has done nothing to 'mprove her appearance'.
Woman's World also suggests that a young man's parents want for him "a girl who is sober to near stupidity, very simple to a fault and very obedient to near servitude. She must be very respectful. In short, they want somebody who cannot stand in their way during their exploitative visits to the couple". (February 1974).

husband. This, in turn, is probably why much of the space in women's magazines is devoted entirely to social matters and why both they and leading newspapers deal largely with matters of etiquette. For example, where her husband invites friends, his wife must be present. She should not stay in the kitchen, but is warned against meeting guests in her kitchen clothes. The would-be hostess is also advised to have food prepared in readiness for guests and to see that utensils and tumblers were clean. It is good manners to say 'thank you' for gifts and when leaving one's seat in a cinema, a church, or when a person admires one's clothes. When entering a room full of people who are seated, one should go round and shake hands with those present, starting from left to right. When attending a party of different nationalities, one should try to mix freely, and one should not rush to greet a friend when one is in a group. One must not chew gum or smoke in public. The enquiries answered also include such apparently trivial questions as how much food a person who is a guest can leave untouched on her plate; when is it proper for a veil a bride wears over her face to be lifted, etc. *(ibid.)*

Fashion notes and dress-making hints are also provided as a regular feature and there are numerous photographs of the wives of prominent politicians showing the kind of clothes that these socially prominent women and other well-known 'socialites' wear at public functions. Further pictures of African women illustrate the use and effects of cosmetics, and advice about deportment is also offered. It is explained, for example, how a women can sit elegantly on a low seat while wearing a tight skirt, or sit cross-legged on a straight seat. Readers are warned against standing akimbo as it displays too much of the hips. *(ibid)*

In addition to these practical hints, the women's magazines naturally pay a great deal of attention to relationships between the spouses. True, a great deal is said about the 'unreliability' and 'infidelity' of men in general and of husbands in particular;[12] but it is also explained how a stable and harmonious relationship may be maintained. It necessitates give and take from both sides and so the advice given to the wife is sociologically significant as well as instructive. She is encouraged to keep her husband's interest alive. In addition to her always being tidily dressed and well groomed, particular emphasis is laid on the avoidance of "nagging", especially in the case of sexual peccadiloes. These, it is implied, are just male human nature. Consequently, if a woman has a good husband, she should sink her pride and be just like a "mother" to him.[13] Wives, therefore, are urged to turn a blind eye, to be 'understanding' and even tolerant[14] so long as the husband's liaisons are conducted with reasonable consideration for their position.

---

[12]Among professional groups in Freetown, Harrell-Bond found that married couples argued twice as often about such matters as any other single subject. Dinan's many case-studies also include much evidence of this. (Dinan, n.d.).

[13]The implication that the emotional bonds between a man and his mother are stronger than the conjugal relationship has been commented on by a number of writers. See Bond, *op. cit*. p. 237, and Fraenkel, *passim*, among others.

[14]In one of its pages, *Ideal Woman* advises wives who are 'unduly jealous' to see a psychisatrist.

(Ideal Woman and *Chit Chat, passim)*. "Better the devil you know, than the devil you don't" is the advice given; and wives who are less philosophical are told to regard a husband's "bad" behaviour as punishment for their own previous misdemeanours.

It is also stressed that not only does an etiquette attach to extra-marital relations but that this applies to the part played in such liaisons by women as well as by men. Thus, although it is wrong for a jealous wife to embarrass her husband by publicly displaying her resentment, it is also incumbent on the mistress to be discreet. *Ideal Woman* invited its readers to comment on the following 'typical' situation.

'Mary', the wife, went home to have a baby. During her absence, 'John', the husband, has been entertaining his mistress, 'Barbara', in the house and he is expecting her next visit. 'Mary', however, returns unexpectedly. 'John' is angry because he considers she should have informed him of her coming. He hurried off to tell 'Barbara' not to call and does not see her during the next fortnight. This worries 'Barbara'. She writes to 'John' addressing the letter to his home, where it is opened by 'Mary', 'John' himself having gone on trek. 'Mary' telegraphs 'Barbara' in 'John's' name to the effect that she, 'Mary', is away again and so 'Barbara' should call that evening. When 'Barbara' arrives, 'Mary' slaps her face and generally beats her up in full view of the neighbours. Three days later, 'John' files a petition for divorce.

Opinions were expressed by both male and female readers and the view mainly taken was that the wife, 'Mary' was principally to blame. Points made were that the last thing a married woman should do is to contrive to meet her husband's mistress. It was very wrong of 'Mary' to entice the other woman to the house, and to beat her up was very "unladylike". She should at least have warned 'Barbara' off. Instead, she disgraced herself and probably humiliated her husband. 'Mary's' behaviour was also ill-considered because her husband's affair should not have come as a surprise; and especially as 'John' had not bothered about 'Barbara' in the meantime, she should have had more patience and given him an opportunity to deny the liaison.

'John' was wrong in carrying on with a mistress, but he was right to keep her away from the house. 'Barbara' was criticized on the grounds that she should have called at 'John's' office instead of writing to his home. It would also serve 'Barbara' right if 'John' married her, for then she would know how it felt to have another woman go after one's own husband.

What is the wife's best way of warding off predatory attacks? It is most important, the magazines suggest, that she should never allow herself to be 'drawn' by the "other woman". If, for example, the latter telephones when the husband is out, this may be a deliberate attempt to start a quarrel between the spouses, because no responsible married man will let his girl friend call his own home. This wife's reaction should therefore be dignified. She should avoid rudeness at any cost because, for one thing, she can't be sure that it is a girl friend. For another, her husband is the most likely person to stop her, if it is. She should simply say her husband is out and the "other woman" will eventually tire of telephoning a never-stay-at-home boy friend *(Ideal Woman,* passim*)*.

The "other woman's" aim may be to supplant the wife. If so, this objective is less likely to be achieved if the wife retains her composure, and is not provoked into openly displaying resentment and suspicion of any attention paid by her husband to other women. Above all, she should avoid any attempt on the part of the "other woman" directly to confront her or to force her into publicity recognizing the outside relationship.[15] Instead she should give extra attention not only to her husband's comfort, but to the creation of an attractive home. The children should be well-fed, nicely dressed and the husband encouraged to imagine himself as the father of future judges, doctors, economists and professors. He should be made to feel that these things can never come about if he dissipates money and energy on other women. The wife should also seek to satisfy her husband's sexual needs but should not be too demanding herself. In fact, female as well as male contributors to the magazines go out of their way to stress the wife's subordinate position.

Woman's World, for example, interviewed its own "ideal" woman—a young Nigerian student of music. Though considering that both men and women "have to work as complementary (sic) as possible for co-existence", this undergraduate believed that "nature has made it from the beginning that women are to be under men by all standards". (November 1973). Somewhat similarly another correspondent said that both husband and wife should have respect for each other; however, the greater respect should be for the husband and so if he is unfaithful, the wife should never try to emulate him, or turn to her boss for consolation. The latter is only interested in 'sex' and will never marry her *(op. cit.* March 1974).

This, then, is the kind of picture of male-female relationships that the magazines convey. How far does this situation as ideologically conceived correspond with the actual social reality? One important thing is that legally—at least in theory[16]—the wife's position is in some respects stronger than these magazines usually suggest. For example, statutory (Ordinance) marriage makes her free of her husband's lineage. It gives her the right to sue him on the grounds *inter alia* of adultery as well as the right to inherit property from him. Also, as already indicated, thanks to the urban-industrial economy there are increasing opportunities for women to earn their own living, especially if well-educated. Hospitals and schools, in particular, offer a relatively good salary and status and so these senior nurses and teachers as well as professional women have potentially within their grasp a by no means negligible sources of economic power. The same applies to women who develop a successful business.

---

[15]See also Bond, *op. cit.* pp. 226-7, in this connection.
[16]We say in "theory" for reasons described briefly in Little, 1976, and at length in Little, 1973, chapter 7. See also Harrell-Bond, *passim. et alii.*

An upshot of this is that whereas it was previously solely a male prerogative, there is now a tendency for women as well to postpone marrying.[17] Those who make this decision want first to be sufficiently established in their own right before facing the uncertainties described. Quite often, they have especially their own children's future in mind. This emerges very clearly from Dinan's numerous case-studies of the 'single' woman in Accra (n.d.) and the importance of this 'power' in marriage itself has been demonstrated cogently by Oppong. Her samples consisted of Ghanaian senior civil servants and their families, and Oppong discovered significant differences between the 'Power relationships' of couples in which the wife makes an economic contribution, on the one hand, and couples in which she makes a medium or high contribution on the other. It was not merely a question of the wife's influence increasing in wage-earning, but that joint financial provision was associated with joint decision-making. Little, too, has found that young educated Ghanaian women regard their training as an economic resource. It is something that in the view of many may be employed, if necessary, to help secure the kind of marital relationship they want. (1976, *op. cit.*). Data from the Ivory Coast provides further evidence of this sort of attitude (Little, n.d.).

Oppong's investigation was carried out among an elite section of Ghanaian society and that of Little involved the expectations of university girls. The norms governing behaviour among such groups are generally very 'modern' compared with those of the wider community. This consideration might therefore be an important factor irrespective of whether the wife contributes or not. On the other hand, among a particular high status group studied by Oppong it was the husband who made the main decisions. This occurred in the case of doctors whose wives also had a high level of education. What is significant, however, is that more of the latter were housewives alone than in the rest of Oppong's sample.

This is why it is necessary to look more closely at the educated wife's position. Its further examination is required because egalitarianism being a sign and a symbol of elite social behaviour, a man should not treat his wife *in public* as an inferior. If he does, he risks being spoken of as 'bush' and losing esteem. (Little, 1973, pp. 173-6). How he acts in private, however, is another matter. He may even beat his wife and perhaps use physical force in order to obtain his conjugal rights.[18] Also, a husband may accept his wife's financial contribution but fail to consider her point of view in return. If he thus reneges on the 'deal' to whom can the wife appeal?

This question arises because in the event of marital disharmony an educated woman may, paradoxically, be at a greater disadvantage than an illiterate one

---

[17]We refer here of course to statutory marriage. It is still the practice of many young men to take 'customary law' wives until such time as they are in a position to marry an educated woman. Incidentally, Dinan's data also show that the deliberate postponement of marriage described is not necessarily confined to the educated category of women with whom we are here mainly concerned.
[18]Here, as well as elsewhere, the parallelism with the wife's position in English Victorian society seems very close.

under 'rural' conditions. In the latter situation, a wife might be given the immediate support of relatives, women's associations, and even of co-wives. As a member of the 'new' type of nuclear family, however, she is in urban circumstances
much more isolated and so, less able to handle an unsatisfactory husband on her
own. This is made clear by the constant reminder that if she herself takes the
initiative and calls her husband out, she cannot necessarily expect other women's
sympathy. Her difficulty is the greater because 'nominally' she is her husband's
'partner'. It was she who chose him and opted, moreover, for the kind of marriage—in statutory terms—over which her own family have no direct control.[19] The
wife, in other words, requires a good deal more room to manoeuvre than the part
voluntarily cast for herself affords.

This is an additional reason why the matrimonial situation of literate women
is complicated. True, there are such marriages in which the joint enterprise of
making a home is spontaneously achieved to the satisfaction of both spouses. In
other such marriages a relatively harmonious and stable relationship is established
largely through the wife's economic strategy. The latter is probably facilitated by
a high level of education, but there are socially ambitious wives who in many
cases are only able to read and write.

How, then, given the above 'urban' situation, does the latter category of
person cope with the drawbacks? Often, she does well in trade, but how does she
obtain the 'modern' status desired—the personal satisfaction of being treated with
respect and consideration as well as the prestige of being referred to as "Mrs" or
"Madame"?

The answer, we suggest, may consist in supplementing the economic strategy
with an attitude of surrender. This additional tactic is needed to counteract the
stereotypes described above. These, as the following further example demonstrates, characterize as a special danger, women who are 'uppity':

> Generally, it has been observed that a woman becomes a lioness in any
> house where there is no other madam to put her back a bit. When a woman
> is made special by a man, she takes the prestige to a climax. She talks with
> such an authority as if the date has been fixed to end the world. She behaves
> abnormally without fear of contradiction, simply because she is one, and 'no
> other woman'. Worse still, she talks without respect to her mother-in-
> law.[20]

Such prejudices can be safely disregarded by women who already are judges,
top civil servants, successful barristers, doctors and the like. The great majority

---

[19]See Harell-Bond *passim* and Little, 1973, chapters 9 and 10 for an elaboration of this point.
[20]A male contributor to *Woman's World*, February 1974.
    Another male contributor to *Woman's World* (January 1976) wrote: 'A man finds his own
wife too intelligent to fault because she always proves she knows better...She bases their existence
as husband and wife "on theory not on practice" because she follows the legality of marriage to
the letter. She has failed to take "our peculiar situation, ethos and norms into consideration".
She is so much engulfed in a completely foreign culture.'
    Wipper (1971 and 1972) has described male stereotypes of 'uppity' women at some length, but
in an East African context.

of women, obviously are not, and the woman who lacks paper qualifications is particularly vulnerable to the charge of being brash and too clever by half. She cannot ignore this because in the last analysis this kind of individual's amour-propre often depends not so much on what actually goes between her and her husband as on public opinion's interpretation of it. The verdict is most likely to be favourable if instead of challenging him the wife apparently conforms with traditional norms and seems to be entirely mild, modest, and governable.

This may be done by *outwardly* accepting the husband's domination. It means that instead of seeking to reverse the traditional role the wife turns its symbols to her own use. In other words, rather than oppose the husband the wife should :

Let him order,
Let him command...
Bluff him...
Shut your mouth,
and be shy.

Never answer back.
Walk like a cat.
Let him not
Hear your footsteps.
He will feel honoured —
Respected and obeyed.

He will boast
Among her friends;
He is the head,
He is the spokesman,
You are under him,
He controls you......

(Likimani, 1974)[21]

This apparent submissiveness thus preserves the husband's public prestige. The advantage is that while making him in consequence more amenable, perhaps, to personal persuasion, it may also undermine his position in the event of a marital 'palaver' being put to the test of community opinion. For example, by no means all husbands are agreeable to their own wife working outside the house: they dislike, among other things, the idea of her being under another man's autho-rity. By taking a 'traditional' position, however, the wife can probably point to the customary right and even the obligation of a mother to provide for her own child. She is thus able to claim a 'legitimate' reason for what she wants to do. Also as already implied, some men who welcome a wife's contribution to household

---

[21]This poem *What Does a Man Want ?* provides, in addition to the above advice a general 'scenario' of the wife's situation. The author is a Kenyan but the East African context described is so similar in many respects to the West African one that one thinks it is legitimate to cite the above illustration.

expenses, object to her retaining the remainder of her earnings. A wife claiming 'equality' might find it difficult to contest this objection if the husband replied that 'equality' meant a complete sharing of common economic resources. He is on less firm ground if the wife not only accepts a subordinate status but the social distance between spouses that this usually involves.

Conclusion

This article has focussed both ideologically and sociologically on the use of tactics in matrimony among urban women, principally in Anglophone West Africa. The idea that women as well as men employ strategies is not new. A simple example is the dowry. Quite often women bring this to marriage in peasant societies, and it gives many of them an effective voice in domestic decisions. Also, divorce itself is sometimes employed. Among the Kanuri of Bornu, for instance, there is competition between co-wives for goods and services from the husband and each wife attempts to build a uterine family at the expense of her co-wives' children. Where influence over the husband fails, a wife may force a divorce through insubordination and return to her father's or brother's compound until remarriage. If subsequent marriages are equally unbearable, there is always the knowledge that her son or other male kinsmen will provide a place to live after her final divorce where she will have a fair amount of respect and influence. (Lamphere, 1974).

The context of the above situation is 'traditional'. Under modern urban conditions the position of the wife as we have explained, is much more equivocal. It is ambiguous because community ideas of women's role have not kept pace with other structural changes. True, this lack of institutionalisation exists in other sections of society as well. There is, for example, a conflict in norms when, for instance, a civil servant has to choose between his kinship obligations and his official responsibilities. The difference is that as individuals women are very much more on their own. A civil servant who decides to be nepotic will have at least his own family's support, but in the matrimonial situation, the notion of female solidarity has only limited validity. True, there is almost a consensus that wives are ill-used, and that women should in the common interest be loyal to each other in their dealings with men. What, however, the above data suggest is that except, perhaps, among close friends and relatives, the latter ideal is far from being realised in actual practice.[22] Rather is it the case that women, including wives themselves, do not always scruple at poaching on each other's preserves. Indeed, some of the women who complain most strongly of male infidelity are among those who mostly encourage it. (Dinan, n.d.). They do so because in this situation and in the matrimonial one generally, a good deal of women's behaviour has often of necessity to be opportunistic. It takes the form of what has been

[22]This observation has also been made in more general terms by Jane Kiano, who heads the influential women's organisation, *Maendeleo Ya Wanawake* in Kenya. Mrs. Kiano said — "Women are their own worst enemy. They try to undermine each other. They quarrel among themselves. They seem to be jealous of one another... Most of their problems are not problems, but lack of a united front" — in the Kenya women's magazine *Viva*.

called situational selection. This is an ability not only to move smoothly between one social system and another but to manipulate either system to one's own purposes. The wife's 'submissiveness' is an example of the deference deliberately shown by the latter's university trained 'bin-to'[23] sister to her elderly and illiterate in-laws when she wants their goodwill.[24]

This being the case it may be useful also, methodologically, to see the strategies described within a general context of adaptation. This means — in simple and popular terms — "playing things by ear". The predicament of the unmarried girl provides an illustration because competition for eligible husbands being keen, she has in addition to finding the one she wants, to divert his interest in other women to her. She will be prudent during the courtship to behave with propriety. This may not be difficult if he is emotionally responsive to her alone. If he is not the girl may feel it necessary to adapt to the situation in a different way. This may take the form of either permitting and even encouraging sexual intimacy, or of ostensibly finding other male attentions more attractive. There is a risk, especially if in the event of pregnancy the man is suspicious,[25] but in expediency it may be a matter of deciding between the three above tactics.

There are also various subtleties that the wife herself may practise if, for instance, an open display of economic power fails. Thus, as explained above, an upwardly mobile man often requires a wife with modern savoir-faire to back him. Her role is to impress the husband's senior colleagues and other potential patrons. Her company, thererefore at official receptions and elite social parties may from his point of view be almost essential. But what if the wife in popular parlance, goes on strike ? Since family ceremonies of her own have to be attended she has this extra card available if, in return for co-operation, she is not given the kind of *quid pro quo* she regards as reasonable.

Our specific conclusion, therefore, reiterates what has been stated in more general terms elsewhere (Little, 1976). It is that the question of African women's position in the 'new' urban society needs to be empirically approached. A prevalent idea is that in it only specially privileged and educationally equipped women stand to benefit individually from participation. Such women truly start with a considerable advantage; but in the light of the above discussion the corollary of this is less certain. This is the implication that although changes in women's position are processive,[26] the speed of such changes is contingent on male alterations of the social structure.

What we have tried to show, using 'matrimony' as a case-study is that the

---

[23]The term 'bin-to', although less common today, refers to a person who has travelled overseas and completed his or her education there, usually at a British university.

[24]For examples of situational selection in other sectors of African society, including politics, see Little (1955) and (1974) pp. 52-54.

[25]A frequent allegation among educated young men is that girls deliberately allow themselves to become pregnant in order to force marriage. See Ike's novel (1965) for a satirical comment on this situation.

[26]Using 'processive' in the sense that Mitchell (1966) distinguishes between change in the system as a whole and change in the situation of a given individual.

conventional approach to West African women's status is not sufficiently elastic. Not only do such women have their own goals, but their attitudes are pragmatic. Taking their antecedent difficulties for granted they employ various strategems and tactics to overcome them and to gain what they want. The result, in consequence, is that to the formal concept of role has to be added an extra dimension.

This, in turn, has significance for methodology. It makes it obligatory for the analyst to look beyond ordinary structuralist models. These may sometimes afford a conceptual framework for African society in general; but for the dynamism to be subsumed in women's contemporary role they are an inadequate guide.

REFERENCES

Dinan, Carmel
    n.d.   Unpublished manuscript. *A Study of the 'Single' Girl in a West African City.*

Fraenkel, Merran
    1964   *Tribe and Class in Monrovia.* London, Oxford University Press for International African Institute.

Harrell-Bond. B.E.
    1975   *Modern Marriage in Sierra Leone: A Study of the Professional Group.* Paris, Mouton.

Ike, Vincent Chukwuemeka
    1965   *Toads for Supper*, London, Harvill.

Lamphere, Louise
    1974   "Women in Domestic Groups in Rosaldo, Michele Zimbalist and Lamphere, Louise (eds.) *Woman, Culture and Society*, Stanford, Stanford University Press.

Likimani, Muthoni
    1974   *What Does a Man Want?* Nairobi, East African Literature Bureau.

Little, Kenneth
    1955   'Structural Change in the Sierra Leone Protectorate', *Africa*, 25.3.
    1966   "Attitudes toward marriage and the family among educated young Sierra Leoneans" in P.C. Lloyd (ed.) *New Elites of Tropical Africa*. London. Oxford University Press for International African Institute.
    1973   *African Women in Towns: An Aspect of Africa's Social Revolution.* Cambridge, Cambridge University Press.
    1974   *Urbanization as a Social Process: As Essay on Movement and Change in Contemporary Africa.* Routledge & Kegan Paul, London.
    1975   "Some Methodological Considerations in the Study of African Women's Urban Roles" in *Urban Anthropology*, Vol. 4, No. 2, Summer 1975. pp. 107-121.
    1976   "A Question of Matrimonial Strategy? A Comparison of Attitudes between Ghanaian and British University Students" in *Journal of Comparative Family Studies*, VII, 1 Spring, 1976.
    n.d.   'Some Ivorian School girls' Atttitudes to Marriage and Work.' Unpublished ms.

Mitchell, J. Clyde
    1966   'Theoretical Orientations in African Urban Studies', in M. Banton (ed.) *The Social Anthropology of Complex Societies*, London, Tavistock.

Omari, Peter
    1962   *Marriage Guidance for Young Ghanaians*, Edinburgh, Nelson.

Oppong, Christine
    1975   *Marriage Among a Matrilineal Elite.*   Cambridge, Cambridge University Press.

Riviere, Claude
    1968   "La promotion de la femme guinéene", in *Cahiers d' Etudes Africaines,* 8 (3).

Schwarz, Alf
    1972   Illusion d'une emancipation et alienation realle de l'ouvriere Zairoise' in *Canadian Journal of African Studies*, 6 (2).

Wipper, Audrey
    1971   'The Politics of Sex', in *African Studies Review*, 14, 3.

    1972   'African Women, fashion and scape-goating' in *Canadian Journal of African Studies,* 16. 2.

Notes on Official View with Regard to Mate Selection and Marital Happiness in Family in People's Republic of China

LUCY JEN HUANG*

For the past two decades information on marriage and the family in People's Republic of China had been relatively limited. This research note is based on official documents and Party propaganda via such mass media as editorials and reports from the Mainland China press and magazines. It is to be remembered that even if the articles or letters were written by readers, the selection of such documents may have been made by regime leaders to correspond with the official views of the government.

New Concept of Happiness

Editorials of a major bi-monthly magazine for Chinese Youth, *China Youth* (Chung-Kuo Ch'ing-nien) in the 1960's decided to guide young people concerning the vital philosophy of happiness in a socialist society (cf. Hu, 1963 a). A collection of articles proclaimed that the greatest happiness consisted not in material enjoyment, but in the service for others. The realization of Communism should be regarded as life's greatest happiness (cf. Hu, 1963 b) and not the pursuit of such bourgeois thoughts as dressing and eating well (cf. Li, 1963). To love comfort was to kill ambition (cf. Chu, 1963) and to pursue fame and expertise was dangerous (cf. Li, 1963). It was further stated that egoistic desire was insatiable (cf. Yao, 1963) and that the struggle for the happiness of man was in reality the struggle for the liberation of labor, of society and of mankind (cf. Wu, 1963). It was the struggle for building a new world where there would be no imperialism, capitalism or any exploitative system. However, Communism did not mean adequate food, clothing, footwear and living quarters for each person (cf. Wei, 1963). Chinese youth were warned that indulging in material pleasure would destroy one's fighting spirit (cf. Hsu, 1963). " Can there be in the world any greater happiness than the dedication of one's all to our noble ideal of thoroughly liberating mankind—the communist cause ?" the readers were asked (cf. Hsing, 1963). It was reported that 10,000 letters were received by *China Youth* editors from April to July 1963 participating in the discussion of the new concept of happiness. The concensus of opinions was consistent with the teachings of Chairman Mao that there was infinite joy in struggling against Heaven ; struggling against Earth ; and struggling against

---

*Associate Professor, Dept. of Sociology, Illinois State University, U. S. A.

man. The above sentiment provided an incisive discourse on the proletariat conception of happiness (cf. Kao, 1965 b). The "survival philosophy" in which one would live only for fame, position, money, marriage and child-birth was severely criticized as too pitiful, selfish and ugly, for happiness of the people was considered true happiness (cf. Shen, 1967).

To sum up the above discussion of communist conception of happiness, it is based on spiritual rather than material enjoyment; it is based on public rather than private interest; it is based on collective welfare rather than individual happiness, and it champions service for the people and the revolution over the cause of self-actualization and the welfare of one's own family.

Changing Values in Mate Selection and Age for Marriage

In the selection of one's mate, the leaders often directed the youth of Mainland China to avoid bourgeois values and to uphold socialistic enthusiasm. An ideal bridegroom, according to commune members, was like Wang Liu-yun of the production team, a hero to be cherished by all eligible girls. "He is always working, now with a hoe and now with a plane, and he is ready to help others...every time an election is held for 'five-good' commune members, he is sure to be elected. Many girls have on their own initiative offered to marry him." (See Young Communist League *China Youth Daily*, 1962a). One girl gave three conditions if she were to pick a husband: (1) that he has good thought; (2) that he labors actively; and (3) that he loves the collective body. (See Young Communist League *China Youth Daily*, 1962 b).

In order to illustrate the importance of selecting a mate with political enthusiasm in socialism, regime leaders often published novels and plays to warn against bourgeois ideology and selfish sentiment. A typical bourgeois way of life was described as when one thinks he "should be with the loved one, arm-in-arm and shoulder-to-shoulder, either in the park and street, or in the cinema house, ballroom and restaurant, billing and cooing and talking about love." (cf. Chang, 1964 a) When one girl selected the wealthier and more attentive suitor of the two who showered her with gifts and dinners, the leaders of her organization began to hold conferences with her, advising her to adopt a "correct attitude toward the question of love and marriage" and urging her "to give first place to politics when choosing a husband" (cf. Kung, 1964).

Since the early years of the communist regime, young people have been criticized for marrying as soon as they reached legal age, 18 for women and 20 for men (cf. Yang, 1959 a). Party leaders observed that young people had taken this law seriously. Some of them got married before they left school in order to be assigned to the same location for work assignments later. Prolific couples often found themselves unable to cope with problems in housekeeping, child care, marital adjustment and full time participation in labour. According to *Women of China*, "Early marriage seriously affects their (young people's) health and progress...The girls, 19 or 20 years of age, are already with children, and many have more than two when they are 24 or 25 years of age, bearing three children every four years as a rule." (*Women of China*, 1957: 14–15).

A campaign against early marriage was launched by China Youth Daily in 1962 inviting readers to discuss the disadvantages of early marriage and to present cases of unhappy marriages. (Editorial, *China Youth Daily*, 1962) (cf. Liu, 1962) (cf. Hsu, 1962) (cf. Hsia, 1962). According to the Dean of the Department of Health of Peking Medical College, due to physiological and intellectual maturity, the best age for a girl to get married is between 23 to 27, and for a man is between 25 to 29. Dr. Lin Chiao-jih, a woman physician, stated that from the standpoint of obstetrics and gynecology, the best marriage age for girls is around 25. (cf. Lin, 1957). A shining example was one Miss Hao, a teacher who persisted in studying culture and political theories and got married at the age of 27. She was said to be good at her work, her studies, enjoying good health and taking good care of her child. (See A Letter from a Reader, Peking *Jen-min Jih-pao*, 1962 *People's Daily*). According to a Washington HTNS report (see The Telegraph, 1964) the Chinese People's Republic was said to be forbidding marriage of men under 30 and women under 25, and punishing those who disobey by refusing to legitimize their children, thus denying state food rations to the infants. The third children were considered "superfluous" and any above that number were political "errors." Heroines such as Wang and Wan were written up on the pages of *Women of China* for rejecting proposals and delaying marriages several times until they were in their late twenties due to their devotion to their work and study. (cf. Salisbury, 1967: 166).

Relative to mate selection and marriage, regime leaders launched a strong drive toward simple and frugal weddings. The traditional Chinese cultural patterns of elaborate ceremonies and expensive feasts continued to emerge in the early years of the communist regime much to the alarm of Chinese officials on the Mainland. (cf. Li, 1962 a). Debates via the pages of China Youth were carried on to encourage young people not to be extravagant, lest the bride might be dressed in silk but eat loaves made of chaff. (cf. Kuang, 1962). It was reported that the girl's family often demanded bridal gifts and dowry such as "a bicycle, a sewing machine, a big leather chest, a guilt with silk surfaces, etc." before marriage. (Young Communist League *China Youth Daily*, 1962). Betrothal presents in cash, cloth and meat were often requested by the bride's parents as in the pre-Communist days. (cf. Shih and Shih, 1964). However, progressive parents of the new era have been lauded for "not asking for a cent" when marrying off a daughter. (cf. Chang, 1966). Other exemplary parents were those who gave their daughter "a hoe, a sickle, a pick and a rake" as wedding presents. ("New Ways of Handling New Things," *China Youth Daily*, 1962). A progressive bride was the girl who asked for three items for her dowry, "a rifle, a nightsoil pail, and a copy of Chairman Mao's Quotations." (cf. Taylor, 1966 : 97).

New Accent on Marital Happiness

One of the relatively effective means in the remoulding of marital relationships in Mainland China was the legislation of new marriage laws. (C. K. Yang, The Chinese Family in the Communist Revolution, 1959 b). The status of both women and children has been promoted to a large extent under the new regime. Fictional literature in the 1950's contributed much in the shaping of new attitudes regarding family bliss and marital happiness. In a story called "The New Home" the wife was gradually indoctrinated not to resent the husband's long hours in his factory work. (cf. Ai, 1953: b).

In "The Wife," (cf. Ai, 1957) a worried wife was convinced finally that the only way to recapture her husband's affection was by studying hard and helping her husband in his work instead of worrying about her own appearance. It was shown that a husband no longer was impressed with the traditional role of a wife and mother but instead, the new role of a productive worker and a committee woman. (cf. Ju, 1959). It is when the wife is able to share her husband's dedication to the Socialist cause that marital happiness can be secured. The ideal wives in the literature are "always public-minded, they are above the temptation of lust, greed, and self-destruction and superior to sadistic and masochistic schemes for unashamed and selfish happiness." (cf. Hsia, 1963 : 174). Political compatibility and service to the people instead of individualistic interest are highly recommended by regime leaders via various means of mass communication media. The wife of a pastor reported that her husband and her two teenage children had been so busy studying and working at different shifts that they rarely saw one another at home at the same time, so they left notes for one another to report what they were doing. "This has become the most convenient way of family communication in the Great Leap Forward. How delightful our family life is !" (See as recorded in *China Bulletin,* 1960).

During the 1950's, official views on marriage and the family were spread on pages of Mainland press and magazines. Fears and doubts were expressed by readers concerning the breaking up of the family, especially after the establishment of the commune system. An editorial (See Editorial, *Women of China,* 1958 : 27-28, 32) was duly published to ease the anxiety of concerned readers. Organized household chores, mass dining halls and nurseries should not be considered threats to the family, they said, as the family life of city dwellers had long been socialized. Such new devices were to help mothers better serve Socialism and achieve greater sexual equality. Many women, unfortunately, had to go through a political struggle and a new awakening before they could achieve the approved concept of marital happiness. Separating from her husband a week at a time due to work assignments in different locations, the wife of a school teacher stated,

> In the midst of production I would reminisce walking down the street with my husband. I was intoxicated in my sweet married life. I often argued for time to be with (my husband) him. When I went to work Mondays I would wish it were Sunday again. Six days' parting was too long for me. I gradually felt that my work was standing in the way of my happiness. (See *Women of China,* 1960a : 23).

Much to her surprise she found that resigning from her work to stay at home as a full time wife did not bring her happiness. Instead, her husband began to look down on her for her "backwardness." She became bored, grouchy and envious of her colleagues in the factory. Her marital happiness was complete when her organization supervisor granted her request to return to work. She put her children in the nursery, seeing them once a week, finding them "grown more in body and intelligence" each time. Her husband no longer quarrelled with her. "We live peacefully, we work together, we progress together and encourage each other. Our love grows deeper....I would never be able to get such happiness if I locked myself in my small family," she concluded.

The election of national heroes and heroines in early 1960's further encouraged young married couples to place group welfare and contribution to the state above that of personal and family happiness The image of such a heroine is seldom short of superhuman, performing Herculean tasks and endowed with saintlike characteristics. A mother of seven children was said to be so interested in her work that she forgot food and sleep, increasing her production rate of electric fan buttons up to ten times her previous rate. " On Sundays and holidays, after taking care of her seven children, she would visit twelve comrades. Under her persuasion the production of her small group continued to progress." (See *Women of China*, 1960b : 22). Another mother of five children admitted that she had never been absent from work in five years. Another heroine stated that she and her husband never allowed their five children to affect their work. " We do not think family happiness is a matter of eating well and dressing well." (See *Women of China*, 1960c : 27–28). The general theme of marital happiness was eloquently summed up by the editors of *Women of China* when they stated that one ought to put the career of revolution first and individual family matters second. " We must be concerned with the warmth of our people's large family. We must be concerned with the warmth of the whole world's people's family." (See *Women of China*, 1960d : 29, 31).

In the new definition of marital happiness, the emphasis on public service rather than personal interest further led Mainland Chinese wives to enjoy sexual equality and freedom never before experienced by women in the Chinese history. As early as 1961 a report showed that there were 10,000 women doctors in Peking, about 40 per cent of the city's total. (cf. Johnson, 1961 : 351). The newly emancipated woman was vividly reflected in the attitude of a girl interpreter of a visiting western writer in China. After learning that she was able to accompany him on a three day trip, the author apologized for taking her away from her family. Her comment was that " her duty to me came first. Besides her mother-in-law would take care of the children. And as for the cooking and housework, her husband always did that anyway." (cf. Taylor, 1966b : 92).

One of the most important ingredients the regime encourages in the ideal spousal relationship is that of political compatibility. The vastly changing roles of marital partners can be attributed to the relatively successful indoctrination and propaganda of the government concerning the importance of joint enthusiasm in political ideology and activities. Spouses may me incompatible in their occupational status, socio-economic standing, educational achievement and other background characteristics, but as long as they are both politically enthusiastic, they are considered ideal in their marital union. (cf. Huang, 1962). According to editors, " The husband and the wife must impose exacting demands on themselves with respect to political ideology, and not until they have first of all overcome their own shortcomings can they reduce the distance between them." (cf. Shih, 1964b). The confession of a grateful wife describing her marital happiness in spite of her inability to bear children after her cancer operation is a case in point. " As our love is built on the foundation of common struggle for the revolutionary cause, we are not only husband and wife but also comrades-in-arms. Therefore, when I experienced misfortune on the road of livelihood, his love for me was never shaken." (cf. Hai, 1964). In general, however, it is the sentiment of regime leaders that compared with revolutionary work, marriage and love is really a

" small matter."   An ambitious young man, according to Party officials, must have a supreme purpose of life, concentrating his principal energy in work, study, progress and in socialist undertakings and putting marriage and love in a minor position of his whole life.   Only this kind of life is meaningful and can be forever stimulating and actively progressing.   (cf. Yang, 1962). According to communist morality, a husband and wife love each other, help and take care of each other, and seek improvement together.   Marital happiness does not rest upon physical beauty but political equality.   It is only the beauty of political equality, sentiments, thinking and acting which represent the true everlasting beauty.   Love that is built on this basis will forever bloom.   Marital happiness based on communist morality advocates egalitarianism in dealing with every phase of married life.   The wife is no longer considered a " slave " or duty-bound to do all the housework.   As long as the husband treats her as a revolutionary comrade as well as a life-companion, joint responsibility and shared obligation in household chores as well as other areas of life will produce great happiness.   Whether a couple can live happily or not does not rest on who obeys whom, or who waits on whom, or who does a bigger share of household work, "but it rests on whether they will understand each other, care for each other and help each other from the revolutionary point of view." (See Editorial, *Women of China*, 1964).

The official view of the People's Republic of China on mate selection and marital happiness can be illustrated by the marriage of Wei Feng-ying and Lu Chi-chong.   They fit well the ideal socialist version of what a progressive family ought to be.   They met in the meeting of delegates for progressive producers of the city group.   Wei had been so involved in her factory work that she often forgot her date with Lu.   Instead of being angry, Lu thought to himself, "Feng-Ying had been so busy and faithful with the matters of the Party that she even forgot me, isn't she lovable ? " (cf. Mei-Mei, 1958 : 20-21).   Both of them had been so busy that they had not seen one another for a long time, for every thing they did was for socialism.   Love should not interfere with work, study and association with the people.   Due to their work responsibility they had postponed their marriage until both of them were twenty-six yeard old.   After marriage, they wished to have more time to study, so they arranged to eat at the mass dining hall.   On Sundays both fought to do household chores. They continued to support their aged parents. As they wished to have two children, they practised birth control so they could devote more time to work for socialism.   "Due to her work with her successful experimenting of new equipments and techniques, Feng-Ying was said to have increased production rate from 800 to 12,000.   In four months she completed five years' work."

Summary

From the above citations of Chinese press and magazines one finds a dramatic change in officially prescribed values and attitudes with regard to mate selection and marital relationships.   What constitutes happiness in marriage and the family has taken a drastic turn from the familial to the collective, from the private to the public, and from the self-centered to the state-centered.   The long history of the consanguineal Chinese family may have facilitated a relatively easier transition than would be possible in a society characterized by nuclear families.   The Communist regime in the People's

Republic of China, capitalizing on the group-centered culture of the past, may not have found too strong a resistance among the masses against broadening the family loyalty to that of patriotism and devotion to the "larger family of revolution", i. e. the state. It is to be hoped that in the future, when there is a possibility of exchanging scholars and researchers between the United States and the People's Republic of China, we may be able to compare the official views on marriage and the family documented above with the actual behavior patterns, values and attitudes of the masses.

REFERENCES

Ai Ming-chih
    1957. "The Wife," *Literary Monthly* (February)

Ai Wu
    1953. "The New Home," *People's Literature* (October) p. 6.

Chang Chi
    1966. "Doing Away with Betrothal Money," *China Youth Daily*, No. 2 (January 16)

Chang Ta-peng
    1964a. "Uphold the Revolutionary Philosophy of Life When Looking at the Question of Love and Marriage," *Women of China*, No. 5 (May 1)

China Bulletin
    1960. Vol. X, No. 10 (May 9)

Chu Yun-shu
    1963. "Love for Comfort is Sure to Kill Ambition," *China Youth*, Nos. 10-11 (May 18)

Editorial
    1964. "What Attitude a Husband Should Take Toward His Wife," *Women of China*, No. 10 (October 1)

Editorial
    1962. "Campaign Against Early Marriages," *Peking China Youth Daily*, (May 10)

Editorial
    1958. "With Reference to the Family," *Women of China*, No. 18, (December) pp. 27-28, 32

Hai Ch'ao
    1964. "Those Who Love Their Work and Study Are Not Fools," *Women of China*, No. 7 (July 1)

Hsia, C. T.
    1963. "Residual Feminity: Women in Chinese Communist Fiction," *The China Quarterly*, No. 13 (January-March) p. 174.

Hsia Yen
    1962. "Handle the Marriage Problem From Long-Range Consideration," *Peking China Youth Daily*, (May 10)

Hsing Yen-tzu
    1963. "My Happiness Knows No Bounds," *China Youth*, Nos. 14-15 (July 28)

Hsu Hsueh-hui
    1963. "The Greatest Happiness Lies in Serving the People Whole-Heartedly," *China Youth*, Nos. 14-15 (July 28)

Hsu Shang-hsi
    1962. "I Do Not Want Early Marriage," *Peking China Youth Daily* (May 10)

Hu Tung-yuan
    1963a. "How Should Young People Approach the Question of Happiness?" *China Youth*, No. 7 (April 1)

Hu Tung-yuan
    1963b. *Ibid.*

Huang, Lucy Jen
    1962. " Communist Chinese Attitude Toward Inter-Class Marriage," *The China Quarterly* (October-December)

Johnson, Hewlett
    1961. The Upsurge of China, Peking, *New World Press*, p. 351.

Ju Cih-Chuan
    1959. " The Warmth of Spring," *People's Literature* (October)

Kao Tze-hung
    1965b. " Proletarian Conception of Happiness is Struggle for Revolution," *China Youth*, No. 4 (February 16)

Kuang Hai
    1962. " Thrifty Weddings Are Good," *Peking China Youth Daily* (February 22)

Kung Kuei-hua
    1964. " Give First Place to Political Conditions," *Women of China*, No. 5 (May 1)

A Letter From a Reader
    1962. " Early Marriage Hinders My Work and Study," *Peking Jen-min Jih-pao* (April 4)

Li Chih-wen
    1963. " One Must Lead a Noble Spiritual Life," *China Youth*, Nos. 10-11 (May 18)

Li Ho
    1963. " Pursuit of Fame or the Name 'Expert' is Dangerous," *China Youth*, Nos. 10-11 (May 18)

Li Pu-ch'en
    1962a. " The Debate on Wedding Feasts," *Southern Daily of Canton* (April 6)

Lin Chiao-jih
    1957. " The Best Marriageable Age from the Physiological Standpoint," *Women of China*, No. 4 (April)

Liu Fa
    1962. " The Pain Brought By Early Marriage," *Peking China Youth Daily* (May 10)

Mei-mei
    1958. " The Happy Home of a Couple of Progressive Producers," *Women of China*, No 8 (July 16) pp. 20-21.

" New Ways of Handling New Things "
    1962. *Peking China Youth Daily* (April 24)

Salisbury, Harrison E.
    1967. *Orbit of China*, New York, Harper and Row, p. 166

Shen Yu-ying
    1967. " Thoughts on Creative Study and Application of Chairman Mao's Works in Struggle, Ten Questions Raised and Answered," *Rural Youth*, No. 13 (July 10)

Shih-Mei-mei
    1964b. " What Are the Criteria for Choosing a Husband," *Women of China*, No. 7 (July 1)

Shih Yen and Shih Feng
    1964. " Is Betrothal Present a Means of Showing Gratitude for Parental Upbringing ? " Canton, *The Southern Daily* (December 25)

Taylor, Charles
    1966a. *Reporter in Red China*, New York, Random House, p. 97

Taylor, Charles
    1966b. *Reporter in Red China*, New York, Random House, p. 92

The Telegraph
   1964. Painesville, Ohio (Wednesday, March 4)

Wei Wei
   1963. "The Flower of Happiness Blooms for the Valiant," *China Youth*, Nos. 20-21
   (October 20)

Women of China
   1957. (March) pp. 14-15

Women of China
   1960a. No. 10 (May) p. 23

Women of China
   1960b. No. 10 (May) p. 22

Women of China
   1960c. (June) pp. 27-28

Women of China
   1960d. (September) pp. 29, 31

Wu Ch'iang
   1963. "What Kind of A Conception of Happiness Should the Youth Have?" *China
   Youth*, No. 18 (September 16)

Yang, C. K.
   1959a. *The Chinese Family in the Communist Revolution*, the Technology Press, p. 221.

Yang, C. K.
   1959b. *The Chinese Family in the Communist Revolution*. The Marriage Law of the People's
   Republic of China, Promulgated by the Central People's Government on May 1,
   1950, Cambridge, The Technology Press, Appendix.

Yang Hsiu
   1962. "Adopt a Careful Attitude Toward Your Matrimonial Question," *China Youth*,
   Nos. 15-16 (September 14)

Yao Po-ch'u
   1963. "Egoistic Desire is Insatiable," *China Youth*, Nos. 10-11 (May 18)

Yeh Kung-shao
   1962. "What is the Most Suitable Age for Marriage?" *China Youth Daily* (April 12)

Young Communist League, *China Youth Daily*
   1962a. "The Correct Approach to One's Own Marriage," Peking (April 24)

Young Communist League, *China Youth Daily*
   1962b. *Ibid.*

Marriage Ceremonies:
An Exploratory Cross-Cultural Study*

PAUL C. ROSENBLATT** AND DAVID UNANGST***

Around the world, marriage ceremonies are common for first marriages. In a random sample of 50 cases from a universe of representative, well described societies, the 200 'best described' societies in each of the 200 clusters of societies in Murdock's 'World Sampling Provinces' (1968), 38 of the 44 societies (86%) that could be evaluated reliably were judged to have ceremonies for typical first marriages. For activities centered on a marriage to be considered ceremony, they had to involve publicity, routinized procedures, and recognition of a change of marital status or of a forthcoming change in marital status. In some cases the principle or only marriage ceremony might properly be called a betrothal ceremony, and in two cases marriage ceremonies were explicitly combined with adolescent initiation. The typical marriage ceremonies of a society might be multiple, and they might not coincide with the onset of sexual intercourse or legal sexual intercourse or coresidence of man and woman.

Ratings of marriage ceremonies were made independently by two raters who worked with extracts of standard ethnographic sources. The most valuable sources are listed in a Supplementary Reference list appended to this article. Forty-four of the 50 societies were jointly classified by the raters into one of four categories of marriage ceremony — marriage ceremonies absent, marriage ceremonies present but minimal, marriage ceremonies present and substantial or very elaborate in attendance and expenditure of wealth, and marriage ceremonies present. Into the last of the four categories fell 11 cases for which the raters agreed that ceremonies were present but not ratable in terms of degree of elaboration and eight cases for which both raters thought ceremonies were present but for which only one rater thought degree of elaboration was ratable. Of the six societies that had to be dropped, three were judged unratable by one or both raters (Crow, Iban, and Arusi - Galla); for one no relevant information could be found (Cocama), and two were dropped because the raters did not agree on whether ceremonies were present (Majuro Marshallese and modern Papago). Hence, for the 44 societies rated by both raters there was precise agreement on categorization for 36 cases and agreement on presence of ceremonies in eight more.

---

*   This research was supported in part by the University of Minnesota Agricultural Experiment Station. Ratings of marriage ceremonies were made by Elizabeth A. Syme and Paul C. Rosenblatt. Elizabeth L. Skoogberg provided bibliographic assistance.

**   Professor, Family Social Science, University of Minnesota, St. Paul, Minnesota, U.S.A.

***   1374 W. 37th, San Pedro, California, U.S.A.

The presence of marriage ceremonies for first marriages in 38 of 44 societies that could be reliably rated is interesting. This suggests that ceremonies at first marriages serve valuable but not universally necessary functions. Undoubtedly marriage ceremonies serve to promote and certify status and role transitions, but in what follows in this paper it is argued that an important amount of the variance in presence of and elaboration of marriage ceremonies is attributable to the role of marriage ceremonies in facilitating and protecting wealth and alliance stakes in a marriage.

It has been suggested that sex norms for betrothed persons are used to protect marital arrangements that have substantial wealth and alliance implications (Rosenblatt, Fugita and McDowell, 1969). Marriage ceremonies, with attendant formal agreements, publicity, and symbols of relationship also seem more useful, and hence more likely to be used, where marriage has important implications for property and alliances. We assume, with Goody (1970), that the value of marriage prestations is correlated with the degree to which rights over persons are transferred as a concomitant of marriage, and we assume also that the importance of alliances is associated with magnitude of prestations. Consequently, we use magnitude of prestations as an imperfect but serviceable indicator of the stakes in a marriage. We hypothesize that where marriage is responsible for large dowry or bridewealth or gift transfers, or where marriage has implications for rights to substantial land or livestock, ceremonies will be more likely to be present and more likely to be relatively elaborate. Goody (1969) has suggested such a relationship but provides no theoretical rationale. It seems to us more useful in cases of substantial wealth transfer that members of the various kin groups involved know of the marriage and associated prestations, agreements, and expectations, accept them and are committed to them. For protecting interests the primary value of ceremonies may lie in their publicity and in the effort required to carry them out.

One value of publicity is that public commitments are likely to be stronger and more enduring than private commitments (Brehm and Cohen, 1962:8; Kiesler, 1971:33). To back down on a commitment that many people know one made is relatively difficult. Furthermore, disputes about agreements and transactions may be more easily resolved if these agreements and transactions have had numerous witnesses. Hence, to protect relations and agreements based on a marriage it is useful to publicize agreements and transactions through public ceremony, and it is more useful the more important are the financial dealings, the alliances, and the relationship changes promoted by a marriage.

In theory, effort can also promote commitment to relationships and to agreements (Brehm and Cohen, 1962:29 ff.; Kiesler, 1971:171 - 172). The more effort people have exerted toward some end the more unwilling they can be expected to be to back down from their commitment to that end. Hence, the effort involved in preparation, engaging in complicated and difficult or tedious ceremonial activity, and expending large amounts of wealth on such things as feasting, musicians, and gifts for an elaborate ceremony can be seen as committing people more to the financial, property, alliance, and other stakes hinging on the marriage relationship. Such effortful commitment would be of more use where there are relatively great stakes riding on the marriage. This is because when stakes are great, some people have a lot to lose or gain, more people may be affected by commitments, and the likelihood is higher that reneging on agreements will produce substantial anger and aggression.

The argument we are making in this paper is that ceremonies make it less likely that problems will arise over inheritance and wealth transfer agreements. However, whether marital stability is necessary to protect wealth interests is more problematic. A crucial variable that may promote marriage stability may be uncorrelated or even negatively correlated with elaborateness of marriage ceremonies; it is degree of volition of the couple being married. A commitment that is coerced may really be no commitment at all (Brehm and Cohen, 1962:206 ff.). Thus, whether an elaborate ceremony stabilizes marriages may not be knowable without data on the degree to which crucial people, particularly the man and woman being married, are voluntarily committed to the marriage. Volitional factors affecting the commitment of the couple being married include both their volition in deciding to marry and their volition in deciding to marry the particular person being married. If running away from an undesirable marriage is an option and is not chosen, their volition would be greater. Performing ceremonial acts indicating acceptance of a relationship, even if these acts are relatively coerced, may be committing. At any rate, the kinsmen of a couple being married may become committed to a financial arrangement or an alliance without the integrity of that commitment being dependent on the persistence of a particular marital relationship. Of course, their commitment may lead them to work to stabilize a linking marriage, but it need not for their wealth and power interests to be protected.

The magnitude of wealth transferred as a concomitant of marriage can be evaluated using the Ethnographic Atlas of the journal *Ethnology,* which has rated for all the societies in our sample the amount of wealth involved as a concomitant of marriage. Although a measure of wealth expenditure relative to means might be more sensitive, the absolute ratings of the Atlas still seem useful. With these ratings we can compare societies that lack wealth transfers or have transfer of minimal value with those that have substantial bride-wealth, dowry, or gift exchange.

Table 1 presents the tabulation of the data. The letters following the names of the societies refer to Ethnographic Atlas ratings of 'mode of marriage', most of which are translatable into wealth transfer terms. In the Atlas *(Ethnology,* 1962: 115-116),

> B refers to "Bride-price or bride-wealth, i.e., transfer of a substantial consideration in the form of livestock, goods, or money from the groom or his relatives to the kinsmen of the bride".
>
> D refers to "Dowry, i.e., transfer of a substantial amount of property from the bride's relatives to the bride, the groom, or the kinsmen of the latter".
>
> G refers to "Gift exchange, i.e., reciprocal exchange of gifts of substantial value . . . or a continuing exchange of goods and services . . ."
>
> O refers to "Absence of any significant consideration, or bridal gifts only".

S refers to "Bride-service, i.e., a substantial material consideration in which the principal element consists of labor or other services rendered by the groom . . ."

T refers to "Token bride-price . . ."

An additional category, "X Exchange, i.e., transfer of a sister or other female relative of the groom in exchange for the bride", did not seem translatable into wealth transfer terms. Excluding that category eliminates one of the 44 societies from the sample for the analysis summarized in Table 1, the Tiv.

TABLE 1.   MARRIAGE CEREMONIES AND MAGNITUDE OF
                             WEALTH TRANSFERRED

		Marriage Ceremonies		
	Absent	Minimal	Present	Substantial
Substantial Bridewealth, Dowry or Gift Exchange			Ashanti B	Burmese D
			Bamileke B	Egyptians of Silwa B
			Barabra B	
			Cambodians B	Fang B
(B, D, or G)			Lau Fijians G	Fulani B
			Lesu B	Ganda B
			Maori G	Herero B
			Otoro B	Khalka Bd[1]
			Riffians B	Maria Gond B
			Rural Irish D	Turks B
Minimal or No Wealth Transfer	Bohogue Shoshoni S	Creek T	Ancient Babylon Td[1]	Javanese T
		Huichol O		Koreans O
	Chippewa O	Nicobarese O	Cagaba S	Spaniards O
	Kaska S	Seneca Iroquois O	Haitians O	Zapotec O
(O, T, or S)	Siriono O		Jivaro S	
	Yabarana S	Trukese O	Katab T	
	Zuni O		Ontong Javanese O	
			Pawnee O	
			Siamese T	
			Timbira S	

[1]Lower-case letters following a capital indicate alternative modes of marriage or supplementary practices.

In Table 1 we classified societies rated B, D, and G together as societies with large amounts of wealth transferred as a concomitant of marriage and societies rated O, S, and T as societies with minimal or no wealth transferred. A word about why societies with bride-service are classified in the category of minimal wealth transfer might be in order. The labor of one man seems to us to be insubstantial if the man is young and his labor was not previously very important to his kin group or if the man's kin group is large. Moreover, bride-service may in many cases function more as a trial marriage than as a payment; thus, for the people of the society, it may not be as salient that something like a payment is going on. Even with societies classified as S in Table 1 removed, the basic statistical relationship between wealth transfer and ceremonial elaborateness remains.

In Table 1 magnitude of wealth transfer is associated with presence of and degree of elaboration of marriage ceremonies. By Fisher's exact probability test each of the following cuts of the data in that table produces an association that could occur by chance fewer than five times in 100: no ceremony versus all three presence categories combined, no ceremony versus the two categories of cases ratable on degree of elaboration, no and minimal ceremonies versus substantial ceremonies.

The data appear to indicate that where wealth transfer as a concomitant of marriage is substantial, ceremonies are more likely to be present. However, there are several alternative interpretations of the data which deserve attention. One is that the association is a mere artifact of random cultural diffusion. All the societies in the ceremonies - absent category are from the Americas, as are three of the five in the minimal - ceremonies category. Only six of the other 32 societies are from the Americas (and all fall in the minimal or no wealth transfer category). It could be argued that the data merely represent joint, accidental diffusion of two culture traits. However, we believe that if culture traits diffuse jointly and are retained jointly there is a substantial likelihood of functional links between them. That is, we think it unlikely that a culture would adopt or long retain ceremony that was not functionally linked to other aspects of the culture. Non-random patches of associations between culture traits can thus be seen primarily as a result of non-random patches of cultural ecologies that place certain functional demands on a society. Nonetheless, the functional argument deserves further test with data that help to evaluate the role of random, non-functional cultural diffusion.

A second alternative interpretation of the association in Table 1 argues that it is not possible to transfer substantial wealth without some ceremony, especially if anything has to be carried and given. From this viewpoint, publicity, formality, and the involvement of substantial numbers of people might result from a need to have many people participating in wealth transfer acts. However, even if carrying and giving coerce some formality and some amount of attendance, these then function to validate the transactions and to help bind the participants. Furthermore, wealth transfers are often spread over a long time span, longer than seems necessary merely to transfer some wealth, and in many instances ceremonies clearly involve a great deal more than a mere act of transfer.

Large wealth transfer commonly requires many kinsmen to contribute or to do without some resources. A large scale ceremony may be useful in these cases to certify obligations to these consanguineal kin and to reward their assistance with feasting, alcohol, dancing or other ceremonial benefits. From this it might be argued that marriage ceremonies have more to do with the operations of consanguineal kingroups than with the building of affinal relations. Although we have no reason to reject the assertion that marriage ceremonies serve functions for consanguineal kin groups, again we argue that these ceremonies serve to validate transactions involving groups being united by marriage and serve to bind the prospective affinals. If the primary function of marriage ceremonies was to promote relations within consanguineal groups, we believe that ceremonies would then not bring together large numbers of people from the two groups being united by marriage. Although there are instances where there is marked inequality in attendance by people from the kin groups being united, we think those instances are in the minority.

A final possibility is that the wealth transfer ratings from the Atlas are contaminated by considerations of ceremonial elaboration or that the elaboration ratings are contaminated by considerations of wealth transfer. Perhaps when attendance is heavy it seems as though wealth transfer is great simply because it takes a lot of wealth to feed the attendants. Perhaps when wealth transfer is great it is possible to mistake the mere act of transfer for elaborate ceremony. With these and the other alternative interpretations of Table 1, it seems important to probe the role of ceremonies as certifiers and protectors of wealth arrangements from a different angle.

An alternative attack on the question of the role of marriage ceremonies in the protection of stakes to wealth and power is to consider the amount of wealth to which marriage may establish rights. An imperfect but not invalid indicator of such wealth is the degree to which the people of a society rely on agricultural and herding activities (as opposed to hunting, gathering, and fishing) for subsistence. Where land and herds are important, one would expect in general that there is more wealth to transmit as a result of agreements surrounding a marriage and more concern with legitimacy of offspring and with intergroup agreement about inheritance rights for the future offspring of a marriage. In Goody's (1970) list of important rights which may be acquired through marriage, these rights seem to us the ones whose importance is most likely to covary with the importance of inheritable property in a society.

The Ethnographic Atlas of *Ethnology* rates the importance of five types of subsistence activities. For each society a total of 10 units is distributed among the five types of activity. A subsistence activity rated 10 would provide almost all or all of subsistence. An activity rated 0 would provide no subsistence. We compared the importance of herding and agriculture for societies differing in presence of and elaboration of marriage ceremonies. We assume that the higher the sum of scores on herding and agricultural activities, the more likely rights to wealth, property and derivative power are to be important to a people. Table 2 presents the tabulation of the data. The mean importance of herding and agricultural activities is lowest for societies that lack ceremonies and highest for societies that have substantial ceremonies. Comparing the three categories of ceremonies absent, ceremonies minimal, and ceremonies substantial the pattern of results is statistically significant (F = 22.03 with 2 and 22 degrees of freedom, p. < .001, est. ν^2 = .63). Thus, it appears that ceremonies are associated with the importance of rights to property.

TABLE 2.   ELABORATION OF MARRIAGE CEREMONIES AND IMPORTANCE
OF HERDING AND AGRICULTURE

No Ceremonies	Minimal Ceremonies	Ceremonies Present	Elaborate Ceremonies
Zuni 8	Huichol 6	Cagaba 10	Fulani 10
Yabarana 4	Nicobarese 6	Bamileke 9	Spaniards 10
Chippewa 2	Tiv 6	Barabra 9	Egyptians of Silwa 9
Siriono 1	Trukese 5	Haitians 9	Javanese 9
Kaska 0	Creek 4	Rural Irish 9	Khalka Mongols 9
Shoshoni 0	Seneca Iroquois 4	Ancient Babylonians 8	Turks of Anatolia 9
			Zapotec 9
		Otoro 8	Burmese villagers 8
		Riffians 8	Ganda 8
		Siamese 8	Korean villagers 8
		Ashanti 7	Maria Gond 7
		Cambodians 7	Fang 6
		Jivaro 6	Herero 6
		Katab 6	
		Lau Fijians 6	
		Lesu 5	
		Ontong Javanese 5	
		Pawnee 5	
		Maori 4	
		Timbira 4	
Mean 2.50	5.17	7.00	8.31

There are other interpretations of the relationship between presence or absence of marriage ceremonies (or degree of elaboration of ceremonies) and importance of inheritable property. Again, being in the New World is associated with ceremonial elaboration and the variable with which it is associated. Again we would argue that joint diffusion, if it has occurred systematically, is likely to represent functional association more often than accident.

Another alternative interpretation of the relationship between ceremonies and the importance of agriculture and herding is that agriculture and herding may enable the accumulation of surplus wealth and larger population concentrations, either of which might promote ceremony directly. Moreover, larger population concentrations may make ceremonies more necessary in that the larger population prevents immediate dissemination of knowledge of changes in relationship and status and of agreements about wealth transfer. However, economic surplus may enable a society to establish dowry, bridewealth, or substantial gift exchange, which may in turn promote ceremony. It is difficult to trace causal links with the data available; it is, of course, possible that the many different strands of causation coexist within societies or among them.

Markedly deviant cases seem to us to be important theoretical challenges. If one's hypotheses cannot account for them and further examination of data from them reveals no significant error of measurement, no substantial signs of dysfunction, and no plausible explanation for their deviance that fits the assumptions underlying one's hypotheses, the hypotheses become less interesting. The Zuni, a society without ceremonies but in which the importance of herding and agriculture is rated 8, is such a society.

How do the Zuni manage without ceremonies? One answer is that although they lacked ceremony at the time of description by Smith and Roberts (1954), they also lacked privacy for the various stages of relationship building leading up to what might be called marriage (John M. Roberts, personal communication, February 19, 1972). Affairs at various stages of commitment were known to the whole community. Thus, relationships had publicity without need of ceremonial publicity. The literature we extracted on the Zuni (see supplementary bibliography) did not indicate that serious problems of property rights following a death or divorce ever arose. This may be partly because several lines of inheritance were open to males and because it was comparatively easy to bring new land into cultivation (Bunzel, 1932: 477). Apparently marrying had little effect on who would inherit anything. Finally, the construction of alliances seem much less a necessity among the tightly knit Zuni.

The analysis of this one strongly deviant case suggests that it is not deviant from theoretical assumptions. In part the Zuni deal with potential problems by informally publicizing movement into a marital type of relationship and in part they have less need for ceremony because property rights problems are reduced in several ways and alliances are not particularly problematic for them.

There are no cases deviant in the direction of having substantial ceremony but lacking substantial stakes as we measure stakes. Such cases would not in our opinion be threats to our theoretical analysis. They would only indicate that our measures of stakes are imperfect or that ceremonies serve other functions. We know our measures of stakes are imperfect. For example, we have no direct measure of the degree to which marriage affects alliances or inheritance. But since there are no deviants with elaborate ceremonies and without substantial stakes to protect, we believe that we are working with the phenomena and the theoretical concepts that are keys to the understanding of the value of marriage ceremonies cross-culturally.

The modal anthropologist comes to topics such as marriage ceremonies with an epistemology different from ours and, as a consequence, a different idea of what is now known or what a paper like this one contributes. An anthropologist reading this paper might well say "I suppose this kind of article has its uses. I myself am unhappy about it. Surely it has already been clear since the days of Radcliffe-Brown and Malinowski that where there is an economic surplus it is most likely to be used for ceremonial." We would reply to that, first of all, that case studies establish nothing of generality. Moreover, we would argue that establishing the fact of expenditure of wealth on ceremony leaves us short of understanding why wealth gets spent on ceremony. Why not spend it for parties or on art objects or to get greater leisure? Why not destroy wealth conspicuously? If people are spending their wealth on ceremonies, why are they doing it? We think we have provided part of the answer to that question, and we think that documenting an answer to that question with a large sample, comparative investigation moves us substantially beyond where we are when all we have is an uncompiled and unsystematic collection of case studies, however insightful they seem to be.

A second complaint an anthropological reader might make about this article is that "I could quote many cases from around the world where the authors' arguments do not apply." Whether contrary cases can be quoted is first of all dependent on whether the variables are assessed by the critic as they are in this article. If this is done and there *are* contrary cases they are certainly of theoretical interest, but the fact remains that we have documented the generality of marriage ceremonies and winnowed alternative interpretations of the functional significance of ceremonies. Admittedly much could be gained from a discussion of specific contrary cases. Perhaps there are functional alternatives to ceremonies or perhaps our concept of ceremonial elaboration could be refined or clarified or perhaps we have missed something terribly important about marriage ceremonies, but any re-evaluation of ceremonies and their functions must contend with the data we have presented. Case studies may well be the source of most of the ideas on which large sample cross-cultural investigations are founded. Nonetheless, we hold it illegitimate to argue that some apparently contrary case or handful of cases, if such can be found, is of as great epistemic significance as our large sample comparative study.

A third complaint an anthropological reader might make is that "there are a number of ethnographic examples where it is the ceremonies that make it more and not less likely that problems will arise over inheritance and wealth." It is true that disputes may arise at ceremonies or over the transactions at ceremonies, but we argue that disputes over wealth transfer and over rights to wealth and power are less likely and are less intense on the average because of ceremonies. The facts that would refute this are not the facts of dispute where ceremonies occur. Rather, the facts that would refute this are *comparative* data, data on dispute rates in societies high in stakes but differing in whether ceremonies have occurred or dispute rates within societies where ceremonies are the mode but where some marriages come off without ceremony due to external factors such as epidemic or severe weather. Data might also come from cultures where magnitude of stakes or of ceremonies has changed due to exogenous factors such as colonial law, cattle epidemic, or the influence of missionaries. Do such societies have very high dispute rates and intense disputes when stakes are great and ceremonies are minimal or absent? Do such societies move toward a level of consistency between stakes and ceremonies? We think they would.

It seems clear that marriage ceremonies are more likely to be present and well developed where marriage has important wealth, rights, and alliance implications. Ceremony can be interpreted as a device for publicizing (and thereby protecting) rights and agreements, and for committing members of both groups being united by marriage to these rights and agreements. However, wealth transfer is associated with size of local population, a surplus-producing technology, and other things that may also contribute to the development of ceremony. The issues are complicated and not resolvable at this time, but it does not seem implausible to us to argue that ceremonies reduce problems that might arise where the stakes associated with a marriage are high.

REFERENCES

Brehm, Jack W. and Arthur R. Cohen
    1962   Explorations in Cognitive Dissonance. New York: Wiley.

Bunzel, R.L.
    1932   "Introduction to Zuni ceremonialism." Annual Report of the Bureau of American Ethnology, 1929-1930: 467-544.

Goody, J.R.
    1969   "Inheritance, property, and marriage in Africa and Eurasia." Sociology 3 (January): 55-76.

    1970   "Marriage prestations, inheritance and descent in pre-industrial societies." Journal of Comparative Family Studies 1 (Autumn): 37-54.

Kiesler, Charles A.
    1971   The Psychology of Commitment. New York: Academic Press.

Murdock, G.P.
    1968   "World sampling provinces." Ethnology 7 (July): 305-326.

Rosenblatt, P.C., S.S. Fugita, and K.V. McDowell
    1969   "Wealth transfer and restrictions on sexual relations during betrothal." Ethnology 8 (July): 319-328.

Smith, W. and J.M. Roberts
    1954   "Zuni law: a field of values." Papers of the Peabody Museum of American Archaeology and Ethnology, Harvard University 43 (1): 1-175.

SUPPLEMENTARY ETHNOGRAPHIC REFERENCE LIST

Arusi Galla
Huntingford, G.W.B.
1955   The Galla of Ethiopia. London: International African Institute.

Paulitschke, Phillip V.
1893 - Ethnographie Nordost-Afrikas. Volume 1. Die Materielle Cultur der Danakil,
1896   Galla, und Somal. Berlin: D. Reimer.

Ashanti
Fortes, M.
1950   "Kinship and Marriage Among the Ashanti." Pp. 252-284 in A.R. Radcliffe-
        Brown and D. Forde (eds.), African Systems of Kinship and Marriage. London:
        Oxford University Press. Pp. 258, 261-264, 268-273, 276, 278-283, 279-280.

Manoukian, Madeline
1950   Akan and Ga-Adangme Peoples of the Gold Coast. London: International Af-
        rican Institute. Pp. 30-31.

Rattray, R.S.
1927   Religion and Art in Ashanti. Oxford: Clarendon Press. Pp. 76-77, 79, 81,
        85.

Babylonians
Delaporte, Louis J.
1925   Mesopotamia. New York: Knopf. Pp. 74-76, 80, 85.

Bamileke
Littlewood, M.
1954   "Bamum and Bamileke". In M. McCulloch (ed.), Peoples of the Central Cam-
        eroons. London: International African Institute. P. 122.

Barabra
Herzog, Rolf
1957   Die Nubier. Berlin: Akademie Verlag. Pp. 91-95.

Bohogue Shoshoni
Steward, J.H.
1938   "Basin-plateau aboriginal sociopolitical groups". Bulletin of the Bureau of
        American Ethnology 120: 1-346. Pp. 213-216.

1943   "Culture element distributions: Northern and Gosiute Shoshoni". Anthropol-
        ogical Records 8 (3): 263-392. Pp. 278-279, 337. ·

Burmese
Brant, C.S., and M.M. Khaing.
1951   "Burmese kinship and the life cycle: An outline". Southwestern Journal of
        Anthropology 7(4): 437-454. Pp. 450-451.

Scott, J.G.
1882   The Burman. Volume 1. London: Macmillan. P. 57.

Cagaba
Reichel-Dolmatoff, Gerardo
1950   "Los Kogi". Revista del Instituto. Etnologico Nacional, No. 4, 2 vols. Bogota:
        Colombia. Editorial Iqueima. Vol. 2. P. 227.

Cambodians
Orans, M.
1955   "The culture and social organization of the Khmer," Pp. 304-354 in M.G.
        Zadrozny (ed.), Cambodia. Chicago: University of Chicago for HRAF. Pp. 315,
        317.

Chippewa

Densmore, F.
1929   "Chippewa customs," Bulletin of the Bureau of American Ethnology 86: 1-204. Pp. 72-73.

Hilger, M.I.
1951   "Chippewa child life and its cultural background." Bulletin of the Bureau of American Ethnology 146: 1-218. Pp. 154-160, 172.

Cocama

Métraux, A.
1948   "South American Indians: Tupian Tribes of the Middle and Upper Amazon." Bulletin of the Bureau of American Ethnology 143: iii, 687-703. Pp. 699-700.

Creek

Swanton, J.R.
1928   "Social organization and social usages of the Indians of the Creek Confederacy." Forty-second Annual Report of the Bureau of American Ethnology, 1924-1925: 23-472, 859-900. Pp. 166, 368-377.

Crow

Lowie, R.H.
1912   "Social life of the Crow Indians." Anthropological Papers of the American Museum of Natural History 9(2): 179-248. Pp. 222-223.

1917   "Mandan, Hidatsa, and Crow social organization." Anthropological Papers of the American Museum of Natural History 21: 53-99.

1935   The Crow Indians. New York: Farrar and Rinehart. P. 50.

Egyptian Fellahin

Ammar, Hamed
1954   Growing Up in an Egyptian Village. London: Routledge and Kegan Paul. Pp. 192-197.

Fang

Alexandre, P., and J. Binet.
1958   Le Groupe dit Pahouin. Paris: Presses Universitaires de France. Pp. 65-66.

Tessman, G.
1913   Die Pangwe: Völkerkundliche Monographie eines West-Afrikanischen Negerstammes. Volume 2. Berlin: Ernst Wasmuth A.-6. Pp. 109-110, 118.

Fulani

Stenning, Derrick J.
1952   Savannah Nomads. London: Oxford University Press. Pp. 112-130.

Ganda

Mair, Lucy P.
1934   An African People in the Twentieth Century. London: Routledge. Pp. 79-91.

Roscoe, John
1911   The Baganda. London: Macmillan. Pp. 87-90, 97.

Haitians

Herskovits, Melville J.
1937   Life in a Haitian Village. New York: A.A. Knopf: Pp. 105, 112-113, 116.

Simpson, G.E.
1942   "Sexual and familial institutions in Northern Haiti." American Anthropologist 44 (October-December): 655-674. Pp. 655-657.

Herero

Vedder, H.
1928   "The Herero," Pp. 153-211 in C.H.L. Hahn, H. Vedder, and L. Fourie (eds.), The Native Tribes of South West Africa, New York: Barnes and Noble. P. 180.

Huichol

Lumholtz, C.
1902 - Unknown Mexico. Volume 2. New York: C. Scribner's Sons. Pp. 91-97.
1904

Zingg, R.M.
1938   "The Huichols: Primitive Artists." University of Denver Contributions to Ethnography 1: 1-826. Pp. 130-134, 136-137.

Iban

Gomes, E.H.
1911   Seventeen Years Among the Sea Dyaks of Borneo. London: Seeley. Pp. 122-123.

Irish

Arensberg, Conrad M.
1937   The Irish Countryman. London: Macmillan. Pp. 41, 77-80.

Javanese

Geertz, Hildred
1961   The Javanese Family. Glencoe, Illinois: Free Press. Pp. 62-71.

Koentjaraningrat, R.M.
1960   "The Javanese of South Central Asia," Pp. 88-115 in G.P. Murdock (ed.), Social Structure in Southeast Asia. Chicago: Quadrangle Books. Pp. 100-102.

Jivaro

Guallart, J.M.
1964   "Los Jibaros del alto Marañon," America Indigena 24: 315-331. P. 320.

Karsten, Rafael
1935   The Head-Hunters of Western Amazonas. Helsinki: Centraltry-Cheriet. P. 193.

Kaska

Honigmann, J.J.
1949   "Culture and ethos of Kaska Society." Yale University Publications in Anthropology 40: 1-365. Pp. 193-194.

Katab

Meek, C.K.
1931   Tribal Studies in Northern Nigeria. Volume 2. London: Kegan Paul, Trench, Trubner. Pp. 20-23, 35-37, 41-43.

Khalka

Vreeland, H.H.
1954   Mongol Community and Kinship Structure. New Haven, Connecticut: HRAF Press. Pp. 76-79.

Koreans

Osgood, C.B.
1951   The Koreans and Their Culture. New York: Ronald Press. Pp. 107-111.

Lau Fijians

Hocart, A.M.
1929   "Lau Islands, Fiji." Bernice P. Bishop Museum Bulletin 62: 1-240. Pp. 34, 156-157.

Lesu
  Powdermaker, Hortense
    1933   Life in Lesu. New York: Norton. Pp. 140-147.

Majuro Marshallese
  Spoehr, A.
    1949   "Majuro, a village in the Marshall Islands." Fieldiana Anthropology 39:
            1-266. P. 214.

Maori
  Best, Elsdon
    1924   The Maori as He Was. Wellington: Dominion Museum. P. 110.

  Biggs, Bruce
    1960   Maori Marriage. Wellington: Polynesian Society. Pp. 41-42.

  Buck, Peter H.
    1950   The Coming of the Maori, Wellington: Whitcombe and Tombs. Pp. 366-368.

Maria Gond
  Grigson, W.V.
    1938   The Maria Gonds of Bastar. London: Oxford University Press. Pp. 244, 247-251.

Nicobarese
  Whitehead, George
    1924   In the Nicobar Islands. London: Seeley, Service. P. 115.

Ontong-Javanese
  Hogbin, H. Ian
    1934   Law and Order in Polynesia. New York: Harcourt, Brace. P. 99.

Otoro
  Nadel, S.F.
    1947   The Nuba. London: Oxford University Press. Pp. 111-115.

Papago
  Joseph, Alice, Jane Chesky, and Rosamund B. Spicer.
    1949   The Desert People. Chicago: University of Chicago Press.

  Underhill, R.M.
    1936   "The autobiography of a Papago woman." Memoirs of the American Anthro-
            pological Association. 46: 1-64. Pp. 36-38, 62-63.

    1965   "The Papago family," Pp. 147-162 in M. Nimkoff (ed.), Comparative Family
            Systems. Boston: Houghton Mifflin. P. 151.

Pawnee
  Dorsey, G.A. and J.R. Murie.
    1940   "Notes on Skidi Pawnee Society." Field Museum of Natural History Anthro-
            pological Series 27 (2): 65-119. Pp. 97-101.

Ramcocamecra Timbira
  Nimuendajú, C.
    1946   "The Eastern Timbira." University of California Publications in American Ar-
            chaeology and Ethnology 41: 1-358. Pp. 122-123, 131.

Riffians
  Coon, C.S.
    1931   "Tribes of the Rif." Harvard African Studies 9:1-417. Pp. 134-142.

Seneca Iroquois
Goldenweiser, A.A.
1912   "On Iroquois work". Pp. 464-475 in Summary Report of the Geological survey of
         Canada. Ottawa: Department of Mines. P. 469.

Morgan, Lewis H.
1901   League of the Ho-Dé-No-Sau-Nee or Iroquois. Volume 1. New York: Dodd,
         Mead. Pp. 312-313, 316-317.

Siamese
Anuman Rajathon, P.
1954   Life and Ritual in Old Siam. New Haven: HRAF. Pp. 4, 8-16.

DeYoung, John E.
1955   Village Life in Modern Thailand. Berkeley: University of California Press. Pp.
         61, 63-64, 164.

Siriono
Holmberg, A.R.
1950   Nomads of the Long Bow. Washington, D.C.: United States Government
         Printing Office. Pp. 49-50, 80, 82.

Spaniards
Kenny, Michael
1961   A Spanish Tapestry: Town and Country in Castile. Bloomington: Indiana Un-
         iversity Press. Pp. 68-69.

Pitt-Rivers, Julian A.
1954   The People of the Sierra. London: Weidenfeld-Nicolson. P. 110.

Tiv
Akiga
1939   Akiga's Story: The Tiv Tribe as Seen by One of Its Members. London: The
         International African Institute. Pp. 113-115.

Bohannan, Paul, and Laura Bohannan.
1953   The Tiv of Central Nigeria. London: International African Institute. Pp. 73-74.

1958   Three Source Notebooks in Tiv Ethnography. New Haven: HRAF Press. P. 73.

Trukese
Goodenough, W.H.
1951   "Property, kin, and community on Truk." Yale University Publications in An-
         thropology 46: 1-192. Pp. 120-122.

Turks of Anatolia
Makal, M.
1954   A Village in Anatolia. London: Vallentine, Mitchell. Pp. 125, 127, 129-130.

Yabarana
Wilbert, Johannes
1963   Indios de la región Orinoco-Ventuari. Caracas: Instituto Caribe de Antropolo-
         gía y Sociología. P. 144.

Zapotec
Fuente, Julio de la
1949   Yalálag: Una Villa Zapoteca Serrana. Mexico: Museo Nacional de Antropolo-
         gía. P. 191.

Parsons, Elsie Clews
1936   Mitla: Town of the Souls. Chicago: University of Chicago Press. Pp. 96-111.

Zuni

Eggan, Fred
  1950   The Social Organization of the Western Pueblos. Chicago: University of
          Chicago Press. P. 193.

Smith, W. and J. M. Roberts
  1954   "Zuni law: A field of values." Papers of the Peabody Museum of American Ar-
          chaeology and Ethnology, Harvard University 43 (1): 1-175. P. 99.

Stevenson, M.C.
  1904   "The Zuni Indians: Their mythology, esoteric fraternities, and ceremonies."
          Annual Report of the Bureau of American Ethnology. 23: 3-608. Pp. 100, 304-
          305.

Determinants of Female Age at Marriage in Rural and Semi-Urban Areas of Four Latin American Countries

T. R. BALAKRISHNAN*

Age at marriage has been an important variable in fertility studies because of its predominant effect on family size. This is especially true in countries where there is little voluntary control of fertility. Later age at marriage decreases fertility levels primarily due to reduced duration of exposure to pregnancy and because it eliminates exposure in the highly fertile years of late teens and early twenties. Formulations of detailed analytical framework for fertility studies have taken age at marriage as an important intermediate variable (Davis and Blake, 1956; Freedman, 1962). Empirical investigations in Latin America and elsewhere in the developing world have examined the effect of delayed marriage on fertility (Miro and Mertens, 1968; Coale and Tye, 1961).

While later age at marriage reduces exposure time and hence fertility, duration in itself cannot explain all fertility differentials by age at marriage. What is equally important is that women who marry late have lower family size ideals, which influence their family planning and fertility behaviour after marriage. In other words, socio-economic factors which motivate a smaller family also tend to increase age at marriage. Thus a better understanding of the variations in age at marriage should help in understanding fertility differentials as well. Many studies while stressing the importance of age at marriage have continued to use it either as an independent variable or control variable in the study of fertility. A plea for more research on the relationship between socio-economic factors and intermediate variables such as age at marriage in contrast to always focussing on fertility as the dependent variable has been recently emphasized (Yaukey, 1969).

*Dept. of Sociology, The University of Western Ontario, London, Canada.

Volume VII, Number 2, (Summer 1976)

Acknowledgements

I would like to thank the Centro Latinoamericano De Demografia of the United Nations in Santiago, Chile, especially Carmen Miro and Arthur Conning for supplying me with the data and giving me the facilities for research during my visit to CELADE in 1973. This research is supported by a grant from the Population Council. However, these organizations are not in any way responsible for the views expressed here which are the author's sole responsibility.

This paper examines female age at marriage and some of its correlates in the rural and semi-urban areas (population less than 20,000) of Mexico, Costa Rica, Columbia, and Peru. The data come from fertility surveys done in these areas under a program of the United Nations Latin American Demographic Center. The surveys interviewed approximately 3,000 women in each country of all marital statuses between the ages 15 and 49 inclusive. The analysis in the paper is restricted to ever married women, as the focus is primarily on age at marriage. Because of a greater incidence of consensual unions in certain Latin American countries, all sexual unions are called marriages, and the age at marriage is defined as "age at first sexual union."

Three independent variables were selected, two to measure rural-urban influence and one to indicate socio-economic status. These were rural-urban classification of places of residence at the time of early socialization and at the time of the survey, and the highest level of education attained by the respondent. Urban influence and education have long been found to be related to fertility declines primarily because they bring about a change in values in female sex roles, activities outside the home, costs and benefits of children and in general attitudes towards family size and family planning. A woman whose childhood socialization took place in a rural setting is likely to be influenced by attitudes that favour a larger family and an early entry into marriage. Similarly a woman with a lower educational level is hypothesized to be more traditional and likely to enter into marriage at an earlier age than her more educated sisters.

Age at Marriage and Completed Fertility

Table 1 presents the number of live births by age at marriage for women who have completed most of their fertility at the time of survey, namely those in the age group 40 to 49. Later age at marriage, primarily due to reduced exposure, has a substantial effect on fertility. Those marrying before age 20 had, on an average, about 1.5 to 2 children more than those marrying in the next age group 20-24 and almost 60 percent more children than those marrying in the age group 25-29.

TABLE 1   NUMBER OF LIVE BIRTHS BY AGE AT MARRIAGE

Age at Marriage	All Women				Women Aged 40-49			
	Mexico	Costa Rica	Columbia	Peru	Mexico	Costa Rica	Columbia	Peru
Less than 19	5.488	5.511	5.420	5.012	8.687	9.373	8.548	8.490
20-24	4.849	5.108	4.834	4.365	7.351	7.822	6.940	6.507
25-29	3.565	4.196	4.083	3.982	5.059	6.032	6.128	5.073
30-49	3.000	3.103	3.065	2.929	3.389	3.364	3.778	3.583
Total Number of Women	2,194	1,465	1,889	1,941	508	293	427	443

Actual Age at Marriage

The mean actual ages for the sample of ever married women included here were 17.72 in Mexico, 18.62 in Costa Rica, 18.72 in Columbia and 19.10 in Peru. Mean actual ages at marriage by the three independent variables selected are presented in Table 2. Mean age increases with level of urbanization and education of women. Differences are greatest by educational categories. Those with some secondary or more education married more than two years later than those with no education. The range was highest in Mexico, where the average age at marriage for women with no education was 17.25, with primary complete was 18.94 and with secondary or more education 20.29. The ranges were somewhat lower but no less noticeable in the other countries.

The differences in mean ages at marriage were lower but in the expected direction for early childhood socialization and rural-urban type of present place of residence. Women whose early childhood socialization took place in a city married later. Similarly women residing in towns larger than 2,500 population had a higher mean age at marriage. Of course many of them lived in the same community as a child, and the relation between place of early socialization and present place of residence is partly a function of lack of mobility.

As urbanization is likely to be related to education it is necessary to examine the differences in mean age at marriage after control. This has been achieved by using Multiple Classification Analysis, which gives adjusted means after removing the influence of other variables.[1] Thus the adjusted means in Table 2 give the average age at marriage after controlling for the other two independent variables. Education of wife remains as the most important variable. Rural, urban influence is minimal, whether we consider place of early socialization or present place of residence. This is consistent for all the four countries. The beta-coefficient indicating the relative importance of education in age at marriage is almost the same, .14 to .16. The combined effect of the three variables as indicated by the multiple correlation coefficient is also very nearly equal across the countries, .14 to .16. The proportion of variance explained by the three independent variables was only 2 to 3 percent in the four countries. Thus, in spite of the clear trends in the expected direction, individual variations within groups are far more significant than the observed differences between group means.

Ideal Age at Marriage

The mean ideal ages at marriage were 20.45 for Mexico, 20.53 for Costa Rica, 20.41 for Columbia and 20.72 for Peru. Mean ideal ages were much closer among the four countries than mean actual ages. Table 3 presents the data for ideal age at marriage. Ideal age at marriage increases with level of urban influence and

---

[1]Basically this is an extention of multiple regression analysis to situations where the independent variables can be either in subclasses or discontinuous variables. In MCA each subclass of an independent variable is a predictor. The technique presents a mean value of the dependent variable for each subclass of each independent variable after controlling for all other predictors (see Andrews, Morgan and Sonquist, 1969).

TABLE 2   MEAN ACTUAL AGE AT MARRIAGE (UNADJUSTED AND ADJUSTED) OF EVER MARRIED WOMEN

	Mexico			Costa Rica			Columbia			Peru		
	Un-adjusted Mean	Adjusted Mean	Number of Women	Un-adjusted Mean	Adjusted Mean	Number of Women	Un-adjusted Mean	Adjusted Mean	Number of Women	Un-adjusted Mean	Adjusted Mean	Number of Women
Early Socialization												
Country	17.55	17.76	1309	18.42	18.53	1043	18.82	18.98	1179	18.92	19.08	1031
Small town	17.90	17.65	740	18.92	18.87	206	18.52	18.29	559	19.80	19.20	678
City	18.52	17.85	137	19.38	18.91	208	18.71	18.28	150	19.47	18.93	208
Beta Coefficient		.03			.06			.08			.02	
Education of Wife												
No education	17.25	17.27	828	18.38	18.42	263	18.17	18.12	515	19.03	19.04	965
Primary incomplete	17.77	17.78	1162	18.44	18.44	939	18.65	18.60	1045	18.52	18.51	629
Primary complete	18.94	18.83	126	18.88	18.81	186	19.75	19 91	179	20.21	20.18	202
Some secondary or more	20.29	20.10	73	21.21	20.99	72	20.02	20.32	145	20.74	20.74	138
Beta Coefficient		.15			.14			.16			.16	
Place of Residence												
Less than 2500	17.50	17.58	1517	18.18	18.24	254	18.70	18.71	1442	19.03	19.07	1650
2500-20000	18.21	18.03	678	18.71	18.70	1211	18.79	18.76	447	19.52	19.22	291
Beta Coefficient		.05			.04			.01			.01	
Multiple Correlation Coefficient (R)		.164			.143			.146			.149	
Proportion of Variance Explained (R²)		2.70%			2.06%			2.14%			2.23%	

Total number of women covered in the tables will differ due to item non-response.

TABLE 3   MEAN IDEAL AGE AT MARRIAGE (UNADJUSTED AND ADJUSTED) OF EVER MARRIED WOMEN

	Mexico			Costa Rica			Columbia			Peru		
	Un-adjusted Mean	Adjusted Mean	Number of Women	Un-adjusted Mean	Adjusted Mean	Number of Women	Un-adjusted Mean	Adjusted Mean	Number of Women	Un-adjusted Mean	Adjusted Mean	Number of Women
Early Socialization												
Country	20.25	20.33	1307	20.36	20.44	1028	20.28	20.37	1208	20.31	20.62	904
Small town	20.68	20.56	742	20.73	20.68	206	20.55	20.43	564	21.12	20.92	642
City	21.10	20.87	137	21.17	20.85	207	20.93	20.70	152	21.33	20.56	205
Beta Coefficient		.08			.06			.03			.04	
Education of Wife												
No education	20.29	20.33	825	20.11	20.15	257	20.08	20.10	538	20.16	20.26	825
Primary incomplete	20.46	20.55	1166	20.48	20.49	930	20.37	20.37	1056	20.69	20.67	602
Primary complete	20.99	20.78	126	20.68	20.62	185	20.77	20.74	181	21.94	21.73	201
Some secondary or more	21.40	21.09	73	22.26	22.04	72	21.57	21.48	145	22.53	22.35	137
Beta Coefficient		.06			.13			.12			.19	
Place of Residence												
Less than 2500	20.30	20.36	1516	20.16	20.20	252	20.35	20.41	1473	20.51	20.60	1486
2500-20000	20.79	20.66	679	20.61	20.60	1196	20.62	20.42	452	21.82	21.34	284
Beta Coefficient		.04			.05			.002			.08	
Multiple Correlation Coefficient (R)		.103			.151			.114			.233	
Proportion of Variance Explained (R²)		1.06%			2.27%			1.29%			5.42%	

Total number of women covered will differ due to item non-response. Non-response on ideal age was especially high in Peru.

education. In all categories, the mean ideal ages are higher than 20, the highest mean ideal age being among the most educated group of women.

Comparison of ideal with actual ages shows that in all categories, ideals are higher than actual.   However, the gap between ideal and actual age at first marriage is greater in less educated rural women.   The gap decreases with education and urbanization.   This is because differences in ideal age at marriage by the different categores are much lower than in the case of actual.   Thus, while norms about age at marriage do not vary too much, behaviours do.

Multiple Classification Analysis on ideal age at marriage reveals another interestng observation.   The differences between countries are more significant than in the case of actual age at marriage.   In Mexico, the variation in ideal age at marriage was lower than in other countries, the variation being highest in Peru.   The multiple correlation coefficient varied from .103 in Mexico to .233 in Peru, wheras the corresponding range in the case of actual age at marriage was much lower.   The proportion of variance explained ranges from 1 per cent in Mexico to 5 per cent in Peru.

Conclusion

As age at marriage is found to be highly important for subsequent fertility, an attempt was made to explain variation in age at marriàge by rural-urban influence and education of wife.   While simple tabular analysis reveals trends in the expected direction, a multi-variable approach shows that only a small proportion of variance in age at marriage can be explained.   The reason for this apparent paradox is that variation within categories is substantial in relation to variation between groups as evident from the relatively high standard deviations (Table 4).

TABLE 4   MEANS AND STANDARD DEVIATIONS ON AGES AT MARRIAGE
                 AND CORRELATION COEFFICIENTS BETWEEN ACTUAL AND
                              IDEAL AGE AT MARRIAGE

	Actual Age at Marriage		Ideal Age at Marriage		Correlation Between Actual and Ideal Age at Marriage
	Mean	Standard Deviation	Mean	Standard Deviation	
Mexico	17.72	3.80	20.45	3.05	.157
Costa Rica	18.62	4.14	20.53	2.92	.186
Columbia	18.72	4.06	20.41	2.97	.190
Peru	19.10	4.11	20.72	3.36	.146

The lack of correspondence between ideal and actual ages at marriage is revealed in the correlations presented in Table 4.   The correlations are low and range between .146 and .190.   Thus while the overall patterns in age at marriage differentials are in the hypothesized direction, the data do not strongly support this, nor the usefulness of ideals in studying actual ages at marriage, consistent with the finding of others in a study of age at marriage in six Latin cities (Yaukey, Thorsen and Onaka, 1972).

REFERENCES

Coale, Ansley, and C.Y. Tye.
1961   "The significance of age patterns of fertility in high-fertility populations." Milbank Memorial Fund Quarterly 39: 631-646.

Davis, Kingsley. and Judith Blake.
1956   "Social structure and fertility: an analytical framework. Economic Development and Cultural Change 4 (April) : 211-235.

Freedman, Ronald.
1962   "The sociology of human fertility." Current Sociology 10/11: 35-121.

Miro, Carmen, and Walter Mertens.
1968   "Influence affecting fertility in urban and rural Latin America." Milbank Memorial Fund Quarterly 46:89-117.

Yaukey, David.
1969   "On theorizing about fertility." American Sociologist 4: 100-104.

Yaukey, David, and Timm Thorsen and Alvin Onaka.
1972   "Marriage at an earlier than ideal age in six Latin American capital cities." Population Studies 26:263-272.

Love as a Factor in Marital Decision in Contemporary Poland

BARBARA LOBODZINSKA*

In the traditional Polish family, marriage occurred within the same social class and within similar economic statuses. While including many traits of patriarchalism, the traditional family in Poland was firmly situated in a definite social class which was determined by the family's standing in the community. Restricted movement from one social class to another and restricted geographic social mobility greatly limited an individual's contact with other eligible partners. Thus, during the nineteenth and at the beginning of the twentieth century, peasant marriages (as well as marriages within the middle and nobility classes) were contracted between partners of the same property and of similar social statuses within the village community. (Even today to some extent, marriages within the peasantry are still contracted on the same principle).

Thus, marriages were contracted primarily on the basis of the economic concerns and needs of the whole family, the kinsmen or the farmer's household and land. The parents made the final decision in the choice of the marital partner while the individual's preferences were usually not considered and, if considered, were not very important. (Examples of this can be found in the classic book of J. Chalasinski [1938] and in other books [cf. Zawistowicz-Adamska, 1948; Duda-Dziewierz, 1938; Wierzbicki, 1963; and *Pamietniki chlopow* (*Peasants' Diaries*)]. 1935-1936.

Thus, the choice of a marital partner required acceptance of the whole family and the village community. Social control comprised the process of mate selection. One might say the family's decision dominated the individual's choice while his own wishes were subordinated. These parental (family) decisions were most often guided by such criteria as social class, economic status, property and sometimes health of the potential spouse.

Objecting to or marrying against parental will entailed the risk of social degradation, the possibility of becoming a social outcast and/or severance from the community heritage even to the extent of religious excommunication and communal condemnation since the social status of both men and women was often affected by marriage. Marriage frequntly meant social advancement for women, and, less frequently, social abasement for men. (An example of social advancement through marriage would be the marriage of a wealthy woman with a bachelor from a formerly-wealthy aristocratic family and in many cases, the motives for such marriages were openly and obviously for social and economic reasons). *The*

*Visiting Scholar, Family Study Center, University of Minnesota, Minneapolis, Minnesota, U.S.A.

Volume VI : Number 1. (Shipping 1975)

concept of love, as a principle for marital choice, *was only a marginal factor*. Thus, love can be treated as a separate category, appearing only accidentally in parentally selected or influenced marital choices.

The above generalizations are described as consistent and representative. However, variations occurred within social class, according to urban and/or rural residential areas, and to economic status, etc.

In most of the rural marriages both spouses were from the same or from neighboring villages. Cross-marriages between land-owners and non-land-owners were exceptions. (Some authors quote no more than about 20% of all the rural marriage cases in their samples). In the group of land-owners about 70% of the couples represent similar kinds of property, similar kinds of area and quality of the land and quantity of the livestock, etc. This indicates a significant trend in homogeneity of economic status between grooms and brides in the rural area. Under such circumstances it is not surprising that matchmakers were parents or other family members and also that sometimes spouses did not know each other before becoming engaged. Marriage contracts would define duties and responsibilities of the husband, wife, parents and parents-in-law in categories of mutual assistance, inheriting land or the home, working on the farm, etc. Marriage contracts were the results of an agreement achieved by both families involved after discussions which had as a goal the protection of the businesses of both negotiations sides.

In contrast to the rural family unit, the urban family unit was not a productive but rather a consumptive unit and the urban families' relations between parents and children were of a more democratic type. While the father was still the only provider, he was no longer the sole manager of the family budget. Thus, in comparison with the marital choices of the rural families, the marital choices of urban families were the results of more personal decisions by the young couples themselves and were less influenced by their parents.

Again in comparison to the rural and urban families, the families of the intelligentsia were characterized by more egalitarian relations.

Nevertheless, most of the families described in different sources of data seemed to be class conscious and cross-marriages occurred rather seldom.

Contemporary Poland has begun the dual-pronged process of equalizing economic standards and eliminating social class differences, both of which are greatly affected by industrialization and urbanization, which in turn influence geographic mobility from rural areas to towns and from one region of Poland to another. In addition to influencing geographic mobility, industrialization and urbanization also appear to be causing a rise in the educational level of the youth as a whole and effecting an increase in the number of professional, specialized and skilled labor jobs. With the appearance of the process of social equalization, the traditional social structure has disappeared, thereby deprecating the importance of personal wealth and increasing the chances of meeting possible spousal candidates without the control of the older generation.

Under the above-mentioned new conditions, the traditional reasons for marriage have undergone revision or rejection and socio-economic motives for marriage have become insignificant while motives involving self-fulfilment, equality and individual worth have become more significant. Free educational opportunities of all kinds and levels continue to diminish social differences and equalize the cultural and intellectual level of underdeveloped communities, thereby establishing the legitimacy of love feelings as a primary criterion for marital choice. Yet, although love is now a common and almost stereotyped basis for marital choice, the meaning of the concept is not uniform for all people. This can cause misunderstanding, conflict and disappointment in conjugal life.

The Social Sphere of Getting Acquainted

In the traditional society there were two institutions giving the youth of both sexes opportunities for social contact : the family and the church. In village communities this sphere of social contact was facilitated by neighbourhood localities which allowed for easy opportunities of cross-sex contact within the community while retaining parental and community supervision, However, new bases for expanded cross-sex interaction of eligible youth evolved through increased geographic and social mobility; increased number of schools and other learning facilities; more highly educated youth; universalization of gainful employment for women; more recreational institutions and the diversification of rest and recreational opportunities. This greater freedom of outside social opportunities thereby limited parental control of the cross-sex contacts of their maturing children.

The country youth (assuming they intend to marry) may be divided into two categories. The first category is composed of the youth who want to stay in the country and cultivate the land or raise animals. These young people are looking for marital partners who have the same or similar aspirations and agricultural qualifications, (i.e., value homogany). The emotional (love feelings) factor, while not being completely omitted, plays only a secondary role in the choice of mate. (B. Tryfan [1968 : 76-91] writes about this phenomenon, pointing out that decisions to marry are based more and more on emotional factors, although this is not spontaneous and is not the only criterion).

The second category of country youth is composed of youth who want to migrate from the country to the city. This involves two factors. The first factor is the accessibility of urban employment opportunities and corresponding lifestyles and the second factor is the possibility of marriage with a resident of the town.

As an example of such migrational endeavor from a rural to an urban residential area, we may consider the 1970 correspondence through a weekly newspaper, "NOWA WIES" ("The New Village") which contains a column analogous to the "Lonely Hearts" columns in the United States. Two thousand letters were sent to a young sailor, lonesome for friends from his homeland (Lobodzinska, 1971). Almost 90% of the letters were written by single girls from the country or from small towns who were hoping to find a potential spouse. Such a marriage could give them the chance to leave the rural community and move to a town. Among others, one reason for marrying a sailor was the lack of alternative marital candidates in the nearest surroundings. The number of possible candidates in a small, local community is limited and the interests of such youth concentrate mainly on rural husbandry. When approval of the young people's choice from their own social environment was lacking, the search for a spouse living and working in a city provided for the possibility of social advancement through urban living. The element of adventure also afforded additional incentive to youth immersed in the monotomy of rural life.

The range of social contacts for urban youth presents another problem. The results of an investigation (Lutynski, 1960) conducted among young couples living in cities posed the question, "Where do these spouses become acquainted?" A non-random sample (the sample were readers of the youth daily, "Sztander Mlodych," [Lutynski, 1960] points out that spouses were introduced: a) 28% by colleagues and acquaintances; b) 19% during work; c) 18% at parties; d) 10% at school or university; e) 4% by parents; f) 3% during sports and tourism; g) 2% at the cinema; h) 1% at a friend's wedding; i) 15% in other situations (on the street, at the beach, at youth organizations).

Matchmakers or arranged dating services are rarely used as a means for becoming acquainted with a potential marital candidate. Most people who look for husbands and wives in this way are those who migrate from the country to towns, thereby lacking colleagues and friends.[1] For these new migrants from the country, matrimonial offers present the chance of getting married in the city, a chance which is synonymous with permanent settlement in the city.

Although city living is highly valued, becoming acquainted with urban residents is difficult for students. An investigation was conducted in 1962 (Wegrzynowski, 1965) on the campus of the University of Lodz, which is located in a large, industrial city. For the students, parties, university classes, board-canteen, sports activities and friends' introductions provided the means of becoming acquainted with potential marital candidates. (However, not all of these acquaintanceships lead to marriage).

Research (Lobodzinska, 1970: 92) conducted on engineers living in Warsaw, the largest Polish center of academic life, indicates how future spouses become acquainted. (See Table I.)

TABLE I: HOW SPOUSES HAVE BECOME ACQUAINTED:
WARSAW ENGINEERS IN PER CENT

Area and Situation	Male Engineers	Female Engineers
School	9.5	10.0
University	9.0	38.0
Work	15.5	27.0
Colleagues and the Family	39.0	15.0
During Vacations, Tourism, Parties at Social Institutions	18.0	9.0
On the Street	7.0	1.0
Total	214=100%	45=100%

[1]The analysis of customers of a matrimonial office in 1961 indicated that 60% were people coming from country but living in cities; 22% were village dwellers; and others were permanent city dwellers. B. Lobodzinska, *Manowce malzenstwa i rodziny (By-Ways of Marriage and Family)*, 1963, pp. 95-108.

For male engineers, the most typical means of becoming acquainted with a future wife is through the assistance of colleagues and family and in more casual situations. For women engineers, the most typical means of becoming acquainted with a future husband is through the school, the university and through work institutions. This may indicate that female engineers 1) find husbands more often in the environment of education and work and 2) pay more attention to the social and professional position of the spouse and 3) care more for having common interests with him (Girard, 1964: 57-72; Burgess and Locke, 1953: 729).

From this data we see that in an urban environment, becoming acquainted with a potential marital candidate occurs more freely than in a rural setting and without the hindrance of adult-supervised interaction. Each partner's choice is relatively independent of family and social pressures. Educational, recreational and social situations provide most of the opportunities for the urban youth's cross-sex contact. Such situations in urban life provide the proper basis for observational access (under acknowledged criteria—also assuming that such criteria exist) to the marital selection process as it occurs.

Motivation for Mate Selection

The question arises, "What criteria are taken for granted in the process of mate selection?" To provide a verbal description of marital motivations is a difficult methodological task. Sometimes the arguments are trivial. In cities, "love" was most often a stereotypical motivation for marriage. However, it is impossible to define what kinds of meanings are given to the concept of love. A 1972 press survey, conducted by the Youth Daily, questioned, "What are motives for marriage?" The questionnaire was answered by 1,648 persons (45.5% males; 54.5% females) in the majority 25 years old and younger, most of whom were unmarried. Sixty five per cent had a middle or high level of education and most lived in large or middle-sized cities. (See Table 2)

This sample cannot be considered as representative of the Polish population. It is, however, a non-random sample of city-dwellers with a higher than average level of education among young adults.

The actual question was, "What are the reasons which incline men and women in general to marry and which incline you to marry?

The question was categorized and the respondents were allowed to choose more than one answer, thus, the percentages total more than 100% since each person could choose as many as three items.

It is possible to conclude the following: 1) Reasons given by men and women are different. 2) Reasons attributed to self are different from reasons attributed to others. These reasons may be considered as indicators of two different measures: 1) motivations and 2) values. It is difficult to judge whether the respondents based their replies more on rational (value) or emotional/impulsive (motivational) considerations. The analysis, therefore, will incorporate both types of response.

The concept of "motive," as used in this article, describes the internal goals of the person upon which that person consciously or unconsciously bases his behavior. The "motive" concept also includes impulses to manifest some beha-

TABLE 2:   REASONS FOR THE INCLINATION TO GET MARRIED

Reasons for Marriage	About Male Reasons			About Female Reasons			About Reasons for Self		
	Answering			Answering			Answering		
	Men	Women	Total	Men	Women	Total	Men	Women	Total
Will to get out from parents home; to have own home.	26.6	18.3	21.9	30.4	42.1	36.8	24.9	28.4	26.8
The proper age to get married has been reached	13.4	16.0	14.8	9.6	8.1	8.8	5.6	3.2	4.2
Partner has a good job, good position	2.8	4.8	3.9	17.7	13.9	15.5	2.1	3.6	2.9
Partner desires the marriage	2.2	1.4	1.8	2.6	1.4	1.9	1.2	1.8	1.5
To secure care	7.1	8.6	7.9	13.8	10.8	12.2	3.7	7.9	6.0
To regulate sexual intercourse	25.2	26.1	25.6	7.0	4.6	5.6	10.7	5.5	7.8
Love to the partner	50.7	45.9	48.0	47.3	60.7	54.8	57.1	66.3	62.1
To change the marital status	1.5	1.8	1.8	7.0	5.8	6.3	2.2	1.9	2.0
To have children	10.4	7.2	8.6	30.1	30.5	30.3	13.4	23.1	18.8
To have mutual relations with beloved person	35.6	33.6	34.5	22.1	26.0	24.2	38.4	34.2	36.0
Partner's physical attractiveness	24.1	30.5	27.7	10.4	5.8	7.9	10.8	3.6	6.9
It makes life easier to get on as a twosome	14.3	8.5	11.1	7.8	8.1	7.9	11.0	6.1	8.2
Parents like the candidate	0.5	0.9	0.7	2.0	1.2	1.6	1.1	0.8	0.9
The character of the candidate is liked	20.3	15.7	17.7	13.6	16.4	15.2	30.0	30.4	30.4
The wish to resign from vocational employment	0.5	0.3	0.4	4.2	1.8	1.8	0.1	0.2	0.2
To make it easier to cope with various everyday necessities/laundry, meals, repairs, etc.	18.7	22.6	20.8	1.8	1.8	1.8	5.8	2.3	3.8
Fear of remaining a a bachelor or spinster	2.3	4.3	3.4	23.4	20.6	21.9	1.1	1.3	1.2
To have someone to share interests	6.9	7.1	7.0	3.2	3.2	3.2	6.0	6.2	6.2
Other reasons	3.4	3.2	3.3	2.6	1.0	1.7	4.2	4.7	4.7
The answer is difficult	2.2	1.4	1.8	1.8	2.6	0.2	1.2	1.1	1.2
No answer	6.0	7.9	7.1	8.9	4.8	6.6	15.1	12.9	13.9

vior caused by a stimulus or a goal. The "value" concept, as contrasted with the "motive" concept is a more generalized concept describing a phenomenon of positive worth of which the individual is aware. Values provide the generalized standards of behavior which are expressed in specific forms in social norms. There are at least three categories of motivations: a) emotional; b) economic; c) familial. These three categories may be viewed in terms of a value continuum from traditional (patriarchal) to modern family values. Linking the two poles of this continuum are certain stable, though modifying values.

TABLE 3 :   MOTIVATION TYPE IN GETTING MARRIED, BY SEX (CUMULATIVE %'S FROM TABLE 2)

About :	Male Motivations		Female Motivations		Own Motivations	
Motivational Category	Answers of : Men	Women	Answers of : Men	Women	Answers of : Men	Women
Emotional	132.9	127.1	96.0	110.3	137.5	136.4
Economic	62.9	54.6	61.9	67.7	43.9	30.6
Familial	60.0	66.1	92.9	81.6	37.3	43.7

The popularity of emotional motivations is significantly greater than either familial or economic motivations. A comparison of the answers of both sexes indicates that each sex attributes to the opposite sex fewer romantic (or less emotional) motivations and more material and familial ones.

Familial motivation is tied in with the consideration of "marriage and family" in terms of such basic functions as care and procreation.

Economic and existential motives are also more often attributed as the motivations of others while motivations for self are more emotional in nature. Males speak of the major female motivation to marry by indicating that the husband has a good job and provides a good social position when marriage allows the wife's resignation from employment. Females speak of the major male motivation to marry by indicating the facilitation for the husband to cope with various everyday necessities, assuming, of course, that the wife will serve her husband.

The emotional motivation constitutes the most popular response is obvious from this summary table: the respondents agree that the emotional motivation is the most common motivation. In describing motivations for self, distinct differences between male and female opinions do not arise. However, a comparison of male and female opinions describing same-sex and cross-sex motivations points out significant differences. Men attribute emotional motivations to males more than women do. However, this attribution applies also to the female sex: women attribute emotional motivations to females more than men do. Both sexes, then, thus indicate an eager trend to identify emotional reasons as the major motivations of one's own sex for marital decisions.

These data provide the basis for concluding that, on the one hand, the general picture of a man and a woman playing marital roles is *differentially* presented and, on the other hand, when describing self motivations for marriage, the differences are slight and without substantive meaning. In a world traditionally divided by two sexes, the sexes do not appear as disparate in the sphere of emotional motivations for self as they do in other spheres of thought and behaviour. Possibly this emotional attitude toward modern marriage is a factor in eliminating differences within marriage and in family sex roles. Emotional motivation for marriage may be the main factor for partnership in modern marriage.

However, when considering economic and familial motivations for marriage, the opinions differ. Males more often choose economic motivations for self as reasons for marriage whereas females more often choose familial motivations for self as reasons for marriage. These choices may be considered as a consequence of traditional norms, given that marriage is an institution of role differentiation (i.e., for males, marriage indicates the role of provider for the household while being served at home by the wife; for females, marriage indicates a rise in social status [from single to married] and performing protective and procreative functions.

In comparing these three types of marital motivations, it must be stressed that emotional responses are valued by men and women equally and are generally given as the most common and universal reasons for men, for women and also for the respondent himself.

In considering what kinds of values may be analyzed as being either traditional or modern, using the classic categorizations of family structure and function, marital values will be characterized on the functional basis of marriage and family.

The traditional patriarchal family manifests a division of labor between husbands and wives, combined with subordination of wife and child. This traditional family is commonly extended, composed of many generations living together. Traditional family functions are linked to 1) social relations among family members and 2) the position of the family in the social community. The traditional family performs several functions which, during the process of social change, are being taken over by other social institutions. For example, the educational function is transferred to schools, to institutions of child care, to kindergartens, etc. The care of the aged is transferred to specialized health service institutions. Nourishment to some extent, is transferred to such institutions as restaurants, canteens, clubs, etc. Health care is transferred to hospitals and infirmaries, and recreational functions are transferred to cultural institutions. (However, with the development of television and radio, recreation returns to the home.) Finally, the liberalization of sexual mores has led to an increased tolerance for premarital and extramarital relations for both sexes.

Despite these limitations and changes, however, it is possible, in terms of continuity, to speak about the fulfilment of basic family functions and the development of new and more specialized family functions pertaining to contemporary life. The present familial functions include: 1) the maintenance of biological continuity (this also applies to the traditional family); 2) the maintenance of cultural continuity; 3) the endowment of a social position for the child; 4) the family's disposal of the part of the national income distributed to individual families (spending money) by government agencies; 5) the satisfaction of emotional needs through intimate relationships and 6) the social control of behavior of family members.

In dealing with values for getting married in the traditional family (with patriarchal elements) 1) "the wish to resign from vocational employment," is taken for granted. This motive is attributed to women because, once they are not employed, they may concentrate upon the duties connected with the household and child care (Table 2). 2) The value, "the partner has a good job or a good position," is also attributed to females on the basis of the division of labor in the home: the role of provider belongs to men. This value, however, appears *not only* as female. In the case of men's demands, it indicates the securing of the family's material existence as a partnership duty. 3) "To change marital status," is valued when the marital status carries higher prestige than the maiden or bachelor status. 4) "The partner is liked by parents", is a value characteristic of situations in which decisions to marry are made for adult children by their parents. (This is distinctly traditional). 5) "Making it easier to cope with everyday necessities", such as laundry, cleaning, cooking, repairs, etc., is a value which refers to sex-based division of labor with the woman performing household duties. (Men attribute this as value for self in marriage).

For values which are consequences of modern relations among family members, we find that satisfaction of emotional needs is the basic family function. These values are linked to expectations of love and affection between spouses, to mutual attractiveness of their personalities. In the same vein, the tendency toward independence and settling one's own home (i.e., nuclearization) may be evaluated as a modern trend. The value, "it makes life easier to get on as a twosome," may be treated as a modern consideration, along with the following: 1) "the candidate's character is well-liked;" 2) "love for the partner;" 3) "partner desires the marriage;" 4) "to have a mutual relationship with a beloved person;" and 5) "to have someone to share interests with".

However, it is not quite clear as to what the relationship is between the family value pattern (i.e., traditional or modern) and the response rate to the reason, "marriage makes life easier to go through as a twosome". Such a reason indicates that both spouses desire to raise the economic standard of the entire family through partnership, but at the same time, this goal can be reached by a traditional division of labor between husband and wife or by the vocational employment and earnings of both of them.

In the traditional family the creation of a new household by a young couple was not equivalent with ending their dependence and subordination to their parents.

The significant "modern" value consists of 1) the desire to move out of the parental home in order to be economically emancipated and 2) the ability to set up one's own home. Such a value is linked to the tendency to create a nuclear family.

Universal values for becoming married include the following: 1) "to secure care;" 2) "the proper age to become married has been reached;" 3) "to regulate sexual intercourse;" 4) "desire for having children;" 5) "sexual attractiveness of partner;" 6) "fear of remaining a bachelor or spinster."

An examination of traditional, modern and universal values for becoming married demonstrates the higher popularity of modern values which are the consequences of adopting the "satisfaction of emotional needs" as the most salient function of the contemporary family.

TABLE 4 :   TRADITIONAL, UNIVERSAL AND MODERN VALUES IN GETTING MARRIED BY SEX. COLLECTIVE INDICATORS : FIGURES DETERMINE THE AMOUNT OF REASONS OF CHOSEN CATEGORY

(See Table 3)

Kind of Values	Male Values, Answers of :		Female Values, Answers of :		Own Values, Answers of:	
	Men	Women	Men	Women	Men	Women
Traditional	24.0	30.6	32.7	23.5	11.3	8.8
Universal	82.5	92.7	94.3	80.4	45.3	44.6
Modern	121.0	96.9	104.9	131.9	130.2	139.2

The above comparison confirms the general trend to become married for universal and modern reasons. It should be emphasized, though, that respondents more often attribute universal values to men and women in general than they do to themselves. Women respondents answering for self show the greatest modernity of values. Women respondents attribute higher value modernity to "Females in General" than to "Males in General." Finally, men respondents attribute less value modernity to "Females in General" than do women respondents, while men respondents attribute greater modernity to "Males in General" than do women respondents.

In this case, given that modernity is positively valued, the tendency to fortify one's own sex as modern is confirmed again. Mention should also be made of the finding that traditional values are few in females' description of values for self. It has been observed that there is a tendency for respondents to avoid those concepts associated with the traditional family which determine the position of males and females as being unequal.

When comparing motives to values the traditional values are generally unpopular, except to a small degree in terms of economic motives (to a small degree). Familial motives are most popular with relation to universal values and least popular with relation to modern values. Emotional motivations are by far the most popular when combined with modern values, and are probably a major substitute for familial motives (at least more so than are economic motives).

TABLE 5:   CROSS-TABULATION OF VALUES & MOTIVES   N=1,648

Motives	Economic			Familial			Emotional		
	Male	Female	Resp.	Male	Female	Resp.	Male	Female	Resp.
VALUES									
Traditional	25.1	19.1	6.9	2.5	7.5	2.9	—	—	—
Universal	—	—	—	60.3	79.0	38.0	27.7	7.9	6.9
Modern	24.8	52.3	29.7	—	—	—	130.9	136.1	163.0

When comparing responses by age category, the following proposition results: the younger the respondent, the more likely is the respondent to be motivated to marriage by emotional motives. However, level of education modifies attitudes toward universal values : the higher the educational level, the more often is marriage precipitated by universal factors (i.e., according to the basic functions). This means that emotional motives characterize marital decisions of younger and less-educated respondents.

An analysis of correlations of the answers given by married and unmarried respondents indicates that marital status does not show a significant difference in the opinions of the two respondent categories (married and unmarried) in the way in which they express emotional motivations. (In the sample, 33.3 of the respondents were married and the remaining percentage of respondents were unmarried.) The single status, however, does seems to be related to respondents of younger age.

Marital decisions as based upon emotional motivations for "Males in General" were given 91.6 points by unmarried respondents and 93.0 points by married respondents. Marital decisions as based upon emotional motivations for "Females in General" were given 83.0 points by unmarried respondents and 86.7 points by married respondents. When the respondents described their own emotional motivations for marital decisions, the unmarried respondents attributed 112.9 points and the married respondents attributed 92.1 point to this reason. In this case, the singles seem to be more romantic than the husbands and wives.

The median age for newlywed couples in Poland (1970) was 24.1 years for the males and 21.7 years for the females. In towns the median age was 24.2 years for the males and 22.0 years for the females and in villages the median age was 24.0 for males and 21.3 for females (see Rocznik Statystyczny, 1970: 92). The majority of newlyweds have attained only primary or vocational educational levels which may indicate that most of these marital decisions were based on emotional motivations. Emotional motivation is the most common marital motivation in Poland.

The Meaning of the Concept of Love as a Motivation to Marry

Asking those "in love" about their feelings is as embarrassing a task as defining the concept of love. Subjective feelings are difficult to rationally analyze, especially so if the analysis is to be done by persons not trained to analyze their own feelings. Thus, in order to facilities such an analysis, the following two questions were used in two different research efforts, 1) Do you think that mutual love is sufficient to achieve success in marriage ? (This question is categorized and close-ended [see Table 6].) (2) Apart from mutual love, what is needed to achieve marital success? (This second question was uncategorized and open-ended; answers were proposed by respondents.)

A questionnaire was published in 1972 in the Youth Daily (*Sztandar Mlodych*) in Warsaw to obtain answers to the first question.

Table 6 indicates that the "love is a necessary, but not the only factor" in marital success is by far the most common response. This means that the majority appreciate the important role of emotional factors in marriage but linked them with other factors which contribute to success in conjugal life.

TABLE 6 :   IS 'MUTUAL LOVE' A SUFFICIENT FACTOR OF MARITAL
                      SUCCESS, (ANSWERING BY SEX)

N=1,648 Persons (in per cent)

	Men	Women	Total
Mutual love is the only and sufficient factor	7.3	7.2	7.2
Mutual love is the necessary factor, but not the only one	81.4	87.7	84.9
Mutual love is desired, but not necessary factor	8.1	3.1	5.3
More important than love are other factors	2.3	1.2	1.7
The answer is difficult; no answer	0.9	0.8	0.9

However, linking the data with other variables manifests somewhat different results. Concerning the age variables, the young, more than the old, are of the opinion that "love is a necessary, but not the only" factor (85.9% for the youngest and 66.7% for the oldest). Yet the response that "love is a desired factor but not necessary one" was much more popular among the oldest (20.0%) than it was among the youngest.

The educational level of the respondents is another modifying variable. The response, "love as a necessary factor but not the only one," is a slightly more common response among the highly educated (82.2 %) than among persons with only a primary educational level (75.8%). The less educated respondents more often gave the response, "love is the only and sufficient factor," further indicating that the younger and less-educated are prone to stress love as a primary factor in marital success.

Psychical more than material factors were mentioned as supplemental to love (see Question Two). These factors include matching of characters, mutual understanding, common interests, esteem and fidelity. (Only 30% of the answers indicated the factors, "security of economic conditions;" "possessing one's own apartment;" and "job security" as factors of marital success). However, since these answers were given as responses to an open question, the results are inconclusive.

All of these expressions were treated as factors associated with love but meaning something other than love. These qualities, however, seem to be those that we commonly identify as "love" qualities. The above mentioned elements of marital success do not indicate "love" for most young people, thus preventing us from discerning exactly their meanings of the "love" concept. We are only informed of what is not considered as love. Perhaps for most loved and loving persons, the concept of love is mysterious, thereby providing the major attraction of this popular feeling.

This notion is acknowledged as typical. In a representative sample of an adult urban population drawn in 1965 by the Center of Public Opinion, similar regularities were observed (Lobodzinska, 1970: 92). 16.3% gave positive response to the statement that "mutual love is the only and sufficient condition for marital success." The majority indicated other conditions, primarily personality factors over material or financial ones. This may mean that the majority of young adults make a distinction between the "love concept" and other characteristics such as appreciation of personality, admiration and shared interests.

The question now arises that if young people are, in their own words, motivated to marry because of love, what is the meaning which they attach to the love concept? The imputation of a deep meditation or a philosophical viewpoint to the love concept is nonsensical, and it may only be guessed here that this love concept is based solely upon emotional or sexual drives.

In a sense, the Latin phrase, "ignotum per ignotum" applies here: they attempt to explain an unknown with another unknown. As an illustration of this statement, a quote is presented from information sent to the youth weekly, *Dookola Swiata* (*Around the World*, No. 14) in 1972.

"The first year of my studies I have spent far from my parents, in another town. Then, there I have met my ideal. I was dreaming during nights about him, my beloved. It is quite obvious that the first impression was a thunder and I fell in love immediately. I felt excited and experienced about life, almost as in paradise. We had dates very often since we studied the same subject at the university. In those days I did not wonder if he was in love with me or if his love came later, reflecting my feelings toward him. At the very beginning my love and infatuation did not allow me sober consideration. It seemed to me, he was a miracle, an ideal, my darling. Now, from the nine years of our marriage I have a perspective. Now I must state, that it does not make sense if one is guided by feelings only. After a while every ideal becomes a common person, and imperfections begin to play an important role. At that time I did not take it for granted. Strictly speaking, I was too young for this kind of knowledge and/or experience. I was 18 and what may such a creature know about real life? After a few years, unfortunately after getting married, I got the chance to be convinced about his self-confidence and selfishness. Nice and well-mannered was only for those whom he needed. My awareness connecting marriage was limited only to very few indications: it is as a duty for the wife to love her husband, she should be faithful and a good organizer of the housekeeping. The husband is obliged to help. The joys and griefs should be shared by both of them. But everything happened completely differently."

Here is another quotation from the same weekly.

"I looked at him in a tramway; he looked at me and we laughed. We observed each other for a while and that day I did not go to the university. This fellow I liked. I was always dreaming about dark hair, blue eyes and a nice body. We went to the cinema instead of to school. Afterwards we took a long walk home. We did not speak too much, but I perceived him watching my legs. We had a date the next day, but he came home with flowers and declared he wanted to marry me. I was very surprised, having no idea how to react. My mother was surprised also. He just came the first time to visit our home. When I was able to speak, I asked him why he acts so rapidly, we do not know each other. He answered, he is in love with me and he does not see any reason to wait. It is obvious to him that sooner or later we will get married. It happened after two years. But first, I experienced a great love. We fell in love. It was a time of passionate kisses and impatient words."

The above cited quotes may be considered as the typical way in which young people imagine love.

Evidently, fates of such excitements vary. Not all lead to marriage, but usually sexual drives and eager decisions of either partner lead to sexual intercourse, as love is generally considered as exaltation.

In this context, we must realize that this type of emotional excitement is essential to young people. Friendship, attachment and rational elements are more commonly attributed to mature, older individuals who "fall in love."

It may be concluded that natural selection is the deciding factor in the majority of marital choices, but it appears to us as a love stereotype. Mate selection is connected with spontaneous feelings and convictions that the selection is free from pressures or constraints. The essential point in these choices is accomplishing them in person, as a result of individual decisions. Parental influence is slight or non-existent in the process of marital choice in contemporary Poland.

Reduction of Parental Authority in Children's Marriages

The "modern" parents try not to express their opinions about the marital decisions of their adult children—such decisions are autonomous choices which cannot be influenced by parental wishes. In some cases this point of view reflects general attitudinal liberalism, but in several others it reflects the parents' belief that objecting to children's plans will probably not change them anyway. This can only function to strain parent-child relationships. It is not an exception for children to fulfil certain desires against their parents' will, be they in terms of marital, educational, vocational or occupational decisions. More traditional parents will sometimes express their opinions, but their viewpoints are seldom taken into consideration by their offspring.

J. Lutynski's research (1960) indicates positive parental attitudes toward daughters' marital plans in 63% of the cases, whereas parental attitudes toward sons' marital plans were positive in 51% of the cases. According to the author's hypothesis, the difference may be explained by the popular notion of a surplus of women compared to the total number of men in the population. This phenomenon lowers the female family's normative standards concerning the overall "quality" of the son-in-law (occupation, character, family background, etc.).

The relative proportion of positive and negative attitudes toward children's marital plans allows us to conclude that numerous marriages were contrary to parental wishes. Thirty-seven per cent of parents were against daughters' marital decisions, while almost 50% of parents were against sons' marital decisions. Despite parental reluctance, their children decided to marry. This means that parental authority in the contemporary Polish family is significantly reduced when compared to relationships within the traditional Polish family.

An analysis of parental attitudes (Lobodzinska, 1970 : 92) in a population of Warsaw engineers gives the basis for a similar deduction. Couples who had been married for many years tried to describe retrospectively their parents' attitudes at the time of their marriage and described them in negative terms. This negative position was especially significant since it was remembered over several years' time.

There are insufficient data to detect if the negative attitude was an important influence in further relations with the married children. It may be assumed that the consequences of objecting to parents' wishes are not as significant in present times. Present-day consequences indicate a lack of cordial relations or are simply neglected while confronting the fact of an existing marriage. We may illustrate with a sample of interviewed engineers.

"The wedding was in the parents'-in-law home. It was performed with grand elegance in spite of their pretensions toward their son (my husband). I was divorced, so we are not allowed a church marriage. They were reluctant toward me in the beginning, but afterwards I was accepted. However, I hardly tried to be accepted and to gain their confidence, I finished my university studies while being employed, after which our son was born. However, it may be assumed that their resignation and acceptance came at the moment they decided to perform the wedding in their own house."

Or—

"My uncle, who helped my mother with finances while I was young, was against my marriage. He emphasized that my husband comes from different surrounding (from the country); but when he realized my determination to get married, he gave up and discontinued his comments. My wedding was in his home, with his support. His housing conditions were the best in the family, but he also expressed his desire to help me in the moment of entering my adult life."

Reluctant attitudes toward marital plans are not exceptions in this population.

The most satisfied parents seem to be parents with daughters who are not engineers but whose husbands are engineers (73%). The least satisfied are parents of daughters who are engineers. This means that the parents of engineers (male or female) are more fastidious than are parents-in-law. They are also more disposed to reveal their negative attitudes toward the marital plans of their children. Finally, the parents-in-law of male engineers expressed the most positive attitudes

TABLE 7 :   PARENTS' ATTITUDE TOWARD MARITAL PLANS—
ENGINEERS' ANSWERS,
214 MEN & 45 WOMEN,
IN PER CENT

Attitude of Parents and Parents-in-Law	Answers			
	Men Engineers'		Women Engineers'	
	Parents	In-Laws	Parents	In-Laws
Good	52.0	73.0	49.0	54.0
Neutral	18.0	10.0	20.0	13.0
Unfavorable	20.5	11.0	29.0	22.0
No Answer, Parents Dead	9.5	6.0	2.0	11.0
TOTAL	100.0	100.0	100.0	100.0

since their daughters were marrying up in terms of occupational and educational background. In comparing parents of female engineers (49%) with parents of females who were not engineers (73%), this difference is due to the fact that the parents of female engineers are more fastidious in accepting a son-in-law of equal or lower occupational status, whereas parents of non-engineer females gladly accept the advancement that their daughters make when marrying an engineer.

Almost half of the parents are unsatisfied or neutral with their children's choices. Despite lack of consensus, however, the young engineers married according to their plans. This shows that engineers' parents do not have great influence in their children's marital decisions. Lutynski's data indicate that this rule has a more universal meaning, and is not specific to the social environment of engineers.

These positive attitudes of engineers' parents toward their children's marriages were based on different premises. One of the premises for acceptance was the set of personality traits associated with their child's future spouse. Another premise was the fact that the several parents had an intimate acquaintance with the parents of the future spouse. realizing that the social and economic position of the latter were similar to, or higher than, their own. The promise of improved housing conditions and standerds of living led to increased acceptance of the future spouse. Finally, in some cases, the parents were anxious to launch the grown-up child from the home, causing them to see the spouse in a more positive light.

The reasons for negative attitudes are more numerous... First, economic and class reasons for negative attitudes are characteristic of societies with high rates of social mobility. Parental reluctance results from the following (1) lack of dowry or possessions; 2) social class differences (such as rural/urban descent or peasant/working class/intelligentia families); and 3) educational level and or professional aspirations of the child's future spouse or the parents.

A second reason for reluctance is the past marital and family status of the future spouse (e.g., if he is divorced, has children from a previous marriage and is not allowed to have the wedding ceremony in the Catholic church). Other kinds of reluctance occurred when the child's future spouse was of a different nationality; when the age gap between the spouses is too big; when the future spouse is too immature or too mature for marriage; or when parents dislike something about the candidate such as his/her character traits, relations to the church and religion, state of health or his family relationships. These parental characteristics just identified are strongly connected with the traditional family value system.

For the "modern" younger generation, it is obvious that parental criteria have been rejected as being useless and old-fashioned. Since parental attitudes have little influence, the most important factor for the young people who marry are their feelings and involvement with their future spouse.

It appears, then, that emotional motivations in marital decisions play the most important role in this population. Some did use the expression "love" but several others attempted to name their feelings in more rational terms. (See Table 8).

Clearly, family pressure has little bearing if it goes against the child's wishes. Sometimes this pressure will strengthen both the child's opposition toward the parent and the child's will to accomplish his or her plans. The engineers emphasize expressive functions of marriage, although they attempt to label them in rational terms, such as love leads to having one's own home, to marriage with a partner who has common interests and to emotional involvement. The marital status is the "proper" one and they tend, therefore, to marry.

TABLE 8:   MARITAL MOTIVES FOR ENGINEERS: SAMPLE (N=259)

Love	44%
Common Interests and Opinions	18%
The Partner Has Good Character	29%
Tendency to Stabilize; to Have Own Home; to Have Children	29%
TOTAL	120% (because more than one response was allowed)

Concluding Remarks

On the basis of data derived from several samples, we may conclude that emotional motivations in marital decisions are common in contemporary Poland. However, the question remains, "If love-motivated marriages increase the chance of securing a compatible mate, will this influence success later on in life ?"

The process of "marital individualization" results from the factor of love as being significant in making the decision to marry. This process is composed of the following elements. 1) Marriage is a private matter for young people. 2) Emotional involvement is the primary motive for marriage 3) The major goal of love-motivated marriage is the creation of a platform for conjugal relations of many kinds (e.g., consensus, cooperation, shared interests, etc.). The emphasis upon child-rearing in traditional families has shifted to an emphasis upon strong conjugal bonds. Marital individualization is a tendency of the younger generation to oppose traditional family customs assuming that contemporary marriage has unique goals. Youth today consciously reject the traditional forms of mate selection. It is still too early and habits and behavior are too new to evaluate clearly if the present trend ef emotional searching will become a standard basis for future marital decision norms.

REFERENCES

Around the World.
1972   (Dookola Swiata.) Number 14.

Burgess, E.W. and H.S. Locke.
1953   The Family. New York : American Book Company.

Chalasinski, J.
1938   The Young Peasant Generation. (Mlode pokolenie chlopow.) Warsaw.

Duda-Dziewierz, K.
1938   Malopolska Village and Emigration to America. (Wies Malopolska a emigracja amerykanska.) Warsaw.

Girard, A.
1964   The Marital Choice in France. (Le choix du conjoint en France.) Paris : Universite de Paris.

Lobodzinska, B.
1963   By-ways of Marriage and Family. (Manowce malzenstwa i rodziny.) Warsaw: Wiedza Powszechna.
1971   "From Research on Customs of Contemporary Youth." ("z badan nad obyczajami wspolczesnej mlodziezy.") Journal of Modern Village (Wies Wspolczesna) : Numbers 9 and 10.
1970   Marriage in the City. (Malzenstwo w miescie.) Warsaw: Panstwowe Wydawnictwo Naukowe.

Lutynski, J.
1960   "Research on Young Marriages." ("Badania mloydymi malzenstwami.") Sociological Survey (Przeglad Socjologiczny) : XIX/1.

Peasants' Diaries. (Pamietniki chlopow.)
1935-1936   Warsaw.

Statistical Yearbook. (Rocznik Statystyczny.)
1972   Warsaw : Glowny Urzad Statystyczny.

Tryfan, B.
1968   The Social Position of the Rural Woman- (Pozycja spoleczna kobiety wiejskiej.) Warsaw : Ksiazka i wiedza.

Wegrzynowski, M.A.
1965   "Customs of Student Youth; Customs of Going Steady." ("Obyczajowosc mlodziezy studenckiej, zwyczaj 'chodzenia'.") Youth in the Process of Change. (Mlodziez epoki przemian.) Warsaw : Nasza Ksiegarnia.

Wierzbicki, Z.
1963   Zmiaca, 50 Years Later. (Zmiaca w pol wieku pozniej,) Wroclaw : Ossolineum.

Zawistowicz-Adamska, K.
1948   Village Community. (Spolecznosc wiejska.) Warsaw : Ludowa Spoldzielnia Wydawnicza.

Comparative Attitudes About Marital Sex Among Negro Women in the United States, Great Britain and Trinidad

ROBERT R. BELL*

In recent years the writer has carried out studies among lower-class Negro families in Philadelphia (United States), Reading (England) and San Fernando (Trinidad).[1] In those studies the major interest was in the lower-class Negro woman and her various family roles. In previous papers the lower-class Negro families in each of the three societies have been examined as to subcultural variations with regard to their dominant societies as well as some aspects of the subcultures compared with respect to one another. The interest in this paper is to look at variations with regard to marital sexual values in the three societies. However, first a brief examination of the family setting in the three societies particularly with regard to their similarities, gives needed background material.

There is a strong body or research evidence to show that in the Negro lower-class in the United States there is limited value attached to marriage.[2] As a result it is very common for the family to be female headed. Even when there is a man present, he is often there for short periods of time and is functionally of limited importance. Furthermore, it is clear that these patterns have been maintained for many years. For example, the significance of the female head family among Negroes has its roots in the slavery system and was further developed and maintained by the caste system of the Negro in the South following the Civil War. As a result, the Negro male was often limited in family involvement because of low economic opportunity and because the climate of racial prejudice made his participation as the family head extremely difficult. An important characteristic of the family in the Negro lower-class continues to be the major role of importance being the mother. This implies that a variety of other role and behavior characteristics are greatly influenced by the importance of the mother in the Negro lower-class.

---

*Professor of Sociology, Temple University, Philadelphia, Penn., U.S.A.

[1]Robert R. Bell, "The One-Parent Mother In The Negro Lower Class," *Eastern Sociological Society*, New York, April 1965; "Lower Class Negro Mother's Aspirations For Their Children," *Social Forces*, May, 1965, pp. 493-500; "The Lower-Class Negro Family In The United States and Great Britain," *Race*, July, 1969, pp. 1173-181; and "Marriage and Family Differences Among Lower Class Negro and East Indian Women in Trinidad," *Race*, June, 1970, pp. 59-73.

[2]See: Bell, "The One-Parent Mother In The Negro Lower Class," *op. cit.*, and Lee Rainwater, *Family Design*, Chicago: Aldine Publishing Co., 1965, pp. 28-60.

The background of the American Negro as related to the plantation system is very familiar to the Negro family in the West Indies. In general, the similarities between the two groups are: both came from African origins into white dominated plantation systems as slaves, and for both groups slavery had the effect of destroying most of the traditional functions of the family.

There have been a number of studies made of the family in the West Indies, but few within the past ten years.[3] In general, the studies agree that the Negro lower-class family in the West Indies is commonly characterized by the female head with generally limited significance of the male in the family and little importance attached to birth legitimacy for either the mother or the child. These patterns are very similar to the ones found in the United States among lower-class Negro families.

However, for many West Indians who migrated to Great Britain there was the feeling and reality of having entered the middle class.[4] When the immigrant is contrasted with the lower-class Negro in the United States, he does not live an isolated life in ghettos. As a result, the West Indian generally feels himself to be a part of Great Britain. While he may feel somewhat different, he does not feel as isolated as does the American Negro. It was found that the West Indian immigrant could get jobs and live in areas in Great Britain that were about the same as was available to the white lower-middle class. As a result he saw himself as being more middle class in Great Britain than he had been in the West Indian country he had migrated from. It appears that for most of the migrants to England, their move represented upward mobility.

---

[3]Judith Blake, *Family Structure in Jamaica*, Glencoe, Illinois: The Free Press, 1961; Edith Clarke, *My Mother Who Fathered Me*, London; George Allen and Unwin, 1957; Yehudi A. Cohen, "Structure and Function: Family Organization and Socialization in a Jamaican Community", *American Anthropologist*, August, 1956; G. E. Cumper, "The Jamaican Family: Village and Estate", *Social and Economic Studies*, March, 1958, pp. 76-108; William Davenport, "The Family System of Jamaica", *Social and Economic Studies*, Jamaica, December, 1961, pp. 452-4; Sidney M. Greenfield, *English Rustics in Black Skin*, New Haven, Conn., College and University Press, 1966; F. M. Henriques, Family and Colour in Jamaica, London, Eyre and Spottiswoode, 1953; Dom Basil Matthews, *The Crisis in The West Indian Family*, University College of the West Indies, 1953; Keith F. Otterbein, "Caribbean Family Organization: A Comparative Analysis", *American Anthropologist*, February, 1965; Hyman Rodman, "Marital Relationships in a Trinidad Village," *Marriage and Family Living*, May, 1961, pp. 166-70; M. G. Smith, *Kinship and Community in Carriacou*, New Haven, Conn., Yale University Press, 1962; M. G. Smith, *West Indian Family Structure*, Seattle, Washington, University of Washington Press, 1962; Raymond Smith, "The Family in the Caribbean", in *Caribbean Studies: A Symposium*, Mona, Jamaica, Institute of Social and Economic Studies, 1957; N. Solien, "Household and Family in the Caribbean", Social and Economic Studies, Jamaica, March, 1960, pp. 101-6; and J. Mayone Stycos and Kurt W. Back, *The Control of Human Fertility* in Jamaica, Ithica, New York, Cornell University Press, 1964.

[4]See R. B. Davidson, *Black British: Immigrants to England*, London, Oxford University Press, for I.R.R., 1966; Mary Dines, "The West Indian Family," *Race*, Vol IX, No. 4, 1968, pp. 522-5; Katrin Fitzherbert, *West Indian Children in London*, Occasional Papers on Social Administration, No. 19, 1967; Ruth Glass, Newcomers: The West Indians in London, London, George Allen and Unwin, 1960; and Sheila Patterson, *Dark Strangers*, Harmondsworth, Penguin Books, 1965.

In general, the lower-class Negro family in Trinidad is similar to the family characteristics of the West Indies. The family tends to be female-centered, with late marriages (when marriages occur), low values placed in the interpersonal nature of marriage and with minimal concern about the legitimacy of offspring. In Trinidad there are no racial ghettos but homogeneous housing areas based on social class. Of the Island's population, 43 per cent are Negro and 37 per cent East Indian, and they frequently live intermingled with one another and share in common a similar social class level.

The people in the samples studied in the three different societies all have similar origins in that they come out of slave backgrounds and their development of adaptive family forms have been very similar. However, only two of the groups, the United States and Trinidad, continue to follow family patterns different from those ideally stated and/or followed by the dominant elements of their societies. In the United States this is due to a combination of racial discrimination and low social class status. In Trinidad it is primarily due to low social class factors. By contrast, the Negroes in Great Britain have reduced their differences from the broader society by being less racially discriminated against than their counterparts in the United States and less lower class restricted than their counterparts in Trinidad. Thus, the Negro in Great Britain is to a great extent a part of the middle class in that country. Given these differences it was therefore hypothesized that: the views about marital sex will be similar among Negro women in the United States and Trinidad and reflect their subcultural values while those of the women in Great Britain will be more conventional and middle class by British standards (as well as by United States and Trinidad standards).

SAMPLES

In the United States the sample was taken from parent lists in three elementary school districts in the city of Philadelphia in 1965. The districts were almost totally Negro, and on the basis of demographic data classified as lower class. There were interviews with 194 mothers who had at least one child in the four to seven year range. The interviewing was done by two Negro graduate students using a schedule consisting of 102 items. The two interviewers had grown up in the same general neighborhood and "could speak the language."

With a few minor changes the same interview schedule was used in the Reading, England study. In 1968 a sample was drawn of 200 West Indian women living in Reading, all of whom had one child under ten years of age. There were no residential records of where the West Indians live in Reading but in consultation with several people who knew the West Indian community, the population distribution in Reading was estimated and divided up by residential areas. The percentage of the total Reading West Indian population in each area was estimated and a proportionate number of interviews were assigned. For each area an interviewer went to a house where she knew the woman would meet the sample requirements. When the interview was finished she would get the names of other eligible West Indian women in that area, add those to the list she already had, and randomly select the next interview. All 200 of the interviews were done by West Indian women who were trained and supervised throughout the interviewing period.

The Trinidad study was carried out in 1969 in central Trinidad. The sample studied was from an area not far from the second largest city on Trinidad, that of San Fernando with a population of about 40,000. However, the area where the respondents lived was primarily rural. To qualify for the sample a woman had to live within the defined area and have at least one child between one and ten years of age. In the area chosen for study, streets were picked at random and the interviewers went to each house on the street and interviewed the woman if she met the requirement of having at least one child under ten years of age. The interviews were done by two trained Negro female interviewers who lived in the area. There were 200 interviews done using the same schedule as used in the United States and Great Britain samples.

BACKGROUND

The ages of the two samples of women in the United States and Great Britain were exactly the same, 30 years old. However, the women in Trinidad were on the average seven years older. About 90 per cent of the women in the United States and Great Britain were Protestants, but neither group showed any strong tendency for church attendance. By contrast, two-thirds of the Trinidad women were Roman Catholics and they were characterized by a high level of church attendance.

TABLE 1

Marital Status (Number and Percent) of the Women in the Three Samples at the Time of the Interview

	United States		Great Britain		Trinidad	
	No.	%	No.	%	No.	%
Single (Never Married)	48	26	16	8	49	25
Married	72	40	177	90	120	60
Widowed, Divorced or Separated	62	34	4	2	31	15
Totals	182	100%	197	100%	200	100%

Table 1 shows the marital status of the women in the three samples. It will be noted that the marriage rate in Great Britain is as high as for that population in general, while in the United States and Trinidad the marriage rate in the two samples is below that found in their overall respective societies. There are also important differences between the three samples on the number of children they have. The mean number of children in the United States was 5.8, in Great Britain 3.2 and in Trinidad 6.3. So the Negro women in Great Britain have a much higher marriage rate and a much lower number of children than did their counterparts in the other countries.

A more positive definition and view of marriage was found among the Great Britain women than among those in the other two samples. For example, 60 per cent of the British sample rated their marriages as "very good" or "good", compared to 48 per cent of the United States women and only 28 per cent of the Trinidad women. For a large number of women in all three groups, there was little positive identification with marriage. To illustrate, over a third of the women in all three samples said they would never marry if they had it to do all over again. There was an even stronger rejection of their specific husbands by the American women (46 per cent) and the Trinidad women (50 per cent) as compared to the British women (35 per cent) who said that if they had it to do all over again they would never marry the same man.

One important consequence of sexual behavior in all societies is the legitimacy or illegitimacy of offspring. An important part of the middle class values common to all three societies is the assumption that legitimacy is very significant. But in the Negro sub-cultures that developed out of slavery this was often an area of irrelevancy. That is, one would ideally marry to make a child legitimate but in reality if one didn't it wasn't very important. Personal experience with illegitimacy was an experience common to many women in all three samples about two-thirds of all the women in each sample had at least one child before they were married. As indicated, this has been a pattern for many generations and as a result social stigma tends to be minimal. This is reflected in several findings. For example, 81 per cent of the women in the United States, 77 per cent in Great Britain and 78 per cent in Trinidad said that within their social setting there were no negative feelings directed at women who were not married and had a child. However, there were some sharp differences among the women to attach some stigma to the illegitimate child. This is reflected in the findings that 36 per cent of the American, 50 per cent of the British and 95 per cent of the Trinidad women felt that it was important for a woman to marry for reasons of making her child legitimate. These findings indicate that for the woman the concern with legitimacy when it occurs is centered on the child rather than the mother. However, the evidence suggests that the Negro woman in Britain was becoming increasingly concerned with legitimizing the role of the mother. In this area at least the pressures of the dominant values of Great Britain appeared to exert a rapid and strong influence on the Negro migrants.

Before looking at some of the specific responses with regard to marital sexuality it is important to discuss some general values in this area. A basic part of marriage is that of the sexual rights and obligations the partners have to one another. In the middle-class in the three societies studied the ideal values restrict all sexual experience in marriage to the partners and any deviance from that is usually seen as extremely threatening to the overall marriage relationship. However, the low expectations associated with marriage role relationships in the Negro lower-class in the U.S. and Trinidad would not lead one to expect there to be very strong values associated with the exclusive nature of sexual expression in marriage. In general, the lower class places much less importance on sexual behavior than does the middle class. This is probably because sex is more open and does not usually take on the highly emotional and psychological dimensions that it does in the middle class. In the lower class, sex is usually engaged in for immediate gratification and not as an expression of a strong emotional commitment between the couple.

It is often assumed that because the lower class is permissive about some heterosexual relations that the subculture is characterized by a general sexual permissiveness. But such is not the case because many types of sexual intimacy common to the middle class are minimized or even rejected in the lower class. For example, extended sexual foreplay and petting are not common sexual patterns in the lower class of the Negro or the White in the U.S. The sexual act tends to be the entire focus, with little foreplay or variation in sexual techniques. In part these limitations are related to the fact that most individuals in the lower class have limited knowledge about sex.

With the greater importance and sense of satisfaction reached by the Reading women in their marriage roles and role relationships than was found for the Philadelphia and Trinidad respondents, it would also be expected that more positive notions about the sexual aspects of marriage would be found among those women than the ones in the other two samples.

TABLE 2

Number and Percent Responses in the Three Samples to the Question: "How Do You Feel About the Importance of Sex in Marriage for the Husband? (and the Wife?)"

For the Husband	United States No.	United States %	Great Britain No.	Great Britain %	Trinidad No.	Trinidad %
Very important	99	54	83	41	147	76
Important	82	45	107	54	47	23
Not Important	2	1	10	5	1	1
Totals	183	100%	200	100%	195	100%
For the Wife						
Very Important	52	28	66	33	66	33
Important	119	65	101	51	90	45
Not Important	11	7	33	16	44	22
Totals	182	100%	200	100%	200	100%

The respondents were asked two questions about the relative importance of sex in marriage for the spouses. They were asked: "How do you feel about the importance of sex in marriage for the husband? and the wife?" Table 2 shows the significant differences given by the three populations for both questions. The Philadelphia women more often said sex was "very important" for the husband (54 per cent) than did the Reading women (41 per cent). However, of the Trinidad women 76 per cent said it was "very important" to the man. The Trinidad women were more apt to define sex as "not important" for the woman (22 per cent) than were the Reading women (16 per cent) or those in Philadelphia (7 pecent).

An examination of Table 2 indicates that the Reading women were more apt to suggest equal importance of sex in marriage for *both* the husband and the wife than were the other two groups of women. In the Philadelphia sample, the women said sex was "very important" for women in only 28 per cent of the cases. Among the Reading and Trinidad respondents it was 33 per cent. This difference is also seen in a related question asking about the relative importance of sex in marriage for the husband and wife. For example, among the Philadelphia sample 42 per cent of the women said sex in marriage was more important for the man as compared to 23 per cent of the Reading and 25 per cent of the Trinidad respondents. Very few in either group suggested sex was more important for the wife. Five per cent in Philadelphia, two per cent in Reading and one per cent in Trinidad. But there was a significantly greater number of women in Reading and Trinidad than in Philadelphia holding to an equalitarian point of view about sex. In the Reading and the Trinidad samples 75 per cent said they thought sex in marriage had about equal importance for both the husband and wife as contrasted to only 53 per cent in the Philadelphia sample.

Extra Marital Sexual Values

For many, if not most, middle class women in the three societies nothing would be more threatening to her marriage than to find that her husband was sexually involved with another woman. If a husband or wife shows a romantic or sexual interest in someone else, this is often viewed as catastrophic to the ego-relationship of marriage. However, in the middle class there are male and female differences. Many middle-class men feel that adultery on the part of the woman is an irreparable blow to their marriage. Women are less inclined to see adultery in the same extreme way. The middle-class husband who has what is seen by the wife as a single sexual encounter may be forgiven; however, if he has an affair of some length, the wife is much more threatened because, to her, a lengthy affair implies that her husband must care about the other woman — thus the "other" woman becomes an emotional threat. In the Negro lower class, marriage has not usually assumed these values and therefore the views about adultery have been quite different from those of the middle class.

A "folk" notion that probably has been common to most cultures of the world is the belief that men are incapable of being sexually monogamous.

This has long been a belief held by many women as well as men in the lower class. Liebow found among the men he studied, that not only was there the belief that men could not be sexually monogamous over time but that they were also incapable of it at any point in time. That is, that no man could be sexually satisfied with only one woman at a time.[5] This belief provides a rationalization for the man not restricting himself to one woman — a kind of folk biological determinism that makes him incapable of being monogamous because it goes contrary to his very biological nature.

The lower-class Negro man in the United States is more apt to also see the rights of sexual freedom for women than is the male in the middle class. Rainwater found that in the Negro lower class the men, when compared to lower-class whites, were more apt to think that a wife would seek sexual gratification elsewhere if relations did not go well.[6] However, there is no complete agreement among Negro men as to how much sexual freedom a woman should have. Liebow found that the men in his study felt that in marriage the man had the right to exclusive sexual access to his spouse. But there was no agreement between the lower-class men on other relationships. "Some streetcorner men feel that a partner in a consensual union has a right to demand exclusive sexual access; others deny this."[7]

Among lower-class Negro women in the United States a common belief is that they have the same sexual rights as the man. And whatever the husband or boy friend does with another woman they have the same right to do with another man. "If the husband indulges himself, they have the right to indulge themselves. If the husband steps out on his wife, she has the right to step out on him." Or as Lewis points out the lower status females show a great deal of sex initiative and independence and often say, "I don't have to worry about no man" or "Anything he can do, I can do."[8] These liberal views about sex in marriage are much less apt to be found in the West Indies, particularly in Trinidad. This is because the Trinidad woman places a high value on eventual marriage and therefore believes in strong monogamous restrictions as to sexual behavior. Also their views are a reflection of the strong conservative sexual values that many of them have as a result of being Catholics. The following discussion shows some of the differences between the three groups in their views about extramarital sexual behavior.

The three groups of women were compared in their responses to questions about restricting sexual expression to marriage. The respondents were asked: "Is there any time when you think a married man is justified

[5]Elliott Liebow, *Tally's Corner*: *A Study of Negro Streetcorner Men*, Boston: Little Brown and Co., 1969, p. 120.

[6]Rainwater, *op. cit.*, p. 116.

[7]Liebow, *op. cit.*, p. 104.

[8]Hylan Lewis, *Blackways of Kent*, Chapel Hill, N.C.: University of North Carolina Press, 1955, p. 83.

in 'running around' with another woman?" The same question was also asked about a married woman ever being justified in "running around."

TABLE 3

Number and Percent Responses in the Three Samples to the Question:
"Is there any time when you think a Married Man, (Woman) is justified in 'running around'?"

Man "Running Around"	United States No.	%	Great Britain No.	%	Trinidad No.	%
Yes	108	59	22	11	62	32
No	75	41	178	89	130	68
Totals	183	100%	200	100%	192	100%
Woman "Running Around"						
Yes	77	41	11	6	45	22
No	109	59	189	94	155	78
Totals	186	100%	200	100%	200	100%

There were very sharp differences in the responses given by the three samples. Fifty-nine per cent of the women in Philadelphia and 32 per cent in Trinidad as compared to only 11 per cent of the Reading women felt men were ever justified in "running around". The same wide difference was also found with regard to married women ever justified in "running around", with 41 per cent of the Philadelphia respondents, 22 per cent in Trinidad and 6 per cent of those in Reading answering "yes". It is of interest that the three groups of women hold to essentially single standards although the standards were different. The Reading women believed that *neither* the married man or woman was justified in "running around", while the Philadelphia women very often believed that *both* the man and woman were often justifield in "running around". The Trinidad women fall in between in having a distinct minority saying *both,* but most of them saying *neither.*

The women were also asked: "Should a wife expect 'running around' at one time or another regardless of how good the husband has been?" And the same question was also asked about the wife. On these questions there were also wide differences in the responses of the women in three samples. As to expecting a husband to engage in "running around" the answer was "yes" by 56 per cent of the Philadelphia women but by only 6 per cent of the women in both the Reading and the Trinidad samples.. There were also significant differences in the responses for expecting "running around" by a wife. In Trinidad 33 per cent said "yes" as compared to 30 per cent in Philadelphia and 12 per cent in Reading. In England there is for most a single standard of not expecting "running around" for either the husband or the wife. However, in Philadelphia there is more a double standard with a greater expectation of "running

around" by the husband than by the wife, while in Trinidad just the opposite is true with greater expectation of the wife than the husband
running around. The findings indicate that the Reading women have
more of a shared or equal view of the sexual aspects of marriage than do
the Philadelphia or Trinidad women.

SUMMARY

The overall findings in all three samples leads to the conclusion that
there is a higher positive view toward marriage among the Reading
women than among the women in the other two samples. This is further
reflected in the evidence suggesting that the Reading women see a greater
equality in the rights and obligations of marriage than do the Negro
women in the other two samples. So the views about sexual rights among
the women in Great Britain can be seen as a part of their changing view
as to the egalitarian nature of marriage. That is, the egalitarian beliefs
that men and women have equal sexual needs and rights in marriage and
these needs are to be met within the exclusive setting of monogamy.

The findings of this study indicate that values about sexual behavior
in marriage are strongly influenced by social class position. All of the
evidence suggests that the West Indians who migrated to Great Britain
shared values very similar to those of the Trinidad women when they
lived in the islands. However, of the three groups of women studied they
were the one group subjected to significant social change. That is, the
women in the the United States and Trinidad were living in a social setting
that for most of them had existed all of their lives and even for at least
several generations. So the women in the United States and Trinidad
followed their life long socialization to sexual values where the women in
Britain were resocialized into the middle class values and as a result
strongly identified with and followed the new values.

TABLE 4

Number and Percent Responses in the Three Samples to the Question:
"Should a wife (husband) expect 'running around' at one time or another regardless of how good the husband (wife) has been?"

Expect of Husband	United States No.	%	Great Britain No.	%	Trinidad No.	%
Yes	102	56	13	6	6	3
No	81	44	187	94	193	97
Totals	183	100%	200	100%	199	100%
Expect of Wife						
Yes	54	30	23	12	66	33
No.	129	70	177	88	134	67
Totals	183	100%	200	100%	200	100%

What generalizations can be made about the three groups? Clearly the historical backgrounds are somewhat different but there is one important sociological difference between the sample in Great Britain and the other two. This is related to the subculture and ghetto-like life patterns found in the United States and Trinidad. In the United States, the women studied lived in the lower class and their ghettos were physical, social and psychological. These women lived in large areas that were almost completely Negro and lower class and were in almost complete isolation from the dominant white world. So the subcultural values were important in her dealing with life as she encountered it. Essentially the same social phenomena was found in Trinidad. However, the one important difference is that the ghetto-like way of life there is not due to racial discrimination, but rather to social class restrictions. By contrast, the Negro in Great Britain is much less isolated either for racial or social class reasons. As a result he feels himself to be a part of Great Britain. While he feels somewhat different, he does not feel as isolated as do the American or the Trinidad lower-class Negroes. Therefore, the acceptance of middle class values about sex in marriage is an indication of the degree of assimilation into society. It also indicates that significant changes may occur with reference to basic family values *if* individuals enter new social patterns that are important and valuable to them.

The Impact of Jewish-Gentile Intermarriage in Canada: An Alternative View*

J. FRIDERES ‡ J. GOLDSTEIN, ‡ ‡

AND R. GILBERT ‡ ‡ ‡

Sociologists have long been concerned with determining the causes and consequences of "intermarriage." Research until the present has concentrated on the former issue. In recent years, however, it has become apparent that the latter issue may be equally (if not more) important. The present research (focusing on Jewish-Jewish and Jewish-Gentile marriages) attempts to measure the impact of religious inter-marriages on offspring in terms of selected social and psychological factors.

Canadian national statistics indicate that the religious inter marriage rate (as measured by nominal faith affiliation) is increasing. (Heer, 1967; Canadian Yearbook, 1957, 1969).

The rate of increase in inter-marriages for Jews has been even higher. In 1951, the intermarriage rate for Jews in Canada was 5.6%; in 1961 this had increased to 7.9% (a 41% increase). Popular literature suggests that inter-marriages are "dysfunctional." (Shanks, 1953; Sklare, 1969: Berman, 1968). Social Scientists have shown that religious inter-marriages have higher separation rates, lower adjustment rates and generally less happy marriages (Landis, 1949, Koening, 1952).

The sociological literature also suggests that religious intermarriage has definite consequences for the offspring of such marriages, specifically it is hypothesized that the offspring from inter-religious marriages are psychologically less well adjusted than offspring in intra-religious marriages, (see Vander Zanden, 1963). However, little systematic research has been undertaken to determine the effects of inter-religious marriages on children. We will now set forth hypotheses relating the effects of Jewish-Gentile inter-religious marriages on offspring with regard to the following characteristics: identity (Religious and Ethnic), alienation, self esteem and anxiety.

* This research was supported by a grant from the Faculty of Graduate Studies, University of Manitoba, Winnipeg, Manitoba.

‡ J. Frideres, Asst. Professor of Sociology, U. of Calgary, Alberta, Canada.

‡‡ J. Goldstein, Asst. Professor, U. of Manitoba, Winnipeg, Canada.

‡‡‡ R. Gilbert. Instructor, John Abbot College, Winnipeg, Canada.

Religious and Ethnic Identity

Ethnic identity, as used in the most general sense, refers to a " universalistic frame of reference for ordering a man's social relationships." (Glaser, 1957 : 31). However, for Jews, identity is not simply a matter of ethnicity. As Rinder (1957), Glaser (1957), Gans (1956), Lazerwitz (1953), and Schoenfeld (1968, 1969) have pointed out, Jewish identity must be viewed as " multifaceted." While all of the above authors disagree as to the total number of components discernable, all agree that there are two major components of Jewish identity : religious and ethnic. The present research will attempt to determine the effects of inter-marriage on these two major components of Jewish identity.

Past research by Baber (1953), Goldstein (1964), Bigman (1957), Kertzer (1967), Goldstein and Goldscheider (1966) has attempted to show that one of the effects inter-marriage has upon offsprings' Jewish identity is to reduce it. Levinson and Levinson (1958), and Rosten (1960) have also suggested that the " mischling " (the offspring of a gentile mother and Jewish father) exists in a " cultureless ' atmosphere and as such would have low Jewish identity[1]. Consequently we formulated the following hypothesis :

1. Offspring from an inter-religious marriage will have less ethnic and religious identity than those from intra-religious marriages[2].

Alienation :

Gordon (1964), Zimmerman and Cervantes (1960) as well as Rosten (1960) have pointed out that offspring of inter-religious marriages can be regarded as somewhat " marginal " in the psychological sense. Our concern centres on what Nettler (1957) and Dean (1961) as well as others refer to as alienation.

While the concept is complex and has been used five different ways (Seeman, 1959), our concern is with only one of the components—self estrangement. Our interest in this component stems from the fact that inter-religious marriages can be viewed as "deviations from the ideal " (which is what self estrangement purports to measure). Thus the general theoretical notion underlying the concept is that the offspring may develop the feeling of being socially isolated and " even being a different person in his behaviour than the self he believes he should be were conditions different." (Clark, 1959 : 849). Thus our second hypothesis is :

2. Offspring from inter-religious marriages will have higher alienation scores than offspring from intra-religious marriages.

Self Esteem

Self Esteem can be viewed as a multidimensional concept (Coppersmith, 1967). For the present research, we are specifically concerned with the " evaluation " dimension. We are concerned with the degree of positive or negative evaluation an individual holds toward himself as an object. Hartman (1958) and Gordon (1964) stated that individuals in " dissonant environments " will have lower self esteem than those in "consonant " ones. Rosenberg (1965) and Gilbert (1971) testing the above claims, found that children raised in a " dissonant religious environment " had slightly more manifest emotional problems than those from "consonant" religious environments. Our test hypothesis is :

3. Offspring from inter-religious marriages will have lower self esteem than those from intra-religious marriages.

Anxiety

Closely related to self esteem is the variable of anxiety. Anxiety is defined as the feeling a child had of being isolated and helpless in a potentially hostile world. Rosenberg (1965), Lipsett (1958), Mitchell (1959) and Crandall and Bellugi (1964) have all pointed out a high negative relationship between self esteem and anxiety. Thus, our last hypothesis dealing with offspring is :

4. Offspring from inter-religious marriages will have higher anxiety scores than those from intra-religious marriages.

The Sample

The community selected was a large mid-western Canadian city with a relatively large number of Jews. A matched pair sample of twenty inter- and intra-religious married couples was selected[3]. Matching was done on the following three characteristics : size of family, SES, and length of marriage.

To obtain the intra-religious married couple, a " complete " list of Jews in the city was obtained by putting together lists from several sources : Canadian Jewish Congress, Bnai Brith, etc. A random sample was then drawn. Letters were sent to the couples explaining the research and stating that they would be contacted by phone within three days to find out if they would participate in the survey. If the subjects agreed to participate, an appropriate time was scheduled for an in-depth interview.

Inter-religious marriages were more difficult to obtain. An initial list was drawn up by local lay leaders as well as rabbis. Additional names were gathered as the research progressed—people calling to volunteer, obtaining names from other inter-married couples, etc. All subjects were interviewed in their home by Jewish males. All offspring between the ages of 6—20 (living in the home at the time of the survey) were included in the sample[4]. However, for the anxiety, self esteem and alienation scales, 6—8 years olds were not included.

Operationalization Procedures

Inter-religious marriage. —The initial operational definition of an " inter-religious marriage " was : any couple which, since the time of marriage until the interview, proclaimed different religious affiliations. Intra-religious marriages were those in which both spouses claimed Judaism as their faith. Inter-religious marriages were those in which the husband was Jewish and the wife Gentile. Intermarriages involving a Jewish wife and a Gentile husband occur much less frequently and are difficult to contact (see Berman, 1968).

Three separate measures were utilized in ascertaining subjects' religious and ethnic identity. The different measures were employed because of the different age levels of the offspring. Subjects were divided into three age groups: 6—8; 9—15; and 16 years or older. A series of short stories and a list of religious terms was presented to the younger group. Ability to "correctly" answer questions about the story and to correctly identify religious terms indicated high religious and ethnic identity. For the older groups, the Rinder (1957) and a modified Rinder scale were used.

A modification of the Dean (1961) alienation scale was used to test for degree of alienation while for the anxiety measure, the Taylor (1953) Manifest Anxiety scale was used. Rosenberg's (1965) Self Esteem scale was utilized to tap this concept.

Results

The first hypothesis was that offspring of inter-religious married couples would have lower religious and ethnic identity than those from intra-religious marriages. Table 1 (A) provides data which partially uphold the hypothesis. A moderate relationship exists between type of marriage and degree of religious identity ($\theta = .28$). For ethnic identity, a similar relationship emerged ($\theta = .22$).

TABLE 1

The relationship between type of marriage (operationalized two ways) and religious and ethnic indentity, alienation, anxiety and self esteem of offspring.

	Religious identity	Ethnic identity	Alienation	Anxiety	Self Esteem
A. Traditional nominal measure	.28	.22	.12	.01	.08
B. Congruency measure	.06	.26	.16	.16	.07

The second hypothesis stated that offspring from inter-religious marriages would be high in alienation than those from intra-marriages. The results in Table I show a θ of .12. Clearly then, the relationship is not that strong. Ability to predict alienation of offspring was not enhanced greatly with knowledge of type of marriage in which they were raised.

Table I also shows that predictability of anxiety and self esteem from type of marriage is very limited. The results suggest that "type of marriage" has little impact on the offspring for these two factors. The question is of course, why? Several alternative answers are possible: (A) the "theory" itself could be wrong; (B) the sample was unique; or (C) operationalization of the concept "inter-marriage" needs to be reviewed. While A and B may account for the negative results, it is our intention to look first at the third possibility. We now turn to operationalizing the concept in a different manner.

Traditional research in intermarriage (as well as the initial definition employed in the present research) assumes that the nominal faiths of the spouses is an indicator of the actual values, and behaviours of these individuals.

Hence, when a couple do not share the same faith, one would predict a greater potential for value conflict between spouses, less consistent socialization of offspring in terms of religion and culture and greater adjustment problems for offspring as a consequence.

The validity of the preceeding assumption is open to challenge (see De Jager, 1970).[6] While a husband and wife may belong to different religious faiths, there may still be a high degree of congruence in their religious and ethnic identities. For any number of reasons an individual may formally belong to a particular faith while actually practising another.

Recognizing that a person's nominal faith may be just that—nominal—it becomes apparent that spouses who belong to different nominal faiths may in actuality be quite congruent in their religious and ethnic identities and vice versa. In light of these comments, it seems appropriate to operationalize the concept of inter-marriage in terms of the actual congruence of the spouses' religious and ethnic identities; and then to determine the relationship between intermarriage and social and psychological characteristics of the children of such marriages.[7]

As previously discussed, all of the husbands in this study were Jewish (nominal faith) while the faith of the wives varied from Jewish to Gentile. Unfortunately no measure of the commitment of non-Jewish wives to their nominal faith was available. Data were available, however, concerning the strength of the non-Jewish wives' religious and cultural identity with regard to Judaism, and these data were used to construct a measure of the congruence of spouses' religious and ethnic identities.

TABLE 2

Relationship between marriage type based on nominal faiths of partners and congruence of spouses' Jewish religious and ethnic identities.

Congruence of spouses' religious and ethnic identities	Nominal Faith	
	Intra-marriage (Jewish-Jewish)	Inter marriage (Jewish-Gentile)
Low	0 (0%)	0 (0%)
Medium	5 (17%)	4 (20%)
High	25 (83%)	16 (80%)
Total	30 (100%)	20 (100%)

N = 100

What is clear from this table is that marriages which were classified as " inter "), on the basis of the nominal faith definition are remarkably similar to those defined as " intra ", in terms of the congruence of the spouses' Jewish religious and ethnic identities.

None of the twenty nominal inter-marriages (or 30 nominal intra-marriages) evidenced a low degree of congruence. Seventeen percent of the nominal intra-marriages fell into the category-medium congruence. The corresponding figure for the nominal inter-marriages fell into the category-medium congruence. The corresponding figure for the nominal inter-marriages was 20% (an insignificant difference considering the small sample size). The remainder of the cases fell (for both nominally "inter" and "intra" into the category of "high congruence." These results suggest a strain toward consistency in beliefs in nominal inter–religious marriages.[9]

These findings would suggest that the assumption that nominal faiths of spouses indicates the degree of conflict between spouses is highly questionable. The use of nominal faiths as a "short hand" method of measuring value conflict (or the potential for such conflict) appears inadequate. An analysis of the actual congruence of spouses' beliefs seems to be a more valid means of assessing actual or potential value conflict.

Our final task is to analyze the consequences of inter–marriage (defined in terms of actual congruence of spouses' religious and ethnic identities) on the previously selected dependent variables. As Table 1 (B) indicates, the relationship between type of marriage and effects on offspring is generally increased (with the exceptions of religious identity and self–esteem). However, the reduction in error in making predictions is not very great—the largest reduction is 15%.

Summary

The above findings suggest that the traditional measure of "inter–religious" marriage is not a sociologically significant measure, i. e., the rules of correspondence are not met. In fact, we view it as a misleading measure. It leads to the unwarranted assumption that all inter–religious marriages involve conflict. Using the model previously discussed (De Jager, 1970), we suggest that a reconceptualization take place.

However it should be pointed out that because of the truncated distribution of scores on the congruence measure, a full test of the suggested model could not be made in this paper. That is, the present sample revealed that most of the marriages were rather highly congruent in terms of spouses' religious and ethnic identities. None of the marriages fell into the category of low congruence. The question of how frequently this latter type of marriage may be observed in reality needs to be answered. Individuals whose religious and ethnic identities are highly incongruent may decide not to marry, or if they do marry, they may not remain together for any extended time period, without reducing the incongruity.

In conclusion, our findings suggest: 1) that inter-religious marriages, *do not* affect children differently than intra–religious marriages, and 2) that the concept of inter–marriage needs to be operationalized in a new fashion. To resolve many of the issues raised in this research a longitudinal study involving a larger and more diversified sample is needed.

FOOTNOTES

1. Their results, however, are clouded by two very important factors: (1) they are ambiguous about the "component (s)" they are investigating and (2) they have no comparative (i. e., intra-religious marriages) data by which to evaluate their results.
2. Inter-religious marriages refer to a Jewish-Gentile marriage while an intra-religious marriage refers to both spouses being Jewish.
3. In addition to selecting the 20 matched pairs, 10 additional intra-marriages were selected.

4. Our pretest found that children under the age of 6 years could not fully comprehend the issues being dealt with.

5. The measure of association used in the analysis is Theta. Theta is appropriate for data which has one ordinal and one nominal variable. It also has the advantage of being interpreted as a P. R. E. measure.

6. De Jager makes a distinction between the following three types of partners: nominal, peripheral and full. Only when there is a maximal difference between partners does he suggest that conflict will occur. Cavan (1970) also notes the importance of considering the actual religiosity of partners in a nominal inter-marriage.

7. We are attempting to " reconceptualize the concept " as suggested by Blumer, 1969; Denzing, 1970; and Willer and Webster, 1970.

8. This congruence measure was arrived at by the following procedure. First, the wife's scores on the Jewish religious identity and ethnic identity scales were summed. Second, the husband's scores on the two scales were summed. The absolute difference between the two scores was then ascertained. The resultant score represented the congruence of the spouses' religious and ethnic identities.

9. While the data presented in table 2 indicates a strain toward consistency in nominal inter-marriages, these data do not reveal the way in which such consistency is produced. It is possible that Jewish males with a weak sense of religious and cultural identity are most likely to marry a non-Jew. On the other hand, it is equally possible that a weak sense of Jewish religious & cultural identity is the result of adjustment to inter-marriage.

REFERENCES

Baber, Ray, 1953, Marriage and The Family, New York, McGraw Hill Co.

Berman, Louis, 1968, Jews and Inter-marriage, New York, Thomas Yoseloff.

Bigᴦan, Stanley, 1957, The Jewish Population of Greater Washington in 1956. Washington, D. C., The Jewish Community Council of Greater Washington.

Blumer, H., 1969, Symbolic Interactionism: Perspective and Method. Englewood Cliffs, New Jersey, Prentice Hall, Inc.

Canadian Yearbook, 1957, Ottawa, Queens Printer 1969.

Cavan, Ruth S., 1970, " Concepts and Terminology in Interreligious Marriage," Journal for the Scientific Study of Religion 9 (Winter): 311–320.

Clark, John, 1959, " Measuring Alienation with a Social System," American Sociological Review 24 (February): 849–852.

Coopersmith, Stanley, 1967, " The Antecedents of Self Esteem," San Francisco, W. H. Freeman and Co.

Crandall, Vaughh and Ursula Bellugi, 1964, "Some Relationships of Interpersonal and Intra-personal Conceptualizations to Personal-social Adjustment," Journal of Personality, 23 (September): 224–232.

Dean, Dwight, 1961, " Alienation: Its Meaning and Measurement," American Sociological Review, 26 (October: 753–758.)

De Jager, H., 1970, " The Socially Mixed Marriage: Some Consideration on Mate Selection and The Transmission of Culture," Sociologia Neerlandica, 6, 2: 14-32.

Denzing, Norman, 1970, " The Research Act " Chicago, Aldine Pub.

Gans, Herbert, 1956, " American Jewry: Present and Future." Commentary 21 (May): 422-431.

Gilbert, Richard, 1971, " Jewish-Gentile Intermarriages : An Empirical Study of its Consequences," unpublished M. A. thesis. University of Manitoba.

Glaser, Nathan, 1957, American Judaism, Chicago, University of Chicago Press.

Goldstein, Sidney, 1964, " Mixed Marriages in the Deep South," Reconstruction, 30 (March): 15-18.

Goldstein, Sidney and Calvin Goldscheider, 1966, " Social and Demographic Aspects of Jewish Inter-marriages," Social Problems 13 (Spring): 386-399.

Gordon, Albert, 1964, Inter-marriage: Interfaith, Interracial, Interethnic, Boston, Beacon Press.

Hartman, Heinz, 1958, " Ego Psychology and the Problem of Adaptation," Journal of American Psychoanalytic Association, Mimeo Series.

Heer, David, 1967, " The Trend of Interfaith Marriages in Canada - -1922-57," American Sociological Review, 27 (April): 245-250.

Kertzer, Morris, 1967, Today's American Jew, New York, McGraw Hill.

Koening, Samuel, 1952, "The Socioeconomic Structure of an American Jewish Community," In Isaque Graebcn and Stewart Henderson Britt (eds.), Jews in a Gentile World, New York, Macmillan.

Landis, Judson, 1949, "Marriages of Mixed and Non-mixed Religious Faith," American Sociological Review, 14 (June): 401-407.

Lazerwitz, Bernard, 1953, "Some Factors in Jewish Identification," Jewish Social Studies. 15 (January): 3-24.

Levinson, Maria and Daniel Levinson, 1958, "Jews Who Inter Marry; Socio-Psychological Bases of Ethnic Identity and Change," Yivo Annual of Jewish Social Science, 12; 103-130.

Lipsett, L. P., 1958, "A Self-Concept Scale for Children and Its Relationship to the Children's Form of the Manifest Anxiety Scale," Child Development. 29 (December): 463-472.

Mitchell, I. U., 1959, "Goal-setting Behaviour as a Function of Self Acceptance Over – and Under – Achievement, and Related Personality Variables," Journal of Educational Psychology. 50 (June): 93-104.

Nettler, Gwynn, 1957, "A Measure of Alienation," American Sociological Review. 22 (December): 670-77.

Rinder, Irwin, 1957, Jewish Identification and Race Relations Cycle, Unpublished Doctoral Dissertation, University of Chicago.

Rosenberg, Morris, 1966, Society and the Adolescent of Self Image. Princeton, New Jersey Princeton University Press.

Rosten Philip, 1960, "The Mischling; Child of the Jewish-Gentile Marriage," Honours paper submitted to the Department of Social Relations, Harvard University.

Schoenfeld, Eugen, 1968, "Jewish Identity and Voting Patterns Among Small Town Jews," Sociological Quarterly, 9 (Spring): 170-174.
1969, "On the Meaning of Alienation," American Sociological Review, 24 (December): 783-791.

Seeman, Melvin, 1959, "On the Meaning of Alienation," American Sociological Review. 24 (December): 783-791.

Shanks, Hershel, 1953, "Jewish-Gentile Intermarriage: Facts and Trends," Commentary, 16, 4: 370-75.

Sklare, 1969, "Intermarriage and the Jewish Future," Commentary, 3, 8, 4: 46-52.

Stinchcombe, Arthur, 1968, Constructing Social Theories, New York, Narcourt, Brace and World.

Taylor, Janet, 1953, "A Personality Scale of Manifest Anxiety," Journal of Abnormal and Social Psychology, 48 (April): 285-290.

Vander, Zanden, 1963, American Minority Relations, New York, Ronald Press Co.

Willer, David and Murray Webster, Jr., 1970: Theoretical Concepts and Obesrvables," Amercian Sociological Review, 35 (August): 748-757.

Zimmerman, Carle and Lucius, Cervantes, 1960, Successful American Families, New York, Pageant Press Inc.

Interracial Marriage in a Southern Area: Maryland, Virginia, and the District of Columbia*

THOMAS P. MONAHAN**

Representing the Southern tradition, Virginia and Maryland in Colonial times enacted strong laws against racial intermarriage, which continued in force until 1967. For over 100 years the District of Columbia, located between Virginia and Maryland at the North-South borderline, allowed the races to marry without legal restriction. Strong social restraints, nevertheless, existed. How frequently mixed marriages occurred in the District in the past, and in all three jurisdictions after 1967, when such marriages could legally take place anywhere in the United States, is a matter of special interest. What change has there been in the extent and nature of interracial marriage in this geographical area?[1]

The Legal Control of Intermarriage

Shortly after the settlement of the English colonies in America, public opinion became antagonistic toward the interbreeding of whites with Negroes, mulattoes, or Indians, and laws were passed to control biological blending and intermarriage of the races (Ballagh, 1902; Johnson, 1919, Guild, 1936; Reuter, 1931:75; Scott, 1930; Wilson, 1965:20; Jordan, 1968:139).

Virginia

Ten years after the importation of a small number of Negro slaves into the colony, the Virginia Assembly in 1630 ordered the sound whipping of one Hugh Davis for lying with a Negress, a heathen (Hening, 1809:I-146; Hurd, 1858:I-229), and in 1640 a Robert Sweet was ordered by the Governor and Council to do penance in church for impregnating a Negro woman, who was to be whipped

* This report was written in the summer of 1976. The collection of the data was supported by a grant from the National Institute of Health, #1-ROI-HD-05137; and assistance in data processing was given by the Villanova University computer center. Annella Lynn made the details of her study available to the writer, although the information developed therefrom is not given in this report, as indicated in footnote 1. Elizabeth H. Monahan rendered editorial and other assistance with the manuscript. Special thanks are also due to Dr. Bettie F. Rogerson, and Mr. Vernon Randall of the Maryland State Department of Health, and to Mr. Deane Huxtable and staff of the Virginia State Department of Health.

**Dept. of Sociology, Villanova University. Villanova, Pennsylvania 19085, U.S.A.

[1]A separate, unpublished analysis has been made by the author on other details of the marriages, such as marital status, age at marriage, ceremony, birthplace, and residence. The literature on the extent of interracial marriage in other parts of the United States is rather well known and documented elsewhere, and therefore will not be cited in this particular article.

(Hening, I-552; Arness, 1966:11). The nature of this very early concern was not merely with miscegenation but rather with the social and moral consequences (Jordan, 1968:78). Subsequently, Virginia passed a law in 1662 against interracial fornication, doubly penalizing the Christian offender (Hening, II-170; Hurd, I-231). However, the behavior was not contained by the law, and, alarmed at the increase in interracial propagation, the first statutory prohibition was approved in 1691 "for prevention of that abominable mixture and spurious issue, which hereafter may increase..." It forbade the marriage of "whatsoever English or other white man or woman being free...with a negro, mulatto, or Indian man or woman, bond or free," under penalty of banishment from the colony "for ever" (Hening, III-86; Hurd, I-236; Arness, 1966:14; Avins, 1966). In illegitimacy cases the white mother of a black child was to be fined 15 lbs., and the child bound to servitude for 30 years; and if the white mother was a servant, her bondage could be extended five more years (Hurd, I-237).

The Virginia laws of 1705 again forbade the intermarriage of any white man or woman with any Negro or mulatto under penalty of 6 months imprisonment for the white person and a fine of 10 lbs., and the officiant became liable to a fine of 10,000 lbs. of tobacco (Hening, III-453; Hurd, I-240; Arness, 1966: 16). Furthermore, any white masters or mistresses who intermarried with any "negro, mulatto, or Indian, Jew, Mahometan, or other infidel" faced the loss of rights over their bonded servants (Hening, III-450; Hurd, I-239). In 1818 a provision was written into the laws to prevent Virginians from marrying elsewhere across racial lines and returning to Virginia (Virginia, 1819:I-Ch. 18). Penalties and fines were raised in 1848 for the white parties to 1 year imprisonment and a $100 fine (Virginia, 1848: Ch. 8; Avins, 1966; Arness, 1966). The law of 1860 declared all marriages between whites and Negroes absolutely void (Virginia, 1860: Ch. CIX), and in 1866 the Negro party became equally punishable (Arness, 1966:22, 27).

Subsequently, in 1878, the parties were faced with imprisonment of 2 to 5 years, and the fine of the officiant was placed at $200 (Virginia, 1877-1878:312). Many court cases arose because of an early definition of a Negro as one who had more than one-half Negro ancestry, and in 1910 the definition was changed to specify one-sixteenth Negro blood (Virginia, 1910: Ch. 357). The last Virginia law, still in effect in 1967, prohibited the marriage of whites with nonwhites, excepting persons who had only one-sixteenth or less Indian blood (Virginia, 1950: Ch. 4, Sec. 20). The parties to an intermarriage now faced a 1 to 5 year jail sentence; the local marriage license clerk a year imprisonment and a $500 fine; and the officiant a $200 fine. The provision that Virginians could not interracially marry in other states was also continued. Court challenges frequently arose, culminating with the classic case of Loving v. Virginia, which, by U.S. Supreme Court decree, led to the invalidation in 1967 of all interracial marriage laws in the United States (Applebaum, 1964; Wadlington, 1964; U.S. Supreme Court, 1966: No 395, and Transcript of Record).

Maryland

Maryland, which prior to 1632 had been part of Virginia, followed the pattern of its parent colony and very early in 1663 sought to deter English women from intermarrying with Negro slaves by defining the offspring as slaves, and requiring the white women to serve the master of such a slave for the lifetime of her husband (Maryland, 1663:533; Hurd, 1858:I-249; Brackett, 1899:33; Norton, 1970). White men were not mentioned, presumably because they did not "marry" Negro women, and because in this case the child's status automatically followed the mother's slave status. In 1681 recognition was taken of the connivance of some masters in encouraging the proscribed behavior of their female white servants, and in cases of this kind the law gave the woman and her children their freedom, while the masters or mistresses were faced with a large fine of 10,000 lbs. of tobacco (Maryland, 1681:204; Hurd, I-250). This 1681 law also enjoined any officiant from performing such a marriage, specifying the same fine.

Stronger laws to control the interbreeding of whites with Negroes were introduced in Maryland in 1700 and later (Hurd, I-251; Dorsey, I-29; Brackett, 1889). White men and women were punished by servitude for 7 years, and free Negro men and women could become slaves again. To prevent intermarriages, the law of 1715 placed a stiff fine on the officiants, which remained in effect until 1967. In the reconstruction period, with the repeal of the "black codes," the Maryland Assembly removed the prohibition against marriage between whites and Negroes, but kept the penalty as to the officiant (Brackett, 1890:355, 406, 412). But in 1884 (Maryland, Ch. 264) it was written into the law again that all marriages of whites and persons of Negro descent to the third generation were declared void, such marriages being termed an "infamous crime" punishable by a prison sentence of from 18 months to 10 years. In 1935 Malays were prohibited from marriage to whites or Negroes, with the same punishment (Maryland, 1935).

District of Columbia

When Maryland and Virginia gave up territory to establish the District of Columbia, it was agreed that the laws of the two states were "to remain in force" in the parts turned over to the Federal government. This can be understood to mean that the Maryland and Virginia laws against miscegenation applied to the District of Columbia (Avins, 1966).

An early code which was proposed for the District in 1819 carried this provision: "if any white man or woman shall intermarry with a negro or mulatto, bond or free, such a white man or woman, and such a negro or mulatto, shall upon conviction or indictment pay a fine of thirty dollars, and suffer six months confinement at hard labour" (District of Columbia, 1819:184). In 1833 another code was drawn up and the intermarriage prohibition repeated, under penalty of one year in the penitentiary (District of Columbia, 1833:222). And again in 1857 another proposed code declared that the marriages of all persons having any Negro blood with whites "shall be void," the penalty being 1 to 5 years, and the fine up to $1,000; issuing a license to marry or officiating at such a marriage meant a fine of $100 and $500, respectively. A marriage evasion clause (out of state) was included, with penalties (District of Columbia, 1857: Ch. 68, Ch. 135, pp. 291, 546). None of these codes, according to Tremain (1892:123), was ever adopted, and technically it might be said that the District never legally prohibited interracial marriage.

In a real sense, however, the "law" in operation, deriving from the systems of the sister states of Maryland and Virginia, probably prevailed down to the 1860's, and Negro marriages with whites were not allowed by custom if not by law. No laws passed in the District following the Civil War contained any proscription against intermarriage, but one Congressman commented in 1867 on their being "prohibited" (Congressional Globe, 1867:39). During the early decades of the 1900's (and as late as 1939) various bills were introduced in the Congress of the United States to make interracial marriages illegal in the District of Columbia (and some others to make it illegal in the United States), but all of these measures failed to pass.

This synopsis indicates how persistently Maryland and Virginia attempted to control racial blending and intermarriage down to 1967. In the beginning the law and the customs of these two states exercised a control over interracial marriage in the District of Columbia, but there has been no legal interdiction in the District for over 100 years. From time to time in Maryland and Virginia, individuals were prosecuted and punished for violating the intermarriage laws of these states (Catterall, 1926). It should be mentioned that during slave days among themselves Negro marriages were of a consensual kind, and the domestic laws gave them no protection or rights.

District of Columbia Intermarriages

Records and Studies

Beginning in 1811 a record of marriage returns was kept by the Supreme Court of the District of Columbia in a ledger-type entry book showing the names of the parties and their color, if not white. Simple licenses to marry were also issued. An examination of this source revealed no identifiable intermarriages. Under the prevailing law in the District at this time, as noted above, mixed marriages were not allowed.

After its founding in 1870, the Health Department initiated a large ledger-type book, listing each marriage return with particulars about the parties, including "color." After 1873 details on the marriage returns were given in the Health Officer's Annual Report to the Commissioners (U.S. Congress, House Miscellaneous Documents). Unfortunately, returns were made to the Health Department for only 40 to 60 percent of the licenses issued, and hence this source is a deficient one. In 1870 the Supreme Court of the District started its own ledger on all licenses issued, and in 1896 expanded the record to include details about the parties in the columnar form, asking also for the "color" of each of the parties. Since the licensing of marriages was a Court matter, the dual reporting of marriages was discontinued in 1902, and the Court continued with its ledger system (later becoming individual documents), but compiled no statistics.

The Court file has been used for several original studies of mixed marriages in the District of Columbia (Herbert, 1939; Hogan, 1943; Shinert, 1952; Lynn,

1953, 1956, 1967). In addition to these studies, other publications have given information on District marriages but no interracial detail (United States, NOVS, 1939, 1940, 1960; Loeb, 1968). From 1963 onwards, unpublished tables have been prepared, based on a 50 percent sample, showing the number of cases in nine categories (a cross tabulation of three racial groups: White, Negro, Other) which have been analyzed by Monahan (1976).

Procedure[2]

For this study the photocopies and record number listings of mixed marriages compiled by Lynn for 1931-1965 were made available to the writer and used to develop additional information on the mixed cases. Unpublished figures for these years were also obtained. In coding and processing these data, some editing was necessary. In addition, selected years were completely searched, including 1960, 1965-1970, and 1973. Except for 1968 and 1973 (for which only tallies were made) the information on all mixed cases was transcribed, coded, and transferred to punch cards for tabulation.

Numerous editing and coding problems as to race arose. Some were resolved by using the names and other information on the record to identify particular races. For instance, some persons reported as "Brown," which the National Center for Health Statistics codes as Negro, could be identified as Filipino. In some instances "Brown" on the record meant Asiatic Indians, but on the other hand, a few others who might have been American Indians could not be correctly classified. "Yellow" and "Oriental" designations could also be identified specifically as Chinese, Japanese, Vietnamese, or other races. A few cases of persons who appear as "White" in the record were assigned their real identity.

It was found that the NCHS unpublished statistics on race for 1965-1970 were 6 percent below the number reported in this article. If NCHS had identified Other-Other mixed races, their number would have been 2 percent higher. For these and other reasons the number of cases in this study may differ slightly from some published figures. The number of unused licenses and the number of white-white and Negro-Negro marriages were determined for selected years for use in calculating proportions intermarried.

---

[2]In supplementing the Lynn data the marriage licenses for the following years were completely searched by the writer: 1874-1875, 1890, 1897, 1900, 1905, 1910, 1915, 1920, 1925, 1930, 1940, 1956, 1960, 1965-1970, and 1973. Herbert (1939:27) and Lynn (1953:20) in searching out interracial couples from the District records found that the Court file was apparently overstating the number of interracial marriages, and this should be kept in mind with respect to the figures assembled here. It might be assumed that in recent decades the information has been more carefully registered. In any case, both applicants are required to read and swear to the document which they sign. In order to determine the number of marriages which took place, separate tallies were made of unused licenses by race. In the early 1920's the figure ranged around 1 to 2 percent. In 1950, 6.5 percent were unused, in 1956 and 1960 the respective figures were 8.3 and 9.3, reaching 12 percent in 1966. Since the introduction of a blood test requirement in 1967, the proportion has fluctuated from 2 to 7 percent. The reasons for this are not really known. The licenses for mixed marriages have shown only a slightly higher tendency to be unused than those for homogamous marriages.

The Trend in Mixed Marriages

In earlier times mixed marriages appear to be rather few and far between. Although the returns were very incomplete, the statistics published by the Health Department (U. S. Congress, Miscellaneous House Documents) show an average of 2 to 3 interracial marriages per year from 1879 to 1891. Proportionally, however, .23 percent of all marriages were mixed, and for Negro marriages, .83 percent mixed. An exception was the 1874-75 fifteen month period when six cases were found in the Health Department register, giving a total proportion of .58 percent mixed, and 1.1 percent for Negro marriages. As shown in Table 1 (and unpublish-

TABLE 1   INTERRACIAL MARRIAGE IN THE DISTRICT OF COLUMBIA
                                                              FOR SELECTED YEARS

Year	Mixed Marriages				Percent (Total) Mixed
	Total	Negro with White	Negro with Other Race	All Other Mixed	
1874-75*	6	6	—	—	.58
1890	2	2	—	—	.16
1897	1	1	—	—	.04
1900	3	3	—	—	.09
1905	4	3	—	1	.10
1910	5	3	—	2	.13
1915	18	13	1	4	.43
1920	14	10	—	4	.20
1925	12	7	2	3	.21
1930	11	1	4	6	.21
1940	29	1	2	26†	.38
1956	92	23	9	61†	1.13

Source : 1874-75, Health Department Register; all other years, a search of the Supreme Court register and documents by the author.
*August 8, 1874 to December 31, 1875.
†The great majority of these are other race males with white females. In 1940, Filipino males with white females, 23 cases: in 1956, Filipino males with white females, 21 cases; and white males with Filipino females, 5 cases.

ed figures), marriages identifiable as interracial for 1910 and years preceding averaged about 3 per year. Even though the number of intermarriages increased after 1910, the proportions remained low, or less than .5 percent. Negro marriages with whites seem to have risen in 1915 and 1920, when 1.0 and .5 percent of the Negro marriages were mixed. It is noteworthy that only one marriage in 1930 and one in 1940 involved a Negro with a white. (See Lynn, 1956:386). In 1956 there was a definite rise in interracial marriages, but nearly two-thirds of them were accounted for by Filipino, Oriental, and other race men marrying white women. Proportionally, 1.1 percent of all marriages in 1956 were mixed, and 1.0 percent of the Negro marriages.

The trend in mixed marriages by yearly periods is given in Table 2. Because

TABLE 2 INTERRACIAL MARRIAGES IN THE DISTRICT OF COLUMBIA
FOR YEARLY PERIODS

Years	Total Marriages*	Mixed Marriages	Percent Mixed
1879-1891@	12,810	30	(.23)
1923-1929	38,773	53	(.13)
1930-1939	58,560	152	.26
1940-1949	116,790	490	.42
1950-1959	85,971	832	.97
1960-1964	44,037	990	2.25
1965-1967	26,104	982	3.76
1968-1970	22,794	762	3.34

*In some early years only marriage license figures were available. But, in recent decades marriages performed according to published totals of the National Office of Vital Statistics (now NCHS) were used, as well as estimates based on tallies of unused licenses. From 1960 onward marriages performed were determined by license tallies.
@Except the year 1885.
Sources: Annual Reports of the District of Columbia Health Department (United States Congress, House Documents, 1870-1902; Leona Herbert, 1923-1929; Annella Lynn, 1930-1965, including unpublished figures; and original compilations in these same and other years. See qualifications upon early data.

of the uncertainties about the data, the first two percentages are offered only suggestively. From the 1930's to the 1960's the proportion of all marriages which were mixed showed a steady rise, peaking at almost 4 percent in 1965-1967, after which, because interracial marriages became allowable in all states, the District had no special attraction to couples wishing to marry across racial lines. For 1968-1970 the percent of all marriages which were mixed declined from 3.8 to 3.3.

Considering the prohibitive laws of Maryland and Virginia down to 1967 against marriages of whites with nonwhites, and the fact that such marriages were effectively excluded from licensing in these two states, it is remarkable that more mixed marriages were not registered in the District of Columbia. Except for 1874-1875, 1890, and 1915 (unpublished data), the proportion of Negro marriages which were mixed was less than .5 percent in the years to 1940. In 1956 a level of 1 percent mixture was reached for all marriages and for Negro marriages. Since 1960 there has been a steady rise in each year down to 1967 in interracial marriage as a whole, and also in Negro with white marriages. The enablement of Negro with white marriages in Maryland and Virginia resulted in hardly any diminution in their number in the District. It should be noted, however, that other nearby states which had no prohibitive law, such as Pennsylvania,

TABLE 3   INTERRACIAL MARRIAGE IN THE DISTRICT OF COLUMBIA IN
                                                                            RECENT YEARS

Year	Marriages*	Mixed Marriages		Percent Mixed	
	Total	Total	Negro with White	Total	Negro with White**
1930	5,355	11	1	.21	.02
1940	7,595	29	1	.38	.01
1956	8,161	92	23	1.13	.28
1960	8,298	148	38	1.78	.46
1961	8,555	171	57	2.00	.67
1962	9,120	196	70	2.15	.77
1963	9,250	203	75	2.19	.81
1964	8,814	272	119	3.09	1.35
1965	9,182	333	172	3.63	1.87
1966	9,416	376	201	4.00	2.13
1967	7,506	273	143	3.64	1.91
1968	7,839	266	166	3.39	2.12
1969	7,745	248	174	3.19	2.25
1970	7,209	248	160	3.44	2.22
1973	5,656	264	140	4.67	2.48

*Marriages are estimated in some years from published NCHS figures, and measured proportions of unused licenses
**This is a percentage of total marriages.

New Jersey, and New York, now and in the past have contributed to the District's pool of non-resident mixed marriages. The usual reasons for migratory marriage can explain this, as well as, perhaps, a special anonimity desired by mixed couples. The Supreme Court decree checked the rise in mixed marriages in the District only temporarily, it seems, because in 1973 a new high was reached in the percentage of interracial unions. (See Table 3).

A somewhat different picture emerges when we examine the marriages of whites and Negroes separately. A sizable proportion of the intermarriages of whites are with Oriental and other races. For the six years 1965-1970, 27 percent of the mixed marriages of whites have been with Other races, 73 percent with Negroes. The overall proportion of mixed marriages has been higher for white than for Negroes. For whites marrying in the District in 1973, 10 percent were interracial, whereas less than 5 percent of the Negro marriages were outside their group. The data for 1973 suggest a renewal of the interracial marriage proclivity for both whites and Negroes. (Table 4).

TABLE 4

PERCENTAGE OF RACIAL MIXTURE IN MARRIAGES IN THE DISTRICT OF COLUMBIA

Year	Total Marriages				Marriages of Whites*				Marriages of Negroes*				Marriages of Other Races		
	Number		Percent Mixed		Number		Percent Mixed		Number		Percent Mixed		Number		Percent Mixed
	Total	Mixed	Total	Negro with white	Total	Mixed	Total	White with Negro	Total	Mixed	Total	Negro with white	Total	Mixed	
1965	9,182	333	3.63	1.87	4,811	300	6.24	3.58	4,437	199	4.49	3.88	261	161	61.69
1966	9,416	376	4.00	2.13	4,704	352	7.48	4.27	4,811	219	4.55	4.18	271	175	64.58
1967	7,506	273	3.64	1.91	3,780	257	6.80	3.78	3,779	158	4.18	3.78	219	130	59.36
1968	7,839	266	3.39	2.12	3,575	240	6.71	4.64	4,319	183	4.24	3.84	203	100	49.26
1969	7,745	248	3.19	2.25	3,416	222	6.50	5.09	4,394	195	4.44	3.96	178	74	41.57
1970	7,209	248	3.44	2.22	3,086	221	7.16	5.18	4,151	180	4.34	3.86	213	88	41.31
1973	5,656	264	4.67	2.48	2,310	232	10.04	6.06	3,394	164	4.83	4.12	208	124	59.62

Source: Original compilation from Court file of marriage records.
*Each group of marriages is separately calculated. These are marriages and not persons.

Changes in Races Intermarrying

   Mixed marriages were few in number and were nearly all whites with Negroes
prior to 1900 (Table 1). In the years following, persons of other races, men
especially, began to intermarry with white women. In the latter part of the
1930's an increasing number of Filipino men and women (prohibited by law from
marriage with whites in Maryland and Virginia) started marrying whites in the
District. In 1940, 76 percent of all mixed marriages were those of Filipino men
with white women, receding to 23 percent in 1956. These high proportions are
a direct result of the legal restrictions in the two neighboring states. When the
prohibition was dropped, the proportion of mixed marriages in the District which
were Filipino with white declined from 17 percent (1965-1966) to 4 percent
(1969-1970). After 1940 races other than Negro and Filipino also began strongly
to affect the intermarriage picture in the District, but the change in the law
did not importantly diminish their proportion of the mixed marriages in the
District because they were party to an intermarriage in 31 percent of the cases
in 1965-1966 and 29 percent in 1969-1970. Related to this shift, in 1965-1966
Negro mixed marriages amounted to 59 percent of the total mixed; in 1969-1970
the figure became 76 percent, with 9 percent of this being Negro with Other
Race marriages. In the 1940 and 1950 decades the proportions of all mixed
marriages which were of the white with Negro types had been only 9 and 23
percent, respectively.

TABLE 5   PERCENTAGE OF MARRIAGES INTERRACIALLY MIXED IN
                                        THE DISTRICT OF COLUMBIA, 1968-1970

Referrent Race*	Marriages Involving Referrent Race			Percentage of Males of Referrent Race in Mixed Marriages	
	Total	Mixed*	Percentage	Total	With Whites
Total	22,793	762	3.34	—	—
White	10,074	680	6.75	35.3	—
Negro	12,864	558	4.34	68.6	71.2
American Indian	41	32	78.05	53.1	62.5
Filipino	153	48	31.37	29.1	36.7
Japanese	48	35	72.92	25.7	22.6
Korean	95	17	17.89	29.4	27.3
Chinese	144	59	40.97	49.2	48.8
Remainder	137	95	69.34	—	64.7

*The marriages for each referrent race were totaled and calculated independently, and are there-
fore not cumulative.

Intermarriage for Particular Races

After June 1967 there was no need for interracial couples to come to the District of Columbia because of restrictive miscegenation laws in their home states. The District records show that in the period 1968-1970 about 3.3 percent of all marriages were interracial. Examined separately, of all Negro marriages 4.3 percent were mixed (90 percent of these with whites), and of all white marriages a higher proportion were mixed, or 6.8 percent (74 percent with Negroes). Of all their marriages, whites had Negro partners in 5.3 percent of the cases. (See Table 5). All other racial groups had even higher proportions of their marriages in the mixed class, increasing from 18 percent for Korean marriages to 31 percent for Filipinos (who prior to 1967 were 70 percent and higher in the District), to 41 percent for Chinese, 73 percent for Japanese, and 78 percent for American Indians. All other miscellaneous races together had a figure of 69 percent mixed. These statistics show that for marriages taking place in the District of Columbia recently, a very considerable proportion were mixed, especially for the minority races.

Percentage of Negro and Other Race Males in Mixed Marriages

Although the 1874-1875 figures for white with Negro marriages showed 5 of the 6 cases to be Negro males, the published statistics of the District of Columbia Health Department indicated a greater number of Negro females were inter-marrying with white men, 14 of the 23 cases (1879-1889). The white male-Negro female combination seems to have prevailed down to 1943, with the years 1915 and 1920 showing 11 out of the 13, and 8 out of the 10 mixed white with Negro marriages to be of this nature. In the period 1930-1939, 13 out of 21 mixed Negro with white marriages showed the male to be white. After 1943 there was a definite shift. The decades 1940, 1950, and 1960 reveal the Negro male with white female to be in the majority, the respective percentages being 66, 62, and 75.

When Other races and whites began to intermarry in the District, among the mixed Filipino marriages it was most often the Filipino man-white woman combination; in the 1930's such was the case for 100 percent of the unions, with the proportion in the later decades diminishing slowly to 99 percent (1940's), 85 percent (1950's), 83 percent (1960-1967). After 1967, the number of Filipino marriages in the District dropped drastically, and of the number who intermarried with whites in 1968-1970 only 37 percent were Filipino males.

Over the years white males and females have tended to marry American Indians at a 50/50 ratio. For all the other races, after a high in the 1930's when 73 percent of the other races married to whites were other race males, the proportion has remained also at the 50 percent level. This is deceptive, however, because when the data are subdivided into specific races we find that whereas in the 1930's and the 1940's for Chinese mixed marriages over 80 percent were Chinese males with white females, from 1960 onward the Chinese female almost equally as often married into the white group. For the Japanese or Korean mixed marriages the story was quite different because in all recent decades the Japanese and Korean females predominated in the marriages of these groups with whites, in the 1960's as much as 65 percent of the time. For the remaining miscellaneous other races, since 1965 they have shown that in 70 percent of the cases it is the other race man who chooses a white bride.

With respect to the Negro group marrying Other Races, it has more often been the Other Race male taking a Negro bride in these mixed marriages. The figure has diminished over the decades from 90 percent prior to 1950, to 65 percent in the 1950's, and 61 percent in the 1960's.

Following the Supreme Court decree in 1967, we find that among the mixed marriages of Negroes with whites in 1968-1970, 71 percent were white women taking Negro husbands. (Table 5). Of all mixed marriages of whites, 35 percent were white males, and of all mixed marriages of Negroes, 69 percent were Negro males. For the other racial groups of mixed marriages, men and women of the particular minority race are about equally involved in Chinese and American Indian marriages (49 and 53 percent in the respective subraces being men). But, in the Filipino, Japanese, and Korean mixed marriages, it was the the females of these groups who were most often intermarrying (71, 74, and 71 percent female, respectively). With reference to the mixed marriages with whites only, these 1968-1970 data suggest that white men more often than white women are choosing Japanese, Korean, and Filipino mates, but the reverse is the case for Negro, American Indian, and miscellaneous other races, in which case it is the white female who is more likely to intermarry with these races. In general, we may observe that for Other races as a whole both sexes participate equally in the mixed marriage exchange, but very substantial subracial differences exist.

Maryland Intermarriages

Because of the strong penalty in Maryland against intermarriage of whites with Negroes, and of Malays with whites or Negroes (and enforcement action against the relatively few who violated the law) not many marriages of these types occurred. However, an interesting study was made which throws light upon the interracial blending that was taking place in the state in spite of the marriage interdiction.

A Study of Interracial Births

Births in the city of Baltimore for the period 1950-1964 were surveyed by Norton (1966) with the finding of a three-fold increase in interracial births from .24 percent in 1950-1954 to .72 percent in 1960-1964. And, in a total of 684 such births (11 percent of which were illegitimate), it was found that 58 percent were to parents not allowed to marry in Maryland at the time. Undoubtedly, most of these parentages derived from marriages of Filipinos and of Negroes performed in other states and abroad. As Norton noted, there was a marked upward movement in mixed parentage in 1960. In the year 1964, 31 percent of the interracial births were of Negro with white parentage, 24 percent of Filipino with white, and 2 percent of Negro with Filipino parentage.

In the entire period (after realigning Norton's data) the father was most often Negro in 58 percent of the births of mixed Negro with white parentage, and for the births of mixed Filipino with white parentages the father was Filipino 85 percent of the time. In the white with Oriental combination, 63 percent of the fathers were white; but in the Negro with Oriental type, 84 percent of the fathers were Negro. American Indians were about evenly split as to the mother or the father being white or American Indian. All through the period these ratios prevailed, except for those of Negro with white parentages: the fathers most often being white up to 1955, and Negro for the rest of the period up to 1964.

The Data

Preceding by three months the U. S. Supreme Court decree, an Act of the Maryland legislature in March 1967 freely allowed interracial marriages for the first time. From June 1, 1967 to July 1. 1970 (when the legislature was prevailed upon to remove racial identification from the marriage record, but not the birth, death, or divorce record), the State of Maryland gathered statistics to show the number and types of such intermarriages (Maryland 1967-69). A detailed report on the interracial marriage picture up to December 1968 has been published by Norton (1970).

All of the marriage records filed with the state office for 1965 were examined by the author to gauge the amount of racial intermarriage just before the legal liberalization. Only two interdicted marriages were found, a Negro male with a white female and a Filipino male with a white female. There were 80 other mixed marriages, however. The overall rate of mixed marriage was .17 percent.

Using a state listing of interracial marriages by record number, the writer transcribed and developed the statistical details on the 1967-1968 cases, and also for the 1969-1970 records (upon which a complete search of the file was made). Some omission of cases was discovered on the state listing, and some corrections of racial identification were necessary in the 1967-1968 group. Exact verification of the state list, the NCHS 10% sample, or the Norton figures was not obtained by the writer. But considering mechanical and coding errors, data interpretation, and sampling (NCHS), the concordance in the sets of figures was very good. For the years 1969 and 1970 a sample of white-white (486) and Negro-Negro (440) marriages was assembled for comparison with the mixed cases.

The Extent of Intermarriage

The new types of intermarriage allowed in 1967 (Negro with white, and Filipino with white and Negro) on a yearly basis increased mixed marriages about three-fold in Maryland. This addition was 23 percent Filipino and 77 percent Negro intermarriages. During 1967-1970 these new interracial marriages accounted for about 70 percent of the total in Maryland.

In the entire year 1967 there were 203 intermarriages (173 after June 1st), 347 in 1968, 463 in 1969, and 272 in 1970 (up to July 1st). In each year the proportion of all marriages which were racially mixed increased progressively from .54 to .68, .88, and 1.09 percent (1970). (Table 6).

TABLE 6   PERCENTAGE OF RACIAL MIXTURE IN MARRIAGES IN
                                MARYLAND IN 1965 AND 1967 to 1970

| | Total Marriages | | | |
| | Number | | Percent Mixed | |
Year	Total	Mixed	Total	Negro with White
1965	47,398	82	.17	@
1967*	31,828	173	.54	.31
1968	51,165	347	.68	.41
1969	52,881	463	.88	.50
1970**	24,951	272	1.09	.65

@One case, Negro male with white female.
*Starting June 1st.
**Ending June 30th.

Calculated in the same way, the percent of all white marriages and of all Negro marriages which were interracial doubled in a span of almost three years, reaching 1.2 and 3.9 percent for the respective groups in 1970 (Table 7). If only white marriages with Negroes are considered, the proportion of the whole is somewhat less. A slightly smaller proportion of all the Negro marriages in 1970 were with whites, 3.7 percent, but a sizable differential is evidenced in the figure on white marriages which were with Negroes, being only .8 percent (vs. 1.2 percent). This is because of the relatively large number of Other race marriages with whites.

If we separately examine the statistics on marriages involving Other races as a group, we find that they have now (as in the past) a high degree of inter-marriage, from 55 to 67 percent for the years 1965 to 1970, mostly with the white group.

Intermarriage for Particular Races

Several observations might be made about the distribution of interracial marriages among the races. From 92 to 95 percent of the Negro mixed marriages were with whites, but altogether these Negro with white marriages constituted somewhat less than 60 percent of all the mixed marriages in Maryland. Over the years from 84 to 91 percent of the Other race marriages have been with whites.

For the year and a half from January 1969 to June 1970 a complete accounting was made of six individual Other race categories with the finding of a wide variation in the proportions of marriage mixture for particular races, the overall average being 64 percent. Calculating each race separately, the highest degrees of out-group marriage were for the Japanese and the American Indians in

TABLE 7   PERCENTAGE OF RACIAL MIXTURE IN MARRIAGES IN MARYLAND IN 1965 AND 1967-1970

| Year[*] | Marriages of Whites** | | | | Marriages of Negroes** | | | | Marriages of Other Races** | | | |
| | Number | | Percent | | Number | | Percent | | Number | | Percent | |
	Total	Mixed	Total	Mixed Negro with White	Total	Mixed	Total	Mixed Negro with White	Total	Mixed	Total	Mixed Negro with White
1965	39,484	74	.19	@	7,846	6	.08	@	147	81	55.10	49.66
1967[″]	26,456	166	.63	.37	5,345	105	1.96	1.83	134	75	55.97	50.75
1968	42,783	326	.76	.49	8,935	227	2.54	2.33	227	139	61.23	52.42
1969	44,592	442	.99	.60	9,010	279	3.10	2.95	295	197	66.78	59.66
1970[″]	20,582	255	1.24	.79	4,453	175	3.93	3.66	183	109	59.56	50.27

*See footnotes to prior table.
**Each group of marriages is separately calculated.   These are marriages not persons.

TABLE 8   PERCENTAGE OF MARRIAGES INTERRACIALLY MIXED IN
                                                                    MARYLAND 1969-1970

Referrent Race*	Marriages Involving Referrent Race		
	Total	Mixed	Percentage
Total	77,832	735	.94
White	65,174	697	1.07
Negro	13,463	454	3.37
American Indian	83	70	84.34
India	17	12	70.59
Filipino	153	92	60.13
Japanese	40	34	85.00
Korean	24	10	41.67
Chinese	112	52	46.43
Remainder	62	49	79.03

*The marriages for each referrent race were totaled and calculated separately, and are therefore not cumulative.

Maryland, with percentages in the 80's. Filipinos had an intermediate ratio in 1969-1970 of 60 percent mixed marriage. The Chinese and the Koreans appear less heterogamous than the others, but even they show over 4 out of every 10 marriages to be interracial. In any case, all of the proportions are quite high compared to the figures of 1 and 3 percent for the whites and the Negroes.

The Race of the Male Partner in Mixed Marriages

In Maryland when Negroes were allowed to marry with whites, the Negro male more often than the Negro female chose a white partner: 73 percent of the time in the period for which there are statistics. To about the same extent the Filipino male married a white female, reaching the 85 percent mark in 1970. The high male sex ratio for the Filipino population, commented upon in the literature (Shinert), and their mobility, has served as an explanation of the Filipino maleness in intermarriages. One might have expected this relationship to have diminished by 1970, as more Filipino females joined the population through births to Filipino parents; yet, the ratio continues very high. On the other hand, the Negro males (for whom the population sex ratio at the marriage ages is not much out of balance) show about as high a ratio of Negro males in the intermarriages with whites. Removing the Filipinos from the Other races group reveals a more evenly divided tendency of the sexes of Other races as a whole to intermarry.

TABLE 9   THE RACE OF THE MALE PARTNER IN INTERRACIAL MARRIAGES
                    WITH WHITES IN MARYLAND, 1965 AND 1967 TO 1970

Year"	Negro with White	Other Race with White	Filipino with White	Other Race with Whire (excl. Fil.)
		Percent of Males*		
	Negro	Other Race	Filipino	Other Race
1965	@	58.9	@	58.2
1967	72.4	58.8	78.6	45.0
1968	66.3	55.1	51.2	57.9
1969	77.4	60.2	80.0	52.4
1970	75.5	64.1	84.8	52.5

@Only 1 case each for Filipino male with white female, and Negro male with white female
*For the period 1967-1970 in marriages with whites, the minority males accounted for the follow-
ing percentages: Negro, 73.2; Asiatic Indians, 94.1; American Indians, 60.5; Filipino, 73.0; Japanese,
32.7; Korean, 33.3; Chinese, 54.3; and miscellaneous other races, 48.4 percent.
"See footnote to prior table.

Breaking down the data into specific races for the period 1967-1970, however,
shows a very considerable variation in the maleness of minority race mixed
marriages with whites. Over 9 out of 10 of the Asiatic Indians who so intermarried were men. For the American Indians, the figure was lower, at 60 percent;
but for the Chinese the ratio was more nearly even. at 54 percent. In contrast,
for the Japanese and Korean marriages in Maryland, it was more often the case
of white men choosing brides of these races, two-thirds of the time.

Virginia Intermarriages

The Virginia miscegenation law, more stringent than that of Maryland, made
marriages of whites with nonwhites within the state all but impossible. Interracial unions, nevertheless, took place and attention was called to this in the state
vital statistics reports (1919-1935) and by Plecker (1925a, b, c; 1934). The Racial
Integrity Law of 1924, which aimed at identifying and thereby preventing racial
intermixture, brought to light "large numbers" of mixed couples who were merely
living together (Virginia, Biennial Report 1925:377; 1926:303). Others falsified
their identities (1929:52). And, some who were denied a marriage license when
their claim to being "Indian" was disallowed, went to other states to be married
(1931:68). The case upon which all state miscegenation laws were declared
unconstitutional by the U. S. Supreme Court was that of two Virginians, a white
man who married a Negro woman in the District of Columbia, and then returned
to live in Virginia. His penalization by the State of Virginia led to the Supreme
Court action (U. S., Loving v. Virginia).

The Data

Virginia began the publication of an interracial table on marriages in 1967, according to a three-way grouping of White, Negro, and Other races. In addition, since 1963 the National Center for Health Statistics has assembled unpublished tables of the same kind on a 10 percent sampling basis for Virginia. State prepared punch cards on all mixed and Other-Other (same race) cases, and magnetic tapes of the statistical data on all marriages for 1969-1970, were made available to the writer. By linking the data cards to the microfilm of the original records, the complete identity of the individual races was determined for 1969 and 1970.

The Extent and Trend in Mixed Marriages

From the last six and one-half months of 1967 through 1974, there was a steady increase in the proportion of racially mixed marriages in Virginia. A very small number of Other Race marriages were of the mixed Other race kind. There was, however, a growing number of Other races who intermarried with Negroes. Prior to June 12, 1967, with a possible exception or two, no white with nonwhite marriages were registered in Virginia. In the rest of the year 1967, .23 percent of all marriages were mixed, becoming .47 in 1970, and 1.20 in 1974 (Table 10).

TABLE 10   PERCENTAGE OF MARRIAGES INTERRACIALLY MIXED IN
                                                                        VIRGINIA, 1967-1974

			Percentage Mixed by Referrent Race@			
Year	All Marriages	White Marriages	Negro Marriages		Other Race Marriages	
			Total	Negro with White	Total	Other with White
1967*	.23	.17	.43	.41	56.5	52.1
1968	.29	.32	.69	.66	47.8	41.3
1969	.42	.48	1.00	.94	61.0	56.6
1970	.47	.53	1.38	1.28	67.9	65.1
1971	.71	.76	2.14	1.77	71.8	66.3
1972	.90	.97	2.81	2.31	72.0	62.9
1973	1.18	1.32	4.18	3.79	71.9	64.8
1974	1.20	1.31	4.56	4.10	70.9	62.3

@The White, Negro, and Other race marriage percentages are independently calculated. Calculations for 1967-1970 were able to take into account a small number of mixed Other-Other races.

*Marriages occurring after June 12 only.

If attention is given to the marriages of whites, Negroes, and the Other races, separately considered, the comparable figures for whites rose from .17 to

1.31 percent mixed, and for all Negro marriages from .43 to 4.56 percent mixed. The Other race marriages have always shown a high proportion to be mixed: 56 percent in 1967 and over 70 percent interracial since 1970.

TABLE 11   PERCENTAGE OF MARRIAGES INTERRACIALLY MIXED IN
                                                    VIRGINIA, 1969-1970

Referrent Race*	Marriages Involving Referrent Race			Percentage of Males of Referrent Race in Mixed Marriages
	Total	Mixed*	Percentage	
Total	104,539	465	.44	—
White	88,679	448	.51	45.1
Negro	15,906	188	1.18	68.6
American Indian	70	54	77.14	46.3
Filipino	149	90	60.40	67.8
Japanese	50	45	90.00	24.4
Korean	34	21	61.76	19.0
Chinese	53	28	52.83	53.6
Remainder	59	52	88.14	34.6

*The marriages for each referrent race were totaled separately.   Hence they are not additive.

Intermarriage for Particular Races

Although the numbers of cases are small, individual other races, as in Maryland and the District of Columbia, show high proportions of mixture. The Chinese marriages in 1969-1970 were 53 percent mixed, the Filipino 60 percent, the Korean 62, and the American Indian 77 percent mixed. Even higher percentages appear for the Japanese, 90, and the miscellaneous Other races, 88 percent.

From 86 to 96 percent of the Other race intermarriages have been with whites, and the remainder with Negroes or other different races. Over the years there has been some shifting in the proportion of mixed white marriages with Negroes, and with Other races. In 1967, 69 percent of the mixed white marriages were with Other races, but by 1974 the figure had dropped to 45 percent, whereas marriages of whites with Negroes rose from 31 percent of the total mixed white marriages in 1967 to 55 percent in 1974   (Unpublished data).

The Race of the Male Partner in Mixed Marriages

In the mixed marriages of Negroes with whites, the groom was Negro in 76 percent of the cases in 1967 in Virginia. (Table 12).   The proportion dropped to 60 percent in 1968, but rose again to 72 percent in 1970 and has tended to hold at

TABLE 12   THE RACE OF THE MALE PARTNER IN INTERRACIAL
                                      MARRIAGES WITH WHITES IN VIRGINIA, 1967-1974

Year	Negro with White Marriages	Other with White Marriages
	Percent of Males	
	Negro	White
1967	76.5	55.3
1968	60.4	53.3
1969	66.2	52.2
1970	71.7	58.4
1971	65.5	61.5
1972	70.4	64.7
1973	74.2	70.4
1974	74.9	69.5

Source: Annual Reports of the Virginia State Department of Health on Vital Statistics, showing three groups (White, Negro, Other).

two-thirds to three-fourths of the mixed marriages. Among the Other race mixed marriages with whites, the white male has always been in the majority, rising from somewhat more than half of the cases in the first few years to 58 percent in 1970, and 70 percent in 1974.

For particular races, however, as illustrated by the figures for 1969-1970, there is considerable variation, although the number of cases is small (Table 11). As to marriages of whites with Other races, the men were Chinese in 52 percent of the 25 Chinese mixed marriages with whites, and in the 88 mixed marriages of Filipinos with whites the male was Filipino 69 percent of the time. Examined in the same way, for all other mixed marriages with whites it was the white man who more often took an Other race bride; 55 percent white males with American Indians; 76 percent with Japanese; 80 percent with Koreans; and 72 percent with the miscellaneous Other races.

The shortage of Filipino, Chinese, and other minority race females, as commented upon in the literature (Hogan, Shinert), has led males in these groups to seek out white females to marry in the past. But it should be noted that for 31 percent of the Filipino marriages with whites in Virginia in 1969-1970, the male was white and the bride Filipino. The imbalance of the sexes within minority races is not as prevailing an influence as it used to be. The differences in the Oriental races is not easily explained, except perhaps on the basis of residential propinquity or availability of women of their race. The marriages of Negroes with Other Races has increased from about 2 percent of the totality of mixed marriages prior to 1970, to 8 percent in 1971-1972, and 5 to 6 percent in 1973-1974. This increase has probably come about as a result of the black man's recent military experience abroad, the growing acceptance of interracial marriage, and increasing social contacts. In these mixed marriages of Negroes with Other races, with some variation since 1970, the male has been a Negro two-thirds to three-fourths of the time.

Concluding Remarks

From Colonial times the laws of Maryland and Virginia rigidly prohibited Negroes and whites from marrying, and later also enjoined other races. Although the control was very strong, as attested to by birth statistics and other information in these states, individuals succeeded in evading the laws, and some interracial blending went on. Legally recognized and registered interracial marriage was another matter, and the extent of it was very minimal. But after 1967 when racial restraints to marriage were abolished and persons became free to marry whomever they wished, the mixed marriage tendency truly burgeoned.

Although the District of Columbia for over 100 years allowed interracial marriages, whereas neighbouring Virginia and Maryland and the rest of the South did not, mixed marriages, especially white with Negro unions, were not frequent in the District. In and around 1920 there was a slight and temporary surge of such mixed marriages. Other races began in 1940 to participate importantly in District intermarriages, notably Filipino men from neighbouring Maryland. And, from 1956 onward, a definite and continuing upward trend developed for all types of mixed marriages. The Supreme Court decree abolishing miscegenation laws in 1967 diminished the flow of migratory marriages to the District and stemmed the growth of interracial marriage there. But, as the 1973 figures show, the upward trend has resumed.

The likelihood of racial intermarriage has been a very sensitive subject in the past, and opponents of civil rights often used this as an argument. It was part of the debate preceding the Supreme Court school desegration decision: Assurance was often given that school integration and social equality would not lead to more intermarriage. There were some perceptive social commentators, however, who said that intermarriages would surely increase. The statistics on the District of Columbia, Virginia, and Maryland give support to the assimilationist position. Unfortunately, Maryland and the District of Columbia no longer ask for the racial identity of persons marrying (Monahan, 1976), so that the future path of mixed marriages cannot be followed in these areas. The recent figures on Virginia indicate that the extent is significant and the rate is continuing to rise. Quite remarkably, in 1973, 10 percent of all marriages of whites in the District of Columbia were mixed, and 5 percent of the Negro marriages.

As a group the marriages of Other races are most likely of all to be interracial, averaging around 50 percent or more in recent years in the three jurisdictions. As to particular races within the Other race category, according to the local circumstances the percentages of mixed marriages for them varies. American Indians and Japanese have very high proportions of intermarriages, whereas the Chinese have a level of 50 percent or lower. The Korean figure varies from place to place, while the Filipino proportion has undergone big changes over time, diminishing as their population approaches a balance in the numbers of men and women. A wholly satisfactory explanation for the differences between particular races is not immediately apparent.

A theory of intermarriage in the United States has been built around the simple preponderance of Negro males in marriages with whites (Monahan and Monahan, 1976). The very early District of Columbia figures show, however, that at one time it was usually the case for white men to marry Negro women, although the numbers were small. In the last few decades the prevailing pattern has most often been one of Negro males marrying white females. The marriages of Filipino males with white females were common for some time, but this situation is now moderating. For instance, in 1973 in the District of Columbia more white males were marrying Filipino females than the reverse combination. Any hypothetical speculation as to why white females tend more often than white males to marry across racial lines cannot be based on such minimal information. An intensive inquiry for each race involved would be needed. In fact, as has been noted in this paper, occasionally it is the white male who may more often be choosing to marry into a particular racial group. The situation is a highly variable and inconstant one when a particular race is studied over a long period of time.

As these statistics show, in terms of marriages contracted, minority races are very much involved in racial mixture. For the Negro group it is no small matter, with about 5 percent of their marriages being interracial. Even the marriages of majority whites, as in the District of Columbia, are evidencing significant and rising proportions of intermarriages with Negroes and Other races. No longer can interracial marriage be called a rare phenomenon.

REFERENCES

Applebaum, Harvey M.
   1964   "Miscegenation statutes: a constitutional and social problem." Georgetown Law
           Review 53 (Fall): 49-91.

Arness, Frank F.
   1966   The Evolution of the Virginia Antimiscegenation Laws. Unpublished master's thesis
           in history, Old Dominion College.

Avins, Alfred
   1966   "Anti-miscegenation laws and the fourteenth amendment: the original intent." Vir-
           ginia Law Review 52 (November): 1224-1255.

Ballagh, James C.
   1902   A History of Slavery in Virginia. Studies in Historical and Political Science, Vol. 24.
           Baltimore: Johns Hopkins University Press.

Brackett, Jeffrey R.
   1889   The Negro in Maryland, A Study of the Institution of Slavery. Studies in Historical
           and Political Science, extra Vol. 6. Baltimore: Johns Hopkins University Press.
   1890   Notes on the Progress of the Colored People of Maryland Since the War. Studies in
           Historical and Political Science, series No. 8-9 (July-August). Studies in Historical
           and Political Science. Baltimore: Johns Hopkins University Press.

Catterall, Helen T.
   1926   Judicial Cases Concerning American Slavery and the Negro. 5 Vols. Washington,
           D.C.: Carnegie Institution.

Congressional Globe. The Official Proceeding of Congress.
    1867   Fourtieth Congress, 2nd Session, Pt. 1. — December 5th.

District of Columbia.
    1819   A Code of Laws for the District of Columbia, Prepared by the Authority of an Act of
            Congress, April 20, 1816. Washington, D.C.: Davis and Force.
    1833   A System of Civil and Criminal Law for the District of Columbia, and for the Organi-
            sation of the Courts Therein. Joint Committee of the U.S. Senate, 22nd Congress,
            2nd Session. Document 85.
    1857   The Revised Code of the District of Columbia. Prepared under the Authority of the
            Act of Congress, Approved March 3, 1855. Washington, D.C.: A.O. P. Nicholson,
            public printer.

Dorsey Clement
    1841   General Public Statutory Law of the State of Maryland, 1692-1839. 3 Vols. Baltimore:
            John Toy.

Guild, June P.
    1936   Black Laws of Virginia. Richmond: Whittet and Shepperson.

Hening, William W.
    1809+   The Statutes at Large: Being a Collection of All the Laws of Virginia, from the First
            Session of the Legislature, in the Year 1619. 16 Vols. Philadelphia, and Richmond—
            1809 to 1823.

Herbert, Leona Anne
    1939   A Study of Ten Cases of Negro-White Marriages in the District of Columbia.
            Unpublished master's thesis, Catholic University of America.

Hogan, William E.
    1943   A Sociological Study of Interracial Marriage by the Chinese in the District of
            Columbia. Unpublished master's thesis, Catholic University of America.

Hurd, John C.
    1858+   The Law of Freedom and Bondage in the United States. 2 Vols. New York: (republi-
            shed) Negro Universities Press, 1968.

Johnson, Franklin
    1919   Development of State Legislation Concerning the Negro. New York: The Arbor
            Press, Inc.

Jordan, Winthrop D.
    1968   White Over Black, American Attitudes Toward the Negro, 1550-1812, Chapel Hill:
            University of North Carolina Press.

Loeb, Ruth
    1968   "A study of age at marriage: the District of Columbia, 1960-61." Demography 5
            (January): 311-317.

Lynn, Anne Q. (Sister Marie Annella)
    1953   Interracial Marriages in Washington, D.C., 1940-1947. Washington, D.C.: Catholic
            University of America-Press.
    1956   "Some aspects of interracial marriage in Washington, D.C." Journal of Negro
            Education 25 (Fall): 380-391.
    1967   "Interracial marriages in Washington, D.C." Journal of Negro Education 36 (Fall):
            428-433.

Maryland, Laws
    1663   Proceedings and Acts of the General Assembly of Maryland, 1637-1664. Archives of
            Maryland. Published in Baltimore, 1883.
    1681   Proceedings and Acts of the General Assembly of Maryland, 1678-1683. Archives of
            Maryland, Published in Baltimore, 1883.
    1884   Laws of Maryland. Chapter 264.
    1935   Laws of Maryland. Chapter 60.

Maryland, Vital Statistics
    1967-1969. Annual Vital Statistics Report. Baltimore: Maryland State Department of
        Health.

Monahan, Thomas P.
    1976   "An overview of statistics on interracial marriage in the United States, with data on
            its extent from 1963-1970." Journal of Marriage and the Family 38 (May): 223-231.

—and Elizabeth H. Monahan
    1976   "The occupational class of couples entering into interracial marriages." Journal of
            Comparative Family Studies, Vol. VII, No. 2 (Summer 1976) 175-92.

Norton, Sidney M.
    1966   "Interracial births in Baltimore, 1950-1964." Public Health Reports 81 (November):
            967-971.
    1968c   Miscegenation Law in Maryland, 1663-1967. Unpublished manuscript.
    1970   "Interracial marriages in Maryland." Public Health Reports 85 (August): 739-747

Plecker, W.A.
    1925a   "Virginia's attempt to adjust the color problem." American Journal of Public
            Health 15 (January): 111-115.
    1925b   "Racial improvement." Pamphlet. Virginia Medical Monthly, October.
    1925c   "The new family and race improvement." Pamphlet. Richmond, Bureau of Vital
            Statistics, State Board of Health.

    1934   "Virginia's effort of preserve racial integrity." A Decade of Progress in Eugenics
            (3rd International Congress) Baltimore: Williams and Wilkins Co.

Reuter, Edmund B.
    1931   Race Mixture: Studies in Intermarriage and Miscegenation. New York: McGraw
            Hill.

Scott, Arthur P.
    1930   Criminal Law in Virginia. Chicago: University of Chicago Press.

Shinert, Gregory E.
    1952   Filipino-White Marriages, A Study of Filipino-White Marriages in the District of
            Columbia, 1940-1947. Unpublished paper. Catholic University of America.

Tremain, Mary
    1892   Slavery in the District of Columbia, The Policy of Congress and the Struggle for
            Abolition. New York: G.P. Putnam's Sons.

United States — Congress.
    1879-1902 Annual Report of the Health Officer, in the Annual Report of the Commissioners
            of the District of Columbia. House Miscellaneous Documents.

—National Office of Vital Statistics.
    1939   Vital Statistics — Special Reports. Vol. 15, No. 8.
    1940   Vital Statistics — Special Reports. Vol. 15, No. 19; Vol. 17. Nos. 9, 13-14, and 22-23.
            Washington, D.C,: Government Printing Office.
    1960   Vital Statistics — Special Reports. "Selected characteristics of marriages: District of
            Columbia, 1956. Vol. 47, No. 7.

—Supreme Court.
    1967   Loving v. Virginia. No. 395, October Term, 1966.
    1967c   Loving v. Virginia. Transcript of Record 388 U.S. 1 (1966) New York: Record
            Press.

Virginia Laws
    1819   Revised Code of Virginia. I, Ch. xviii.
    1848   Acts of Assembly. Ch. viii.
    1860   Code of Virginia. Ch. cix.

1877-78. Acts of Assembly. Page 302.
1910   Acts of Assembly. Ch. 357.
1950   Code of Virginia. Domestic Relations, Ch. 4, Sec 20-50, 20-54.

Virginia Vital Statistics
1919-1935. Biennial Report of the State Board of Health, becoming Annual Report of the State Department of Health.
1967-1974. Annual Vital Statistics Report. Richmond, Virginia.

Wadlington, Walter
1966   "The Loving case: Virginia's antimiscegenation statute in historical perspective." Virginia Law Review 52 (October): 1189-1223.

Wilson, Theodore B.
1965   The Black Codes of the South. University Ata: University of Alabama Press.

PART III

DIVORCE AND REMARRIAGE

The breakdown of marriage is a matter of great concern in modern societies in Europe and America, but it does not have the same meaning in more traditional societies. In some societies, especially where Islam is the dominant religion, divorce is a serious social problem. For the rest of the non-Western family systems, the level of marital stability is much higher than in modern family systems. It is perhaps for this reason that there are few articles dealing with marital instability in non-Western areas.

All of the studies in this section focus on North American family systems, except one which is devoted to African society. The first study by S. P. Reyna, suggests that among the Barma of Chad divorce granted on the grounds of childlessness is consistent with economic rationality. Thus, the marriages that do culminate in divorce are of relatively brief duration. The data in this study indicate that the absence of children is associated with marital instability.

Having children in subsistence economies has great economic advantages, for children provide additional labor. Children are the *major* source of labor in Barma society, and as such, the success or failure of individual firms depends on them. For the Barma, there are no practical alternatives to having children; polygyny and foster children are not substitutes. Children perform all the work expected of their age and sex. There are strong norms urging adult sons to work with their parents. A son who works with his father will be assisted in his marriage, and will receive land, position, and valuables. An errant son is considered "moral leper." Because of cost factors, neither polygyny nor wage labor is a significant source of labor.

Female sterility among Barma women is as high as 25 percent, largely because of the high incidence of venereal disease. Since childless marriage threatens the sole source of labor, divorce is not uncommon. Clearly, then, the children in this poor society represent a crucial labor supply and the absence of children in a marriage is a threat to its stability.

Another interesting dimension of divorce is found among the Eskimos. According to the study by Albert Heinrich, "in most Eskimo societies there is no absolute divorce. Ex-spouses retain a certain connectedness and moral responsibility toward each other and, in addition, have definite responsibilities to their ex-spouses' future marriage partners and future offspring." He also suggests that "polygamy, spouse exchange, and remarriage after the death of a spouse are all rather easily demonstrated as having integrative functions."

According to Heinrich, "even today in many Eskimo communities, connections between two divorced persons do not bring about complete obliteration of connectedness, either terminologically or functionally." As an example, he notes that among the Mackenzie Eskimos, a husband and an ex-husband maintain ritual-cermemonial obligations to each other, much as two men who exchange wives retain a social relationship. Evidently, divorce in Eskimo culture does not sever social connections as completely as it does in many other societies.

Heinrich concludes that, while disruptive, divorce serves as another mechanism for widening the connectedness in the society at large.

The next study in Part III, by Thomas Monahan, deals with interracial marriages and divorces in Kansas. Until 1947, there were legal obstacles to interracial marriages, but after that date, the number of such unions increased steadily. Concurrent with this rise, divorces of racially mixed couples have increased. Among Negroes and Chinese there are more racially mixed marriages than racially mixed divorces, but for Mexicans married to nonwhites the situation is reversed. According to this study, mixed racial marriages have a higher divorce ratio than all marriages (27 to 100 for the whole, and 45 to 100 for the mixed types). Interestingly, mixed Negro-white marriages show more stability than marriages between two Negroes. Monahan concludes that, even though mixed racial marraiges might be more likely to end up in divorce than homogamous ones, the factors affecting the stability of mixed marriages are the particular races intermarrying, social circumstances, and the nature of the marital choice itself.

The next five studies are about the Canadian family. The first explores the reason for marriage breakdown as viewed by a social worker (Sally Palmer). The work is based on an investigation of 291 couples over a two and a half year period; its findings reinforce the results of studies done in the United States.

In the study population, the average age at marriage of couples who were divorced was much younger than average. The majority of the men were under twenty-four years of age and women, under twenty-one. As shown by Palmer, those who marry too young have unrealistic expectations of marriage; they are inexperienced in human relationships and cannot handle crises; and some of them have not yet fully emancipated themselves from their parents. Husbands have distorted notions about their authority in the family and become too demanding; they also have little tolerance for frustration.

Another important factor in divorce in Canada is the rise in teen-age marriages because of premarital pregnancy. If parents and other social pressures force them to get married, such marriages will collapse sooner than later.

People with criminal tendencies are also poor candidates for marriage. Apparently, such unstable people marry in the hopes of attaining stability. Sometimes they end up in jail, and the wife and children suffer.

Money problems is another cause of marriage breakdowns in Canada. Some of the husbands in the study were unemployed or were in low-paying jobs with no prospect of improvement. In an affluent society, those with low incomes can barely survive; the pressures are especially great on young couples who are exposed to the propaganda of commercials in the mass media. Low income also means low status for families, and there are fewer social pressures on them when marriages break up than there are on middle-class families.

Other cases of divorce in the study population involved women who worked to make up for the low income of their husbands. When one partner is forced to work, the marriage becomes more unstable. Working wives expect more decision-making power in the family, especially with regard to money. Hence, in a difficult situation, she would rather end the marriage than endure an unhappy relationship.

Dissimilar socioeconomic backgrounds of husband and wife also lead to marital conflicts. For such couples, the too-early arrival of children will precipitate a crisis. According to the study, the arrival of children will totally break down an already weak relationship.

The next paper, by John Peters, provides valuable data for the reader interested in examining the recent divorce trend in Canada. With the liberalization of divorce laws in Canada in 1967-1968, the divorce rate has increased 7 percent yearly since 1969. The divorce rate is correlated with a province's percent of urban population and city size.

Peters also investigates the alleged grounds for divorce. For those receiving a divorce in Canada between 1970 and 1973, separation for three years or more is the reason most frequently given (35 percent). The next most frequent grounds are adultery, physical cruelty, and mental cruelty. Provinces with a high rural population generally have a lower divorce rate. Peters suggests that the normative change in the interpretation of the Divorce Act of 1968 by younger judges may liberalize the criteria for divorce. The Canadian government has been contemplating "no-fault" divorce but has not yet made a final decision. The provinces of Ontario and Alberta have passed legislation which accepts the principle of equal property division between the spouses when the marriage ends in divorce. It will be interesting to see what effect this legislation will have on marriage rates.

The next three studies deal specifically with remarriage. While divorces are high, remarriages are also increasing in modern societies. All three studies provide some insight into this very important aspect of family life in modern society.

In Paul Kuzel and P. Krishnan discuss some of the demographic aspects of remarriage. Young males under thirty years of age usually remarry without waiting too long. At older ages, widowers have a better chance to marry, but younger widowers have better probabilities than young divorced. Both divorced and widowed men have brighter prospects for remarriage than women.

Widowed women have better remarriage probabilities than divorcees. This pattern differs from that in the United States, possibly because of the greater number of Roman Catholics in Canada and because of an unfavorable distribution in the country with regard to the availability of partners. Canada has almost twice the percentage of Catholics in its population than the United States. The position of the Catholic church on divorce definitely affects remarriage. It is statistically shown that the larger the share of Catholics in a province; the lower the remarriage rate for divorced females.

With divorced men marrying single and widowed women, divorced women find remarriage very difficult. As a result, they have to seek partners from either single or widowed males. It also seems that the marriage market is becoming more favorable to divorced females.

In the article by Benjamin Schlesinger, ninety-six couples in metropolitan Toronto, Canada, who had remarried formed the study population. In the period 1950-1964, an average of 13.1 percent of all marriages were remarriages. Bachelors tended to marry divorced women more than widows; widowers married widows; divorced men married single women; and divorced women married single men.

The sample in this study was white, mostly Protestant, and middle class in terms of income, education, and housing. On the average, the youngest divorced males and females tended to marry single people; the eldest, widowed people; and those in the middle, divorced people. Significantly, 45 percent of the divorced males and 43 percent of the divorced females in the sample had marital separation or divorce in their family background, and 50 percent of the sample had parents or siblings who had remarried at least once. Thus, there was a large experience of family disorganization.

With regard to attitudes toward remarriage, many males and females in the sample expected different qualities in their new spouses than from their first partners, and they emphasized the need for more caution than intuition in planning remarriages. Less than half the male sample and slightly more than half the female sample felt that their sexual experience in the first marriage influenced their sexual adjustment in remarriage. A predominant majority of the males (87.5 percent) and of the females (81.3 percent) reported that their remarriage "very satisfactorily" met their expectations of marriage. In an earlier study of remarriages, conducted in the United States, Jesse Bernard found that remarriages were not less successful than first marriages. She also found that because of the differences in the selection processes involved, the remarriages of the widowed were apparently more successful than those of the divorced. According to Schlesinger, satisfaction with remarriages has also been found by William J. Goode. With regard to the instability of remarriages, Schlesinger cautions that much of the literature on the subject is based on professional social work experience rather than on research projects and that, as a consequence, findings may be biased.[1]

The topic of remarriage in Canada is again taken up in the next article in Part III. In John Peters' study of forty-eight people in Ontario, selected from names in the 1970 and 1971 divorce registry, almost half of the brides were below the age of twenty in their first marriage compared to 28 percent in the national population. This statistic confirms the relationship between too-early marriage and divorce as found in Sally Palmer's study and other works. Almost half of the first marriages were opposed by one or both parents of the spouses, with greater opposition being registered towards the daughters than toward the sons, probably because the girls were younger than the boys. Thus, family support, which is so important to marital stability, was largely lacking for this sample.

Peters suggests premarital counseling as an aid in promoting marital stability. The respondents themselves also made some useful recommendations for the young contemplating marriage: know each other's values, needs, and goals; maintain open communication; don't anticipate changing a partner's personality through marriage; and never rush into marriage at too young an age. (These recommendations are similar to those found in Schlesinger's study.)

The study population showed more rationality in second marriages. Their bitter experiences in their first marriages made them more cautious in their second marriage.

While counseling does not as such prevent marriage breakups, it should be borne in mind that it is often sought too late inasmuch as members of a highly individualistic society are unwilling to let others become involved in their marriage difficulties. In traditional cultures with their extended family system, troubled spouses can readily obtain useful advice from family members. Unlike the case in modern family systems, such counsel is not resented.

In India, for example, social pressures prevent marriage breakdowns: "In India instances of divorce irrespective of economic independence are still very rare. This holds true with most religious groups, as the social pressure on the people prevents any show-down. Education and democratic outlooks have not changed the people very much. The difficulties now encountered to separation or divorce may not necessarily stand the test of time."[2]

The final article in this section, Dorothy M. Stetson's comparison of divorce reform policies in Western democracies, is an interesting cross-cultural study. The countries compared are the United States, Great Britain, Australia, New Zealand, Canada, and Italy.

The Christian concept of marriage is that it is a lifetime commitment. Italy, through the strong influence of the Catholic church, has had the most stringent divorce laws of all the countries in this study. In other countries, divorce could be obtained only in court, when one spouse proved the guilt of the other. Until very recent decades, while there was demand for divorce, lawmakers were very slow to effect any meaningful change. The choice was between living together unhappily or separate without the approval of the law.

In recent years, governments have attempted to give marriage laws the same status as any other laws. As such, the state has no role in preserving standards of family life. It is felt that the government should pass legislation to dissolve marriages which are unworkable. The fault grounds for divorce, however, has been maintained, for no fault divorce is not generally acceptable even in many modern societies.

In its recognition that monogamy may not be lifelong, the modern view of family stability differs from the traditional views. Since strict divorce laws only further disrupt family life, reforms in divorce laws are necessary. Nonetheless, public support of standard monogamy remains.

In the United States, Florida and California have adopted progressive laws based on the breakdown theory without investigation or "no fault" divorce. New York, California, Australia, and New Zealand all have made funds available to assist judges in promoting reconciliation. Most reconciliation efforts are not very successful, however. In practice, breakdown without investigation and separation as proof of marital breakdown mean that new reforms have done little to change past practices. As long as the fault grounds are retained in law, couples will manufacture the evidence to obtain divorce.

It is interesting that the divorce reform policies of the various countries studied are quite similar. The reasons for the similarities are that (1) the opposition of the Anglican and Catholic churches has delayed divorce reform laws (except in Florida and California); (2) legislators have inadequate knowledge about the issues involved and, hence, are unlikely to agree to drastic changes in existing laws; and (3) there has been weak mobilization of interest in changing existing policies.

Stetson concludes that national policies in the area of divorce are characterized by the "lag of public symbols behind social change. . . . [the] gap between public and private norms illustrates the common interests of legislators and moral leaders on these matters. In turn, decision-makers are prevented from officially admitting the effectiveness of traditional norms and values in regulating individual conduct in modern society." This study, with its valuable cross-national comparison, demonstrates the lack of imagination in implementing effective laws that would facilitate the dissolution of unhappy marriages. Such laws are crucial to the happiness of couples as well as children in modern family systems.

Notes

1. Gerald R. Leslie, *The Family in Social Context*, New York: Oxford University Press, 1976, pp. 734-739.

2. George Kurian, *The Indian Family in Transition—A Case Study of Kerala Syrian Christians*, The Hague: Mouton Publishers, 1961, p. 83.

The Rationality of Divorce:
Marital Instability among the Barma of Chad*

S. P. REYNA**

"A woman without children is like a tree without leaves." Chadian Proverb.

Ethnological research on marital instability in traditional sub-Saharan Africa is distinguished by the insistence of British social anthropologists on the importance of descent system variables for understanding divorce rates (Gluckman, 1950; Mitchell, 1961; Fallers, 1957; Lewis, 1962; Goody and Goody, 1967). Other contributions have also emphasized social structural features. Cohen's work among the Kanuri has stressed the role of status distinctions and hierarchical relations (1961, 1971). Gibbs accented 'tightness' or 'looseness' of societal structuring in his work among the Kpelle (1963); while Ackerman, in a cross-cultural test of 62 African populations, has insisted 'on the network of conjunctive affiliations' as the significant determinant of divorce (1963). Only three anthropological contributors on Africa note a relationship between fertility and divorce: Stenning on pastoral Fulani (1959), Ardener (1962) on Bakweri, and Cohen (1971) on Kanuri. All observe that childlessness is an important factor associated with marital instability. None attempts to show systematically why childlessness contributes to divorce in sub-Saharan Africa.[1] Further, the previously cited social structural interpretations ignore the relationship between fertility and divorce. This is unfortunate, because in Africa (Nag, 1968: 204; van de Walle, 1968), high fertility appears to be associated with fragile marriages. This paper considers how the absence of children can threaten a marriage's durability.

Since the late 1950's, a tradition has arisen which interprets the number of children produced in a marriage in terms of some form of rational, economic choice. Reviews of this literature can be found in Hawthorn (1970), Easterlin (1969), and Liebenstein (1974). Rational choices are those where individuals

* Financial assistance for this research was provided by the Population Council (Grant 069.096). Professors L. Cobb, R. Cohen, R. E. Downs, L. Mair, A. Rosman, and M. Straus have commented on versions of this paper. Its shortcomings are the author's.
**Department of Sociology and Anthropology, University of New Hampshire, Durham, New Hampshire 03824, U.S.A.
[1] Cohen's latest study of Kanuri marital instability, employing stepwise discriminant function analysis, found that out of 20 variables, whether or not a union was childless was the most important predictor of marital stability (Cohen, Ibid. : 152). Yet he concluded that '...high divorce is ...based ultimately upon status distinctions and hierarchical relations...' (Ibid. : 179). The relationship between the social structural variables and childlessness is not systematically explored.

rank alternatives open to them in preference orders, and select the most preferred option (Heath, 1976). Economic choices are restricted to production, distribution, and consumption alternatives (Lancaster, 1969). Preference orders are established by the relative costs and benefits of the alternatives. The option providing relatively the greatest benefits at the least cost is the preferred alternative. Rational economic choice is a function of those factors which control the costs and benefits of different economic alternatives. In general, it has been argued for societies with horticultural or agricultural modes of production that high fertility is consistent with rational economic behavior (Caldwell, 1976; Liebenstein, 1957; Nag, 1972; Reyna, 1976, 1977), even when such individual decisions may be maladaptive for the entire society (White, 1975). This paper, assuming the 'economic' interpretation of fertility, demonstrates for one horticultural ethnic group, the Barma of Chad, that divorce under conditions of childlessness is consistent with economic rationality.

The paper consists of five sections. The first presents pertinent Barma ethnographic material. The second documents the high divorce rates. The third, after associating divorce with childlessness, shows why divorce is a rational decision for the childless. The fourth considers potential criticisms of our position. The conclusion examines whether our 'economic' approach is competitive with the previously mentioned 'social structural' studies of marital durability in traditional Africa.

I. Background

Information was collected from August through September, 1963 and from July, 1969 through November, 1970 in the Prefecture of Chari-Baguirmi in the Republic of Chad. Two data collection techniques were utilized. Information from the villages of Bougoumen and Guera is derived from participant observation. Material designated from 'presently married' or 'Northwestern Barma' comes from a survey of married females between the ages of 14 and 59. A total of 208 women were interviewed in six rural villages and the capital, N'djamena. Systematic sampling was employed in the urban area. In the rural areas, every household containing a suitable respondent at the time interviewing was conducted was surveyed. The area sampled was the north-western-most area of Barma habitation. The questionnaire and field procedures employed are described in Reyna (1972: 7-13).

The Barma (numbering about 24,500 in 1970) live along the Chari and Bahr Erguig Rivers between Bousso and N'djamena, in the Sahelo-Sudanic climatic zone. They were the politically dominant ethnic group in the emirate of Baguirmi. Residence patterns prior to French colonization consisted of two supra-familial residence units—town and hamlet. The towns were 'largish' and walled, containing officials and important markets. Surrounding the towns were small, predominantly horticultural hamlets. Colonial administration, begun during the first decade of the 20th century, crippled the operation of the traditional markets and political system, prompting a considerable emigration, especially to N'djamena. As a result, the large towns are today diminished in size, while many of the small hamlets have been deserted. Barma lack descent groups.

The economy resembles that of her Muslim neighbors—the Kanuri and Hausa. Most Barma are extensive subsistence cultivators of cereals, especially sorghum. They keep no cattle, but trade for dairy products with the neighboring pastoralists, Shuwa Arabs and Fulani. Many Barma fish, and trading is a prestigious activity. However, perhaps due to transportation and market constraints, fewer Barma than Kanuri or Hausa commercialize agricultural products, fewer Barma are large-scale traders, and fewer Barma produce craft items. Most Barma, like most Chadians, are exceptionally poor. After immediate individual consumption and cash needs (for taxes) have been satisfied, there is very little surplus. Clearly, the most important commodity produced by the Barma economy is food.

In micro-economics, a firm is the sector of the economy that produces goods for consumption by the household (Schneider, 1974:236). Analytically, the firm, managed by an entrepreneur, consumes the factors of production (land, labor, and capital) to produce goods and services. Among the Barma, as is true in many rural African societies, the domestic group (*bey*) is the firm. It produces horticultural, fishing, and craft goods. Households should be some form of the patrilocal extended family, though compounds may be further extended through the addition of divorced sisters and additional wives. Extended family households were found in 35% of all surveyed northwestern rural Barma. Household members begin regular food production activities as they approach puberty (about age 15), and they tend to stop such work by age 65. Active males work cereal fields and fish. Active females work smaller plots of land, growing okra and peanuts (primarily for the household's subsistence, though occasionally for sale). In extended family households, the nuclear family segments or fragments of such segments pool their labor and *tachita kede* ('work one'). Additional information concerning the organization of economic activities in Barma households can be found in Reyna (1976).

Each household has a head (either *ngolbey* or *malabey*). In nuclear family households, this is the husband. In father-son compounds, it is the father if he is not too feeble. In fraternally extended households, it is normally the most energetic elder brother. The household head is its usual representative in external ritual and political affairs. He is not, however, invariably its entrepreneur. Husbands do not take food production decisions without consulting their wives, so that the ultimate decision a man takes is only after a process of conjugal negotiation. In extended family households there is an elder male (father or brother) who is the nominal entrepreneur. But his decisions are made only after consultation with other adult males in the household who in turn consult with their wives. Each adult male has the possibility of deciding whether it is in their interests to 'work one', or to break off and found their own domestic firms. Married adults, then, face the decisions which may or may not be rational concerning the domestic firms.

II. Barma Marital Instability

Below we examine how frequently Barma females divorce, after what periods of marriage, and at what ages. The measures of divorce frequency are those introduced by Barnes (1949), which are:

(a) the number of marriages ended in divorce expressed as a percentage of all marriages;

(b) the number of marriages ended in divorce expressed as a percentage of all completed marriages; and

(c) the number of marriages ended in divorce expressed as a percentage of all marriages except those that have ended by death.

Divorce ratios for the presently married Barma women are presented in Table 1 (row vii) which compares these ratios to those in African populations

TABLE 1   DIVORCE RATES IN SELECTED HIGH DIVORCE POPULATIONS

	A	B	C
i Kanuri men*	54	81	58
ii Bakweri men*	42	66	54
iii Yao women*	35	68	41
iv Ngoni*	29	56	37
v U.S.A.*	3	22	3
vi Barma (ever mar.)	59	97	61
vii Barma (pres. mar.)	31	89	33

(*Source : Cohen 1971:125)

previously known to exhibit high marital instability. The sample of presently married Barma women indicates a divorce level between that of Ngoni and Yao (the two lowest of the high divorcing populations). The figures in row vii probably under-represent Barma female marital instability because: (1) the data from presently married women include a higher percentage of younger women who, due to their youth, have had less time to divorce; and (2) the data exclude presently divorced and widowed women. A more accurate measure of marital instability would be from a sample of all women who have ever been married. Figures from such a population in Bougoumen and Guera are presented in row vi of Table 1, and indicate the highest level of marital instability reported in the table. Barma, with reason, regard an enduring marriage as something of an oddity.

Table 2 displays by duration of unions, in a manner also suggested by Barnes (1949: *Ibid.*): the percentage of extent marriages, marriages ended in death, marriages ended in divorce, and the total number of unions. The table reveals that about 60% of the total number of marriages last 5.0 to 7.4 years or more; but that 80% of the marriages which terminate in divorce do so by or before 5.0 to 7.4 years of marriage. Marriages culminating in divorce, thus, are of relatively brief duration.

TABLE 2   DURATION-SPECIFIC MARRIAGE AND DIVORCE DATA AMONG THE NORTHWESTERN BARMA

Duration of Union in Yrs.	Extant Unions	% of Total	Acc. %	Deaths	% of Total	Acc. %	Div.	% of Total	Acc. %	Size of Sample	% of Total Sample (314)
0.0— .9	5	2.4	2.4	2	14.3	14.3	5	5.2	5.2	314	100.0
1.0—1.9	13	6.3	8.7	4	28.6	42.9	14	14.6	19.8	302	96.2
2.0—2.9	18	8.8	17.5	—	—	—	13	13.5	33.3	271	86.3
3.0—3.9	14	6.9	24.4	3	21.4	64.3	14	14.6	47.9	240	76.4
4.0—4.9	14	6.9	31.3	—	—	—	9	9.4	57.3	209	66.6
5.0—7.4	26	12.8	44.1	2	14.4	78.7	20	20.8	78.1	186	59.2
7.5—9.9	21	10.3	54.4	—	—	—	8	8.3	86.4	138	44.0
10.0—14.9	44	21.6	76.0	1	7.1	85.8	8	8.3	94.7	109	34.7
15.0—19.9	25	12.3	88.3	1	7.1	92.9	2	2.1	96.8	56	17.8
20.0—24.9	9	4.4	92.7	1	7.1	100.0	2	2.1	98.9	28	8.9
25.0—29.9	7	3.4	96.1	—	—	—	1	1.1	100.0	16	5.1
30.0+	8	3.9	100.0	—	—	—	—	0.0	—	8	2.6
TOTAL	204			14			96				

Table 3 presents the ages of presently married women at the time of their divorces.

TABLE 3   MEAN AGE AT DIVORCE AMONG THE NORTHWESTERN BARMA WOMEN

	Ist Divorce	2nd Divorce	3rd + Divorce	TOTAL
Number	65	16	3	34
Total Ages	1267	390	74	1731
Mean	19 2/5	24 1/4	24 2/3	20 3/5

The mean age at first divorce was about 19; second divorce, 24 years; and third or more divorces, 25 years. Even Barma who have multiple divorces are finished with these on the average by their middle twenties. Barma women, then, divorce frequently, after relatively short marriages, and they do their divorcing while they are young.

III. Hormo, Labor Scarcity, and Rationality

(a) *Hormo*

Male informants, when pressed as to why divorce occurred so frequently, would respond: "*Hormo* gone."[2] *Hormo* is for Barma males the normative principle regulating wifely behavior. If pressed for descriptions as to what exactly *hormo* was, men would sink to their knees, bow humbly, adjust their facial features in a contrite fashion. and silently clap their hands. These are the same features employed in the political arena, when a person of lower status wishes an audienee with a person of higher status. *Hormo*, according to men, is proper wifely conduct, meaning wifely subservience.

The preceeding paragraph describes *hormo* from a male viewpoint. This makes it appear as if only men make divorce decisions. Men's perceptions of divorce decision-making are not inevitably accurate, as the following illustrates. Ali was a phlegmatic, middle-aged man of Bougoumen. Komani was his high-spirited, teenage wife. In principle, women cannot divorce men. In fact Komani, ran away from Ali, the shame of which obliged him to liberate his wife. But Ali did not wish a divorce, and so after a time, he raised a group of his neighbors to plead with Komani's kin for her return. She would not return, however, and soon after, Ali, pursued by unpleasant spirits, ran madly into the bush. He was returned by his co-villagers in a semi-catatonic state. Ali's breakdown suggests how far removed he actually was from the decisions involved in his own divorce.

Ali conceptualized the breakup of his marriage as resultant from the loss of *hormo*. But it is critical to understand that lack of *hormo* did not destroy Ali's marriage, any more than 'not liking' each other breaks up American marriages. We are trying to isolate the reasons why, in Barma marriages, there is no *hormo*

---

[2] *Hormo* is a word probably borrowed from Arabic (Stevenson, 1969:14).

prior to divorce, just as we would like to ascertain why many Americans report that they didn't 'like' each other just before divorce.

One of the areas in which most Barma are in striking agreement is in their love of, and desire for, children. Even so, as crude a research technique as a questionnaire reveals this preference for children. Only 7% of the presently married Barma women surveyed wanted fewer than 5 children (Reyna, 1972:116). Not unsurprisingly, the absence of children in a marriage leads to strains between husband and wife, and male informants were aware that *hormo* was likely to evaporate when children did not appear in a marriage. One lengthy interview with an old man who had had nine wives went as follows:

Question : And why did you divorce Hadidja?
Response : No children, *hormo* fled.
Question : And why did you divorce Pulo?
Response : No children, *hormo* fled.
Question : And why did you divorce Lamana?
Response : No children, *hormo* fled.
etc., etc., etc.

Barma want children and male informants indicated that if children did not enrich a marriage, then the normative basis for marriage was destroyed.

It is accordingly not surprising that there is a strong statistical association between divorce and childlessness. The presently married women gave retrospective marital histories. These were scrutinized to ascertain whether children were or were not produced in a marriage, and whether the marriage ended in divorce. The chi square test was applied to this material, and the results of the test are reported in Table 4. Childlessness was frequent (present in 42% of the

TABLE 4   CHILD PRODUCTION IN MARRIAGE BY MARITAL STABILITY
                                        AMONG THE NORTHWEST BARMA

Marital Stability	Child Production		
	Marriage with No Children	Marriage with Children	Total
Ever-Divorced	65 (50%)	37 (21%)	102
Never Divorced	65 (50%)	141 (79%)	206 (N=308)

$X^2 = 29.1$; P .005
$\phi = .31$ (9% of variance explained)

marriages), and the X^2 resultant from the test indicates a strong non-chance relationship between childlessness and divorce. Note that 21% of the marriages with children ended in divorce, while 50% of the marriages without children ended in divorce. Divorce probability rises from .20 to .50 if the marriage is childless.

These figures indicate that while the absense of children is associated with marital instability, their presence is more strikingly associated with marital stability. Having children acts to stabilize marriage, and not having children tends toward the opposite consequence. Why?

(b) Labor: The Scarce Factor of Barma Food Production

The benefits of children derive not merely from the fact, "universally reported by field researchers" (Caldwell, 1976:339), that they support their parents in old age. Barma children are crucial to the success or failure of individual firms' production decisions. This is true, I content, because Barma society is so organized that children are: *the major source of labor supplied to production units*, and *labor is the only scarce factor of production in Barma society*. These two factors determine the rational entrepreneur's production preference, for the second implies that the *only* strategy available to individual Barma for future production increases is greater inputs of labor, while the first means that the *only* realistic means for increasing labor is to have children. If the contentions are correct, they imply that a childless marriage deprives firms of the sole means of securing the single factor of production capable of raising future production outputs. Data supportive of the two contentions are presented below.

i. Having Children: How Labor is Supplied to Households

The first contention is treated by examining how labor is supplied to all farming, northwest Barma households over short, medium, and long terms. (Short term labor is that supplied for a single, particular chore in a production process; medium term labor is that supplied for an entire production process for a relatively few years; while long term labor is that supplied for relatively many years.) Tables 5 and 6 display the magnitude of each labor source as a percentage of the total farming labor force among the northwest Barma. Concern is with *both* how a particular household may supply its own labor, and how all households are supplied with labor.

TABLE 5   SOURCES OF LABOR IN NORTHWESTERN BARMA FARMING HOUSEHOLDS EXPRESSED AS A PERCENTAGE OF THE TOTAL NUMBER OF LABORERS*

Household Heads	First Wives	Other	Total
33.9	34.1	32	100
147	148	138	433

*The top figure in each cell is the percentage; the bottom figure is the frequency.

Table 5 reports that 68% of the active labor in households is supplied by husbands and first wives. There are nine possible alternative options for supplying the remaining 32% of the labor force. These are:

TABLE 6   SOURCES OF LABOR FOR NORTHWESTERN BARMA FARMING
                      HOUSEHOLDS EXPRESSED AS A PERCENTAGE OF THE
                                    TOTAL NUMBER OF LABORERS

(Excepting Husbands and First Wives)

1	2	3	4	5	6	7	8	9	10	Total
0	28.3	5.7	5.7	0	0	0	1.4	46.5	12.0	100
0	39	8	8	0	0	0	2	64	17	138

Key
*The top figure in each cell is the percentage; the bottom figure is the frequency.
1 = wage labor
2 = adult consanguineal kin of the head
3 = affines of the head
4 = polygynous wives
5 = captured wives
6 = bride service
7 = labor reciprocity
8 = fostered persons
9 = as the result of 'having children'
10 = do not know, or no response, or other

(1) *Wage Labor.* During the entire time that research was conducted, no household relied upon wage labor to perform horticulural or fishing activities. Quantitative estimates of the prevalence of wage labor are available for Bougoumen and Guera, where wage laborers toiled with family workers in three households out of a total of 28 (i.e., in only 11%). Horticultural production requires six major activities in both mens' and womens' fields (clearing, planting, weeding, protection against predators, harvesting, and preparation for storage). The three households which used wage-labor did so in only one of the major horticultural tasks (i.e., 17%). Wage laborers performed none of the fishing chores. Barma informants reported that a reason wage laborers were so rare was their expense. This seems reasonable in light of the fact that the Barma grow no exclusively cash-crops, so that money to pay laborers is in very short supply. Hiring wage labor, then, is not realistic as even a short term alternative for most Barma entrepreneurs.

(2) *Consanguineal Kin from the Entrepreneur's Own Generation.* Barma can add close adult consanguines to their households such as brothers, divorced sisters, or cousins. Approximately 28% of the additional labor supplied to households consisted of adding adult consanguines or the spouses of such kin. Active members of these households perform all the major food producing chores required of their sex. Although adding adult consanguines is a realistic possibility in the

medium run for securing additional household labor inputs, it is risky as a long term strategy. Any labor provided by adult consanguines is ultimately voluntary and there are norms conflicting with consanguine labor cooperatives. Brothers should make their own households for their own offspring, while divorced wives should remarry. An entrepreneur provisioning his household with his brothers, cousins, or divorced sister's labor is aware that these individuals have conflicting goals for the long term disposition of their labor. Thus, the average age of brothers or cousins in fraternally extended households is 32.8 years, and only one of the fraternally extended households surveyed consisted of brothers who were all aged 40 or over. Further, the average time for a woman's remarriage following divoree is one year and seven months.

(3) *Adult Affines.* Barma occasionally recruit affines of the household head in their households. Approximately 5.7% of the labor force beyond that of husbands and wives consisted of affinal relatives of the head. Addition of affines, however, is normatively discouraged, occurring only under exceptional circumstances, i.e., when the head has been obliged to reside uxorilocally, or when some kin of the wife have chosen to live with her temporarily. A man living uxorilocally simply cannot count on cooperation over the long term with his wife's father or brother. Conversely, he cannot expect his wife's siblings or parents to reside with her for long. Addition of affines is therefore a medium term source of labor for only a small number of households.

(4) *Polygyny.* Barma may enlarge their labor supply by taking additional wives. Such women would perform all female productive chores. However, only 5.7% of the labor force beyond that of husbands and wives consisted of polygynally married wives. Barma do not practise the levirate, so wives may be secured only through the payment of bridewealth. Marriage costs were approximately 12,000 CFA in 1969-1970. This is the largest single payment Burma men normally make during their lives, comparable to purchasing a house in the industrial world (Reyna, 1975). Thus increasing labor by taking additional wives is no more realistic an option for the average Barma than buying a number of houses for the average American.

(5) *Wife Capture.* Until 1905, Barma raided to the south for slaves, a fair number of whom ended up in Barma households as wives. Today, however, Barma never capture their labor for three reasons: the populations whom they raided in the past now control the Chadian central government, they are geographically situated close to the capital of the Chadian central government, and they are a distinct minority even within their home region (so that any ethnic group they might raid would be quite capable of resisting). Barma enterpreneurs, then, cannot add to their labor force by capturing it.

(6) *Bride-Service.* When a household has unmarried daughters, prospective suitors may perform bride-service by forming their male age mates into working groups to perform chores, such as weeding or house building. Barma realize that bride-service is an extremely rare source of labor, only available when there are unmarried daughters. (In Bougoumen and Guera, only one bride-service work group was observed during 1969-1970).

(7) *Generalized reciprocity of labor.* Neighbors and kin within a village and between neighboring villages exchange their labor. Such exchanges were observed to be especially common for the threshing of millet and sorghum. When a man wished his grain threshed, he invited neighbors to assist him at the task. He was expected to work later at the threshing of those individuals who had helped him. Such labor is a form of generalized reciprocity (Sahlins, 1972). They may assist the household entrepreneur in performing arduous chores quickly, but they do not usually increase the household labor input because the entrepreneur is expected to repay the labor donated to him with some of his own. Thus, if three men thresh for me one day, I do not increase may household's labor input by three man-days because I or somebody else in my household will have to work at their threshing for a total of three man-days.

(8) *Fostering.* A few Barma households raise children who are not the biological offspring of any members of the compound. Such children are never legally fully incorporated into the family raising them. They acquire limited rights of inheritance from their foster parents. Two factors make fostering a risky long term source of labor. First, low Barma fertility means that there are very few children to foster. Second, the foster child's inheritance situation usually offers little inducement to remain with their foster family, where they will inherit less than the biological offspring. Thus, besides husbands and wives, only 1.4% of the actives in households were fostered persons.

(9) *'Having Children'.* We are left, then, with 'having children' as a way of securing labor. Such children perform all the work expected of their age and sex. There are extremely strong norms urging adult sons to 'work one' with their parents. A son who ignores his parents is likely to be classified as a *malabungo* (a malicious, crazy person), and considered a sorcere (*mbuli*) or one who might have recourse to sorcerers. The inheritance situation is conducive to 'working one' relationships between father and son. The latter's position, cleared fields, and movable property is inherited from his father. Further, his father is under strong obligations to aid him in meeting bridewealth costs. A son who works with his father will be assisted in his marriage, will receive land, position, and valuables. An errant son is a moral leper. The situation is different for daughters. On marriage, a woman's labor is lost to her family of orientation. However, on divorce, if her parents are still alive, a woman is expected to return to her parental household where she will perform all normal adult female tasks. 'Having children' is the largest of the nine additional labor sources. About 47% of the workers in households beyond husbands and first wives were either offspring of the head or spouses of these offspring. Further, it is the only labor source both normatively encouraged and, at least for sons, materially rewarded through inheritance and bridewealth.

Barma, surveying alternative sources of labor for their households, are obliged to make the following observations. Wife capture and bride-service are not reliable labor sources over any term. Due to cost factors, both polygyny and wage labor must be ruled out as significant sources of labor. The addition of the head's affines is a possibility only in exceptional circumstances, perhaps because it is so normatively deviant. Reciprocity permits solution of short term production problems, but must be repaid, so that in the middle and long term, donated labor inputs are returned with labor subtracted from one's own firm. Fostering is impractical as a source of labor for demographic and inheritance reasons. Thus, most Barma husbands and wives are restricted to two choices as to where they may secure additional labor for their domestic firms. They may add adult consanguines of the husband. This is a sound medium term strategy, but as brothers, sisters, and cousins age, their labor is transferred to their families of procreation. For the long term, however, if Barma enterpreneurs want labor, they must 'have children'.

Barma reflecting on how labor is added to any firm observe that workers are added either directly as a result of someone 'having children' in the firm or indirectly as a result of somebody having children in some other firm. Readers may exclaim: "Of course, all labor must be born in all economies!" But in industrial economies, being born does not distribute labor to firms. The wage-market performs this function (Lancaster, 1969: 227). Whereas among the Barma, having children places these individuals into social or kin categories, which are the basis for distributing labor to firms. Household heads add labor by recruiting wives, consanguines, affines, or foster children because someone somewhere had a child who, vis-a-vis the head, corresponds to one of the above categories. From the perspective of entrepreneurs choosing for their firms: 'having children' is the major source of additional Barma labor after husbands and wives; and it is the sole important source of long term labor. From the vantage point of entrepreneurs choosing for all firms: 'having children' increases the number of individuals occupying the kin-based labor sources, thus increasing the labor supply for all. The implication of this paragraph is that Barma marriage in a number of ways is the institution distributing the bulk of the labor used in most households, and it is only by having children that marriage can act as the institution distributing labor to the firm.

ii. *Labor-Scarcity in Barma Food Production*

A factor of production is scarce if it is in limited supply relative to the requirements of a particular production process (Lancaster, 1969). Barma farming and fishing technologies include a very few implements: hoes, axes, machetes, nets weirs, and canoes. Implements used in industrial farming and fishing operations are either unknown or far too expensive for Chad.

This simple capital is not scarce for two reasons. First, if a domestic firm finds itself in need of a tool to farm or fish, it either fabricates it itself, purchases it inexpensively, or receives it from someone in the household's network of generalized reciprocity. (Even the most complicated of Barma capital goods, the dugout canoe, is crafted by male household members using additional labor borrowed from other households.) Simpler tools (axes, weirs, etc.) are home-made or cheaply purchased at the local markets, or immediately borrowed. Thus, if the Barma hausehold needs tools, it can quickly secure what it needs. Essentially, traditional Barma food producing capital is available in unlimited supplies.

It is, in economists' terms, a "free good" (Lancaster, 1969). Second, because technologies are so simple and options so restricted, the food producer can not generally increase land or labor productivity *solely* by investing in new forms of capital.[3] A Barma may choose to increase the capital input by using two axes to clear his land. He may even choose to wield three or four axes. But differences in output (if not demeanor) are trival if one clears with one axe or several per worker. Capital, then, is not a scarce factor of Barma food production because increased total output is never constrained by lack of capital due to the easy availability of the simple tools (though increased productivity is constrained precisely because there are no capital alternatives save for the simple technology).

Nor are land and fishing areas scarce factors of production. This is true of fields both for reasons pertaining to land tenure and to human population density. Barma land tenure excludes the individual buying and selling of land. Existing fields are inherited patrilineally. If one wishes to acquire a new field, one has to establish social relationships with the individual representing the groups with recognized right to control access to the land. For the acquisition of new land, this group is the village, and the person representing it is the head (*ngar*). An individual wishing a new field has simply to inform the village head of his desires. The head lacks authority to refuse the individual's request.

Not only does Barma land tenure not restrict individuals' access to new fields, but population density in the region was low enough in the late 1960's (about 5.0 people/km²) so that there was new land available for fields. Land, then, for Barma farmers, was essentially available in unlimited quantities. The situation was the same for fishing. An individual was allowed to fish wherever he wanted; i.e., his access to fishing areas was unlimited. Thus, the Barma possessed for food production, under the conditions prevailing in 1969-1970, more land than they used, and all the traditional tools they needed, but they had only a small number of workers in their domestic firms. Land and capital exist in effectively unlimited quantities, while labor was available in very restricted amounts. (The mean number of workers for each northwest Barma farming household was 2.9). Labor, then, was the sole scarce factor of production. The implication of the preceding statement is: although additional inputs of land could increase output by bringing new fields and fishing areas into production, and additional inputs of the simple capital tools could increase output by being used in the new fields and fishing areas, they are *only* possible if there are additional inputs of labor. Increased inputs of labor are the *sine qua non* for increased inputs of land and capital. If the benefit one is seeking is increased production, the sole option, and hence the rational preference, is for Barma to increase labor, which they can only do by "having children".

(c) *The Rationality of Divorce*

Previous research has indicated that the incidence of female sterility among northwestern Barma females is high, with 25% of the population surveyed being

---

[3]There is a single exception to this statement. Barma fishermen were aware of a nylon net for sale at certain major markets which increased productivity of fishing.

infertile (Reyna, 1972:90). A high incidence of venereal disease, especially gonorrhea, has been reported within the region occupied by the Barma, and available
data indicate that the high female infertility is due to veneral infections (Reyna,
1975:55-75). This means that many marital unions are likely to be deficient in
their ability to provide potential labor to the firm, which implies that Barma will
be obligated to divorce frequently in order to achieve adequate supplies of labor.

Given the preceding information, Barma divorce levels appear to be consistent with a rationality designed to increase food production. First, we syllogis-
tically show why 'having children' is consistent with rational production increases;
then, why the high divorce level is consistent with the same economic goal.

Increasing production by 'having children'

1: 'having chidren' is the most preferred option for securing labor, because
it is the *only* available option capable of providing this benefit. (The validity
of this proposition is examined in Section III, b, i.)

2: Adding labor, 'by having children' is the most preferred option with
regard to the different factors of production because without it, the benefits of
production increases are unattainable. (The validity of this proposition is
considered in Section III, b, ii.)

Inference 1: If propositions 1 and 2 are correct, 'having children' among the
Barma is consistent with increasing food production in domestic firms, because
it is the sole option for providing labor, which is the sole option whose increase
can provide increased production.

Divorce and increased production

3: There are many childless domestic firms among the Barma. (The validity
of this observation is considered in Section III, c, above.)

4: Divorce permits the formation of new mating pairs, and is the only
choice offering the possibility of 'having children' for the majority of Barma.
The validity of this proposition is considered in Section III, b, i.)

Inference 2: If propositions 3 and 4 are correct, together with inference 1,
then *ceteris paribus,* divorce under conditions of childlessness is consistent
with rationality, for it offers the sole way of securing the single scarce factor
of production.

Corollary 1: Divorce is frequent among the Barma because childlessness is
frequent.

This interpretation accounts for why women's marriages that result in divorce
are relatively short and why women are divorced at young ages. After one or
two years of marriage, childless couples begin to worry about having children.
This precipitates squabbles so that, from the husband's vantage, prudent *hormo*
flees and the marriage flounders. It is in her most youthful, reproductive years
that a women is thought able to bear children. Thus, when she is young and

infertile, a woman is likely to be married and divorced by different men seeking offspring. Wen it becomes clear that no children can be expected from her because she has passed the years when women bear children, her utility is for reasons other than reproductive capacity and marriage is thus likely to be more stable.

Discussion

We are not proposing a single factor explanation of all divorce among the Barma, rather merely trying to understand why Barma divorce frequently under conditions of childlessness. Two potential criticisms of our positions are considered below. First, instead of hypothesizing that childlessness itself leads to divorce, one might argue that 'bad marriages result in childlessness which leads to divorce, i.e., that people who do not get on do not sleep together and ultimately divorce. We might label this the Rocky Marriage Childlessness (RMC) hypothesis.

Barma themselves insist that if a marriage is childless for whatever reason, something must be done to alleviate the situation. Previously married women were asked the open question, "What should be done if a wife is childless?" Of those giving meaningful responses, only 18% thought that nothing should be done, while 77% suggested doing one of two things. The suggestions were either seeking a divorce or addition of another wife (Reyna, 1972:178). Both of the women's suggestions would serve the same function of adding additional offspring to the household, but Barma were aware that polygyny was an expensive option, hence open only to the wealthy.

Barma, then, believe that the condition of childlessness in a marriage is one which must be resolved, and they propose divorce as the solution.

What is proposed, and what is done, are not necessarily identical. There are, however, statistical data supporting the position that childless marriages generate divorce. Table 7 examines the marital stability of women in their first marriages who have been married for at least two years. The reason a period of two years was selected is that such a time span provides a good measure of female infertility. (After two years, it is reported that 90.00% of the women unprotected by contraception who will conceive have already done so (Buxton and Southam, 1958)).

TABLE 7   STABILITY OF FERTILE AND INFERTILE WOMEN'S MARRIAGES
               WHICH LASTED AT LEAST TWO YEARS

(A) Marriage with Offspring		(B) Marriage without Offspring	
divorce	no divorce	divorce	no divorce
15 (15%)	81 (85%)	36 (49%)	38 (51%)

The table reports that 85% of its fertile women's marriages did not end in divorce, while 49% of its infertile women's marriages did end in divorce.

How should one interpret Table 7? To sustain the RMC hypothesis, Table 7 must indicate that 'bad' marriages result in childlessness, while 'good' marriages have children. However, as we have already seen, the table strongly associates stability with children in marriage, and instability with childlessness. Thus, if the RMC hypothesis is to be countenanced we must be able to show that the vast majority of all 'good' first marriages are those *with children* while the vast majority of 'bad' marriages are those *without children*.

We have already learned that infertility among Barma women is largely due to venereal infection. Further, the incidence of such infection is likely to be low and widely distributed for women marrying the first time. Wives are likely to be uninfected at first marriage, contract gonorrhea from their husbands, and then become infertile (Reyna, 1975b:Ibid.). Here is the crux of our argument: if venereal disease is evenly distributed among first marriage women, it means that infertility is equally likely to become evenly distributed among such women, and hence that there is little reason to expect fertile, 'good' marriages and infertile, 'bad' marriages. The information in Table 7 does not support the RMC hypothesis.

A second interpretation of the table is presented below. Most Barma marriages begin in a more or less felicitous state, as the mate selection process pairs roughly compatible spouses. Over time, some marriages are rewarded with children while others are not. Barma set no time span of childless marriage prior to classifying a marriage as sterile, but after two years, they realize that there is a likelihood of infertility. (A manifestation of this concern is that women begin visiting religious specialists, *mallams*, seeking supernatural solutions to their fertility problems.) Table 7 allows us to see what happens when infertility is perceived, because it classifies observed marriages into two groups: those with problems 'having children', (column B), and those free of such problems (column A). The table can be interpreted as providing support for the hypothesis that childlessness leads to divorce among the Barma, because in marriages where the partners perceive there are problems in 'having children', divorce occurs far more frequently than where partners lack such perceptions.

A second criticism of our position is that the reason there is an association between childlessness and divorce is not simply because of the need of the house-hold to supply itself with labor, but because there are other non-economic reasons why children are valued. This could plausibly be argued for the Barma. If one asks people why they want children, sooner or later they will reply: "Because 'Allah' wants us to have to children." This indicates that Barma, like other African populations, are strongly pro-natal, which has been previously reported (Caldwell, 1973: 79-137). The moot question is 'why'? One answer is that pro-natalism is a normative expression of the preferred option in the preference order 'having children' versus 'not having children'. For traditional Africans farming under conditions of abundant land, being chauvinistic pro-natalists is akin to industrialists being jingoistic capitalists: both pursue scarce factors of production—in the former case, labor; in the latter, capital.

The position developed with regard to Barma marital instability might be explored in other traditional African societies. In many areas of sub-Saharan Africa, the domestic group is the firm, and marriage allocates labor to the firm. As earlier noted, there is evidence suggesting that infertility and high marital instability are associated throughout Africa (Nag, Ibid.; van de Walle, Ibid.). It is reported that a major cause of female infertility in Africa is venereal disease (Romaniuk, 1968: 223). Further, the most consistent findings of fertility surveys conducted in West, Central, and East Africa have been that traditional, rural peoples are pro-natal (cf. Caldwell, Ibid. 1973). Hence available studies suggest that the situation reported for the Barma obtains in a number of African populations. In these areas, the following hypothesis should be entertained: childless marriage threatens deficiencies in the sole scarce factor of production in the domestic firm, which the prevalent pro-natalism rejects as intolerable, thus precipitating divorce. This results in the reported association of marital instability and infertility, allowing possible resolution of the labor problems in further marriages.

Conclusion

Are 'social structural' explanations which have dominated interpretations of traditional African divorce competitive with 'economic' accounts? Before proceeding, it should be observed that the present paper has examined intra-societal divorce differentials, while most 'social structural' positions deal with inter-societal divorce differentials. My present concern has been to outline an alternative to 'social structural' explanations, not to pit the two positions against each other.

To design a test of the two approaches, it should be observed that two economic traditions exist: one of pure economists, and one of economic anthropologists. Pure economists and structural functionalists would account for marital instability at different levels of analysis. Social structuralists have emphasized how 'social' *institutional* factors (e.g., those associated with descent group organization of a society, or with the nature of its stratification, etc.) influence marital instability. Pure economists' interests are focused at the *individual* level of decision-making, with actors assumed to be rational. The two levels of analysis are not mutually exclusive. Rather, they compete with different interpretations at their own levels: e.g., is the assumption of rationality sufficient to explain individuals' decisions?, are the institutions identified as important for triggering African divorce the correct institutions?

Recent economic anthropology exploits the strengths of both the above positions by seeking individual rationality within varying institutional contexts (cf. Godelier, 1972; Prattis, 1973). Hence, economic anthropologists turn out to be *very interested* in institutions, but they are concerned with 'economic' ones, for they study how different societies organize the production, distribution, and consumption of goods and services. Economic anthropoligists would insist that 'economic' as well as 'social' institutional factors set the costs and benefits of divorce which determine the rationality of individual marital decision-making. It is with regard to the relative importance of the two categories of institutional factors that the two positions are competitive, with economic anthropologists insisting that 'economic' rather than 'social' institutions are the more important determinants of divorce levels.

Clearly, empirical studies comparing 'social' and 'economic' institutional factors are in order. Ecology should be roughly identical in each society; and they should all be agrarian with land and capital essentially free goods. Different 'social' factors should be examined in societies with high and low fertility. If, regardless of the 'social' institutions present in the societies, high fertility was always associated with low divorce, and low fertility with the reverse, then the 'economic' position presented in this paper would receive important support.

It should be obvious what I believe would be the results of such research. Divorce in Western society is a juridical resolution to marital combat resultant from personal idiosyncrasies. In societies with kin-based economic institutions, the eccentricity of being able to bear children effects economic performance, so such societies may help their members by ranking spousely idiosyncracies. Among the Barma, a childless woman is not preferred. She is, after all, like "...a tree without leaves."

REFERENCES

Ackerman, C
    1963   Affiliations : structural determinants of differential divorce. American Journal of Sociology 69:13-20.

Ardener, E.
    1962   Divorce and Fertility: An African Study. Published for the Nigerian Institue of Socio. and Econ. Research. London: Oxford University Press.

Barnes, J.
    1959   Measures of divorce frequency in simple society. Journal of Royal Anthropological Institute 79:62.

Buxton, C. L. and A. L. Southam
    1953   Human Infertility. New York: Hoeber and Harder.

Caldwell, J.
    1978   Regulation de la fecondite. In Croissance demographique et evolution socio-econo-mique en afrique de l'ouest. J.D. Caldwell et al., eds. The Population Council.
    1976   Toward a restatement of domographic transition theory. Population and Development Review 2, 3:321-367.

Cohen, R.
    1961   Marriage instability among the Kanuri of northern Nigeria. American Anthropologist 63:1231-1249.
    1971   Dominance and Defiance. Washington: American Anthropological Association.

Easterlin, R.
    1969   Towards a socioeconomic theory of fertility: a survey of recent research on economic factors in American fertility. In S.J. Behrman et al., eds. Ann Arbor: University of Michigan Press.

Fallers, L.
    1957   Some determinants of marriage stability in Busoga: a reformulation of Gluckman's hypothesis. Africa 27:106-121.

Gibbs. J.
  1963   Marital instability among the Kpelle: toward a theory of epainogamy. American Anthropologist 65:552-559.

Gluckman, J.
  1950   Kinship and marriage among the Lozi of Northern Rhodesia and the Zulu of Natal. *In* African Systems of Kinship and Marriage. A.R. Radcliffe-Brown and D. Forde, eds. London: Oxford University Press.

Godelier, M.
  1972   Rationality and Irrationality in Economics. New York: Monthly Review Press.

Goody, J.E.
  1967   The circulation of women and their children in northern Ghana. Man 2:226-248.

Hawthorn, G.
  1970   The Sociology of Fertility. London: Collier-Macmillan.

Heath, A.
  1976   Rational Choice and Social Exchange. New York: Cambridge University Press.

Lancaster, K.
  1969   Introduction to Modern Microeconomics. Chicago: Rand McNally.

Liebenstein, H.
  1957   Economic Backwardness and Economic Growth. New York: Wiley.
  1974   An interpretation of the economic theory of fertility: Promising path or blind alley? Journal of Economic Literature XII:457-479.

Lewis, I.M.
  1962   Marriage and the Family in Northern Somaliland. East African Studies 15. Kampala: East African Institute of Social Research.

Michell. J.D.
  1961   Social change and the stability of African marriage in Northern Rhodesia. *In* Change in Modern Africa. A. Southall, ed. London: Oxford University Press.

Nag, M.
  1968   Factors Affecting Human Fertility in Non-Industrial Societies. New York: Taplinger.
  1972   Economic Value of Children in Agricultural Societies: Evaluation of Existing Knowledge and an Anthropological Approach. *In* the Satisfactions and Costs of Children. J. Fawcett, ed. Honolulu: East-West Center.

Radcliffe-Brown, A.R.
  1950   Introduction. *In* African Systems of Kinship and Marriage. A.R. Radcliffe Brown and D. Forde, eds. London: Oxford University Press.

Reyna, S.P.
  1972   The Costs of Marriage. Unpublished Ph.D. Dissertation. New York: Columbia University.
  1975   Age-differential, marital instability, and venereal disease. *In* Population and Social Organization. Moni Nag, ed, Chicago: Aldine.
  1976   The extending strategy: Regulation of the household dependency ratio. Journal of Anthropological Research 32.2:182-198.
  1977   Economics and fertility: Waiting for the demographic transition in the dry-zone of Francophone West Africa. *In* The Persistence of High Fertility. J.C. Caldwell, ed. Canberra: Australian National University Press.

Romaniuk, A.
  1968   Infertility in Tropical Africa. *In* The Population of Tropical Africa. J.C. Caldwell and Okonjo, eds. New York: Columbia University Press.

Sahlins, M.
    1972   Stone Age Economics. Chicago: Aldine.

Schneider, H.K.
    1974b   Economic Man. New York: The Free Press.

Stenning, D.
    Savannah Nomads. London: Oxford University Press.

Stevenson, R.C.
    1969   Baguirmi Grammar Khartoum: Sudan Research Unit, University of Khartoum.

Van de Walle, E.
    1968   Marriage in African censuses and inquiries. *In* Demography of Tropical Africa.
            W. Brass, *et al.*, eds. Princeton: Princeton University Press.

White, B.
    1975   The Economic Importance of Children in a Javanese Village. *In* Population and
            Social Organization. M. Nag, ed. Chicago: Aldine.

Divorce as an Integrative Social Factor

ALBERT HEINRICH*

In Western society we are accustomed to thinking of divorce as the complete abrogation of a marital relationship, and we are, derivatively, accustomed to thinking of this dramatic dissolution of a social connection as having destructive effects on the social order generally. Among Eskimos divorce is not the traumatic affair that it is in our own culture, nor is it as complete and absolute as we conceive it to be in our own social system. In this paper I shall attempt to demonstrate that it is, in fact, a mechanism for maximizing the number of kinship ties, and that it is an integrative mechanism when viewed from the societal point of view.

In most Eskimo societies there is no absolute divorce. Ex-spouses retain a certain connectedness and moral responsibility toward each other and, in addition, have definite responsibilities to their ex-spouses' future marriage partners and future offspring. Examples of this include the following : children born to a man and woman after they become divorced will have strong sibling-like kinship connection with each other, connections which are isomorphic with those that arise from polygamous marriages and from spouse exchanges ; the ex-spouses will be " step-parents " to all the children of each other's subsequent families ; and affines do not become ex-affines, but retain their relationships to in-laws. Since marriage almost inevitably occurs after divorce, the separation and subsequent remarriage of a marital pair to other partners does not lead to societal disorganization, but becomes a source of increased interconnection for the society.

Polygamy, spouse exchange, and remarriage after the death of a spouse are all rather easily demonstrated as having integrative functions. All these institutionalized forms bring about the same or very nearly the same sets of terminologies and interconnections. In making this argument, I will demonstrate that there is a general symmetry underlying all of these social transactions and that divorce—and the subsequent realignment of status and roles—fits into a general pattern. This pattern is explained, in part diagrammatically, below.

ACKNOWLEDGEMENT

A first run of this paper was presented at the American Anthropological Association annual meeting in New York in November 1971 as part of a symposium on Eskimo alliance mechanisms. Subsequently the chairman of the symposium, Dr. Donald Lee Guemple, arranged to have the papers of the symposium published in the Proceedings of the American Ethnological Association, forthcoming 1972. Subsequent to that, I decided that, whereas the proposed AES publication was couched in the jargon of anthropology, it might be of value to the sociological profession if the material were presented to them in revised form. The present paper is the outcome. In discussing the preparation of the AES paper, Dr. Guemple, who is much more conversant with the literature of sociology than I am, made numerous suggestions, most of which I rejected for the SAE article, but a number of which I have incorporated here, usually in altered form. I wish to express here my sincere thanks for his painstaking efforts to improve my paper, but I, of course, take all the credit for any mistakes, crudities and/or boners that the paper contains.

*The University of Calgary, Calgary Alberta, Canada.

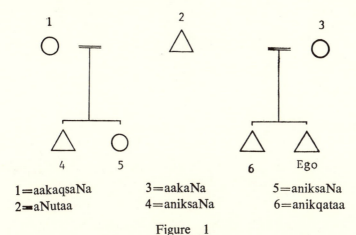

1=aakaqsaNa   3=aakaNa   5=aniksaNa
2=aNutaa   4=aniksaNa   6=anikqataa

Figure 1

Polygyny and its consequences

Figure 1, which is the basis for the explication of the other marital arrangements and rearrangements, shows a straightforward polygynous marriage arrangement and the associated kinship terminology. Half-siblings are terminologically separated from full-siblings, but they are functionally equivalent as far as interaction is concerned. Father's other spouse is classed as a stepmother by Ego. The -*sa*- infix found in the stepmother and half-sibling terms (1, 4, 5) denotes " replacement", " substitute", " material for". "Ersatz", in the German sense of the word, is its best translation. The terminology shown in the diagram is what might be called " recruitment " terminology—the form most often used in reference. These " ascribed " recruitment terms show how, by the actions of others, the designated persons have come to be related to Ego, and as such it "tells " the members of the society how they are interconnected genealogically. These terms are not generally used in encounters, however. In face-to-face situations, " Interactional " terms[1] are generally used as terms of address. They are the terms that Ego and the others use to define their relationships and norms of interaction on any particular occasion. These terms relate to age and sex, and quite expectedly, will be variously applied between the individuals, depending on the situations. Both the reeruitment and the interactional terms are applied to step-and-half-siblings, but only the recruitment set has -*sa*- variables. The international set admits of no equivocation whatsoever. It applies equally well to full-siblings, to step-and half-siblings,[2] whether derived by divorce or by some more " regular " means. All terms given in the diagrams are recruitment terms.

---

[1] The six most commonly used of the interactional terms are: *nukaNa*=younger sibling regardless of sex, Ego either sex (lit., "newer", "younger"="junior"); *aNayua*=older sibling regardless of sex, Ego either sex (from *aNa-*="large", "male"); *nayaa*=female sibling regardless of age, Ego male; *aNutnuna*=male sibling regardless of age, Ego female (from *aNu-*="male", "large"); *aNauzaNa*=older male sibling, Ego either sex (lit., "minor father"); *aakauzaNa*=older female sibling, Ego either sex (lit., "minor mother").

[2] There are also separate recruitment terms for parallel and cross cousins, but the same interactional terms apply for cousins as for siblings.

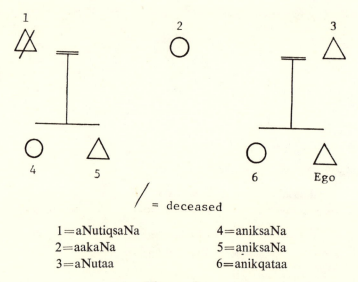

/ = deceased

1=aNutiqsaNa	4=aniksaNa
2=aakaNa	5=aniksaNa
3=aNutaa	6=anikqataa

Figure 2

Death and remarriage

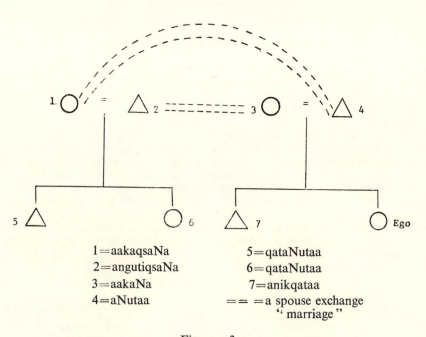

1=aakaqsaNa	5=qataNutaa
2=angutiqsaNa	6=qataNutaa
3=aakaNa	7=anikqataa
4=aNutaa	=== =a spouse exchange " marriage "

Figure 3

Spouse exchange and its consequences

Figure 2 shows the terminology applicable between the offspring of two unions in the case where a woman (No. 2) marries a man (No. 3) after the death of her first husband (No. 1), and where there are children born to both unions. As can be seen, the terminology used for relatives in this situation is the same as that applicable between relatives in the polygynous union shown in Figure 1. The implication is that the status of the siblings linked by complex marriage arrangements is the same, irrespective of whether they are linked through polygyny or through the death of one parent and the remarriage of the other.

Figure 3 shows the terminology that applies in the case where two couples, each having children, exchange spouses. The parental terminology follows that associated with polygynous unions and remarriages. We can clearly see that the term *aakaqsaNa* applies to father's other wife, just as it does in the case of remarriage. The term *qataNutaa*, literally "he who belongs together with him," is another of the recruitment terms, a term for a special sort of sibling in the other family.[3]

The arrangement shown in Figure 3 is perhaps the most frequently misunderstood of all Eskimo institutions, possibly due to bias in observation (see Guemple 1961). The connections attendant upon spouse exchange, often referred to ethnocentrically as wife lending, have been described variously by designations such as para-kinship or putative kinship, presumably because it has been assumed that the spouse exchange relationship was not to be equated in any way with "real" marriage. My analyses have convinced me that Jenness (1922) was correct when he equated spouse exchange with

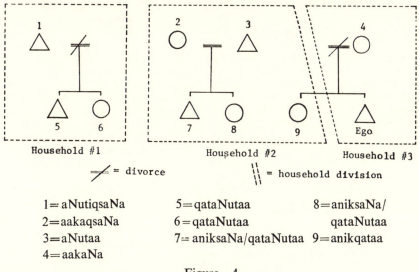

1 = aNutiqsaNa   5 = qataNutaa   8 = aniksaNa/
2 = aakaqsaNa   6 = qataNutaa   qataNutaa
3 = aNutaa   7 = aniksaNa/qataNutaa   9 = anikqataa
4 = aakaNa

Figure 4

Double divorce and remarriage

---

[3] East of Hudson Bay *qataNutaa* is often the term for nuclear family sibling.

marriage. Just as Jenness (1922 : 85) defined a *qataNutaa* as a type of brother or sister [4] ("a curious extension of the family"), I have had informants describe a *qataNutaa* as "brother", "just like a brother", or even a "brother who lives somewhere else." Spouse exchange is a second, or secondary, marriage and is structurally similar to other forms of non-initial marriage. Observation of behavior also leads one to conclude that "other-family" siblings (or sibling substitutes) interact as siblings do, both with respect to the present and with respect to the consequences in future generations. The children of two people who stand in a *qataNutaa* relationship are always cousins, and these cousins are interacted with just as any other cousin, i. e., functionally as siblings (Heinrich 1960). Secondary marriage, for analytic purposes termed spouse exchange here, produces results analogous to any other form of second (secondary) marital union, but with a terminology that has tended to confuse the issue for many observers.

Figure 4 illustrates a case of double divorce and remarriage and shows that the convention of extending kinship terms and roles to the spouses of former marriage partners after their remarriage can be carried to the point where they become problematic to the Eskimo themselves. In the case shown, Ego's mother (No. 4) has divorced Ego's father (No. 3) who has subsequently married a woman (No. 2) already divorced from a former husband (No. 1). A case such as this is by no means unusual for Eskimo, and it nicely illustrates some of the borderline cases of relatedness which can result.

Ego can recognize each of the persons shown in Figure 4 as a relative. His own parents, Nos. 3 and 4, and his own sibling, No. 9, are, of course, relatives to begin with, i. e., before any divorce or remarriage. Relationships with Nos. 1, 5, and 6, being "two jumps over," are optional in the sense that Ego can recognize them as kinsmen if it is mutually satisfying to honour the connection, or he may simply never exploit the relationship. The terminology (but not the relationship) of Ego to Nos. 7 and 8 is ambiguous, not so much for the Eskimo as for the anthropologist. The crux of the matter seems to be the delineation of the semantic fields and the atributes involved. The term *aniksaNa* is a generic term which can cover the whole range of sibling-like presons, i. e., functional sibling substitutes, which includes adoptive sibling, other-family sibling, step—and half-sibling. It is more commonly used to designate the person living in the same household who has the same sociological parents as Ego. The term *qataNutaa*, on the other hand, can only be used to designate the sibling-like person who resides in another household and who has parents who are addressed as "step-parents" by Ego. In this case, Nos. 7 and 8 definitely are *aniksaNa*, but they could alternately be called *quataNutaa*. Regardless of which term would be used, they are functionally siblings.

The matter can perhaps be clarified a bit if we isolate the attributes that are relevant for the terms *anikqataa*, *aniksaNa*, and *quataNutaa* as applied in Figure 4. These are (1) persons with whom Ego shares a common genitor and genitrix ; (2) persons who share one biological parent in common but not both : (3) persons having common sociological parents ; (4) persons who co-reside ; (5) persons whose parent(s) have had previous marital connection

---

[4] Jenness (1922: 85) gives the plural form of the term, spelled somewhat differently, *kataugotit*.

of any sort.   These relationships are, in practice, generally calculated on the
basis of " prepotence."   That is, if the relationship is based on (1), the
term *anikqataa* tends to prevail as the appropriate kinship designation.   If
the relationship is determined on the basis of (2) only, that also resolves the
issue, and *aniksaNa* can be applied unambiguously.   But if the relationship
depends on some combination of (3), (4), and (5), then there is some degree
of uncertainty regarding the appropriate term to be applied.   Finally,
if only (5) obtains, with respect to both sets of parents, then the term
qataNutaa is the only term that is applicable.[5]   In any and all cases, if these
recruitment terms are applicable, then the individuals concerned can activate
the relationship or potential relationship by use of the interactional terminology, and if they do this, then it is a real and genuine relationship, not some
sort of quasi—or luke-warm relationship.

ADDITIONAL DATA

Among most Eskimo groups the " step-parent " terms are constrcuted by
adding the non-final suffix *-sa-* to the parent term (see p. 3, above).
" Mother," for instance, is modified to produce *aakaksaNa* " stepmother."
The latter term designates any of the following :   the stepmother where the
biological mother has died and the father has remarried ;   the stepmother in a
monogamous household where there has been divorce and remarriage and the
children have remained with the father ; father's other wife in a polygynous
household ; father's second wife where the father has left the mother and
children and remarried and set up another household ; the woman of the
conjugal pair with whom Ego's parents have practised spouse exchange. The
case with the " stepfather " designation is analogous.

The male (or the female) members of two conjugal pairs who have
practised spouse exchange have a well-defined relationship to each other.
The terms *muliaqqataa,* " having wives in common," and *uikqataa,* " having
husbands in common " are used in the Bering Straits, and similar terms and
statuses found among other Eskimo groups (cf., *arnauqqataa* and *aNutauqqataa*
among the Copper Eskimos).   These terms, which denote sharing, designate
status and roles that are coupled with the repression of hostility that could
arise in connection with sexual matters ; they enjoin cooperation and
solidarity ; and they also require certain sorts of ceremonial interaction in
recognition of the connection.   These terms, and ideally the entailed
behaviour, obtain also where the " spouse exchange " is instituted as a result
of divorce as disaffection.   Even in cases where the wife has been abducted
and the " divorced " ex-husband decides that prudence is the better part of
valor, the person whose wife is taken from him by force does not need to
seek redress.   He can accept the fact, as there is a ready-made status that he
can fit himself into.

More so in former times, but even today in many Eskimo communities,
connections between two divorced persons do not bring about complete

---

[5]The term for adoptive sibling, *tiguaNa,* is another case in point.   A *tiguaNa* can be, and often is
referred to as an *aniksaNa,* i.e., a sibling substitute.   This would be the case where attributes
(1) and (4) only operate.

obliteration of connectedness, either terminologically or functionally.[6] The terminology is not one that denotes a completely abrogated relationship.   It merely denotes a change in the character of that relationship.   An "ex-husband", for instance, will be termed either *uikluataq* (literally "the ideal or wonderful husband") or *uikluaq* (literally "the no-good husband") in the Bering Straits area.   Neither term designates formerness or complete cessation of connectedness.   Functionally, an "ex-spouse" is considered always to have a certain residual moral obligation toward his or her former mate, especially in cases where the latter falls upon hard times.   And among the Mackenzie Eskimos, at least, a husband and an ex-husband had ritual-ceremonial obligations to each other in the same way that two men who have exchanged wives have a continuing social relationship.

An additional, and I think very telling indication that divorce does not bring about complete cessation of relatedness is the fact that formal affinal relationships are not appreciably disturbed by divorce.   A male in-law, for instance, usually continues to be referred to by his former parents-in-law and siblings-in-law as *niNaunga*.   He will only occasionally be identified as *niNaukluataq* or as *niNaukluaq* (the "good" and "no-good" son-in-law, respectively).   And older Eskimos when speaking English will never use any term other than son-in-law, daughter-in-law, sister-in-law etc. when referring to former in-laws.   The explanation that was often given to me was that the two who used to live together as married partners can be expected to have their personal differences, and if they chose to split it is their business, but "They only divorced each other, they did not divorce me."   (To the Eskimo the strange and not quite comprehensible English term "divorce" apparently carries only the connotation of ceasing to cohabit.)

Most instructive of all is the usage prevailing with respect to relationships that come into being after separation.   Not only do nephews and nieces continue to be nephews and nieces across the "broken" marriage bond, but future relationships can be validated via a broken marriage tie : the former wife's children subsequent to the break in marriage relationships are Ego's "step-children"; the children of these "step-children" will be grand-children to Ego ; the children born to the sister of Ego's former wife, *subsequent* to the breakup of the marriage, will be nephews or nieces, too, and are expected to interact with Ego in much the same fashion as if they were "regular" nephews and nieces.   Very evidently divorce in Eskimo culture is not the complete breakage of social connections that it is in many societies. It entails some tensions and a very severe diminution of interaction for the two individuals concerned, but it also creates additional siblings, parents, and spouses.   And for the society it not only continues to be a valid and viable link in the kinship network, but makes for an expanded and more intricately interconnected social network.

DISCUSSION

Marriage, however it may be defined cross-culturally, takes several forms among the Eskimos.   There is, first, the "regular" form of monogamous sexual and economic union.   There is, secondly, the similarly "regular",

[6]Acculturation most certainly has taken place, and there most certainly has been a shift in behavioral norms among a great many Eskimos, especially among third and fourth generation Christians. The present tense is used throughout the article to represent the "ethnographic present" that was still the norm 20 years ago and which is still reality for many Eskimos today.

though not very common, form of polygamous (usually polygynous) marriage. Somewhat removed from this is the third form, which I call non-residential marriage, i. e., spouse exchange. Intermediary between the third form, exchange marriage, and the second, polygamous, form is yet another structural arrangement, the fourth form, i. e., the type of marriage bond that remains after the separation of a former conjugal pair. My conclusion is that this latter still is a marital union, but shorn of its cohabitational and economic aspects. The first two forms, monogamous and polygamous unions, which I like to consider "primary" forms of marital unions have the factors of residential and economic togetherness, plus sexual interaction. The third and the fourth forms, exchange marriage and the "residual" marriage that remains after separation, which I term non-residential forms of marriage, have in common former legitimate sexual interaction and continued moral obligations plus continued recognition by the whole of society that a valid affinal bond continues to exist. The second, third and fourth forms have in common the fact that the relationships stemming from these unions are isomorphic and in fact, merely terminological elaborations of the status resulting from primary monogamous marriage. All four have in common the fact that they constitute, FOR THE SOCIETY, a valid kinship link in the social structure. We can then, for our purpose at least, define Eskimo marriage as any socially recognized sexual interaction that produces kinship connections (moral obligations) for the two persons concerned AND for all the consanguinials of both of the contracting parties. We can also conclude most definitely that, though a marriage connection can be entered into by choice, it can never be completely broken ; once contracted, it remains a valid connection so far as members of the society other than the erstwhile marital pair are concerned and it remains as a source of existing and future social interconnectedness.

CONCLUSIONS

Many of the features of most Eskimo social systems operate to maximize the number of connections among the group and also with neighbouring groups. Flipper relationships, dance and song partnerships, trading partnerships, spouse exchange relationships and the kinship statuses that are set up upon this practice, wrestling partnerships, namesake relationships, all operate to widen the network of connectedness of the individual and to increase the amount and degree of interconnectedness found within the society. The characteristics of Eskimo divorce are merely another manifestation of this general characteristic, or theme, of Eskimo culture. Divorce, though it undeniably has disruptive aspects for those closely involved, serves in a wider sense, as another mechanism for widening and increasing the connectedness found in the society at large. Given the fact that, in aboriginal Eskimo culture, remarriage usually occurs soon after separation from a former mate, divorce, just as is the case with spouse exchange and with death and remarriage, functions to increase social integration.

BIBLIOGRAPHY

Guemple, D. L.
    1961. *Inuit Spouse Exchange*, Department of Anthropology, University of Chicago.
Heinrich, Albert
    1960. "Structural features of northwestern Alaskan Eskimo kinship", *Southwestern Journal of Anthropology*, 16: 1–110.
Jenness, Diamond
    1922. "The life of the Copper Eskimo", *Report of the Canadian Arctic Expedition 1913-1918*, Ackland, Ottawa, XII: Pt A.

Interracial Marriage and Divorce in Kansas and the Question of Instability of Mixed Marriages

THOMAS P. MONAHAN*

PREFATORY NOTE

Although broadly theoretical and interpretive articles have been written upon interracial, interethnic, and intercaste marriages (Davis, 1941;; Merton, 1941; van den Berghe, 1960), the statistical basis for such studies is rather fragmentary and selective material (Monahan, 1970a, 1970b). On the whole, even though individual countries have at times assembled such data, factual information is sparse, and none appears in the *1968 Demographic Yearbook* of the United Nations. A cross-cultural comparison of the demographic concomitants of this phenomenon requires sets of carefully drawn data, analyzed first within their separate cultural contexts. As part of a larger study of the past and present situation in the United States, information about interracial marriage and divorce in the mid-American state of Kansas should add a segment to our understanding of the American pattern.

In their recent book on *Marriage and Divorce* (1970:129), Carter and Glick propose that the number of interracial marriages, while "extremely small," has shown an upward trend and in the coming decades will register substantial increases. Their findings are also interpreted to support the theory that mixed marriages are relatively unstable as compared to homogamous ones (pp. 124-125). Unfortunately these hypotheses are based on 1960 Census data, about which there are serious doubts as to accuracy and significance, acknowledged in part by the authors (Carter and Glick, 1970:424-426; Monahan 1970a:462). It would seem that answers to these questions on the trend and instability of interracial marriages in the United States should be derived from statistics on marriage and divorce occurrences, rather than from secondary Census information showing marital status of the population.

Reliance upon Census data is to some extent due to the lack of national statistics on marriage and divorce in depth and in detail. Also, because they are based upon a very small sample of state records, the marriage data of the National Center for Health Statistics are not very meaningful as to interracial marriage trends, as yet; and, with respect to interracial divorce, only a few states have records by race for a sufficient number of years. Indeed, race-or-color has been poorly defended as a statistical item and has been obliterated from the marriage records in some major population areas (California, Maryland, Michigan, and New York) by civil rights protagonists, thus making objective findings on interracial marriage more difficult.

---

*Professor of Sociology, Villanova University, Villanova, Pennsylvania, U.S.A.

There does exist, however, some information (not cited by Carter and Glick) which portrays for a number of states a recent and a gradual rise in the incidence of interracial marriage(Burma, 1963; Heer, 1966; Lynn, 1967; Monahan, 1970a, 1970b). And, in respect to divorce, some exceptions have been found for Hawaii and Iowa (Monahan, 1966, 1970a) to the proposition that interracial marriages are uniformly more unstable.

KANSAS STATE DATA

The present study seeks to develop some new information upon another midwestern state, hitherto unreported in the literature. With the help of Mr. Irvin G. Franzen, the Kansas State director of health statistics, a number of published and unpublished tables on interracial marriage and divorce were edited and compiled, and a set of basic data for recent years was assembled.

Accuracy and Other Problems

In addition to the problems of racial identification and accuracy of reporting "race or color," the failure to report any race at all on vital records raises a degree of uncertainty as to the complete picture. In Kansas the non-reporting of race on marriage records has been relatively insignificant, less than 0.4 per cent, although in the very early years under study it seems, because no "not stated" cases appear in the numerical tables, that race was statistically assigned when the item was missing. In the divorce records the omissions of race were exceptionally high, amounting to about 25 per cent of all records. This was due primarily to the failure to complete the registration reports fully in the largest county of the state, where unfortunately a high percentage of the states' non-whites resided. This situation was corrected and from 1964 onward only 6 per cent of the state reports did not specify race, and the distribution of these was random and not in any one locality. The question always remains, however, as to whether the "not stated" group contains a higher than average proportion of mixed cases. As revealed in Chart 2, after 1963 there was only a very moderate alteration in the percentage of cases mixed, and it may be presumed that the dubiousness coming from unreported information is not a major issue.

Another ambiguity arising in the use of state data is the possible unequal migration into or out of a state of the mixed-race marriages and divorces, especially those of a truly evasive or "migratory" kind. This perplexity applies particularly when marriages within a state are compared to divorces occurring there. However, unless some unusual circumstances obtained, the migratory flow of such cases could be totally counterbalancing in effect. If military marriages had an above average interracial component, this would serve to inflate the divorce picture in the state.

The Legality of Interracial Marriage in Kansas

Antecedent to the entry of Kansas into the Union in 1861, there had been interracial marriage prohibitions in this part of the country. The

Spanish *Leyes de Las Siete Partidas,* promulgated in 1343 and governing the Province of Louisiana in the frontier days, permitted slaves to marry free persons. Prior to the French accession, in 1800, some decrees were passed which restricted the marriages of blacks (Love, 1970). Following the Louisiana Purchase by the United States, among the Acts passed by the first legislature of the Territory of Orleans in 1806, one finds a provision in that section called the "Black Code" which "Forbids marriages of whites with slaves and concubines with whites and manumitted or free-born blacks with slaves, and imposes penalties" (Fortier, 1904:I-88; Art. VI of code.) The 1807 version of the Laws (Ch. XVII, p. 102) was that "Free persons and slaves are incapable of contracting marriage together, celebration of such is forbidden, and the marriage is void." Then in 1808 (Title IV, Ch. 2, Art. 8), another provision was appended, saying, "It is the same with respect to the marriages contracted by free white persons with free persons of color." In the Missouri Territory no prohibition was found in a search of the laws until 1835, when "All marriages of white persons with negroes or mulattoes are declared to be illegal and void" (Rev. Statutes, Sec. 2., p. 401), and violation of this law was deemed a misdemeanor for the parties and the officiant, who were subject to a fine or imprisonment. No regulations were found in the Indian Country (1834) or Indian Territory laws (1840).

The Kansas Territory was formed in 1854, and in 1855 the Laws of the Territory of Kansas (Ch. CXVIII, Sec. 3, p. 488) specifically provided that "All marriages of white persons with negroes or mulattoes are declared to be illegal and void," violation of which was a misdemeanor of an "infamous character," punishable by a fine or imprisonment, or both, for the officiant and the parties (Sec. 4). Other legal provisions in 1855 (Crimes and Punishments, Ch. 53, Sec. 10, p. 284) made the officiant possibly liable to a $500 fine and/or imprisonment in the county jail for one year, if he solemnized any marriage with a legal impediment. However, the Statutes of the Territory (Sec. 12, p. 489) also provided that "All marriages which have been heretofore solemnized in this territory, are declared as valid and binding, as if made in pursuance of this act," which could be interpreted as a non-retroactive clause.

In 1858 the above interracial marriage prohibition was dropped from the laws (Sess. Laws, Ch. LXIX, p. 325). Hence, before statehood, it appears that the Kansas territory had a prohibition only against Negro-white marriages (unless the 1807 prohibition against slave marriages with free persons is interpreted to include Indians, slave or free). But, no such law has existed since 1858, and citizens of Kansas were free to marry whom they chose.

In the absence of law, the pressure of social custom in Kansas, as in other parts of the United States, was probably against mixed racial marriages. Indeed, prior to 1946, the Kansas Legislature had before it the question of miscegenation on a number of occasions, but took no action (communication from Richard F. Hayse, Assistant Attorney General).

The Trend in Interracial Marriage

Statistics assembled for Kansas from 1947 to 1969 show a rather steady rise in the per cent of all nonwhite marriages which were of a mixed nature. This is true whether Mexicans are counted as a separate "racial" group or not. (Table 1, Chart 1). The proportion mixed has increased from less than 5 per cent to 15 per cent by the end of the period. Negroes separately considered show a correspondingly steady rise in intermarriage from 1 per cent in the 1950's to over 7 per cent of all Negro marriages in recent years.

TABLE 1

Per Cent of Marriages and Divorces Which Are Mixed

KANSAS

| | Marriages | | | | Divorces | |
| | NONWHITES | | | NEGROES | NONWHITES | |
YEAR	Counting Mexican as Nonwhite	Mexican as White	Total	Negroes with Whites Only	Counting Mexican as Nonwhite	Mexican as White
1947	5.3	3.8	1.5	1.2	—	—
1948	3.6	3.1	1.2	1.0	—	—
1949	4.2	3.2	1.0	1.0	—	—
1950	3.2	2.0	0.7	0.6	—	—
1951	4.1	2.8	1.1	0.5	—	—
1952	4.4	3.4	1.7	1.5	3.7	2.2
1953	4.5	3.4	1.4	1.0	3.0	1.7
1954	4.4	2.5	1.0	0.9	2.9	2.4
1955	6.4	4.7	3.0	2.7	1.5	1.2
1956	5.9	3.9	2.3	1.6	6.8	5.2
1957	7.2	5.3	2.3	1.7	3.8	2.8
1958	8.2	5.0	2.5	2.4	6.0	4.2
1959	9.6	6.8	3.7	2.6	6.2	4.6
1960	7.9	5.9	2.8	2.5	8.8	7.1
1961	9.5	7.4	4.0	3.7	6.2	5.2
1962	9.8	7.0	3.9	3.3	7.7	6.3
1963	10.1	7.2	4.6	4.0	10.6	7.8
1964	12.9	8.4	4.2	8.6	12.5	10.4
1965	14.4	10.5	7.3	6.9	10.9	9.4
1966	13.2	10.0	7.0	6.7	9.8	8.3
1967	15.2	10.3	6.3	5.8	9.3	5.9
1968	—	16.4	6.4	—	—	15.5
1969	—	18.3	8.3	—	—	12.0

Note: Mexicans were no longer classified separately after 1967.

It also appears that only one-fifth to one-third of the mixed marriages in Kansas involved Negroes, depending upon whether Mexican-white marriages are counted as mixed. (See Table 3). This figure has changed, so that in the last decade or so since the Civil Rights movement Negroes

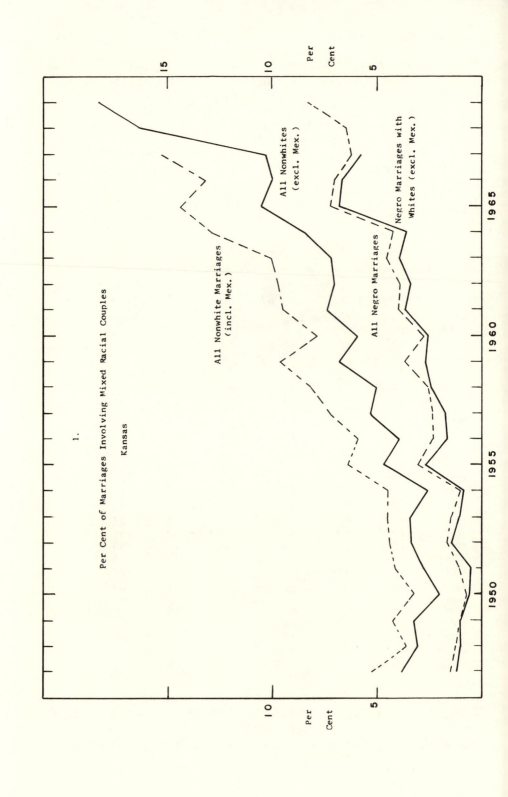

1.

Per Cent of Marriages Involving Mixed Racial Couples

Kansas

All Nonwhites (excl. Mex.)

All Nonwhite Marriages (incl. Mex.)

All Negro Marriages

Negro Marriages with Whites (excl. Mex.)

Per Cent

Per Cent

have increasingly accounted for more of the mixed-race marriages. The reporting of race on marriage records in Kansas has been nearly complete, but some part of the rise, it might be allowed, could have been due to improved identification and a willingness of the parties in Negro-white marriages to so identify themselves.

The total of *all* marriages of Indians, Chinese, Japanese, and Other Races was a little more than one-twentieth (6 per cent) of the number of Negro marriages, and yet their total number in *mixed* marriages was greater than for Negroes in mixed marriages — with Indian mixed marriages accounting for more than half the Other minorities' total (excluding Mexican). From 1947 to 1969 only 0.5 per cent of all marriages in Kansas were mixed, counting Mexican-white as mixed. In the same period of time, the figures for each race *separately* derived on marriages which were mixed amounted to 3 per cent for Negroes, Mexicans 35 per cent, Chinese 44, Indians 62, Other Races 74, and Japanese 91 per cent.

TABLE 2

Per Cent of Marriages and Divorces Which are Mixed
3-Year Average

KANSAS

	Marriages				Divorces	
	NONWHITES		NEGROES		NONWHITES	
YEAR	*Counting Mexican as* Nonwhite	*White*	Total	Negroes with Whites Only	*Counting Mexican as* Nonwhite	*White*
1948	4.6	3.5	1.3	1.1	—	—
1949	3.7	2.8	1.0	0.9	—	—
1950	3.9	2.7	0.9	0.7	—	—
1951	3.9	2.7	1.1	0.9	—	—
1952	4.3	3.2	1.4	1.0	—	—
1953	4.4	3.1	1.4	1.1	3.2	2.1
1954	5.2	3.6	1.9	1.6	2.5	1.8
1955	5.6	3.8	2.1	1.8	3.8	2.9
1956	6.5	4.6	2.6	2.0	4.1	3.1
1957	7.1	4.7	2.4	1.9	5.5	4.1
1958	8.4	5.7	2.8	2.3	5.3	3.8
1959	8.6	5.9	3.0	2.5	7.0	5.3
1960	9.1	6.7	3.5	2.9	7.1	5.7
1961	9.1	6.8	3.6	3.2	7.6	6.2
1962	9.8	7.2	4.2	3.7	8.2	6.5
1963	11.0	7.6	4.2	3.7	10.4	8.4
1964	12.5	8.7	5.3	4.8	11.4	9.4
1965	13.5	9.6	6.2	5.7	11.0	9.4
1966	14.2	10.3	6.8	6.4	10.0	7.8
1967	—	12.4	6.6	—	—	10.3
1968	—	15.3	7.0	—	—	11.4

Note: Mexicans were not classified separately after 1967.

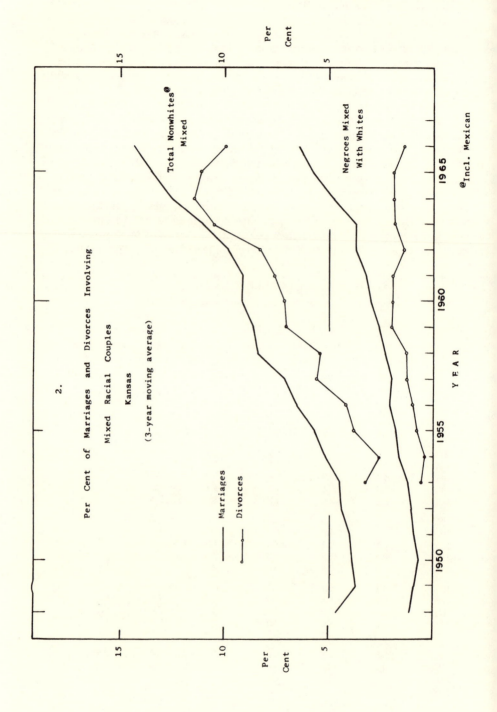

2.

Per Cent of Marriages and Divorces Involving

Mixed Racial Couples

Kansas

(3-year moving average)

Marriages

Divorces

Total Nonwhites@ Mixed

Negroes Mixed With Whites

Y E A R

1950   1955   1960   1965

Per Cent

@Incl. Mexican

Cross Race Marriages by Sex

In two out of three cases of mixed marriages the female was white, counting Mexican-white marriages as mixed, and somewhat less if Mexican-white is not counted as mixed. (Table 3). In recent years there were about as many Indian and all Other Races of men who married nonwhite women of a different race as married white women. In the case of Orientals, whatever the explanation, there were half as many more male Chinese in cross race marriages than there were female Chinese so intermarrying; but for the highly intermarrying Japanese, female Japanese accounted for 2½ times as many of these mixed marriages as did Japanese men. As to Negro marriages, 87 per cent were with whites and an additional 7 per cent with Mexicans. Within the Negro mixed marriages 82 per cent were male Negroes; for Negro-Mexican combinations there was less Negro male predominance, only 62 per cent; but for Negro-white mixed marriages 85 per cent of the male spouses were Negro men.

TABLE 3

Marriages of Whites with Mexicans and Other Races

KANSAS

YEAR	No. of CASES	Per Cent of Total* Negro	Per Cent of Total (excl. Mex.) Negro	Total*	Per Cent of Cases Where Females Were White Where Spouse Was			
					Mex.	Other (Indian) &c.	Negro or Other	Negro
1947-49	171	22.8	33.6	68.4	65.5	61.0	69.8	87.2
1950-54	192	21.4	33.3	62.0	58.0	51.9	65.8	92.7
1955-59	379	28.8	48.9	64.6	62.8	47.4	65.9	85.3
1960-64	496	31.0	49.0	62.5	52.7	57.5	68.2	79.2
1965-69	745	—	45.4	—	—	47.2	64.7	85.8

*Counting Mexican-white marriages as mixed. Mexicans were not separately identified in the statistics after 1967.

Mixed Marriages Ending in Divorce

Concomitant with the rise in mixed marriages there has been a similar increase in divorces of couples who were racially intermarried. (See Tables 1 and 2, and Chart 2). The yearly figures are a little erratic, and in some cases the divorce percentages (mixed) exceed the marriage percentages (mixed). However, as witnessed in Chart 2, when a 3-year moving average is used, the proportions of mixed divorces are uniformly exceeded by the mixed marriage proportions. This is especially evident for the Negro-white group. In fact, as disclosed in the study of Iowa data (Monahan, 1970a) the deficiency in the divorce percentage which is mixed is growing.

Compacting the time period and subdividing the races further (Table 4), the total figures tend to show the same underrepresentation of mixed

marriages in the divorce picture. The Mexican component shows an irregular effect, which may indicate imprecision in the identification of
Mexicans in the data. Indians follow the general pattern. Negro mixed
marriages taken as a totality, or considered separately as to marriages
with whites only (excluding Mexicans), definitely show the same underrepresentation of mixed marriages in divorce as appears in Chart 2.

TABLE 4

Per Cent of Marriages and Divorces Which Are Mixed
by Racial Groups

KANSAS

MARRIAGES

YEAR	ALL NONWHITES		MEXICAN		NEGROES		INDIANS
	Counting Mexican as Nonwhite	White	Total	With Nonwhites	Total	With Whites*	Total
Cases	23,598	24,192	2,092	2,069	22,785	20,591	865
1947-49	4.6	3.5	21.5	3.8	1.3	1.1	53.0
1950-51	3.7	2.4	18.3	3.4	0.9	0.6	59.1
1952-54	4.4	3.1	25.4	2.4	1.4	1.1	59.7
1955-59	7.4	5.1	35.0	6.2	2.8	2.2	59.7
1960-64	10.1	7.2	44.8	4.5	3.9	3.4	53.5
1965-69	—	13.5	—	—	7.1	—	70.5

DIVORCES

Cases	5,844	6,561	356	356	6,114	5,208	248
1952-54	3.2	2.1	26.8	5.4	0.8	0.6	55.6
1955-59	4.9	3.6	27.0	3.6	1.4	1.1	35.7
1960-64	9.4	7.6	44.3	7.0	2.7	1.9	48.1
1965-69	—	10.6	—	—	3.1	—	73.9

Note: Mexicans were not tabulated separately after 1967.
*Whites as separately identified from Mexicans prior to 1967.

Taking the entire set of data together (Table 6), all nonwhite marriages
(counting Mexicans in this group) show 8.8. per cent mixed, and divorces
7.0 per cent mixed. If Mexicans are tallied with the white group, the
marriage and divorce percentages are alike. Mexicans separately show
contrasting figures of 35 and 38 per cent in mixed marriages and divorces, but Mexicans with other-nonwhites only — 4.2 versus 6.5 per cent.
The proportions for the other minorities were Indians 61 per cent each;
Japanese 91 versus 93 per cent; Chinese 44 as compared to 93 per cent;
and Other Races 74 and 77 per cent. Although 3.4 per cent of the Negro
marriages were mixed as to race, only 2.2 per cent of the Negro divorces
were mixed; while Negroes married to whites (Mexican excluded) tallied
3.0 versus 1.3 per cent, correspondingly. Besides the statistical identification problem, the possible unequal losses of mixed marriages due to
migration from Kansas and a similar net gain of divorces by an unequal

TABLE 5

Per Cent of Each Race Which is Male in Mixed Marriages
and in Mixed Divorces

KANSAS

Year	MARRIAGES					DIVORCES				
	All Mexican	Mexican with Nonwhite	All Negro	Negro with White	Indian	All Mexican	Mexican with Nonwhite	All Negro	Negro with White	Indian
No. of Cases	739*	87*	780	534*	532	135*	23*	134	68*	150
					Per cent					
All Years	56.7	48.3	81.9	84.5	54.0	71.9	69.6	83.6	83.8	51.3
1947-49	66.7	72.7	76.6	87.2	55.7	—	—	—	—	—
1950-51	55.3	42.9	75.0	90.0	53.8	—	—	—	—	—
1952-54	51.9	100.0	76.3	93.6	51.2	62.5	100.0	62.5	66.7	10.0
1955-59	61.8	55.9	81.0	85.3	45.8	83.3	75.0	81.8	88.2	46.7
1960-64	50.5	30.0	80.7	79.2	57.6	68.6	62.5	85.7	83.3	57.7
1965-69	56.3*	10.0*	84.4	85.9*	51.6	71.1*	62.5*	85.5	86.7*	57.6

*Mexicans were not shown separately after 1967.

TABLE 6

Per Cent of Marriages and Divorces of Each Race§
Which Were Mixed

KANSAS

RACE	Marriages 1947-69		Divorces 1952-69	
	Number of Cases	Per Cent	Number of Cases	Per Cent
All Nonwhite Races				
Incl. Mexican*	26,198	8.8	5,844	7.0
Excl. Mexican	22,536	6.8	6,251	6.7
Mexican	2,088	35.3	355	38.0
Negro	22,785	3.4	6,114	2.2
Indian	865	61.5	248	60.5
Chinese	173	43.9	15	93.3
Japanese	115	90.6	68	92.6
Mexican + Other Non-whites*	2,088	4.2	355	6.5
Negro + Whites, Excl. Mex.	20,591	3.0	5,208	1.3

§Counting each race separately.
*Counting Mexicans as a separate race, not so indentified after 1967.

in-movement of mixed divorces, all of which qualify any interpretation, a crude conclusion would be that Negroes and Chinese tend to show more racially mixed marriages than racially mixed divorces, but for the Mexicans married to non-whites the position is reversed.

The Predominance of Minority Males in Mixed Marriages and Divorces

Mexican men are more often found in mixed-race divorce cases than in mixed marriages of Mexicans as shown in Table 5, especially when they are married to nonwhites. For Indians, and for all Negro mixed marriages (or for marriages with whites only), no such sex imbalance importantly evidences itself. Hence, from this set of Kansas figures one cannot adduce that the sex of the intermarrying party uniformly contributes to the divorce outcome.

The Divorce Ratio by Race of Husband Compared to Race of Wife

When the per cent of mixed-race marriages is rising, it is improper to compare the divorce proportions which are mixed with the marriage proportions which are mixed *in the same years*: for the reason that the increasingly higher percentages of mixed marriages require time to show themselves in the divorce picture. To adjust for this condition, divorces should be referred to a prior set of marriage figures; in other words there should be a lag in the method of calculation. If not, the divorce outcome of mixed-race marriages will be underestimated.

There is, of course, no simple way of doing this. First, one needs to know what is the pattern of average duration of marriage to divorce, and this may not be the same for same-race as for mixed-race marriages. Secondly, if the detailed data were at hand, an intricate case-by-case or *duration specific* weighting procedure is probably unwarranted, even if technically precise, considering the lack of precision in racial counting. Thirdly, if one lags marriage data more than two or three years behind divorce data, then there could result a serious loss in measurement of the effect of any mixed marriage increase upon the divorces following — because divorces peak early in marriage (Monahan, 1962). A five year lag would mean that the immediate effect of a mixed marriage increase would not enter into the measurement until five years had elapsed.

In trying to allow for the delayed impact of the rise in mixed marriage upon the divorce outcome in Kansas, a series of relative ratios were calculated. With no time lag the mixed Negro-white marriages showed a lower divorce ratio than the white-white and the Negro-Negro couples, with the latter having a figure double that for the mixed group. With a five year lag in the calculation the divorce ratio of the Negro-white marriages takes a position midway between the white-white and the Negro-Negro marriages. It should be particularly noted that the mixed Negro-white marriages, even in this case, have a lower divorce ratio than the homogamously married Negroes. As between the Negro male-white female, and the Negro female-white male types there is not much difference, although the latter of the two shows a slightly higher ratio.

TABLE 7

Divorce Ratio
Race of Husband by Race of Wife
Divorces 1952-69 / Marriages 1949-66‡

Race of Husband		**Race of Wife**						
	Total	*Mixed*	*White and Mexican*	*Negro*	*Indian*	*Chinese*	*Japanese*	*Other*
Total	26.6		25.9	36.6	47.2	10.3	120.0	122.6
Mixed		44.8	31.7	23.6§	49.6	*	(127.1)	(161.2)
White and Mexican	26.0	67.2	25.9	23.2§	48.5	*	(134.2)	(152.3)
Negro	36.4	26.2	21.1	36.7	*	—	*	*
Indian	49.7	55.9	57.6	*	45.6	—	—	—
Chinese	28.0§	(25.0)	(26.1)	*	—	1.6§	*	*
Japanese	28.0§	*	*	*	—	—	*	—
Other	64.8	54.7§	54.2§	*	*	*	*	(79.5)

‡All not stated cases excluded. This is a 3-year lag calculation.
§50 to 100 cases of marriages
( )Less than 50 cases
*Less than 20 cases
—No cases
Note: Because Mexican was not separately identified after 1967, rates in this
    table could not be calculated for them.

A 3-year lag, chosen as a reasonable compromise, shows the mixed Negro-white marriages with a divorce ratio below that for white couples. (Table 7). In this calculation the racially mixed marriages of Negro males have a slightly higher divorce ratio than mixed marriages of Negro females, but not at all as divergent as was the case in Iowa (Monahan, 1970a). In general, mixed-race marriages as a totality have a higher divorce ratio than the whole: the ratio of divorces to marriages was 27 to 100 for the whole, and 45 to 100 for the mixed types. Vagary appears in the data, some of it because of classification and other identity problems, and some of it probably due to migration of couples, particularly military personnel who were married abroad. For instance, there were only 38 white males enumerated who were married to Japanese females in the period, but 51 divorces were allocated to the same group. Chinese couples (62 cases) showed a very low divorce outcome, but American Indian couples (215 cases) showed a dissolution ratio approaching fifty per cent. Nevertheless, mixed-Chinese and mixed-Indian couples *both* evidence more break up of marriage than do couples of the same-race.

Concluding Remarks

There is undoubtedly an upward swing in interracial marriage in the United States, definitional and statistical problems notwithstanding, as is witnessed by these Kansas State and other data (Burma, 1963; Heer, 1966; Lynn, 1967; Monahan, 1970a, 1970b).

Of the minority groups, Negroes are the least intermarried in Kansas; and, excluding the Mexican-white cases, although Negroes are far more numerous than other nonwhites, they account for less than one-half of the racial intermarriages. From the viewpoint of the majority, perhaps the extent of this is extremely small, but from the minority groups' viewpoint interracial marriage is of a sizeable proportion, ranging from 7 per cent for Negroes in Kansas to much higher proportions (60 per cent for Indians) for other groups. It is surely more fitting to refer to the impact of intermarriage upon the identity of the lesser group. How these mixed marriages and divorces differ from the rest is the subject of another inquiry.

The theme of relative instability of cross race marriages is an interesting one, and requires much more detailed and comprehensive national figures than are currently available in the United States. Contrary to popular and sociological belief in the past, for which there was no objective and quantitative proof, mixed Negro-white marriages in Kansas (as in Iowa) have not evidenced any special proclivity to divorce, but rather probably somewhat more stability than obtains for homogamously married Negroes. It has yet to be demonstrated whether this is due to special partner selectivity in a demographically favorable sense, or whether there is a special attitudinal and value consensus of Negro-white couples which contributes to the marital survival. It would be interesting to discover why other racial intermarriages do and do not show less favorable outcomes. (Monahan 1966, 1970a). So, even though the totality of mixed racial marriages might show more likelihood to wind up in divorce than do homogamous ones, whether or not a certain type of mixed-race marriage will endure (from the information now available), would seem to depend upon the particular races intermarrying, the social circumstances surrounding them at the time, and the nature of the marital choice itself.

REFERENCES

Burma, J. H., 1953. "Interethnic Marriage in Los Angeles, 1948-1959." *Social Forces* 42 (December): 156-165.
Carter, H. and P. C. Glick, 1970. *Marriage and Divorce: A Social and Economic Study.* Cambridge: Harvard University Press.
Davis, K., 1941. "Intermarriage in Caste Societies." *American Anthropologist* 43 (July-September): 388-395.
Encyclopedia of the Social Sciences, 1937. "Miscegenation." Vol. V.
Foner, L., 1970. "The Free People of Color in Louisiana and St. Domingue." *Journal of Social History* 3 (Summer): 406-430.
Fortier, A., 1904. *A History of Louisiana.* New York: Manzi, Joyant, & Co. Vol. 1: 86-88.
Heer, D. M., 1966. "Negro-White Marriage in the United States." *Journal of Marriage and the Family* 27 (August): 262-273.
Kansas, Division of Vital Statistics, State Department of Health. 1947+ *Annual Report.*
Kansas, 1855+. Laws of the Territory of Kansas.
1862. Compiled Laws of Kansas.
Louisiana, 1820. *The Laws of Las Siete Partidas.* Translated by L. M. Lislet and H. Carleton, authorized by the Legislature. New Orleans.

Love, E. F., 1970. "Legal Restrictions on Afro-Indian Relations in Colonial Mexico." *Journal of Negro History* LV (April): 131-139.

Lynn, Sister M. Annella, 1967. "Interracial Marriages in Washington, D.C." *Journal
of Negro Education* 36 (Fall): 428-433.

Merton, R. K., 1941. "Intermarriage and the Social Structure: Fact and Theory."
Psychiatry 4 (August): 361-374.

Missouri, 1835. *Laws of the Territory of Missouri.*

Monahan, T. P., 1962. "When Married Couples Part: Statistical Trends and Relationships in Divorce." *American Sociological Review* 27 (October): 625-633.

1966. "Interracial Marriage and Divorce in the State of Hawaii." *Eugenics
Quarterly* 13 (March): 40-47.

1970a. "Are Interracial Marriages Really Less Stable?" *Social Forces* 48
(June): 461-473.

1970b. "Interracial Marriage: Data for Philadelphia and Pennsylvania."
Demography 7 (August): 287-299.

Orleans, The Territory of (New), 1806. *Acts Passed at the First Legislature,* January 25, 1806.

1807. *An Act Concerning the Celebration of Marriages.* Ch. XVII: 102.

1808. *Digest of Laws Now in Force in the Territory of Orleans.* Ch. 2, Art.
8:24.

Peterson, W., 1969. "The Classification of Subnations in Hawaii: An Essay in the
Sociology of Knowledge." American Sociological Review 34 (December): 863-
877.

van den Berghe, P. L., 1960. "Hypergamy, Hypergenation, and Miscegenation."
Human Relations 13 (February): 83-91.

Reasons for Marriage Breakdown: A Case Study in Southwestern Ontario (Canada)

SALLY E. PALMER*

Marriage breakdown is a subject on which many people have strong opinions and do not hesitate to express themselves. Their opinions usually come from personal experience in marriage and they are inclined to generalize about other marriages as being similar to their own. An example is the husband who thinks all marriage breakdown has a sexual basis because this is the main point of dissatisfaction in his own marriage. Another type of opinion arises from concern about the stability of family life as the basis of our society and is characterized by a negative attitude toward any behaviour which detracts from family solidarity. Some proponents of family solidarity feel that religion is the one answer to a successful marriage ("The family that prays together, stays together").

Actually, families which break up have some common characteristics which set them apart from other married couples and which make their life together very difficult from the outset. Conditions such as lack of religion and an unsatisfactory sex life cannot be discounted, but they are shown in proper perspective when a number of other handicaps are discovered in a large group of couples seeking divorce.

These handicaps can generally be described as youth, premarital pregnancy, antisocial tendencies, economic weakness, working mothers, incompatible backgrounds, and the early arrival of children. These were all found to be present in a group of marriages which were on the brink of divorce.

Description of the Study

The reason for studying this group of divorcing couples was to see whether any characteristics could be identified which would set them apart from other married couples. It was reasoned that the discovery of areas in which significant differences existed would give some insight into the causes of marriage breakdown. Some of these areas had already been indentified by previous studies (e. g. the age at which marriage is undertaken) and this study served only to confirm previous findings. Other points had not been given much attention (e. g. the mother's employment) and the findings were rather striking.

---

*Director, Family and Children's Services of London and Middlesex County.

It was decided to include in the study all couples with children who began divorce proceedings during a 2 1/2 year period in Middlesex County, Southwestern Ontario.[1] There were 291 couples involved, a large enough number to allow for the findings to be satistically significant. The rationale for generalizing from this group was provided by the similarity they showed with divorcing couples in Ontario generally, according to statistics collected by the Official Guardian's Department. There is also a similarity between married couples in Middlesex and those in Canada generally, according to D. B. S. figures on age at marriage, education and income.

Too Young for Marriage

The average age at marriage of couples who later divorce is much younger than that of married couples generally as shown on Table 1 and 2. Those who marry when they are exceptionally young cannot be realistic in their expectations of marriage. The picture of married life they are given, mostly through advertising, is romantic and unreal; they fasten their hopes on this rather than on the real-life marriages they see around them. There is usually no one (except an occasional parent who is dismissed as prejudiced) who tries to hold them back, as the idea of young marriage seems to have a sentimental appeal. With such high expectations, the young couples are quickly disillusioned by the first setback or the beginnings of tedium.

TABLE 1

Comparison of Divorcing Wives with all Married
Wives by Age at Marriage

Age	Divorcing Wives (Middlesex)		Married Wives (Canada)[2]	
Under 21	193	70%	66,310	50%
21 and over	82	30%	66,309	50%
Total	275[3]	100%	132,619	100%

P=.001

TABLE 2

Comparison of Divorcing Husbands with all Married
Husbands by Age at Marriage

Age	Divorcing Husbands (Middlesex)		Married Husbands (Canada)	
Under 24	183	75%	66,552	50%
24 and over	61	25%	66,552	50%
Total	244	100%	133,104	100%

P=.001

[1]They were seen by the author in the course of investigations for the Official Guardian, a prerequisite to divorce in Ontario when children are involved in a divorce. Both husband and wife were interviewed separately, except for a few who refused.

The subsequent research was supported by the national Welfare Grants program, Department of National Health and Welfare, Canada.

[2]Median age at first marriage in 1965 was 21.2 for women and 23.7 for men, as shown in Canada yearbook 1968, P. 284.

[3]Totals of divorcing wives and husbands less than total sample because one partner refused interview in these cases.

The inexperience of young people in human relationships is another handicap. They have not had time to develop the personality strengths needed in marriage. For example, they lack skill in handling crises, so they tend to panic, to confront each other head-on and to say things they later regret.

Many young people in their late teens have not completed their emancipation from parents. This shows up in the young wife as overt dependency on her family. With young husbands it comes out indirectly in a distorted view of how a husband and father should behave: they are overly authoritarian, copying their own fathers whom they perceived as dominating them. They try to prove their manliness by being the "head" of the new family. There is much evidence of husbands being inappropriately aggressive in quarrels with their wives.[4] This behaviour could be seen as simply a facet of an aggressive personality. Yet the men who were reported as abusive by their wives usually turned out to be quite submissive, immature and lacking in self-confidence.. Their behaviour seemed to arise from frustration when they felt they were not given the respect they deserved. They felt inadequate as adults, so they attacked the person who reinforced this feeling.

Another characteristic of very young couples is their low tolerance of frustration–they are readier to give up if the marriage does not give immediate satisfaction. If a marriage fails, the separation comes much faster for younger brides and grooms than for older ones as shown on Table 3 and 4.

TABLE 3

Length of Marriage Related to Wife's Age at Marriage

Wife's Age	Long Marriage (4 years or more)	Short Marriage (Less than 4 years)	% of Long Marriages
Under 20	102	50	67%
20 or more	98	25	80%
Total	200	75	P = .01

TABLE 4

Length of Marriage Related to Husband's Age at Marriage

Husband's Age	Long Marriage (4 years or more)	Short Marriage (Less than 4 years)	% of Long Marriages
Under 22	100	37	73%
22 or more	88	19	82%
Total	188	56	P = .04

Premarital Pregnancy

The most frequent reason for marrying young is premarital pregnancy. A high percentage of the divorcing couples seen had begun their marriages

---

[4] 18% of wives complained of physical abuse by their husbands.

this way.[5] They might not have succumbed to the pressure to get married if they were older, but parental influence is still strong at 18 and a girl "in trouble" is afraid of her parents' reaction if she does not get married.

One typical case illustrates the disadvantages of youth and forced marriage. This was a 17 year old girl who got married because of pregnancy and was unable to accept the restrictions of marriage and motherhood. She persisted in going out alone and became involved with other men. Her husband realized she had never had enough freedom before marriage and was not ready to settle down—he too was pushed into marriage by the premarital pregnancy. Thus circumstances influenced her to take on responsibilities which she could not meet and the baby, on whose behalf the marriage was undertaken, was soon left with only one parent.

The premarital pregnancy which draws couples into early, unsuitable marriages is often itself a result of the girl's unhappiness at home. Girls who feel unappreciated by their parents or are used by their mothers to take on much of the work in the home, look for some way of escape. Many teenagers have enough intelligence and educational opportunities to give them direction. The average girl in the group which eventually gets divorced does not have these opportunities because she comes from a low socio-economic level in the community (to be shown later). She cannot imagine moving out into a job, as a boy might, and marriage seems to be the only way of escape.

Thus the type of girl who is least ready for marriage is most likely to get caught in the inevitable sequence leading to marriage and early motherhood. It is not surprising that many of them find themselves unequal to the demands and the marriage ends in divorce.

Antisocial Tendencies

A man's respect for society's rules has a bearing on whether he will be a good husband. Men with ciminal records are likely to be impulsive, wilful and to feel alien to community standards–qualities which make them poor candidates for marriage. Yet young men who feel alien to society are often attracted by the security of marriage, seeing it as a place where they will be given love and respect. Unfortunately their marriages are risky undertakings. There is a much higher rate of criminal activity among couples who divorce than the general population (including unmarried men and women) as shown on Table 5.

The worst effect of criminal activity on married life is the result when the husband is caught and punished (7% of the men in the families studied had been in jail during the marriage). These men are forced to desert their families physically and financially; the family is left to face the shame of a "jail-bird" husband or father and they will resent him for putting them in this position. Even a wife who understands and forgives her husband for criminal activity will not have the same respect for and trust in him after a jail sentence. The entire family has to learn to get along without the father and they will be reluctant to become too dependent on him again. Thus the husband returns to a weaker union, if his wife accepts him back at all.

---

[5] 33% had their first child in 7 months.

TABLE 5

Comparison of Divorcing with Non-Divorcing
Population by Rate of Criminal Charges per 100 People

Population Group	Number of Charges		Total Population aged 16–59 yrs.		Rate of Charges Per 100 people	
	1963	1964	1963	1964	1963	1964
Non-Divorcing (London)[6]	860	880	99,480	101,732	0.9	0.9
Divorcing Husbands[7]	14	7	366	162	4.4	4.3
Divorcing Wives	2	...				

P=.001

In choosing a partner who has been in trouble with the law, a woman may be fully aware of the circumstances; she feels either that he will not repeat his past behaviour or that she can accept the consequences to the marriage if her husband is fined or jailed. The over-representation of these men in the divorcing group however indicates that they are not good marriage risks.

Economic Unreadiness

The husband's ability to support a family is another aspect of readiness for marriage. People whose marriages end in divorce have a lower than average education (see Table 6) occupational level (see Table 7) and income,[8] all of which contribute to dissatisfaction and eventual break-up.

TABLE 6

Comparison of Divorcing Husband's Education
with Married Men in General

Grade Completed	Divorcing Men		Married Men[9]	
Grade 10 or less	165	68%	22,888	57%
More than grade 10	80	32%	17,365	43%
Totals	245	100%	40,253	100%

P=.001

---

[6] Charges obtained from Police Records for of City London. Population figures obtained from City Hall London.

[7] Total population of divorcing group includes only husbands and wives seen after December 31, 1963, as police records for 1963 were not complete for those seen after this date. For the same reason, total population for 1964 includes only those seen after December 31, 1964.

[8] Average income for the divorcing husbands was $73. per week compared to $86. per week for the average male family head husband in London (latter figure represents 40,253 husbands living with their wives, earning an average of $4,511 per year, shown in Catalogue 93-516, Bulletin 2.1-7, p. 74-12): the 95% confidence interval for this difference is 13% ± 5%; p-value = .001.

[9] These figures are for the London Metropolitan area, from unpublished data of the 1961 Census of Canada, D. B. S.

TABLE 7

Occupational Representation of Divorcing Husbands
Compared to Married Men in General

Occupation	Divorcing Husbands		Married Men[10]	
Professional, managerial and skilled	117	48%	683,756	57%*
Labourers	44	18%	59,260	5%*
Others	83	34%	476,397	38%
Totals	244	100%	1,219,413	100%

P=.001

There is a two way connection between economic inadequacy and marriage failure. Marriages with these disadvantages are more likely to dissolve, also the early acceptance of responsibility by the husband means he can no longer improve himself as a wage earner. He is not as free to move around seeking better opportunities, to take a low paying job with a chance for advancement or to continue his education.

There are some divorcing husbands whose income is erratic because they have frequent job changes and periods of unemployment. Yet a significant group stay at the same low-paying job year after year, presumably because of their family responsibilities and their lack of transferable skills.[11]

Low Income: The strain of low income on family living is obvious. It causes irritation, quarrelling about priorities and worry about necessities such as clothing and rent. A family trying to get along on an income which is below average for its community is like a worker with poor tools. The job can be done but it requires much more patience and skill; also there is a chronic sense of being at a disadvantage compared to other people.

If the parents' expectations exceed their income, they will envy the living standards of others. Sometimes they live by their expectations rather than their income and the marriage is burdened with debts and unpaid bills. A wife is bound to resent her husband for his inability to earn an average income; the husband, on his part, may well blame his low earning power on the early marriage and arrival of children which held him in an un-skilled job.

A financial crisis can precipitate the breakup of a marriage. One family was evicted due to non-payment of rent; the husband and wife had to find separate places to stay with relatives and were never reunited. The effect of low income on the families is aggravated by the early arrival of children (discussed below). The family is reduced at a very early stage to one sub-average income, unless the wife decides to combine a job with motherhood, which puts another kind of strain on the marriage (to be discussed later).

[10]These figures are for Ontario from the 1961 Census of Canada, Households and Families, Bulletin 2.1-11, P. 93-14; all husbands in husband-wife families are included except those 65 years and over.

[11]44% of the 168 men who gave employment histories had been at the same job all their working lives; another 26% had been in one job over half their working lives.

Tension about low income is also created by the husband's guilt when he is unable to provide a comfortable living for his family. He is unlikely to talk about this but instead blames the economy or accuses his wife of expecting too much. Underneath he feels inadequate and can find only destructive ways of handling this feeling. As mentioned above, drinking and staying away from the home are common defenses; in extreme cases, the husband deserts.[12]

Families with below average incomes almost never own their own homes, so they have one less tie to hold them together. The families who were seen rated even lower in home ownership than income compared to the general population.[13] Home ownership is psychologically important to a family as a symbol of stability and success. It provides a focus for united effort, as husband and wife plan for their own home and work on making it attractive. It also lessens mobility, which is shown below as a destructive influence on marriage.

Low Status: The level of the husband's job has an effect on his marriage aside from the obvious one of income. A man who is at the low end of the occupational scale knows he can easily be replaced; he has to worry about losing his job if he is sick or incapacitated. His working conditions may be demoralizing, as he is vulnerable to criticism by the people above him but the line of authority ends at him. Sometimes he comes home and takes out his frustration on the family—or he may go out "with the boys" and drink his troubles away. Even if he is fairly submissive and accepts his position in life, he does not return home from work in an expansive mood, as does a husband with a challenging job who derives a sense of achievement from his work. It is a strain on the entire family when the husband is bored and apathetic about his job.

Also, a man's occupation determines his family's status and the influence that community attitudes will have in keeping the family together. Public opinion acts as a deterrent to men in business or professional life and the prospect of losing status makes separation more difficult to contemplate. A couple which is already at the bottom of the status scale, because the husband has a low-paid, unskilled job, have little to lose in this respect if they decide to separate. The cumulative effect of job insecurity, lack of challenge and low standing in the community can make a significant contribution to family instability.

Employment of the Mother

One consequence of the father's inability to earn an average income is that the mother continues to work. This puts a strain on marriage from a number of directions; the cumulative effect is a high percentage of working mothers among divorcing couples as shown on Table 8.

---

[12] 5% of husbands deserted, apparently feeling their families would be better off without them.

[13] 29% of the families seen owned real estate at a time when over 66% of dwelling units in Canada were occupied by their owners, according to the D. B. S., Bulletin 93-523, 1961, quoted in Frederick Elkin, *The Family in Canada* (Ottawa: The Vanier Institute of the Family, 1964), P. 83.

TABLE 8

Comparison of Divorcing Wives with Married Women re Employment

Employed[14]	Divorcing Wives		Married Women[15]	
Yes	125	50%	182,370	22%
No	123	50%	642,304	78%
Totals	248	100%	824,674	100%

P = .001

It could be argued that, rather than their employment causing marriage breakdown, these wives were at work because their marriages were unhappy. Surveys have shown, however, that most working wives are employed for financial reasons.[16, 17] Most of those who worked felt it was absolutely necessary. Many were saving for the downpayment on a house which they would otherwise never have; most of the others simply could not manage on their husbands' low incomes.

The most important influence of the wife's outside work on marriage breakdown comes from her attitude toward her husband. She feels he should have been able to support the family at a certain level without her having to work.[18] Wives who work are much more likely to express dissatisfaction about economic matters. The working wife also feels there should be some compensation from her husband for the extra work she does, but most husbands do not take an equal share in housework and child care[19]. Besides the wife's unmet expectations of her husband, there is the strain of doing two jobs. One wife said she was brought to the point of separation by her depression and irritability over a double workload.

There are other aspects of an outside job which make a wife less satisfied with her husband. If she works in an office she is usually treated with respect and consideration by the men there, while her husband takes her for granted at home. She also wants to have more decision-making power about how the family money is spent; in this she comes into conflict with her husband about their priorities.

---

[14] These women were employed most or all the time during their marriages (part-time or occasional employment not included).

[15] These were Ontario wives with dependent children as shown in the *1961 Census of Canada, Households and Families*, Bulletin 2. 1—11, Table 93—13.

[16] Money was the reason for working given by the majority of working wives in a U. S. survey according to Nye and Hoffman, *op. cit.*, p. 22.

[17] A trans-Canada survey showed that 78.7% of wives worked for economic reasons, 10.5% for non-economic reasons and 19.8% for a combination of the two, in *Canadian Government Department of Labour, Married Women Working for Pay in Eight Canadian Cities* (Ottawa: Queen's Printer, 1958).

[18] Complaints about the husband as a provider were made by 88% of wives who worked compared to 71% of wives who did not work: the 95% confidence interval for the difference is 17% ± 11%; p-value = .001.

[19] A study of married couples in Florida showed that poor marital adjustment was likely when the husband did not respond to his wife's increased work load, in Nye and Hoffman, *op. cit.*, p. 287.

The independence of having her own income frees a wife of some of the fear she might otherwise feel about a contemplated separation. Socially she is more confident about her ability to get along apart from her husband. A housewife usually has few friends apart from those she and her husband make as a couple; the working wife however has a set of colleagues who are friends or potential friends and who treat her as a separate individual.

Thus, the experiences which are part of an outside job cause the wife to appreciate her husband less and to view separation as more feasible both socially and financially. A couple who feel that it is economically necessary for the wife to work should cosider the effect this has on their total relationship. Unless the husband can reciprocate for her greater contribution to the partnership, he is going to find his wife expecting more of him than before and being more critical if he does not meet these expectations.

Different Backgrounds

The decision to marry is filled with emotion—both romantic idealism and sexual attraction—but there is usually an underlying logic in the choice of partner. A woman is not likely to marry a man whose job and income potential are lower than those of her original family. Also, she usually picks someone who is at least equal to her in intelligence so that she can respect him and depend upon his judgment. A man too seeks a wife who is compatible with his social and economic level—someone who fits in with the wives and girl friends of his friends and colleagues; he will avoid someone whose economic standards he thinks he cannot meet. Such expectations, however, seem to be much less important to the husband than to the wife;[20] the high level of dissatisfaction of wives over economic matters is discussed in the next chapter.

The instability of marriages in which social and economic compatibility is lacking has been supported by research.§ An important factor in compatibility is the similarity in education between husband and wife. Among divorcing couples, the wife's education is more likely to exceed the husband's than in the general population as shown on Table 9. Although there are numerous reasons unrelated to intelligence why a man may have ended his education before his wife did, this does leave him with less training and general information, fewer job opportunities and more limited social aspirations than his wife. He is likely to feel somewhat inferior to her when the question of education or intelligence comes up; he will also be sensitive about having his decisions challenged by his wife.

---

[20]Only 4% of husbands complained that their wives were inadequate homemakers; 5% felt their wives' economic goals were too low and 4% said their wives made excessive material demands.

§425 divorced couples were compared to a national sample in relation to the similarity in occupational level between the husband and the wife's father; it was found that marriages where there was a similarity contributed less than their share of divorces.

TABLE   9

Comparison of Husband's and Wife's Education

Wife had	Divorcing Couples		Married Couples‡	
More	88	39%	11,346	29% *
Equal	72	32%	16,873	41% *
Less	65	29%	12,034	30%
Totals	225	100%	40,253	100%

* p=.001

These differences between the husband and the wife or their original families seem unimportant at the dating stage, when personal charm and sexual attraction are paramount. They take on much more importance after marriage, however, when the wife sees her friends with husbands who have higher incomes or when she objects to the way her husband manages their affairs.

As mentioned above, economic considerations play an underlying part when young people are free to choose a partner. Unfortunately, with marriages which end in divorce, the dating stage has often led into marriage without much further thought about suitability; when a girl becomes pregnant, her boyfriend's economic prospects seem much less important than the fact that he is the baby's father. The instinct for choosing a compatible person does not have a chance to work for these couples.

Arrival of Children

As mentioned earlier, children tend to arrive much earlier to couples whose marriages end in divorce.[21] The harmful effect of early pregnancy on marriage begins even before the baby is born. During pregnancy most wives have mood swings and make more demands on their husbands for understanding. Unfortunately the husband has come to the marriage with some expectations of his own—he may well resent getting extra demands in place of the extra attention he expected from his wife. Their sex life is also affected by physical changes in the wife which can make either of them less interested in sex. These disadvantages are not hard to accept for a couple who have planned and waited eagerly for their first child; but it is different for those who were not ready for a baby.

When children arrive too soon the early marriage relationship between the couple is interrupted. The baby demands the wife's attention and energy at a point when the couple are still unsure of each other as husband

---

‡These were all couples in this London Metropolitan area ; figures were obtained from unpublished material of the 1961 Census of Canada.

[21]The average (median) time for the first baby to be born was nine months after marriage. The only available figures for the general population was for the United states where the average baby arrived 18 months after marriage giving parents twice as long to prepare. The latter figure was from Paul C. Glick, "Demographical Analysis of Family Data ", in H. J. Christensen, ed., *Handbook of Marriages and the Family* (Chicago : Rand McNally, 1964), p. 301,

and wife. They need time together to deepen their relationship by long discussions, even by arguments. If the baby cries when they are having a talk or an argument, they cannot finish because the baby's needs take priority. There is also some jealousy over the attention each one gives the child if they are still unsure of each other.

As more children are added to the family, they continue to distract the couple from their one-to-one relationship. Meals become centered around the children and the parents no longer have time to talk over coffee, because children have to be supervised, bathed and put to bed. The husband is likely to feel especially left out—he works for the family all day, but finds himself very low in priority when he gets home. All this improves as children grow older, but most separations come while they are still very young.[22] The interference of children with the development of a good marital relationship was confirmed by the trends in separation. Those couples who separated very early in marriage (before the third year) had been burdened with children at a very early point—the slower-producing marriage lasted longer.[23] The quick producing marriages seemed to have never taken hold. Either the children interfered with the parents' private relationship or the couple had married only because of pregnancy and had soon regretted this.

Another set of conditions which suggested that couples could not absorb children into their marriage, without overloading it, was the association of separation with the birth of an additional baby. It is obvious that the baby's first year is the worst time to separate—the mother needs her husband's support most when the child is most helpless, yet this is a common time for families to break up.[24] The association of separation with a baby's birth suggests that the family's resources were all used up before the last baby arrived and the strain of this extra responsibility was more than the marriage could take. The reason for this would be similar to those in the above discussion—diversion of the parents' energy and attention away from each other in order to meet the demands of parenthood. The birth of a baby is a critical point in family life and a weak family collapses during a crisis. Aside from the immediate demands of a new baby, there is a commitment demanded of the parents which they know will last for many years ; the realization of this by parents who are already having doubts about their marriage can bring on a strong need to run away from increased responsibility.

These patterns indicate that more birth control is needed in shaky marriages, because the addition of one child too many can be the breaking point. The first pregnancy is often underway before the couples realize the full consequences, but after marriage they might be able to prevent separation by having no more children until their marriage has a sound basis. Babies

---

[22]The most common time for separation was between the 3rd and 4th year of marriage.

[23]All couples who separated before the third year of marriage had two children by the time they separated or at least one during the first year. Those couples who had their first child after one year all stayed together at least 3 years.

[24]Almost 50% of the couples who built up their families quickly had separated within a year of the time their last child was born. These were families who had 2 children born in the first 3 years of marriage or 3 in the first 6 years ; this occurred in 119 families.

appeal to the imagination ; many couples let nature take its course because pregnancy and birth adds excitement to their lives. By the time the duller stage of caring for the baby comes along with its hard work and frustrations, it is too late to discover that the marriage could not absorb another child.

In the two main jobs of marriage—providing the necessities of life for a family and raising children—most divorcing couples show evidence of weakness, although they themselves may give far different reasons why their marriages failed. There has usually been destructive behaviour in many areas by the time the final break comes, but the majority of couples seen at the point of divorce have been unable to make their marriages work as partnerships in the business of sustaining family life.

SUMMARY

Unreadiness for marriage is characteristic of those who divorce. They tend to marry young—with the accompanying high expectations, dependency on parents, inexperience, low frustration tolerance and restlessness characteristic of youth.

They are often premaritally pregnant—pushed into marriage by parents, rebelling or trying to escape from home. The incidence of anti-social behaviour is higher. They are economically unprepared in terms of education and job level. This causes frustration and guilt for the husband, leading to escapist behaviour, sometimes desertion. Attempts to solve financial problems, by dependency on in-laws or by the mother working, bring other complications which have a destructive effect on the marriage.

Some couples are poorly matched, in education and economic expectations. The wife's expectation of companionship, adequate financial resources and the husband's hopes for a satisfying sex life are frequently not met.

The arrival of children coincides with marriage breakdown in two respects. Families who have children quickly tend to break up quickly. Also the first part of a child's life is likely to be the time the parents separate.

The tasks of keeping the family financially viable and bringing up children are basic to marriage. A couple who cannot do this without great strain on their resources are likely to give the marriage up as a bad job. Unfortunately most of the conditions which make the job relatively difficult or easy are pre-determined : maturity, compatibility, earning power and arrival of children (the last being unplanned rather than pre-determined). No amount of effort by the couple can make up for serious handicaps in these areas. They have the final decision about whether to struggle on with a difficult marriage, but they have little control over how pleasant or frustrating their life together will be ; the conditions discussed above are the controlling factors.

Divorce in Canada: A Demographic Profile

JOHN F. PETERS*

The Divorce Act 1967-68, which liberalized divorce laws in Canada, has stimulated considerable comment from both the academic and popular sectors. A special Commission is presently examining the existing Divorce Laws. Until very recently, research on the subject of divorce in Canada has been sparse. Statistical data for such research was also restricted prior to 1969. However, this picture is changing. Roberts and Krishnan (1973) have attempted to relate the variables of working women and "youth" to the divorce rate. The remarriage probability for the divorced in Canada has been studied by Kuzel and Krishnan (1974). Reed has addressed selected legal aspects of divorce proceedings in recent years (1975) while Pike has presented a socio-historical analysis of the incidence of divorce (1975). Palmer (1971) indicates the social variables precipitating divorce in a southwestern Ontario region.

With the divorce rate as the independent variable this Canadian study examines the social variables (dependent) of age at first marriage, age at time of marriage, duration of marriage and divorces involving dependent children. The divorce rate is correlated with a province's per cent urban population and city size. Trends in the alleged grounds used for divorce are also investigated. In this study the most recent published divorce statistics (1973) are used, and trends generally are based upon the 1970-1973 year period.

Divorce Rate

Canada's divorce rate was 54.8 per 100,000 population in 1968, and had exceeded that figure previously only twice: in 1946 and 1947, the years of the post-War divorce (Table 15, p. 73)[+]. After the new divorce laws the divorce rate in Canada climbed an abrupt 126 per cent and generally continued to climb in all provinces except P.E.I., which has had a general decline (Table 16. p. 74). The most radical percentage change in 1969 took place in the provinces which had no federal jurisdiction of divorce. Newfoundland and Quebec did not receive legislation to issue divorces until 1968, and their divorce increases were 567 per cent and 382 per cent respectively the following year. P.E.I. established her divorce courts in 1945. This province showed a 405 per cent increase in divorces in 1969. Canada has averaged a yearly increase of 7.7 per cent in the divroce

*Department of Sociology and Anthropology, Wilfrid Laurier University, Waterloo, Ontario, Canada.
+Where table and page numbers are used the source is *Vital Statistics*, Vol. II, Marriage and Divorces, 1973, (84-205), Ottawa, Information Canada, 1975.

rate between 1969 and 1974. During that period N.S. and Quebec have shown the largest percentage increase in 1972 and 1973.

There were a total of 36,704 divorces in a population of 22,095,000, or one for every 5 marriages in the year 1973. There has been considerable variation in the divorce rate between provinces: 41.4 for Nfld. and 263.5 for Alberta in 1973 (per 100,000 population).

Of all divorces granted between 1970 and 1973, approximately 5.5 per cent were granted to individuals who had previously been divorced (Table 18, p. 75).

Marriage Rate and Divorce

The marriage rate for Canada in 1973 was 9.0 per 1,000 population (Table 5, p. 46). This rate was higher in the 1940's, then declined to a low of 6.9 in 1973, and since has increased. This rate now seems to have stabilized. Quebec has generally had a lower marriage rate (8.5 in 1973), and the province of New Brunswick a relatively high marriage rate (9.8 in 1973). The range between provinces is relatively small (S.D.=.42). A more careful analysis would compare the population of eligibles for marriage). There is no correlation between a province's marriage rate and divorce rates (r=.28).

Age at First Marriage and Divorce Rate

In the early 1940's the average age of the bride and groom at first marriage was 24.4 and 27.7 years respectively (Table 6, p. 48). There was an average difference of 3.3 years between bride and groom. Since that time there has been a gradual lowering of the average age, to 22.3 and 24.7 years of age for bride and groom, respectively. The average age difference between the spouses now ranges between 2.2 and 2.4 years. The decrease in the age difference of spouses suggests a greater potential similarity in interests between spouses, a factor which would curb the divorce rate. The trend of a younger age at first marriage might indicate an increase in the divorce rate in the future due to the limitation in life experience and exposure of the couple previous to the marital bond. Nfld., N.B. and Sask. have a relatively low age at marriage for brides and grooms, and their divorce rate is comparatively low. In B.C., Ontario and particularly in Quebec the average age of bride and groom at first marriage is higher than other provinces, yet their divorce rates vary from moderate to high in Canada. There is no relationship between a province's divorce rate and the average age at marriage for brides (r=.35). There appears to be some relationship between a province's divorce rate and the average age at marriage of grooms in that province (r=.64, level of significance .024).

In 1973, 28 per cent of all brides and 8 per cent of all grooms who married were under 20 years of age (Table 1). In the same year (1973) 43 per cent of all women and 13 per cent of all men who divorced were first married under 20 year of age (Table 2). These figures show a disproportionately high percentage of divorce coming from young marriages.

Those marrying in the 20-24 age cohort represented 46 per cent and 50 per cent of al marriages for brides and grooms respectively. Thirty-nine and 52 per

TABLE 1   BRIDES AND GROOMS OF ALL MARRIAGES, BY AGE COHORTS,
                                              CANADA, 1973*

Age	Bride %	Groom %
Under 20 years	28.4	8.1
20-24 years	45.9	50.3
26-25 years	12.4	22.4
30-34 years	4.2	6.9
35-39 years	2.2	3.3
40+ years	6.9	9.0
	100.0	100.0

*Data taken from Vital Statistics 1973, 84-205, Table 10, pp. 59, 62.

TABLE 2   DIVORCES BY MALES AND FEMALES BY AGE COHORT
                                     AT TIME OF MARRIAGE, CANADA, 1973**

Age	Females %	Males %
Under 20 years	43.2	13.1
20-24 years	38.8	52.3
25-29 years	8.4	19.8
30-34 years	2.9	6.0
35-39 years	1.4	2.7
40-44 years	0.8	1.4
45-49 years	0.6	0.8
50+ years	0.7	1.0
Not stated	3.2	2.9
	100.0	100.0

**Vital Statistics 1973, 84-205, Table 19, p. 82.

cent of all males and females who divorced in 1973 originally married in the 20-24
age cohort.

Age of Husband and Wife at Time of Divorce

The average age of husband and wife at the time of divorce in Canada in
1973 was 38.6 and 35.6 respectively (Table 22, p. 83). There has been a gradual
decrease in the average age since 1969. Alberta, the province with the highest
divorce rate, has the highest per cent of husbands and wives divorcing under 20
and between 20-24 years of age (Table 3).

TABLE 3   AGE COHORTS OF HUSBAND AND WIFE AT TIME OF DIVORCE
                 IN PERCENTAGE OF THAT PROVINCE'S TOTAL DIVORCES
                                    CANADA, 1973*

Age	Canada	Nfld.	P.E.I.	N.S.	N.B.	Que	Ont.	Man.	Sask.	Alta.	B.C.	Yukon	N.W.T.
					Husbands								
Under 20	.1	—	1.9	.16	—	.03	.05	.20	.10	.2	.05	1.70	—
20—24	5.6	7.1	14.8	6.4	7.1	2.8	5.6	6.4	6.8	9.0	5.6	5.0	2.4
25—29	20.0	22.3	18.5	20.2	23.9	16.6	21.2	21.1	20.4	21.5	20.5	18.3	14.3
30—34	19.3	16.5	14.8	18.5	19.0	20.6	19.0	16.7	18.7	19.9	19.2	28.3	19.0
35—39	14.7	17.0	9.3	17.7	11.0	16.6	14.1	15.0	12.0	14.5	13.4	15.0	23.8
40—44	12.8	16.0	9.3	11.8	12.0	15.0	12.2	11.7	12.0	10.7	13.1	6.7	11.9
45—49	9.7	6.7	11.1	8.4	8.7	11.1	9.9	8.8	8.7	8.8	8.9	8.3	11.9
50+	17.8	14.3	20.4	16.8	18.3	17.1	17.8	20.1	21.2	16.1	19.3	16.7	16.7
not stated	—	—	—	—	—	—	—	—	—	—	—	—	—
Total	36,704	224	54	1,249	574	8,091	13,781	1,620	887	4,435	5,687	60	42
					Wives								
Under 20	.58	.90	—	.70	.30	.01	.50	.80	.70	1.40	.60	—	—
20—24	12.8	13.8	20.4	12.0	17.4	7.9	12.9	14.0	15.9	17.7	14.4	18.3	14.3
25—26	24.0	28.6	24.0	25.3	24.4	22.5	25.2	23.3	23.0	24.0	23.0	26.7	19.0
30—34	17.6	15.6	14.8	18.4	15.3	19.9	16.8	16.2	14.8	17.0	17.7	20.0	19.0
35—39	12.8	14.7	11.1	14.7	11.3	15.0	12.1	12.8	12.2	12.0	11.5	6.7	14.3
40—44	10.9	11.2	13.0	9.8	10.1	13.4	10.6	10.5	9.9	9.7	9.8	8.3	16.7
45—49	8.7	5.8	7.4	6.9	9.6	9.8	8.8	8.5	8.9	7.0	8.6	6.7	7.1
50+	12.7	9.4	9.3	12.2	11.5	11.2	13.1	13.9	14.7	11.2	14.5	13.3	9.5
not stated	—	—	—	—	—	—	—	—	—	—	—	—	—
Total	36,704	224	54	1,249	574	8,091	13,781	1,629	887	4,435	5,687	60	42

*Information from Statistic Canada. Percentages are correct to within 1%.

Quebec, a province with a current moderate divorce rate, has the lowest percentage of husbands and wives divorcing under 20, 20-24, and 25-29 years of age. This is somewhat influenced by the higher average age found in Quebec for both brides and grooms at the time of the first marriage. (Nfld. and N.B. also have a low percentage for grooms under 20). In contrast, Quebec has a high comparative percentage of husbands and wives who divorce between 40 and 44, and 45 to 49 years of age. The provinces of B.C. and Sask. have a relatively high percentage of brides and grooms divorcing after age 45.

One might assume that provinces which evidence a relatively high divorce rate have a higher proportion of divorces of wives under 24 years of age. These variables were cross tabulated and shown to have no relationship ($r=.09$). Similarly the provinces' divorce rate was cross tabulated with the percentage of divorces for wives over 40 years of age. There was no relationship ($r=.17$).

Duration of Marriage for the Divorced

On the average, marriages which terminated with divorce in Canada lasted approximately 12 years (Table 4). Divorces taking place after less than five years marriage duration comprise 15 per cent of all divorces, while marriages of less than 10 years duration comprise 41 per cent of all divorces (1970-1973). The modal year of marriage duration of the divorced is five years, though the years between four and nine years of marriage duration are each fairly comparable. Canada's duration of marriage for the divorced is somewhat higher than the statistics in the United States, a median of 7 years in 1967. Many divorces in Canada are preceeded by two and three years of separation (see Alleged Grounds for Divorce) giving evidence of marriage breakdown long before the legal divorce. The trend between 1970 and 1973 has been a gradual increase in absolute numbers

TABLE 4   DIVORCES BY DURATION OF MARRIAGE AND MEDIAN DURATION OF MARRIAGE, CANADA, 1970-1973*

Divorces in Years	1970		1971		1972		1973		1970-73	
	Divorces	Percent	Divorces	Percent	Divorces	Percent	Divorces	Percent	Divorces	Percent
Under 1 year	58	0.2	75	0.3	84	0.3	99	0.3	316	0.2
1 year	390	1.3	472	1.6	524	1.6	645	1.8	2,031	1.6
2 years	834	2.9	931	3.1	1,022	3.2	1,165	3.2	3,952	3.1
3 years	1,094	3.7	1,258	4.2	1,465	4.5	1,712	4.5	5,529	4.3
4 years	1,406	4.8	1,638	5.5	1,948	6.0	2,152	5.8	7,144	5.6
1-4 years	3,724	12.7	4,299	14.4	4,959	15.3	5,674	15.5	18,656	14.6
5 years	1,388	4.7	1,687	5.7	2,020	6.2	2,403	6.6	7,498	5.9
6 years	1,430	4.9	1,586	5.3	1,924	4.9	2,237	6.1	7,177	5.6
7 years	1,479	5.1	1,468	4.9	1,717	5.2	2,146	5.8	6,810	5.3
8 years	1,350	4.6	1,471	5.0	1,523	4.7	1,900	5.2	6,244	4.9
9 years	1,251	4.3	1,270	4.3	1,465	4.6	1,774	4.5	5,650	4.4
5-9 years	6,898	23.6	7,482	25.2	8,649	26.7	10,350	28.2	33,379	26.1
10-14 years	5,655	19.3	5,631	18.9	5,905	18.2	6,490	17.7	23,681	18.6
15-19 years	4,401	15.1	4,290	14.5	4,442	13.7	4,930	13.4	18,063	14.1
20-24 years	3,615	12.4	3,438	11.6	3,518	10.9	3,896	10.6	14,467	11.3
25-29 years	2,510	8.6	2,307	7.8	2,445	7.6	2,734	7.4	9,996	7.8
30+ years	2,319	7.9	2,123	7.2	2,323	7.2	2,502	6.8	9,267	7.2
Not stated	58	0.2	27	0.1	39	0.1	29	0.1	152	0.1
Total	29,238	100.0	29,672	100.0	32,364	100.0	36,704	100.0	127,978	100.0
Median duration of Marriage	13.5		12.6		12.1		11.8		12.5	

*Vital Statistics, Marriage and Divorces, 84-205, Table 23, p. 84.

of divorces in all years of marriage duration (Table 23, p. 84). There has been a percentage increase in divorces in each of the years of marriage duration under 10.

One may assume that the provinces with a high divorce rate do have a higher proportion of marriages ending in divorce in less than five years. This is only true for Alberta. The provinces with a relatively low divorce rate did have a higher proportion of divorces with marriages of at least 25 years duration. In 1973 these provinces were Nova Scotia, New Brunswick, Quebec and Saskatchewan.

Divorce and Dependent Children by Province

The percentage of divorces with dependent children is now 56.7 per cent, an increase of two per cent in the past three years (Table 24, p. 84). There were at least 42,900 dependent children of parents who divorced in 1973.

The provinces with the highest percentage of divorces with dependents were N.S., Man., Que., Nfld., Sask. and Alta. (all over 60 per cent of that province's divorces). The provinces with the lowest percentage of divorces with dependents were P.E.I. and B.C. (Table 5). It may be noted that there is no relationship between a province's divorce rate and the percentage of divorces with dependents ($r = .14$). Alberta had a high divorce rate and a high percentage of divorces with dependents.

TABLE 5   DISTRIBUTION OF DIVORCES BY PERCENT OF DEPENDENT CHILDREN BY PROVINCE, 1973.*

	Number of Dependents				
	0	1	2	3	4+
Canada	43.3	22.4	18.6	9.2	6.5
Newfoundland	38.4	19.2	21.0	7.1	14.3
Prince Edward Island	48.1	27.8	14.8	3.7	5.6
Nova Scotia	36.4	23.6	19.7	11.5	8.8
New Brunswick	40.6	21.4	19.5	10.1	8.4
Quebec	38.9	24.9	18.9	9.6	7.7
Ontario	46.4	22.0	17.6	8.5	5.5
Manitoba	37.6	23.9	19.8	9.9	8.8
Saskatchewan	39.2	19.8	24.0	10.5	6.5
Alberta	39.3	22.2	20.1	10.6	7.8
British Columbia	49.7	19.4	18.0	8.6	4.3
Yukon	28.3	28.3	25.0	10.0	8.4
North West Territories	38.1	23.8	21.4	7.2	9.5

*From personal correspondence with Statistics Canada.

The majority of the divorces with dependents involve one (22.4 per cent) or two (18.6 per cent) dependents. Combining divorces with one and two dependents, the provinces of Sask. and Que. have the highest percentage (43.8 per cent). Both of these provinces have a divorce rate lower than the Canadain average.

Alleged Grounds for Divorce

The Canadian divorce law which preceded the Divorce Act 1968 originated from the British Divorce and Matrimonial Causes Act of 1857. Divorce was granted on grounds of adultery, cruelty and desertion. Cruelty referred to danger of life, limb or health, either bodily or mentally, and was interpreted very conservatively. Desertion had reference to a minimum period of two years. Originally divorces were only granted federally, which made procedings costly, time consuming and restrictive. By the 1930's most provinces issued their own divorces, but it was not until the Divorce Act 1968 that the Supreme Courts in Quebec and Newfoundland became responsible for their own divorce cases (Pike, 1975). This history of Canadian divorce law has undoubtedly flavoured the present divorce courts, and will witness considerable change in values with respect to divorce in the years ahead.

The alleged grounds of separation for not less than three years was the reason most frequently given (35 per cent) for those receiving a divorce in Canada between 1970 and 1973 (Table 24, p.85). This grounds for divorce (separation) shows a marked decline from 41.6 to 33.1 per cent of all divorces between 1969 and 1973. The new Divorce Law allowed for other options of grounds to divorce by the petitioner.

Adultery as a grounds for divorce is the second most frequently stated, representing 29 per cent between 1970 and 1973. Other alleged grounds often used were physical cruelty (13 per cent) and mental cruelty (14.6 per cent). Mental cruelty as a grounds for divorce is showing a gradual increase since 1969. Desertion by petitioner not less than 5 years is also showing a decline: from 8 to 3.7 per cent of all divorces between 1961 and 1973.

Between 1970 and 1973, 64 per cent of all divorces were granted to females (Table 6). Quebec had the lowest percentage of females being granted divorces (59 per cent) and Alberta the highest (72.8 per cent).

TABLE 6   DIVORCES IN PERCENTAGES GRANTED TO MALES AND FEMALES
CANADA AND PROVINCES, 1970-1973*

	Females	Males
Canada	63.7	36.3
Newfoundland	62.5	37.5
Prince Edward Island	69.4	30 6
Nova Scotia	64.7	35.3
New Brunswick	63.4	36.6
Quebec	59.0	41.0
Ontario	63.3	36.7
Manitoba	64.7	35.3
Saskatchewan	65.0	35.0
Alberta	72.8	27.2
British Columbia	63.2	36.8
Yukon	58.5	41.5
North West Territories	65.8	34.2

*From Vital Statistics, (84-205) 1973, Table 17, p. 75

Between 1970 and 1973 when the wife petitioned for the custody of the children, she was granted custody in 89 per cent of the cases, while the husband was granted custody in 39 per cent of the cases, when he was the petitioner (Table 26, p.85).

Rural-Urban Variations in the Divorce Rate

Research on divorce in Western societies has generally indicated a higher rate in urban areas than in rural areas. Table 7 indicates the urban-rural distribution of Canada and the percentage of those who have the marital status of divorced, 1966 and 1971. Except for the urban populations between 100,000 and 499,999 in 1971 and the populations between 10,000 and 29,999 in 1966 there is a consistent trend showing a decrease of those with the status of divorced in the less populated areas. These two exceptions show only a slight reverse trend.

TABLE 7   URBAN-RURAL SIZE AND PERCENTAGE IN MARITAL STATUS   OF
DIVORCED, CANADA, 1971*

Locality	% Divorced 1971
Canada	.81
Urban	.94
500,000 and over	1.12
100,000 to 499,999	1.14
30,000 to 99,999	7.4
10,000 to 29,999	6.7
5,000 to 9,999	5.5
2,500 to 4,999	5.0
1,000 to 2,499	4.3
Rural	4.2
Non farm	4.7
Farm	2.5

*Vital Statistics, Population, 1973, 92-731.

Though Canada does have an urban population of 76 per cent which is comparable to many industrial countries, there is great variation in this urban percentage from province to province (Table 8). The provinces with an urban population of 60 per cent or less in 1966 and 1971 are Nfld., P.E.I., N.S., N.B., and Sask. Except for N.S. in 1966 these provinces show a divorce rate of at least 67 per cent lower than that of the Canadian average. Therefore, Canadian provinces with a large percentage of rural population do have a lower divorce rate.

Divorced Populations in Urban Centres

The divorced population in the large cities is consistent with the divorce rates in the respective provinces (Table 9). Edmonton, Calgary and Vancouver have a comparatively high divorced population (over 2.5) as well as a high divorce rate.

TABLE 8   PER CENT URBAN AND DIVORCE RATE BY PROVINCE 1966, 1971

Localitity	% Urban		Divorce Rate	
	1966	1971	1966	1971
Canada	73	76	51.2	137.6
Newfoundland	54	54	2.2	28.7
Prince Edward Island	37	37	16.6	54.7
Nova Scotia	58	58	53.7	91.6
New Brunswick	51	51	25.1	76.1
Quebec	78	78	17.1	86.3
Ontario	80	80	58.9	158.5
Manitoba	67	67	54.4	140.1
Saskatchewan	49	49	33.6	88.1
Alberta	69	69	107.1	224.6
British Columbia	75	75	113.4	225.6
Yukon	47	47	146.0	255.4
North West Territories	40	40	10.4	71.8

TABLE 9   MARRIED AND DIVORCED POPULATIONS IN SELECTED CANADIAN
                                          CITIES, 1973*

City	Population Married	Population Divorced	% Divorced of Married Population
Montreal	1,243,930	18,585	1.49
Toronto	1,271,965	30,515	2.39
Vancouver	520,495	21,810	2.59
Winnipeg	253,700	6,125	2.40
Hamilton	242,670	4,630	1.90
Edmonton	226,160	8,145	3.60
Quebec	199,540	1,330	.66
Calgary	186,660	7,410	3.96
London	131,865	3,305	2.50
Kitchener	110,065	1,995	1.81
Halifax	99,865	2,080	2.08
Regina	64,210	1,390	2.16
St. John's	56,640	335	.61
St. John	46,505	885	1.90

*Statistics Canada, Populations, Marital Status by Age Group, 92-730.

Cities in eastern Canada have a relatively low or moderate (Halifax) population
with the status of divorced. It may be noted that in the province of Quebec,
Montreal has a divorced population of 1.49 per cent of the married population
while the city of Quebec has an even lower percentage of .55 per cent. The percentage of the population which are non-French and non-Catholic in Montreal
are considered relevant influencing variables.

Provincial Average Income and Divorce Rate

Divorce rates are generally found to be high among less privileged groups (Goode, Bossard, Glick, Burgess and Cottrell) in the United States. The stress of limited economic resources, a lower than average education, an unskilled or low skilled occupation, and restricted or confined space; characteristics commonly found in lower class peoples, mitigate against a stable marriage. In Canada there is considerable variation in average income from province to province (Table 10). The provinces with a low average family income do not have a high divorce rate. Ontario, Quebec, Alta. and B.C. have relatively high average incomes, but their divorce rates are comparatively moderate or high. There is a positive relationship between a province's divorce rate and its average income ($r=.83$, Level of significance .001). One is reminded of committing the ecological fallacy in the use of analyzing these statistics. It is felt that in Canada many couples with little or no income separate rather than divorce. This position has been affirmed in conversations the author has had with academics, and social workers in Canada.

TABLE 10   AVERAGE INCOME OF FAMILIES BY PROVINCE, CANADA, 1973*

	Average Income
Canada	$12,716
Newfoundland	9,400
Prince Edward Island	8,572
Nova Scotia	10,575
New Brunswick	9,873
Quebec	12,024
Ontario	13,912
Manitoba	11,389
Saskatchewan	11,032
Alberta	12,405
British Columbia	13,942

*Source: Statistics Canada, Catalogue 13-207 Annual Income Distributions by size in Canada, 1973, p. 34-25.

Divorce Rate and Remarriage of the Divorced

Generally the provinces with a low and average Canadian divorce rate also have a low and moderate rate of remarriage for the divorced respectively (Table 11). One exception is Quebec, which had a moderate divorce rate in 1973, but a low remarriage rate. Alberta, with a high divorce rate, had a high remarriage rate of the divorced, but this was not the case for B.C. The remarriage rate of the divorced was comparatively low. An analysis of those two variables should consider the number of marriageable eligibles, particularly in the 20-30 age cohort.

In Canada there were fewer divorced females who remarried than divorced males. (For a detailed analysis of remarriage rates between 1961 and 66, see Kuzel

TABLE 11   PERCENTAGE OF BRIDES AND GROOMS PREVIOUSLY DIVORCED,
                MARRYING AND DIFFERENCE FROM AVERAGE CANADIAN
                PERCENTAGE, CANADA AND PROVINCES, 1973*

	% Grooms Previously Married	Grooms' Differences from National Percentage	% Brides Previously Married	Brides' Differences from National Percentage
Canada	9.5		8.6	
Newfoundland	2.1	—7.4	1.5	—7.1
Prince Edward Island	4.1	—5.4	4.2	—4.4
Nova Scotia	8.3	—1.2	7.6	—1.0
New Brunswick	5.7	—3.8	4.9	—3.7
Quebec	4.6	—4.9	3.5	—5.1
Ontario	11.2	+1.7	10.2	+1.6
Manitoba	9.2	— .3	8.5	— .1
Saskatchewan	6.0	—3.5	6.0	—2.6
Alberta	14.3	+4.8	14.2	+5.6
British Columbia	5.1	—4.4	5.5	—3.1
Yukon	24.2	+14.7	21.9	+13.3
North West Territories	9.3	— .2	10.6	+2.0

*From Vital Statistics, Marriages and Divorces, 84-205, Table 11, p. 62-67.

and Krishnan). This pattern is consistent in every province, with the exception of Sask. (same), P.E.I. (.1 per cent more brides), and B.C. (.4 per cent more brides).

Little research has been done in the area of racial and religious exogamy and divorce in Canada. The Heer and Hubey study shows an increase in the percentage of interfaith exogenous marriages between 1922 and 1972 (1975). Religious value differences between spouses are generally considered an area of potential disagreement and tension. Peters' more recent research of the divorced remarried, using a non-random sample, indicated an increase from "religious" to "non-religious" between the first and second marriage of the divorced (1975). There is a higher percentage of civil marriages for remarriages, than for first marriages, according to U.S. research (Carter and Glick, 1970, 53).

Divorced Status

Canada had a population of 154,005 with the status of divorced in 1971. This is 1.8 per cent of the total married population. With the increase in the divorce rate since 1968, it is anticipated that this percentage has increased, though the remarriage rate of the divorced is also increasing for both males and females (Table 11, p.62). The divorced in any age cohort in Canada do not exceed 2.1 per cent for the females or 1.8 per cent for the males (Table 12). This percentage is highest for females in the 25-44 age cohorts. For the men it is in the 40-49 age cohorts. The percentage of those divorced decreases considerably after age 64.

TABLE 12   STATUS OF DIVORCED IN PERCENTAGE, BY FIVE YEAR
                                 AGE GROUPS, PROVINCES, AND CANADA, 1971*

Ages	Canada	Nfld.	P.E.I.	N.S.	N.B.	Que.	Ont.	Man.	Sask.	Alta.	B.C.	Yukon	N.W.T.
15-19	.04	.01	—	.02	.04	.04	.04	.03	.03	.08	.05	—	—
20-24	.4	.13	.3	.3	.3	.2	.4	.4	.4	.9	.74	.3	.3
25-29	1.2	.3	.8	1.0	.8	.6	1.3	1.1	1.0	2.3	2.1	1.3	.8
30-34	1.6	.4	1.0	1.4	1.1	1.0	1.8	1.5	1.2	2.6	2.8	1.9	1.2
35-39	1.7	.4	1.0	1.4	1.2	1.1	1.9	1.8	1.3	2.8	3.2	2.2	1.2
40-44	1.8	.5	1.0	1.0	1.2	1.0	2.0	1.8	1.3	2.4	3.4	3.1	1.6
45-49	1.8	.3	1.1	1.1	1.2	.9	2.0	1.7	1.2	2.9	3.4	3.4	1.9
50-54	1.7	.3	.9	.9	1.1	.8	1.9	1.8	1.3	2.8	3.6	4.4	2.5
55-59	1.6	,3	.7	.7	1.1	.7	1.7	1.7	1.2	2.6	3.3	3.7	2.0
60-64	1.4	.2	.6	.6	.9	.6	1.5	1.5	1.1	2.3	3.1	4.1	1.7
65-69	1.1	.2	.8	.8	.9	.4	1.2	1.2	.9	1.8	2.4	4.1	1.5
70-74	.8	.1	.5	.5	.6	.4	.8	.9	.7	1.3	1.9	4.3	—
75-79	.6	.1	.2	.2	.4	.2	.5	.7	.6	1.2	1.4	6.3	—
80-84	.5	.1	.3	.3	.4	.2	.4	.6	.4	.9	1.1	—	—
85-89	.4	—	.6	.6	1.4	.2	.4	.4	.3	.9	.8	—	—
90-94	.3	—	—	—	.5	.2	.3	.3	.2	.7	.7	—	—
95+	.6	—	—	—	—	.4	.2	1.2	—	1.1	1.6	—	—

*From Statistics Canada, Population, 92-730, Table 2, p.1-6.

The percentage divorced in specific age cohorts varies considerably from province to province. This percentage is generally gradual in increase and decline, reaching a peak in the 40-44 age cohort as mentioned above. The provinces which have a comparatively high divorce rate, such as Alta. and B.C. have a dispropotionately higher percentage in the 45-54 age cohorts. This may indicate that a smaller percentage remarry, but it also suggests some who divorce at 30 or 40 retain the status of divorced.

There are more females with the status of divorced than men, until the 65-69 age cohort, at which time the reverse takes place. This trend is generally true for most provinces.

Summary and Conclusion

The average age at marriage has decreased in the past for both bride and groom, while the difference in age between the bride and groom has similiarly decreased. Canada's marriage rate has shown a gradual increase in the past decade, but more recently has seemingly stabilized.

Canada's divorce rate abruptly climbed with the new Divorce Act of 1968. It has continued to show an average 7 per cent yearly increase since 1969. Alberta and B.C. have the highest divorce rate, and Ontario generally approximates the Canadian rate.

There is no relationship between a province's relatively high marriage rate and divorce rate. Provinces with a relatively low averge age at first marriage have a comparatively low divorce rate.

The average age at time of divorce is decreasing. Canada has a disproportionately high percentage of divorces of those who first married under 20 years of age. However provinces with a high divorce rate do not necessarily have a high proportion of divorces in the lower age cohorts. The average duration of marriage for the divorced is 12 years, a figure relatively high for western countries. The trend in Canada is toward an increasing percentage of divorces for marriages below 10 years duration, and a decreasing percentage after that period of marriage. There has been a gradual increase in the percentage of divorces involving children and this is likely to continue. Fifty-seven per cent of all divorces in 1973 involved dependent children. There is no relationship between a province's divorce rate and the percentage of divorces involving dependent children.

Separation and adultery were the grounds most frequently used in obtaining a divorce. Because of other legal alternatives, separation as grounds for divorce is currently decreasing. The use of mental cruelty as grounds is increasing. Divorce petitions are made primarily by women.

Provinces with a high rural population generally have a lower divorce rate when compared to provinces with a high urban population. The greater the population of an urban centre, the higher the divorce rate.

There is inconclusive evidence that income is inversely related to the divorce rate in Canada. Unstable marriages among those with very low income frequently leads to separation rather than divorce. More research in this area is necessary.

Provinces with a relatively high percentage of divorced do not necessarily have a comparable high remarriage rate for the divorced. Quebec and B.C. show a relatively low remarriage rate for the divorced. Provinces with a high divorce rate have a relatively high percentage with the status of divorced in the 45-54 age cohort. More divorced males than females remarry.

Canada's divorce rates in the past two decades do not follow patterns of divorce as found in other western countries. The history of the divorce laws, the ethnic mosaic, the religious representation and the varied population density all mitigate against some uniform pattern. This research has indicated some of this diversity. Provinces with a high non-Catholic population and a highly urban and industrial base, do however, show a comparatively higher divorce rate. Canada is likely to see continued provincial variance in the divorce rate because of differences in legal accessibility and the time normally involved in the divorce process (Reed, 1975). Similarly there will be regional differences due to major social changes within a relatively short space of time, yielding a type of moral confusion or anomie (Pike, 1975). Boom towns, and some regions of the N.W.T. are examples of this description.

The populous and high urban province of Quebec is of particular interest in divorce research in Canada. Quebec has a higher than Canadian average age at first marriage for both bride and groom. This province's remarriage rate is relatively low. There is a relatively higher percentage of males petitioning and being granted divorces when compared to other provinces. It has shown an unusually large increase in the divorce rate in 1969, and a consistently high increase annually since that date. Traditions and Catholicism have had a negative influence upon divorce in the past, but these restrictions do not seem to be as significant in the present decade. An indication of this change is the high (30 per cent) percentage of cohabitation reportedly practised by all classes in the 30-35 age cohort among residents in the city of Quebec. Quebec's divorce rate may soon approximate the Canadian average.[1]

A number of social factors suggest a continued increase in the divorce rate in Canada. Normative changes in the interpretation of the Divorce Act 1968 by younger judges may liberalize the criteria for divorce. It is generally felt that when children are involved in a broken marriage, a divorce with the possibility of remarriage is much more beneficial for the children. This is a change from the former stance of "keep the marriage for the sake of the kids." Companionship, happiness and individual growth are now considerd as strong reasons for marriage. When these characteristics are not achieved, or do not continue to develop, the marital bond may be terminated. The rapid changes within society in general, and with the individual's interests, values and aspirations in particular, all mitigate against an enduring marriage at all costs. Some suggest the current trend of increasing heterosexual cohabitation further encourages divorces (Peters, 1976). As more married people come in contact with those who have been divorced, the likelihood of divorce becomes an increasing possibility.

BIBLIOGRAPHY

Bossard, J.H.S., "Spatial Distribution of Divorced Women," *American Journal of Sociology,* 40, (1935), 503-507.

Burgess, Ernest W. and Cottrell, Leonard, S. Jr., *Predicting Success or Failure in Marriage,* New York, Prentice Hall, 1939.

Carter, Hugh, and Glick, Paul C., *Marriage and Divorce,* a Social Economic Study, Cambridge, Harvard Press, 1970.

Divorce, Working Paper 13, Law Reform Commission of Canada, Ottawa, 1975.

Finlay, H.A. (ed.), *Divorce, Society and the Law,* Melbourne, Butterworths, 1969.

Glick, Paul C., *American Families,* New York, Wiley, 1957.

Goode, William J., "A Cross-Cultural Class Analysis of Divorce Rates" *International Social Science Journal,* Vol. 14, No. 3 (1962), 507-526.

Heer, David, and Hubay, Charles A., "The Trend of Interfaith Marriages in Canada: 1922-1972", in *Marriage, Family and Society,* S.P. Wakil (ed.) Toronto, Butterworths, 1975, 85-96.

Kuzel, Paul and Krishnan, P., "Changing Patterns of Remarriage in Canada, 1961-1966", *Journal of Comparative Family Studies,* Vol. IV, No. 2, 215-224.

Palmer, Sally E., "Reasons for Marriage Breakdown: A Case Study in Southwestern Ontario", *Journal of Comparative Family Studies,* Vol. 2 (1971), 251-262.

Peters, John F., "Mate Selection and Marriage of the Remarried Divorced", unpublished paper, 1975.

---

[1]Statistics released since the writing of this paper indicate that Quebec had a divorce rate of 199.8 in 1974, an increase of 50 per cent over 1973. Canada's 1974 divorce rate was 200.3.

——*Divorce in Canada*, 1976 (book in progress).

Pike, Robert, "Legal Access and the Incidence of Divorce in Canada: A Socio-Historical Analysis" in *Canadian Review of Sociology and Anthropology*, Vol. 12, No. 2, 1975.

Reed, Paul, "A Preliminary Analysis of Divorce Actions in Canada, 1969-1972", paper presented at the Canadian Sociology and Anthropology Association meetings, May, 1975.

Roberts, Lance and Krishnan, P., "Age Specific Incidence and Social Correlates of Divorce in Canada," Population Research Laboratory, U. of Alberta, Edmonton, 1973.

Stetson, Dorothy M., "The Two Faces of Policy: Divorce Reform in Western Democracies," *Journal of Comparative Family Studies*, Vol. VI, No. 1, (Spring) 1975, 15-30.

Statistics Canada, *Vital Statistics, Marriage and Divorces*, Vol. II, 1973, (84-205) Information Canada, Ottawa, 1975.

Statistics Canada, *Vital Statistics Preliminary Annual Report*, 1973, (84-201) Information Canada, Ottawa, 1974.

Statistics Canada, *Population*, Marital Status by Age Group, 1971, (92-730) Information Canada, Ottawa, 1973.

Changing Patterns of Remarriage in Canada, 1961-1966*

PAUL KUZEL** AND P. KRISHNAN***

INTRODUCTION

Marriage, separation, divorce, and widowhood are demographic events that influence the course of population growth (Bogue, 1969). In view of this, there is considerable interest on the part of demographers and family sociologists to develop marriage and nuptiality tables for studying the dynamics of marriage patterns (Charles, 1941; Grabill 1945; Jacobson, 1959; Laing and Krishnan, 1972; Mertens, 1965; Saveland and Glick, 1969).

Studies on remarriages are available only on a small scale for the United States (Carter, 1965; Jones, 1962) and for New Zealand (New Zealand Dept. of Statistics, 1970). The National Centre for Health Statistics publications on trends and characteristics of marriages in the United States throw some light on this topic. But the analysis attempted in these publications is rather sketchy and not comprehensive. For Canada, even though published data are available, the present writers have not been able to come across many studies on remarriages. The main objective of this paper is to develop remarriage probability tables for males and females in Canada for 1961 and 1966 and examine the changing patterns, if any, in remarriages. Since the risk populations for remarriages are those whose marriages have been disrupted, the remarriage tables presented here will be based on the widowed and the divorced segments of the Canadian population.

*Revised version of a paper presented at the annual meetings of the Canadian Sociology and Anthropology Association, Montreal, May-June, 1972.

**Graduate Student in the Department of Sociology, University of Alberta, Edmonton, Alberta, Canada.

***Assistant Professor, and Director, Population Research Laboratory, Department of Sociology, University of Alberta, Edmonton, Alberta, Canada.

The authors are grateful to the referees for their comments and criticism.

METHODOLOGY

We make use of the life table technique for this exercise. The life table technique is a useful tool in several areas of research, other than mortality, where decrement is a part of the process under investigation. For detailed discussion on life tables and their construction reference may be made to Barclay (1958).

The tables are based on the remarriage experiences in 1961 and 1966 for the whole of Canada. Two approaches are considered. A hypothetical cohort of persons is followed through, as it is exposed to the forces of decrement resulting from remarriage and mortality. In the first approach, only marriage as a force of decrement is considered. This gives "gross" tables. In the second approach, we follow the cohort as it is diminished not only by marriage but also by deaths. This yields "net" tables. For comparing remarriage patterns of two populations, it is better to use gross tables, since in the net tables the differences may be caused by differential mortality or nuptiality patterns, or by a mixture of both.

DATA AND FINDINGS

Data for this exercise were taken from the censuses of 1961 and 1966 and from the marriage registration tabulations for the same years. (Dominion Bureau of Statistics, 1963; 1968; 1972). As there were only a negligibly small number of people reported as widowed or divorced for ages less than 20, we present here the remarriage probability tables for males and females in Canada for ages 20 and above. Since the number of males or females who will remarry beyond age 80 is small and not very important from a socio-demographic perspective, we have truncated the tables at age 80 (Krishnan, 1971). This truncation will not in any way affect the results from the point of view of interpretation.

SOME TECHNICAL PROBLEMS

We encountered some problems when calculating q_x ($= 1 - p_x$) values for divorced men and women for both 1961 and 1966. The simple approximation and also the Greville approximation for q_x from the age-specific remarriage rate M_x[1], calculated from marriage-registration data, resulted

---

[1]Based on reasonably large risk (base) populations. Still the bases for the calculation of remarriage rates for divorced females/males are not very large. This may be one reason for the difficulty in q_x computation. In the construction of working life tables, two consecutive values of age specific participation rates are averaged to estimate the probability of work force participation at the beginning of an age interval, excluding the first age group. If such a procedure is followed, the age specific remarriage probabilities of divorced females will be a little higher, by about 2 or 3 percent, than those of widowed females for the age groups 25-29 through 30-39. This difference being rather small, we did not use this approach. The conclusions would have remained the same in view of: a) divorced females in 20-24 had smaller probability of remarriage, as measured by the central rate, in comparison to widowed females and b) from age 40 onwards, widowed females had greater chances of remarriage as compared to divorcees, even after employing the averaging procedure.

in values greater than unity for the first three age groups for both the male and female tables. A negative exponential curve was fitted to the q_x values of the other age groups and then the probabilities for the first three age groups estimated by extrapolation. The fit was good, but the estimated probabilities for the first three age groups again turned out to exceed unity. The Canadian registration system is considered to be quite good and hence we cannot attribute this to data deficiencies. Since it was not easily possible to obtain q_x values from M_x values for the construction of remarriage tables for the divorced population, we decided to use the M_x values themselves as proxies for the q_x values. It should be realized that this is a very crude way of approximating the remarriage probabilities.

REMARRIAGE EXPECTATIONS BY MARITAL STATUS AND SEX

Detailed gross and net remarriage tables are comprehensive and complex[2]. The kind of results that can be gleaned from these tables are presented in this and the following sections.

Demographers and family sociologists will be interested to know the expected time of stay in a marital status before remarriage. Since the expectation of life is very high in Canada, we present the results on the expected number of years of stay in a marital status for males and females in Canada, ignoring mortality. These are given in Table 1.

Table 1. Expected Years of Remaining in Widowed/Divorced State Before Remarriage, by Sex and Age: Canada 1966

EXPECTED YEARS

	DIVORCED		WIDOWED	
Age	Male	Female	Male	Female
20	3.6	10.7	6.1	8.5
25	3.5	18.5	4.6	14.6
30	8.5	24.3	6.3	21.0
40	19.7	29.5	11.2	26.0
50	22.1	26.7	14.3	24.7
60	18.2	19.3	14.2	18.7
70	9.7	9.9	9.1	9.9

(Source: Gross remarriage tables prepared by the writers)

Differentials by sex and marital status in the remarriage patterns are clear from the above findings (Table 1). Young males, who are less than 30 years old and divorced, have not to wait much to get married. But when the males are older than thirty years, it is the widowed people who stand a better chance in the marriage market than the divorced. It is observed that the remarriage probabilities of young divorced males are higher than those of young widowers.

[2]The detailed tables can be obtained from the senior author or, the Population Research Laboratory, Department of Sociology, University of Alberta, Canada.

It is also clear that chances of remarriage are brighter for men (widowed or divorced) as compared to women in all age groups. But it is worthwhile to note the huge differential between the divorced and the widowed females. Widowed females at every age have a greater chance of remarriage than divorced females, the differentials declining, from age 30 onwards, with age. This is quite different from the pattern observed in the United States (Carter, 1965), where the divorcees always have a higher remarriage chance as compared to the widowed females. Some explanation for this pattern in Canada as compared to the U.S. is given elsewhere in the paper. Results for 1961 are on similar lines. One more point has to be stressed here. From Table 1, we see that the expected number of years before remarriage are lower for men than those for women.

PROSPECTS OF EVENTUAL REMARRIAGE

Prospects of eventual remarriage can be gauged in several ways. An easy method of discerning this aspect will be to look at the probability of ever getting remarried within the limits imposed by the truncation (that is, by age 80). These probabilities are presented in Table 2.

Table 2. Probability of Ever Getting Remarried by Age 80, by Sex and Marital Status: Canada 1966

Age	DIVORCED		WIDOWED	
	Males	Females	Males	Females
20	.998	.911	.997	.947
25	.991	.773	.995	.851
30	.927	.620	.982	.711
40	.625	.336	.889	.457
50	.330	.145	.683	.242
60	.115	.046	.377	.092
70	.033	.008	.127	.019

(Source: Tables prepared by the writers)

These probabilities are high for males, whether divorced or widowed, up to age 40. The widowers still have a good chance of 2 in 3 for remarriage even at the age of 50. For females, whether widowed or divorced, the chances are bright till 30 years and then there is a steep fall in the probability of ever getting married. The decline in the remarriage chances is sharp for divorced females as compared to the widowed. The results seem to support the principle of cumulative inertia (McGinnis, 1968) that, if a male or female, divorced or widowed, does not remarry soon, the probability of remarriage declines with the time spent in the divorced/widowed state tending to zero in the limit.

CHANGING PATTERNS OF REMARRIAGE

It is of considerable interest to us to examine whether the patterns of re-marriage have changed during the period 1961-66. There are several indi-cators which can be studied to discern the changes, if any. We present here two indicators:

(a) the age-specific remarriage probabilities. These are shown in Table 3.

(b) expected years of stay in a state before remarriage.

Table 3. Age Specific Remarriage Probabilities and Expected Years of Stay Before Re-marriage, by Sex and Marital Status: Canada 1961 and 1966

DIVORCED

	Male			Female		
Age	1961	1966	% Increase over 1961	1961	1966	% Increase over 1961
20-24	.643	.826	+28.5	.643	.612	- 4.8
25-59	.671	.880	+31.1	.456	.402	-11.8
30-34	.516	.656	+27.1	.301	.295	- 2.0
35-59	.359	.444	+23.7	.182	.190	+ 4.4
40-44	.239	.278	+16.3	.117	.135	+15.4
50-54	.117	.164	+40.2	.050	.062	+24.0
60-64	.050	.057	+14.0	.024	.029	+20.8
70-74	.010	.027	+170.0	.005	.006	+20.0

WIDOWED

	Male			Female		
Age	1961	1966	% Increase over 1961	1961	1966	% Increase over 1961
20-24	.535	.492	- 8.0	.644	.649	+ 0.8
25-59	.744	.759	+ 2.0	.491	.485	- 1.2
30-34	.629	.676	+ 7.5	.395	.325	-17.7
35-39	.551	.495	-10.2	.271	.212	-21.8
40-44	.334	.429	+28.4	.188	.171	- 9.0
50-54	.284	.322	+13.4	.095	.101	+ 6.3
60-64	.187	.216	+15.5	.045	.048	+ 6.7
70-74	.088	.105	+19.3	.017	.016	- 5.9

(Source: Tables prepared by the writers)

It is obvious that the remarriage chances have increased over time for the males, whether divorced or widowed. The only exceptions are provided by the age-groups 20-24 and 35-39 for the widowed males. But interestingly enough, the changes in the chances of remarriage for females are not one-sided in direction. In the case of widowed females the remarriage chances have declined for almost every age group. But for divorced females, the remarriage chances have increased for ages 35 and above, while they have declined for ages less than 35. These results are rather surprising. With the present state of our knowledge, we are unable to account for these declining probabilities of remarriage for young females.

Now we look at the other indicator, viz. the expected number of years of stay in divorced or widowed state before remarriage. These are shown in Table 4.

Table 4. Expected Years of Stay in Divorced/ Widowed State Before Remarriage

	DIVORCED				WIDOWED			
	Male		Female		Male		Female	
Age	1961	1966	1961	1966	1961	1966	1961	1966
20	6.1	3.6	9.7	10.7	5.5	6.1	8.0	8.5
25	7.6	3.5	17.5	18.5	3.9	4.6	12.9	14.6
30	12.9	8.5	25.1	24.3	7.1	6.3	17.9	21.0
40	23.1	19.7	31.0	29.5	13.7	11.2	25.6	26.0
60	21.7	18.2	19.4	19.3	14.8	14.3	14.5	18.7
70	9.9	9.7	10.0	9.9	9.3	9.1	9.9	9.9

(Source: Tables prepared by the authors)

Our earlier analysis is reinforced by this indicator. The expected stay for males in divorced state has sharply declined. The widowed males have to tell the same story, but there is a small increase in expected stay for the first two age-groups. The females, whether widowed or divorced, on an average, have to wait longer to get married.

A PLAUSIBLE EXPLANATION FOR THE CANADIAN PATTERN

An attempt is being made in this section to explain at least partially the Canadian pattern of remarriage of the widowed and the divorced females. It is conjectured that the Canadian pattern is different from that in the U.S. on account of: (a) higher incidence of Catholicism, (b) unfavorable distribution with regard to availability of partners, and (c) combination of both of the above factors.

According to a current population survey estimate (U.S. Bureau of Commerce, 1969), about 25.7 per cent of the population in the United States are

Table 5. Index Numbers of Remarriage Rates of Divorced and Widowed
Females: Canada and Provinces, 1961

Province	INDEX NUMBERS OF RE-MARRIAGE RATES FOR FEMALES		PER CENT POPULATION CATHOLIC
	Divorced	Widowed	
Quebec	100	100	88.2
Nfld.	149	104	35.7
P.E.I.	129	72	46.1
N.S.	174	92	35.4
N.B.	255	109	52.0
Ont.	180	114	30.8
Man.	178	107	29.2
Sask.	146	91	30.0
Alta.	235	149	25.0
B.C.	193	136	17.9
CANADA	180	112	46.8

(Source: Computed from D.B.S. data)

Catholics, while in Canada the 1961 Census enumeration showed the Catholic component of the population as 46.8 per cent. The attitude of the
Catholic Church toward divorce is well known and needs no documentation.
To see the effect of the adherence of a population to Catholic teachings,
it will be worthwhile to look at the situation in the different Canadian provinces. Index numbers of remarriage rates of divorced females in 1961 taking
Quebec as the base (Quebec value = 100) along with the per cent population Catholic in the provinces are shown in Table 5.

It is clear from the above Table that larger the share of Catholics in a
province, lower the remarriage rate for divorced females. Index numbers of
remarriage rates for widowed females, shown also in Table 5, do not reveal
such a negative association with the Catholic component in the population.
Thus there is strong evidence to infer that the high degree of adherence to
Catholicism and Catholic teachings is one of the factors responsible for low
remarriage rates among divorcees in Canada.

The imbalance in the distribution of males and females in the marriage
market adds, it seems to us, to this unfair situation. If the like marry the
like, we can expect a good proportion of divorced females marrying divorced
males and vice versa. This would ensure greater chances of remarriage for
the divorcees. If some factors such as religious proscription prevent divorced
males marrying divorced females, the former may go for marrying single
or widowed females creating a vacuum of potential like-partners for the di-

vorced females resulting in imbalanced   distribution and less remarriage
chances. The divorcees will then have to seek partners from either single or
widowed males. Schlesinger's (1970) findings confirm this point.

Now let us look at the per cent distribution of brides' by the marital status
categories of their grooms for the years 1961, 1966, and 1970 (Table 6).

Table 6. Per Cent Distribution of Brides by Marital Status of Grooms: Canada, 1961,
1966, and 1970

MARITAL STATUS OF BRIDES

		Single			Widowed Per Cent Distribution			Divorced		
		1961	1966	1970	1961	1966	1970	1961	1966	1970
MARITAL	Single	95.8	95.6	94.6	38.6	34.5	28.8	60.9	55.6	58.7
STATUS	Widowed	1.7	1.3	1.0	50.2	52.1	48.8	11.4	10.7	0.9
OF	Divorced	2.5	3.1	4.4	11.2	13.4	22.4	27.7	33.7	40.4
GROOMS	Total	100.0	100.0	100.0	100.0	100.0	100.0	100.0	100.0	100.0

(Source: Computed from D.B.S. data)

A perusal of Table 6 reveals that the like marrying the like is true for
single and widowed females in the span 1961-1970. But divorced females,
during this period and particularly in 1961-1966, took their partners mostly
from single males. This means that they had to compete with single females,
who stood always better chances, in the marriage market resulting in probably high selectivity. This could have lowered the remarriage chances of
the divorcee population as a whole. It is important to note that the distributions of divorced brides by the marital status categories of grooms are under-
going shifts in this time span. The shifts in single and widowed female distributions are rather small. The 1970 distribution reveals that 40.4 per cent
of the grooms is divorced males while the share of single males is 58.7 per
cent, with the widowed males being phased out of the scene. The implication is that the marriage market is becoming favourable to divorced females.
In view of this, we can expect an increase in remarriage rates and a decrease in waiting time before marriage for divorcees in Canada in the future.

CONCLUSIONS

We can make broadly the following conclusions:

(1)   Remarriage patterns are changing over time.

(2)   The changing remarriage patterns are favourable to men and not to women now.

(3)   The shifting distributions of divorced brides with respect to the marital status of grooms reveal that the marriage market is likely to become favourable to divorced females in the future.

REFERENCES

Barclay, G.W.
1958   Techniques of Population Analysis. New York: John Wiley and Sons.
Bogue, D.J.
1969   Principles of Demography. New York: John Wiley and Sons.
Carter, H.
1965   Recent changes in remarriage of women of child bearing age in the United States. Paper presented at the World Population Conference, Belgrade.
Charles, E.
1941   The nuptiality problem with special reference to Canadian marriage statistics. Canadian Journal of Economics and Political Science 7: 447-465.
Dominion Bureau of Statistics
1972   Vital Statistics 1970. Ottawa: Queen's Printer.
1968a   1966 Census of Canada. Marital Status by Age Group and Sex. Catalogue No. 92-613. Ottawa: Queen's Printer.
1968b   Vital Statistics 1966. Ottawa: Queen's Printer.
1963a   1961 Census of Canada, Population, Marital Status by Age Groups Bulletin 1.3-1. Ottawa: Queen's Printer.
1963b   Vital Statistics 1961. Ottawa: Queen's Printer.
Grabill, W.H.
1945   Attrition life tables for the single population. Journal of the American Statistical Association 40: 364-375.
Jacobson, P.H.
1959   American Marriage and Divorce. New York: Rinehart and Company.
Jones, J.P.
1962   Remarriage Tables based on experience under O.A.S.D.I. and U.S. Employees Compensation Systems: Social Security Administration Actuarial Study No. 55. Washington, D.C.: U.S. Department of Health, Education and Welfare.
Krishnan, P.
1971   Divorce tables for females in the United States, 1960. Journal of Marriage and the Family 33: 318-320.
Laing, L., and P. Krishnan
1972   First-marriage decrement tables for males and females in Canada, 1961-66. Paper presented at the annual meetings of the Canadian Sociology and Anthropology Association, Montreal.
McGinnis, R.
1968   A stochastic model of social mobility. American Sociological Review 35: 712-722.
Mertens, W.
1965   Methodological aspects of the construction of nuptiality tables. Demography 2: 319-348.

New Zealand Department of Statistics, 1970. New Zealand: Widowhood and remarriage of
        widows, 1965-67. Wellington: Government Printer-Abstract in Population Index
        37, 110.
Saveland, W., and P.C. Glick
    1969   First-marriage decrement tables by color and sex for the United States in 1958-
                60. Demography 6: 243-260.
Schlesinger, B.
    1970   Remarriage as family reorganization for divorced persons — a Canadian study.
                Journal of Comparative Family Studies 1: 101-118.
U.S. Bureau of Commerce
    1969   Statistical Abstract of the United States 1969. Washington, D.C.: U.S. Bureau
                of Commerce.

Remarriage as Family Reorganization
for Divorced Persons
—A Canadian Study

BENJAMIN SCHLESINGER*

Very little attention has been paid by family sociology to the Institution of Remarriage in North America. The available published studies have been annotated by Schlesinger (1969: 104 - 106), and a summary of findings of American studies related to the topic has been reviewed by the same author (Schlesinger, 1968). A search of family studies in Canada (Elkin, 1964; Vanier Institute of the Family, 1967), has not been able to discover one study on Remarriage. An analysis of remarriage rates in Canada up to 1964 has been completed by Schlesinger and Macrae (1970).

Remarriage is a social institution; that is, it is an established pattern of operating which serves both public and private interests in an orderly, accepted, enduring way. In Western society the nuclear family predominates, and marriage, the recognized union of husband and wife, constitutes its foundation. The changes which inhere in our age of acceleration demand that human beings and the structures which they create adjust and accommodate themselves. The modern family unit derives its sustenance and stability from the love and satisfaction of its members. Consequently, family living is more tenuous, more problematic, more significant. Finally, as an institution which serves both human and social needs, remarriage manifests basic similarities to marriage, and as a specialized form of marriage it possesses its own constructs, characteristics and possibilities. A remarriage contains a valuable combination: the reality of a disruption of some kind and degree, and an attempt at reorganization. In short, as one of several solutions to family breakdown, it warrants examination per se.

The phenomenon of remarriage cannot be simplified; those persons who are remarried are not easily classified or categorized. We realize that there are eight types of remarriage:

1) divorced man remarried to a single woman
2) divorced man remarried to a widowed woman
3) divorced man remarried to a divorced woman
4) single man remarried to a divorced woman

---

*Professor, School of Social Work, University of Toronto, Toronto, Canada.

TABLE I

MARITAL STATUS OF BRIDEGROOMS, BY MARITAL STATUS OF BRIDES
CANADA — 1950-1964

Year	Total marriages	Marriages between												
		Bachelors				Widowers				Divorcees			
		Total	Spinsters	Widows	Divorcees	Total	Spinsters	Widows	Divorcees	Total	Spinsters	Widows	Divorcees
1950	125,083	113,880	108,319	2,834	2,727	6,463	2,886	3,090	487	4,740	3,176	524	1,040
1951	128,408	117,567	112,152	2,834	2,581	6,474	2,818	3,154	502	4,367	2,871	490	1,006
1952	128,474	117,361	111,847	2,768	2,746	6,518	2,762	3,246	510	4,595	2,912	540	1,143
1953	131,034	119,844	114,269	2,700	2,875	6,432	2,645	3,280	507	4,758	2,966	603	1,189
1954	128,629	117,688	112,090	2,646	2,952	6,228	2,504	3,229	495	4,713	2,938	603	1,172
1955	128,029	117,403	111,833	2,537	3,033	6,019	2,374	3,118	527	4,607	2,872	598	1,137
1956	132,713	122,032	116,430	2,618	2,984	5,847	2,233	3,077	537	4,834	2,922	654	1,258
1957	133,186	122,437	116,844	2,491	3,102	5,700	2,230	3,002	468	5,049	3,052	631	1,366
1958	131,525	120,957	115,234	2,538	3,185	5,696	2,112	3,065	519	4,872	2,966	625	1,281
1959	132,474	121,367	115,760	2,439	3,168	5,892	2,088	3,211	593	5,215	3,111	680	1,424
1960	130,338	119,449	113,801	2,506	3,142	5,771	2,022	3,217	532	5,118	3,013	662	1,443
1961	128,475	117,597	112,089	2,505	3,003	5,816	1,993	3,258	565	5,062	2,963	732	1,367
1962	129,381	118,508	113,117	2,386	3,005	5,651	1,887	3,206	558	5,222	2,974	763	1,485
1963	131,111	119,884	114,357	2,437	3,090	5,771	1,858	3,313	600	5,456	3,020	752	1,684
1964	138,135	126,272	120,604	2,424	3,244	5,818	1,863	3,382	573	6,045	3,367	851	1,827

5) single man remarried to a widowed woman
6) widowed man remarried to a single woman
7) widowed man remarried to a widowed woman
8) widowed man remarried to a divorced woman

Further variations occur in terms of a union which involved children:

1) father, father's own children and new mother
2) mother, mother's own children and new father
3) father, father's own children and mother, mother's own children.

These combinations are increased if the spouses have children after their second marriage.

CANADIAN STATISTICS

The effect of the lack of studies in Canada on remarriage is felt particularly in the area of statistical knowledge. The sources are limited. Probably the most comprehensive study ever published in Canada appeared in 1967 under the aegis of the Dominion Bureau of Statistics (1967). This report provides basic data on marriage extending from 1921 to 1964 for all of Canada. The number of marriages annually, crude marriage rates, average age for brides and bridegrooms, nationally and by provinces, are included. The report also provides an analysis of marital status, religious denomination, age and sex for the years 1950 to 1964.

The statistical picture of the remarriage rate in Canada can best be viewed in the context of the total marriage situation as illustrated in Table I.

In this period, an average of 13.1 percent of all marriages were *remarriages*. Table I shows that nationally, bachelors tended to marry divorced women more than widows. The trend of the former after 1952 is upward from 2.18 percent (2,727) in 1950, to a high of 2.34 percent (3,244) in 1964. The average per year was 2.29 percent. Marriages of bachelors and widows decreased over the period from 2,834 in 1950 and 1951 (2.26 percent) to 2,424 in 1964. The yearly average was 1.97 percent.

Widowed men tended to wed widows in this period. A slight increase is noted from 1950 (3,090) to 1964 (3,382), averaging at 2.44 percent of total marriages per year. Widowers' second choice were single women. There is a general decline in the number of these marriags from a high of 2.3 percent (2,886) to 1.34 percent (1,863). The average is 2 percent. The marriages of widowers and divorced women remained less than one half of one percent in any one year and averaged .4 percent. The low occurred in 1951 (468), the high in 1963 (600).

Divorced men in this period chose single women in preference to both widows and divorced women; i.e., the number of these divorced - single unions in any one year was greater than the total of the other two. The rate of remarriage for the first category remained approximately 3,000 per year, averaging at 2.3 percent, the high occurring in 1964 (3,367). Divorced women were second choices, averaging one percent per year. An upward trend is noted from 1,040 (1950) to 1,827 (1964). Marriages of divorced men and widows accounted for slightly less than one half of one percent of the total number of marriages, on the average, per year.

TABLE II

AVERAGE RATE OF REMARRIAGE IN PERCENT FORM OF TOTAL MARRIAGES BY MARITAL STATUS OF BRIDEGROOMS AND BRIDES CANADA 1950-1964

Men	Women		
	Single	Widowed	Divorced
Single		2.0	2.3
Widowed	2.0	2.4	.4
Divorced	2.3	.5	1.0

In terms of the remarriage picture alone, Table III gives the average percentage of the various combinations of remarriage in the period under discussion.

TABLE III

AVERAGE RATE OF REMARRIAGE IN PERCENTAGE FORM AMONG REMARRIED MEN AND WOMEN BY MARITAL STATUS CANADA 1950-1964

Men	Women		
	Single	Widowed	Divorced
Single		15.5	18.1
Widowed	13.8	19.1	3.1
Divorced	18.1	3.8	8.0

In summary, then, in 87 out of every 100 marriages in Canada during 1950 - 1964, both brides and grooms were single. Widowers tended to marry widows and divorced men tended to marry single women, while divorced women tended to marry single men. In each year in approximately 35 percent of all marriages involving a widowed person, the partner selected was also widowed. Similarly, in each year throughout the period under examination, approximately 60 percent of each of the divorced men and women selected a single partner for their remarriage. An overall view shows that single brides comprised 91.5 percent of all brides, on the average, during 1950 - 64; widows, with 4.9 percent; and divorcees, with 3.6 percent accounted for the remainder of the brides. The situation has been much the same for bridegrooms during this period;

single bridegrooms comprised 91.6 percent of all bridegrooms while widowers and divorcees, with 4.6 percent and 3.8 percent respectively, accounted for the remainder of the bridegrooms.

THE SAMPLE

In 1968 we conducted a study of 96 couples (192 persons) in Metropolitan Toronto, Canada[1]. Table IV contains a breakdown of the marital composition of our sample. In selecting our sample we asked that at least one of the partners should have been married previously.

Our sample was white, predominantly Protestant, and middle class in terms of income, education and housing. We obtained our sample by advertising in the major daily newspapers, and realize that this fact presents us with a major limitation of our study. However, we feel that the findings are still pertinent and consider the study an exploratory one, which will hopefully lead to further investigations. Each couple was visited by two interviewers, who saw the husband and wife separately. Information was obtained by using a structural interview schedule which contained a selected number of open - ended questions. Table V contains the marital status of husbands and wives in their second union.

TABLE IV
MARITAL COMPOSITION OF COUPLES WHO REMARRIED

Male	Female	Total
Widowed	Divorced	5
Widowed	Widowed	6
Single	Divorced	23
Single	Widowed	8
Divorced	Single	16
Divorced	Divorced	20
Divorced	Widowed	6
Widowed	Single	12
TOTAL		96

TABLE V
MARITAL STATUS OF HUSBANDS AND WIVES AT TIME OF REMARRIAGE

	Husband	Wives	TOTAL	Percentage
Single	31	28	59	31
Divorced	42	48	90	47
Widowed	23	20	43	22
TOTAL	96	96	192	100

[1]The research group included: Judith Bamiling, Edythe Jacobson, Jewell Lanterman, Alex Macrae, Brendon Montgomery, Dee Osachoff, Elizabeth Smith and Eugene Stasiuk.

Thirty - one percent of the sample were single at the time of remarriage. Of these, 53% were male and 47% were female. Among the 47% previously divorced, 47% were male and 53% were female. Twenty - one percent of the sample were widowed at the time of remarriage, of which 53% were male and 47% were female.

THE DIVORCED IN REMARRIAGE

Among the 70 couples which contained at least one divorced person, there were 42 males and 48 females who were divorced. At the time of our study, the divorced persons had been married for the second time on the average of 5 years. The males had been married on the average of 11 years during their first marriage and the females averaged 8.5 years during their first union. The average lapse between the final divorce decree and the second marriage was two years for both males and females. At the time of remarriage our males were on the average 36.5 years old and our females 33.5 years old.[2] The divorced males brought 10 children into the second union, while the divorced females brought 42 children to their second marriage. A breakdown of sex of these children indicated 22 boys and 30 girls. Sixty children were born into the second marriage to couples which contained at least one divorced spouse. In examining remarriage patterns of the divorced persons we found that on the average the youngest divorced males and females tended to marry a single person the second time, the eldest remarried widowed people, and those in the middle tended to choose divorced spouses. The male who remarried a single person was, on the average, 11 years younger than the male who remarried a widowed person. For females the average age gap was 6.5 years.

FINDINGS

We will present a selected number of findings related to the divorced in remarriage.

Forty - five percent of the divorced males and 43% of the divorced females in our sample had been indirectly involved in marital separation or divorce in their family of orientation. Fifty percent of the sample had parents or siblings who had been remarried at least once. Thus, nearly one half of the sample had experience with family disorganization and reorganization. This finding raises the question of whether people from divorced homes conceive of marriage as being an explosive and temporary arrangement, whether they have learned that marriage is chaotic by nature. It is in this area, perhaps, that our finding that divorced women tend to marry divorced men is significant. Why do they not remarry single men? This perpetuation of life style by divorced people, particularly by females, is worthy of study.

---

[2]Average age of first marriage in Canada in 1964: Females — 24.5 years, Males — 27.3 years.

We asked our sample whether they had experienced any lowering of self - esteem or status in the community as the result of their divorce. On the part of the males, 17 of the 41 who answered (41.5%) said they had; of these, 6 answered "yes" to both loss of self - esteem and status, giving us a total of 23 answers. Six males experienced loss of self - esteem only, and 11 males only felt a loss in community status.

There were 26 "yes" answers for the females (56.5%); 9 females felt a loss in self-esteem only, 17 females experienced a loss in community status only, and 8 females answered "yes" to both. Those who said that their self - esteem had been lowered because of the divorce most often explained their feelings in terms of guilt and failure. One male said, "You feel guilty when you can't talk about your past in the presence of others." Another male talked of the "sense of failure I felt." A female subject said, "You feel like a complete failure; it was a real blow to my self-esteem". Another female spoke of how she "felt very ashamed, even degraded". The subjects who spoke of feeling their social status lowered generally were more verbal. A thread of bitterness runs through most answers. One of the male respondents said, "You have to move out of your old circle of friends because of detrimental remarks and unbased opinions". Another male said, "My parents wouldn't talk to me after the divorce", while a third male explained, "My business and social life were disrupted. I was discredited by the Church and nearly everyone else except my immediate relatives".

On the whole, the females were more expressive than the males in answering this question, and they frequently mentioned the myth that still seems to surround the divorcee. One woman answered, "A divorcee is assumed to be going to bed with every man she dates, and most men she dates assume she will go to bed. Some former married women friends now consider you a threat to their home; and when a married man friend, within a week of your divorce, presents himself at your door to proposition you, you *know* without a doubt that your status has been lowered to that of sexual opportunist". Another woman said, "A divorced woman in this community (Toronto) is not accepted socially, not even after three and a half years of successful remarriage." Finally, a female replied, "Community attitudes to a divorcee are still old - fashioned. It was almost as if I were a leper". For those who felt neither a loss in self - esteem nor in social status, the following are representative answers. One male said, "I consider it a part of growing up, unfortunate, but a fact". A couple of females felt just the opposite to what the people quoted above felt. One said, "I felt like a marked woman while I was married, because of my spouse's behaviour, but not after. I felt better at having divorced him". Thus, slightly less than one - half of the males and slightly more than one - half of the females in our sample felt that their self - esteem and/or their status in the community had been lowered as a result of divorce.

We asked our sample whether they had looked for the same or different qualities in their second mates as those possessed by their first mates. Both males and females who wanted different qualities emphasized the following attributes as those desired: higher intelligence in new mate than in old (more males looked for this factor than females), emotional maturity, greater sense of responsibility, deeper sense of affection and understanding, desire on the part of new mate to have children (more males looked for this than females), greater similarity in background encompassing mutual values and interests, and a deeper sense of integrity and self-respect. Slightly over one - half of the males and more than three - quarters of the females felt that the reasons for the breakup of the first marriage influenced their selection of a second mate. What was overtly implied by these respondents is that they see themselves as having learned something from the experience of the marriage breakdown and divorce, and that they have been able to channel this knowledge into a maturing episode rather than a destructive one. Only one male and one female looked for qualities in their second mate similar to those possessed by the first mate. This reinforces the observation that the subjects not only avoided making the same mistake, and were more cautious the second time, but it also partially shatters the publicly - held belief that divorced persons tend to remarry the same type of person. Furthermore, when asked whether they compare spouses, most replied that they did not because there was no basis for comparison. Those who did almost invariably said their present spouse rated favourably. This seems to be further evidence that divorced people tend not to remarry the same type of person and that they are not unhappy in remarriage.

We asked the subjects whether they approached their second marriage with the same attitudes as they did the first. The reasons given for their approach to second marriages revolve around three main themes: being more cautious the second time; being more mature as the result of experiences in first marriage; and the pressing need to make the second marriage successful. One man said, "I approached my second marriage more carefully; I was determined to compromise and avoid pitfalls." Another male answered, "I learned how to meet problems in my first marriage and this helped me lose the idealism I had about marriage. I came prepared to put a big effort into making this one work". A third male, addressing himself to the need to make his remarriage successful, said, "I had the feeling that I must make this one work or I'd lose my self - respect. A second failure would be disastrous in my own self - opinion". A few women explained their increased maturity in remarriage by saying they saw their first union as a "challenge" or "adventure", but now, as one woman said, "I am more realistic, not so influenced by surface features like good looks or sensuousness. I've also tried to keep the mystery in this marriage by always making myself look good". One female said that the basis for her difference in approach to remarriage was that, "I had two children, so I was looking for a father". Representative of the males who approached remarriage with the same attitudes as they did the first was the man who said, "I think I approached the second a bit wiser, but not with a different attitude". One female replied, "I'm childish enough to have thought love and companionship important both times". The overall picture is one of changed attitudes on the part of those who remarry.

The most common reply by both males and females to the question "Why did you decide to remarry"? was "needed or found love". Eight women listed both "preference for family life" and "companionship". Although it was the most popular response of the males, "needed or found love" received the nod of only one man more than the second most numerous response, "preference for family life". The reason "I found the right mate" was the third most numerous explanation. Other responses were: A need for security (four times as many males as females), a liking for the institution of marriage, loneliness, to provide a parent for children (5 females, no males), convenience, and for social life. In conclusion, the reasons given by the males and females for remarrying were very similar. The most prominent reason was the same for both sexes, while the second and third most frequent reasons for the females were the third and second reasons for the males.

The advice given by our sample to divorced persons who are planning to remarry is extensive and covers a wide area. Generally, there is agreement, but there are contradictions as well. Many males and females emphasized the necessity of being more cautious and less intuitive when planning remarriage. One of our males said, "Take your time in selecting a new partner. Be sure of yourself. Don't be led by false feelings; analyze yourself, and be sure you didn't cause the problem in your first marriage and might do the same again". Another male replied, "First, you have to know the person well. Also, after a disaster in the first marriage, you must work hard to accept the person's faults to have a successful marriage". A female answered, "Find out why your first marriage was unsuccessful. Don't marry on the rebound or because you have to prove you can get another husband. Think it over, give it a lot of calm and rational consideration, and don't do the same wrong things again". More respondents felt that first marriages should not be discussed between partners, or even thought of, than felt they should be. One female advised, "Never refer to your first marriage and don't compare your spouses; be lenient, don't expect perfection, have a sense of humour and don't take things too seriously". A male said, "Don't let your first marital experience get into your new marriage. Don't compare; make it a new life". However, another male offered just the opposite advice: "Don't be afraid to discuss first marriage — no skeletons in the closet makes it more healthy". One woman's advice, representative of a number of people, was, "They should live with each other before getting married; at least get the sex thing straightened around so there is more to the relationship than that". Among other various types of responses there runs the theme of "be realistic, don't expect miracles". Finally, two opposing replies, one optimistic, the other pessimistic. One male said, "My advice is don't be afraid to remarry — one failure doesn't mean at all that your second marriage won't work". Another gentleman advised, however, "Don't remarry! We've been lucky and it's very hard work. Most people probably couldn't do it — there's little chance of success for most people because a marriage relationship is too close and intense for most people".

We wondered if those in our divorced sample felt more self - conscious in remarriage than they did in their first marriage. Only 10 males and 15 females felt more self -conscious. One gentleman said, "I don't want to make any mistakes like I did before, so I watch myself carefully. I try to think before speaking and acting". One of the females answered, "I'm trying not to make whatever mistakes I made in my first marriage. I'm more on my guard so that I don't do something stupid. Therefore, I am more uneasy". Another woman explained, "sometimes when friends talk about someone, they refer to her as 'well, she was divorced anyway', and I feel uncomfortable". The majority, those who did not feel more self - conscious, tended to refer to the first marriage as the uncomfortable one. A male replied, "I feel more confident in this marriage, I feel more mature". One of the females said, "I feel that I am myself now, proudly a woman. In the first marriage I felt like a nonentity". Most of our respondents, therefore, felt less self - conscious in remarriage than they did in their first marriage.

Somewhat less than half of the male sample (40%) and slightly more than half of the female sample (51.1%) felt that their sexual experience in the first marriage influenced their sexual adjustment in remarriage. Most of these people (13 of the 16 males and 18 of the 23 females) felt that the influence was of a positive or maturing nature. One man said, "Since the breakdown of my first marriage, I have a more mature outlook towards sex and more consideration for my partner". Another man replied, "The more experienced you are, the more you enjoy it". One of the females explained, "I was very inexperienced when I first got married, but this time I knew more about what to expect — both from my husband and from myself. I wasn't as nervous". A second female said, "It's easier to spot problems before they develop now, and I know how to keep a loving relationship going". For the subjects who felt that the sexual experience of the first marriage had been detrimental to their sexual adjustment in remarriage, the following quotes are representative of how they answered this question. A male said, "My first wife's infidelity upset my values and threw my self - confidence into doubt, and I'm only now getting normally aggressive again." Another male replied, "After a number of years of mating with the 'wrong' spouse, one's responses are altered. I'm slowly beginning to readjust." A female answered, "I didn't have a good sexual experience with my first husband, so my spouse (present) had to convince me and show me how to enjoy myself". Another female said, "I wasn't too happy with my first husband, and this made it hard for me in this marriage. I was scared, and felt, at that time, that I could do without sex in my marriage".

Faced with the question, "What advice would you give someone who plans to remarry in the area of sexual adjustment". A great number of subjects replied that they would advise that the couple sleep together beforehand. One female said, "Have pre - marital relations to find out whether you like each other's skin, temperament, emotional temperature, and attractiveness". A male replied, "Sleep with everyone you can. Try to experience many relationships — you learn skills and learn about yourself and what you can offer in order to please". A large number of people also advised that a person planning to remarry should simply enjoy the sex to come. One female said, "Relax and enjoy it," while another advised, "Don't be afraid of it; if you love somebody enough, it will work out without any problem". Other suggestions included advice to please your spouse as much as possible, to try and forget about past upsetting experiences, and to be realistic, i.e. not expecting the ideal in sex.

An impressive majority of the sample — 85.7% of the males and 81.3% of the females — felt that their present marriage meets their expectations of marriage "very satisfactorily". Four males and 5 females felt their marriage rated as "satisfactory" while 2 males (4.8% of the males) and 4 females (8.3% of the females) felt their marriage was "unsatisfactory" in terms of meeting their expectations of marriage. One male explained that the success of his marriage was partly due to the fact that he was made to feel like an individual, like a person. "It has love, respect and consideration". Another male replied, "I deeply believe in our marriage. We find comfort in each other in adversity, but it isn't adversity that's kept us together". A male who rated his remarriage as unsuccessfully meeting his expectations of marriage said, "Our intellectual rapport is not good; I enact in life while my wife reacts". A female who rated her marriage as "very satisfactory" explained, "We love doing things together; we sense what each other feels and we meet each other's needs". Another woman referred to the little things that she didn't have before, "like security, regularity, dependability, so they seem extra important now". A woman who rated her marriage as "unsatisfactory" referred to the conflict between her spouse and the child of her first marriage — "he thinks I place the child first and him second and he's never really accepted her".

The subjects were asked what advice they could give to people who were planning to remarry about the involvement of friends, relations, and parents in the planning. Only a very small proportion of the sample felt that the opinions and advice of friends and family should be heeded. The vast majority stated, usually in strong terms, that any such advice should be dismissed or ignored. The following answers were given by those who favoured listening and responding to such advice. One man said, "Listen to them and try to come to an objective conclusion". Another male advised, "Seek the advice of honest friends and take it seriously. Consider their social, political and medical aspects". One female said, "Parents and families have an important effect on marriage, and this must be sorted. Friends also influence your life and activities, so consider this carefully and be aware of the effect this will have." For the majority who favoured ignoring the involvement and advice of others in planning to remarry, the type of things they said are as follows. One male said, "Keep away from them because marriage has the greatest chance of success with total separation; you have enough problems without their contradictory advice". Another male replied, "Be as realistic as possible regarding expected results for you and your children, and disregard almost all outside influences". More advice along this vein came from the man who said, "Stay away from the whole lot of them and tell them to mind their own business. They mean well, but they can only confuse everything. It's your life, and it's a decision only you can make." Similarly, one female replied, "The couple should make the decisions themselves because it's their lives. You're alone with your problems, and although they may be very sympathetic, you have to live with your decision".

A very significant finding is that only 6 people felt that their remarriage did not satisfactorily meet their expectations of marriage. Previous reports on the success of remarriages have ranged from statements to the effect that remarriages do not work out to hesitant suggestions that perhaps they are as successful as marriages. The unknown element in the present study is the possibility that remarried couples who are not happy did not volunteer to have interviewers come in and stir up the already muddy waters; however, some couples did participate for the express hope of finding help, and this indicates that the assumption must not be entirely true. In short, then, a pronounced majority of the respondents (more males than females) felt that their attitudes to marriage were favourable after divorce.

The replies of most of our respondents to the question, "What would you say are the most important components of a successful marriage?" can be classified into ten categories. They are understanding, tolerance, patience and compassion; financial security; maturity; good communication; honesty, sharing problems and showing feelings; compatibility and complimentarity; a good sexual relationship; love; common interests, goals, attitudes, beliefs; mutual respect. Some of the answers are quite interesting. A female said, "A couple should be honest with each other; in the second marriage one may recognize danger points and things should be talked out before they become magnified". Another woman explained, "Mutual appreciation of individual differences which will contribute to confidence in and for each other must exist. You must be sure you want a relationship and find enjoyment from it. Have some perspective of the relationship in terms of its workability and value in small things. You must have relative, not absolute, values". A male said the components were "the same as for first marriage. In remarriage, though, you have a better chance of knowing why you're getting married. Make sure you've learned from your previous experiences; be able to answer the question, 'What makes me think this will be better than the last one?"

Another male referred to "a desire to be married rather than single, and a strong belief that marriage between the right partners, under reasonable circumstances, can be the most satisfactory mode of living, despite previous problems".

By far the most salient finding of a review of the literature on Remarriage is the dearth of scientific studies and material. The only extensive study of Remarriage in the United States was undertaken by Jessie Bernard, (1956) and that was more than a decade ago. Other references usually relate only to statistical analyses; the *International Bibliogrphy of Research in Marriage and the Family* (Aldous and Hill, 1967) lists only 19 items directly related to Remarriage, and of these, 6 are statistical items. In Canada, where about 13% of all marriages are remarriages on the average, there has never been a study on Remarriage, and consequently, Canadian literature on the subject is meagre. In spite of the inadequacy of research in this area, however, Remarriage has indeed received some literary attention. It is axiomatic, though, that most writings concentrate on divorce and widowhood and seem to deal with Remarriage as only one of a number of possible "solutions" to the tribulations of these unfortunate conditions. The lack of objective studies in this field may partially explain why a number of the publications reflect the findings and feelings of the authors' professional experiences in Social Service Agencies. This raises the question of whether those remarried couples who do not seek professional help, and thus are assumed to be relatively happy in their Remarriages, are even considered in the literature, or whether the reader is exposed to only those who are in trouble. This surely would be further evidence that the behavioural sciences seem to be almost exclusively concerned with abnormal behaviour.

Depending upon the individual situation, the process of divorce may constitute a cataclysmic juncture or merely serve as legal notice of an already long - since defunct marriage. Regardless of the degree of consent of the two partners for divorce, however," . . . there are religious conflicts, unrealistic legal requirements, implications of blame and wrong - doing, and widespread evasion of the law . . .". (Schwartz, 1968: 215). After any crisis which produces a significant fundamental change in one's condition of life, the problem of reintegration becomes acute. Willard Waller, in his book, *The Old Love and The New*, (Waller, 1967), discussed six major problem areas requiring reintegration for the divorced person. Of these, the resolution of personality conflicts resulting from the general upheaval of the divorce's world seems the most peculiar to divorce. Waller sees the act of divorce as such a blow to one's pride, and feels that there are so many things to avoid if one is to assimilate a divorce in a healthy manner that ". . . one who succeeds in working out a thoroughly sane adjustment finds himself in select company." (Waller, 1967: 297). However, there are indications that the widowed person must also undertake personality reorganization. A study of twelve widowed and divorced women was conducted by Ilgenfritz at the Guidance

Center of New Rochelle in Westchester County, New York, in 1958, (Ilgenfritz, 1961). She found the most common problems to be fear of loneliness, practical problems of living, specific concerns about their children, concern for their loss of self - esteem as women, and hostility towards men who considered them "fair game". The over - riding problem was that of loneliness, which is the result of role disturbance, and the more specialized the roles of a person in marriage, the greater the disturbance. The feelings of failure and self-depreciation are most prominent in the divorced person, but the widowed may experience feelings of guilt as well. All writers emphasize the impact of grief upon the widowed person and it is this acute response to deprivation that probably distinguishes widowhood from divorce more than any other single reaction.

Out of all this, however, and in contradiction to Waller's belief that adjustment is nigh - well impossible, M. H. Hunt, in his book, *The World of the Formerly Married,* (Hunt, 1966), presents a more optimistic viewpoint. He feels that this period of crisis may trigger health - producing mechanisms, personality growth and re-organization. The formerly married person can become galvanized, aware of his power to survive, to experience grief, but move toward re-adjustment. Whether a formerly married person should seek professional assistance in coping with his adjustment difficulties and/or his plans for remarriage is a matter of increasing concern. Goode found that only a minority of the divorced women in his study received help along the lines of marital counselling (Goode, 1956), and that Roman Catholics and those of a median amount of education were most likely to have obtained it. From all appearances, it would seem that the divorced person occupies an awkward position in our society. One American author refers to ". . . the somewhat confused, contradictory, double - bind messages it gives to its members." (Schwartz, 1968: 215). What she refers to is that although divorce is widespread and has lost the taboo it had even two generations ago, it is doubtful that our feelings and thoughts have kept up with the realities of our behaviour. Thus, lip - service is paid to divorce as a means of terminating an unfortunate marital relationship, but the deeper feeling is that "Pure unmarriage . . . is unnatural and has been since the dawn of man", (Egleson and Egleson, 1961: 216), and that by being divorced, a person is somehow a repudiation of this belief. If this is a value of our society, can a formerly married person, divorced or widowed, ultimately feel a sense of worth or social acceptance? Most writers agree that social condemnation contributes to the formerly married's view of himself as a failure, a defective, a selfish and immature person. Countless reports and testimonials refer to the divorced persons' embarrassing experiences at social gatherings where they were the only single person. It seems that the partnered world has yet to form a cohesive set of attitudes toward the divorcee; she may be respected, admired, even envied — but she does not fit snugly into other peoples' private lives. Speculation raises the possibility that the divorcee may be anathema to married couples because she embodies the tensions they are feeling within their own marriage.

Being thus subtly isolated by society, the divorced person must tolerate gossip, but even more difficult, she must cope with the uncomfortable questions of how to act with old friends, her attitude to them and their attitude to her, and what she should tell them. Worthy of note is a finding by Goode that is contradictory to the popular belief that the divorcee encounters a prejudiced society; he found that 70% of the women in his project reported no experience of discrimination against them as divorcees and that fewer people care about the personal traumas and difficulties than was expected, (Goode, 1956: 184). Any change in financial status resulting from change in marital status usually depends upon the role of the deceased or departed person. Where he has been the breadwinner, the remaining spouse may experience a worsening of his economic status. Bitterman found that a second marriage "occasionally" improves the economic standing of the family members, but that usually spending power is decreased, with resulting resentments and frustrations, (Bitterman, 1968:219). In support of this finding, Bernard found the adjustment to the spending of family income in remarriage to be one of the most difficult adjustments the new family has to make, (Bernard, 1956:244).

Péter Marris conducted an Institute of Community Studies survey in the working class district of London's East End. Of the 72 widows studied, 12 had remarried; he concluded that the appeal of remarriage for these widows appeared to be the companionship it offered and in providing a second parent for the children, (Marris, 1958:61). However, Marris did conclude that a remarriage would generally be under a greater strain than the first marriage. He states of remarriage for the widowed, "It restores to them the status, income and companionship that a wife enjoys. But, it is clear from their repudiation of anything more than friendship and companionship, that those who remarried could not commit themselves whole - heartedly to the new relationship, (Marris, 1958:65)." For the remarried divorced person, the most popular point of view seems to be that second marriages most often are a repetition of first marriages, and therefore probably doomed to failure, (Bitterman, 1968:218). It is conceded that mistakes in the first marriage may be corrected in a second marriage if the person has had an opportunity for personal growth and can evaluate the breakdown that occurred in the first marital relationship, although most writers are pessimistic about such probabilities. The less popular, but more adequately researched point of view is exemplified by Bernard and Goode. Bernard concludes her study that remarriages are not less successful than first marriages. She also found that because of differences in the selective processes involved, the remarriages of the widowed seem more successful than those of the divorced, (Bernard, 1956: 108-111). In Goode's study, 87% of the remarried divorced mothers stated that their present life was "much better" than the former and 8% claimed it was a "little better", (Goode, 1956:238).

In the basic nature of the relationships involved, remarriage is like all marriage, but is compounded by its especial characteristics. It is a heterogeneous group, having three major sources of difference within the group:

(1) previous marital status of spouses; (2) presence or absence of children from previous marriage; and (3) significance of first or subsequent marriages. The literature on adjustment falls into three main areas: relationships of the partners with ex-spouses and/or members of the previous families; attitudes in remarriage toward each other; and, adjustment difficulties centering around the children. "Whether the first marriage was terminated by death or divorce, many unresolved feelings are often carried over into the new marriage, by both parents and children," (Bitterman, 1968:218). Divorced persons especially may continue to be somewhat emotionally bound to their former spouse in ways that could be harmful to themselves and their families, particularly if the former spouse does not remarry and if he lives in close proximity to the new family. The difficulties of the formerly widowed relationship to the former spouse largely hinged on community and family affiliation and interaction with the former spouse. The more interaction, the more the new spouse was seen as an intruder in Bernard's study.

Waller feels that the emotional participation of the divorced person in his second marriage depends in large part upon the completeness of the transference which he is able to make to his new mate, and that "Where one has contracted a second marriage without being sufficiently free of the first, the results may well be disastrous," (Waller, 1967:151). This viewpoint is expanded by Bitterman, when she states that although some spouses had come to grips with the causes of the imbalance in the first marriage before they entered the second, the majority appeared to move into the second marriage ". . . almost as impulsively as they had contracted the first," (Bitterman, 1968:218). In other words, the second marriage became part of a continuum rather than a distinct step. Again, it should be remembered that much of what is written about the instability of remarriages comes from professional social work experience rather than from research projects, and that findings may be consequently biased. It also is interesting and characteristic that there is little information concerning widowed courtship time and remarriage relationships.

The establishment of a dynamic equilibrium in remarriages involving children is an important area of adjustment, and has received the most attention. Underlying all adjustments is the crucial task of establishing a new pattern of family relationships that will build toward solidarity within the new family unit. The step-parent is expected to fill a role that is both conducive to the child's sound personality development and, at the same time, compatible with the role of the other parent. How is this to be accomplished? Anne Simon advised the step - father not to try to be a good father so much as a good friend, (Simon, 1964:184). That is, he should not strive to compete with the image the child holds of his biological father, which may be idealistic, for he would stand a good chance of falling short of the child's standards. The crux of the matter is whether or not the step - father is a strong enough individual to adapt himself to the new role he has in the step - famiy, and to act accordingly. Bowerman and

Irish found in their study that step - fathers appear to fare better in comparison with the real fathers than do step - mothers in contrast with mothers in normal homes, in terms of the adjustment of the step-children to the parents, (Bowerman and Irish, 1962). Most authors would seem to agree that the step - mother in particular gets caught in a dichotomy of role in which she is treated as a confidante one day, and an "outsider" the next. This can be confusing for the step - mother, and can create tensions and conflicts. Thomson suggests that the step - mother should attempt to be as honestly pleasant and good to the children as possible without forcing herself to meet demands that are beyond her emotionally, (Thomson, 1966). What seems to be the key issue when there is a new parent in the family is, "Who is the intruder?". The new parent is the intruder for the children, while the children are the intruders for the new marriage. If not handled adequately, this can become the focus of competition within the new family. Jessie Bernard also distinguishes between interpersonal and sociological conflict. Interpersonal conflict can be expressed through favouritism, discipline, material goods or life - values. Sociological conflict exists when a family has not established a we - feeling and the children turn to other ties, (Bernard, 1956:314).

In general, the successful step - parent of a happy remarriage will contribute his share to the functioning of the total family and will baulk at being inveigled into making alliances with certain members of the family to the detriment of the family unit. In the area of child adjustment, the step - child long seems to have borne the stereotypic image of suffering from neglect and cruel treatment, and this concept is perpetuated by findings like that of Thomas P. Monahan which summarize that children of remarriages ". . . seems to show double the rate of early mental illness than in the general population," (Monahan, 1952). However, limited personality testing shows that children of remarried parents have a slightly better than normal score in stability and self - sufficiency, and Bernard concludes that the idea of damage to the child's personality through family disintegration and remarriage may not be as valid as our society thinks. One study concluded that adolescents in broken homes adjust easier to new parents than children in unhappy unbroken homes, (Nye, 1957). Nye also found that reconstructed families, those into which a step - parent had been incorporated, often enhanced the child - parent adjustments. Recent evidence indicates that step - parents are seldom able to attain the same level of affection and degree of closeness with step-children as had the real parents, (Bowerman and Irish, 1962), and that the adjustment of the step - children to their parents is more difficult and at a less harmonious level than is that of the child in a normal home. This is a considerably less distressing finding than that of Monahan. Bowerman and Irish found that children of divorced remarried adults tend to adjust to their step - parents both better and worse than those of parents who had experienced widowhood. It is clear that we have little scientific information available in the area of remarriage. In one way, it is surprising when we balance this against studies in mate selection and marriage. Family sociologists would do well to tap this source in order to obtain valid data in this important area of family life.

CONCLUSIONS:

An exploratory study of 90 divorced persons in second unions has examined some of the characteristics related to remarriage of divorced persons. Selected findings related to personal adjustment in second unions have been presented. The limitations of this study have been noted, in that it is a self-selected sample; however, the findings can be used as a springboard to varied investigations into the neglected field of Remarriage.

REFERENCES:

Aldous, Joan and Reuben Hill, 1967. International Bibliography of Research in Marriage and the Family, 1900-1964. Minneapolis: University of Minnesota Press.

Bernard, Jessie, 1956. Remarriage. New York: Dryden Press.

Bitterman, Catherine M., 1968. "The Multimarriage Family", Social Casework, 49 (April), 218-221.

Bowerman, Charles E., and Donald P. Irish, 1962. "Some Relationships of Stepchildren to their Parents", Marriage and Family Living, 24 (May), 113-121.

Dominion Bureau of Statistics, 1967. Nuptiality 1950-1964. Ottawa: Catalogue No. 84-523.

Egleson, Jim, and Janet Egleson, 1961. Parents Without Partners. New York: E. P. Dutton.

Elkin, Frederick, 1964. The Family in Canada. Ottawa: Vanier Institute of the Family.

Goode, William J., 1956. Women in Divorce. New York: MacMillan C.

Hunt, H. M., 1966. The World of the Formerly Married. New York: McGraw-Hill.

Ilgenfritz, Marjorie, 1961. "Mothers on their Own — Widows & Divorcees", Marriage and Family Living, 23 (February), 38-42.

Marris, Peter, 1958, Widows and Their Families. London: Routledge and Kegan Paul.

Monahan, Thomas P., 1952. "How Stable are Remarriages." American Journal of Sociology, 58 (November), 102-103.

Nye, Ivan, 1957. "Child Adjustment in Broken and in Unhappy Broken Homes", Marriage and Family Living, 19 (November), 356-361.

Schlesinger, B., 1968. "Remarriage: An Inventory of Findings." The Family Coordinator, 17 (October), 248-250.

——, 1969. The One-Parent Family: Perspectives and Annotated Bibliography. Toronto: University of Toronto Press.

Schlesinger, B., and A. Macrae, 1970. "Remarriage in Canada: Statistical Trends." Journal of Marriage and the Family, 32 (May), 300-304.

Simon, Ann, 1964. Step-child in the Family. New York: Odyssey Pres.

Schwartz, Anne C., 1968. "Reflectives on Divorce and Remarriage." Social Casework, 49 (April), 213-217.

Thomson, Helen, 1966. The Successful Step-parent. New York: Harper and Row.

Vanier Institute of the Family, 1967. An Inventory of Family Research and Studies in Canada — 1963-1967. Ottawa: Vanier Institute of the Family.

Waller, Willard, 1967. The Old Love and the New. Carbondale: Southern Illinois University Press.

A Comparison of Mate Selection and Marriage in the First and Second Marriages in a Selected Sample of the Remarried Divorced

JOHN F. PETERS*

Mate selection studies have focused upon the highly eligible first marriageable. The researcher anticipated that the experience of the first marriage and the maturing process would affect mate selection as well as the perception of marriage. The results of the questionnaire, used with a sample of remarried divorced in a medium sized Canadian city, indicate that "parent image" and propinquity are significant in both marriages. Rationalism is higher in the second marriage. Religious affiliation declines between the first and second marriage. Respondents gave evidence that the second marriage is generally considered as "happy". A number of very young married couples had unsatisfactory relationships within the first year of marriage. There was evidence of "doubt" of the marriage in both the first and the second marriage.

The popular topic of choosing one's mate seems to consist of myth as much as fact. Each culture and subculture may have a customary pattern in the way one's marriage partner is chosen but there will also be unique and deviant aspects of this process. Any research on the subject has been done with those in the age of prime first marriage eligibility. Often research in mate selection has been done on a university campus, evidencing a biased sample of the young and usually middle class. It is conceivable that when remarriage has taken place, the mate selection process is different, when compared to the first marriage. A comparison between mate selection and the first and second marriage is the focus of investigation in this research.

Related Research

Theories of mate selection include explanations which are individual, psychological, and sociological in orientation. In some societies the bride is chosen for the groom by the parents, or an uncle, but this practice is rare in Western society (Peters, 1971). The selection of a mate is sometimes attributed to instinct or cupid. Others suggest that a person seeks a mate who has some characteristics found in his/her own parent. The theory of "like attracts like" seems satisfactory as a means of explanation for some, while "opposites attract" appears to be acceptable to others. In the mid fifties the complimentary needs theory had gained considerable interest (Winch, 1955).

* Department of Sociology & Anthropology, Wilfrid Laurier University, Waterloo, Ontario.

One other rationale for the choice of a mate is propinquity — the proximity of residence between the two individuals (Eshleman 1974, 295-298). Propinquity is significant for the choice of a mate, but may vary with ethnicity, region and religion. Bernard's research on the remarried, done in the mid fifties shows that dating and engagement periods are shorter for those who are divorced and remarry (1956, 39).

Two characteristics which affect the mate selection process in varying degrees are romanticism and rationalism. Romanticism is generally viewed as wholesome in a heterosexual relationship, but an over abundance is considered detrimental. Rationalism is generally viewed as valuable because it is pragmatic and consistent with our production and economic-conscious society. It avoids the flutter and temporality often found in romanticism. Greenfield (1965) suggests that both these orientations harmonize within the social structure of our society. Christensen (1958) and Kephart (1961) found that romanticism was found to be greater for males than for females before marriage. Kanin and Clark (1970), however, found that males develop love feelings earlier in a relationship; but, once in love, females were more likely than males to experience the emotional or euphoric dimensions of romantic love. Hobart (1958) found that males increased in romanticism, with a change from the non-dating to the going steady stage of involvement. Females did not change. Knox and Sporakawski (1968: 641) showed that once people are engaged they are more realistic in their attitude toward love. Their research also indicates that "females tend to be more realistic or conjugal in their attitude toward love" (1968: 639). Spanier's research (1972) suggests that romanticism does not appear to be harmful to the marriage relationship.

Schlesinger's research (1975) with a sample of 96 remarried divorced and widowed couples indicated that the remarrying wife sought different characteristics than that found in the first husband. Infidelity of wives was a frequent complaint by the husbands. A number of divorced remarried women kept separate bank accounts after remarriage, which may be interpreted as a type of alternative security. Ninety-four percent of the women indicated they were satisfied with their marriage.

Sampling and Data Gathering
The initial intent of the research was to take a random sample of a population which had been married and divorced. A city in southwestern Ontario was selected from which sixty names out of the 1970 and 1971 divorce registry furnished the sample, randomly chosen from the county court house. Because of the sensitivity of the data, interviewing was chosen as the data gathering technique. The trained interviewers sought to contact this sample of 60, but was confronted with numerous problems: change of name or address, suspicion, and reluctance to recount the traumatic experience of divorce when the present marriage was satisfactory. Thus, only six persons were interviewed, and this data was included in the final sample of 48.

Because of the lack of success in the interview population, the researcher resorted to the use of questionnaires with a selective sample. Names were obtained by means of advertising in local newspapers, an announcement over "As It Happens" (CBC, Canada) the organization of Parents Without Partners and personal contact. Forty-two responded to the mailed questionnaire of 100 questions. Only a small percentage (N=4) of the sample came from other than southwestern Ontario. Fifty-two percent of the respondents were female. The ages of the respondents ranged between 24 to older than 60 years, with a mean of 34 years.

All respondents had been divorced and were now remarried or about to be remarried (N=2). The average duration of the first marriage was about 6 years (considerably below the Canadian average of 12 years), and the average length of time of the second marriage was 2½ years. In one half of all cases the time between the divorce and the second marriage was under two years. Sixty percent of the sample was Protestant while 21 percent were Catholics. Almost ¾ of the sample had children in their first marriage.

Findings and Discussion

First Marriage

In this sample 48 percent of the brides and 18 percent of the bridegrooms had first married while younger than 20 years of age. This compares to 28 and 8 percent of all first marrying Canadian brides and grooms respectively, under age 20 in 1973 (*Vital Statistics, 1973, 59*). This positive relationship between early marriage and a high incidence of divorce is consistent with other studies on divorce. Forty-six percent of the males and 36 percent of the females had first married between the ages of 20 and 22. This age at marriage is still considerably lower than the average age at first marriage for males and females in Canada in 1970.

Forty-eight percent of the first time marriages were opposed by one or both of the parents of the marriage partners, while an equal percentage were "favourable" or "very favourable" to the marriage. The parents did not differ considerably in their opposition (mothers 43%, fathers 43% to daughter and 20% and 16% respectively to son) or their favourability (mothers 30%, fathers 20% to daughter and 50% and 47% respectively to son) toward the marriage. Opposition was decisively stronger toward the daughter's than toward the son's marriage. This may be partially explained because the bride's age at marriage was younger than that of the bridegroom. It may also suggest that parents feel the bride has more at stake in marriage than does the bridegroom. In any case couples who marry young do confront a peculiar problem in marital adjustment if parents disapprove of the marriage.

In most cases (75%) friends and associates accepted the pair as partners in the first marriage. In 11 and 23 percent of the cases the couples had known one another for under 6 and 12 months respectively. They first met each other through friends (21%), social activities, the church or school. They were living under 20 miles away from one another in 80 percent of the cases thus affirming the significance of propinquity. Seventeen percent responded that they were attracted to the spouse because he/she had some characteristic of their own parent of the same sex (parent image). Among the Protestant respondents, 72 percent married endogamously and among the Catholic respondents, 80 percent married within their own faith. Among the nonreligious, 62.5 percent married endogamously. Fifty-six percent indicated that they had actual doubts about marriage at the time of the first marriage. The engagement period was less than four months in 35 percent of the cases. The respondents were initially attracted to their first spouse for physical (35%) and/or personality characteristic factors (38%). In 38 percent of the cases their first year of marriage was considered "extremely happy" or "happy". In 31 percent of the cases the marriage was considered "unhappy" or "very unhappy" during the first year. This statistic suggests that some marriages are somewhat fragile from the beginning. Premarital counselling might have prevented the unfortunate relationship. A prolonged marriage in many of these cases would undoubtedly do little to ameliorate this unhappiness.

There was social class endogamy among 75 percent of the spouses who considered themselves lower class and 82 percent among the middle class in the first marriage. Rationalism with respect to marriage was viewed as "high" or "extremely high" in 21 percent of the cases. Romanticism during courtship was "high" or "very high" in 36 percent of the cases. The most important characteristics which led to the choice of the first spouse were: personality characteristics (26%), compatibility (9%), physical attraction, "love and attention", and "will make a good spouse".

Among the problems these couples reportedly encountered in their first marriage were: finances (18%), sex (13%), different goals and priorities (11%), alcoholism, conflict with in-laws, arguments, and absence of spouse from home. Adultery was mentioned as a reason for divorce more frequently by the wife (64%) than by the husband (36%). Forty-two percent had counselling before divorce.

The respondents had several recommendations to make for young people considering marriage. They felt it was essential that prospective marriage candidates should know each other's values, needs and goals. Communication should be free and complete. Couples should not anticipate changing their partner's personality through marriage. They should not rush into marriage at too young an age.

Second Marriage

Most of the second marriages (60%) in the sample took place within a year after the divorce. A high proportion married within 6 months (42%). In 63 percent of our sample, parents were "favourable" or "very favourable" to the second marriage (Table 1). In 10 and 21 percent of the cases the couples had known one another for under 6 and 12 months respectively. These figures do not vary considerably from the first marriage. Possibly the maturity at the time of the second marriage would allow for the brief time of association. They first met one another through work (25%), social activities (25%), or friends (23%). They had been living within 20 miles of one another in 83 percent of the cases, again an evidence of propinquity. Twenty-seven percent said that they had been

TABLE 1

COMPARISON OF FIRST AND SECOND MARRIAGES

Characteristic	First Marriage %	Second Marriage %
Marriage opposed by parent(s)	48	27
Marriage "favourable" or "very favourable" (as viewed by parent(s))	48	63
Known one another: under 6 months	11	10
between 6 and 11 months	23	21
between 12 and 23 months	23	27
Distance between one another before marriage under 1 mile	16	31
between 1 and 5 miles	29	31
between 5 and 20 miles	31	21
Attracted because of parent characteristic	17	27
Doubts of the marriage at time of marriage	56	25
Engágement period: less than 4 months	38	56
between 4 and 8 months	31	20
First year marriage: "happy" or "very happy"	38	85
"unhappy" or "very unhappy"	31	12
Religion by respondent: Protestant	62	48
Roman Catholic	21	14
Non-religious	17	34
Class endogamy: Lower	75	60
Middle	82	95
Rationalism in decision to marry: "high" or "extremely high"	21	69
no rationalism	35	6
Ramonticism in courtship: "high" or "extremely high"	37	60
no romanticism	9	6
Marriage veiwed as most romantic	23	60
Marriage viewed as most rational	10	75

attracted to their second spouse because of some parent image. In the second marriage the percentage of religious endogamous marriages by respondent was: Protestant 68 percent, Catholic 33 percent and nonreligious 67 percent. A considerable number of Protestants (decrease of 14%) and Catholics (decrease of 7%) had changed their religious views between the first and second marriage. There was social class endogamy in 60 percent of those who considered themselves in the lower class and 95 percent among the middle class (Table 1).

Some 25 percent had doubts about their second marriage at the time of marriage. This percentage may appear high but is one half the percentage of doubt found in the first marriages. The engagement period was less than four months in 56 percent of the cases (compared to 38% in the first marriage.)

In 85 percent of the cases the first year of marriage was considered "extremely happy" or "happy". In 12 percent of the cases the marriage was considered "unhappy" or "very unhappy" during the first year. Sixty-nine percent of the respondents considered their decision to marry the second time as "extremely high" or "high" in rationalism (compared to 21% in the first marriage). Romanticism during courtship was "high" or "very high" in 60 percent of the cases. When asked in which marriage the decision to marry was more romantic, 60 percent indicated the first marriage. Twenty-three percent said the second marriage was less romantic. When comparing rationalism to many in the first and second marriage, 75 percent indicated the second marriage as more rational.

The respondents generally experienced little or no social pressure to marry the second time. those who had custody of children from the first marriage gave consideration to child-step-parent relationships in the choice of the second partner.The vast majority (81%) felt their second marriage met their expectations and 85 percent considered their second marriage as "happy".

In the final question of the questionnaire, respondents were asked their views on the institution of marriage.Responses varied from "a need for a less romantic view of marriage," "more counselling", "make it more difficult" to "abolish *legal* marriage." The most repeated theme was the recognition and need for *growth* in the marital relationship.

Comment

This research has considerable limitation, primarily due to the small sample size of 48, the sample selection of those who were generally middle class, a high proportion of parents, a second marriage experience which was relatively brief in time, and a second marital experience which was fairly satisfactory.

The research does confirm the positive relationship between an early marriage and a high divorce rate. Young couples undoubtedly face more financial strain and have a smaller reservoir of experience to cope with tension and stress than do older marrying couples. This research suggests limited emotional support for the young nuptial couple from the parents; a significant variable for marriage stability. This sample had a high proportion of couples who had known one another for a brief period before the first marriage, a variable generally considered positively related to a high divorce rate. This sample also showed a brief "knowing" period and a brief engagement period for the second spouse.

Propinquity seems to apply to both first and second marriages, though this study did not isolate intervening variables such as ethnicity and religion. The study also indicated that endogamous marriages by social class are still dominant in both first and second marriages and that religious endogamy is common in the first marriage. The "parent image" is present to some degree in both first and second marriages.

The study showed that religious association between the first and second marriage depreciated considerably. The degree of religiosity at the time of the first marriage was not researched. It may be that religious institutions are viewed by the respondents as failing to address the problems of marriage adjustment, intraspouse tension and failing to consider divorce as an option to marriage dissatisfaction. This may explain the decline in religious affiliation after marriage difficulties arise in the first marriage.

Parents were more approving of the son's marriage than of the daughter's marriage. This may be evidence of the double standard, although the sample indicates a relatively high proportion of very young brides over grooms. This data may suggest that the female has fewer sidebets (Becker) in the institution of marriage than does the male. Despite the fact that divorcees have a higher divorce rate than previously non divorced couples, the second marriage can be happy. The myth of the divorcee as a loser is not substantiated. Eighty-five per cent in this sample considered themselves happily married.

Respondents in this research gave evidence that more rationality was found in the decision to marry the second time than in the first marriage. Undoubtedly the additional years of experience and the trauma of the first marriage gave impetus to a much more cautious decision in the second marriage.

Romanticism was viewed as higher in the second marriage than the first. This term was not defined in the study, and therefore left to a subjective interpretation; a limitation of the study. If the respondent viewed romanticism as a negative phenomenon to the marriage experience, romanticism would tend to show itself in the first marriage. Similarly, if romanicism was viewed as an enduring real love experience which complimented a relationship, it was likely not to be found in the first marriage. This term should have been clarified.

Practical Application of the Research

Despite the fact that a fair percentage had counselling previous to the actual legal breakup, the relationship terminated in divorce. Hence, counselling service is not necessarily an assurance of marriage repair.

The high percentage of unhappy first-year marriages suggests that a bad marriage may show itself rather early. In such cases could counselling rehabilitate the fractured relationship? Do we not have a societal responsibility of ameliorating the "marriage shock" by exposing youth to the reality of marriage in a more institutionalized fashion than is presently done?

A very high percentage of respondents had doubts concerning their marriage at the initial stages of the first (56%) and second (26%) marriage. Though this might indicate a realization of the responsibility of marriage and family by the couple, several alternative research questions are suggested. Is the divorce sample any different with respect to doubt than a non divorce sample? Is not doubt inevitable in the second marriage when the first marriage did not prove successful? How strong a doubt trait will affect an otherwise successful marriage? Will the young couple in our contemporary society with a marriage relationship of "until love do us part" change one's attitude of doubt? Would premarital counselling remove or diminish the doubt of marriage with young couples? Possibly some doubt at marriage is inevitable due to the very nature of the risk and unpredictability of marriage. More research is necessary.

The recommendations to young people contemplating marriage are noteworthy. The respondents suggest one should not rush into marriage, should communicate openly and freely and should not anticipate restructuring the spouse's personality after marriage. Knowing each other's values, goals and needs was stressed. It was considered crucial that both spouses have opportunity for continual growth in the new relationship, a characteristic expected in the companionship marriage of to-day.

BIBLIOGRAPHY

Becker, Howard S.
    1960   "Notes on the Concept of Commitment," American Journal of Sociology, 66 (July), 35.

Bernard, Jess
    1956   Remarriage, New York, Dryden.

Christensen, Harold
    1958   Marriage Analysis, New York, Ronald Press.

Eshleman, J. Ross
    1974   The Family: An Introduction, Boston, Allyn and Bacon.

Fengler, Alfred P.
    1974   "Romantic Love in Courtship: Divergent Paths of Male and Female Students", Journal of Comparative Family Studies, Vol. V, No. 1 (Spring), p. 135-139.

Greenfield, Sidney M.
    1965   "Love and Marriage in Modern America: A Functional Analysis," Sociological Quarterly, 6 (Autumn), p. 361-377.

Hobart, Charles
    1960   "Attitude Changes During Courtship and Marriage." Marriage and Family Living 22 (Nov.), p. 352-359.

    1958   "The Incidence of Romanticism During Courtship." Social Forces, 36 (May), p.362-367.

Kanin, Eugene Davidson and Clark, Sonia
    1970   "A Research Note on Male-Female Differentials in the Experience of Heterosexual Love" in Intimate Life Styles: Marriage and Its Alternatives, Joann S. and Jack R. Delora (eds.) Pacific Palisades, California, Goodyear Publishing.

Kephart, William
    1961   The Family, Society and the Individual, Boston, Houghton Mifflin.

Knox, David and Sporakowski, Michael
    1968   "Attitudes of College Students Toward Love," Journal of Marriage and the Family, 30 (Nov.), p. 638-642.

Messinger, Lillian
    1976   "Remarriage Between Divorced People with Children From Previous Marriages", Journal of Marriage and Family Counselling.

Peters, John F.
    1971   "Mate Selection Amongst the Shirishana of North Brazil," Practical Anthropology, Vol. 20.

and Hunt, Chester L.
    1975   "Polyandry Among the Yanomama Shirishana," Journal of Comparative Family Studies, Vol VI, No. 2.

Schlesinger, Benjamin
    1970   "Remarriage as Family Reorganization for Divorced Persons — A Canadian Study," Journal of Comparative Family Studies, Vol. I, No. 1.

    1975   "Women and Men in Second Marriages", in Marriage, Family and Society, (Wakil, ed.) Scarborough, Butterworth, p. 317-339.

Spanier, Graham B.
    1972   "Romanticism and Marital Adjustment," Journal of Marriage and the Family, August, p. 481-487.

Winch, Robert F.
    1955   "The Theory of Complementary Needs in Mate Selection: A Test of One Kind of Complementariness," American Sociological Review, 20 (Feb.), p. 52-56.

The Two Faces of Policy:
Divorce Reform in Western Democracies

DOROTHY M. STETSON*

Divorce reform in western states has two faces : official policy symbols and expedient policy implementation. The statutes that have recently been adopted to reform divorce practices purport to take a realistic official stance toward preserving marriage and family stability and thus improve laws which have become out of date with social needs.[1] Yet the probable effect of these statutes on private action will be to remove government further from discretionary involvement in regulating families through divorce policy. The goal of divorce reform is to enable government to be realistic and effective in protecting the family; the prevailing divorce policy in the West as a result of reforms is divorce by consent.

This paper reports on the comparison of recent divorce reforms in a number of Western democratic states. The goal of the research is to characterize the changes in divorce laws and to explore the reasons for contradictory divorce reform policies. Policy changes in the United States (Florida, California, New York), Great Britain, Australia, New Zealand, Canada, and Italy will be examined.[2]

A number of questions will be considered : Why have the policies of so many governments followed a similar course ? Why have systems been unable or unwilling to adopt policies that provide effective means to achieve family stability ? Or, if this is impossible, why do governments continue to express public goals they are unable to meet ? What are the implications of such ineffective family policy on the interaction between public goals and private norms ?

* Asst. Professor Department of Political Science Atlantic University Boca Raton Florida, U.S.A.

[1]There is disagreement among scholars, lawyers, legislators and the public about the definition of family stability and its relation to divorce. Traditional views associated divorce rates with the breakdown of the family. But, contemporary lawyers and sociologists argue that families break down regardless of divorce laws and whether a divorce is available will not keep unhappy people together. Divorce rates are a legal expression of broken marriages. Similarly, families may be more unstable and detrimental to welfare of children when unhappy couples seek to remain together rather than divorce. In this paper, goals of family stability are defined as the lawmakers define them. They no longer see divorce as equal to instability yet seek to ensure stable responsible monogamy.

[2]It may appear that this list is unrepresentative, since all but one of the countries are in the English-speaking tradition. These are the nations which have recently undertaken major reforms in laws. Divorce laws in other Western systems are as follows : Scandinavian countries reformed divorce laws in the 1920's. France and Belgium are considering reforms. Spain and Portugal have not passed reforms to date. Germany's current law was passed in 1946, with minor recent revisions. Nearly half the U.S. states have passed reforms (see note 11 for details of substance of these reforms). The policies selected for detailed study here are representative of the early reforms in the U.S. and offer the most interesting information on the legislative process.

Divorce law can be viewed as part of regulatory family policy along with laws governing family formation, equality of sexes, marriage, matrimonial property, sexual relationships, birth control, child bearing, custody and rearing, and inheritance. Reforms in individual laws ultimately should be considered in terms of their relationship to and impact upon other areas of family policy. Findings concerning the political process of divorce reform may be applicable to the politics of reform in other areas of family regulation.

Traditional Divorce Policy

Divorce has not always been a public problem. In Western countries governments did not pass divorce statutes until the 18th and 19th centuries when churches and ecclesiastical courts could no longer handle the demand. The first statutes reflected traditional values and practices of Catholic and Protestant Churches.

The Christian philosophy of marriage provided a common basis for laws in all countries being studied : marriage should be for life and divorce should be very difficult to obtain.[3] Italian law prohibited divorce altogether, in accordance with the Catholic Church. Other countries harbored divorce only when one spouse was able to prove the guilt of the other spouse in court. Since the common law did not provide many guidelines on the subject, English divorce statutes in 1857 and later were based on previous practices of the Church of England, allowing divorce when fault was proved (Rheinstein, 1972; Martinson; Morris). Australia, Canada, and the United States, with no tradition of ecclesiastical rule, left the matter to constituent state governments rather than having a national policy. Although there were variations, in general these laws resembled the English law, based on the fault principle. New Zealand had a law similar to the English pattern with one important exception : a 1920 amendment introduced divorce based on separation on a limited basis.[4]

All these divorce policies set out certain grounds for divorce, that is, the types of offenses thought to be so heinous as to justify the termination of marriage. For a time adultery was the only ground, but later other grounds, such as cruelty and desertion, were added without changing the basic philosophy or intent of the law.[5]

Demands for Reform

Demands for reform of these laws have come from feminists (Blake, 1962),

---

[3] Church regulation is especially attributed to the admonition of Jesus in Mark 10 : 2-12, *The Bible*. As pressure for divorce increased within the Church, the nullity provisions were liberalized. Such revisions by the Pope have continued into the 1970's. Luther is attributed with viewing marriage as a worldly thing, and interpreting Matthew 5 : 32 to permit a man to divorce his wife for adultery (Max Rheinstein, 1972 : 22).

[4] Laws in the United States, Britain and the Commonwealth countries became, of course, quite complicated as they evolved from the first divorce statutes. At one time 32 different grounds for divorce were found in the United States. A number of monumental studies catalog the variations: Graveson and Crane (eds.); Vernier; American Association of Law Schools.

[5] One faultless ground, insanity, was amended to these laws in several nations. Later, reformers were to challenge the inviolability of the fault principle on this ground : if marriage were for life, regardless of the strains placed upon it, it was contradictory to allow divorce for insanity that was due to no one's willful guilt.

lawyers (Sayre, Hurst, Vernier), sociologists (Lichtenberger) and socialists (Engels) for nearly 100 years. The reformers agreed that private values about marriage and divorce had become incongruent with official policy based on fault. Although demands for divorce increased, legislators failed to reform the laws.[6] As a result, couples resorted to collusion, perjury and faking of evidence to obtain necessary grounds. They found the "mental cruelty" provision to be the most malleable part of the law. By the 1960's most of the divorces in Western countries were uncontested (Rheinstein, 1972).[7] The law did not change but the processes of implementation adapted to increased demands for divorce.

The problem for law makers centers on the contradictions between public mores and private values. Publicly, the family is not only a social phenomenon but a public good. Government must support this public good and therefore must act to preserve families, by making divorce dfficult. Privately, even though divorces are difficult to obtain, marriages and families continue to break down (Archbishop of Canterbury, 1966). People may continue to live together unhappily or they may separate and form new families regardless of the law.

In solving the contradiction between public and private values, legislators have three choices : (1) to satisfy individuals' demands for divorce by recognizing that marriage is a private matter, thus abandoning the view the family stability is a public good; (2) to achieve material stability by strictly enforcing divorce laws and increasing powers and resources for implementation; (3) to adopt a public stance in support of family stability, but fail to enforce any provisions that would make divorce difficult, thereby adopting policy provisions that are inconsistent with policy goals.

Four specific policy alternatives have been suggested by reformers that conform to the choices described. *Divorce by consent* would remove the government from an enforcement role with regard to divorce (Choice 1). *Breakdown with investigation* is an attempt to provide the necessary resources to achieve family stability (Choice 2). *Breakdown without investigation* and *separation added to fault grounds* retain public goals of preserving marriage without necessary enforcement powers and resources (Choice 3).

Policy Alternative

Consent

The most drastic change from the traditional role of government with regard to divorce is the proposal to treat marriage as having the same status as any other legal contract. As such, marriage, which requires the mutual consent of the parties, would be dissolved by spouses (one or both) formally expressing the wish to be

---

[6]Since the 19th century the rise in divorce frequency has been steady except for a dip during the depression and a bulge after World War II. See Statistical Abstract of the U.S., 1970.
[7]In the U.S. by 1950, 58.7% of divorces were on mental cruelty grounds and 17% for desertion. (Jacobsen, 1959 : 121). In California 90% of the divorces were based on cruelty and 94% were uncontested prior to divorce reform, according to the Governor's law commission. In Australia, 1959 figures indicate 61% were granted on basis of desertion (Turner). The overwhelming majority of divorces in England (93%) were uncontested, according to the Law Commission Report 8, 18, Cmnd, 3123, 1966. Ninety per cent of divorces in Canada were uncontested according to the Report of the Special Joint Committee on Divorce Reform, 1961.

relieved of their obligations. The role of the state would be to register marriages and divorces, keeping track of the alliances and giving marriage a legal status. The state would have no role in preserving standards of family life.[8]

The various study commissions which have been formed to advise Western legislatures on divorce reform have advised against adopting consent theory as the basis for divorce (Canada, 1967; California, 1966; New York, 1966; England, 1966). The reasons for rejecting this alternative reflect the wide acceptance of the importance of the family to the public good and the necessity for the government to be publicly involved. To adopt divorce by consent as official policy would be a drastic switch in the official position of government with regard to marriage and the family.

Breakdown with Investigation

The breakdown theory defines marriage as a complex human relationship that ideally should be for life, but which is under stress in modern society. It does recognize that when marriages fail, as they may, it is not due to the sins of one spouse combined with the innocence of the other, but to the dismal failure of a relationship in which both spouses are deeply involved. The government should do everything possible to revive sick marriages, but when they die, they should be given decent, dignified, quick burials. It is up to the government to facilitate divorce when it determines that the marriage has irrevocably broken without hope for reconciliation (Archbishop of Canterbury's Group, 1966).

The courts would have the responsibility to determine, with the assistance of trained investigators, whether a particular marriage had broken down. Counseling services would be available to help the courts in finding ways to reconcile couples with marital problems. In this way, the government would more realistically approach its policy goals by helping couples to maintain stable families, rather than spending resources punishing errant spouses.[9]

While the consent alternative has received little support, the breakdown theory is the basis for reform most preferred by legal scholars (Friedman, 1972; Smith, 1947). It embodies what reformers argue is a realistic view of the current social norms regarding marriage and still recognizes the values of government in trying to preserve the stability of marriage.

Breakdown without Investigation

This policy is often referred to as "no fault" divorce (none of the policy alternatives described are based on spousal fault, however). The concept of marital breakdown would be incorporated into the law as the basis for divorce without

---

[8]The consent idea is expressed in the writings of socialists, especially Engels, who argued that traditional marriage and divorce policies are used by governments to protect private property rights and perpetuate inequality. In a communist system, there would be no private property and thus the interest of the state in marriage would vanish. After the Revolution, the Soviet Union adopted a consent policy which remained in effect until the Stalinization of the 1930's. Rheinstein (1972) traces the consent theory of divorce back to the Greeks and Romans.

[9]The California report (1966) presents a wide ranging proposal for a comprehensive family court system in line with enforcing the breakdown principle. Such family courts currently operate in several Ohio cities and California cities.

the investigative and counseling requirements.[10] The courts would continue to have the power to deny divorce if the evidence were not compelling. A couple seeking a divorce must prove to the court that their marriage is irretrievably broken.

Separation Added to Other Grounds

This policy combines, in principle, fault and breakdown. The fault grounds are retained and a means by which legal proof of marital breakdown can be demonstrated is added : a period of separation usually more than six months and less than five years. Retaining fault grounds reflects the belief that an innocent spouse might be forced into divorce against his or her will and must be protected. According to this argument, such a wronged spouse might be denied the right to an immediate divorce and compensation for injuries caused by the other spouse if breakdown is the only basis for divorce.

Proponents of this alternative also recognize, however, that some marriages break down without any wrong-doing, and traditional laws do not provide outlets for them. The solution is for government to maintain and perhaps increase the number of grounds for divorce under the fault concept and add a "no fault" ground to the existing law : the granting of divorce to a couple which has been continuously separated for a considerable time. Separation provides little discretion or power to courts in seeking to maintain marriage, since once this provision is met, the divorce is granted.

Recent Divorce Policies

Divorce reform in the mid-twentieth century has taken place in the English-speaking countries and Italy. In most cases the final policies were determined after extensive debate among legal scholars and churchmen, lengthy studies by legislative commissions, and repeated introduction of bills.

Divorce reform laws (Table I) were enacted to achieve two official goals : (1) to modernize the family law code in light of changes in society and culture; and (2) to maintain marriage and family stability by involving government more effectively in regulating family life.

The main goal in Australia and New Zealand was to make divorce laws uniform throughout each federal system.   Many of the provisions of these divorce reforms were based on state laws. In debates it was necessary to convince all states that provisions would be advantageous to family stability.

In Florida and New York, divorce laws had been on the books for 143 and 179 years, respectively, so reforms were advocated in order to bring laws up to date. In Canada and Great Britain, law commissions criticized the old laws as being harsh and unfair when they were administered in courts. In Italy, the prohibition of divorce was criticized by reformers as old fashioned.

In at least five of the cases, divorce reforms were explicitly sought to maintain the stability of the family. It is likely, however, that definitions of stability varied

---

[10]The main proponents of breakdown without investigation and separation are legislative study commissions (England, 1966; New York, 1967; Canada, 1966) and legislators.

TABLE I[11] :   DIVORCE REFORMS

Country and Act	Effective Date	Provisions
United States		
Florida		
Divorce Act	1971	Breakdown without investigation (fault grounds taken into account in property settlement). Court can order counseling.
New York		
Divorce Act	1967	Separation added to fault grounds. Court can order conciliation.
California		
Divorce Act	1970	Breakdown without investigation. Court can order counseling. Family court possible.
Great Britain		
Divorce Reform Act	1971	Separation added to fault (as proof of breakdown). Court can order counseling.
New Zealand		
Matrimonial Proceedings Act	1963	Separation added to fault. Conciliation.
Australia		
Matrimonial Causes Act	1959	Separation added to fault. Conciliation.
Canada		
Divorce Act	1968	Separation added to fault. Court can order counseling.
Italy		
Divorce Act	1971	Separation as proof of breakdown Court can order counseling.

slightly from system to system.   In Britain, the Law Commission outlined the purpose of divorce reform :

> (1) to buttress, rather than undermine, the stability of marriage;
> (2) when, regrettably, a marriage has irretrievably broken down, to enable the empty legal shell to be destroyed with maximum fairness and minimum bitterness, distress and humiliation. (para. 15).

---

[11]Divorce Reforms in U.S. : While other federal systems studied have adopted national policies, the U.S. continues to vary policies by state. Three states have been selected which had reforms in divorce laws early : California, New York, and Florida. However, a number of other states have made changes in their laws as well. They have either adopted breakdown without investigation as the main grounds or added separation or breakdown provisions to fault grounds between 1965 and 1974.

Breakdown without investigation, sole grounds :

California	Arizona	Nebraska
*Florida	Colorado	Washington
Iowa	Kentucky	*Indiana
Oregon	Michigan	

*insanity also

Separation breakdown added to fault and increased grounds :

Connecticut	Nevada	North Dakota	Maine
Illinois	Alabama	Ohio	Texas
New York	South Carolina	Hawaii	Georgia
New Jersey	West Virginia	Montana	Idaho
			Missouri

Similarly, in Florida, the stated purpose of the Act is :

(a) to preserve the integrity of marriage and to safeguard meaningful family relationships;

(b) to promote the amicable settlement of disputes that have arisen between parties to a marriage;

(c) to mitigate the potential harm to spouses and their children caused by the process of legal dissolution of marriage. (Ch. 71-241, Laws of Florida, 1971).

In California, the governor's commission advocated that the government get involved in the "creative maintenance of the family" through dissolution of marriage and the elaborate family court system: "If by proper handling of troubled families we can reduce the human wreckage of family disruption, the expense will be more than justified (1966, p. 13). In New York, legislative leaders whose version of the divorce bill finally passed argued that the reform would strengthen family life and protect innocent children (NYT, Mar. 24, 1966).

These goals are in congruence with cultural traditions of monogamy. The modern view of family stability differs from the traditional view in the recognition that monogamy may not be lifelong. Older laws were based on the idea that divorce itself was dangerous. Reformers argue that lifelong monogamy and difficult divorce may lead to instability if unhappy parents are forced to live together, or face grueling abuses in court fights. Another result of strict divorce laws disturbing to legislators was the large number of illegal unions which deprive children of legal family organization indefinitely (as was noted in New York, Britain and Italy). Thus, divorce reform was to promote stability by encouraging happy legal monogamous relationships and, for those who are unable to live together, amicable divorce proceedings. The traditional standard of monogamy remains central to public values of family life.

In all the statutes courts are given the final authority for determining whether a family relationship has broken down and in every case are admonished to postpone proceedings, appoint counselors, or order conciliation to ensure that the state has made every effort to save marriages and prevent divorce. Both the goals and this requirement of satisfying the court seem to support the conclusion that these statutes were all intended to continue to involve government in maintaining family stability through the administration of the divorce statutes. None of these systems which have adopted policies have provided for enforcement powers consistent with official goals.

In five systems, separation has been added to fault grounds, and in a sixth, Italy, it is the only basis for divorce. The official position in these systems is to view the separation provision as compatible with public values about the importance of marriage to society. At the same time, in practice, it provides an outlet in the law for divorce by consent. In this sense, the separation provision is more in line with private goals and relieves the courts of manipulation often associated with "fault" divorce. In effect, it contradicts the public standards of divorce policies set forth in the process of passing the new laws.

Florida and California have adopted laws based on breakdown without investigation or "no fault" divorce.[12] These laws give responsibility to the courts to determine when a marriage has "irretrievably broken." A couple seeking a divorce presents all the evidence as to the failure of the marriage and the courts must dissolve the marriage if both spouses consent. In those few cases where one spouse petitions and the other refuses to corroborate the failure, the court may seek additional evidence or order spouses to attempt a reconciliation for several months.

In both types of reforms, separation and dissolution due to irrevocable breakdown, the statutes provide for the judge to delay proceedings and order counseling to satisfy himself that all efforts at keeping the marriage together have been exhausted. In New York, California, Australia and New Zealand, funds have been committed to assist judges in promoting reconciliation in those cases where it may be possible. In general, these conciliation efforts are not effective in achieving the official goals. In New York, the conciliation program is understaffed (McLaughlin). In California, family courts and staffs have been established in a few cities where there is evidence of unusually high divorce rates, and especially to protect children rather than help couples. There are courts in 14 of the 58 counties (Rheinstein, 1972).

In Australia studies of conciliation offices with adequate staff indicate that they have little effect on divorce, since the service is usually brought into the process after the marriage has ended and divorce proceedings have been started (Turner; 909). Judges and lawyers do not push use of conciliation procedures to couples seeking divorce (Finlay).

To have an impact on maintaining marriages and to assist couples and families with problems to stay together, a complete staff of psychologists and social workers would probably be necessary. In most statutes, however, the judge has the power only to order an already estranged couple to consult a marriage counselor, usually at their own expense. Yet, even though it is inadequate, these minimal reconciliation features were crucial to the passage of the reform in New York where legislative leaders rewrote the original legislative committee bill to provide more requirements for counseling. Florida's governor vetoed a first reform bill in order to obtain stronger conciliation measures. And in Australia, according to one study, conciliation was adopted as a result of "political compromise" (Selby).

It may be concluded, than, that with limited exceptions noted above, divorce reform policies provide for an official stance in support of family stability (however defined) yet continue the trend away from effective governmental involvement in maintaining the stability of the family through divorce law. Breakdown without investigation and separation as proof of breakdown in practice mean new reforms have done little to change past practices.

---

[12]A number of states in the U.S. have very recently added a breakdown provision to fault policies. These are similar in theory to separation provisions, although less specific. None of them provides the basis for investigation that would adequately achieve marital stability goals.

In the first place, the retention of old fault grounds is likely to maintain the practice of granting uncontested divorces to couples who manufacture the necessary evidence of mental cruelty.   Secondly, the separation grounds adopted as proof of breakdown in most states give less discretion to government in granting divorces than the fault grounds do.   Thirdly, in those American states which have adopted dissolution policies based on the breakdown theory without investigation, courts are forced to accept the testimony of the couple that the marriage is irretrievably broken.   Fourthly, although courts are given authority to delay divorce and encourage reconciliation, few resources are provided to effectively assist families in resolving marital difficulties other than to allow them to divorce.

Therefore, although the new laws do not mention the consent theory, they do not provide powers to the courts or any other agency that would involve the government in a realistic way in preserving marriages.   Reforms have succeeded only in enforcing conformity of couples to certain procedures in order to legally end their marriages.   Officially, most governments support the goal of family stability.   Whether or not a marriage actually ends is, ultimately, a private decision of the spouses involved.

Reasons for Policies

Divorce policies in the political systems studies are similar in the following respects :   (1) they set forth a policy goal of modernizing divorce law through effective government action to maintain the stability of the family; (2) they fail to provide effective means for achieving goals; (3) these policies place the decision to divorce largely in the hands of the couples involved, restricting the government involvement to definition of procedures.   They fall short of expectations and recommendations of advocates of divorce reform.

The intriguing questions about these policies are not in explaining the *differences* in laws, but determining the reasons for the *similarities.*   There are, of course, reasons peculiar to each situation — United States, England, Canada, Italy, Australia, and New Zealand — that would help account for the particular policy in each state, (See Strickland, 1972 ; Halden, 1971: Turner. 1969; Puxon, 1971; Rheinstein, 1972).   However, this study is concerned with those reasons which are applicable to understanding divorce reform in a number of the systems, that is, those circumstances which are common to most of the cases.

Reform policies are the direct result of the legislative process.   Information on this process leading toward the adoption of divorce reforms was gathered from newspapers, journals and public documents.[13]   In examining the processes three factors seems to be central to understanding the similarities in policy : (1) the changing influence of churches, (2) lack of knowledge of actual marital practices, (3) weak mobilization of interest and lack of clientele.   Each will be discussed in detail.

Changing Influence of Churches

Catholic and Anglican Churches are dominant influences in all but Florida

---

[13]Data for study comes from materials cited in References.   Especially important were law commission reports, case studies, and the *New York Times*, 1965-71; *Miami Herald*, 1969-71.

and California. In Canada, New York, Australia and New Zealand, Catholic minorities are influential in politics. In Great Britain and Italy, Anglican and Catholic churches are dominant, respectively. The opposition of these religions has hampered divorce reforms for many years. The fact that divorce reforms have been possible is due to the change in posture of the churches toward divorce laws.

After Vatican II, the Roman Catholic Church tempered its absolute opposition to divorce reform in New York, Italy and Canada, although the church did not support reform or remain officially neutral. The local bishops did not mount the strong compaigns against reforms that had been so effective in the past. In New York, for example, the Bishops' Conference maintained its public opposition to any change, but did not lobby against the bill. Their weak position depended on the New York legislature adopting a moderate bill that did not change government's traditional position toward marriage but retained the fault grounds. In Italy, the controversy was much more vehement, with proponents staging hunger strikes while the Pope voiced verbal opposition to the change. Observers maintained that no reform would have been possible at all in Italy without the tacit consent of the Vatican (*New York Times* 1970). In both cases, groups of prominent Catholics openly supported the divorce reform. The relaxation of Church opposition may be attributed to the decision of Vatican II in accepting religious freedom and not requiring that all secular laws be in total agreement with Church dogma (Vongrimler, V. IV, 1969). The Church, of course, still retains it official prohibition against divorce for Catholics.

The Anglican Church went even further in separating its own laws from secular law. The change in the Church's position culminated with the reports of the Archbishops' Group, *putting asunder* (1966). They advocated the adoption of the breakdown theory as the sole basis for government divorce policy. The Group argued that such a change would be more human and would not contradict the Church's traditional opposition to divorce. None of the systems under the influence of the Anglican Church went so far as to base divorce on breakdown with investigation as the Church advocated. The Church's new position was considered very seriously in both Canada and England (it came too late for Australia and New Zealand). The change in the influence of both the Catholic and Anglican Churches helps account for reforms in several systems being passed at all. Yet the Church continued to demand the government take responsibility for regulating the stability of the family, and make divorce difficult whether by retaining fault grounds or by making a serious effort to determine whether marriages have irrevocably broken down.

Lack of Knowledge of Marriage and Divorce

When legislators are faced with an issue about which they have little information they are not likely to opt for drastic changes in existing laws (Anderson, 1971) This seems to be particularly true when considering such personal and potentially ethical matters as divorce reform. Marriage is a changing institution (Martinson, Morris, Bernard). Statisticians offer data indicating great increases in the frequency of divorce (U.S. Vital Statistics, 1969). But there appears to be little information for legislators about the complexity of family patterns today. Data on the types of living arrangements and their frequency is not regularly gathered.[14] Legislative study commissions that recommended policy revisions depended for the most part on the assumptions of their members about the increase in consensual unions and the actual breakdown of traditional marriage.

Some information came from testimony taken about individuals who were suffering under existing laws. The prominent British investigators talked about the certainty that large numbers of illegitimate children were being victimized because some vindictive wives clung to their marital status in name only and refused to grant their husbands divorces so they could marry the mothers. In New York, the evidence included a description of the suffering of a young woman who could not divorce her husband, a scoundrel who was only out of prison long enough to come home, take her money, beat her and the children, and squander the resources on his bad habits before being sent back to prison. The legislative studies are full of references to vindictive wives, innocent mothers, husbands who toss over aged wives for younger models, wives clinging to marriage as the only basis of status, "other women," lotharios, worthless bums, and so on: emotional language for discussing a policy of such widespread effect. It is not surprising that new policies did not stray very far from existing ones.[15]

Weak Mobilization of Interest

There was little organized support for changing existing implementation procedures for divorce by allocating resources appropriate for policy goals. In most cases such funds were not even seriously considered. In Italy, England, Canada, Florida, New York and California, public debate included the issue of committing resources for helping preserve marriage. Proposals ranged from mandatory conciliation for couples with court-appointed marriage counselors to an elaborate family court system covering the range of family problems. When the dust had cleared, only New York and California provided some limited conciliation facilities at public expense.

The policy process in Australia and New Zealand differed somewhat from the other systems. In both cases, the Attorneys General introduced the divorce reforms on behalf of the Government. The Government then took an active part in promoting the reform and in both cases advocated the establishment of conciliation apparatus at government expense. In the other cases, where the leadership of the legislature took less initiative in reform movement, conciliation features are very limited or missing altogether.

---

[14]The U.S. Bureau of the Census, in a mid-decade survey for 1975, planned one question on marital status and several pages of items on occupation, education, conditions of employment and wages. A question included in the 1970 Census to determine number of communes did not reveal enough useful information, according to the Bureau, to warrant retaining it. The monthly census surveys from time to time include information on the incidence of divorce and remarriage of a very general nature.

[15]In the U.S., the Uniform Marriage and Divorce Act (1970) may have been helpful in the Florida reform and to future legislators who must change policy with little information to guide them (Paulson and Wadlington, 1971).

In most cases there was little mobilization of interest to support the commitment of resources that must be allocated to provide effective administration of marital conciliation and protection of family stability in the absence of commitment by Executive. Certainly, interest groups gathered, such as the Committee of Catholic Citizens to Support Divorce Reform (New York), New York City Bar Association, and the Italian Divorce League, to promote law reform. But, to be successful, they found it necessary to bump aside institutionalized economic pressure groups in competing for scarce revenue. The reform groups, although they claimed to speak for great numbers of people, in fact, the public interest, had small specialized professional membership. Their greatest appeal was to the consciences of the legislators, not to their purse strings. Expenditure to save marriages, when there is little knowledge of marriage patterns and much doubt whether marriage is susceptible to salvation, quickly dissipates under current pressures to limit overall government spending. Therefore, the inclination was against setting up bold programs; with few powerful interests in support, the allocation of money to achieve the goals of the policy received little serious consideration.

In addition, lawmakers probably had a difficult time identifying a clientele that would use and benefit from the services, as is possible when providing other sorts of services. Marriage cuts across all classes, races, economic groups, educational groups, regional groups, and professional organizations that serve as a basis for seeking public support. Divorced people and people who will seek divorce in the future do not have an organized base for lobbying.

This does not mean that the clientele has no influence on divorce policy outputs, however. Individually, they figure prominently in each divorce case in each court. Together with their counsel, they have sought changes in the administration of the law; and the courts, over time, have been fairly responsive to individual interests by relaxing controls on evidence and perjury. Legislatures have done little more than follow on the heels of court action without providing additional resources for effective administration of official goals. The wide-spread acceptance of the new provisions of divorce by separation or dissolution may reduce the burdens on existing judicial structures.

Conclusion

Although divorce laws are, on the surface, quite varied with regard to details, language, and procedures, the alternatives available to married couples seeking divorce are quite similar in Western democracies. It may be quicker in Florida than in France, and more painful in England than in Sweden, it may require a longer separation in Italy than in Australia, and it may cost more in Germany than in California, but in all cases governments are currently powerless to save troubled marriages regardless of the circumstances and despite reforms.

In the traditional agrarian culture, marriages were considered religious matters and they were well regulated. The belief in religion provided the Church with power over marriage and enabled it to exert meaningful sanctions over those who would attempt to dissolve their marriages. Since governments assumed control of divorce from the Church, individuals have obtained divorces with increasing frequency and the state has not effectively intervened to slow the process. These laws, based on traditions of indissolubility, guilt, and innocence, were not in line with individual goals and personal norms of marital happiness. Therefore, there has been a trend away from effective government regulation of divorce.

Some of the important challenges have come from the wealthy and articulate. Historically, relief from strict regulation of marriage by the Church was sought through parliamentary dispensation. When government took over control of divorce, along ecclesiastical lines, the wealthy and articulate no longer had an outlet. They led the society in manipulating the law through the courts, obtaining fast divorces in other states or countries, and ignoring the law. People too poor to manipulate the law formed illegitimate unions, separated, or suffered in broken marriages.

New laws are still guided by traditional norms and standards of marital indissolubility, family stability and the need for government to enforce these standards. As such they represent a continuation of the trends away from effective regulation of divorce. The revisions in the law have added new alternatives to freedom of divorce, although in effect they contradict the overall intent of the legislature. There continues to be increasing freedom of divorce in line with modernizing society and pluralistic personal values while, at the same time, the public authorities maintain a symbolic posture based on traditional morality.

The process and impact of policy output in the area of divorce is characterized by the lag of public symbols behind social change. The demands for more freedom and consent in divorce have been answered in an informal way at the level of divorce courts, in the interaction among couples, lawyers, and judges. The legislatures tacitly accept this pattern by refusing to adopt new means to enforce divorce. Yet, the prevalence of traditional norms in stated public policy of legislatures continues and is supported by churches and lawyers' organizations.

The gap between real output and symbolic output in modern states has been elaborated by Murray Edelman in *The Symbolic Uses of Politics*. Symbols are used by governments for the general public, according to Edelman, in place of real distribution or regulation. The organized groups are regulated and receive the distributed goods, services, and privileges. The case of divorce policy represents an interesting reversal of the Edelman thesis. The symbolic government action appears to be for the benefit of the organized groups—churches and the bar associations. The effective policy output—divorce by consent—occurs for individuals in the general public at the court level. This change occurs even before organized groups begin to pressure legislatures for reform. Policy change is begun at the lower levels—at the level of impact of policy output on individuals—and is eventually transmitted to legislators. Legislatures adhere to symbolic output for the benefit of the moral leaders of society. This gap between public and private norms illustrates the common interests of legislators and moral leaders on these matters. In turn, decision-makers are prevented from officially admitting the ineffectiveness of traditional norms and values in regulating individual conduct in modern society.

Divorce laws are part of the regulatory family policy of a government. Moral, religious, and legal norms and political processes similar to those found in this study of divorce policies may be associated with reforms in other areas of family policy, such as birth control laws, abortion reform, matrimonial property laws, and laws regulating sexual activities and equality between the sexes. The effect of these norms and processes on the gap between real output and symbolic outputs may also apply to other areas of family policy. Further study of family policy reforms that have been passed in Great Britain, New Zealand, California, New York, and Florida will test the applicability of findings in this study to a broader policy area and contribute to development of theory explaining the impact of public policy on the family.

REFERENCES

American Association of Law Schools
    1950   Essays in Family Law. New York.

Anderson, C.
    1971   "Comparative Policy Analysis : A Design of Measures," Comparative Politics, 4 : 117-132.

Archbishop of Canterbury's Group
    1966   "Putting Asunder : A Divorce Law for Contemporary Society."

Bernard J.
    1972   The Future of Marriage. New York : World Book.

Blake, N.M,
    1962   The Road to Reno : A History of Divorce in the United States. New York : Macmillan.

Bradway, J.S.
    1969   "Progress in Family Law," The Annals, 383 : 1-144.

California
    1966   Report of the Governor's Commission on the Family.

Canada
    1967   "Report of the Special Joint Committee of the Senate and the House of Commons on Divorce," June.

Cohen, N.E. and Conery, M.
    1967   "Government Policy and the Family," Journal of Marriage and the Family, 24 : 6-17.

Durkheim, E.
    1947   The Division of Labor in Society. Glencoe. The Free Press.

Edelman, M.
    1967   Symbolic Uses of Politics. Urbana : University of Illinois Press.

England
    1966   "Law Commission Report 8."

Engels, F.
    1942   The Origin of the Family, Private Property and the State. New York : International Press.

Finlay, H.A.
            "Australian Divorce Law and Marriage Conciliation," Family Law Quarterly, V. 3 (December, 1969) 344-370.

Foster
    1969   "The Future of Family Law," The Annals, 383 : 142.

Friedman, W.
    1972   Law in a Changing Society, 2nd Edition. New York : Columbia University Press.

Graveson, R.H. and Crane, F.R. (Ed).
   1957   A Century of Family Law : London : Sweet and Maxwell.

Hogan, J.D. and Ianni, F.
   1965   American Social Legislation. New York : Harper.

Holden, A.C.
   1971   "Divorce in the Commonwealth," International and Comparative Law Quarterly, 20 : 58-74.

Hurst, J.W.
   1960   Law and Social Process in U.S. History. Ann Arbor : University of Michigan Law School.

Lichtenberger, J.P.
   1931   Divorce : A Social Interpretation. New York : McGraw-Hill.

Litvak, E.
   1956   "Three Ways in Which Law Acts as a Means of Social Control : Divorce as a Case," Social Forces, 34 : 217-23.

Martinson, F.M.
   1970   Family in Society. New York : Dodd, Mead.

Mc Laughlin, Jon M.A.
           "Court-connected Marriage Counseling and Divorce : The New York Experience, Journal of Family Law, V. 11 (1972) 517-556.

Miami Herald
   1969-71

Morris, D.
   1971   The End of Marriage. London : Cassell.

New York
   1966   "Report of the Joint Legislative Committee on Matrimonial and Family Laws to the Legislature of New York." March 31.

New York Times
   1966-71

Nimkoff, M.F.
   1947   Marriage and the Family. Boston : Houghton, Mifflin.

Paulson, M.G. and Wadlington, W. (Ed.).
   1971   Statutory Materials on Family Law. Minneola, New York : The Foundation Press.

Puxon, M.
   1971   Family Law. Middlesex, Great Britain : Penguin.

Ranney, A.
   1968   Political Science and Public Policy. Chicago : Markham.

Rheinstein, M.
   1953   "Trends in Marriage and Divorce Law in Western Countries," Law and Contemporary Problems, 18 : 3-19.

Rheinstein, M.
   1972   Marriage Stability, Divorce and the Law. Chicago : University of Chicago Press,

Rowland, D.
   1971   "Matrimonial Law in England," American Bar Association Journal, 57 : 981-5.

Sayre, P.
   1950   Selected Essays in Family Law. Minneola, New York : Foundation Press.

Selby

"The Development of Divorce Law in Australia," Modern Law Review (1966) 473.

Smith, R.H.
1947   "Dishonest Divorce," Atlantic Monthly, 153 : December.

Tonnies, F.
1937   Community and Society. East Lansing, Michigan : Michigan State University Press.

Struckland, S. (Ed.).
1972   Florida Family Law, 2nd Edition. Florida Bar Association.

"Symposium on No Fault Divorce."
1971   Florida Bar Journal, November.

Turner, J.N.
1969   "Divorce : Australian and German Breakdown Provisions Compared," International Comparative Law Quarterly, 18 : 869-983.

U.S. Department of H.E.W. Divison of Vital Statistics
1969   "Divorce : Analysis of Changes."

Vernier, C.
1932   American Family Laws, v. 2. Stanford : Stanford University Press.

Vongrimler, H.
1969   Commentary on the Documents of Vatican II. New York : Herder and Herder.

Statutes

Australia
    Australian Matrimonial Causes Act, 1959, 1966.

California
    The Family Law Act, 1970; Title 3 : Dissolution of Marriage Section, 4500.

Canada
    Divorce Act, 1967-68. Ch. 24, s. 1.

Florida
    Dissolution of Marriage, Chapter 71-241, Laws of Florida 1971.

Great Britain
    Divorce Reform Act, 1969. Laws, Ch. 55.

Italy
    Leggi 1 December 1971, no. 898. Disciplina del casi di scioglimento del matrimonio Gazzetta Ufficiale della Repubblica Italiana, N. 306.

New York
    Divorce Reform Law, 1966. Laws, Ch. 254.

New Zealand
    Matrimonial Proceedings Act of 1963, no. 71; Matrimonial Proceedings Amendment Act, 1966, 1968, 1970.

Selected Bibliography

Abrasiekong, E. M. "Attitudes of Graduating Secondary School Students in Nigeria Toward Intertribal Marriage." *International Journal of Sociology of the Family*, 1976, 6, 1, 13-20.

Ahmed, Feroz. "Age at Marriage in Pakistan." *Journal of Marriage and the Family*, 1969, 31, 41, 799-807.

Aldridge, D. P. "The Changing Nature of Interracial Marriage in Georgia, A Research Note." *Journal of Marriage and the Family*, 1973, 35, 4, 641-42.

Alston, J. P. "Three Current Religious Issues, Marriage of Priests, Intermarriage and Euthanasia." *Journal for the Scientific Study of Religion*, 1976, 15, 1, 75-78.

Alston, J. P., Mcintosh, W. A., and Wright, L. M. "Extent of Interfaith Marriages Among White Americans." *Sociological Analysis*, 1976, 37, 3, 261-64.

Anspach, D. F. Kinship and Divorce," *Journal of Marriage and the Family*, 1976, 38, 2, 323-30.

Arkoff, A., Meredik, G., and Dong, J. "Attitudes of Japanese-American and Caucasian-American Students Toward Marriage Roles." *Journal of Social Psychology*, 1963, 59, February, 11-15.

Ayres, B. "Bride Theft and Raiding for Wives in Cross-Cultural Perspective." *Anthropological Quarterly*, 1974, 47, 3, 238-52.

Baade, H. W. "The Form of Marriage in Spanish North America." *Cornell Law Review*, 1975, 61, 1, 1-89.

Banerjee, S. N. "Effect of Changes in Age Patterns of Marriage on Fertility Rates in Bilar. 1961-85." *Man in India*, 1973, 53, 3, 262-75.

Bates, D. G. "Normative and Alternative Systems of Marriage Among the Yoruk of Southeastern Turkey." *Anthropological Quarterly*, 1974, 47, 3, 270-87.

Bean, F. D. and Aiken, L. H. "Intermarriage and Unwanted Fertility in the United States." *Journal of Marriage and the Family*, 1976, 38, 1, 61-72.

Bean, L. L. and Afzal, M. "Informal Values in a Muslim Society, A Study of the Timing of Muslim Marriages." *Journal of Marriage and the Family*, 1969, 31, 3, 583.

Bell, R. R. "Religious Involvement and Marital Sex in Australia and the United States." *Journal of Comparative Family Studies*, 1974, 5, 2, 109-16.

Berreman, G. D. "Pahari Polyandry: A Comparison." *American Anthropologist*, 1962, 64, February, 66-75.

Bhatia, P. "Change in Matrimonial Values, A Study of Matrimonial Advertisements." *Eastern Anthropologist*, 1973, 26, 3, 271-77.

Birchnell, J. "Some Possible Early Family Determinants of Marriage and Divorce." *British Journal of Medical Psychology*, 1974, 2, 121-28.

Bolas, D. M. "No Fault Divorce, Born in the Soviet Union." *Journal of Family Law*, 1975, 14, 1, 31-66.

Boon, J. A. "The Balinese Marriage Predicament—Individual, Strategical, Cultural. *American Anthropologist*, 1976, 3, 2, 191-214.

Brandes, S. H. "Wedding Ritual and Social Structure in a Castilian Resort Village." *Anthropological Quarterly*, 1973, 46, 2, 65-74.

Brigham, J. C., Woodmansee, J. J., and Cook, S. W. "Dimensions of Verbal Racial Attitudes, Interracial Marriage and Approaches to Racial Equality." *Journal of Social Issues*, 1976, 32, 2, 9-22.

Brown, C. H. "Formal Semantic Analysis of Huastec Kinship Terminology, A Case of Unusual Marriage Rule." *Anthropological Linguistics*, 1973, 15, 6, 259-66.

Brukman, J. "Stealing Women Among the Koya of South India." *Anthropological Quarterly*, 1974, 47, 3, 304-13.

Cannon, C. A. "The Awesome Power of Sex, The Polemical Campaign Against Mormon Polygamy." *Pacific Historical Review*, 1974, 43, 1, 61-82.

Carlow, W. R., Reynolds, R., Grean, L. W., and Khan, N. J. "Underlying Sources of Agreement and Communication Between Husbands and Wives in Dacca, East Pakistan." *Journal of Marriage and the Family*, 33 (1971): 3, 571.

Cassin, R. W., and Gregory, R. J. "Kinship in Tanna, Southern New Hebrides, Marriage Rules and Equivalence Rules." *Anthropological Linguistics*, 1976, 18, 4, 168-82.

Chakrabarti, T. K. "Attitudes Reflected in Matrimonial Advertisements." *Australian and New Zealand Journal of Sociology*, 1974, 10, 2, 142.

Chakrabarti, T. K. "Student Attitudes Towards Inter-Caste Marriage, A Sample Survey in Calcutta." *Australian and New Zeland Journal of Sociology*, 1975, 1, 1, 67.

Chandra, R. "Types and Forms of Marriage in a Kinnaur Village." *Man in India*, 1973, 53, 2, 176-87.

Chatterjee, Mary. "Conjugal Roles and Social Networks in an Indian Urban Sweeper Locality." *Journal of Marriage and the Family*, 1977, 39, 1, 193.

Chen, K. H., Wishik, S. M., and Scrimshaw, S. "Effects of Unstable Sexual Unions on Fertility in Guayaquill, Ecuador." *Social Biology*, 1974, 21, 4, 353, 59.

Chester, Robert, and Streather, Jane. "Cruelty in English Divorce: Some Empirical Findings." *Journal of Marriage and the Family*, 1972, 34, 4, 706.

Christensen, H. T., and Gregg, C. F. "Changing Sex Norms in America and Scandinavia." *Journal of Marriage and the Family*, 1970, 32, 4, 616-27.

Colbert, Helen. "First Marriage Decrement Tables for Women in Western Canada, 1966." *Journal of Comparative Family Studies*, 1976, 7, 2, 283-94.

Cole, C. L., and Powers, E. A. "Industrialization and Divorce, A Cross-Cultural Analysis." *International Journal of Sociology of the Family*, 1973, 3, 1, 42-47.

Conklin, G. H. "Urbanization, Cross-Cousin Marriage and Power of Women, A Sample from Dharwar." *Contributions to Indian Sociology*, 1973, 7, 53-63.

Connant, F. P. "Frustration, Marriage Alternatives and Subsistence Risks Among the Pokot of East Africa: Impressions of Covariance." *Anthropological Quarterly*, 1974, 47, 3, 314-27.

Corween, A. Lauren. "Caste, Class and the Love Marriage—Social Change in India." *Journal of Marriage and the Family*, 1977, 39, 4, 823-32.

Cottrell, A. R. "Cross National Marriage as an Extension of an International Life Style, A Study of Indian-Western Couples." *Journal of Marriage and the Family*, 1973, 35, 4, 739-41.

Das, V. "The Structure of Marriage Preferences, An Account from Pakistani Fiction." *Man*, 1973, 8, 1, 30-45.

Das, V., and Madan, T. N. "Marriage and Kinship in India, *Two Recent Studies.*" *Contributions to Indian Sociology*, 1973, 3, 135-43.

David, K. "Until Marriage Do Us Part, A Cultural Account of Jaffna Tamil Categories for Kinsmen." *Man*, 1973, 8, 4, 521-35.

Day, L. H. "Divorce in Australia." *Australian Quarterly*, 1976, 48, 2, 61-73.

DeRuyter, B. "Ethnic Differentials in Age at First Marriage, Canada, 1971." *Journal of Comparative Family Studies*, 1976, 7, 2, 159-66.

Devi, B. "The Rarhi Brahmans of Chakdaha, A Study on Their Marriage Structure and Distance." *Man in India*, 1973, 53, 1, 63-75.

DeVos, George." The Relation of Guilt Toward Parents to Achievement and Arranged Marriage Among the Japanese." *Psychiatry*, 1960, 23, 287-301.

Dodinval, P. A. "Distribution of Matrimonial Migrations in Belgium." *Human Heredity*, 1973, 23, 1, 59-68.

Eastwell, H. "Dilemmas of Aboriginal Marriage in East Arnhem Land, North Australia." *Australian and New Zealand Journal of Sociology*, 1974, 8, 1, 49-54.

Eberstein, J. W., and Frisbie, W. P. "Differences in Marital Instability Among Mexican Americans, Blacks and Anglos, 1960-1970." *Social Problems,* 1976, 23, 5, 609-21.

Ekechi, F. K. "African Polygamy and Western Christian Ethnocentrism." *Journal of African Studies*, 1976, 3, 3, 329-50.

Farid, S. M. "Cohort Nuptiality in England and Wales." *Population Studies*, 1976, 30, 1, 137-52.

Fernando, D.F.S. "Changing Nuptiality Patterns in Sri Lanka, 1901-1971." *Population Studies*, 1975, 29, 2, 179-190.

Festy, P. "Canada, United States, Australia and New Zealand, Nuptiality Trends." *Population Studies*, 1973, 27, 3, 479-92.

Fix, A. G. "Neighbourhood Knowledge and Marriage Distance, The Semai Case." *Annals of Human Genetics*, 1974, 37, 3, 327-32.

Fleming, P. H. "The Politics of Marriage Among Non-Catholic European Royalty." *Current Anthropology*, 1973, 14, 3, 231-42.

Fonesca, C. "I Didn't Choose My Husband—An Enquiry on the Situation of Women Villagers in Upper Volta." *Unesco Courier*, 1975, 8, 5-12.

Fox, G. L. "Love Match and Arranged Marriage in Modernizing Nation, Mate-Selection in Ankara, Turkey." *Journal of Marriage and the Family*, 1975, 37, 1, 180-93.

Fredlund, E. V., and Dyke, B. "Measuring Marriage Preference." *Ethnology*, 1976, 15, 1, 35-46.

Freed, S. A., and Freed, R. S. "Status and the Spatial Range of Marriages in a North Indian Area." *Anthropological Quarterly*, 1973, 46, 2, 92-99.

Freiden, A. "The United States Marriage Market." *Journal of Political Economy*, 1974, 82, 2, 834-53.

Frideres, J. A., and Goldstein, J. E. "Jewish-Gentile Intermarriages, Definitions and Consequences." *Social Compass*, 1974, 21, 1, 69-84.

Frideres, J. S., Nye, F. I., and White, L. "Preliminary Theory of Marital Stability, Two Models." *International Journal of Sociology of the Family*, 1973, 3, 1, 102-22.

Friedl, J., and Ellis W. S. "Celibacy, Late Marriage and Potential Mates in a Swiss Isolate." *Human Biology*, 1976, 48, 1, 23-25.

Fulton, P. N. "Setting of Social and Status Advancement Through Marriage, A Study of Rural Women." *Rural Sociolgy*, 1975, 40, 1, 45-54.

Glendon, M. A. "The French Divorce Reform Law, 1976." *American Journal of Comparative Law,* 1976, 24, 2, 199-228.

Glenn, N. D., Ross, A. A., and Tully, J. C. "Patterns of Intergenerational Mobility of Females Through Marriage." *American Sociological Review*, 1974, 39, 5, 683-99.

Goldschmidt, W. "The Bride Price of Sebei." *Scientific American*, 1973, 19, 4, 577-84.

Goldschmidt, W. "The Economics of Bride Price Among the Sebei and in East Africa." *Ethnology*, 1974, 13, 4, 311-31.

Gregon, T. A. "Publicity, Privacy and Mehinacu Marriage." *Ethnology*, 1974, 13, 4, 333-49.

Grossbard, A. "An Economic Analysis of Polygyny, The Case of Maidugri." *Current Anthropology*, 1976, 17, 4, 701-707.

Hall, F. "A Raw Power Question/Interracial Marriage." *Psychology Today*, 1973, 29, 2, 67-81.

Harral-Bond, B. E. "Stereotypes of Western and African Patterns of Marriage and Family Life." *Journal of Marriage and the Family*, 1976, 38, 1, 177-82.

Hartley, S. M. "Illegitimacy Among "Married" Women in England and Wales." *Journal of Marriage and the Family*, 1969, 31, 41, 793.

Hassan, R., and Benjamin, G. "Ethnic Outmarriage in Singapore, the Influence of Traditional Socio-cultural Organization." *Journal of Marriage and the Family*, 1973, 35, 4, 731-38.

Hobart, C. W. "The Social Context of Morality Standards Among Anglophone Canadian Students." *Journal of Comparative Family Studies*, 1974, 5, 1, 26-40.

Holcomb, B. K. "Oromo Marriage in Wallage Province, Ethiopia." *Journal of Ethiopian Studies*, 1973, 11, 1, 107-42.

Iro, M. I. "The Pattern of Elite Divorce in Lagos, 1961-1973." *Journal of Marriage and the Family*, 1976, 38, 1, 177-82.

Kandel, B. Denise B., and Lesser, S. Gerald. "Marital Decision Making in American and Danish Urban Families: A Research Note." *Journal of Marriage and the Family*, 1972, 34, 1, 134.

Kaplan, J. O. "Endogamy and the Marriage Alliance, A Note on Continuity in Kindred Based Groups." *Man*, 1973, 8, 4, 555-70.

Katz, J. S., and Katz, R. S. "The New Indonesian Marriage Law, A Mirror of Indonesia's Political, Cultural, and Legal Systems." *American Journal of Comparative Law*, 1975, 23, 4, 653-81.

Keyser, M.M.B. "The Middle Eastern Case, Is there a Marriage Rule." *Ethnology*, 1974, 76, 2, 312-18.

Kikumura, A., and Kitano, H.H.L. "Interracial Marriage, A Picture of the Japanese Americans." *Journal of Social Issues*, 1973, 29, 2, 67-81.

Kim, C. S. "The Yon-Jul-Hon or Chain Form of Marriage Arrangement in Korea." *Journal of Marriage and the Family*, 1974, 36, 3, 575-79.

Kim, M., Rider, R. V., Harper, P. A., and Yong, J. M. "Age at Marriage, Family Planning Practices, and Other Variables as Correlates of Fertility in Korea." *Demography*, 1974, 11, 4, 641-56.

Kooy, G. A. "The Declining Age of Marriage in the Netherlands in the Sixties, A Possible Sociological Explanation." *Sociologica Neerlandica*, 1975, 11, 1, 21-40.

Kooy, G. A. "Force Marriages in the Netherlands, A Macrosociological Approach to Marriage Contracted as a Consequence of Unintended Pregnancy." *Journal of Marriage and the Family*, 1975, 37, 4, 954-65.

Kopp, P.A.M. "Age of Marriage and Divorce Trends in Amsterdam During the Period 1911-71." *Journal of Biosocial Science*, 1976, 8, 2, 137-44.

Korson, J. H. "Student Attitudes Towards Mate Selection in a Muslim Society: Pakistan." *Journal of Marriage and the Family*, 1969, 31, 1, 153.

Krige, E. J. "Asymmetrical Matrilateral Cross-Cousin Marriage, The Lovedu Case." *African Studies*, 1975, 34, 4, 231-58.

Krige, E. J. "Women and Marriage, with Special Reference to the Lovedu, Its Significance for the Definition of Marriage." *Africa*, 1974, 44, 1, 11-37.

Kudat, A. "Institutional Rigidity and Individual Initiative in Marriage of Turkish Peasants." *Anthropological Quarterly*, 1974, 47, 3, 288-303.

Kunzel, R. "The Connection Between the Family Cycle and Divorce Rates, An Analysis Based on European Data." *Journal of Marriage and the Family*, 1974, 36, 2, 379-88.

Kuo, E.C.Y. "Collectivism in Communist China, A Case Study of Mate Selection and Marriage." *Wisconsin Sociologist*, 1973, 10, 1, 3-16.

Kuo, E.C.Y., and Hassan, R. "Some Social Concomitants of Interethnic Marriage in Singapore. "*Journal of Marriage and the Family*, 1976, 38, 3, 549-59.

Lapierre, Adamcyk E., and Rurch, T.K. "Trends and Differentials in Age at Marriage in Korea." *Studies in Family Planning*, 1974, 5, 8, 255-60.

Larsen, K. S. "An Investigation of Sexual Behaviour Among Norwegian College Students. A Motivation Study. *Journal of Marriage and the Family*, 1971, 33, 1, 219.

Lasswell, M. F. "Is There a Best Age to Marry. An Interpretation." *The Family Co-ordinator*, 1974, 23, 3, 237-42.

Lastry, J. C., Bloomfield-Schacht. "Jewish Intermarriage in Montreal, 1962-1972." *Jewish Social Studies*, 1975, 37, 3-4, 267-78.

Laughlin, C. D., Jr. "Maximization, Marriage and Residence Among the So." *Canadian Review of Sociology and Anthropology*, 1973, 10, 3, 199-213.

Lee, C. F., Potvin, R. H., and Verdieck, M. J. "Interethnic Marriage as an Index of Assimilation, The Case of Singapore." *Social Forces*, 1974, 53, 1, 112-19.

Leon, J. J. "Sex Ethnic Marriage in Hawaii, A Nonmetric Multidimensional Analysis." *Journal of Marriage and the Family*, 1975, 37, 4, 475-81.

Locke, H. J., and Karlson, G. "Marital Adjustment and Prediction in Sweden and United States." *American Sociology Review*, 1952, 17, February, 10-17.

Lockwood, W. G. "Bride Theft and Social Maneuverability in Western Bosnia." *Anthropological Quarterly*, 1974, 47, 3, 253-69.

Maher, V. "Divorce and Property in the Middle Atlas of Morocco." *Man*, 1974, 9, 1, 103-22.

Maller, A. S. "Jewish-Gentile Divorce in California." *Jewish Social Studies*, 1975, 37, 3-4, 279-90.

Maller, A. S. Mixed Marriage and Reform Rabbis." *Judaism*, 1975, 24, 1, 39-48.

Mandeville, E. "The Formality of Marriage, A Kampala Case Study." *Journal of Anthropological Research*, 1975, 31, 3, 183-95.

McCreery, J. L. "Women's Property Rights and Dowry in China and South Asia." *Ethnology*, 1976, 15, 2, 153-74.

Miao, G. "Marital Instability and Unemployment Among Whites and Non-whites, The Moynihan Report Revisited, Again." *Journal of Marriage and the Family*, 1974, 36, 1, 77-86.

Michel, Andree. "Wife's Satisfaction with Husband's Understanding in Parisian Urban Families." *Journal of Marriage and the Family*, 1970, 32, 3, 351.

Michielutte, R., Vincent, C. E., Cochrane, C. M., and Maney, C. A. "Censensual and Legal Marital Unions in Costa Rica." *International Journal of Comparative Sociology*, 1973, 14, 1-2, 119-28.

Momeni, D. A. "The Difficulties of Changing the Age at Marraige in Iran." *Journal of Marriage and the Family*, 1972, 34, 3, 545.

Momeni, D. A. "Polygyny in Iran." *Journal of Marriage and the Family*, 1975, 37, 2, 453-56.

Monahan, T. P. "Marriage Across Racial Lines in Indiana." *Journal of Marriage and the Family*, 1973, 35, 4, 632-40.

Monahan, T. P. "The Occupatonal Class of Couples Entering into Inter-racial Marriages." *Journal of Comparative Family Studies*, 1976, 7, 2, 175-92.

Monahan, T. P. "An Overview of Statistics on Inter-racial Marriage in the United States, with Data on Its Extent from 1963-1970." *Journal of Marriage and the Family*, 1976, 38, 2, 223-31.

Monahan, T. P. "Some Dimensions of Inter-religious Marriages in Indiana, 1962-1967." *Social Forces,* 1973, 7, 1, 27-57.

Msereko, D. O. "The Nature and Function of Marriage Gifts in Customary African Marriages." *American Journal of Comparative Law*, 1975, 23, 4, 682, 704.

Mukherjee, D. P. "Patterns of Marriage and Family Formation in Rural India and Genetic Implications of Family Planning." *Journal of Indian Anthropological Society*, 1973, 812, 131-45.

Muller, J. C. "On Preferential Prescriptive Marriage and the Function of Kinship Systems, The Rukuba Case/Benuc Plateau Site/Nigeria." *American Anthropologist*, 1973, 75, 5, 1563-76.

Muller, J. C., and Sangree, W. H. "Irigwe and Rukuba Marriage—A Comparison." *Canadian Journal of African Studies*, 1973, 7, 1, 27-57.

Olusanya, P. O. "A Note on Some Factors Affecting the Stability of Marriage Among the Yoruba of Western Nigeria." *Journal of Marriage and the Family*, 1970, 32, 1, 150.

Oppong, C. "Conjugal Power and Resources: An Urban African Example." *Journal of Marriage and the Family*, 1970, 32, 4, 676.

Oppong, C. "Marriage Among a Matrilineal Elite, Family Study of Ghanian Senior Civil Servants." *Cahiers D'Etudes Africaines*, 1975, 15, 3, 550.

Oppong, C. "Note on Attitudes to Jointness of Conjugal Role Relationship and Family Size, Study of Norms Among Ghanian Students." *Human Relations*, 1975, 28, 9, 801-10.

Pakrasik, Malaker C. "Interval Between Age at Marriage and First Birth in India." *Social Biology*, 1973, 20, 1, 103-10.

Parvez, Wakil S. "Campus Dating, An Exploratory Study of Cross-national Relevance." *Journal of Comparative Family Studies*, 1973, 4, 2, 286-94.

Patel, G. V. "A Study of Marital Happiness in Hindu Gujerati Women." *Indian Journal of Psychiatric Social Work*, 1974, 3, 37-40.

Peters, J. F., and Hunt, C. L. "Polyandry Among the Yanoma of Shirishana." *Journal of Comparative Family Studies*, 1975, 6, 2, 197-208.

Plunkett, F. T., "Royal Marriages in Rajasthan." *Contributions to Indian Sociology*, 1973, 7, 65-80.

Pool, D. I., and Bracher, M. C. "Aspects of Family Formation in Canada." *Canadian Review of Sociology and Anthropology*, 1974, 11, 4, 308-23.

Porterfield, E. "Mixed Marriage or Inter-racial Marriage." *Psychology Today*, 1973, 6, 8, 71-78.

Raju, M.V.T. "Illitan Marriage, Marriage by Adoption in Telengana." *Eastern Anthropologist*, 1976, 29, 3, 301-02.

Rao, M. K. "Rank Difference and Marriage, Reciprocity in South India, An Aspect of the Implications of Elder Sister's Daugher's Marriage in a Fishing Village in Andhra." *Contributions to Indian Sociology*, 1973, 7, 16-35.

Rheinstein, Max. "Trends in Marriage and Divorce Laws of Western Countries." *Source Book of Marriage and the Family* (edited by M. Sussman), 2d ed., Boston: Houghton Mifflin, 1963, 669-78.

Rosman, A., and Rubel, P. G. "Marriage Rules and the Structure of Relationships Between Groups in New Guinea Societies." *Social Science Information*, 1975, 14, 5, 109-25.

Rusicka, Lado T. "Premarital Pregnancies in Australia." *Journal of Marriage and the Family*, 1977, 39, 2, 387.

Sackett, L. "Marriage Alliance in the Western Desert of Australia." *Ethnology*, 1976, 15, 2, 135-49.

Sage, Z. "Dissolution of the Family Under Swedish Law." *Family Law Quarterly*, 1975, 9, 2, 375-404.

Salaff, J. W. "The Status of Unmarried Hong Kong Women and the Social Factors Contributing to Their Delayed Marriage." *Population Studies*, 1976, 39, 3, 391-412.

Salisbury, R. "Asymmetrical Marriage Systems." *American Anthropologist*, 1956, 58, 4, 639-55.

Schlesinger, Yaffa. "Sex Roles and Social Change in the Kibbutz." *Journal of Marriage and the Family*, 1976, 39, 4, 771-80.

Schmidt, R. C. "Age and Race Differences in Divorce in Hawaii." *Journal of Marriage and the Family*, 1969, 31, 1, 48.

Schmidt, R. C. "Recent Trends in Hawaiian Inter-racial Marriage Rates by Occupation." *Journal of Marriage and the Family*, 1971, 33, 2, 373.

Schoenfeld, E. "Intermarriage and the Small Town." *Journal of Marriage and the Family*, 1969, 31, 3, 551.

Serjeanton, S. "Marriage Patterns and Fertility in Three Papua New Guinean Populations." *Human Biology*, 1975, 47, 4, 399-413.

Singer, Alice. "Marriage Payments and the Exchange of People." *Man*, 1973, 8, 1, 80-92.

Singh, G. B. "Hindu Marriage, Symbolism and Change." *Social Welfare*, 1973, 20, 3, 13-15.

Singh, K. P. "Women's Age at Marriage." *Sociological Bulletin*, 1974, 23, 2, 236-44.

Singh, N. R. "Marriage by Elopement Among the Meiieis of Manipur." *Man in India*, 1973, 53, 2, 135-52.

Skarsten, S. "Family Desertion in Canada." *The Family Co-ordinator*, 1974, 23, 1, 19-25.

Spicer, J. W., and Hampe, G. D. "Kinship Interaction After Divorce." *Journal of Marriage and the Family*, 1975, 37, 1, 113-19.

Spiro, M. E. "Marriage Payments, A Paradigm from the Burmese Perspective." *Journal of Anthropological Research*, 1975, 31, 2, 89-115.

Stoeckel, J. Tuladhar, J. M., and Gubhaju, B. B. "Marital Structure and Birth Rate in Nepal." *Journal of Biosocial Science*, 1976, 8, 2, 79-84.

Strange, H. "Continuity and Change, Patterns of Mate Selection and Marriage Ritual in a Malay Village." *Journal of Marriage and the Family*, 1976, 38, 3, 561-71.

Stuart, R. J. "Natality, Fertility and Marriage Status in Sepik River Population of New Guinea." *Tropical and Geographical Medicine*, 1974, 26, 4, 399-413.

Tien, H. Y. "Fertility Decline via Marital Postponement in China." *Modern China*, 1975, 1, 4, 447-62.

Tinker, J. N. "Intermarriage and Ethnic Boundaries, The Japanese American Case." *Journal of Social Issues*, 1973, 29, 2, 49-66.

Trilin, A. D. "Western Samoan Marriage Patterns in Auckland." *Journal of Polynesian Society*, 1975, 84, 2, 153-76.

Trost, Jan, "Attitudes Toward and Occurrence of Cohabitation Without Marriage," *Journal of Marriage and the Family*, 1978, 40, 2, 393-400.

Undeutsch, U. "Comparative Incidence of Premarital Coitus in Scandinavia, Germany and the United States." *Sexual Behaviour in American Society* (edited by J. Himelhock and S. Fava), New York: W. W. Norton, 1955, 360-63.

Upadhaya, H. "Incidences of Separations in Hindu Joint Family as Depicted in Bhojpuri Folk Songs." *Folklore*, 1975, 17, 3, 77-81.

Vanderveen, K. W. "Marriage and Hierarchy Among the Anavil Brahmans of South Gujerat." *Contributions to Indian Sociology*, 1973, 7, 36-52.

Van Horn, L. F. "Recruitment and Preferred Second Marriage Among the Kwaktutl." *Anthropological Journal of Canada*, 1974, 12, 1, 24-25.

Vetscher, T. "Bethrothal and Marriage Among the Minas of South Rajasthan." *Man in India*, 1973, 53, 4, 387-413.

Wagatsuma, H., and DeVos, George. "Attitude Toward Arranged Marriage in Rural Japan." *Human Organization*, 1962, 21, 187-200.

Walsh, B. M. "Marital Status and Birth Order in a Sample of Dublin Males." *Journal of Biosocial Science*, 1973, 5, 2, 187-93.

Walter, Mahb. "Kinship and Marriage in Mualevu, A Dravidian Variant in Fijis." *Ethnology*, 1975, 14, 2, 181-96.

Watson, C. "Marriage and Sexual Adjustment in Guajiro Society." *Ethnology*, 1973, 12, 2, 153-61.

Weiss, M. S. "Selective Acculturation and the Dating Process: The Patterning of Chinese-Caucasian Inter-racial Dating." *Journal of Marriage and the Family*, 1970, 32, 2, 273.

Weissleder, W. "Amhara Marriage, The Stability of Divorce." *Canadian Review of Sociology and Anthropology*, 1974, 11, 1, 67-85.

Williams, S. J., Murtly, N., and Berggren, S." Conjugal Unions Among Rural Haitian Women." *Journal of Marriage and the Family*, 1975, 37, 4, 1022-31.

Yaukey, David, and Thorsen, Timm." Differential Female Age at First Marriage in Six Latin American Cities." *Journal of Marriage and the Family*, 1972, 34, 2, 375.

Yinon, Y. "Authoritarianism and Prejudice Among Married Couples with Similar or Different Ethnic Origin in Israel." *Journal of Marriage and the Family*, 1975, 37, 1, 214-20.

Author Index

Subject Index

About the Editor

George Kurian, professor of sociology at the University of Calgary, Alberta, Canada, is the founder and editor of the JOURNAL OF COMPARATIVE FAMILY STUDIES. He has written THE FAMILY IN INDIA and THE INDIAN FAMILY IN TRANSITION as well as articles published in scholarly journals.

81-225

HQ
734
.C93   Cross-cultural
        perspectives of
        mate-selection and
        marriage